D0086014

Economics USA

Eighth Edition

Economics USA

Eighth Edition

NARIMAN BEHRAVESH

IHS Global Insight

W. W. Norton & Company has been independent since its founding in 1923, when William Warder Norton and Mary D. Herter Norton first published lectures delivered at the People's Institute, the adult education division of New York City's Cooper Union. The firm soon expanded its program beyond the Institute, publishing books by celebrated academics from America and abroad. By midcentury, the two major pillars of Norton's publishing program—trade books and college texts—were firmly established. In the 1950s, the Norton family transferred control of the company to its employees, and today—with a staff of four hundred and a comparable number of trade, college, and professional titles published each year—W. W. Norton & Company stands as the largest and oldest publishing house owned wholly by its employees.

Copyright © 2014, 2005, 2001, 1998, 1995, 1992, 1989, 1986 by W. W. Norton & Company, Inc.

All rights reserved
Printed in Canada

Editor: Jack Repcheck
Project Editor: Rachel Mayer
Editorial Assistant: Theresia Kowara
Manuscript Editor: Janet Greenblatt
Managing Editor, College: Marian Johnson
Managing Editor, College Digital Media: Kim Yi
Production Manager: Ashley Horna
Media Editor: Cassie del Pilar
Associate Media Editor: Carson Russell
Assistant Media Editor: Michelle Salyga
Marketing Manager, Economics: Janise Turso
Design Director: Rubina Yeh
Photo Editor: Stephanie Romeo
Permissions Manager: Megan Jackson
Composition: Cenveo® Publisher Services
Manufacturing: TransContinental

Permission to use copyrighted material is included in the credits section of this book, which begins on page 703.

ISBN: 978-0-393-91969-1

W. W. Norton & Company, Inc., 500 Fifth Avenue, New York, NY 10110-0017
wwnorton.com

W. W. Norton & Company Ltd., Castle House, 75/76 Wells Street, London W1T 3QT

1 2 3 4 5 6 7 8 9 0

Contents in Brief

PART SIX   International Economics

Contents

PART 2   Economic Decision Making: The Firm, the Consumer, and Society

CHAPTER 3   The Business Firm: Organization, Motivation, and Optimal Input Decisions   71

CHAPTER 7   Monopoly and Its Regulation   164

CHAPTER 8   Monopolistic Competition, Oligopoly, and
Antitrust Policy   192

PART 3   The Distribution of Income and the Role of Government in Markets

CHAPTER 14 Public Goods and the Role of the Government   329

CROSS CHAPTER CASE: PART 3 U.S. Health Care Reform: The Twin Challenges of Universal Coverage and Cost Control   351

CHAPTER 23   Productivity, Growth, and
Technology Policy   544

CHAPTER 24   Surpluses, Deficits, Public Debt, and the
Federal Budget   563

CHAPTER 25   Monetary Policy, Interest Rates, and Economic Activity   587

CHAPTER 26   Controversies over Stabilization Policy   618

PART 6   International Economics

Preface

The approach used in this text is to teach introductory economics by using actual economic events to motivate the study of the fundamental ideas of the field. I believe, and the numerous instructors who use this text confirm, that this is the best way to help students understand the complex and dynamic American economy.

Based on feedback from instructors who have used this book in the past, there have been some major changes between the 7th and 8th editions. First, the chapters on microeconomics have been moved to the first half of the book, and the chapters on macroeconomics have been moved to the second half of the book. Second, new case studies have been added. Third, new material has been developed (both in the text and in the cross-chapter case studies) on the important topics of the 2008–2009 financial crisis, health care, and climate change.

This book has been prepared as both a stand-alone text and one that accompanies the Annenberg Lerner multimedia, distance-learning course entitled *Economics U$A: 21st-Century Edition*. The Annenberg distance-learning course is designed to use economic events in America and the world, present and past, to teach the core principles of economics. More information about this course can be found at http://www.learner.org/series/econusa/.

I am grateful to the following teachers, who commented in detail on the manuscript: Robert C. Augur, Pasadena City College; Carlos Aguilar, El Paso Community College; Gary Arbogast, Glenville State College; Susan Bell, Seminole State; David Black, University of Toledo; Clifton Chow, Massachusetts Bay; James E. Clark, Wichita State University; Curtis Clarke, Eastfield College; Peter Dorman, Evergreen State College; Dorsey Dyer, Davidson County Community College; Clinton Greene, University of Missouri–St. Louis; Paul Grimes, Mississippi State University; Dan Harrison, Murray State University; Ralph F. Lewis, Economics Research, Inc.; Chuck Nugent, Pima Community College; Doborah Paige, Santa Fe Community College; James Phillips, Cypress College; Tom Porebski, Triton University; Victor H. Rieck, Miami-Dade Community College;

Larry Ross, University of Alaska; Steve Smith, Rose State College; John Somers, Portland Community College; and Michael Vaughan, Weber State College. In addition I would like to thank my editor, Jack Repcheck, along with Ashley Horna, Theresia Kowara, Rachel Mayer, and Carson Russell of Norton for their efficient handling of the publishing end of the work.

Lexington, MA   N.B.

Economics USA

Eighth Edition

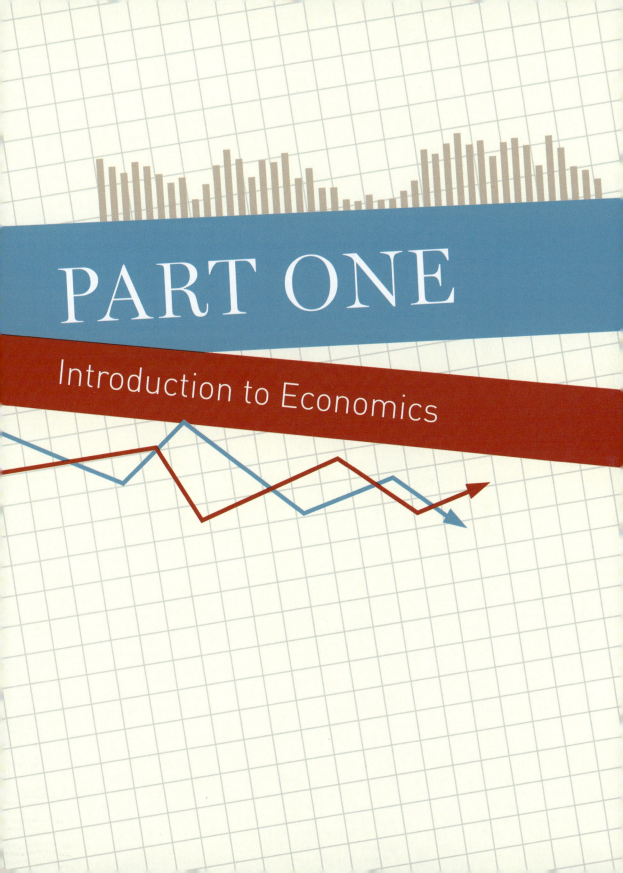

PART ONE

Introduction to Economics

Economic Problems

A Sampler

George Bernard Shaw, the great playwright, once said, "The only time my education was interrupted was when I was in school." Fortunately, economics, if properly presented, can contribute mightily to your education—and you can learn it without leaving school. To help you understand the pervasive importance of economics, we begin by looking at a sample of the major problems economists deal with. Each of these problems can have a big effect on your life. More generally, economic and market forces will determine what types of jobs will be open to you, what kinds of choices you can make about where and how you live, what you do with your leisure time, and what you own.

Financial Crises

Most Americans are painfully aware that in 2008–2009, the United States suffered through a major financial crisis and economic downturn, the likes of which had not been seen since the Great Depression of the 1930s. The unemployment rate rose from 4.4 percent in March 2007 to 10.1 percent in October 2009. House prices in some cities (for example, Las Vegas and Phoenix) dropped by 50 to 60 percent. Roughly $17 trillion in household wealth was wiped out, including retirement and college savings. Families found it very difficult to qualify for home mortgages, car loans, and student loans.

Our first example of an economic problem is this: *What causes financial crises, and what can be done to prevent them?* Unfortunately, financial crises are nothing new. In the words of the late economic historian Charles Kindleberger, they are a "hardy perennial," occurring on a regular basis over the past several hundred years. In each case, there is a fairly predictable sequence of events. Optimism about future increases in the prices of certain assets (such as real estate and stocks) encourages a large number of people to invest in those assets. Prices go up and more people invest. Many people borrow the funds to make these investments. Eventually, prices get so high that they are no longer justified by market "fundamentals"

FIGURE 1

Evidence of a U.S. Housing Bubble

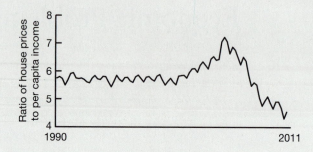

(supply, demand, people's incomes, and so on). At some point, market sentiment turns, and people worry that prices are no longer going to rise but are likely to fall. They start to sell. Panic sets in and the vast majority of investors try to unload their assets. For those who borrowed the money to invest, the depressed value of the assets is often less than the value of the loan. For some investors, this can mean bankruptcy.

The U.S. housing bubble of the 2000s was a classic case in point. A lot of families were caught up in the euphoria, expecting that house prices would rise forever. Many people who had never owned a home before became homeowners. Banks and other financial institutions relaxed their lending standards so that individuals who previously were denied mortgages were able to qualify. House prices rose so much that the value of the average American home relative to the average American income was at historic highs—and ultimately unsustainable (see Figure 1).

When the U.S. housing bubble finally burst, millions of new homeowners were "under water"; the value of their homes was less than the value of their mortgages. Many of these homeowners walked away from their homes, leaving hundreds of thousands of homes standing empty.

Why did this happen? There is plenty of blame to go around. Some fault the Federal Reserve for keeping interest rates "too low for too long." Others point the finger at the U.S. Congress for passing legislation that made it easier for Americans to own homes. Yet others accuse the banks for irresponsible lending practices. Unfortunately, part of the problem is human nature. It is very easy for even ordinary people to get caught up in a bubble mentality.

Economics has a lot to say about what kinds of policies can minimize the risk of financial crises and what kinds of policies can limit the economic damage from financial crises. It is important to point out, though, that on these important topics there is disagreement among economists.

Unemployment and Inflation

Unemployment

There can be large fluctuations in economic activity and also in **unemployment**. In periods when output has fallen, thousands, even millions, of people have been thrown out of work. In the Great Depression of the 1930s, for example, nearly 25 percent of the labor force was unemployed (see Figure 2).

Our second example of an economic problem is this: *What determines the extent of unemployment in the U.S. economy, and what can be done to reduce it?* This problem is complicated by a related phenomenon: The level of prices may

Inflation

rise when we reduce the level of unemployment. In other words, **inflation** may occur. Therefore, the problem is not only to curb unemployment but to do it without producing an inflation so ruinous to the nation's economic health that the cure proves more dangerous than the ailment. Consequently, another question we must ask is this: *What determines the rate of inflation, and how can it be kept under control?* As Figure 3 shows, we have experienced considerable inflation since 1930; the dollar has lost over 90 percent of its purchasing power during the past 85 years. Moreover, in the 1970s and early 1980s, our economy was bedeviled by "stagflation"—a combination of high unemployment and high inflation. While inflation does not seem to be the most pressing economic issue in the second decade of the twenty-first century, it remains a problem in many parts of the world and could, depending on the circumstances, become an economic challenge in the future.

FIGURE 2

Unemployment Rates, United States, 1930–2012

The unemployment rate has varied substantially from year to year. In the Great Depression, it reached a high of over 24 percent. In 2000, it hit a low of 3.8 percent.

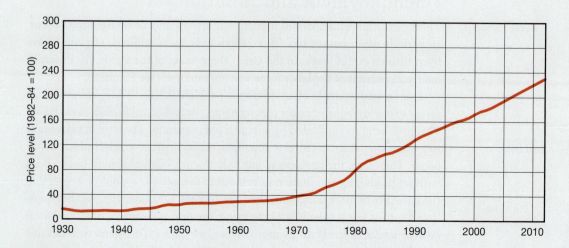

FIGURE 3

Changes in Price Level, United States, 1930–2012

The price level has increased steadily since the 1930s and is now almost ten times higher than it was in 1950.

During the past six decades, economists have learned a great deal about the factors that determine the extent of unemployment and inflation. As a responsible citizen, you need to understand what has been learned. But you also need to be aware of the differences of opinion among leading economists on this score. To understand many of the political issues of the day and vote intelligently, you need to be equipped with this knowledge. And to understand the fallacies in many apparently simple remedies for the complex problems in this area, you need to know some economics.

Labor Productivity and Rising Standard of Living

Believe it or not, the history of the U.S. economy is for the most part a story of growth, not business cycles. Our output—the amount of goods and services we produce annually—has grown rapidly over the years, giving us a standard of living that could not have been imagined a century ago. For example, the output per person in the United States was about $48,000 in 2011; in 1900, it was much, much smaller—about one-tenth as big, after adjusting for inflation. The rise in our standard of living is closely correlated with how productive we are.

Labor productivity is defined as the amount of output that can be obtained per hour of labor. All countries are interested in increasing labor productivity, since it is intimately related to a country's standard of living. Many factors, including new technologies like the Internet and biotechnology, influence the rate of increase of labor productivity. Historically, labor productivity has increased relatively rapidly in the United States.

However, beginning in the late 1960s, U.S. labor productivity rose at a slower pace. At first, it was unclear whether this slowdown was only temporary, but during the 1970s, the situation got worse, not better. Between 1977 and 1980, labor productivity in the United States actually declined. (In other words, less was produced per hour of labor in 1980 than in 1977!) During the 1980s and early 1990s, productivity growth picked up but was still slower than it was in the 1960s.

In the 1970s, 1980s, and early 1990s, many observers worried about the poor productivity performance of the United States relative to other industrialized countries, especially Japan and Germany. There was much talk of a "competitiveness problem" in the United States. However, by the late 1990s, productivity growth was strong again, thanks, in part, to large investments in information technologies earlier in the decade and the explosive growth of the Internet. During the 2000s, productivity growth remained strong and continued to do so through the Great Recession.

Our third example of an economic problem is this: *What determines the rate of increase of labor productivity? Why did productivity growth slow down in the 1970s and 1980s? Why did it accelerate in the 1990s? What can be done to sustain high growth rates of productivity?* Economics provides a considerable amount of information on this score. Not only does economics tell us a good deal about the broad factors influencing national productivity levels; it also provides rules and principles that are useful in increasing the productivity and efficiency of individual firms and government agencies.

Challenges Facing Emerging Market Economies

In 1900, per capita income in the United States was about 10 times greater than that of the poorest country, after adjusting for differences in purchasing power. By 2011, that gap had widened so that the typical American earned over 100 times as much as the typical Ethiopian. Nevertheless, some emerging market economies, notably those in East Asia, made significant strides in closing the gap. In 2011, Singapore and Hong Kong's per capita income levels were, respectively, 88 and 77 percent of the U.S. level. Other emerging markets, such as Chile and Mexico, have also succeeded in closing the gap in the past 30 years.

Unfortunately, even for those countries that have been successful in engineering rapid improvements in living standards, the path has been a very bumpy one. Latin America suffered through a debt crisis in the early 1980s. In 1994 and 1995, Mexico suffered through its worst recession in 50 years, triggered by a currency crisis. Between 1997 and 2002, many of the East Asian economies, Russia, Brazil, and Argentina were dragged down by financial crises. In 2013, a milder financial panic engulfed emerging markets such as India, Indonesia, and South Africa.

Our fourth example of an economic problem is this: *Why do some countries grow much faster than others? Why has the economic growth rate in emerging markets been so volatile in recent years? What can be done to improve living standards worldwide?* In recent years, economic research has highlighted the value of high levels of educational attainment and national savings (to fund investments in productivity capacity) as key determinants of growth. Just as crucial are free trade and unencumbered access to global capital. The recent emerging market crises have also underlined the importance of stable macroeconomic policies, well-regulated banking systems, and the rule of law, especially the enforcement of property rights.

Eliminating Poverty

As pointed out by Philip Wicksteed, a prominent twentieth-century British economist, "A man can be neither a saint, nor a lover, nor a poet, unless he has comparatively recently had something to eat."[1] Although relatively few people in the United States lack food desperately, about 45 million—approximately

Poverty

15 percent of the population—live in what is officially designated as **poverty**. These people have frequently been called *invisible* in a nation where the average yearly income per family is about $60,000; but the poor are invisible only to those who shut their eyes, since they exist in ghettos in the wealthiest U.S. cities, like New York, Chicago, and Los Angeles, as well as in thousands of small towns. They can also be found in areas where industry has come and gone, as in the former coal-mining towns of Pennsylvania and West Virginia, and in areas where decades of farming have depleted the soil.

Table 1 shows the distribution of income in the United States in 2009. Clearly, income levels differ very substantially among families. Indeed, the cats and dogs of the very rich eat better than some human beings. You, as a citizen and human being, need to understand the social mechanisms underlying the distribution of income, both in the United States and in other countries, and judge how reasonable and just they are.

Our fifth example of an economic problem is this: *Why does poverty exist in the world today, and what can be done to abolish it?* To help the poor effectively, we must understand the causes of poverty.

---

[1] Philip H. Wicksteed, *The Common Sense of Political Economy* (London: Macmillan, 1910).

TABLE 1	Money Income (dollars)	Percent of All Households*
Percentage Distribution of Households, by Annual Money Income, United States, 2009	Under 15,000	9
	15,000–24,999	9
	25,000–34,999	10
	35,000–49,999	14
	50,000–74,999	19
	75,000–99,999	13
	100,000 and over	26
	Total	100

Source: U.S. Bureau of the Census, 2011.

*This represents the percent of total income that each income group receives.

Looking Ahead

Despite the problems described here, the U.S. economy is among the most prosperous in the world. The average U.S. family has plenty of food, clothing, housing, appliances, and luxuries of many kinds; and the average U.S. worker is well educated and well trained. The tremendous strength and vitality of the U.S. economy should be recognized, as well as its shortcomings. Nothing is gained by overlooking either the strengths or the weaknesses of our system.

As a first step toward understanding why we are so well-off in some respects and so lacking in others, we need to understand how our economy works. Of course, this is a big task. Indeed, you could say that this whole book is devoted to discussing the subject. So, we do not try to present a detailed picture of the operation of the U.S. economy at this point. Instead, in the following chapters, we will give a basic blueprint of what an economic system must do.

What Is Economics?

LEARNING OBJECTIVES

➤ To define economics and explain the concepts of resources, scarcity, and choice

➤ To identify the four basic tasks that must be accomplished by any economic system

➤ To understand the concept of opportunity cost

➤ (Exploring Further) To explain what a production possibilities curve shows and why the curve is important

A political battle has raged for years over the extent to which our natural resources should be commercially exploited. Why did Congress in 1980 ban the exploitation of over 100 million acres of Alaskan wilderness? Why in 2011 did President Obama delay the building of a pipeline to bring Canadian oil into the United States? One purpose of this chapter is to answer questions like these.

In this chapter, we will define economics, identify the basic questions that economists ask about any economic system, and explain the basic methodology of economics.

What Is Economics?

Economics

According to one standard definition, **economics** is the study of how resources are allocated among alternative uses to satisfy human wants. This definition is fine, but it does not mean much unless we also define human wants and resources. What do these terms mean?

Human wants

Human wants are the things, services, goods, and circumstances people desire. Wants vary greatly among individuals and over time for the same individual. Some people like sports, and others like books; some want to travel, and others want to putter in the yard. An individual's desire for a particular good during a particular period of time is not infinite, but in the aggregate, human wants seem to be insatiable. In addition to the basic desires for food, shelter, and clothing, which must be fulfilled to some extent if the human organism is to survive, wants stem from cultural factors. For example, society, often helped along by advertising and other devices to modify tastes, promotes certain images of the good life, which frequently entail owning an expensive car and living in a million-dollar house in the suburbs.

Resources
Economic
resources
Free
resources

Resources are the things or services used to produce goods, which then can be used to satisfy wants. **Economic resources** are scarce; **free resources**, such as air, are so abundant they can be obtained without charge. The test of whether a resource is an economic resource or a free resource is price: Economic resources command a price; free resources do not. The number of free resources is quite limited. For instance, although the earth contains a huge amount of water, water is not a free resource for typical urban or suburban homeowners, who must pay a local water authority for providing and maintaining their water supply. In a world where all resources were free, there would be no economic problems, since all wants could be satisfied.

Economic resources can be classified into three categories:

1. *Land.* A shorthand expression for natural resources, land includes minerals as well as plots of ground. Clearly, land is an important and valuable resource in both agriculture and industry. Think of the fertile soil of Iowa or Kansas, which produces such abundant crops. Or consider Manhattan Island, which supports the skyscrapers, shops, and theaters in the heart of New York. In addition, land is an important part of our environment, and it provides enjoyment above and beyond its contribution to agricultural and industrial output.

2. *Labor.* Human efforts, both physical and mental, are included in the category of labor. When you study for a final examination or make out an income tax return, this is as much labor as if you were digging a ditch. In 2013, over 155 million people were employed (or looking for work) in the United States. This vast labor supply is, of course, an extremely important resource, without which our nation could not maintain its current output level.

3. *Capital.* All the buildings, equipment, inventories, and other nonhuman producible resources that contribute to the production, marketing, and distribution of goods and services fall within the economist's definition of capital. Examples are machine tools and warehouses. But not all types of capital are big or bulky; for example, an iPad, or a pen for that matter, is a type of capital. Workers in the United States have an enormous amount of capital to work with. Think of the oil refineries in New Jersey and Texas, the electronics factories near Boston and San Francisco, the aircraft plants in California, and the host of additional types of capital that we have in this country. Without this capital, the nation's output level would be a great deal less than it is.

Technology and Choice

As already pointed out, economics is concerned with the way resources are allocated among alternative uses to satisfy human wants. An important determinant of the extent to which human wants can be satisfied from the amount of resources at hand is technology. **Technology** is society's pool of knowledge concerning the industrial arts. It draws on the knowledge of engineers, scientists, artisans, managers, and others concerning how goods and services can be produced and includes, for example, the best ways to design and operate an automobile plant. The level of technology sets limits on the amounts and types of goods and services that can be derived from a given amount of resources.

Technology

Suppose, for example, that engineers do not know how to produce an automobile using less than 500 hours of labor in its manufacture. Clearly, this sets limits on the number of automobiles that can be produced with the available labor force. Or suppose that scientists and engineers do not know how to produce a ton of steel using less than a certain amount of capital in its manufacture. This sets limits on the amount of steel that can be produced with the available quantity of capital.

Given the existing technology and the scarcity of resources, only a limited amount of goods and services can be produced. In other words, the capacity to produce goods and services is limited—*far more limited than human wants.* Hence, the necessity for choice arises. Somehow or other, a choice must be made as to how the available resources are used (or if they will be used at all). And somehow or other, a choice must be made as to how the output produced from these resources is distributed among the population.

Economics is concerned with how such choices and tradeoffs are made. Economists spend a great deal of time, energy, and talent trying to determine how such choices *are* made in various circumstances and how they *should* be made. Indeed, as we will see in the next section, the basic questions that economics deals with are problems of choice—at the individual (household and business) level and at the national level.

Central Questions in Economics

Economists are particularly concerned with four basic questions regarding the working of any economic system, ours or any other:

1. What determines what and how much is produced?
2. What determines how it is produced?
3. What determines how the society's output is distributed among the members?
4. What determines the rate at which the society's per capita income will grow?

These questions lie at the core of economics because they are directed at the most fundamental characteristics of economic systems. And as stressed in the previous section, they are problems of choice.

To illustrate the nature and significance of these questions, suppose that, because of war or natural catastrophe, your town is isolated from the adjoining territory. No longer is it possible for the town's inhabitants to leave or for people or goods to enter. (Lest you regard this as fanciful, it is worth noting that during Hurricane Katrina in 2005, the city of New Orleans was cut off from the rest of the country for many days.) In this situation, you and your fellow townspeople must somehow resolve each of the four questions. You must decide what goods and services are produced, how each is produced, who receives what, and how much provision is made for increased output in the future.

In a situation of this sort, your very survival depends on how effectively you answer these questions. If a decision is made to produce too much clothing and too little food, some townspeople may starve. If a decision is made to allot practically all the town's output to friends and political cronies of the mayor, those who oppose the mayor may have a very rough time. And if a decision is made to eat, drink, and be merry today and not worry about tomorrow, life may be very meager in the days ahead.

Because we are considering a relatively small and isolated population, the importance of these questions may seem more obvious than in a huge country like the United States, which is constantly communicating, trading, and interacting with the rest of the world. But the truth is that these questions are every bit as important to the United States as to the isolated town. And for this reason, it is important that we understand how these decisions are made and whether they are being made effectively. Just as in the hypothetical case of the isolated town, your survival depends on these decisions; but in the United States, the situation is not hypothetical!

Opportunity Cost: A Fundamental Concept

We have previously emphasized that economics is concerned with the way resources are allocated among alternative uses to satisfy human wants. To help determine how resources should be allocated, economists often use the concept of opportunity cost. We turn now to a brief discussion of this concept.

Because a specific case is more interesting than abstract discussion, we return to the case of the town isolated from the adjoining territory because of war or natural catastrophe. Suppose you are a member of the town council that is organized to determine how the town's resources should be utilized. To keep things simple, suppose that only two goods—food and clothing—can be produced. (This is an innocuous assumption that allows us to strip the problem to its essentials.) You must somehow figure out how much of each good should be produced. How can you go about solving this problem?

CASE STUDY 1.1

LAND USE IN ALASKA

In November 1980, the Alaska National Interest Lands Conservation Act declared more than 100 million acres of Alaskan wilderness off-limits to extensive mining and resource exploitation. Interior Secretary Cecil Andrus and Arizona senator Morris Udall supported the bill, but Alaskan representatives, including Senator Mike Gravel, sought to have the federally owned lands opened for development.

The bill was the culmination of the environmental battle that started when the conservationists inserted conditions for the preservation of the wilderness in the 1958 Alaska Statehood Act. Environmentalists believed that the value of the land as wilderness—the preservation of the habitat of many plant and animal species and the use of the land by backpackers—greatly exceeded the potential value of its soil or minerals. Those who sought to postpone the act, including the majority of people in Alaska, argued that the value of the land for mining or logging should be assessed first. They argued in particular that the potential oil reserves should be estimated in light of the then-recent doubling in the price of oil caused by the 1979 oil shortage. It would be foolhardy, they said, to reduce artificially the amount of oil available for domestic consumption when the dependence of the United States on foreign oil caused so much harm in terms of inflation and unemployment.

The vote in Congress implicitly maintained that the benefit of keeping the land as wilderness was greater than that of any alternative use. The bill that President Jimmy Carter signed into law sought to "protect the resources of Alaska's crown jewels in perpetuity as national parks, wildlife refuges, forests and wild and scenic rivers." Put in the language of this chapter, the opportunity cost of keeping the land as wilderness was regarded as less than the benefits of doing so.

However, in 1991, President George H. W. Bush proposed opening for oil exploration the 1.5-million-acre coastal plain of the Arctic National Wildlife Refuge in Alaska. The proposal included many restrictions and regulations to protect animals and their environment in the refuge, but environmentalists argued that oil drilling should not occur there. Obviously, President Bush felt that the opportunity cost of keeping this land as wilderness was greater than the benefits of doing so. The environmentalists disagreed. Arguments of this sort between developers and environmentalists have continued into the twenty-first century and are an important illustration of the role of opportunity costs in discussions of public policy.

Clearly, the first step toward a solution is to list the various resources contained within the town. Using the technology available to the townspeople, each of these resources can be used to produce either food or clothing. Some of these resources are much more effective at producing one good than the other. For example, a tailor probably is better able to produce clothing than food. Nonetheless, most resources can be adapted to produce either good. For example, a tailor can be put to work on a farm, even though he or she may not be very good at farming.

After listing the various available resources and having determined how effective each is at producing food or clothing, the next step is to see how much food the town could produce per year if it produced nothing but food and how much clothing it could produce per year if it produced nothing but clothing. Also, you should determine the maximum amount of clothing that the town can produce per year when various amounts of food are produced per year. For example, if the town produces 100 tons of food per year, what is the maximum amount of clothing it can produce per year? If the town produces 200 tons of food per year, what is the maximum amount of clothing it can produce per year? And so on.

Having carried out this step, suppose that the results are as shown in Table 1.1. According to this table, the town can produce (at most) 200 tons of clothing per year if it produces nothing but clothing (possibility *A*). Or it can produce (at most) 400 tons of food per year if it produces nothing but food (possibility *E*). Other possible combinations (labeled *B*, *C*, and *D*) of food output and clothing output are specified in Table 1.1.

Table 1.1 puts in bold relief the basic problem of choice facing you and the other members of the town council. Because the town's resources are limited,

TABLE 1.1 **Combinations of Output of Food and Clothing That the Town Can Produce per Year**	Possibility	Amount of Food Produced per Year (tons)	Amount of Clothing Produced per Year (tons)
	A	0	200
	B	100	180
	C	200	150
	D	300	100
	E	400	0

the town can produce only limited amounts of each good. There is no way, for example, that the town can produce 200 tons of clothing per year and 200 tons of food per year. This is beyond the capacity of the town's resources. If the town wants to produce 200 tons of clothing, it can produce no food—hardly a pleasant prospect. And if the town wants to produce 200 tons of food per year, it can produce 150 (not 200) tons of clothing per year. Table 1.1 shows which combinations of food and clothing outputs are attainable.

More Food Means Less Clothing

A very important fact illustrated by Table 1.1 is that whenever the town increases its production of one good, it must cut back its production of the other good. For example, if the town increases its production of food from 100 to 200 tons per year, it must cut back its production of clothing from 180 to 150 tons per year. Therefore, the cost to the town of increasing its food output from 100 to 200 tons per year is that it must reduce its clothing output from 180 to 150 tons per year. Economists refer to this cost as the **opportunity cost** (or **alternative cost**); it is one of the most fundamental concepts in economics. The opportunity cost of using resources in a certain way is the value of what these resources could have produced had they been used in the best alternative way. In this case, the opportunity cost of the extra 100 tons of food per year is the 30 tons of clothing per year that must be forgone. This is what the town must give up to get the extra 100 tons of food.

Opportunity cost

Alternative cost

Why is opportunity cost so important? For you and the other members of the town council to determine which combination of food and clothing is best, you need to compare the value of increases in food output with the opportunity costs of such increases. For example, suppose the town council is considering whether to increase food output from 100 tons per year to 200 tons per year. To decide this question, the council should compare the value of the extra 100 tons of food with the opportunity cost of the extra food (which is the 30 tons of clothing that must be given up). If the town council feels that the extra 100 tons of food is worth more to the town's welfare than the 30 tons of clothing given up, then the extra food should be produced. Otherwise it should not be produced.

The concept of opportunity cost is just as important at an individual level. When you choose to do one activity, that choice prevents you from doing something else during that same time and with the money you are spending on that activity. If you go to a football game, you won't be able to go to dinner and a movie. So the opportunity cost of the football game is not going to dinner and a movie. Or if you choose to be a lawyer, you cannot also choose to be a doctor (or at least most people can't). The point is that for every choice you make, there are opportunity costs and tradeoffs. The key to having a fulfilling life is to be able to make well-informed, well-thought-out, and deliberate decisions that take into account these opportunity costs and tradeoffs.

The Impact of Economics on Society

Economics has influenced generations of political leaders, philosophers, and ordinary citizens and has played a significant role in shaping our society today. Skim through the articles in a daily newspaper. Chances are you will find a report of an economist testifying before Congress, perhaps on the costs and benefits of a program to reduce unemployment among minority teenagers in the Bedford-Stuyvesant area of New York City or on the steps to be taken to make U.S. goods more competitive with those of Japan, Germany, or China. Still another economist may appear on the editorial page, perhaps discussing the pros and cons of various proposals for reducing the federal deficit or advising how to prevent the next financial crisis.

Economics plays a key role at the highest levels of our government. The president, whether a Democrat or a Republican, relies heavily on economic advisers in making the decisions that help shape the future of the country. In Congress, too, economics plays a major role. Economists are frequent witnesses before congressional committees, staff members for the committees, and advisers to individual members of Congress. Many congressional committees focus largely on economic matters, and members of Congress spend large chunks of their time wrestling with budgetary and tax questions.

Economic theories are not abstract constructs that only see the light of day in the halls of academia. Rather, they are often formulated in response to pressing social problems and get tested via economic policies soon after they are formulated.

Positive Economics versus Normative Economics

Positive economics

From the outset, it is essential to distinguish between positive economics (what is) and normative economics (what should be). **Positive economics** contains descriptive statements, propositions, and predictions about the world. For instance, an economic theory may predict that increasing the amount of money in circulation will lead to inflation. Positive economics tells us only what will happen under certain circumstances. It says nothing about whether the results are good or bad or what we should do. **Norma-**

Normative economics

tive economics, on the other hand, makes statements about what ought to be or what a person, organization, or nation ought to do. An example of normative economics is the conviction that the federal government should end poverty.

Clearly, positive economics and normative economics must be treated differently. Positive economics is science in the ordinary sense of the word. Propositions in positive economics can be tested by comparisons with facts. In a nonexperimental science like economics, it is sometimes difficult to get the facts you need to test particular propositions. For example, if the income per

ELIMINATING BROWN LUNG DISEASE

Perhaps as many as 150,000 Americans suffer from brown lung disease. The disease is brought on by inhaling the particles of cotton dust and fiber that are a by-product of textile manufacturing. Growing public awareness of brown lung disease was a prime force behind the passage of the Occupational Safety and Health Act in 1970. But over the next decade, as competition increased and profits shrank, managers, workers, and the government wrestled with the question, How much more should we spend to protect our workforce? This question involves *normative economics*, and the answer you get depends on your values or preferences.

Throughout the 1970s, the U.S. textile industry was locked in a fierce struggle against foreign competition. Asian competitors were undercutting U.S. mills. The U.S. textile industry was spending millions to protect workers' health. The Asian textile industries spent almost nothing. Faced with this competition, the U.S. industry looked for ways to cut costs. Then along came the Occupational Safety and Health Administration (OSHA), telling business that it had to spend more money, not less.

Indeed, OSHA proposed tough new standards for cotton dust in the mills. The industry claimed that the new regulations would require it to spend $2 billion on new equipment and that it could achieve almost the same result by spending $1.49 per worker on dust masks. The Amalgamated Clothing and Textile Workers Union disagreed. Workers still died from brown lung disease, and dust masks would not eliminate the risk. The union argued fiercely for the tougher standards, but many in Washington sided with the industry.

The textile industry sued OSHA, arguing that the new regulations would impose a relatively high cost to protect a relatively small number of lives. They argued that eliminating all risk of brown lung disease would destroy the ability of the industry to survive against overseas competition and that the most effective dollars had already been spent. Late in 1980, the Supreme Court heard arguments from both sides. In June 1981, the Court agreed with the union that Congress had intended the question of worker health to be considered first, above all other considerations of cost.

By 1985, most U.S. textile companies had installed the new equipment to meet the cotton dust regulations. Brown lung disease had virtually disappeared, but so had 300,000 jobs in the textile mills. Many in the industry argued that regulations of this sort were to blame.

person in the United States does not rise by 10 percent, it may be difficult to tell what the effect of such an increase would be on the price of copper. Moreover, even if per capita income does increase by this amount, it may be difficult to separate the effect of the increase in income per person on the price of copper from the effects of other factors. Nonetheless, we can, in principle, test propositions in positive economics by an appeal to the facts.

In normative economics, however, this is not the case. In normative economics, the results you get depend on your values or preferences. For example, if you believe that reducing unemployment is more important than maintaining the purchasing power of the dollar, you will get one answer to certain questions; if you believe that maintaining the purchasing power of the dollar is more important than reducing unemployment, you are likely to get a different answer to the same questions. This is not at all strange. After all, if people desire different things (which is another way of saying that they have different values), they may well make different decisions and advocate different policies. It would be strange if they did not.

The Methodology of Economics

Model Building in Economics

Model

Like other types of scientific analysis, economics is based on the formulation of models. A **model** is a theoretical framework. It is composed of a number of assumptions from which conclusions—or predictions—are deduced. An astronomer who wants to formulate a model of the solar system might represent each planet by a point in space and assume that each would change position in accord with certain mathematical equations. On the basis of this model, the astronomer might predict when an eclipse would occur or estimate the probability of a planetary collision. Economists proceed along similar lines when they set forth a model of economic behavior.

Several important points concerning models should be noted:

1. *To be useful, a model must simplify the real situation.* The assumptions made by a model do not need to be exact replicas of reality. If they were, the model would be too complicated to use. The basic reason for using a model is that the real world is so complex that masses of detail often obscure underlying patterns. The economist faces the familiar problem of seeing the forest as distinct from just the trees. Other scientists must do the same; physicists work with simplified models of atoms, just as economists work with simplified models of markets. However, this does not mean that *all* models are good or useful. A model may be so oversimplified and distorted that it is utterly useless. The trick is to construct a model so that irrelevant and unimportant considerations and variables are neglected, but the major factors—those that seriously affect the phenomena the model is designed to predict—are included.

2. *The purpose of a model is to make predictions about the real world; in many respects, the most important test of a model is how well it predicts.* A model that predicts the price of copper within plus or minus 1 cent a pound

is better than a model that predicts it within plus or minus 2 cents a pound. Of course, this does not mean that a model is useless if it cannot predict very accurately. We do not always need a very accurate prediction. For example, a road map is a model that can be used to make predictions about the route a driver should take to get to a particular destination. Sometimes, a very crude map is good enough to get you where you want to go, but such a map would not, for instance, serve hikers who need to know the characteristics of the terrain through which they plan to walk. How detailed a map you need depends on where you are going and how you want to get there.

3. *To predict the outcome of a particular event requires the use of the model that predicts best, even if that model does not predict very well.* The choice is not between a model and no model; it is between one model and another. After all, a person who must make a forecast uses the most accurate device available, and any such device is a model of some sort. Consequently, when economists make simplifying assumptions and derive conclusions that are only approximately true, it is somewhat beside the point to complain that the assumptions are simpler than reality or that the predictions are not always accurate. This may be true, but if the predictions based on the economists' model are better than those based on other models, their model must and will be used until something better comes along. Thus, if a model can predict the price of copper to within plus or minus 1 cent per pound and no other model can do better, this model will be used even if those interested in the predictions bewail the model's limitations and wish it could be improved.

Economic Measurement

To utilize and test their models, economists need facts of many sorts. For example, suppose that an economist constructs a model that predicts that a household's annual clothing expenditure tends to increase by $60 when its income increases by $1,000. To see whether this model is correct, the economist must gather data concerning the incomes and clothing expenditures of a large number of households and study the relationship between them. Suppose that the relationship proves to be as shown in Figure 1.1. The line represents an average relationship between household income and household clothing expenditure. Judging by Figure 1.1, the model is reasonably accurate, at least for households with incomes between $30,000 and $60,000 per year.[1]

Measurements like those in Figure 1.1 enable economists to *quantify* their models; in other words, they enable them to construct models that predict *how much* effect one variable has on another. If economists did not quantify their models, they (and their models) would be much less useful. For example, the economist in the

---

[1] Although it is useful to see how well a model would have fit the historical facts, this is no substitute for seeing how well it will predict the future. According to one old saying, "It's a darned poor person who can't predict the past."

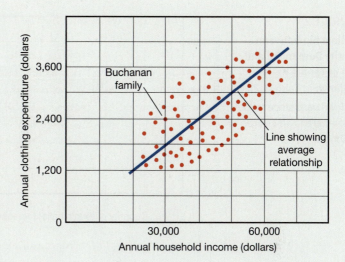

FIGURE 1.1

Relationship between Annual Clothing Expenditures and Annual Household Income

Each family is represented by a dot. The line does not fit all families exactly, since all the points do not fall on it. The line does, however, show average clothing expenditure for each income level.

previous paragraph might have been content with a model that predicts that higher household income results in higher household clothing expenditure, but this model would not have been interesting or useful, since you do not need an economist to tell you that. A more valuable model is one that is quantitative, that predicts how much clothing expenditure would increase if household income rises by a certain amount. This is the sort of model that economists usually try to construct.

Graphs and Relationships

Graphs can be a convenient way of illustrating or validating economic models. In particular, visualizing the relationship between various economic variables (for example, income and spending) can be extremely useful. We conclude our brief discussion of economic methodology with the basics of constructing and interpreting graphs:

1. A graph has a horizontal axis and a vertical axis, each with a scale of numerical values. For example, in Figure 1.1, the horizontal axis shows a household's annual income, and the vertical axis shows the annual amount spent by the household on clothing. The intersection of the two axes is called the *origin* and is the point where both the variable measured along the horizontal axis and the variable measured along the vertical axis are zero. In Figure 1.1, the origin is at the lower left-hand corner of the figure, labeled 0.

2. To show the relationship between two variables, we can plot the value of one variable against the value of the other variable. In Figure 1.1, each family is represented by a dot. For example, the dot for the Buchanan family is in the

FIGURE 1.2

Relationship between Quantity Demanded and Price of Tennis Balls (as Shown in Table 1.2)

The downward slope tells us that there is an inverse relationship.

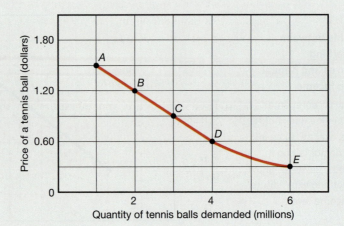

position shown in Figure 1.1 because its income was $30,000 and its clothing expenditure was $2,400. Clearly, the line showing the average relationship does not fit all the families exactly, since all the points do not fall on the line. This line does, however, give the average clothing expenditure for each level of income: it shows the average relationship.

3. The relationship between two variables is *direct* if, as in Figure 1.1, the line of average relationship slopes upward. In other words, if the variable measured along the vertical axis tends to increase in response to increases in the variable measured along the horizontal axis, the relationship is direct. On the other hand, if the line of the average relationship slopes downward, as in Figure 1.2, the relationship is *inverse*. In other words, if the variable measured along the vertical axis tends to decrease in response to increases in the variable measured along the horizontal axis, the relationship is inverse.

To illustrate how to graph a relationship between two variables, consider Table 1.2, which shows the quantity of tennis balls demanded in a particular

TABLE 1.2

Quantity of Tennis Balls Demanded at Various Prices

Price of Tennis Ball (dollars)	Quality of Tennis Balls Demanded (millions)
1.50	1
1.20	2
0.90	3
0.60	4
0.30	6

market at various prices. Putting price on the vertical axis and quantity demanded on the horizontal axis, we can plot each combination of price and quantity in this table as a point on a graph, which is precisely what has been done in Figure 1.2 (points A to E).

The Tasks of an Economic System

Having discussed the nature and quantification of economic models, we conclude by describing what an economic system must do. Basically, as we saw earlier in this chapter, any economic system must perform four tasks:

1. *An economic system must determine the level and composition of society's output.* That is, it must answer questions like these: To what extent should society's resources be used to produce new aircraft carriers and missiles? To what extent should they be used to produce sewage plants to reduce water pollution? To what extent should they be used to produce swimming pools for the rich? To what extent should they be used to produce low-cost housing for the poor? Pause for a moment to think about how important—and how vast—this function is. Most people simply take for granted that somehow it is decided what we as a society are going to produce, and too few people think about the social mechanisms that determine the answers to such questions.

2. *An economic system must determine how each good and service is to be produced.* Given existing technology, a society's resources can be used in various ways. Should the skilled labor in Birmingham, Alabama, be used to produce cotton or steel? Should a particular machine tool be used to produce aircraft or automobiles? The way questions of this sort are answered determines the way each good and service is produced. In other words, it determines which resources are used to produce which goods and services. If this function is performed badly, society's resources are put to the wrong use; this results in less output than if this function is performed well.

3. *An economic system must determine how the goods and services produced are to be distributed among the members of society.* In other words, how much of each type of good and service should each person receive? Should there be a considerable amount of income inequality, the rich receiving much more than the poor? Or should income be relatively equal? In a market-based economic system, your income depends on your skills, the property you own, how hard you work, and prevailing prices. This function of the economic system has generated and will continue to generate heated controversy—as evidenced by the Occupy Wall Street movement in 2011. Some people favor a relatively egalitarian society, where the amount received by one family varies little from that received by another family of the same size. Other people favor a society where the amount a family or person receives can vary a great deal. Few people favor a thoroughly egalitarian society, if for no other reason than that

ADAM SMITH, FATHER OF MODERN ECONOMICS

To illustrate the importance of economic ideas, consider some of the precepts of Adam Smith (1723–1790), the man often called the father of modern economics. Much of his masterpiece, *The Wealth of Nations*, seems trite today because it has been absorbed so thoroughly into modern thought, but it was not trite when it was written in 1776. On the contrary, Smith's ideas were revolutionary. He was among the first to describe how a free, competitive economy can function—without central planning or government interference—to allocate resources efficiently. He recognized the virtues of the "invisible hand" that leads the private interest of firms and individuals toward socially desirable ends; and he was properly suspicious of firms sheltered from competition, since he recognized the potentially undesirable effects on resource allocation.

Adam Smith

In addition, Smith, with the dire poverty of his times staring him in the face, was interested in the forces that drive the economy—the forces that determine the rate of growth of the average income per person. Although Smith did not approve of avarice, he believed that saving is good because it enables society to invest in machinery and other forms of capital. Accumulating more and more capital would, according to Smith, allow output to grow. In addition, he emphasized the importance of increased specialization and division of labor in fostering economic progress. By specializing, people can concentrate on the tasks they do best, with the result that society's total output is raised.

All in all, Smith's views were relatively optimistic. Leave markets alone, said Smith, and beware of firms with too much economic power and government meddling. If this is done, Smith argued, there is no reason why considerable economic progress cannot be achieved. Smith's work has been modified and extended in a variety of ways over the last two centuries. Some of his ideas have been challenged and in some cases discarded. But his influence on modern society has been enormous.

some differences in income are required to stimulate workers to do certain types of work.

4. *An economic system must determine the rate of growth of per capita income.* An adequate growth rate has come to be regarded as an important economic goal, particularly in the developing countries of Africa, Asia, and Latin America. There is very strong pressure in these countries for changes in technology, the adoption of superior techniques, increases in the stock of capital resources, and better and more extensive education and training of the labor force. These are viewed as some of the major ways to promote the growth of per capita income.

EXPLORING FURTHER[2]

A Simple Introductory Model of the Economic System

The Production Possibilities Curve: Determining What Is Produced

Earlier we said that economists use models to throw light on economic problems. At this point, we try our hand at constructing a simple model to illuminate the basic functions any economic system, ours included, must perform. To keep things simple, suppose that society produces only two goods, food and tractors. This, of course, is unrealistic, but as we stressed previously, a model does not have to be realistic to be useful. Here, by assuming that there are only two goods, we eliminate a lot of unnecessary complexity and lay bare the essentials. In addition, we suppose that society has at its disposal a certain amount of resources and that this amount is fixed for the duration of the period in question. This assumption is quite realistic. So long as the period is relatively short, the amount of a society's resources is relatively fixed (except, of course, under unusual circumstances—if a country annexes additional land, for example).[3] Finally, suppose as well that society's technology is fixed. So long as the period is relatively short, this assumption, too, is realistic.

Under these circumstances, it is possible to figure out the various amounts of food and tractors that society can produce. Specifically, we can proceed as we did at the beginning of this chapter when we determined the amounts of food and clothing that an isolated town could produce. We begin with how many tractors society can produce if all resources are devoted to tractor production. According to Table 1.3, the answer is 15 million tractors. Next, we consider the opposite extreme, where society devotes all its resources to food production. According to Table 1.3, it can produce 12 million tons of food in this case. Next, we consider cases where both products are being produced. Such cases are represented by

---

[2] Exploring Further sections are optional.
[3] For example, in 1990, Iraq tried to take over Kuwait but was driven out by the United States and its allies.

TABLE 1.3

Alternative Combinations of Outputs of Food and Tractors That Can Be Produced

Possibility	Food (millions of tons)	Tractors (millions)
A	0	15
B	2	14
C	4	12
D	6	10
E	8	7
F	10	4
G	12	0

possibilities *B* to *F* in the table. As emphasized earlier in this chapter, the more of one good that is produced, the less of the other good that can be produced. Why? Because to produce more of one good, resources must be taken away from the production of the other good; this lessens the amount of the other good produced.

Figure 1.3 shows how we can use a graph to show the various production possibilities society can attain. It is merely a different way of presenting the data in Table 1.3. The output of food is plotted on the horizontal axis and the output of tractors on the vertical axis. The curve in Figure 1.3, which shows the various combinations of output of food and tractors that society can produce, is called the **production possibilities curve**.

The production possibilities curve sheds considerable light on the economic tasks facing any society. It shows the various production possibilities open to

Production possibilities curve

FIGURE 1.3

Production Possibilities Curve

This curve shows the various combinations of tractors and food that can be produced efficiently with given resources and technology. Point H is unattainable.

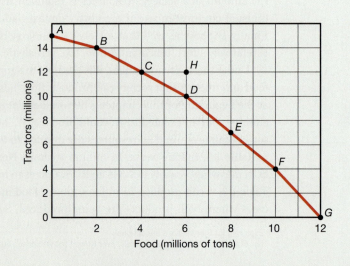

society. According to Figure 1.3, society can choose to produce 4 million tons of food and 12 million tractors (point *C*) or 6 million tons of food and 10 million tractors (point *D*), but it cannot choose to produce 6 million tons of food and 12 million tractors (point *H*). Point *H* is inaccessible with this society's resources and technology. Perhaps it will become accessible if the society's resources increase or if its technology improves, but for the present, point *H* is out of reach.

If resources are fully and efficiently utilized, the first function of any economic system (to determine the level and composition of society's output) is really a problem of determining at which point along the production possibilities curve society should be. Should society choose point *A*, *B*, *C*, *D*, *E*, *F*, or *G*? In making this choice, one thing is obvious from the production possibilities curve: You cannot get more of one good without giving up some of the other good. In other words, you cannot escape the problem of choice. So long as resources are limited and technology is less than magic, you must deal with the fact that more of one thing means less of another. The old saying "You don't get something for nothing" is hackneyed but true, so long as resources are fully and efficiently utilized. The production possibilities curve is a good way to visualize the concept of opportunity cost and tradeoffs introduced earlier in this chapter.

The Production Possibilities Curve: Determining How Goods Are Produced

We turn now to the second basic function of any economic system: to determine how each good and service should be produced. In Table 1.3, we assume that society's resources would be fully utilized and that the available technology would be applied in a way that would get the most out of the available resources. In other words, we assume that the firms making food and tractors are as efficient as possible and that there is no unemployment of resources. But if there is widespread unemployment of people and machines, can society still choose a point on the production possibilities curve? Clearly, the answer is no. If society is not using all its resources, it cannot produce as much as if it used them all. Therefore, if there is less than full employment of resources, society must settle for points *inside* the production possibilities curve. For example, the best that society may be able to do under these circumstances is to attain point *K* in Figure 1.4. Point *K* is a less desirable point than *C* or *D*, but that is the price of unemployment.

Suppose, on the other hand, that there is full employment of resources but that firms are inefficient. Perhaps they promote relatives of the boss, regardless of their ability; perhaps the managers are lazy or not very innovative; or perhaps the workers take long coffee breaks and are unwilling to work hard. Whatever the reason, will society still be able to choose a point on the production possibilities curve? Again, the answer is no. If society is not getting as much as it could out of its resources, it will not be able to produce as much as it would

FIGURE 1.4

Production Possibilities Curve

Point *K* is less desirable than point *C* or *D* because less output is produced at this point. But because of unemployment or inefficiency, society may wind up at point *K*.

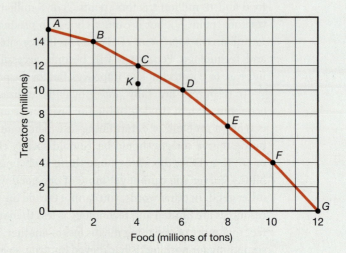

if its resources were used efficiently. Hence, if resources are used inefficiently, society must again settle for points inside the production possibilities curve. Perhaps, in these circumstances, too, the best society can do may be point *K* in Figure 1.4. This less desirable position is the price of inefficiency.

At this point, it should be obvious that our model at least partially answers the question of how each good and service should be produced. The answer is to produce each good and service in such a way that you wind up on the production possibilities curve, not on a point inside it. Of course, this is easier said than done, but at least our model indicates a couple of villains to watch out for: unemployment of resources and inefficiency. When these villains are present, we can be sure that society is not on the production possibilities curve. Also, the old saying is wrong, and it *is* possible to "get something for nothing" when society is inside the production possibilities curve. That is, society can increase the output of one good without reducing the output of another good in such a situation.

The Production Possibilities Curve, Income Distribution, and Growth

The third basic function of any economic system is to distribute the goods and services produced among the members of society. Each point on the production possibilities curve in Figure 1.4 represents society's total pie, but to deal with the third function, we must know how the pie is divided among society's members. Because the production possibilities curve does not tell us this, it cannot shed light on this third function.

PRODUCING BOTH GUNS AND BUTTER, 1939–1941

Production of munitions during World War II

Throughout the 1930s, massive amounts of productive resources were wasted. In 1938, even after the economy had recovered from the worst years of the Depression, the unemployment rate was 19 percent, more than 10 million people could not find jobs, and the capacity utilization rate for the nation's plants and equipment was very low.

With the outbreak of war in Europe in 1939, the demand for U.S. goods jumped sharply. Orders flowed in, and U.S. firms put their dormant factories to work and increased their hiring. Real national output increased 7.7 percent in 1939, 7.6 percent in 1940, and 16 percent in 1941. Munitions production went from almost zero in 1938 to $3 billion by the end of 1940 and $10 billion by the end of 1941 (all figures are in 1943 dollars).

Because consumer income had increased along with the recovery, the demand for consumer goods also grew. But with the diversion of so much of the labor force and factories into war-related production, what happened to the production of consumer goods? Consumer expenditures increased from $58 billion in 1938 to $70 billion in 1941. By putting existing resources to work, the U.S. economy was able to increase production of *both* guns *and* butter in the early years of the war. Why? Because the United States had been operating at a point inside its production possibilities curve.

By the end of 1941, when the United States officially entered the war, the economy was already producing close to its potential. The unemployment rate had fallen to 4 percent, and capacity utilization had improved dramatically. Only by extending work hours and upgrading and expanding the nation's capital stock could the economy grow. The United States continued to produce more and more every year of the war, but the gains in both guns and butter were no longer possible. Munitions production increased from $10 billion in 1941 to $64 billion by the end of the war, but there was no further growth in civilian consumption after 1941. In fact, the production of some civilian goods, such as autos and appliances, was halted completely, and others, such as tires, sugar, and coffee, were rationed. By 1942, after having taken up the slack of the Depression years, the economy had to face the classic tradeoff between guns and butter.

Fortunately, the production possibilities curve is of more use in analyzing the fourth basic function of any economic system: to determine the society's rate of growth of per capita income. Suppose that the society in Figure 1.4 invests a considerable amount of its resources in developing improved processes and products. It might establish agricultural experiment stations to improve farming techniques and industrial research laboratories to improve tractor designs. As shown in Figure 1.5, the production possibilities curve is pushed outward. This is the result of improved technology, allowing more food or more tractors, or both, to be produced from the same amount of resources. Therefore, one way for an economy to increase its output—and its per capita income—may be to invest in research and development.

Another way is for the economy to devote more of its resources to the production of capital goods than to the production of consumer goods. **Capital goods** consist of manufacturing plants and equipment used to make other goods; **consumer goods** are items that consumers purchase, like clothing, food, and

Capital goods

Consumer goods

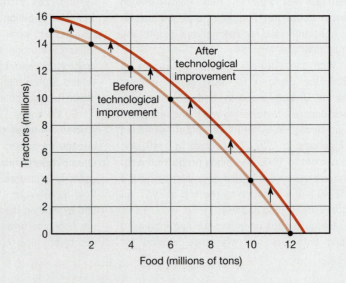

FIGURE 1.5

How Improving Technology Affects the Production Possibilities Curve

An improvement in technology results in an outward shift of the production possibilities curve.

FIGURE 1.6

How an Increase in Capital Goods Affects the Production Possibilities Curve

An increase in the amount of capital goods results in an outward shift of the production possibilities curve. The choice of point *C* means the production of more capital goods than the choice of point *F*.

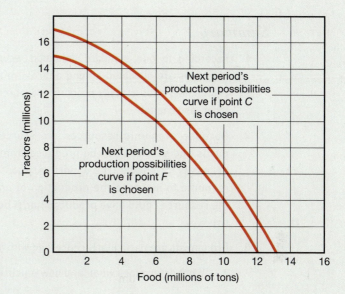

drink. Since capital goods are themselves resources, a society that chooses to produce lots of capital goods and few consumer goods pushes out its production possibilities curve much farther than a society that chooses to produce lots of consumer goods and few capital goods.

To illustrate this point, consider our simple society that produces food and tractors. The more tractors (and the less food) this society produces, the more tractors it has in the next period; and the more tractors it has in the next period, the more of both goods (food and tractors) it can produce. Thus, the more tractors (and the less food) this society produces, the farther out it pushes its production possibilities curve—and the greater the increase in output (and per capita income) that it achieves in the next period. If this society chooses point *F* (shown in Figures 1.3 and 1.4), the effect is entirely different than if it chooses point *C*. If it chooses point *F*, it produces 4 million tractors, which we assume to be the number of tractors worn out each year. So if it chooses point *F*, it adds nothing to its stock of tractors; it merely replaces those that wear out. Since it has no more tractors in the next period than in the current period, the production possibilities curve does not shift out at all if point *F* is chosen. But if point *C* is chosen, the society produces 12 million tractors; this means that it has 8 million additional tractors at the beginning of the next period. Therefore, as shown in Figure 1.6, the production possibilities curve is pushed outward. By producing more capital goods (and fewer consumer goods), the society has increased its production possibilities and its per capita income.

REVIEW AND PRACTICE

Summary

1   According to one standard definition, economics is the study of how resources are allocated among alternative uses to satisfy human wants. Economists often classify economic resources into three categories: land, labor, and capital.

2   Because economic resources are scarce, only a limited amount of goods and services can be produced from them, and there arises the necessity for choice. The opportunity cost (alternative cost) of using a resource to increase the production of one good is the value of what the resource could have produced had it been used in the best alternative way.

3   Economists are particularly concerned with four basic questions:

     1.   What determines what (and how much) is produced?

     2.   What determines how it is produced?

     3.   What determines how the society's output is distributed among its members?

     4.   What determines the rate at which the society's per capita income will grow?

4   Economists often distinguish between positive economics and normative economics. Positive economics contains descriptive statements, propositions, and predictions about the world; normative economics contains statements about what ought to be or what a person, organization, or country ought to do.

5   The methodology used by economists is much the same as that used in any other kind of scientific analysis. The basic procedure is the formulation and testing of models. A model must simplify and abstract from the real world. Its purpose is to make predictions concerning phenomena in the real world, and in many respects the most important test of a model is how well it predicts these phenomena.

* 6[4]   The production possibilities curve, which shows the various production possibilities a society can attain, is useful in indicating the nature of the economic tasks that any society faces. Society has to recognize that it cannot get more of one good without giving up some of another good if resources are fully and efficiently used.

---

[4]Starred (*) items refer to material covered in Exploring Further.

* 7 The task of determining how each good and service should be produced is, to a considerable extent, a problem of keeping society on its production possibilities curve rather than at points inside the curve. By doing research and development or producing capital goods (rather than consumer goods), society may push its production possibilities curve outward, thus increasing its per capita income.

Problems and Questions

* 1 Suppose that a society's production possibilities curve is based on the following data:

	OUTPUT (PER YEAR)	
Possibility	Food (Millions of Tons)	Tractors (Millions)
A	0	30
B	4	28
C	8	24
D	12	20
E	16	14
F	20	8
G	24	0

(a) Is it possible for the society to produce 30 million tons of food per year?

(b) Can it produce 30 million tractors per year?

(c) Suppose this society produces 20 million tons of food and 6 million tractors per year. Is it operating on its production possibilities curve? If not, what factors might account for this?

* 2 Plot the production possibilities curve in question 1 on a graph. At what point along the horizontal axis does the curve cut the axis? At what point along the vertical axis does the curve cut the axis?

* 3 Suppose that, because of important technological improvements, the society in question 1 can double its production of tractors at each level of food production. If so, is this society on its new production possibilities curve if it produces 20 million tons of food and 16 million tractors? Plot the new production possibilities curve. At which point along the horizontal axis does the new curve cut the axis? At which point along the vertical axis does it cut the axis?

4   Suppose that the quantity of corn demanded annually by U.S. consumers at each price of corn is as follows:

Price (dollars per bushel)	Quantity of Corn (millions of bushels)
1	2.0
2	1.0
3	0.5
4	0.4

How much will farmers receive for their corn crop if it is 2 million bushels? If it is 1 million bushels? If you owned all the farms producing corn, would you produce 2 million bushels? Why or why not?

5   Plot the relationship between price and quantity demanded in question 4 on a graph. Is the relationship direct or inverse? On the basis of your graph, estimate how much corn is likely to be demanded if the price is (a) $1.50, (b) $2.50, and (c) $3.50.

Key Terms

economics

human wants

resources

economic resources

free resources

technology

opportunity cost

alternative cost

positive economics

normative economics

model

production possibilities curve

capital goods

consumer goods

Viewpoint for Analysis

In the 2003 Economic Report, the administration of President George W. Bush affirmed: "Formal education is a direct way to invest in human capital, and there is some evidence of a positive relationship between national income and educational attainment. In 2000, the average duration of schooling in low-income countries was 4.4 years (3.3 years for females), compared with 10 years in high-income countries (9.8 years for females). In a cross-country analysis of 98 developing and developed countries covering 1960–1985, a 1-percentage-point increase in the primary school enrollment rate was associated with a 2.5-percentage-point increase in the growth in income per capita."[5]

(a) Suppose that an economy produces only two things: food and education. What would the production possibilities curve for such an economy look like? Draw its general shape on a graph.

(b) Can this production possibilities curve tell us whether all the citizens in this economy have access to a high-quality education? Why or why not?

(c) Can this production possibilities curve indicate the cost of raising educational attainment? Why or why not?

[5] *Economic Report of the President* (Washington, DC: U.S. Government Printing Office, 2003), pp. 239–240.

Markets and Prices

LEARNING OBJECTIVES

➤ To explore market demand and market supply curves

➤ To distinguish between shifts in a commodity's demand or supply curve and changes in the quantity demanded or supplied

➤ To recognize the significance of the equilibrium price

➤ To explain how the price system accomplishes the four basic tasks of an economic system but also recognize some general limitations of the price system

➤ *(Exploring Further)* To analyze the effects of shifts in the demand and supply curves

Politicians, industrialists, and consumers frequently lament the fact that low-cost housing is so hard to find in the United States, especially in the era of McMansions. After World War II, a builder named William Levitt produced a lot of low-cost houses and offered them for sale. What determined whether his venture succeeded? One purpose of this chapter is to answer this question.

Market-based economies use the price system to perform the four basic tasks any economic system must carry out. However, the U.S. economy is a mixed capitalist system, not a pure one. Both government and private decisions are important. This does not mean that the price system is unimportant. On the contrary, the price system plays a vital role in the U.S. economy, and to obtain even a minimal grasp of the workings of our economic system, we must understand how the price system operates. This chapter takes up the nature and functions of the price system and applies our theoretical results to some real-life problems.

Consumers and Firms

We begin by focusing on consumers and firms, the basic building blocks of the private (nongovernment) sector of the economy. What is a consumer? Sometimes—for example, when a person buys a beer on a warm day—the consumer is an individual. In other cases—for example, when a family buys a **Consumers**   new car—the consumer is an entire household. **Consumers** purchase the goods and services that are the end products of the economic system.

There are over 10 million firms in the United States. About 90 percent of the goods and services produced in this country are produced by firms. (The rest are provided by government and not-for-profit institutions, such as **Firm**   universities and hospitals.) A **firm** is an organization that produces a good or service for sale. In contrast to not-for-profit organizations, firms attempt to make a profit. It is obvious that our economy is centered around the activities of firms.

Like consumers, firms are extremely varied in size, age, power, and purpose. Consider two examples: Chris Venier's Theatre Pharmacy, in suburban Boston, and the Apple Corporation. Venier's drugstore is known in the retail drug trade as an independent because it is not affiliated with a chain store organization. In contrast, Apple is one of the giants of the U.S. economy. It manufactures computers (iMacs), cell phones (iPhones), tablets (iPads) and music players (iPods). Despite its many ups and downs in the past three decades, it is viewed as an American success story.

Markets

Consumers and firms come together in a market. The concept of a market is not quite as straightforward as it may seem, since most markets are not well defined geographically or physically. For example, the New York Stock Exchange is an atypical market because it is located principally in a particular building (although most stock transactions these days are done electroni-**Market**   cally). For our purposes, a **market** can be defined as a group of firms and consumers in touch with each other to buy or sell some good. Of course, not every consumer or firm in a market has to be in direct contact with every other consumer or firm in the market. Consumers or firms are part of a market even if they are in contact with only a subset of the other persons or firms in the market.

Markets vary enormously in their size and procedures. For some goods, like toothpaste, most people (assuming they have their own teeth and are interested in keeping them) are members of the same market; for other goods, like Picasso paintings, only a few connoisseurs (dealers, collectors, and museums in certain parts of the world) may be members of the market. And for still other goods, like lemonade sold by neighborhood children for a quarter a glass at a sidewalk stand, only people who walk by—and are brave enough to try the stuff—are members of the market. Basically, however, all markets consist primarily of buyers and sellers, although third parties, like brokers and agents, may be present as well.

Markets also vary in the extent to which they are dominated by a few large buyers or sellers. For example, in the United States for many years, there was only one producer of aluminum. This firm, the Aluminum Company of America, had great power in the market for aluminum. In contrast, the number of buyers and sellers in some other markets is so large that no single buyer or seller has any power over the price of the product. This is true in various agricultural markets, for example. When a market for a product contains so many buyers and sellers that none of them can influence the price, economists call the market *perfectly competitive*. In these introductory chapters, we make the simplifying assumption that all markets are perfectly competitive. In later chapters, we will look at markets that are dominated either by one company or only a few companies.

The Demand Side of a Market

Market demand curve

Every market has a demand side and a supply side. The demand side can be represented by a **market demand curve**, which shows the amount of the commodity buyers would purchase at various prices. Consider Figure 2.1, which shows the demand curve for wheat in the U.S. market in 2011.[1] The figure shows that about 2.3 billion bushels of wheat would be demanded annually if the farm price were $7.40 per bushel, about 2.4 billion bushels would be demanded annually if the farm price were $7.00 per bushel, and about 2.5 billion bushels would be demanded annually if the farm price were $6.60 per bushel. The total demand for wheat is of several types: to produce bread and other food products for domestic use; to provide feed for livestock; to export out of the country; and to use in industry. The demand curve in Figure 2.1 shows the total demand, including all these components, at each price.

Take a good look at the demand curve for wheat in Figure 2.1. This simple, innocent-looking curve influences a great many people's lives. After all, wheat is the principal grain used for direct human consumption in the United States. To states like Kansas, North Dakota, Oklahoma, Montana, Washington, Nebraska, Texas, Illinois, Indiana, and Ohio, wheat is a very important cash crop. Note that the demand curve for wheat slopes downward to the right. In other words, the quantity of wheat demanded increases as the price falls. This is true of the demand curve

[1] The U.S. Department of Agriculture provided this information. Of course, these numbers are only approximations, but they are good enough for our purposes here.

FIGURE 2.1

Market Demand Curve for Wheat, 2012

The curve shows the amount of wheat buyers would demand at various prices. At $6.60 per bushel, about 9 percent more wheat can be sold than at $7.00 per bushel.

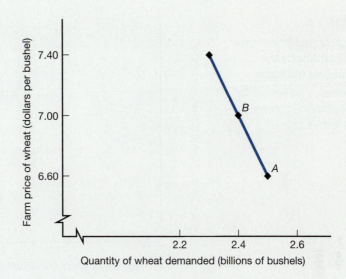

for most commodities: They almost always slope downward to the right. This makes sense; we would expect increases in a good's price to result in a smaller quantity demanded.

Any demand curve is based on the assumption that the tastes, incomes, and number of consumers, as well as the prices of other commodities, are held constant. Changes in any of these factors are likely to shift the position of a commodity's demand curve:

➤ *Consumer tastes.* If consumers show an increasing preference for a product, the demand curve shifts to the right; that is, at each price, consumers desire to buy more than previously. On the other hand, if consumers show a decreasing preference for a product, the demand curve shifts to the left, since at each price, consumers desire to buy less than previously. Take wheat; if consumers become convinced that foods containing wheat prolong life and promote happiness, the demand curve may shift, as shown in Figure 2.2. The greater the shift in preferences, the larger the shift in the demand curve.

➤ *Income level of consumers.* For some types of products, the demand curve shifts to the right if per capita income increases; for other types of commodities, the demand curve shifts to the left if per capita income increases (these are typically called "inferior" goods because people demand less of them when they become richer). Economists can

FIGURE 2.2

How Increased Preference for Wheat Affects the Market Demand Curve

An increased preference for wheat shifts the demand curve to the right.

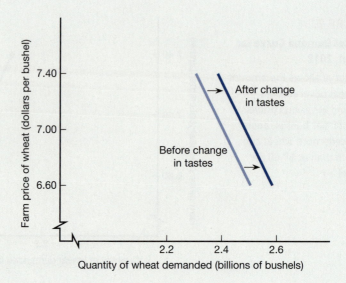

explain why some goods fall into one category and other goods fall into the other, but at present this need not concern us. All that is important here is that changes in per capita income affect the demand curve, and the size and direction of this effect vary from product to product. In the case of wheat, a 10 percent increase in per capita income would probably have a relatively small effect on the demand curve, as shown in Figure 2.3.

➤ *Number of consumers in the market.* Compare Austria's demand for wheat with that of the United States. Austria is a small country with a population of about 8.5 million; the United States is a huge country with a population of around 320 million. Clearly, at a given price of wheat, the quantity demanded by U.S. consumers greatly exceeds the quantity demanded by Austrian consumers, as shown in Figure 2.4. Even if consumer tastes, income, and other factors are held constant, this still is true simply because the United States has so many more consumers in the relevant market.[2]

➤ *Level of other prices.* A commodity's demand curve can be shifted by a change in the price of other commodities. Whether a change in the price of one good shifts the demand curve for another good depends

---

[2] Note that no figures are given along the horizontal axis in Figure 2.4 because we have no reasonably precise estimates of the demand curve in Austria. Nonetheless, the hypothetical demand curves in Figure 2.4 are close enough to the mark for present purposes.

FIGURE 2.3

How an Increase in Income Affects the Market Demand Curve for Wheat

An increase in income shifts the demand curve for wheat to the right, but only slightly.

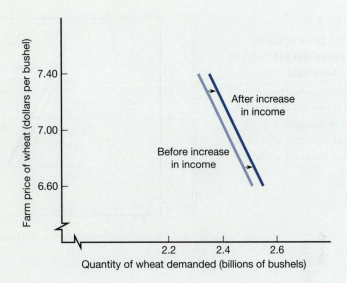

on the relationship between the two goods. Consider the case of corn and wheat. If the price of corn goes up, more wheat is demanded, since it is profitable to substitute wheat for corn. If the price of corn drops, less wheat is demanded, since it is profitable to substitute corn for wheat. As shown in Figure 2.5, increases in the price of corn shift

FIGURE 2.4

Market Demand Curve for Wheat, Austria and the United States

Because the United States has many more consumers than Austria, the demand curve in the United States is far to the right of Austria's.

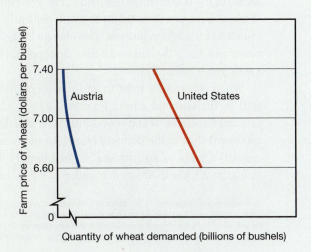

FIGURE 2.5

How the Price of Corn Affects the Market Demand Curve for Wheat

A price increase for corn shifts the demand curve for wheat to the right. A price decrease for corn shifts the demand curve for wheat to the left.

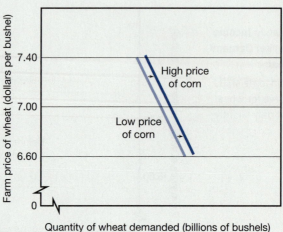

the demand curve for wheat to the right, and decreases in the price of corn shift it to the left.[3]

Change in Demand versus Change in the Quantity Demanded

It is essential to distinguish between a shift in a commodity's demand curve and a change in the quantity demanded of the commodity. A shift in a commodity's demand curve is a change in the relationship between price and quantity demanded. Figures 2.2, 2.3, and 2.5 show cases where such a change occurs. A change in the quantity demanded of a commodity may occur even if no shift occurs in the commodity's demand curve. For example, in Figure 2.1, if the price of wheat increases from $6.60 to $7.00 per bushel, the quantity demanded falls from 2.5 to 2.4 billion bushels. This change in the quantity demanded is due to a movement along the demand curve (from point *A* to point *B* in Figure 2.1), not to a shift in the demand curve.

When economists refer to an increase in demand, they mean a rightward shift in the demand curve. Figures 2.2, 2.3, and 2.5 show increases in the demand for wheat. When economists refer to a decrease in demand, they mean a leftward shift in the demand curve. An increase in demand for a commodity is not the same as an increase in the quantity demanded of the commodity. In Figure 2.1, the quantity demanded of wheat increases if the price falls from

---

[3] If two goods are complements, an increase in the price of one good shifts the demand curve for the other good to the left. For example, an increase in the price of chips is likely to shift the demand curve for salsa to the left. Why? Because chips and salsa tend to be used together. The increase in the price of chips reduces the quantity of chips demanded; this, in turn, reduces the amount of salsa demanded.

FIGURE 2.6

Market Supply Curve for Wheat, 2012

The curve shows the amount that sellers would supply at various prices. At $7.40 per bushel, about 18 percent more wheat would be supplied than at $6.60 per bushel.

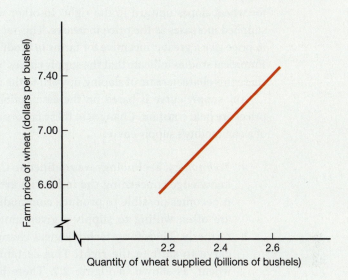

$7.00 to $6.60 per bushel, but this is not due to an increase in demand, since there is no rightward shift of the demand curve. Similarly, a decrease in demand for a commodity is not the same as a decrease in the quantity demanded of a commodity. In Figure 2.1, the quantity demanded of wheat decreases if the price rises from $6.60 to $7.00 per bushel, but this is not due to a decrease in demand, since there is no leftward shift of the demand curve.

The Supply Side of a Market

Market supply curve

So much for our first look at demand. What about the other side of the market: supply? The supply side of a market can be represented by a **market supply curve** that shows the amount of the commodity sellers would offer at various prices. We continue with the case of wheat. Figure 2.6 shows the supply curve for wheat in the United States in the mid-1990s.[4] According to the figure, about 2.2 billion bushels of wheat would be supplied if the farm price were $6.60 per bushel, about 2.4 billion bushels if the farm price were $7.00 per bushel, and about 2.6 billion bushels if the farm price were $7.40 per bushel.

Look carefully at the supply curve shown in Figure 2.6. Although it looks innocuous enough, it summarizes the potential behavior of thousands of U.S. wheat farmers, and their behavior plays an important role in determining

[4]The U.S. Department of Agriculture provided these estimates. Although rough approximations, they are good enough for present purposes.

the prosperity of many states and communities. Note that the supply curve for wheat slopes upward to the right. In other words, the quantity of wheat supplied increases as the price increases. This seems plausible, since increases in price give a greater incentive for farms to produce wheat and offer it for sale. Empirical studies indicate that the supply curves for a great many commodities share this characteristic of sloping upward to the right.

Any supply curve is based on the assumption that technology and input prices are held constant. Changes in these factors are likely to shift the position of a commodity's supply curve:

> ➤ *Technology.* Technology was defined in Chapter 1 as society's pool of knowledge concerning the industrial arts. As technology improves, it becomes possible to produce commodities more cheaply, so firms are often willing to supply a given amount at a lower price than formerly. Therefore, technological change often causes the supply curve to shift to the right. This certainly occurred in the case of wheat, as shown in Figure 2.7. There have been many important technological changes in wheat production, ranging from advances in tractors to the development of improved varieties, such as semi-dwarf wheats.

> ➤ *Input prices.* The supply curve for a commodity is affected by the price of the resources (labor, capital, and land) used to produce it. Decreases in the price of these inputs make it possible to produce commodities more cheaply, so firms may be willing to supply a given amount at a lower price than formerly. Thus, decreases in the price of inputs may cause

FIGURE 2.7

How Technological Change Affects the Market Supply Curve for Wheat

Improvements in technology often shift the supply curve to the right.

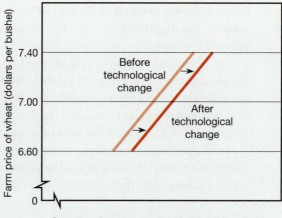

Quantity of wheat supplied (billions of bushels)

FIGURE 2.8

How an Increase in Farm Wage Rates Affects the Market Supply Curve for Wheat

An increase in the wage rate might shift the supply curve to the left.

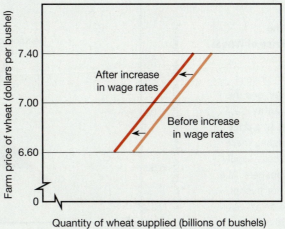

the supply curve to shift to the right. On the other hand, increases in the price of inputs may cause it to shift to the left. For example, if the wage rates of farm labor increase, the supply curve for wheat may shift to the left, as shown in Figure 2.8.

An increase in supply is defined as a rightward shift in the supply curve; a decrease in supply is defined as a leftward shift in the supply curve. A change in supply should be distinguished from a change in the quantity supplied. In Figure 2.6, the quantity of wheat supplied increases from 2.2 to 2.4 billion bushels if the price increases from $6.60 to $7.00 per bushel, but this is not due to an increase in supply, since there is no rightward shift of the supply curve in Figure 2.6.

Equilibrium Price

The two sides of a market, demand and supply, interact to determine the price of a commodity. Prices in a market-based system are important determinants of what is produced, how it is produced, who receives it, and how rapidly per capita income grows. It behooves us, therefore, to look carefully at how prices are determined in a market-based system. As a first step toward describing this process, we must define the equilibrium price of a product. At various points in this book, you will encounter the concept of equilibrium, which is very important in economics, as in many other scientific fields.

FIGURE 2.9

Determining the Equilibrium Price of Wheat, 2012

The equilibrium price is $7.00 per bushel, and the equilibrium quantity is 2.4 billion bushels. At a price of $7.40 per bushel, there would be an excess supply of 300 million bushels. At a price of $6.60 per bushel, there would be an excess demand for 300 million bushels.

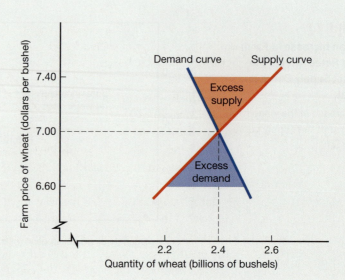

Equilibrium price

When something is in a state of equilibrium, there is no tendency for change; in other words, it is a situation that can persist. Therefore, an **equilibrium price** is a price that can be maintained. Any price that is not an equilibrium price cannot be maintained for long, since basic forces are at work to stimulate a change in the price. The best way to understand what we mean by an equilibrium price is to consider a particular case, such as the wheat market. Let us put the demand curve for wheat (from Figure 2.1) and the supply curve for wheat (from Figure 2.6) together in the same diagram. The result, shown in Figure 2.9, helps us determine the equilibrium price of wheat.

We begin by seeing what would happen if various prices were established in the market. For example, if the price were $7.40 per bushel, the demand curve indicates that 2.3 billion bushels of wheat would be demanded, while the supply curve indicates that 2.6 billion bushels would be supplied. Hence, if the price were $7.40 a bushel, there would be a mismatch between the quantity supplied and the quantity demanded per year, since the rate at which wheat is supplied would be greater than the rate at which it is demanded.

Excess supply

Specifically, as shown in Figure 2.9, there would be an **excess supply** of 300 million bushels. Under these circumstances, some of the wheat supplied by farmers could not be sold, and as inventories of wheat built up, suppliers would tend to cut their prices to get rid of unwanted inventories. Therefore, a price of $7.40 per bushel would not be maintained for long; hence, $7.40 per bushel is not an equilibrium price.

If the price were $6.60 per bushel, on the other hand, the demand curve indicates that 2.5 billion bushels would be demanded, while the supply curve indicates that 2.2 billion bushels would be supplied. Again we find a mismatch between the quantity supplied and the quantity demanded per year, since the rate at which wheat is supplied would be less than the rate at which it is demanded. Specifically, as shown in Figure 2.9, there would be an **excess demand** for 300 million bushels. Under these circumstances, some consumers who want wheat at this price would have to be turned away empty-handed. There would be a shortage. Given this shortage, suppliers would find it profitable to increase the price, and competition among buyers would bid the price up. Therefore, a price of $6.60 per bushel could not be maintained for long, so $6.60 per bushel is not an equilibrium price.

Excess demand

The equilibrium price must be the price where the quantity demanded equals the quantity supplied. Obviously, this is the only price at which there is no mismatch between the quantity demanded and the quantity supplied, and consequently, it is the only price that can be maintained for long. In Figure 2.9, the price at which the quantity supplied equals the quantity demanded is $7.00 per bushel, the price where the demand curve intersects the supply curve. Therefore, $7.00 per bushel is the equilibrium price of wheat under the circumstances visualized in Figure 2.9, and 2.4 billion bushels is the equilibrium quantity.

Actual Price

The price that counts in the real world, however, is the actual price, not the equilibrium price; and it is the actual price that we set out to explain. In general, economists assume that the actual price approximates the equilibrium price; this seems reasonable enough, since the basic forces at work tend to push the actual price toward the equilibrium price. Thus, if conditions remain fairly stable for a time, the actual price should move toward the equilibrium price. Nevertheless, at any given time, the actual price may diverge from the equilibrium price because of drought, consumer fads, or other factors.

So long as the actual price exceeds the equilibrium price, there is downward pressure on price. Conversely, so long as the actual price is less than the equilibrium price, there is upward pressure on price. Thus, there is always a tendency for the actual price to move toward the equilibrium price. But it should not be assumed that this movement is always rapid. Sometimes it takes a long time for the actual price to get close to the equilibrium price.

In fact, the actual price may *never* get to the equilibrium price because by the time it gets close, the equilibrium price has changed (because of shifts in the demand curve, the supply curve, or both). All that we can safely say is that the actual price moves toward the equilibrium price. But, of course, this information is of great value, both theoretically and practically. For many purposes, all that is needed is a correct prediction of the direction in which the price moves.

How the Price System Determines What Is Produced

Having described how prices are determined in free markets, we can now describe how the price system performs the four tasks that face any economic system (described in the previous chapter). We begin by considering how society determines what to produce. How does the price system carry out this task?

A product's demand curve is an important determinant of how much firms produce of the product, since it indicates the amount of the product demanded at each price. From the producers' point of view, the demand curve indicates the amount they can sell at each price. In a capitalist economy, firms are in business to make money: the manufacturers of any product turn it out only if the amount of money they receive from consumers exceeds the cost of putting the product on the market. Acting in accord with the profit motive, firms are led to produce what consumers desire. We saw in a previous section that if consumer tastes shift in favor of foods containing wheat, the demand curve for wheat shifts to the right, which increases the price of wheat. (If this is not obvious, see Exploring Further in this chapter.) Given the shift in the demand curve, it is profitable for firms to raise output. Acting in their own self-interest, they are led to make production decisions geared to the wants of the consumers.

Thus, the price system uses the self-interest of the producers to get them to produce what consumers want. Consumers register what they want in the marketplace by their purchasing decisions, which can be represented by their demand curves. Producers can make more money by responding to consumer wants than by ignoring them. Consequently, they are led to produce what consumers are willing to pay for. (In addition, as we have seen, the level of production costs as well as demand determines what is produced.) Note that producers are not forced by anyone to do anything. They can produce air conditioners for Eskimos if they like and are prepared to absorb the losses. The price system uses prices to communicate the relevant signals to producers and metes out penalties and rewards in the form of losses and profits.

CASE STUDY 2.1

LOW-COST HOMES AFTER WORLD WAR II

When World War II was over, millions of ex-GIs came home, fell in love, got married, and started families. And there was one thing they all needed: homes. But homes were not easy to come by. Depression and war had put home building on hold for almost 20 years. What housing there was was beyond the means of most young vets with new jobs and new families. Young families were looking for low-cost housing. Home builders needed customers. It was demand in search of supply.

For most people, the "American dream" included a house and a car. Henry Ford had made the dream come true for cars. Were there any Henry Fords in the postwar home-building business? William Levitt rose to the challenge. Backed by the promise of VA and FHA mortgages, Levitt put his money where his judgment was. He laid out 6,000 lots on low-cost Long Island potato fields and poured 6,000 concrete slabs. Specialized construction teams hit Levittown streets like commandos. But, as with Ford's Model T, assembly-line methods could mean assembly-line sameness. In a nation dedicated to individualism, would mass-produced houses have mass appeal?

The houses were built. The ads were placed. The case went to the jury. The verdict was not slow in coming in. It was the unprecedented demand by

Suburban development after World War II in Levittown, New York

World War II veterans for affordable housing that drew William Levitt and thousands of other builders into the low-cost housing market and built one of the foundations for postwar prosperity.

How the Price System Determines How Goods Are Produced

Next we consider how society determines how each good and service is produced. How does the price system carry out this task? The price of each resource gives producers an indication of how scarce this resource is and how valuable it is in other uses. Clearly, firms should produce goods and services at minimum cost. Suppose there are two ways of producing tables: technique *A* and technique *B*. Technique *A* requires 4 hours of labor and $10 worth of wood per table, whereas technique *B* requires 5 hours of labor and $8 worth of wood. If the price of an hour of labor is $10, technique *A* should be used, since a table costs $50 with this technique, as opposed to $58 with technique *B*.[5] In other words, technique *A* uses fewer resources per table.

The price system nudges producers to opt for technique *A* rather than technique *B* through profits and losses. If each table commands a price of $65, then by using technique *A*, producers make a profit of $65 – $50 = $15 per table. If they use technique *B*, they make a profit of $65 – $58 = $7 per table. Therefore, producers, if they maximize profit, are led to adopt technique *A*. Their desire for profit leads them to adopt the technique that enables society to get the most out of its resources. No one commands firms to use particular techniques. Government officials do not order steel plants to substitute the basic oxygen process for open hearths or petroleum refineries to substitute catalytic cracking for thermal cracking. It is all done through the impersonal marketplace.

You should not, however, get the idea that the price system operates with kid gloves. Suppose all firms producing tables used technique *B* until this past year, when technique *A* was developed; in other words, technique *A* is based on a new technology. Given this technological change, the supply curve for tables shifts to the right, and the price of a table falls. (If this is not obvious, see Exploring Further in this chapter.) Suppose the price drops to $57. Any firm that insists on sticking with technique *B* will lose money at the rate of $1 a table; and as these losses mount, the firm's owners become increasingly uncomfortable. The firm will either switch to technique *A* or go bankrupt. The price system leans awfully hard on producers who try to ignore its signals.

How the Price System Determines Who Gets What

We now turn to the way society's output is distributed among the people. How does the price system carry out this task? The amount of goods and services people receive depends on their money income, which in turn is determined under the price system by the amount of various resources that they own and the price of each resource. Thus, under the price system, each person's income is determined in the marketplace: people come to the marketplace with certain resources to sell, and their income depends on how much they can get for these resources.

[5] To obtain these figures, note that the cost with technique *A* is 4 labor-hours times $10 plus $10, or $50, while the cost with technique *B* is 5 labor-hours times $10 plus $8, or $58.

WHY DO SOME SPORTS STARS EARN MORE THAN THE PRESIDENT OF THE UNITED STATES?

Why do star athletes earn so much? The answer is simple: there are few of them around and their "product" is highly valued by the market. The laws of supply and demand that affect the price of products like wheat also affect the price of our services—our wages and salaries. If public demand is high for certain kinds of rare skilled labor—long-ball hitters, rock stars, neurosurgeons—then customers and employers will be willing to pay a lot extra. Unfortunately, the market, operating in this way, does not always produce a result we find personally agreeable. Should a baseball player earn four or five times as much as the president of the United States? Markets are potent but not always ideal. Moreover, as we will learn in later chapters, not all markets work perfectly. For example, the salaries of many professional athletes are determined through collective bargaining, which may or may not fully reflect the forces of supply and demand.

The question of who gets what is solved at two levels by the price system. Consider an individual product—for example, the tables discussed in the previous section. If the price of these tables is at its equilibrium, the quantity demanded equals the quantity supplied. Consumers willing and able to pay the equilibrium price (or more) get the tables, while those unwilling or unable to pay it do not get them. It is as simple and impersonal as that. It does not matter whether you are a nice guy or a scoundrel or whether you are a connoisseur of tables or someone who doesn't know good workmanship from poor. All that matters is whether you are able and willing to pay the equilibrium price.

Now let's consider the question of who gets what at a somewhat more fundamental level. After all, whether consumers are able and willing to pay the equilibrium price for a good depends on their money income. As we have already seen, consumers' money income depends on the amount of resources that they own and the price that they can get for them. Some people have lots of resources: they are endowed with skill and intelligence and industry or they have lots of capital or land. Other people have little in the way of resources. Moreover, some people have resources that command a high price, whereas others have resources that are of little monetary value. The result is that under the price system, some consumers get a lot more of society's output than others.

The Price System and Economic Growth

We turn now to the task of determining a country's rate of growth of per capita income. How does the price system do this? A country's rate of increase in per capita income depends on the rate of growth of its resources and the rate of increase of the efficiency with which they are used. First consider the rate of growth of society's resources. The price system controls the amount of new capital goods produced, much as it controls the amount of consumer goods produced. Similarly, the price system influences the amount society invests in educating, training, and upgrading its labor resources. To a considerable extent, the amount invested in such resource-augmenting activities is determined by the profitability of such investments, which is determined in turn by the pattern of prices.

Next consider the rate of increase of the efficiency with which a society's resources are used. Clearly, this factor depends heavily on the rate of technological change. If technology is advancing at a rapid rate, it should be possible to get more and more out of a society's resources. But if technology is advancing rather slowly, it will be difficult to get much more out of the resources. The price system affects the rate of technological change in a variety of ways: it influences the profitability of investing in research and development, of introducing new processes and products into commercial practice, and of accepting technological change (as well as the losses involved in spurning it).

The price system establishes strong incentives for firms to introduce new technology. Any firm that can find a cheaper way to produce an existing product or a way to produce a better product has a profitable jump on its competitors. Until its competitors can do the same thing, this firm can reap higher profits than it otherwise could. Of course, these higher profits eventually are competed away as other firms begin to imitate this firm's innovation. But lots of money can be made until then. These profits are an important incentive for the introduction of new technology.

The Circular Flow of Money and Products

So far, we have been concerned largely with the workings of a single market. But how do all of the various markets fit together? Perhaps the best way to begin answering this question is to distinguish between product markets and resource markets. As their names indicate, **product markets** are markets where products are bought and sold, and **resource markets** are markets where resources are bought and sold. We first consider product markets. As shown in Figure 2.10, firms provide products to consumers in product markets and receive money in return. The money the firms receive is their receipts; to consumers, on the other hand, it is their expenditures.

Product markets

Resource markets

FIGURE 2.10

The Circular Flow of Money and Products

In product markets, consumers exchange money for products and firms exchange products for money. In resource markets, consumers exchange resources for money and firms exchange money for resources.

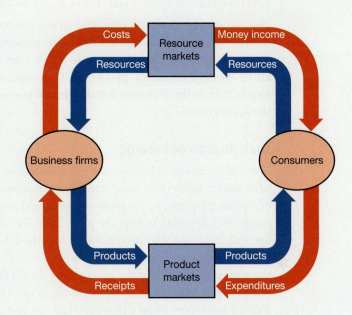

Next we consider resource markets. Figure 2.10 shows that consumers provide resources, including labor, to firms in resource markets, and they receive money in return. The money the consumers receive is their income; to firms, on the other hand, it is their costs. Note that the flow of resources and products in Figure 2.10 is counterclockwise: consumers provide resources to firms, which in turn provide goods and services to consumers. On the other hand, the flow of money in Figure 2.10 is clockwise: firms pay money for resources to consumers, who in turn use the money to buy goods and services from the firms. Both the flow of resources and products and the flow of money go on simultaneously and continuously.

So long as consumers spend all their income, the flow of money income from firms to consumers is exactly equal to the flow of expenditures from consumers to firms. As a first approximation, this is a perfectly good model. But capitalist economies have experienced periods of widespread unemployment and severe inflation that this model cannot explain. Also, note that the simple economy in Figure 2.10 has no government sector. In later chapters, we bring the government into the picture. Under pure capitalism, the government would play a limited role in the economic system, but in the mixed capitalistic system we have in the United States, the government plays an important role indeed.

Limitations of the Price System

Despite its many advantages, the price system suffers from limitations. Because these limitations are both significant and well known, no one believes that the price system, left to its own devices, can be trusted to solve all of society's economic problems. To a considerable extent, the government's role in the economy has developed in response to the limitations of the price system.

Distribution of Income

There is no reason to believe that the distribution of income generated by the price system is *fair* or, in some sense, *best*. Most people feel that the distribution of income generated by the price system should be altered to suit humanitarian needs—in particular, to help the poor. Both liberals and conservatives tend to agree on this score, despite arguments over the extent to which the poor should be helped and the conditions under which they should be eligible for help. But the general principle that the government should step in to redistribute income in favor of the poor is generally accepted in the United States today. Also, the wealthy have more money to spend than the poor, and the sorts of goods and services that society produces reflect this fact. Luxuries for the rich may be produced in larger amounts, and necessities for the poor in smaller amounts, than some critics regard as sensible and equitable. This is another frequently encountered criticism of the price system.

Public Goods

Some goods and services cannot be provided through the price system because there is no way to exclude citizens from consuming the goods whether they pay for them or not. For example, there is no way to prevent citizens from benefiting from national expenditures on defense, whether they pay money toward defense or not. Consequently, the price system cannot be used to provide such goods; no one would pay for them, since all receive them whether they pay or not. Further, some goods, like the quality of the environment and national defense, can be enjoyed by one person without depriving others of the same enjoyment. Goods **Public goods** with these characteristics are called **public goods**. Government provides many public goods. Such goods are consumed collectively or jointly, and it is inefficient to try to price them in a market. They tend to be indivisible; that is, they cannot easily be split into pieces and bought and sold in a market.

External Economies and Diseconomies

In cases where the production or consumption of a good by one firm or consumer has adverse or beneficial uncompensated effects on other firms or consumers, the price system does not operate effectively.

THE FOOD STAMP PROGRAM AND THE ALLOCATION OF RESOURCES

Although the free market encourages an efficient allocation of resources, it responds only to those who have money to spend. If people are willing and able to spend money to fulfill a *need* for a good, there is an *effective demand* for that good, and the market automatically responds to that need. Needs that are not backed up by spending power, however, are not met by the market.

Clearly, the market system does not ensure that everyone has money. Income depends primarily on being able to sell one's services in exchange for a wage. Those who cannot or will not sell their labor services, such as children, the adults who must care for young children, the aged, or the disabled, have small incomes under the market system. Their needs are not translated into effective demands, so the market does not, by itself, provide for these people.

The government has set up programs that provide varying degrees of assistance to those who have an income below the poverty level. One of the largest, the Food Stamp program, began as a pilot program in 1961 and was greatly expanded under the Johnson administration in the Food Stamp Act of 1964. Any low-income households meeting the basic eligibility requirements could buy food stamps at a price below their market value. By 1969, 3.2 million people were using food stamps at a cost to the government of $272 million.

The Food Stamp program was expanded in 1971 under President Richard Nixon. By the early 1980s, about 1 out of every 11 Americans was a food stamp recipient, and the program cost $11.3 billion. The rapid growth of the program made it a focus of controversy, and the Reagan administration sought to reduce the growth in outlays. Part of the debate concerned the perennial question of the extent of the federal government's responsibility to help the poor. Should government programs be only a safety net for the truly needy, or should the government create programs of such scope that they would have a major impact on income distribution?

In 1996, significant changes were made to the Food Stamp program as part of a major overhaul of the welfare system in the United States. The most significant change required able-bodied food stamp recipients between the ages of 18 and 50 who did not have dependents to work an average of at least 20 hours per week or participate in a state-approved work, training, or workfare program. Otherwise, they could receive no more than three months of food stamps out of every three years. This was part of an overall attempt to reduce the disincentives to work in the welfare system.

In the late 1990s, the numbers of both welfare and food stamp recipients fell. How much of this was due to the economic boom of the 1990s versus the work incentives is still being debated. During the economic downturn in the early 2000s, the number of people applying for food stamps increased again, but still remained below the levels in 1996, suggesting that the changes made to the Food Stamp program (including the work incentives) may have had a long-term impact.

During the deep recession of 2008–2009, the number of food stamp recipients soared from about 26 million to 36 million. By 2012, the number of recipients had risen to over 47 million. In October 2008, the Food Stamp program was renamed the Supplemental Nutritional Assistance Program, or SNAP. Unfortunately, in late 2013 Congress cut SNAP benefits by an average of 57% per family.

External economy

An **external economy** is said to occur when consumption or production by one consumer or firm results in uncompensated benefits to another consumer or firm. Thus, an external economy exists when fundamental research carried out by one firm is used by another firm. To cite one such case, there were external economies from the Bell Telephone Laboratories' invention of the transistor. Many electronics firms, such as Texas Instruments and Fairchild, benefited considerably from Bell's research. The Internet is another example. Without early funding by the Department of Defense, the Internet may never have been created. It is generally agreed that where external economies exist, the price system produces too little of the good in question and the government should supplement the amount produced by the private sector. This is the basic rationale for much of the government's huge investment in basic science.

External diseconomy

An **external diseconomy** is said to occur when consumption or production by one consumer or firm results in uncompensated costs to another consumer or firm. A good example of an external diseconomy is when a firm dumps pollutants into a stream and makes the water unfit for use by firms and people downstream. It is generally agreed that where activities result in an external diseconomy, the price system tolerates too much of these activities and the government should curb them.

EXPLORING FURTHER

Shifts in the Demand and Supply Curves

The ancient Greek philosopher Heraclitus said you cannot step in the same stream twice: everything changes, sooner or later. We need not be a disciple of Heraclitus to recognize that demand and supply curves shift. Indeed, we have already seen that demand curves shift in response to changes in taste, income, population, and prices of other products, and supply curves shift in response to changes in technology and input prices. Any supply and demand diagram, such as the one in Figure 2.9, is essentially a snapshot of the situation during a particular period of time. The results in Figure 2.9 are limited to a particular period because the demand and supply curves in the figure, like any demand and supply curves, pertain only to a certain period.

Shifts in the Demand Curve

What happens to the equilibrium price of a product when its demand curve changes? This is an important question, because it sheds a good deal of light on how the price system works. Suppose that consumer tastes shift in favor of foods containing wheat, causing the demand curve for wheat to shift to the right, as shown in Figure 2.11. It is not hard to see the effect on the equilibrium price of wheat. Before the shift, the equilibrium price is P. But when the demand curve shifts to the right, a shortage develops at this price; that is, the quantity demanded exceeds the quantity supplied at this price. (This shortage is equal to $Q'_1 - Q$ in Figure 2.11.) Consequently, suppliers raise their prices. After some testing of market reaction and trial-and-error adjustments, the price tends to settle at P_1, the new equilibrium price, and the quantity tends to settle at Q_1.

On the other hand, suppose that consumer demand for wheat products falls off, perhaps because of a great drop in the price of corn products. The demand for wheat now shifts to the left, as shown in Figure 2.12. What is the effect on the equilibrium price of wheat? Clearly, the equilibrium price falls to P_2, where the new demand curve intersects the supply curve.

In general, a shift to the right in the demand curve results in an increase in the equilibrium price, and a shift to the left in the demand curve results in a decrease in the equilibrium price. This is the lesson of Figures 2.11 and 2.12.

FIGURE 2.11

How a Shift to the Right of the Market Demand Curve Affects the Equilibrium Price

This shift of the demand curve to the right results in an increase in the equilibrium price from P to P_1 and an increase in the equilibrium quantity from Q to Q_1.

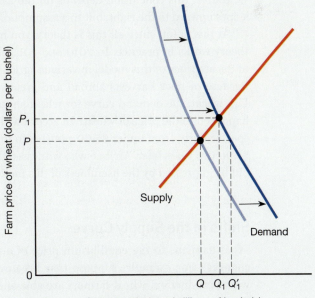

FIGURE 2.12

How a Shift to the Left of the Market Demand Curve Affects the Equilibrium Price

The shift of the demand curve to the left results in a decrease in the equilibrium price from P to P_2 and a decrease in the equilibrium quantity from Q to Q_2.

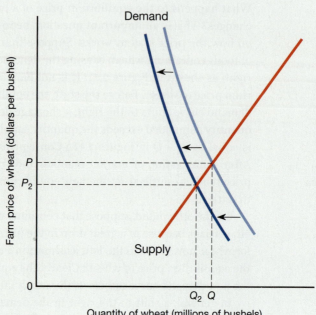

Of course, this conclusion depends on the assumption that the supply curve slopes upward to the right, but this assumption is generally true.

At this point, since all this is theory, you may be wondering how well this theory works in practice. In 2010 and 2011, there was a vivid demonstration of the accuracy of this model in various agricultural markets, including wheat. Because of poor harvests abroad and greatly increased foreign demand for U.S. wheat, the demand curve for wheat shifted markedly to the right. What happened to the price of wheat? In accord with our model, the price increased spectacularly, from under $5.00 a bushel in the early summer of 2009 to over $7.00 two years later. Anyone who witnessed this phenomenon could not help but be impressed by the usefulness of this model.

Shifts in the Supply Curve

What happens to the equilibrium price of a product when its supply curve changes? For example, suppose that because of technological advances in wheat production, wheat farmers are able and willing to supply more wheat at a given price than they used to, with the result that the supply curve shifts

FIGURE 2.13

How Shifts in the Market Supply Curve Affect the Equilibrium Price

The shift of the supply curve to the right results in a decrease in the equilibrium price from P to P_3. The shift of the supply curve to the left increases the equilibrium price from P to P_4.

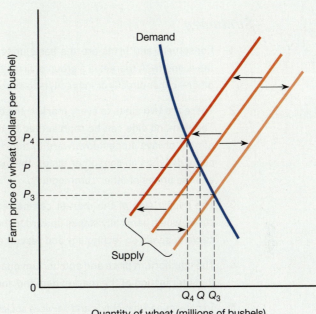

to the right, as shown in Figure 2.13. What will be the effect on the equilibrium price? Clearly, it will fall from P (where the original supply curve intersects the demand curve) to P_3 (where the new supply curve intersects the demand curve).

On the other hand, suppose that the weather is poor, with the result that the supply curve shifts to the left, as shown in Figure 2.13. What will be the effect? The equilibrium price increases from P (where the original supply curve intersects the demand curve) to P_4 (where the new supply curve intersects the demand curve).

Some of the increase in the price of wheat in 2010 and 2011 was due to droughts in many parts of the world, most importantly in Russia. This resulted in a leftward shift in the supply curve and helped to propel prices to record highs.

In general, a shift to the right in the supply curve results in a decrease in the equilibrium price, and a shift to the left in the supply curve results in an increase in the equilibrium price. Of course, this conclusion depends on the assumption that the demand curve slopes downward to the right, but this assumption is generally true.

REVIEW AND PRACTICE

Summary

1 Consumers and firms are the basic units composing the private sector of the economy. A market is a group of firms and consumers in touch with each other—either directly or indirectly— to buy or sell some commodity or service.

2 There are two sides to every market: the demand side and the supply side. The demand side can be represented by the market demand curve, which almost always slopes downward to the right. The position of the demand curve depends on consumer tastes, the number and income of consumers, and the prices of other commodities.

3 The supply side of the market can be represented by the market supply curve, which generally slopes upward to the right. The position of the supply curve depends on technology and resource prices.

4 The equilibrium price and equilibrium quantity of a commodity are given by the intersection of the market demand and market supply curves.

5 To determine what goods and services society produces, the price system sets up incentives for firms to produce what consumers want. Also, the price system sets up strong incentives for firms to produce goods at a minimum cost.

6 To determine who gets what, the price system results in people receiving an income that depends on the quantity of resources they own and the prices that these resources command. The price system also establishes incentives for activities that result in increases in a society's per capita income.

7 There is a circular flow of money and products in a capitalist economy. In product markets, firms provide products to consumers and receive money in return. In resource markets, consumers provide resources to firms and receive money in return.

8 The price system, despite its many virtues, suffers from serious limitations. There is no reason to believe that the distribution of income generated by the price system is equitable or optimal. Also, there is no way for the price system to handle public goods properly, and because of external economies or diseconomies, the price system may result in too little or too much of certain goods being produced.

*9[6] Changes in the position and shape of the demand curve—in response to changes in consumer taste, income, population, and prices of other commodities—result in changes in the equilibrium price and equilibrium output of a product. Similarly, changes in the position and shape of the

---

[6] Starred (*) items refer to material covered in Exploring Further.

supply curve—in response to changes in technology and resource prices, among other things—also result in changes in the equilibrium price and equilibrium output of a product.

Problems and Questions

1   Assume that the market for electric toasters is competitive and that the quantity supplied per year depends on the price of a toaster:

Price of a Toaster (dollars)	Number of Toasters Supplied (millions)
12	4.0
14	5.0
16	5.5
18	6.0
20	6.3

Plot the supply curve for toasters. Is this relationship direct or inverse? Do supply curves generally show direct or inverse relationships?

2   Suppose that the quantity of toasters demanded per year depends on the price of a toaster:

Price of a Toaster (dollars)	Number of Toasters Demanded (millions)
12	7.0
14	6.5
16	6.2
18	6.0
20	5.8

Plot the supply and demand curves for toasters. If the price is $14, is there an excess demand for toasters? If the price is $20, is there an excess demand? What is the equilibrium price of a toaster? What is the equilibrium quantity?

3   Suppose that the government imposes a price ceiling on toasters. In particular, suppose that it decrees that a toaster cannot sell for more than $14. Would the quantity supplied equal the quantity demanded? What sorts of devices may come into being to allocate the available supply of toasters to consumers? What problems would the government encounter in keeping the price at $14? What social purposes, if any, might such a price ceiling serve?

4 Suppose that the government imposes a price floor on toasters. In particular, suppose that it decrees that a toaster cannot sell for less than $20. Would the quantity supplied equal the quantity demanded? How would the resulting supply of toasters be taken off the market? What problems would the government encounter in keeping the price at $20? What social purposes, if any, might such a price floor serve?

Key Terms

consumer

firm

market

market demand curve

market supply curve

equilibrium price

excess supply

excess demand

product markets

resource markets

public goods

external economy

external diseconomy

Viewpoint for Analysis

In a speech delivered at the American Bar Association, William Brewer said: "The suggestion was put forth in a newspaper article some years ago that to solve the problem of the oversupply of attorneys, the government should pay lawyers $500,000 each to turn in their bar cards. It was proposed as a sort of a 'farm subsidy' solution . . . whereby the government would pay lawyers *not* to practice law. So instead of say, wheat, the uncultivated crop in the fallow north forty would be litigation."[7]

(a) Is there a market for lawyers? If so, what determines the location and shape of the demand curve? Of the supply curve?

(b) If the market for lawyers were perfectly competitive, could there be an oversupply in the sense that the quantity of lawyers supplied exceeded the quantity demanded? Under conditions of equilibrium, could such an oversupply exist? Why or why not?

(c) If the government were to pay lawyers $500,000 to leave their profession, would this influence the demand curve for lawyers? Would it influence the supply curve? Would it influence the wage paid to lawyers? Do you favor such a policy? Why or why not?

[7]William A. Brewer III, "The Breakdown of the Monopoly of the Bar Card: The Game Is Over," *Vital Speeches of the Day*, March 1, 1993, 318.

THE KEY ROLE OF SAVING AND INVESTMENT IN RAISING PER CAPITA INCOME

Spinning jenny

In the first 10,000 years of human development, there was almost no economic growth to speak of, and per capita income in Europe in the 1600s was barely higher than in the time of the Roman Empire. However, in the late 1700s and early 1800s, something began to change. In the intervening two centuries, European per capita income (after adjusting for inflation) rose almost 15-fold! What happened?

One of the most remarkable developments in human history was the Industrial Revolution. Until the middle of the eighteenth century, industry (as distinct from agriculture or commerce) played a small role in the economies of Europe and America. But during the late eighteenth and early nineteenth centuries, a host of important technological innovations, such as James Watt's steam engine and Richard Arkwright's spinning jenny, made possible a very rapid growth in the output of industrial goods (like textiles and pig iron). And accompanying this growth of industrial output was the advent of the factory, a social and economic institution taken for granted today but largely unknown prior to the Industrial Revolution.

The Industrial Revolution was characterized by major improvements in technology and a large increase in the amount of capital resources available to society. Thanks mainly to the improvements in technology, the standard of living in England, as measured by per capita income (total income divided by population), grew at an unprecedented rate. As the Industrial Revolution spread, a similar rise in living standard occurred on the European continent and in the United States; it remained one of the lasting effects of industrialization.

The Industrial Revolution was characterized by considerable increases in capital, largely brought about through saving and investment. In other words, people had to set aside some of their resources and say in effect, "These resources will *not* be used to satisfy the current needs of our population for food, clothing, and other forms of consumption. Instead, they will be used to produce capital—factories, machines, equipment, railroads, and canals—that will increase our future productive capacity." Much more is said about this saving process in subsequent chapters. For now, the essential point is that saving was one of the necessary conditions for the Industrial Revolution.

Turning from the Industrial Revolution to the present, one reason for Japan's remarkable increase in output during the period since World War II has been the very high Japanese savings rate. During the 1960s and early 1970s, when output in Japan was growing at about 10 percent per year, the Japanese were saving about 25 percent of their income. Like their counterparts during the Industrial Revolution, the Japanese said in effect, "These resources will be used for factories, equipment, and other forms of investment, not for consumption." Thanks to the liberalization of trade and the rapid transfer of technology, the improvement in living standards in East Asian countries in recent decades was even faster than in Europe and the United States during the Industrial Revolution. In the 1800s, it took five decades for per capita output to double in Britain and the United States. In recent years, South Korea and China accomplished the same feat in one-fifth the time! As in Japan, saving rates in East Asia were an important factor.

Questions

1 Did the major improvements in technology in the late eighteenth and early nineteenth centuries, such as Watt's steam engine and Arkwright's spinning jenny, have an effect on the production possibilities curve in England? Why or why not?

2 If these inventions had an effect on the production possibilities curve in England, did they shift it to the left or to the right? Explain.

3 Why did these inventions result in an increase in the standard of living in England? Did they alone accomplish this, or were increases in the amount of capital resources important, too?

4 Why couldn't the Industrial Revolution have occurred without considerable increases in capital?

5 In Japan after World War II, did the Japanese invent lots of new techniques, as the English did at the beginning of the Industrial Revolution? If not, where did they get the advanced technology required to transform their economy?

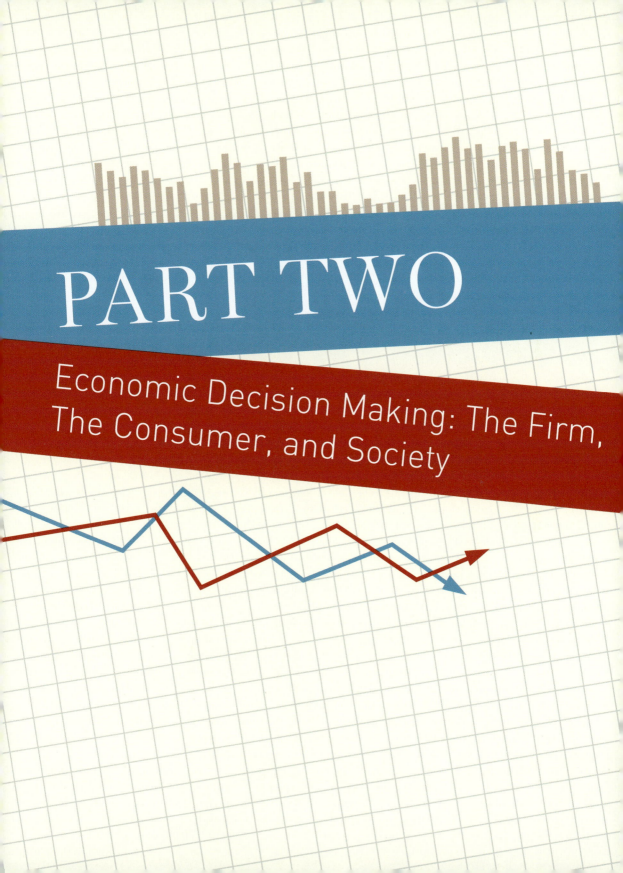

PART TWO

Economic Decision Making: The Firm, The Consumer, and Society

The Business Firm

Organization, Motivation, and Optimal Input Decisions

LEARNING OBJECTIVES

➤ To explore the pros and cons of various types of business organizations (proprietorships, partnerships, corporations)

➤ To understand what a production function is

➤ To describe the law of diminishing marginal returns

➤ To explain how firms should make input decisions if they want to maximize profit

Consider the challenges faced by the owners of a large corn farm in Illinois. Among other things, they must decide how much of various inputs (like fertilizer, land, labor, and capital) to use to produce their corn. How can they solve this problem? One purpose of the chapter is to answer this question.

It is hard to overstate the importance of business firms in the U.S. economy. They produce the bulk of our goods and services, hire most of the nation's workers, and issue stocks and bonds that represent a large percentage of the nation's wealth. Judged by any yardstick—even less complimentary ones like the responsibility for environmental pollution—business firms are an extremely important part of the U.S. economy.

In this chapter, we will look closely at the decision-making process within the firm. We begin by discussing the organization, motivation, and technology of the firm, then focus particular attention on the following central question: If a firm wants to maximize profits, what production technique— that is, what combination of inputs—should it choose to produce a particular quantity of output? Two points should be noted at the outset. First, when finding the optimal input combination, we will take as a given the quantity of output the firm will produce. In subsequent chapters, we will discuss how the firm should choose this output quantity. Second, an important purpose of this chapter and Chapters 4 and 5 is to show how a product's supply curve can be derived. In this chapter, we present some of the concepts and findings required for this purpose.

General Motors: A Study

In Chapter 2, when we first discussed the role of the business firm in the U.S. economy, we cited two examples: Chris Venier's Theatre Pharmacy, a small independent drugstore, and the Apple Corporation, a huge enterprise. Now that we are considering the business firm in more detail, we will look closely at another large U.S. company: General Motors Corporation (also known simply at GM).

The Early Years

General Motors was formed in 1908 by William C. Durant, an energetic and imaginative entrepreneur who made over a million dollars in the carriage business before he was 40. After taking over the bankrupt Buick Motor Company in 1904, Durant built it into a very successful operation. Then, in 1908, he gained control of a number of small automobile companies (including Cadillac and Oldsmobile), several truck firms, and 10 parts and accessory firms. The resulting amalgamation was General Motors.

In 1910, General Motors's sales fell, and Durant lacked the funds to pay his workforce and suppliers. To get the money he needed, he went to a banking syndicate, which lent him $15 million but required him to turn over the management of the company. By 1915, Durant had acquired another auto producer, Chevrolet, and had picked up formidable financial allies in the DuPonts, the owners of the famous chemical firm. Using both these levers, Durant regained full control of General Motors in 1916, and between 1916 and 1920, he concentrated on expanding the productive capacity of the General Motors Corporation. A man of extraordinary vision, he recognized, as few of his contemporaries did, a great potential demand for moderately priced cars; and he devoted his energy to putting General Motors in a position to satisfy this demand.

Reorganization of the Firm

Although Durant was a man of great vision, he was not the sort of administrator who created a tidy organizational structure. The General Motors Corporation under Durant was a large agglomeration of companies in a variety of product lines, with somewhat tangled lines of communication and diffuse control. When automobile sales did not come up to expectations in 1920, the firm suffered a reduction in profits. The resulting crisis led to Durant's retirement as president of General Motors and the firm's adoption of a new organizational plan created by Alfred Sloan, a young MIT-trained engineer who soon became GM's president.

Sloan's plan divided General Motors into a number of divisions: the Buick division, the Chevrolet division, the accessory division, and so forth. Each division was given considerable freedom, but greater attention was devoted to central control and coordination than under Durant's more anarchic organization. Sloan's organizational plan, an important innovation in its day, remained in effect with little change for many years.

Prosperity and New Challenges

During the 1920s, General Motors prospered. Its sales rose from $600 million in 1920 to $1.5 billion in 1929, and its profits rose from about $38 million in 1920 to about $248 million in 1929. The next decade was different. The 1930s were the years of the Great Depression, when sales and profits of most firms, including General Motors, were hard hit. But during the 1940s, General Motors entered another period of prosperity and growth. Its sales rose from about $1.8 billion in 1940 to about $5.7 billion in 1949, and its profits rose from about $196 million in 1940 to about $656 million in 1949. During the 1950s and 1960s, GM's prosperity continued. Of course, there were short intervals when sales and profits fell, but the trend was upward, in part because of population growth and in part because higher incomes meant increased automobile sales. The firm experienced no prolonged period of low profits or considerable excess capacity, as was the case in the 1930s.

In the 1970s, however, trouble began to appear in the form of imported Japanese cars. By 1981, the trouble was serious, as evidenced by GM's third-quarter loss of about $500 million. Quotas on Japanese imported cars helped the firm get back into the black, and in 1984, the firm seemed healthier than it had been. But in 1987, its profits were less than Ford's, its smaller rival, and from 1990 to 1992, it racked up a total of almost $10 billion in losses. During the rest of the 1990s, General Motors became profitable once again. By 2000, its net income was back to $4.4 billion. However, the recession of 2001 and the terrorist attacks of September 11, 2001, hurt sales and profits that year. The company responded very aggressively by offering generous incentives on each of its cars, including 0 percent financing. By 2003, both sales and profits had recovered once again.

STUDEBAKER AND THE LOW-VOLUME TRAP

In this case study, we turn from General Motors to another major auto producer, Studebaker, which, after having had its ups and downs before World War II, started off the postwar period in good shape. Flush with cash, Studebaker capitalized on the pent-up demand of the war years by being the first to come out with a new model, a streamlined car of the future. The firm prospered in the late 1940s and early 1950s, and in 1952, it had its best year ever.

As the seller's market of the early postwar years disappeared, however, serious weaknesses in Studebaker's position became obvious. The auto industry was very competitive in the mid-1950s. There were eight major manufacturers (today's Big Three and Studebaker, plus Nash, Hudson, Packard, and Willys). Studebaker suffered from bad management and high-cost labor, but one of its major problems could not have been easily solved by either management or labor—its inability to capture the cost savings that result from large-scale production. General Motors and the other large manufacturers had begun to introduce new models every year. While these firms could spread the costs of new model development (about $30 million) over the 1 to 2 million units they produced each year, Studebaker was selling fewer than 300,000 cars a year. The company could not reach the minimum cost per car possible through large volume. In 1953, it scheduled production of 350,000 cars but built only 186,000. By 1954, Studebaker had set its breakeven point at 108,000 per year and was trying to reduce the figure still further.

Bankruptcy and Revival

Unfortunately, the troubles for General Motors were not over. In 2008, because of the global financial crisis and the deep recession that followed, the company was pushed into bankruptcy. Because of the importance of GM to both the U.S. automotive industry and the U.S. economy, the administrations of both George W. Bush and Barack Obama agreed to help with a combined bailout of nearly $55 billion. In return, General Motors agreed to undergo a massive restructuring, which included deep cuts in its workforce. In 2009, GM emerged from bankruptcy and returned to profitability—even posting a record annual profit in 2011.

However, General Motors will have to continue working hard to compete successfully against both its domestic rivals and Japanese imports. The stakes are high, since the somewhat jumbled organization that William Durant assembled in 1908 is still one of the biggest industrial companies in the United States and in the world.

U.S. Firms, Large and Small

General Motors is an economic colossus, a huge organization with around 200,000 employees. Of course, it is not typical of U.S. business firms. If we broaden our focus to take in the entire population of business firms in the United States, the first thing we note is their tremendous number: according to government statistics, about 29 million. The vast majority of these firms, as we would expect, are very small. There are lots of grocery stores, gas stations, auto dealers, drugstores (like Venier's), clothing shops, restaurants, and so on. You see hundreds of them as you walk along practically any downtown city street, the main drag of most small towns, or a suburban shopping mall.

Firms, large or small, can be classified into three types: proprietorships, partnerships, and corporations. What do these terms mean?

Proprietorships

Proprietorship

A proprietorship is the most common and also the simplest legal form of business organization. Specifically, a **proprietorship** is a firm owned by a single individual. Over 75 percent of the nation's small businesses are proprietorships. The corner drugstore may well be one. If so, it has a single owner, say, Rita Sanchez. She hires the people she needs to wait on customers, deliver orders, do the bookkeeping, and so forth. She borrows, if she can, whatever money she feels she needs. She reaps the profits or incurs the losses. All her personal assets—her house, her furniture, her car—can be taken by creditors to meet the drugstore's bills; she has unlimited liability for the debts of the business.

Pros. What President Lincoln said about common men and women applies as well to proprietorships: God must love them, or he wouldn't have created so many. If proprietorships did not have certain advantages over other legal forms of business organization, there would not be so many of them. What are these advantages? First, the owner of a proprietorship has complete control over the business. There is no need to negotiate with partners or other co-owners; the proprietor is the only boss. Anyone who has been in a position of complete authority knows the satisfaction it can bring. Many proprietors treasure this feeling of independence. Second, a proprietorship is easy and inexpensive to establish: all you have to do is hang out your shingle and announce that you are in business. This, too, is a great advantage.

Cons. But proprietorships have important disadvantages as well, and for this reason they are seldom found in many important industries. One disadvantage is that it is difficult for a proprietor to put together enough financial resources to enter an industry as big as the automobile or steel industry. No one in the world has enough money to establish, by himself or herself, a firm like General Motors. Another disadvantage is that proprietors are liable for all of the debts of the firm. If their business fails, their personal assets can be taken by their creditors, and they can be completely wiped out.

Partnerships

Partnership

A partnership is more complicated than a proprietorship. As its name implies, a **partnership** is a form of business organization where two or more people agree to own and conduct a business. Each partner agrees to contribute some proportion of the capital and labor used by the business and to receive some proportion of the profits or losses. There are many types of partnerships. In some cases, one or more of the partners may be "silent partners," who put up some of the money but have little or nothing to do with the operation of the firm. The partnership is a common form of business organization in some industries and professions, such as the law. But partnerships are found less frequently than proprietorships or corporations in the United States.

Pros. A partnership has certain advantages. Like a proprietorship, it can be established without great expense or legal red tape. (However, if you ever go into a partnership with someone, you would be well advised to have a good lawyer draw up a written agreement establishing such things as the salary of each partner and how profits are to be shared.) In addition, a partnership can avoid some of the problems involved in a proprietorship. It can usually put together more financial resources and specialized know-how than a proprietorship, and this can be an important advantage.

Cons. But the partnership also has certain drawbacks. First, each partner is liable without limit for the bills of the firm. For example, even if one partner of a law firm has only a 30 percent share of the firm, she may be called on to pay all the firm's debts if the other partners cannot do so. Second, there is some red tape in keeping a partnership in existence. Whenever a partner dies or withdraws or whenever a new partner is admitted, a new partnership must be established. Third, although preferable to a proprietorship, the partnership is still not a very effective way to obtain the large amounts of capital required for some industries. A modern automobile plant may cost $500 million, and not many partnerships could assemble that much capital. For these reasons, as well as others discussed in the next section, the corporation has become the dominant form of business organization in the United States.

Corporations

Corporation

A far more complicated form of business organization than either the proprietorship or partnership, the **corporation** is a fictitious legal person, separate and distinct from its owners. A corporation is formed when lawyers draw up the necessary papers stating (in general terms) what sorts of activities the owners of the corporation intend to engage in. The owners of the corporation are the stockholders. Stock, pieces of paper signifying ownership of the corporation, is issued to the owners, generally in exchange for their cash. The corporation's board of directors, which is responsible for setting the overall policy for the firm, is elected by the stockholders. Ordinarily, each share of stock gives its owner one vote. The firm's owners can, if they are dissatisfied with the company's policies or think they have better opportunities elsewhere, sell their stock to someone else, assuming, of course, that they can find a buyer.

Pros. The corporation has many advantages over the partnership or proprietorship. In particular, each of the corporation's owners has limited, not unlimited, liability. If I decide to become one of the owners of General Motors and if a share of General Motors stock sells for $25, I can buy 10 shares of General Motors stock for $250. And I can be sure that if General Motors falls on hard times, I cannot lose more than the $250 I paid for the stock. There is no way that I can be assessed beyond this. Moreover, the corporation, unlike the partnership or proprietorship, has unlimited life. If several stockholders want to withdraw from the firm, they simply sell their stock. The corporation goes on, although the identity of the owners changes. For these reasons, the corporation is clearly a better device for raising large sums of money than the partnership or proprietorship. This is an enormous advantage of the corporation, particularly in such industries as automobiles and steel, which could not otherwise finance their operations. This is one reason why companies such as Google and Facebook have "gone public," offering to sell ownership stakes in their company to the public at large and allow their shares to be traded on one of the stock exchanges (such as NASDAQ).

Cons. Without question, the corporation is a very important social invention. It permits people to assemble the large quantities of capital required for efficient production in many industries. Without limited liability and the other advantages of the corporation, it is doubtful that the opportunities and benefits of large-scale production could have been reaped. This does not mean that the corporate form will work for all firms. If a firm requires only a modest amount of capital, there is no reason to go to the trouble and expense of establishing a corporation. Moreover, one disadvantage of the corporation is double taxation of income, since corporations themselves pay income taxes. Therefore, every dollar earned by a corporation and distributed to stockholders is taxed twice by the federal government—once when it is counted as income by the corporation and once when it is counted as income by the stockholders.

CASE STUDY 3.2

THE COLLAPSE OF ENRON AND THE IMPORTANCE OF CORPORATE GOVERNANCE

1400 Smith Street

On December 2, 2001, Enron (an energy trading company headquartered in Houston, Texas) declared bankruptcy. Enron had been one of the superstars of the 1990s boom. Its spectacular demise—one for the record books—was the result of too much debt and unusually risky investments. On top of that, the senior executives of the company had practiced creative accounting and hidden serious financial problems; in other words, they committed fraud. Unfortunately, Enron was not alone. Other large corporations, such as Dynegy, World-Com, and Tyco, were also discovered to have engaged in questionable and illegal accounting practices in an attempt to make their profits look much better than they actually were.

The collapse of Enron and the investigations into the other corporations sent a shock wave through financial markets, pushing down stock prices and creating a crisis of confidence about U.S. corporate governance. Not only were the corporations themselves implicated, but auditors (who were supposed to catch fraud), banks (which were lending money to these corporations), and elected officials (who were supposed to be the ultimate watchdogs) all had a complicit role in these scandals.

Corporate governance may seem like a dull topic, but it is at the heart of the system of trust that is an integral part of modern capitalism. The 2003 *Economic Report of the President* devoted a whole chapter to the topic, which began by saying:

> Corporate governance is the system of checks and balances that guides the decisions of corporate managers. As such,

it affects the strategy, operations, and performance of business firms over a large segment of the U.S. economy. Corporate governance also affects the ability of those outside the corporation—including investors—to monitor the quality of management and its decisions, and to influence and even control some of those decisions. This observability, or transparency, can greatly enhance a corporation's ability to raise funds from outside investors. It can also make it easier for other outsiders, including suppliers and customers, to transact with the corporation, by making the incentives and abilities of its managers and other employees more clear.*

In response to the wave of corporate scandals, the U.S. Congress passed the Sarbanes-Oxley Act in July 2002. The principal goal of this act is to strengthen U.S. corporate governance rules in three areas. First, it requires that both accuracy of and access to information about the financial health of corporations be improved. Second, it tightens the standards of accountability for corporate officers, especially chief

executive officers (CEOs) and chief financial officers (CFOs). Any restatement of profits following earlier inflated estimates can result in heavy fines. Third, it strengthens auditor independence and, in particular, tries to minimize any conflict of interest on the part of the auditor. Specifically, it forbids auditors from engaging in other types of business with the corporations they audit, keeping the auditors more objective in their assessments.

In response to the corporate scandals and the Sarbanes-Oxley Act, the quality of the financial statements (as well as the profits themselves) of U.S. nonfinancial corporations improved and with it investor confidence.

U.S. financial companies had their "year of infamy" in 2008, when many of them failed spectacularly as a result of taking on too much debt and making a lot of bad investments, especially in housing. This, in turn, led to the passage of the Dodd-Frank Act, one of whose aims is to improve governance in banks and other financial sector companies.

Economic Report of the President, 2003 (Washington, DC: U.S. Government Printing Office, 2003), 73.

Motivation of the Firm

Profit maximization

Profit

What determines the behavior of the business firm? Economists generally assume that firms are primarily motivated by a desire for **profit maximization**. A **profit** is defined as the difference between the firm's revenue and its costs. In other words, economists generally assume that firms try to make as much money as possible. This assumption does not seem unreasonable; most businesses appear to be interested in making money. Nonetheless, the assumption of profit maximization oversimplifies the situation. Although businesses certainly want profits, they are interested in other things as well. Some firms claim that they want to promote better cultural activities or better racial relations in their community. At a less lofty level, other firms say that their aim is to increase their share of the market. Whether or not we take these self-proclaimed goals very seriously, it is clear that firms may be interested in more than just making money.

Technology, Inputs, and the Production Function

The decisions a firm should make to maximize its profits are determined by the current state of technology.

Technology

Technology is the sum total of society's knowledge concerning the industrial arts. Just as consumers are limited by their income, firms are limited by the current state of technology. If the current state of technology is such that we do not know how to produce more than 40 bushels of corn per year from 1 acre of land and 2 units of labor, then this is as much as the firm can produce from this combination of land and labor. In making its decisions, the firm must take this into account. Similar assessments need to be made in the production of much more complex products, such as smartphones and tablets, which have thousands of parts produced in many parts of the world. Unlike the technology geared to agriculture, the technology around the design and production of such high-tech devices changes very rapidly, creating a different set of challenges for companies such as Apple, Motorola, and Samsung.

Input

In constructing a model of the profit-maximizing firm, economists must somehow represent the state of technology and include it in the model. As a first step toward this end, we must define an input. Simply put, an **input** is anything the firm uses in its production process. On a corn farm, some of the inputs might be seed, land, labor, water, fertilizer, and various types of machinery, as well as the time of the people managing the farm.

Production function

Having defined an input, we can now describe how economists represent the state of technology. The basic concept economists use for this purpose is the production function. For any commodity, the **production function** is the relationship between the quantities of various inputs used per period of time and the maximum quantity of the commodity that can be produced per period of time. More specifically, the production function is a table, graph, or equation showing the maximum output rate that can be achieved from any specified set of usage rates of inputs. The production function summarizes the characteristics of existing technology at a given point in time. It reflects the technological constraints the firm must reckon with.

To see more clearly what we mean by a production function, consider the Milwaukee Machine Company, a hypothetical machine shop that produces a simple metal part. Suppose we are considering a period of time that is so short that the firm's basic plant and equipment cannot be altered. For simplicity, suppose the only input whose quantity can be altered in this period is the amount of labor used by the machine shop. Suppose that the firm collects data showing the relationship between the quantity of its output and the quantity of labor it uses. This relationship, given in Table 3.1, is the firm's production function. It shows that when one worker is employed, 100 parts are produced per month; when two workers are employed, 210 parts are produced per month; and so on.

TABLE 3.1

Production Function, Milwaukee Machine Company

Quantity of Labor Used per Month (number of workers employed)	Output per Month (number of parts)
0	0
1	100
2	210
3	315
4	415
5	500

(You will soon learn why the company's incremental output can rise initially and then fall.) Information concerning a firm's production function is often obtained from the firm's engineers, as well as from its artisans and technicians.

Types of Inputs

In analyzing production processes, we can classify all inputs into two categories: fixed and variable.

Fixed input

A **fixed input** is one whose quantity cannot change during the period of time under consideration. This period varies. It may be six months in one case, six years in another case. Among the most important inputs often included as fixed are the firm's plant and equipment: its factory and office buildings, machinery, tools, and transportation facilities. In the simple example of the wheat farm in Table 3.2, land is a fixed input, since its quantity is assumed to be fixed at 1 acre.

Variable input

A **variable input** is one whose quantity can be changed during the relevant period. It is generally possible to increase or decrease the number of workers engaged in a particular activity (although this is not always the case, since they may have long-term contracts). Similarly, it is frequently possible to alter the amount of raw material used. In the case of the wheat farm in Table 3.2, labor clearly is a variable input, since its quantity can be varied from 0 to 5 units.

TABLE 3.2

Relationship Between Labor Input and Output on a 1-Acre Wheat Farm

Number of Units of Labor	Bushels of Wheat Produced per Year
0	0
1	30
2	70
3	100
4	125
5	145

The Short Run and the Long Run

Short run

Long run

Whether an input is considered variable or fixed depends on the length of the period under consideration. The longer the period, the more inputs are variable, not fixed. Although the length of the period varies from case to case, economists have found it very useful to focus special attention on two time periods: the short run and the long run. The **short run** is defined as the period of time in which at least one of the firm's inputs is fixed. More specifically, since the firm's plant and equipment are among the most difficult inputs to change quickly, the short run is generally understood to mean the length of time during which the firm's plant and equipment are fixed. On the other hand, the **long run** is that period of time in which all inputs are variable. In the long run, the firm can make a complete adjustment to any change in its environment.

To illustrate the distinction between the short run and the long run, consider General Motors. Any period of time during which GM's plant and equipment cannot be altered freely is the short run. A period of one year is certainly a case of the short run, because General Motors could not vary the quantity of its plant and equipment in a single year. It takes longer than a year to construct an automotive plant or alter an existing plant to produce a new kind of automobile. Also, because some of its existing contracts with suppliers and workers extend for more than a year, GM cannot vary all its inputs in a year without violating these contracts. On the other hand, any period of time during which GM can vary the quantity of all inputs is the long run. A period of 50 years is certainly a case of the long run. Whether a shorter period of time (10 years, say) is also a long-run situation depends on the problem at hand. If all the relevant inputs can be varied, it is a long-run situation; if not, it is a short-run situation.

A useful way to look at the long run is to consider it a planning horizon. While operating in the short run, the firm must continually be planning ahead and deciding its strategy for the long run. Its decisions concerning the long run determine the sort of short-run position the firm will occupy in the future. Before a firm makes the decision to add a new type of product to its line, it is in a long-run situation (with regard to the new product), since it can choose among a wide variety of types and sizes of equipment to produce the new product. But once the investment is made, the firm is confronted with a short-run situation, since the type and size of equipment is, to a considerable extent, frozen.

Average Product and Marginal Product of an Input

Average product of an input

To determine which production technique—that is, which combination of inputs—a firm should use, it is necessary to determine the average product and marginal product of an input. The **average product of an input** is the firm's total output divided by the amount of input used to produce this amount of output.

The average product of an input can be calculated from the production function. Consider the wheat farm in Table 3.2. The average product of labor is 30 bushels per unit of labor when 1 unit of labor is used, 35 bushels per unit of labor when 2 units are used, 33⅓ bushels per unit of labor when 3 units are used, and so forth.

As the amount of labor used on the farm increases, so does the farm's output; but the amount of extra output from the addition of an extra unit of labor varies, depending on how much labor is already being used. The extra output from the addition of the first unit of labor is 30 − 0 = 30 bushels per unit of labor. The extra output due to the addition of the second unit of labor is 70 − 30 = 40 bushels per unit of labor. And the extra output from the addition of the fifth unit of labor is 145 − 125 = 20 bushels per unit of labor. The **marginal product of an input** is the addition to total output due to the addition of the last unit of input, the quantity of other inputs used being held constant. Therefore, the marginal product of labor is 30 bushels when between 0 and 1 unit of labor are used, 40 bushels when between 1 and 2 units of labor are used, and so on.

Marginal product of an input

Table 3.3 shows the average and marginal products of labor at various levels of utilization of labor; Figure 3.1 shows the same thing graphically. The data in both Table 3.3 and Figure 3.1 concerning the average and marginal products of labor are derived from the production function. Given the production function, shown in Table 3.2 and reproduced in Table 3.3, the average and marginal products at each level of utilization of labor can be determined in the way we have indicated.

In Figure 3.1, as in the case of most production processes, the average product of the variable input (labor in this case) rises, reaches a maximum, then falls. The marginal product of labor also rises, reaches a maximum, and

TABLE 3.3 Average and Marginal Products of Labor on a 1-Acre Wheat Farm	Number of Units of Labor	Total Output (bushels per year)	Marginal Product (bushels per unit of labor)	Average Product (bushels per unit of labor)
	0	0		—
			30	
	1	30		30
			40	
	2	70		35
			30	
	3	100		33½
			25	
	4	125		31¼
			20	
	5	145		29

FIGURE 3.1

Average and Marginal Products of Labor on a 1-Acre Wheat Farm

The marginal product of the first unit of labor (which, according to Table 3.3, equals 30 bushels per unit) is plotted at the midpoint between 0 and 1 unit of labor. The marginal product of the second unit of labor is plotted at the midpoint between 1 and 2 units of labor. The marginal product curve connects these and other points showing the marginal product of various amounts of labor.

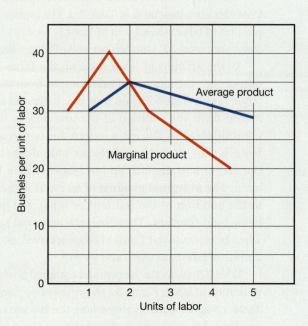

falls. This, too, is typical of many production processes. Why do average and marginal products behave in this way? Because of the law of diminishing marginal returns, to which we now turn.

The Law of Diminishing Marginal Returns

Law of diminishing marginal returns

Perhaps the best-known (and possibly least understood) law of economics is the so-called **law of diminishing marginal returns**. This law states that if equal increments of an input are added, the quantities of other inputs being held constant, the resulting increments of product will decrease beyond some point; that is, the marginal product of the input will diminish.

Suppose that a small factory that manufactures a metal automobile component has eight machine tools, each capable of performing a different task. If this firm hires only one or two workers, total output and output per worker will be quite low. These workers will have a number of quite different tasks to perform, and the advantages of specialization will be sacrificed. Workers will spend considerable time switching from one machine to another, and many of the eight machine tools will be idle much of the time. What happens as the firm increases its workforce? As more and more workers are added, the marginal product (that is, the extra product) of each tends to rise as the workforce grows

CASE STUDY 3.3

TO OFFSHORE OR NOT? THAT IS THE QUESTION

Under the pressures of competition and the market, businesses cut costs in many ways. They often substitute less expensive inputs for more expensive ones. In the case of PrintPOD—a small printing company in New Jersey—this meant less expensive labor and machinery in India for more expensive ones in the United States. However, there are limits to this substitution. Consider the following example. If Indian workers' wages are 10 percent of those in the United States, but the marginal product (productivity) of labor is 20 percent of that in the United States, then it is cost-effective for a company such as PrintPOD to produce books in India. However, as more Indian workers are employed, their marginal product (productivity) will decline because of diminishing returns. Once the marginal product of Indian workers falls below 10 percent of their American counterparts—the same percentage of the Indian-to-American wages—then there is no advantage in using Indian rather than American workers. This type of "input optimization," as economists call it, helps to keep businesses profitable and to keep prices down for consumers.

to the point where it can operate the fixed amount of equipment effectively. However, if the firm continues to increase the number of workers, the marginal product of a worker eventually begins to decrease. Why? Because workers have to wait in line to use the fixed number of machine tools, and the extra workers have to be assigned to less and less important tasks. Eventually, if too many workers are hired, they may get in each other's way to such an extent that production may grind to a halt.

Returning to the wheat farm discussed in the previous section, Table 3.3 shows that the law of diminishing marginal returns applies in this case, too.

The third column of this table indicates that beyond 2 units of labor, the marginal product of labor falls. Certainly, it seems entirely reasonable that as more and more of a variable input (in this case, labor) is combined with a fixed amount of another input (in this case, land), the additional output to be derived from an additional unit of the variable input eventually decreases. In the case of a 1-acre wheat farm, we would expect that as more and more labor is added, the extra workers' functions eventually become less and less important and productive.

The law of diminishing marginal returns plays a major part in determining the firm's optimal input combination and the shape of the firm's cost functions. But we need to clarify several points about this law. First, it is assumed that technology remains fixed. If technology changes, the law of diminishing marginal returns cannot predict the effect of an additional unit of input. Second, at least one input must be fixed in quantity, since the law of diminishing marginal returns is not applicable to cases where there is a proportional increase in all inputs. Third, it must be possible to vary the proportions in which the various inputs are utilized. This is generally possible in industry and agriculture.

The Optimal Input Decision

Now we are in a position to answer the question posed at the beginning of this chapter: If a firm wants to maximize profits, what production technique—that is, what combination of inputs—should it choose to produce a particular quantity of output? Note first that if the firm is to maximize its profits, it must minimize the cost of producing this quantity of output. This seems obvious enough. But which combination of inputs minimizes the firm's costs? The answer can be stated like this: The firm minimizes cost by combining inputs in such a way that the marginal product of a dollar's worth of any one input equals the marginal product of a dollar's worth of any other input used. Another way to say the same thing is this: The firm minimizes cost by combining inputs in such a way that for every input used, the marginal product of the input is proportional to its price.

This principle is best illustrated by the example given in Case Study 3.3. A firm can minimize costs by offshoring to India if the relative cost of Indian labor (say, 10 percent of U.S. labor costs) is less than the relative marginal product (say, 20 percent of U.S. productivity). When—from a cost minimization point of view—does it make sense to stop offshoring? It makes sense to bring production back to the United States when the relative cost of Indian labor and the relative marginal product of Indian labor converge. This can happen in a number of ways: the marginal product of Indian labor can fall, the cost of Indian labor can rise, the cost of American labor can fall, and so on. So when the relative cost and relative marginal product of Indian labor are the same (say, 10 percent), then a company can no longer minimize costs by offshoring to India.

TABLE 3.4
Determining the Optimal Input Combination

AMOUNT OF INPUT USED		MARGINAL PRODUCT		MARGINAL PRODUCT ÷ PRICE OF INPUT		
Labor (units)	Land (acres)	Labor (units)	Land (acres)	Labor (units)	Land (acres)	Total Cost (dollars)
0.5	7.0	50	5	50 ÷ 4,000	5 ÷ 1,000	9,000
1.0	4.1	40	10	40 ÷ 4,000	10 ÷ 1,000	8,100
1.5	3.0	30	30	30 ÷ 4,000	30 ÷ 1,000	9,000
2.5	2.0	20	50	20 ÷ 4,000	50 ÷ 1,000	12,000

The Wheat Farm: A Numerical Example

To provide another illustration of this rule, we take a numerical example from the wheat farm cited earlier. Suppose that the farm can vary the amount of labor and land it uses. Table 3.4 shows the marginal product of each input when various combinations of inputs able to produce the specified quantity of output are used. Suppose that the price of labor is $4,000 per unit and the annual price of using land is $1,000 per acre. (We assume that the farm takes the prices of inputs as given and can buy all it wants of the inputs at these prices.) For each combination of inputs, Table 3.4 shows the marginal product of each input divided by its price. Based on the rule, the optimal input combination is 4.1 acres of land and 1 unit of labor, since this is the only combination (capable of producing the required output) where the marginal product of labor divided by the price of labor equals the marginal product of land divided by the price of land.

Is this rule correct? Does it really result in a least-cost combination of inputs? Looking at the cost of the various input combinations in Table 3.4, we see that the first combination (0.5 unit of labor and 7 acres of land) costs $9,000; the second combination (1.0 unit of labor and 4.1 acres of land) costs $8,100; and so on. An examination of the total cost of each input combination shows that the input combination chosen by our rule (1.0 unit of labor and 4.1 acres of land) is indeed the least-cost input combination, the one for the profit-maximizing farm to use.

EXPLORING FURTHER

How to Produce Kansas Corn

To illustrate the practical payoff from the sort of analysis discussed in this chapter, we consider how a distinguished agricultural economist, Earl Heady, of Iowa State University, used these methods to help farmers make better

TABLE 3.5	AMOUNT OF INPUT USED		Marginal Product of Fertilizer ÷
Combinations of Fertilizer and Land Required to Produce 82.6 Bushels of Corn, and the Ratio of Marginal Products at Each Combination	**Fertilizer (pounds)**	**Land (acres)**	**Marginal Product of Land**
	0	1.19	0.0045
	20	1.11	0.0038
	40	1.04	0.0030
	60	0.99	0.0019
	80	0.96	0.0010
	100	0.95	0.0003

production decisions. Table 3.5 shows the various amounts of land and fertilizer that produce 82.6 bushels of corn on Kansas Verdigras soil. As you can see, this amount of corn can be produced if 1.19 acres of land and no fertilizer are used, if 1.11 acres of land and 20 pounds of fertilizer are used, if 0.99 acre of land and 60 pounds of fertilizer are used, and so forth.

The third column of Table 3.5 shows the ratio of the marginal product of a pound of fertilizer to the marginal product of an acre of land when each of these input combinations is used. For example, when 1.19 acres of land and no fertilizer are used, this ratio is 0.0045. Using the optimal input rule, a farm can minimize its costs by setting the ratio in the third column equal to the ratio of the price of a pound of fertilizer to the price of an acre of land. Why? Because the optimal input rule stipulates that the farm should choose an input combination so that

$$\frac{\text{Marginal product of fertilizer}}{\text{Price of fertilizer}} = \frac{\text{Marginal product of land}}{\text{Price of land}}$$

So if we multiply both sides of this equation by the price of fertilizer and divide both sides by the marginal product of land, we get

$$\frac{\text{Marginal product of fertilizer}}{\text{Marginal product of land}} = \frac{\text{Price of fertilizer}}{\text{Price of land}}$$

To minimize costs, a farm should set the ratio in the third column of the table equal to the ratio of the price of fertilizer to the price of land.

Heady and his coworkers, having obtained the results in the table, used this technique to determine the optimal input combination farmers should use to minimize their costs.[1] The optimal input combination depends on the price of land and the price of fertilizer. Suppose a pound of fertilizer costs 0.003 times as much as an acre of land. Under these circumstances, the least-cost input combination would be 40 pounds of fertilizer and 1.04 acres of land, since, as shown in the table, this is the input combination where the ratio of the marginal product of fertilizer to the marginal product of land is 0.003. No matter what the ratio of the price of fertilizer to the price of land may be, the least-cost input combination can be derived this way.

Such results are of considerable practical value to farmers. Moreover, the same kind of analysis can be used by organizations in other sectors of the economy, not just agriculture. Studies of how the Defense Department can reduce its costs have utilized concepts and techniques of essentially this sort. In a more peaceful vein, this same kind of analysis has been used by various manufacturing firms. For example, steel firms have made many such studies to determine least-cost ways to produce steel, and auto firms have made similar studies to reduce their costs.

REVIEW AND PRACTICE

Summary

1   There are three principal types of business firms: proprietorships, partnerships, and corporations. Some advantages of the corporation are limited liability, unlimited life, and greater ability to raise large sums of money.

2   Economists generally assume that firms attempt to maximize profits. Economists are interested in the theory of the profit-maximizing firm because it provides rules of behavior for firms that want to maximize profits.

3   To summarize the characteristics of existing technology at a given point in time, economists use the concept of the production function, which shows the maximum output rate of a given commodity that can be achieved from any specified set of usage rates of inputs.

4   Inputs can be classified into two categories: fixed and variable. A fixed input is one whose quantity cannot be changed during the period of time under consideration. A variable input is one whose quantity can be changed during the relevant period.

---

[1] E. Heady and L. Tweeten, *Resource Demand and Structure of the Agricultural Industry* (Ames: Iowa State University Press, 1963). It is assumed that a certain amount of labor is used; this amount is proportional to the number of acres of land.

5 Whether an input is considered variable or fixed depends on the length of the period under consideration. The longer the period, the more inputs are variable, not fixed. The short run is defined as the period of time in which some of the firm's inputs (generally its plant and equipment) are fixed. The long run is the period of time in which all inputs are variable.

6 The average product of an input is the firm's total output divided by the amount of input used to produce this amount of output. The marginal product of an input is the addition to total output due to the addition of the last unit of input, the quantity of other inputs used being held constant.

7 The law of diminishing marginal returns states that if equal increments of an input are added (and the quantities of other inputs are held constant), the resulting increments of product decrease beyond some point; the marginal product of the input diminishes.

*8[2] To minimize its costs, a firm must choose its input combination so that the marginal product of a dollar's worth of any one input equals the marginal product of a dollar's worth of any other input used. Put differently, the firm should combine inputs so that for every input used, the marginal product of the input is proportional to its price.

Problems and Questions

1 Suppose that a cost-minimizing firm in a perfectly competitive market uses two inputs: labor and capital. If the marginal product of capital is twice the marginal product of labor and the price of a unit of labor is $4, what must be the price of a unit of capital?

2 In Figure 3.1, the marginal product of labor equals its average product when the average product is at a maximum. Do you think that this is generally the case? Why or why not? (*Hint:* If the marginal product of an extra amount of labor exceeds the average product, will the average product increase? If it is less than the average product, will the average product decrease?)

3 A firm uses two inputs: capital and labor. The firm's chief engineer says that its output depends on the amount of labor and capital it uses in the following way:

$$Q = 3L + 4C$$

where Q is the number of units of output produced per day, L is the number of units of labor used per day, and C is the amount of capital used per day. Does this relationship seem sensible? Why or why not?

[2]Starred (*) items refer to material covered in Exploring Further.

4 In the previous problem, suppose that the price of using a unit of labor per day is $50 and the price of using a unit of capital per day is $100. What is the optimal input combination for the firm if the relationship in the previous problem is valid? Does this seem reasonable? Why or why not?

Key Terms

proprietorship	production function
partnership	fixed input
corporation	variable input
corporate governance	short run
profit maximization	long run
profit	average product of an input
technology	marginal product of an input
input	law of diminishing marginal returns

Viewpoint for Analysis

Dexter Baker, former head of Air Products and Chemicals, Inc., gave a speech at Hilton Head Island, in which he said: "I believe we in the business community as stewards of our nation's wealth-creating processes have a special responsibility to ensure that the value systems upon which our business operates are based upon the highest ethical standards we can conceive. . . . Furthermore, [adherence to] sound ethical standards is not just a pious way to conduct one's affairs, it is also the most remunerative in the long run."[3]

(a) Does the goal of profit maximization ever conflict with high ethical standards? If so, give some examples.

(b) When economists assume that a firm maximizes profit, do you think that they make the tacit assumption that profit maximization occurs given the constraint that the firm observes reasonably high ethical and legal standards? For example, do you think they assume that the firm stays within federal and state laws?

(c) Are high ethical standards more likely to be remunerative in the long run than in the short run? If so, why?

[3] Dexter Baker, "Ethical Issues and Decision Making in Business," *Vital Speeches of the Day*, January 15, 1993, 211–212.

Getting behind the Demand and Supply Curves

LEARNING OBJECTIVES

➤ To understand consumer behavior

➤ To understand the concept of marginal utility

➤ To explain the relation between an individual's demand curve and the market demand curve

➤ To describe the nature of the cost curves that underlie firms' decisions on supply

Droughts have been a recurring problem in California. In 1991, after five consecutive dry years, residents of Los Angeles were required by city ordinance to reduce water usage by 15 percent. What sorts of principles should be applied to determine which kinds of water use should be cut back most severely? One purpose of this chapter is to answer this question.

In a market economy, consumers decide how much to buy based on their income, their tastes, and market prices; firms decide how much to produce on the basis of their costs and what they can charge for their products. In this chapter, we look behind the individual's demand curve and the firm's supply curve by outlining, first, the basic model of consumer demand and, second, the role that costs play in a firm's decision of how much to produce (that is, supply). In Chapters 5 and 6, we will expand our discussion of supply and demand and consider what determines the characteristics of market demand and supply.

The Demand Curve

To a considerable extent, consumers, voting with their pocketbooks, are the masters of our economic system. No wonder, then, that economists spend much of their time describing and analyzing how consumers act. In addition, economists are interested in determining how consumers, as well as other decision-making units, should go about making rational choices. In this chapter, we present the basic model that economists use to analyze consumer behavior.

Consumer Expenditures

The Martins of Jacksonville

Because we are concerned here with consumer behavior, we begin by looking at the behavior of a particular consumer. It is hard to find any consumer who is "typical." There are hundreds of millions of consumers in the United States, and their behavior varies enormously. But how does one particular U.S. family—the Martins, of Jacksonville, Florida[1]—spend its money? Janet and Mike Martin are about 40 years old, are both married for the second time, and have three children (by his first marriage). They own their own home, and both work. Mike is a computer programmer, and Janet is a product manager. Together the Martins make about $120,000 a year.

How do the Martins spend their money? For most consumers, we cannot answer this question with any accuracy, because people usually do not tell anyone what they do with their money. But because the Martins and their buying habits were scrutinized in a series of articles in a national magazine, it is possible to describe quite accurately where their money goes. As shown in Table 4.1, the Martins, who own their own home, spend about $1,800 a month (about 18 percent of their income) on housing. They spend about $500 a month (about 5 percent of their income) on food and drink. About $1,300 a month (about 13 percent of their income) goes for child support and education.

In addition, the Martins spend about $1,300 a month (about 13 percent of their income) on entertainment and clothing. Medical, dental, and insurance expenses consume about $400 a month (about 4 percent of their income); another $400 a month (again, about 4 percent of their income) is spent on transportation. Finally, the Martins allocate about $1,500 a month (about 15 percent of their income) to other expenditures and about $2,900 a month (about 29 percent of their income) to taxes and savings.

This, in a nutshell, is how the Martins spend their money. The Martins exchange their resources (mostly labor) in the resource markets for $120,000

---

[1] For obvious reasons, we changed the name and residence of the family in question. Otherwise, however, the facts given in the following paragraphs are as they were stated in a series of articles in a national magazine. To correct for inflation, we increased the figures in the articles by the (approximate) percentage by which the price level has risen since the article appeared.

TABLE 4.1

Monthly Spending Pattern of Janet and Mike Martin, of Jacksonville, Florida

Item	Amount (dollars)	Percent of Income
Housing	1,800	18
Food and drink	500	5
Child support and education	1,300	13
Entertainment and clothing	1,300	13
Medical, dental, and insurance expenses	400	4
Transportation	400	4
Other expenditures	1,500	15
Taxes and savings	2,900	29
Monthly income	10,000	100*

*Because of rounding errors, the percentages do not sum to 100.

a year. They take this money into the product markets and spend about three-fourths of it for the goods and services just described. The remaining one-fourth of their income goes for taxes and savings. The Martins, like practically every family, keep a watchful eye on where their money goes and what they are getting in exchange for their labor and other resources.

Aggregate Data for the United States

How does the way that the Martins spend their money compare with consumer behavior in general? In Table 4.2, we provide data on how all consumers allocated their aggregate income in 2012. These data tell us much more about the typical behavior of U.S. consumers than our case study of the Martins. Note, first of all, that U.S. households paid about 11 percent of their income in taxes. This, of course, is the price of government services. In addition, U.S. households saved about 4 percent of their income. In other words, they refrained from spending 4 percent of their income on goods and services; instead, they put this amount into stocks, bonds, bank accounts, or other such channels for saving. Also, about 4 percent of their income went for interest payments to banks and other institutions from which they had borrowed money.

They spent the remaining 81 percent of their income on goods and services. Table 4.2 makes it clear that U.S. consumers allocated much of their expenditures to housing, food and drink, and transportation. Spending on housing, furniture and other household equipment, and other durable goods accounted

TABLE 4.2

Allocation of Income by U.S. Households, 2012

Item	Percent of Total
Personal Taxes	11
Personal Savings	4
Interest Payments	4
Consumption Expenditures	
Autos and parts	4
Furniture and household equipment	3
Other durable goods	4
Food and drink	6
Clothing and shoes	3
Gasoline and oil	3
Other nondurable goods	8
Housing	15
Transportation	3
Medical care	13
Recreation	8
Other services	11
Total Income	100

Source: Survey of Current Business, Bureau of Economic Analysis, U.S. Department of Commerce.

for about 22 percent of U.S. consumers' total income. Spending on food and beverages accounted for about 6 percent of their total income. Spending on automobiles and parts, gasoline and oil, and other transportation accounted for about 10 percent of their total income. Thus, taxes, savings, housing, food and drink, and transportation accounted for about half of the total income of all households in the United States.

The data in Table 14.2 make it obvious that the Martin family is not very typical of U.S. consumers. For example, the Martins spend a much larger percentage of their income on entertainment and education than consumers as a whole do and a smaller share on medical expenses. To a large extent, this reflects the fact that people want and need different things. Looking around you, you see considerable diversity in the way consumers spend their money. Take your own family as an example. It is a good bet that your family spends its money quite differently from the nation as a whole. If you like to live in a big house, your family may spend much more than the average family on housing.

Or if you like to go to sports events, your expenditures on such entertainment may be much higher than average.

A Model of Consumer Behavior

Model of consumer behavior

Why do consumers spend their money the way they do? The economist answers this question with the aid of a **model of consumer behavior**, which is useful for both analysis and decision making. To construct this model, the economist must consider consumer tastes, which certainly influence how much consumers purchase of a particular commodity. Some people like beef; others like pork. Some people like the opera; others would trade an opera ticket for a ticket to an NFL game any day of the week.

In Chapter 1, we pointed out that to be useful, a model must omit many unimportant factors, concentrate on the basic factors at work, and simplify in order to illuminate. To focus on the important factors at work here, we assume that there are only two goods, food and clothing. This is an innocuous assumption, since the results we obtain can be generalized to include any number of goods. For simplicity, food is measured in pounds, and clothing is measured in number of pieces of clothing.

Consider how Janet Martin makes choices for her family. Undoubtedly, she regards certain market baskets—that is, certain combinations of food and clothing (the only commodities)—to be more desirable than others. She certainly regards 2 pounds of food and one piece of clothing to be more desirable than 1 pound of food and one piece of clothing. For simplicity, suppose that it is possible to measure the amount of satisfaction that she gets from each market basket by its utility. **Utility** is a number that represents the level of satisfaction the consumer derives from a particular market basket. For example, the utility attached to the market basket containing 2 pounds of food and one piece of clothing may be 10 utils, and the utility attached to the market basket containing 1 pound of food and one piece of clothing may be 6 utils. (A *util* is the traditional unit in which utility is expressed.)

Utility

Marginal Utility

Total utility
Marginal utility

It is important to distinguish between total utility and marginal utility. The **total utility** of a market basket is the number described in the previous paragraph; the **marginal utility** measures the additional satisfaction derived from an additional unit of a commodity. To see how marginal utility is obtained, we take a close look at Table 4.3. The total utility the Martin family derives from the consumption of various amounts of food is given in the middle column of this table. (For simplicity, we assume for the moment that the Martins consume only food.) The marginal utility, shown in the right-hand column, is the extra utility derived from each amount of food over and above the utility derived

TABLE 4.3

Total Utility and Marginal Utility Derived by the Martins from Consuming Various Amounts of Food per Day*

Pounds of Food	Total Utility	Marginal Utility
0	0	3(=3 – 0)
1	3	4(= 7 – 3)
2	7	2(= 9 – 7)
3	9	1(= 10 – 9)
4	10	

*This table assumes that no clothing is consumed. If a nonzero amount of clothing is consumed, the figures in this table will probably be altered, since the marginal utility of a certain amount of food is likely to depend on the amount of clothing consumed.

from 1 less pound of food. Thus, it equals the difference between the total utility of a certain amount of food and the total utility of 1 less pound of food.

For example, as shown in Table 4.3, the total utility of 3 pounds of food is 9 utils, which is a measure of the total amount of satisfaction that the Martins get from this much food. In contrast, the marginal utility of 3 pounds of food is the extra utility obtained from the third pound of food, that is, the total utility of 3 pounds of food less the total utility of 2 pounds of food. Specifically, as shown in Table 4.3, it is 2 utils. Similarly, the total utility of 2 pounds of food is 7 utils, which is a measure of the total amount of satisfaction that the Martins get from this much food. In contrast, the marginal utility of 2 pounds of food is the extra utility obtained from the second pound of food, that is, the total utility of 2 pounds of food less the total utility of 1 pound of food. As shown in Table 4.3, it is 4 utils.

The Law of Diminishing Marginal Utility

Economists generally assume that as a person consumes more and more of a particular commodity, beyond some point, the extra satisfaction derived from the last unit of the commodity consumed declines. For example, if the Martins consume 2 pounds of food in a particular period of time, it may be just enough to meet their basic physical needs. If they consume 3 pounds of food in the same period of time, the third pound of food is likely to yield less satisfaction

FIGURE 4.1

Total and Marginal Utility from Food Consumption, Martin Family

The marginal utility of the first pound of food (which, according to Table 4.3, equals 3 utils) is plotted at the midpoint between 0 and 1 pound of food. The marginal utility of the second pound of food (which, according to Table 4.3, equals 4 utils) is plotted at the midpoint between 1 and 2 pounds of food. The marginal utility curve connects these and other points, showing the marginal utility of various amounts of food consumed.

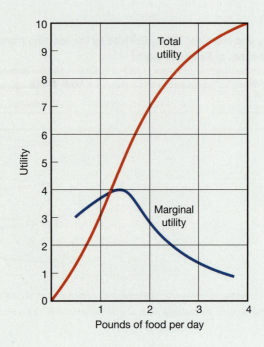

than the second. If they consume 4 pounds of food in the same period of time, the fourth pound of food is likely to yield less satisfaction than the third. And so on. To use another food example, when you are hungry, a hot dog tastes great. Maybe even two hot dogs taste great. But for most people, the third hot dog is much less satisfying.

Law of diminishing marginal utility

This assumption, or hypothesis, is often called the **law of diminishing marginal utility**. This law states that as a person consumes more and more of a given commodity (the consumption of other commodities being held constant), the marginal utility of the commodity eventually tends to decline. The figures concerning the Martin family in Table 4.3 are in accord with this law, as shown in Figure 4.1, which plots the marginal utility of food against the amount consumed. Once the daily consumption of food exceeds about 1.5 pounds, the marginal utility of food declines.

The Equilibrium Market Basket

Preferences alone do not determine how consumers behave. We must also know their income and the prices of commodities to predict which market basket they will buy. A consumer's money income is the amount of money the consumer can spend per unit of time, and this amount constrains the consumer's choice of a market basket. For example, although Mike Martin may regard an Austin Reed as his favorite suit, he may not have sufficient income to buy it. The prices of commodities also influence the consumer's choice of a market basket. If the Austin Reed suit were offered by a discount store at $300, rather than at its list price of $800, Mike might purchase it after all.

Economists assume that consumers generally attempt to maximize utility. In other words, consumers are assumed to be rational in the sense that they choose the market basket—or more generally, the course of action—most to their liking. As previously noted, consumers cannot choose whatever market basket they please. Instead, they must maximize their utility subject to the constraints imposed by the size of their money income and the nature of commodity prices.

What is the optimal market basket, the one that maximizes utility subject to these constraints? It is the one where the consumer's income is allocated among commodities so that for every commodity purchased, the marginal utility of the commodity is proportional to its price. Therefore, in the case of the Martin family, the optimal market basket is the one where

$$MU_F/P_F = MU_C/P_C \qquad\qquad (4.1)$$

where MU_F is the marginal utility of food, MU_C is the marginal utility of clothing, P_F is the price of a pound of food, and P_C is the price of a piece of clothing.

Why Is This Rule Correct?

To understand why the rule in equation 4.1 is correct, it is convenient to begin by pointing out that MU_F/P_F is the marginal utility of the *last dollar's worth* of food and that MU_C/P_C is the marginal utility of the *last dollar's worth* of clothing. To see why this is so, take the case of food. Since MU_F is the extra utility of the last pound of food bought and P_F is the price of this last pound, the extra utility of the last dollar's worth of food must be MU_F/P_F. For example, if the last pound of food results in an extra utility of 4 utils and this pound costs $2, then the extra utility from the last dollar's worth of food must be 4/2, or 2 utils. In other words, the marginal utility of the last dollar's worth of food is 2 utils.

Since MU_F/P_F is the marginal utility of the last dollar's worth of food and MU_C/P_C is the marginal utility of the last dollar's worth of clothing, what equation 4.1 really says is that the rational consumer will choose a market basket where the marginal utility of the last dollar spent on all commodities purchased is the same. To see why this must be so, consider the numerical example in Table 4.4, which shows the marginal utility that the Martins derive from various amounts of food and clothing. Rather than measuring food and clothing in physical units, in Table 4.4 we measure them in terms of the amount of money spent on them.

TABLE 4.4
Marginal Utility Derived by the Martins from Various Quantities of Food and Clothing

| | MARGINAL UTILITY (UTILS) PER DOLLARS WORTH | | | | |
Commodity	1	2	3	4	5
Food	20	16	12	10	7
Clothing	12	10	7	5	3

Given the information in Table 4.4, how much of each commodity should Janet Martin buy if her money income is only $4 (a ridiculous assumption but one that helps make our point)? Clearly, the first dollar she spends should be on food, since it will yield her a marginal utility of 20. The second dollar she spends should also be on food, since a second dollar's worth of food has a marginal utility of 16. (Hence, the total utility derived from the $2 of expenditure is 20 + 16 = 36.)[2] The marginal utility of the third dollar is 12 if it is spent on more food and 12, too, if it is spent on clothing (since it would be the first dollar spent on clothing). Suppose that she chooses more food. (The total utility derived from the $3 of expenditure is 20 + 16 + 12 = 48.) What about the final dollar? Its marginal utility is 10 if it is spent on more food and 12 if it is spent on clothing; so she will spend it on clothing. (The total utility derived from her expenditure of $4 is then 20 + 16 + 12 + 12 = 60.)

Equilibrium market basket

Therefore, Janet Martin, if she is rational, will allocate $3 of her income to food and $1 to clothing. This is the **equilibrium market basket**, the market basket that maximizes consumer satisfaction. The important thing to note is that this market basket demonstrates the principle set forth earlier in equation 4.1. As shown in Table 4.4, the marginal utility derived from the last dollar when it is spent on food is equal to the marginal utility derived from the last dollar when it is spent on clothing (both are 12). Thus, this market basket has the characteristic described previously: the marginal utility of the last dollar spent on all commodities purchased is the same.

The Consumer's Demand Curve

Individual demand curve

In analyzing consumer behavior, economists often use the concept of an individual demand curve. Like the market demand curve, the **individual demand curve** is the relationship between the quantity demanded of a good and the good's price. But whereas the market demand curve shows the quantity demanded in the *entire market* at various prices, the individual

---

[2] Since the marginal utility is the extra utility obtained from each dollar spent, the total utility from the total expenditure must be the sum of the marginal utilities of the individual dollars of expenditure.

FIGURE 4.2

Janet Martin's Individual Demand Curve for Food

The consumer's individual demand curve for a commodity shows the amount of the commodity the consumer will buy at various prices.

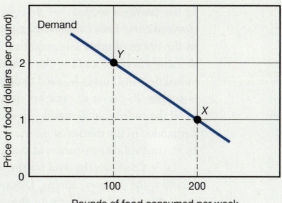

demand curve shows the quantity demanded by a *particular consumer* at various prices. By applying the theory of consumer behavior presented earlier, we can derive a particular consumer's demand curve for a particular good. To see this, we return to Janet Martin and show how we can derive the relationship between the price of food and the amount of food she buys per month.

Assuming that food and clothing are the only goods, that Janet's weekly income is $400, and that the price of clothing is $40 per piece of clothing, we confront her with a variety of prices of food. First, we confront her with a price of $1 per pound of food. How much food will she buy? Next, we confront her with a price of $2 per pound of food. How much food will she buy? The theory of consumer behavior shows how, in each of these circumstances, she allocates her income between food and clothing. From equation 4.1, we know that she will choose an allocation where the marginal utility of the last dollar spent on food equals the marginal utility of the last dollar spent on clothing. Suppose she buys 200 pounds of food when the price is $1 per pound and 100 pounds of food when the price is $2 per pound. These are two points on Janet's individual demand curve for food, those corresponding to prices of $1 and $2 per pound. Figure 4.2 shows these two points, *X* and *Y*.

It is no trick to obtain more points on her individual demand curve for food. All we have to do is confront her with other prices of food and see how much food she buys at each price. Plotting the amount of food she buys against the price, we obtain new points on her individual demand curve for food. Connecting all these points, we get her complete individual demand curve for food, shown in Figure 4.2.

Deriving the Market Demand Curve

In the previous section, we described how to derive a consumer's individual demand curve for a commodity, given the consumer's tastes and income as well as the prices of other commodities. Suppose we have obtained the individual demand curve for each of the consumers in the market. How can these individual demand curves be used to derive the market demand curve? The answer is simple. To derive the market demand curve, we obtain the horizontal sum of all the individual demand curves. In other words, to find the total quantity demanded in the market at a certain price, we add up the quantities demanded by the individual consumers at that price.

Table 4.5 shows the data for the individual demand curves for food for four families: the Joneses, Kleins, DiNardis, and Martins. For simplicity, suppose these four families constitute the entire market for food. Then the market demand for food is shown in the last column of Table 4.5. Figure 4.3 shows the four families' individual demand curves for food as well as the resulting market demand curve. To illustrate how the market demand is derived from the individual demands, suppose that the price of food is $1 per pound. From Table 4.5, we see that the total quantity demanded in the market is 102 hundreds of pounds per month, since this is the sum of the quantities demanded at this price by the four families (50 + 45 + 5 + 2 = 102).

Because individual demand curves for a commodity almost always slope downward to the right, it follows that market demand curves, too, almost always slope downward to the right. (Why? Because the market demand curve is the horizontal sum of all the individual demand curves.) However, the shape and location of the market demand curve vary greatly from commodity to commodity and from market to market. Market demand curves, like people, do not look alike.

TABLE 4.5

Individual Demand and Market Demand for Food

Price of Food	INDIVIDUAL DEMAND				Market Demand
(dollars per pound)	Jones	Klein	Dinardi	Martin	
	(hundreds of pounds per month)				
1.00	50.0	45.0	5.0	2.0	102
1.20	43.0	44.0	4.2	1.8	93
1.40	36.0	43.0	3.4	1.6	84
1.60	30.0	42.0	2.6	1.4	76
1.80	25.0	41.4	2.4	1.2	70
2.00	20.0	41.0	2.0	1.0	64

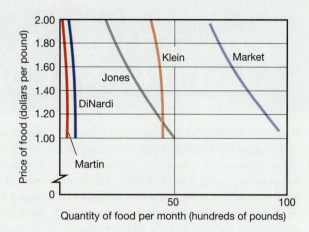

FIGURE 4.3

Individual Demand Curves and the Market Demand Curve for Food

The market demand curve is the horizontal sum of all the individual demand curves.

The Supply Curve

We now turn from the demand curve to the supply curve. When we look behind the supply curve, it is clear that a firm's decision about how much to produce depends on its costs. In the rest of this chapter, we analyze a firm's costs in some detail. Then, in Chapter 6, we will show how the results enable us to derive the market supply curve.

What Are Costs?

Cost

What do we mean by cost? Although this question may seem foolishly simple, it is in fact tricky. Fundamentally, the **cost** of a certain course of action is the value of the best alternative course of action that could have been adopted instead. The cost of producing automobiles is the value of the goods and services that could be obtained from the resources used currently in automobile production if those resources were no longer used to produce automobiles. In general, the costs of a firm's inputs (that is, anything the firm uses in its production process) are their values in their most valuable alternative uses. This is the **opportunity cost** (or **alternative cost**) doctrine (recall the discussion of opportunity cost in Chapter 1).

Opportunity cost
Alternative cost

Suppose that a firm's owner devotes 50 hours a week to the firm's business and that, because he is the owner, he pays himself no salary. According to the usual rules of accounting, the costs of his labor are not included in the firm's income statement. But according to the economist's opportunity cost doctrine, the cost of his labor is by no means zero. Instead, this cost equals whatever

CONSERVING WATER IN A CALIFORNIA DROUGHT

From 1975 to 1977, California suffered a series of droughts. Many communities embarked on water conservation programs. Washing cars and watering lawns were forbidden. Farmers were notified that there might be a cutback of 25 percent in water allotment for the spring and that they should reduce planting. Marin County, a wealthy community just north of San Francisco, was one of the hardest hit California communities. By the second year of the drought, residents were rationed to 46 gallons per day, one-third their normal usage.

To maintain rationing quotas, stiff new water rates were imposed. The basic rate was doubled; anyone who used twice the quota paid more than 8 times the old rate, and usage beyond that amount cost 40 times the predrought rate. People reduced their water consumption by 25 percent in the first year and by 65 percent in the second. Water was saved for its most-valued uses. Low-volume shower heads were installed as well as other apparatus to reduce water usage in toilets and sinks.

Torrential rains in the final days of 1977 marked the end of this drought, but its legacy lingered on. Several conservation measures were written into law, and the people of Marin County continued to pay—and pay willingly—more for water than they had before the drought. Total water usage stayed well below the predrought levels for years, both because the higher price of water reduced the quantity demanded and because the demand curve for water had shifted to the left.

The California drought is a good illustration of marginal utility. As water became scarce, its marginal utility to the average consumer rose. People cut back on uses of water that added little to their satisfaction, such as washing cars and watering lawns, and the available water was used in ways that had a high marginal utility: drinking, cooking, and bathing.

amount he could obtain if he worked 50 hours a week for someone else. Both economists and accountants agree that opportunity costs are the relevant costs for many types of problems and that the failure to use the proper concept of cost can result in serious mistakes.

Costs for the individual firm are the necessary payments to the owners of resources to get them to provide these resources to the firm. To obtain these resources as inputs, the firm must bid them away from alternative uses. The payments made to the owners of these resources may be either explicit or implicit costs. If a payment is made to a supplier, laborer, or some other resource owner who is not the firm's owner, this is an **explicit cost**, which is paid for in an explicit way. But if a resource is owned by the firm's owner, there may be no explicit payment for it, as in the case of the labor of the owner who paid himself no salary. The costs of such owner-supplied resources are **implicit costs**,

Explicit cost

Implicit costs

which are equal to what these resources could bring if they were used in their most valuable alternative ways. And the firm's profits (or losses), as defined by economists, are the difference between the firm's revenues and its total costs, both explicit and implicit.

Short-Run Cost Functions

Cost functions

To maximize its profits, a firm must determine the least-cost combination of inputs to produce any quantity of output. The previous chapter showed how this least-cost input combination can be found; with this information, it is easy to determine the minimum cost of producing each quantity of output. Knowing the (minimum) cost of producing each quantity of output, we can define and measure the firm's **cost functions**, which show how various types of costs are related to the firm's output.

A firm's cost functions vary, depending on whether they are based on the short run or the long run. As we saw from the previous chapter, the short run is the period of time in which at least one of the firm's inputs is fixed. On the other hand, the long run is that period of time in which all inputs are variable. In the long run, the firm can make a complete adjustment to any change in its environment.

In the following sections, we will concentrate on the short run, where the firm cannot vary the quantities of plant and equipment it uses. These are the firm's fixed inputs, and they determine the scale of its operations. Three kinds of costs are important in the short run: total fixed cost, total variable cost, and total cost.

Total Fixed Cost

Total fixed cost

Total fixed cost is the total expenditure by the firm per period of time for fixed inputs. Since the quantity of the fixed inputs is unvarying (by definition), the total fixed cost is the same whatever the firm's level of output. Among the firm's fixed costs in the short run are property taxes and interest on bonds issued in the past. If the firm has contracts with suppliers and workers that cannot be renegotiated (without dire consequences) in the short run, the expenses involved in meeting these contracts are also fixed costs.

Consider a hypothetical firm, the HighNote Music Box Company. This firm produces a high-priced line of music boxes. Table 4.6 shows that HighNote's fixed costs are $300 per day; the firm's total fixed cost function is shown in Figure 4.4.

Total Variable Cost

Total variable cost

Total variable cost is the firm's total expenditure on variable inputs per period of time. Since, by definition, a firm cannot vary its fixed inputs in the short run,

TABLE 4.6	Number of Boxes Produced Per Day	Total Fixed Cost	Total Variable Cost	Total Cost
Fixed, Variable, and	0	300	0	300
Total Costs per Day,	1	300	60	360
HighNote Music Box	2	300	110	410
Company (in dollars)	3	300	160	460
	4	300	200	500
	5	300	260	560
	6	300	360	660
	7	300	510	810
	8	300	710	1,010
	9	300	1,060	1,360

it has to increase its variable inputs if it wants to increase its output. And since higher output rates require greater utilization of variable inputs, they mean a higher total variable cost. So if HighNote increases its daily production of music boxes, it must increase the amount it spends per day on metal (for the components), wood (for the outside of the boxes), labor (for the assembly of the boxes), and other variable inputs. Table 4.6 shows HighNote's total variable costs at various output rates; Figure 4.5 shows the firm's total variable cost function.

Beyond an output rate of four music boxes per day, total variable cost increases at an increasing rate. It is important to understand that this

FIGURE 4.4

Total Fixed Cost per Day, HighNote Music Box Company

The total fixed cost function is always a horizontal line, since fixed costs do not vary with output.

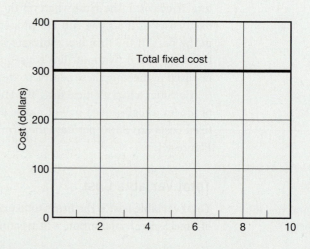

FIGURE 4.5

Total Variable Cost per Day, HighNote Music Box Company

Total variable cost is the total expenditure per period of time on variable inputs. Because of the law of diminishing marginal returns, total variable cost increases first at a decreasing rate and then at an increasing rate.

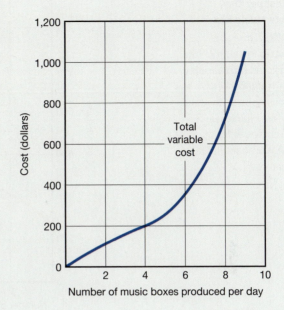

characteristic of the total variable cost function results from the operation of the law of diminishing marginal returns. This law states that if equal increments of an input are added, the quantities of other inputs being held constant, the resulting increments of product decrease beyond some point; that is, the marginal product of the input diminishes. At small output rates, increases in the utilization of variable inputs may bring about increases in their productivity and cause total variable cost to increase with output but at a decreasing rate. Beyond a point, however, there are diminishing marginal returns from the variable input, with the result that total variable costs increase at an increasing rate.

Total Cost

Total cost

Total cost is the sum of total fixed cost and total variable cost. Therefore, to obtain HighNote's total cost at a given output, we need only add its total fixed cost and its total variable cost at that output. The result is shown in Table 4.6, and the corresponding total cost function is shown in Figure 4.6. Because the total cost function and the total variable cost function differ by only a constant amount (equal to total fixed cost), they have the same shape, as shown in Figure 4.7, which brings together all three of the total cost functions (or cost curves, as they are often called).

FIGURE 4.6

Total Cost per Day, HighNote Music Box Company

Total cost is the sum of total fixed cost and total variable cost. The total cost curve has the same shape as the total variable cost curve, since the two curves differ by only a constant amount (equal to total fixed cost).

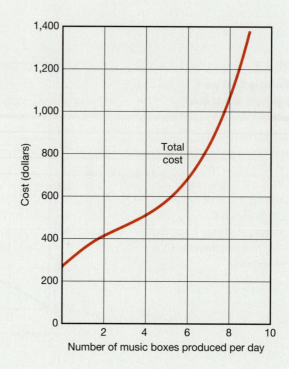

FIGURE 4.7

Fixed, Variable, and Total Costs per Day, HighNote Music Box Company

All three cost functions, presented in Figures 4.4 to 4.6, are brought back for a curtain call.

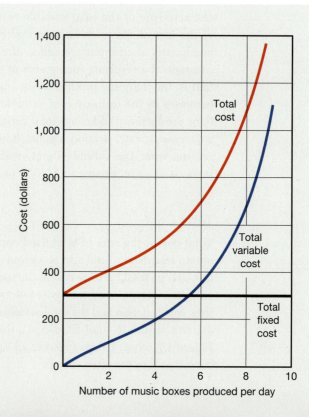

Average Costs in the Short Run

HighNote's CEO unquestionably cares about the average cost of a music box as well as the total cost incurred; so do economists. Average cost tells how much a product costs per unit of output. There are three average cost functions, one corresponding to each of the three total cost functions.

Average Fixed Cost

Average fixed cost

We begin with **average fixed cost**, which is simply the total fixed cost divided by the firm's output. Table 4.7 and Figure 4.8 show the average fixed cost function for the HighNote Music Box Company. Average fixed cost must decline with increases in output, since it equals a constant (total fixed cost) divided by the output rate.

Average Variable Cost

Average variable cost

The next type of average cost is **average variable cost**, which is total variable cost divided by output. For HighNote, the average variable cost function is shown in Table 4.7 and Figure 4.9. At first, increases in the output rate result in decreases in average variable cost, but beyond a point, they result in a higher average variable cost, owing to the law of diminishing marginal returns. As more and more of the variable inputs are utilized, the extra output they produce declines beyond some point, so the amount spent on variable inputs per unit of output tends to increase.

Average Total Cost

Average total cost

The last type of average cost is **average total cost**, which is total cost divided by output. For HighNote, the average total cost function is shown in Table 4.7 and Figure 4.10. At any level of output, average total cost equals average fixed cost plus average variable cost.

The fact that average total cost is the sum of average fixed cost and average variable cost helps explain the shape of the average total cost function. If, as the output rate goes up, both average fixed cost and average variable cost decrease, average total cost must decrease, too. But beyond some point, average total cost must increase, because the increases in average variable cost eventually more than offset the decreases in average fixed cost. However, average total cost achieves its minimum after average variable cost, because the increases in average variable cost are for a time more than offset by decreases in average fixed cost. (To see this visually, look ahead to Figure 4.12.)

CASE STUDY 4.2

OIL PRICE SWINGS AND DRILLING ACTIVITY

In the decade prior to 1973, independent domestic oil producers found it increasingly difficult to compete with OPEC's low world oil prices. Domestic oil production had leveled off, and many suppliers had left the industry. In the wake of the 1973–1974 oil embargo and the quadrupling of oil prices, new producers and speculative investors were spurred to jump into the oil patch, and existing companies expanded their drilling. The new price and profit potential were the main motivating factors for this expansion. The lust for undiscovered "new" oil was greater than ever.

In 1979, the Carter administration announced the gradual phaseout of control on domestic oil prices. The new high price for oil and government decontrol were the financial carrots needed to lure new suppliers back into domestic oil production. The number of active rigs had gone from under 1,000 in 1971 to over 4,000 in 1981. Over 16,500 wildcat wells were drilled in 1982, as opposed to 7,000 in 1971. As one producer put it, "Just about anywhere you went in that period, you stumbled over someone behind a bush, drilling." In the decade following the first oil crisis in 1973, oil exploration almost doubled. Independent companies, "wildcatters," accounted for roughly 90 percent of the drilling. In accord with the basic economic models presented in this text, the amount of drilling activity increased in response to higher oil prices, which acted both as signals and as incentives for such resource reallocation.

The marginal cost of extracting additional barrels of oil rises steeply after a point. Drillers have to resort to more expensive techniques for secondary and tertiary recovery, that is, recovering hard-to-reach oil from a given well. As the price of oil rose, these more expensive techniques became more affordable. Similarly, the drilling of new, deeper, and more expensive wells could be justified because the higher costs could be covered by the higher price of oil.

What goes up must come down—and go up and come down again. In late 1985, the price of oil fell rapidly because of overproduction and weak demand. Drilling came to a virtual standstill, and many existing wells were closed. Production in the United States fell, and import dependence rose again. In 1990, when the price of oil rose after Iraq invaded Kuwait, there were signs of renewed interest in drilling in the United States. After the Gulf War, drilling activity dipped a little and then remained steady until the end of the 1990s. In 1998, oil prices collapsed in the wake of the Asian financial crisis. Once again, drilling activity dried up. By 2000, oil prices had recovered. In late 2002 and early 2003, oil prices hovered between $35 and $40 a barrel, mostly because of the uncertainty that preceded the Iraq War. After the war, oil prices fell again, but not by much, then rose again—and kept rising—until 2008, when they hit a record $150 a barrel. But as a consequence of the financial crisis that year and the deep recession that followed, oil prices fell to $40 a barrel by early 2009. But the story does not end there. As the economic recovery got under way, oil prices rose again, reaching $125 a barrel by early 2012. The rise and fall of oil prices was matched by a similar pattern in the rig count, as higher prices made drilling more profitable and lower prices made drilling less profitable.

TABLE 4.7

Average Fixed Cost, Average Variable Cost, and Average Total Cost per Day, HighNote Music Box Company (in dollars)

Number of Boxes Produced per Day	Average Fixed Cost	Average Variable Cost	Average Total Cost
1	300(=300 ÷ 1)	60(=60 ÷ 1)	360(=360 ÷ 1)
2	150(=300 ÷ 2)	55(=100 ÷ 2)	205(=410 ÷ 2)
3	100(=300 ÷ 3)	53(=160 ÷ 3)	153(=460 ÷ 3)
4	75(=300 ÷ 4)	50(=200 ÷ 4)	125(=500 ÷ 4)
5	60(=300 ÷ 5)	52(=260 ÷ 5)	112(=560 ÷ 5)
6	50(=300 ÷ 6)	60(=360 ÷ 6)	110(=660 ÷ 6)
7	43(=300 ÷ 7)	73(=510 ÷ 7)	116(=810 ÷ 7)
8	38(=300 ÷ 8)	89(=710 ÷ 8)	126(=1,010 ÷ 8)
9	33(=300 ÷ 9)	118(=1,060 ÷ 9)	151(=1,360 ÷ 9)

Marginal Cost in the Short Run

Marginal cost

No one can really understand the operations of a business firm without understanding the concept of **marginal cost**, the addition to total cost resulting from the addition of the last unit of output. To see how marginal cost is calculated, look at Table 4.8, which shows data for the total cost function of the HighNote Music Box Company. When output is between zero and one music box per day, the firm's marginal cost is $60, since this is the *extra cost* of producing the first music box per day. In other words, $60 equals marginal cost in this situation,

FIGURE 4.8

Average Fixed Cost per Day, HighNote Music Box Company

Average fixed cost is the total fixed cost divided by the firm's output. Because it equals a constant (total fixed cost) divided by the output rate, it must decline with increases in output.

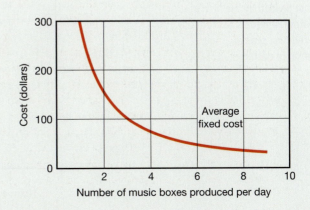

FIGURE 4.9

Average Variable Cost per Day, HighNote Music Box Company

Average variable cost is total variable cost divided by the firm's output. Beyond a point (in this case, about four music boxes per day), average variable cost rises with increases in output because of the law of diminishing marginal returns.

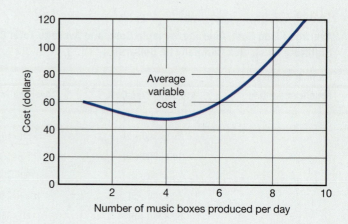

FIGURE 4.10

Average Total Cost per Day, HighNote Music Box Company

Average total cost is the total cost divided by the firm's output. It equals average fixed cost plus average variable cost.

because it is the difference between the total cost of producing one music box per day ($360) and the total cost of producing zero music boxes per day ($300, which is the firm's total fixed cost).

In general, marginal cost varies, depending on the firm's output level. As Table 4.8 shows, HighNote's marginal cost is $50 when the firm produces

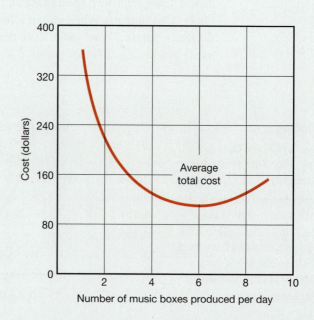

TABLE 4.8

Calculation of Marginal Cost per Day, HighNote Music Box Company (in dollars)

Number of Music Boxes Produced per Day	Total Cost	Marginal Cost
0	300	
		60(= 360 − 300)
1	360	
		50(= 410 − 360)
2	410	
		50(= 460 − 410)
3	460	
		40(= 500 − 460)
4	500	
		60(= 560 − 500)
5	560	
		100(= 660 − 560)
6	660	
		150(= 810 − 660)
7	810	
		200(= 1,010 − 810)
8	1,010	
		350(= 1,360 − 1,010)
9	1,360	

between one and two music boxes per day, $100 when the firm produces between five and six music boxes per day, and $350 when the firm produces between eight and nine music boxes per day. Table 4.8 (and Figure 4.11, which shows the marginal cost function graphically) indicates that marginal cost, after decreasing with increases in output at low output levels, increases with further increases in output. In other words, beyond some point, it becomes more and more costly for the firm to produce yet another unit of output.

Increasing Marginal Cost and Diminishing Returns

The reason why marginal cost increases beyond some output level is found in the law of diminishing marginal returns. If (beyond some point) increases

FIGURE 4.11

Marginal Cost per Day, HighNote Music Box Company

The marginal cost of the first unit of output (which, according to Table 4.8, is $60) is plotted at the midpoint between 0 and 1 unit of output. The marginal cost of the second unit of output is plotted at the midpoint between 1 and 2 units of output. The marginal cost function connects these and other points, showing the marginal cost of various amounts of output.

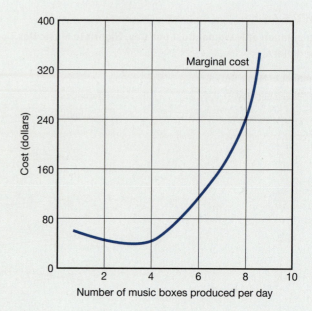

in variable inputs result in less and less extra output, it follows that a larger and larger quantity of variable inputs must be added to produce an extra unit of output. Therefore, the cost of producing an extra unit of output must increase.

Relationship between Marginal Cost Function and Average Cost Function

Figure 4.12 shows the marginal cost curve together with the three average cost curves. Note that the marginal cost curve intersects both the average variable cost curve and the average total cost curve at their minimum points. The reason for this is simple. If the extra cost of a unit of output is greater (or less) than the average cost of the units of output already produced, the addition of the extra unit of output clearly must raise (or lower) the average cost of production. Therefore, if marginal cost is greater (or less) than average cost, average cost must be rising (or falling). And if this is so, average cost can be at a minimum only when it equals marginal cost. (The same reasoning holds for both average total cost and average variable cost and for the short and long runs.)

To clarify this point, consider the following numerical example. Suppose that the average total cost of producing 4 units of output is $10 and that the

FIGURE 4.12

Average Fixed Cost, Average Variable Cost, Average Total Cost, and Marginal Cost per Day, HighNote Music Box Company

All of the curves presented in Figures 4.8 to 4.11 are brought together for review. Note that the marginal cost curve intersects both the average variable cost curve and the average total cost curve at their minimum points.

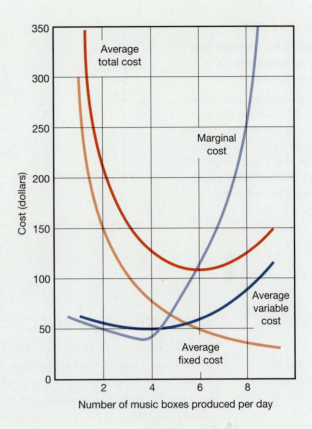

marginal cost of the fifth unit of output is less than $10. Will the average total cost be less for 5 units of output than for 4 units? It will be less, because the fifth unit's cost pulls down the average. On the other hand, if the marginal cost of the fifth unit of output is greater than $10, the average total cost for 5 units of output is greater than for 4 units of output, because the fifth unit's cost pulls up the average. Hence, average total cost falls when it is above marginal cost and rises when it is below marginal cost. Consequently, when it is at a minimum, average total cost must equal marginal cost, as shown in Figure 4.12.

At this point, you might wonder about the relevance of concepts such as average cost and marginal cost to firms such as HighNote, which have to make day-to-day decisions about how to manage their costs and how much to produce. While not all firms go through such rigorous analysis, concepts such as fixed costs (in business jargon, sunk costs or overhead) and marginal costs (in business jargon, variable costs) are crucial when it comes to figuring out how profitable a company is and how to improve profitability.

FIGURE 4.13

Short-Run Average Cost Curves and Long-Run Average Cost Curve

The short-run average total cost functions for three plants—small, medium, and large—are *AA'*, *BB'*, and *DD'*. The long-run average cost function is *AUVD* if only these three types of plants can be built.

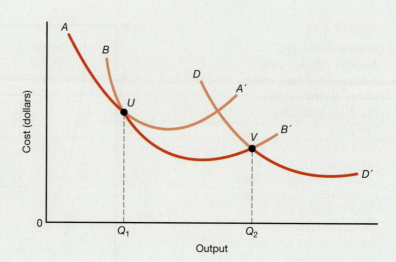

Long-Run Average Cost Function

Long-run average cost function

We held for last an additional kind of cost function that plays a very important role in economic analysis. This is the firm's **long-run average cost function**, which shows the minimum average cost of producing each output level when any desired type or scale of plant can be built. Unlike the cost functions discussed in the previous sections, this cost function pertains to the long run, a period long enough that all inputs are variable and none are fixed. In the long run, a firm can make any adjustments in its production techniques to suit changes in its environment.

Suppose a firm can build plants of three sizes: small, medium, and large. The short-run average total cost functions corresponding to these plants are *AA'*, *BB'*, and *DD'* in Figure 4.13. If the firm is still in the planning stage of plant construction, it can choose whichever plant has the lowest costs. Consequently, the firm chooses the small plant if it believes that its output rate will be smaller than Q_1, the medium plant if it believes that its output rate will be above Q_1 but below Q_2, and the large plant if it believes that its output rate will be above Q_2. Therefore, the long-run average cost curve is *AUVD'*. And if, as is generally the case, there are many possible types of plants, the long-run average cost curve looks like *LL'* in Figure 4.14. (Only a few of the short-run average cost curves are shown in Figure 4.14.)

Returns to Scale

Production function

What determines the shape of the long-run average cost function in a particular industry? Its shape must depend on the characteristics of the **production function**, which shows the most output that existing technology permits the

FIGURE 4.14

Long-Run Average Cost Curve

If many types of plants can be built, the long-run average cost function is *LL'*.

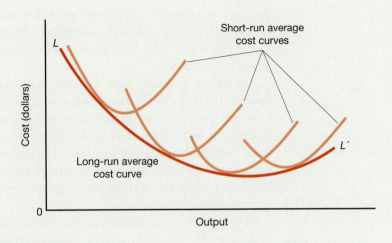

firm to extract from each quantity of inputs. Specifically, the shape of the long-run average cost function depends in part on whether there are *increasing*, *decreasing*, or *constant* returns to scale. To understand what these terms mean, consider a long-run situation and suppose that the firm increases the amount of all inputs by the same proportion. What will happen to output? If output increases by a larger proportion than each of the inputs, this is a case of **increasing returns to scale**. If output increases by a smaller proportion than each of the inputs, this is a case of **decreasing returns to scale**. If output increases by the same proportion as each of the inputs, this is a case of **constant returns to scale**.

At first glance it may seem that constant returns to scale must always prevail. After all, if two factories are built with the same equipment and use the same type and number of workers, it seems reasonable that they can produce twice as much output as one such factory. But things are not that simple. If a firm doubles its scale, it may be able to use techniques that could not be used at the smaller scale. Some inputs are not available in small units; for example, we cannot install half a robot. Because of indivisibilities of this sort, increasing returns to scale may occur. Hence, although a firm could double its size by simply building two small factories, this may be inefficient. One large factory may be more efficient than two smaller factories of the same total capacity because it is large enough to use certain techniques and inputs that the smaller factories cannot use.

Increasing returns to scale can also stem from certain geometrical relations. For example, the volume of a box that is 3 × 3 × 3 feet is 27 times as great as the volume of a box that is 1 × 1 × 1 foot and thus can carry 27 times as much as the smaller box. But since the area of the six sides of the larger box is

Increasing returns to scale

Decreasing returns to scale

Constant returns to scale

54 square feet and the area of the six sides of the smaller box is 6 square feet, the larger box requires only 9 times as much wood as the smaller box. Greater specialization also can result in increasing returns to scale. As more workers and machines are used, it is possible to subdivide tasks and allow various inputs to specialize.

Decreasing returns to scale can also occur, and the most frequently cited reason is the difficulty of coordinating a large enterprise. It can be difficult even in a small firm to obtain the information required to make important decisions; in a large firm, the difficulties tend to be greater. It can be difficult even in a small firm to be certain that management's wishes are being carried out; in a larger firm, these difficulties, too, tend to be greater. Although the advantages of a large organization seem to have captured the public fancy, there are often very great disadvantages as well.

Whether there are increasing, decreasing, or constant returns to scale in a particular situation must be determined case by case. Moreover, the answer is likely to depend on the particular range of output considered. Frequently, increasing returns to scale accrue up to some level of output, then perhaps constant returns to scale up to a higher level of output, beyond which there may be decreasing returns to scale. This pattern is responsible in part for the U-shaped long-run average cost function in Figure 4.14. At relatively small output levels, there are increasing returns to scale and long-run average cost decreases as output rises. At relatively high output levels, there are decreasing returns to scale and long-run average cost increases as output rises.

The U-shaped pattern is not found in all industries. Within the range covered by the available data, there is little or no evidence in many industries that long-run average cost increases as output rises. But this may be because the data do not cover a wide enough range. Eventually, long-run average cost should rise because of problems of coordination, increased red tape, and reduced flexibility. Firms as large as General Motors or Exxon are continually bedeviled by the very real difficulties of enormous size.

REVIEW AND PRACTICE

Summary

1 Utility is a number that represents the level of satisfaction derived by the consumer from a particular market basket. Market baskets with higher utility are preferred over market baskets with lower utility.

2 The model of consumer behavior recognizes that preferences alone do not determine the consumer's actions. Choices are dictated by the size

of the consumer's money income and the nature of commodity prices. These factors, as well as the consumer's preferences, determine choice.

3   If consumers maximize utility, their income is allocated among commodities so that for every commodity purchased, the marginal utility of the commodity is proportional to its price. In other words, the marginal utility of the last dollar spent on each commodity is made equal for all commodities purchased.

4   The individual demand curve shows the quantity of a good demanded by a particular consumer at various prices of the good. The individual demand curve for practically all goods slopes downward and to the right. Its location depends on the consumer's income and tastes and the prices of other goods.

5   To derive the market demand curve, we obtain the horizontal sum of all the individual demand curves of the people in the market. Since individual demand curves for a commodity almost always slope downward to the right, it follows that market demand curves, too, almost always slope downward to the right.

6   The cost of a certain course of action is the value of the best alternative course of action that could have been pursued instead. This is the doctrine of opportunity cost, or alternative cost.

7   Three kinds of total cost functions are important in the short run: total fixed cost, total variable cost, and total cost. In addition, there are three kinds of average cost functions (corresponding to each of the total cost functions): average fixed cost, average variable cost, and average total cost.

8   Marginal cost, the addition to total cost due to the addition of the last unit of output, is of enormous significance in the firm's decision-making process. Because of the law of diminishing marginal returns, marginal cost tends to rise beyond some output level.

9   The firm's long-run average cost curve shows the minimum average cost of producing each output level when any desired type or scale of plant can be built. The shape of the long-run average cost curve is determined in part by whether there are increasing, decreasing, or constant returns to scale.

10   Suppose that a firm increases the amount of all inputs by the same percentage. If output increases by more than this percentage, this is a case of increasing returns to scale. If output increases by less than this percentage, this is a case of decreasing returns to scale. If output increases by this same percentage, this is a case of constant returns to scale.

Problems and Questions

1 Suppose that the total utility attached by Elaine Johnson to various quantities of hamburgers consumed (per day) is as follows:

Number of Hamburgers	Total Utility (utils)
0	0
1	5
2	12
3	15
4	17
5	18

Between three and four hamburgers, what is the marginal utility of a hamburger? Between four and five hamburgers? Do these results conform to the law of diminishing marginal utility?

2 If Elaine maximizes her satisfaction and the marginal utility of a hot dog is twice that of a bottle of beer, what must the price of a hot dog be if

(a) the price of a bottle of beer is $0.75.

(b) the price of a bottle of beer is $1.

(Assume that Elaine consumes both beer and hot dogs.)

3 Suppose that the data for a firm's short-run total cost function are as follows:

Output (number of units per year)	Total Cost per Year (dollars)
0	20,000
1	20,100
2	20,200
3	20,300
4	20,500
5	20,800

What are the firm's total fixed costs? What are its total variable costs when it produces 4 units per year?

4 In question 3, what is the firm's marginal cost when between 4 and 5 units are produced per year? Does marginal cost increase beyond some output level?

5 In question 3, what is the firm's average cost when it produces 1 unit per year? 2 units per year? 3 units per year? 4 units per year? 5 units per year?

Key Terms

model of consumer behavior	total fixed cost
utility	total variable cost
total utility	total cost
marginal utility	average fixed cost
law of diminishing marginal utility	average variable cost
equilibrium market basket	average total cost
individual demand curve	marginal cost
cost	long-run average
opportunity cost	cost function
alternative cost	production function
explicit cost	increasing returns to scale
implicit costs	decreasing returns to scale
cost functions	constant returns to scale

Viewpoint for Analysis

In a 2012 editorial in the *Wall Street Journal*, Ed Morse, of Citigroup, said, "The United States has become the fastest-growing oil and gas producer in the world, and is likely to remain so for the rest of this decade and into the 2020s."[3]

(a) What does this statement imply about the costs (fixed and variable) of producing oil and natural gas in the United States?

(b) What will likely happen to the supply of natural gas and oil in North America and, as a consequence, the price of each?

(c) At what point will it become unprofitable to extract more oil and gas? (*Hint:* It has to do with the average and marginal cost of extracting and producing extra volumes of natural gas and oil.)

[3] Ed Morse, "Move Over OPEC—Here We Come," *Wall Street Journal*, March 19, 2012.

Market Demand and Price Elasticity

LEARNING OBJECTIVES

➤ To explain how a good's price elasticity affects demand

➤ To describe the income elasticity of demand

➤ To define product substitutes and product complements

➤ *(Exploring Further)* To describe the market conditions that present ongoing problems for farmers

Airlines like American or United and aircraft manufacturers like Boeing or Airbus must forecast the demand for air travel 5 or 10 years ahead. An important factor influencing the quantity of air tickets demanded is the price of a ticket. If this price falls by 15 percent, what will be the effect on the quantity of tickets demanded? One purpose of this chapter is to show how the price elasticity of demand (a concept we will define later) can be used to answer this question.

In a free market economy, market demand is a fundamental determinant of what is produced and how. The market demand curve for a commodity plays an important role in the decision-making process within each firm that produces the commodity, as well as in the economy as a whole. It is no exaggeration to say that firms spend enormous time and effort trying to cater to, estimate, and influence market demand.

Market Demand Curves

**Market
demand curve**

Let us review what a **market demand curve** is. You will recall from Chapters 2 and 4 that a commodity's market demand curve shows how much of the commodity will be purchased during a particular period of time at various prices. Figure 5.1 ought to be familiar; it is the market demand curve for wheat in 2011, which figured prominently in our discussion of the price system in Chapter 2. Among other things, it shows that during 2011, about 2.5 billion bushels of U.S. wheat would have been purchased per year if the price were $6.60 per bushel, that about 2.4 billion bushels would have been purchased per year if the price were $7.00 per bushel, and that about 2.3 billion bushels would have been purchased if the price were $7.40 per bushel.

The market demand curve reflects what consumers want and are willing to pay for. When the market demand curve for wheat shifts upward to the right, this indicates that consumers want more wheat at the existing price. On the other hand, when the curve shifts downward to the left, this indicates that consumers want less wheat at the existing price. Such shifts in the market demand curve for a commodity trigger changes in the behavior of the commodity's producers. When the market demand curve shifts upward to the right, the price of wheat tends to rise, inducing farmers to produce more wheat, because they find that given the price increase, their profits will increase if they raise their output levels. The same process occurs in other parts of the economy. Shifts in the demand curve reflecting the fact that consumers want more

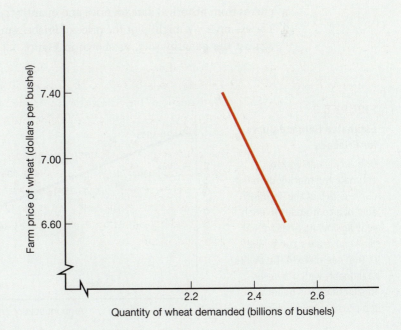

FIGURE 5.1

Market Demand Curve for Wheat, 2011

This curve shows how much wheat would be purchased per year at various prices.

(or less) of a commodity set in motion a sequence of events leading to more (or less) production of the commodity.

Measuring Market Demand Curves

To be of practical use, market demand curves must be based on careful measurements. Various techniques are used to estimate the market demand curve for particular commodities. It might seem that a quick and easy way to estimate the demand curve might be to interview consumers about their buying habits and intentions. However, simply asking people how much they would buy of a certain commodity at particular prices is not usually very useful, since off-the-cuff answers to such questions are rarely very accurate. Therefore, marketing researchers and econometricians interested in measuring market demand curves have been forced to use more complex procedures.

One such procedure is the direct market experiment. Although the designs of such experiments vary greatly and are often quite complicated, the basic idea is simple: see the effects on the quantity demanded of actual variations in the price of the product. (Researchers attempt to hold other market factors constant or take into account whatever changes may occur.) The Parker Pen Company conducted an experiment a number of years ago to estimate the demand curve for their ink, Quink. They increased the price from $0.15 to $0.25 in four cities and found that the quantity demanded was quite insensitive to the price. Experiments like this are frequently carried out to try to estimate a product's market demand curve.

Still another technique is to use statistical methods to estimate demand curves from historical data on price and quantity purchased of the commodity. For example, we might plot the price of Frisbees in various periods in the past against the quantity sold, as shown in Figure 5.2. Judging from the results,

FIGURE 5.2

Estimated Demand Curve for Frisbees

One very crude way to estimate the market demand curve is to plot the amount sold of a commodity in each year against its price in that year and draw a curve, like *D*, that seems to fit the points reasonably well. However, this technique is generally too crude to be reliable.

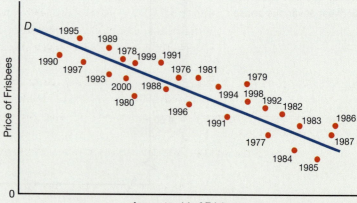

FIGURE 5.3

Market Demand Curves, Beef and Cotton

The quantity demanded of beef is much more sensitive to price than is the quantity demanded of cotton.

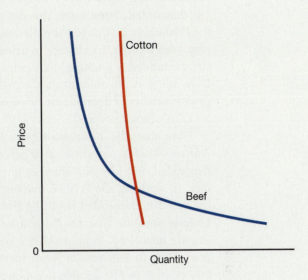

curve *D* in Figure 5.2 seems a reasonable approximation to the demand curve. Although this simple analysis provides some insight into how statistical methods are used to estimate demand curves from historical data, it is a vast oversimplification. For one thing, the market demand curve may have shifted over time, so that curve *D* is not a proper estimate. Fortunately, modern statistical techniques recognize this possibility and allow us to estimate the position and shape of this curve (at each point in time) in spite of it.

Price Elasticity of Demand

As Figure 5.3 shows, the quantity demanded of some commodities, such as beef, is fairly sensitive to changes in the commodity's price; that is, changes in price result in significant changes in quantity demanded. On the other hand, the quantity demanded of other commodities, such as cotton, is very insensitive to changes in the price; large changes in price result in small changes in the quantity demanded.

To discuss this subject more rigorously, we must have some measure of the sensitivity of the quantity demanded to changes in price. The measure customarily used for this purpose is the **price elasticity of demand**, defined as the percentage change in quantity demanded resulting from a 1 percent change in price.[1] For example, suppose that a 1 percent

Price elasticity of demand

[1] What if price does not change by 1 percent? Then the price elasticity of demand is defined as the percentage change in quantity demanded divided by the percentage change in price. This definition is used in the next section. Put in terms of symbols, the price elasticity of demand equals $(-\Delta Q/\Delta P) \times (P/Q)$, where *P* is price, ΔP is the change in price, *Q* is quantity demanded, and ΔQ is the change in the quantity demanded.

reduction in the price of Frisbees results in a 2 percent increase in quantity demanded. Then using this definition, the price elasticity of demand for Frisbees is 2. (Convention dictates that we give the elasticity a positive sign even though the change in price is negative and the change in quantity demanded is positive.) The price elasticity of demand is likely to vary from one point to another on the market demand curve. For example, the price elasticity of demand for Frisbees may be higher when a Frisbee costs $4 than when it costs $1.

Note that the price elasticity of demand is expressed in terms of *relative*—that is, proportional or percentage—changes in price and quantity demanded, not *absolute* changes in price and quantity demanded. Therefore, in studying the Frisbee market, we look at the *percentage* change in the quantity demanded resulting from a 1 *percent* change in price. This is because absolute changes depend on the units in which price and quantity are measured. Suppose that a reduction in the price of a commodity from $100 to $99 results in an increase in the quantity demanded from 200 pounds to 210 pounds per month. If price is measured in dollars, the quantity demanded of the commodity seems quite sensitive to price changes, since a decrease in price of 1 results in an increase in quantity demanded of 10. On the other hand, if price is measured in cents, the quantity demanded seems quite insensitive to price changes, since a decrease in price of 100 results in an increase in quantity demanded of 10. By using relative changes, we avoid this problem. Relative changes do not depend on the units of measurement. The percentage reduction in the price of the commodity is 1 percent, regardless of whether price is measured in dollars or cents. And the percentage increase in the quantity demanded is 5 percent, regardless of whether it is measured in pounds or tons.

Calculating the Price Elasticity of Demand

The price elasticity of demand is a very important concept and one that economists use often, so it is worth spending some time explaining exactly how it is computed. Suppose we have a table showing various points on a market demand curve. For example, Table 5.1 shows the quantity of wheat demanded at various prices in 2011. Given these data, how do we go about computing the price elasticity of demand for wheat? Since the price elasticity of demand for any product generally varies from point to point on its market demand curve, we must first determine at what point on the demand curve we want to measure the price elasticity of demand.

Let us assume that we want to estimate the price elasticity of demand for wheat when the price of wheat is between $7.40 and $7.80 per bushel. To do this, we can use the following equation:

TABLE 5.1	Farm Price of Wheat (dollars per bushel)	Quantity of Wheat Demanded (billions of bushels)
Market Demand for Wheat, 2011	5.80	2.7
	6.20	2.6
	6.60	2.5
	7.00	2.4
	7.40	2.3
	7.80	2.2

Price elasticity = percentage change in quantity demanded

÷ percentage change in price

$$= \frac{\text{change in quantity demanded}}{\text{original quantity demanded}} \div \frac{\text{change in price}}{\text{original price}}$$

Table 5.1 shows that the quantity demanded equals 2.3 billion bushels when the price is $7.40 and 2.2 billion bushels when the price is $7.80. But should we use $7.40 and 2.3 billion bushels as the original price and quantity? Or should we use $7.80 and 2.2 billion bushels as the original price and quantity? If we choose the former, then

$$\textit{Price elasticity} = -\frac{(2.2 - 2.3)}{2.3} \div \frac{(7.8 - 7.4)}{7.4} = 0.80$$

The price elasticity of demand is estimated to be 0.80. (The minus sign at the beginning of the right side of this equation is needed because convention dictates that elasticity be given a positive sign.)

But we could just as well have used $7.80 and 2.2 billion bushels as the original price and quantity. If this had been our choice, then

$$\textit{Price elasticity} = -\frac{(2.3 - 2.2)}{2.2} \div \frac{(7.4 - 7.8)}{7.80} = 0.88$$

which is somewhat different from our earlier answer.

To get around this difficulty, we use the average values of price and quantity as the original price and quantity. In other words,

$$\text{Price elasticity} = \frac{\text{change in quantity demanded}}{\text{sum of quantities}/2} \div \frac{\text{change in price}}{\text{sum of prices}/2}$$

Arc elasticity of demand

This is the **arc elasticity of demand**. In the specific case we are considering, the arc elasticity is

$$\text{Price elasticity} = -\frac{(2.2 - 2.3)}{(2.2 + 2.3)/2} \div \frac{(7.80 - 7.40)}{(7.80 + 7.40)/2} = 0.83$$

Thus, the answer to our problem is 0.83.

Determinants of the Price Elasticity of Demand

Studies have been made of the price elasticity of demand for particular commodities. Table 5.2 reproduces the results of some of them. Note the substantial differences among products. For example, the estimated price elasticity of demand for women's hats is about 3.00, whereas for cotton it is only about 0.12. Think for a few minutes about these results, and try to figure out why these differences exist. Chances are that you will agree that the following factors are important determinants of whether a commodity's price elasticity of demand is high or low.

➤ *Number and closeness of available substitutes.* If a commodity has many close substitutes, its demand is likely to be highly elastic; that is, the price elasticity is likely to be high. If the price of the product increases, a large proportion of its buyers turn to the close substitutes available. If its price decreases, a great many buyers of substitutes switch to this product. Naturally, the closeness of the substitutes depends on how narrowly the commodity is defined. In general, we would expect that as the definition of the product becomes narrower and more specific, the product has more close substitutes and its price elasticity of demand is higher. Therefore, the demand for a particular brand of motor oil is more price elastic than the overall demand for oil, and the demand for oil is more price elastic than the demand for fuel as a whole. If a commodity is defined so that it has perfect substitutes, its price elasticity of demand approaches infinity. For example, if one farmer's wheat is exactly like that grown by other farmers and the farmer raises the price slightly (to a point above the market level), the farmer's sales will be reduced to nothing.

TABLE 5.2	Commodity	Price Elasticity
Estimated Price Elasticities of Demand for Selected Commodities, United States	Women's hats	3.00
	Gasoline	0.30
	Sugar	0.31
	Corn	0.49
	Cotton	0.12
	Hay	0.43
	Potatoes	0.31
	Oats	0.56
	Barley	0.39
	Buckwheat	0.99
	Refrigerators	1.40
	Airline travel	2.40
	Radio and TV sets	1.20
	Legal services	0.50
	Pleasure boats	1.30
	Canned tomatoes	2.50
	Newspapers	0.10
	Tires	0.60
	Beef	0.92
	Shoes	0.40

➤ *Importance in consumers' budgets.* It is often asserted that the price elasticity of demand for a commodity is likely to depend on the importance of the commodity in consumers' budgets. The elasticity of demand for commodities like pepper and salt may be quite low. Typical consumers spend a very small portion of their income on pepper and salt, and the quantity they demand may not be influenced much by changes in price within a reasonable range. However, although a tendency of this sort is often hypothesized, there is no guarantee that it always exists.

➤ *Length of the period.* Every market demand curve pertains to a certain time interval. In general, demand is likely to be more sensitive to price over a long period than over a short one. The longer the period, the easier it is for consumers and business firms to substitute one good for another. If, for example, the price of oil should decline relative to other fuels, oil consumption in the month after the price decline would probably increase very little. But over a period of several years, people would have an opportunity to take advantage of the price decline in choosing the type of fuel to be used in new and renovated houses and businesses. In the longer period of several years, the price decline would have a greater effect on the consumption of oil than in the shorter period of one month.[2]

Price Elasticity and Total Money Expenditure

Many important decisions hinge on price elasticity. The price elasticity of demand determines whether a given change in price increases or decreases the amount of money spent on a commodity—often a matter of great importance to firms and government agencies. We look more closely at how the price elasticity of demand determines the effect of a price change on the total amount spent on a commodity.

Price elastic
Price inelastic

Unitary elastic

As a first step, we must define three terms: price elastic, price inelastic, and unitary elastic. The demand for a commodity is **price elastic** if the price elasticity of demand is *greater than 1*. The demand for a commodity is **price inelastic** if the price elasticity of demand is *less than 1*. And the demand for a commodity is **unitary elastic** if the price elasticity of demand *equals 1*. As you will see, the effect of a price change on the total amount spent on a commodity depends on whether the demand for the commodity is price elastic, price inelastic, or unitary elastic.

Case 1. Demand Is Price Elastic

In this case, if the price of the commodity is *reduced*, the total amount spent on the commodity *increases*. To see why, suppose that the price elasticity of demand for high-definition television sets is 2 and the price of the high-definition television sets is reduced by 1 percent. Because the price elasticity of demand is 2, the 1 percent reduction in price results in a 2 percent increase in the quantity of high-definition television sets demanded. Since the total amount spent on high-definition television sets equals the quantity demanded times the price, the 1 percent reduction in price is more than offset by the 2 percent increase in quantity demanded. The result of the price cut is an increase in the total amount spent on high-definition television sets.

On the other hand, if the price of the commodity *increases*, the total amount spent on the commodity *falls*. For example, if the price of high-definition television sets is raised by 1 percent, this reduces the quantity demanded by 2 percent.

[2] For durable goods like automobiles, the price elasticity of demand may be smaller over a long period than over a short one. If the price of autos increases, the quantity demanded is likely to fall substantially because many people postpone buying a new car. But as time goes on, the quantity of autos demanded tends to rise as old autos wear out.

CASE STUDY 5.1

INSTABILITY OF FARM PRICES AND THE PRICE ELASTICITY OF DEMAND

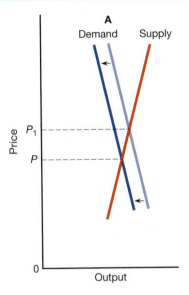

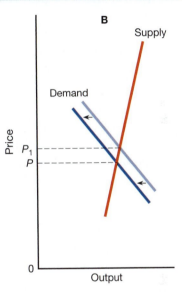

Between the summer of 1997 and the end of 1998, the price of soybeans fell a staggering 50 percent. This was the result of deep recessions in Asia, Russia, and Latin America. While the demand for other products, such as automobiles, fell as well, the prices of these products did not decline anywhere near as much. What explains the volatility in agricultural prices?

One of the most difficult problems for farmers is that in a free market, farm incomes vary enormously between good times and bad, much more than nonfarm incomes. This is so because although farm prices vary a great deal between good times and bad, farm output is much more stable than industrial output. Why is agriculture like this?

The answer lies in considerable part with the price elasticity of demand for farm products. Food is a necessity with few good substitutes. Therefore, we would expect the demand for farm products to be price inelastic. And as Table 5.2 suggests, this expectation is borne out by the facts. Given that the demand for farm products is price inelastic—and that the quantity supplied of farm products is also relatively insensitive to price—it follows that relatively small shifts in either the supply curve or the demand curve result in big changes in price. This is why farm prices are so unstable. Panel A in the accompanying figure shows a market where the demand curve is much more inelastic than in panel B. As you can see, a small shift to the left in the demand curve results in a much larger drop in price in panel A than in panel B.

The instability of farm prices was once again evident in 2010 and 2011 when a series of bad weather events around the world raised the prices of many crops. In the case of soybeans, prices rose from around $6 to around $12 per bushel in a matter of months.

The 2 percent reduction in the quantity demanded more than offsets the 1 percent increase in price and results in a decrease in the total amount spent on television sets.

Case 2. Demand Is Price Inelastic

In this case, if the price is *reduced*, the total amount spent on the commodity *decreases*. To see why, suppose that the price elasticity of demand for corn is 0.5 and the price of corn is reduced by 1 percent. Because the price elasticity of demand is 0.5, the 1 percent price reduction results in a 0.5 percent increase in the quantity demanded of corn. Since the total amount spent on corn equals the quantity demanded times the price, the 0.5 percent increase in the quantity demanded is more than offset by the 1 percent reduction in price. The result of the price cut is a decrease in the total amount spent on corn.

On the other hand, if the price of the commodity *increases*, the total amount spent on the commodity *increases*. For example, if the price of corn is raised by 1 percent, this reduces quantity demanded by 0.5 percent. The 1 percent price increase more than offsets the 0.5 percent reduction in quantity demanded and results in an increase in the total amount spent on corn.

Case 3. Demand Is Unitary Elastic

In this case, a price increase or decrease results in no difference in the total amount spent on the commodity. Why? Because a price decrease (or increase) of a certain percentage always results in a quantity increase (or decrease) of the same percentage, so the product of the price and quantity is unaffected.

Table 5.3 summarizes the results of this section and should help you review the findings.

Industry and Firm Demand Curves

Up to this point, we have been dealing with the market demand curve for a commodity. The market demand curve for a commodity is not the same as the demand curve for the output of a single firm that produces the commodity unless, of course, the industry is composed of only a single firm. If the industry is composed of more than one firm, as is usually the case, the demand curve

TABLE 5.3

Effect of an Increase or Decrease in the Price of a Commodity on the Total Expenditure on the Commodity

| | EFFECT ON TOTAL EXPENDITURE OF | |
Commodity's Price Elasticity of Demand	Price Decrease	Price Increase
Price elastic (elasticity is greater than 1)	Increase	Decrease
Price inelastic (elasticity is less than 1)	Decrease	Increase
Unitary elastic (elasticity equals 1)	No change	No change

for the output of each firm producing the commodity usually is quite different from the market demand curve for the commodity. The demand curve for the output of Farmer Brown's wheat is quite different from the market demand curve for wheat.

In particular, the demand curve for the output of a particular firm is generally more price elastic than the market demand curve for the commodity, because the products of other firms in the industry are close substitutes for the product of this firm. As pointed out earlier, products with many close substitutes have a relatively high price elasticity of demand.

If many firms are selling a homogeneous product, the individual firm's demand curve becomes *horizontal*, or essentially so. To see this, suppose that 100,000 firms sell a particular commodity and all these firms are of equal size. If any one of these firms were to triple its output and sales, the total industry output would change by only 0.002 percent, too small a change to have any perceptible effect on the price of the commodity. Consequently, each firm can act as if variations in its output, within the range of its capabilities, have no real impact on market price. In other words, the demand curve facing the individual firm is horizontal, as in Figure 5.4.

FIGURE 5.4

Demand Curve for Output of an Individual Firm: The Case of a Great Many Sellers of a Homogeneous Commodity

If many firms are selling a homogeneous product, the demand curve facing an individual firm is horizontal.

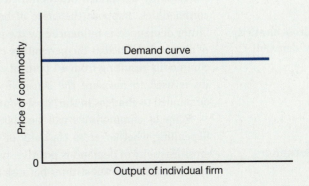

Income Elasticity of Demand

So far, this chapter has dealt almost exclusively with the effect of a commodity's price on the quantity demanded of it in the market. But price is not, of course, the only factor that influences the quantity demanded of the commodity. Another important factor is the level of money income among the consumers in the market. The sensitivity of the quantity demanded to the total money income of all of the consumers in the market is measured by the **income elasticity of demand**, defined as the percentage change in the quantity demanded resulting from a 1 percent change in total money income (all prices being held constant).

Income elasticity of demand

A commodity's income elasticity of demand may be positive or negative. For many commodities, increases in income result in increases in the amount demanded. Such commodities, like steak or caviar, have a positive income elasticity of demand. For other commodities, increases in income result in decreases in the amount demanded. These commodities, such as poor grades of vegetables, have a negative income elasticity of demand; economists call these types of goods "inferior goods." However, be careful to note that the income elasticity of demand of a commodity is likely to vary with the level of income under consideration. For example, if only families at the lowest income levels are considered, the income elasticity of demand for poor grades of vegetables may be positive.

Luxury items tend to have a higher income elasticity of demand than do necessities. Indeed, one way to define luxuries and necessities is to say that luxuries are commodities with a high income elasticity of demand, and necessities are commodities with a low income elasticity of demand.

Business owners do not want to leave money on the table, so they are always trying to learn how sensitive consumers are to price changes and to figure out the ideal price for maintaining business while maximizing profits.

Cross Elasticity of Demand

In addition to the price of the commodity and the level of total money income, the quantity demanded of a commodity also depends on the prices of other commodities. Suppose the price of butter is held constant. The amount of butter demanded is influenced by the price of margarine. The **cross elasticity of demand**, defined as the percentage change in the quantity demanded of one commodity resulting from a 1 percent change in the price of another commodity, is used to measure the sensitivity of the former commodity's quantity demanded to changes in the latter commodity's price.

Cross elasticity of demand

Pairs of commodities can be classified as substitutes or complements, depending whether cross elasticity of demand is positive or negative. If the cross elasticity of demand is positive, two commodities are **substitutes**. Butter and margarine are substitutes because a decrease in the price of butter results

Substitutes

Complements

in a decrease in the quantity demanded of margarine. On the other hand, if the cross elasticity of demand is negative, two commodities are **complements**. For example, gin and tonic may be complements since a decrease in the price of gin may increase the quantity demanded of tonic. The reduction in the price of gin increases the quantity demanded of gin and therefore increases the quantity demanded of tonic, since gin and tonic tend to be used together.

Many studies have been made of the cross elasticity of demand for various pairs of commodities. After all, it is frequently important to know how a change in the price of one commodity will affect the sale of another commodity. For example, what would be the effect of a 1 percent increase in the price of pork on the quantity demanded of beef? According to estimates by the late Herman Wold, a distinguished Swedish economist, the effect would be a 0.28 percent increase in the quantity demanded of beef, since he estimated that the cross elasticity of demand for these two commodities is 0.28. This means that the cross elasticity of beef and pork is quite weak. What effect would a 1 percent increase in the price of butter have on the quantity demanded of margarine? According to Wold, the effect would be a 0.81 percent increase in the quantity demanded of margarine, since he estimated that the cross elasticity of demand for these two commodities is 0.81. This estimate suggests that the cross elasticity of butter and margarine is quite strong.

EXPLORING FURTHER

The Farm Problem

Agriculture is an enormously important sector of the U.S. economy. Even though its size has been decreasing steadily for many decades, agriculture still employs about 1.2 million Americans. Its importance, moreover, cannot be measured entirely by its size. You need only think about how difficult it would be to get along without food to see the strategic role that agriculture plays in our economic life. Also, agriculture is one of the most technologically progressive parts of the U.S. economy. The efficiency of U.S. agriculture is admired throughout the world.

Nonetheless, U.S. farmers have had serious problems. Historically, the clearest indication of these problems has emerged from a comparison of U.S. farmers' per capita income with per capita income among the rest of the population. Frequently, the average income of farm families has been 20 percent or more below the average income of nonfarm families. Moreover, a large proportion of the rural population has been poor.

This farm problem is nothing new. Farmers enjoyed relatively high prices and high incomes during the first two decades of the twentieth century. But in 1920, the country experienced a sharp depression that jolted agriculture as well as the rest of the economy. Whereas the Roaring Twenties saw a recovery and boom in the nonfarm sector of the economy, agriculture did not recover as completely, and the 1930s were dreadful years; the Great Depression resulted in a devastating decline in farm prices and farm incomes. World War II brought prosperity to agriculture, but in the postwar period, farm incomes have often been well below nonfarm incomes. From 1973 to 1975, prosperity returned to farms because of soaring commodity prices. However, in the late 1970s and throughout the 1980s, farmers again complained about prices and incomes. The boom years of the 1990s helped farm incomes, and rapid growth in Asia with its large population made that region a major market for U.S. farm products; however, the Asian financial crisis in 1998 brought with it a sharp drop in farm prices. Fortunately, in the first decade of the twenty-first century, Asia resumed its strong growth, and demand for U.S. farm products soared once again. Farm incomes also rose during the first decade of the twenty-first century, alleviating some of the rural poverty mentioned earlier. Nevertheless, given the short-run inelasticity of both food supply and demand, the volatility in food prices is, unfortunately, something we are likely to see more of in the future.

Characteristics of Demand and Supply Curves for Farm Products

We start with the market demand curve for farm products. This market demand curve must have two important characteristics. First, its shape must reflect the fact that food is a necessity and the quantity demanded does not vary much with the price of food; in other words, the demand curve is price inelastic. Second, the market demand curve for food is unlikely to shift to the right very much as per capita income rises, because consumption of food per capita faces natural biological and other limitations. In other words, consumption of food is income inelastic as well.

Next, consider the market supply curve for farm products. Again, be aware of two important characteristics of this market supply curve. First, the quantity of farm products supplied tends to be relatively insensitive to price (it is price inelastic) because the farmers have only limited control over their output. (Weather, floods, insects, and other factors are important.) Second, because of rapid technological change, the market supply curve has been shifting markedly and rapidly to the right.

Decline in Relative Price of Food Products

If you understand these simple characteristics of the market demand curve and market supply curve for farm products, it is no trick to understand why we have had the sort of farm problem just described. Figure 5.5 shows the market demand and market supply curves for farm products at various points in time. As you would expect, the market demand curve for farm products shifts rather slowly

FIGURE 5.5

Shifts over Time in the Market Demand and Supply Curves for Farm Products

The market demand curve has shifted rather slowly to the right (from D to D_1 to D_2), whereas the market supply curve has shifted rapidly to the right (from S to S_1 to S_2), with the result that the equilibrium price has declined (from P to P_1 to P_2).

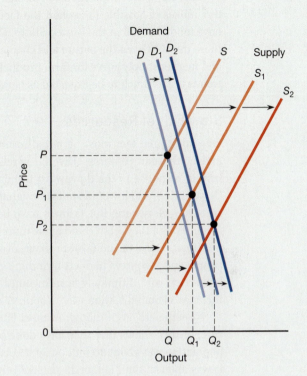

to the right as incomes (and population) grow over time. Specifically, the market demand curve shifted from D in the first period to D_1 in the second period to D_2 in the third period. On the other hand, the market supply curve for farm products shifted rapidly to the right as technology improved over time. It shifted from S in the first period to S_1 in the second period to S_2 in the third period.

What was the consequence of these shifts in the market demand and supply curves for food products? Clearly, the equilibrium price of food products fell (relative to other products). Specifically, the equilibrium price fell from P to P_1 to P_2 in Figure 5.5. This price decrease was, of course, a large part of the farm problem. If we correct for changes in the general level of prices (which have tended to rise over time), there was, in general, a declining trend in farm prices; agricultural prices generally fell, relative to other prices, in the last 70 years. Moreover, given this fall in farm prices, farm incomes tended to fall, because although lower prices were associated with greater amounts sold, the reduction in price was much greater than the increase in quantity sold, as we can see in Figure 5.5.[3]

---

[3] The amount farmers receive is the amount they sell times the price. In Figure 5.5, the amount farmers receive in income is $P \times Q$ in the first period, $P_1 \times Q_1$ in the second period, and $P_2 \times Q_2$ in the third period. Clearly, since the price is decreasing much more rapidly than the quantity is increasing, farm incomes are falling.

Therefore, the simple model of market behavior described in previous chapters makes it possible to explain the fact that farm prices and farm incomes have tended to fall in the United States. Certainly, nothing is mysterious about these trends. Given the nature and characteristics of the market demand curve and market supply curve for farm products, our simple model shows that these trends are as much to be expected as parades on the Fourth of July.

Slow Exit of Resources

One additional fact must be noted to understand the farm problem: people and nonhuman resources have been relatively slow to move out of agriculture in response to the downward trends. The price system uses such trends (lower prices and lower incomes) to signal producers that they should use their resources elsewhere. But farmers have been loath to move out of agriculture (even though they often could make more money elsewhere), and this has been a primary cause of the farm problem over most of the past 50 years. If more people and resources had left farming, agricultural prices and incomes would have risen, and ultimately farm incomes would have come closer to nonfarm incomes. (Poor education was, of course, a significant barrier to migration.)

Nonetheless, even though farmers have been slow to move out of agriculture, history shows that they have done so in the long run. In 1930, the farm population was about 30 million, or 25 percent of the total population; in 1950, it was about 23 million, or 15 percent of the total population; and in 2010, it was about 1.2 million, less than 1 percent of the total population. Thus, the price system has had its way. Resources have been moving out of agriculture in response to the signals and pressures of the price system. This movement of people and nonhuman resources unquestionably has contributed to greater efficiency and prodution for the nation as a whole.

Government Aid to Agriculture

Farm policy often has more to do with politics than economics. Traditionally, farmers have had a disproportionately large amount of political clout. It is no surprise that the farm programs introduced by successive administrations were timed to have maximum impact on elections. The politics of agriculture is also big in Europe and Japan, where some of the agricultural programs are even more wasteful and counterproductive than in the United States.

The political power of farmers derives from two fundamental fears. The first is the security of the food supply. Few countries want to depend too much on foreign suppliers of food or be ill prepared in the face of the whims of Mother Nature. Second, many countries, including the United States, would like to preserve the way of life of the small family-owned farm, which has often been highly romanticized.

Well intentioned as government farm programs may be, they usually are hugely expensive and inefficient. Often, the price paid for saving a farm, either in higher food prices or higher taxes to support farmers, is many times the cost of farmers' incomes. Also, programs intended to save small farms often end up subsidizing much larger farms, which do not need to be saved.

The United States is blessed with such a productive agricultural sector that food security is not a serious problem. This leaves the protection of small farmers, especially the poor ones. Fortunately, the history of farm programs in the United States shows that there are cost-effective ways of helping poor farmers during the lean years. These programs are so effective, in fact, that according to the U.S. Department of Agriculture, in 2012 the average U.S. farm household's net worth was around $1.2 million (though most of that was tied up in land).

REVIEW AND PRACTICE

Summary

1 The market demand curve is the relationship between the price of a commodity and the amount of the commodity demanded in the market. The shape and position of a product's market demand curve depend on consumer tastes, consumer incomes, the price of other goods, and the number of consumers in the market.

2 The price elasticity of demand, defined as the percentage change in quantity demanded resulting from a 1 percent change in price, measures the sensitivity of the amount demanded to changes in price. Whether a price increase results in an increase or decrease in the total amount spent on a commodity depends on the price elasticity of demand.

3 The market demand curve for a commodity is not the same as the demand curve for the output of a single firm that produces the commodity unless the industry is composed of only one firm. In general, the demand curve for the output of a single firm is more elastic than the market demand curve for the commodity. Indeed, if many firms are selling a homogeneous commodity, the individual firm's demand curve becomes horizontal.

4 The income elasticity of demand, defined as the percentage change in quantity demanded resulting from a 1 percent change in total money income, measures the sensitivity of the amount demanded to changes in total income. A commodity's income elasticity of demand may be positive or negative. Luxury items are generally assumed to have a higher income elasticity of demand than necessities.

5 The cross elasticity of demand, defined as the percentage change in the quantity demanded resulting from a 1 percent change in the price of another

commodity, measures the sensitivity of the amount demanded to changes in the price of another commodity. If the cross elasticity of demand is positive, two commodities are substitutes; if it is negative, they are complements.

*6[4] The demand for farm products grew slowly, while rapid technological change meant that the people and resources currently in agriculture could supply more and more farm products. Because people and resources did not move out of agriculture as rapidly as the price system dictated, farm incomes in the United States often tended to be relatively low. Nevertheless, a variety of farm subsidy and support programs have helped to alleviate rural poverty.

Problems and Questions

1 Professor Kenneth Warner, of the University of Michigan, has estimated that a 10 percent increase in the price of cigarettes results in a 4 percent decline in the quantity of cigarettes consumed. For teenagers, he estimated that a 10 percent price increase results in a 14 percent decline in cigarette consumption. Based on his estimates, what is the price elasticity of demand for cigarettes? Among teenagers, what is the price elasticity of demand? Why is the price elasticity different for teenagers than for the public as a whole?

2 Suppose that each of the four corners of an intersection contains a gas station and that the gasoline is essentially the same. Do you think that the price elasticity of demand for each station's gasoline is above or below 1? Why? Do you think that it is less than or greater than the price elasticity of demand for all gasoline in the United States?

3 The High Note Music Box Company is convinced that an increase in its price will reduce the total amount of money spent on its product. If the company is correct, can you tell from this whether the demand for its product is price elastic or price inelastic?

4 Suppose that the relationship between the price of aluminum and the quantity of aluminum demanded is as follows:

Price (dollars)	Quantity
1	8
2	7
3	6
4	5
5	4

[4] Starred (*) items refer to material covered in Exploring Further.

What is the arc elasticity of demand when price is between $1 and $2? Between $4 and $5?

5   Is each of the following statements true, partly true, or false? Explain.

   (a) If a good's income elasticity of demand is less than 1, an increase in the price of the good will increase the amount spent on it.

   (b) The income elasticity of demand will have the same sign (+ or –) regardless of the level of income at which it is measured.

   (c) If Mr. Miller spends all his income on steak (regardless of his income or the price of steak), his cross elasticity of demand between steak and any other good is 0.

6   What is the sign (+ or -) of the cross elasticity of demand for each of the following pairs of commodities?

   (a) Tea and coffee

   (b) Tennis rackets and tennis balls

   (c) Whiskey and gin

   (d) Fishing licenses and fishing poles

   (e) Nylon rugs and wool rugs

Key Terms

market demand curve
price elasticity of demand
arc elasticity of demand
price elastic
price inelastic

unitary elastic
income elasticity of demand
cross elasticity of demand
substitutes
complements

Viewpoint for Analysis

According to Henry Ford, "It is better to sell a large number of cars at a reasonably small margin than to sell fewer cars at a larger margin of profit. Bear in mind that when you reduce the price of the car without reducing the quality you increase the possible number of purchases."[5]

(a) In 1909, Ford introduced the Model T at a price of $900; sales were 58,000 cars. In 1914, the price was $440; about 470,000 cars were sold. If the demand

[5] John B. Rae, ed., *Henry Ford* (Englewood Cliffs, NJ: Prentice-Hall, 1969), 112.

curve for the Model T remained constant during 1909–1914, what was the price elasticity of demand?

(b) Do you think that the demand curve remained constant during 1909–1914? If not, do you think that it shifted to the right or to the left? Why?

(c) Do price reductions always result in higher profits? For example, if the demand for a firm's product is price inelastic, will the firm increase its profits by cutting its price? Explain.

Economic Efficiency, Market Supply, and Perfect Competition

LEARNING OBJECTIVES

➤ To describe the conditions defining a perfectly competitive market structure

➤ To explain the golden rule of output determination for a perfectly competitive firm

➤ To understand the concept of economic profits

➤ To describe the long-run equilibrium position for a perfectly competitive firm

An important determinant of how a society's resources are used is the organization of its markets—whether the market for wheat contains few sellers or many, for example, or whether 20 firms provide telephone service in Chicago rather than a single firm. Economists have no simple formulas that will eliminate all social waste. But on the basis of existing models and evidence, some forms of market organization tend to minimize social waste, whereas other forms seem to promote it.

Perfect competition

In this chapter, we will examine the way resources are allocated and prices are set under **perfect competition**. This type of market organization—or market structure, as it is often called—is a polar case that seldom, if ever, occurs in a pure form in the real world. But it is an extremely useful model that sheds much light on a market structure's effects on resource allocation. Anyone who wants to understand how markets work in a capitalistic economy or why our public policies toward business are what they are must understand perfect competition as well as the other market structures we take up later.

Market Structure and Economic Performance

Having studied the workings of various markets, many economists have come to the conclusion that, from society's point of view, certain kinds of market organizations are better than others. Despite considerable controversy on this score, there is a majority view that market structures should be as close as possible to perfect competition.

Economists have generally found it useful to classify markets into four broad types: *perfect competition, monopolistic competition, oligopoly*, and *monopoly*. Each is a particular type of market structure or organization. Table 6.1 provides a capsule description of each type of market, highlighting how these market structures differ.

Number of Firms

The economist's classification of market structures is primarily based on the number of firms in the industry that supplies the product. In perfect competition and monopolistic competition, there are *many* sellers, each of which produces only a small part of the industry's output. In monopoly, on the other hand, the industry consists of only a *single* seller. Oligopoly is an intermediate case where there are *a few* sellers. For example, since NSTAR is the only supplier of electricity for Boston, it is a monopoly. And since there are only a small number of laptop computer manufacturers, the market for laptops is an oligopoly.

TABLE 6.1

Types of Market Structure

Market Structure	Examples	Number of Producers	Type of Product	Power of firm over Price	Barriers to Entry	Nonprice Competition
Perfect competition	Parts of agriculture are reasonably close	Many	Standardized	None	Low	None
Monopolistic competition	Retail trade	Many	Differentiated	Some	Low	Advertising and product differentiation
Oligopoly	Autos, steel, machinery	Few	Standardized or differentiated	Some	High	Advertising and product differentiation
Monopoly	Public utilities	One	Unique	Considerable	Very high	Advertising

Type of Product

Market structures also differ in the extent to which the firms in an industry produce standardized (identical) products. All firms in a perfectly competitive market produce *identical* products. Farmer Brown's corn is essentially the same as Farmer Smith's. In a monopolistic competitive industry like dress manufacturing, firms produce *somewhat different* products. One firm's dresses differ in style and quality from another firm's dresses. In an oligopolistic industry, firms *sometimes*, but not always, produce identical products. And in a monopolistic industry, there can be *no difference* among firms in their products, since there is only one firm.

Control over Price

Market structures differ considerably in the extent to which an individual firm has control over price. A firm under perfect competition has *no control* over price. For example, a wheat farm (which is close to being a perfectly competitive firm) has no control over the price of wheat. On the other hand, a monopolist is likely to have *considerable control* over price. In the absence of public regulation, NSTAR would have considerable control over the price of electricity in Boston. A firm under monopolistic competition (say, an apparel manufacturer) or oligopoly (a computer company, for example) is likely to have *more* control over price than a perfectly competitive firm and *less* control over price than a monopolist.

Barriers to Entry

Barriers to entry

The ease with which firms can enter the industry differs from one market structure to another. In perfect competition, **barriers to entry** are *low*. Only a small investment is required to enter many parts of agriculture. Similarly, there are *low* barriers to entry in monopolistic competition. But in oligopolies such as autos and steel, there tend to be *very considerable* barriers to entry because, among other reasons, it is so expensive to build an auto or steel plant. In monopoly, entry is blocked; once another firm enters, the monopolist is an ex-monopolist.

Nonprice Competition

Market structures also differ in the extent to which firms compete on the basis of advertising and differences in product characteristics, rather than price. In perfect competition, there is no nonprice competition. In monopolistic competition, there is *considerable* emphasis on nonprice competition. Dress manufacturers compete by trying to develop better styles and by advertising their product lines. Oligopolies also tend to rely heavily on nonprice competition. For example, auto firms try to increase their sales by building better and more attractive cars and by advertising. Monopolists also engage in advertising to increase their profits, although this advertising is not directed at reducing the sales of other firms in the industry, since no other firms exist.

Perfect Competition

When business executives speak of a highly competitive market, they often mean one in which each firm is keenly aware of its rivalry with a few others and in which advertising, styling, packaging, and other such commercial weapons are used to attract business away from them. In contrast, the basic feature of the economist's definition of perfect competition is its *impersonality*. Because so many firms are in the industry, no firm views another as a competitor any more than one small tobacco farmer views another small tobacco farmer as a competitor. A market is perfectly competitive if it satisfies three conditions.

Condition 1. Homogeneity of product. The product of any one seller must be the same as the product of any other seller. This condition ensures that buyers do not care from which seller they purchase the goods, so long as the price is the same. This condition is met in many markets. As pointed out earlier, Farmer Brown's corn is likely to be essentially the same as Farmer Smith's.

Condition 2. Many buyers and sellers. There must be a large number of buyers and sellers. Each participant in the market, whether buyer or seller, must be so small in relation to the entire market that he or she cannot affect the product's price. All buyers and sellers must be "price takers," not "price makers." A firm under perfect competition faces a horizontal demand curve, since variations in its output (within the range of its capabilities) have no effect on market price.

Condition 3. Mobility of resources. All resources must be capable of switching readily from one use to another, and consumers, firms, and resource owners must have complete knowledge of all relevant economic and technological data.

No industry in the real world, now or in the past, satisfies all these conditions completely; therefore, no industry is perfectly competitive. Some agricultural markets may be reasonably close, but even they do not meet all the requirements. But this does not mean that it is useless to study the behavior of a perfectly competitive market. The conclusions derived from the model of perfect competition have proved very helpful in explaining and predicting behavior in the real world. Indeed, as we shall see, they have permitted a reasonably accurate view of resource allocation in many important segments of our economy.

The Output of the Firm

What determines the output rate in the short run of a perfectly competitive firm? Since the firm is perfectly competitive, it cannot affect the price of its product, and it can sell any amount it wants at this price. And since we are

TABLE 6.2

Costs and Revenues per Week, Adagio Piano Company (in dollars)

Output per Week (pianos)	Price	Total Revenue (price × output)	Total Fixed Cost	Total Variable Cost	Total Cost	Total Profit
0	1,000	0	1,000	0	1,000	−1,000
1	1,000	1,000	1,000	200	1,200	−200
2	1,000	2,000	1,000	300	1,300	700
3	1,000	3,000	1,000	500	1,500	1,500
4	1,000	4,000	1,000	1,000	2,000	2,000
5	1,000	5,000	1,000	2,000	3,000	2,000
6	1,000	6,000	1,000	3,200	4,200	1,800
7	1,000	7,000	1,000	4,500	5,500	1,500
8	1,000	8,000	1,000	7,200	8,200	−200

concerned with the short run, the firm can expand or contract its output rate by increasing or decreasing its utilization of its variable inputs but not its fixed inputs. (We consider the situation in the long run in a later section.)

What Is the Profit at Each Output Rate?

To see how a firm determines its output rate, suppose that you take over the family business, the Adagio Piano Company. Your first problem is to decide how many pianos (each with a price of $1,000) the firm should produce per week. Having a good deal of economic intuition, you instruct your accountants to estimate the company's total revenue (defined as price times output) and total costs (as well as, separately, fixed and variable costs) at various output levels. The results are shown in Table 6.2. Subtracting the total cost at a given output rate from the total revenue at this output rate, you obtain the total profit at each output rate, which is shown in the last column of Table 6.2.

Finding the Maximum-Profit Output Rate

As the output rate increases from zero to four pianos per week, the total profit *rises*. As the output rate increases from five to eight pianos per week, the total profit *falls*. Therefore, the *maximum* profit is achieved at an output rate between four and five pianos per week.[1] (Without more detailed data, we cannot tell precisely where the maximum occurs, but this is close enough

---

[1] This assumes that the output rate can be varied continuously and there is a single maximum. These are innocuous assumptions.

FIGURE 6.1

Costs, Revenue, and Profit, Adagio Piano Company

Profit equals the vertical distance between the total revenue curve and the total cost curve. The distance is maximized when the output rate is between four and five pianos per week. At this output rate, profit (measured by the vertical distance) is somewhat more than $2,000.

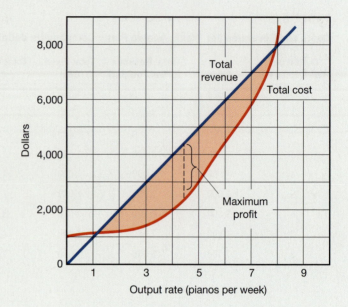

for our purposes here.) Since the maximum profit is obtained at an output of between four and five pianos per week, this is the output rate you choose.

Figure 6.1 gives a more vivid picture of the firm's situation by plotting the relationship between total revenue and total cost, on the one hand, and output, on the other. At each output rate, the vertical distance between the total revenue curve and the total cost curve is the amount of profit the firm earns. Below an output rate of about one piano per week and above a rate of about eight pianos per week, the total revenue curve lies below the total cost curve, indicating that profits are negative; that is, there are losses. Both Table 6.2 and Figure 6.1 show that the output rate that maximizes the firm's profits is between four and five pianos per week. At this output rate, the firm makes a profit of over $2,000 per week, which is more than it can make at any other output rate.

There is an alternative way to analyze the firm's situation. Rather than looking at total revenue and total cost, we can look at price and marginal cost. Table 6.3 and Figure 6.2 show the product price and marginal cost at each output rate. The maximum profit is achieved at the output rate where price equals marginal cost. Both Table 6.3 and Figure 6.2 indicate that price equals marginal cost at the profit-maximizing output rate of between four and five pianos per week. This raises a question: Will price usually equal marginal cost at the profit-maximizing output rate, or is this merely a coincidence?

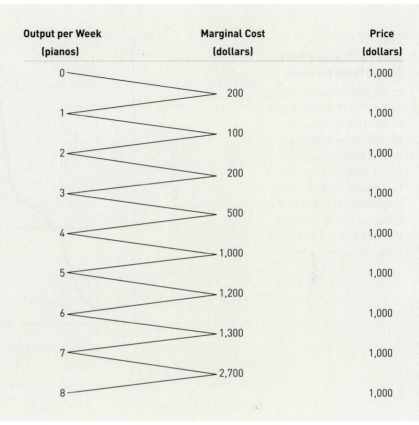

TABLE 6.3

Marginal Cost and Price, Adagio Piano Company

Output per Week (pianos)	Marginal Cost (dollars)	Price (dollars)
0		1,000
	200	
1		1,000
	100	
2		1,000
	200	
3		1,000
	500	
4		1,000
	1,000	
5		1,000
	1,200	
6		1,000
	1,300	
7		1,000
	2,700	
8		1,000

The Golden Rule of Output Determination

The equality of marginal cost and price at the profit-maximizing output rate is no mere coincidence. It usually is true if the firm takes the price of its product as given. Indeed, the golden rule of output determination for a perfectly competitive firm is this: *Choose the output rate at which marginal cost is equal to the price.*

To prove that this rule maximizes profits, consider Figure 6.3, which shows a typical short-run marginal cost function. Suppose that the price is P_1. At any output rate less than Q_1, price is greater than marginal cost. This means that increases in output increase the firm's profits, since they add more to total revenue than to total cost. Why? Because an extra unit of output adds an amount equal to price to total revenue and an amount equal to marginal cost to total cost. Therefore, since price exceeds marginal cost, an extra unit of output adds more to total revenue than to total cost. This is the case for the Adagio Piano Company when it produces three pianos per week. As shown in Table 6.3, the extra cost of producing a fourth piano is $500, while the revenue brought in by

FIGURE 6.2

Marginal Cost and Price, Adagio Piano Company

At the profit-maximizing output rate of between four and five pianos per week, marginal cost (which is $1,000 when the output rate is between four and five) equals price ($1,000). Recall from Figure 4.11 that marginal cost is plotted at the midpoint of the range of output to which it pertains.

FIGURE 6.3

Short-Run Average and Marginal Cost Curves

If price is P_1, the profit-maximizing output rate is Q_1. If price is P_2, the profit-maximizing output rate is Q_2, even though the firm incurs a loss. If the price is below P_3, the firm discontinues production. (Note that regardless of what the price is, the demand curve facing the firm is a horizontal line at this price.)

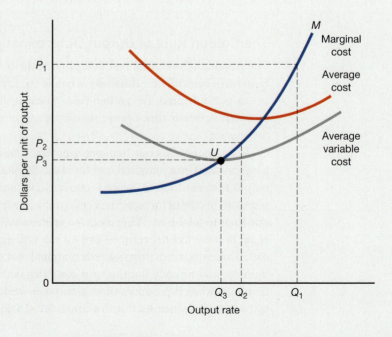

producing and selling it is $1,000. Consequently, it pays for the Adagio Piano Company to produce more than three pianos per week.

At any output rate above Q_1, price is less than marginal cost. This means that decreases in output increase the firm's profits, since they subtract more from total cost than from total revenue. This happens because one fewer unit of output subtracts an amount equal to price from total revenue and an amount equal to marginal cost from total cost. Since price is less than marginal cost, one fewer unit of output subtracts more from total cost than from total revenue. Such a case occurs when the Adagio Piano Company produces seven pianos per week. As shown in Table 6.3, the extra cost of producing the seventh piano is $1,300, while the extra revenue it brings in is $1,000. So it pays for the Adagio Piano Company to produce fewer than seven pianos per week.

Because increases in output increase profits if output is less than Q_1 and decreases in output increase profits if output is greater than Q_1, it follows that profits must be maximized at Q_1, the output rate at which price equals marginal cost. After all, if increases in output up to Q_1 result in increases in profit but further increases in output result in decreases in profit, Q_1 must be the profit-maximizing output rate. For the Adagio Piano Company, this output rate is between four and five pianos per week.

Does It Pay to Be a Dropout?

All rules have exceptions, even the golden rule we just mentioned. Under some circumstances, the perfectly competitive firm does not maximize its profits if it sets marginal cost equal to price. Instead, it maximizes its profits only if it becomes an economic dropout by discontinuing production. The first important point is that even if the firm is doing the best that it can, it may not be able to earn a profit. If the price is P_2 in Figure 6.3, short-run average cost exceeds the price P_2 at all possible output rates. Thus, the firm cannot earn a profit whatever output it produces. Since the short run is too short for the firm to alter the scale of its plant, it cannot liquidate its plant in the short run. Its only choice is to produce at a loss or discontinue production.

Under what conditions does the firm produce at a loss, and under what conditions does it discontinue production? If there is an output rate where price exceeds average variable costs, it pays for the firm to produce, even though price does not cover average total cost. If there is no such output rate, the firm is better off producing nothing at all. This is true because even if the firm produces nothing, it must pay its fixed cost. If the loss resulting from production is less than the firm's fixed cost, the firm is better off producing than not producing. On the other hand, if the loss resulting from production is greater than the firm's fixed cost, the firm is better off not producing.

To illustrate the conditions under which it pays for a firm to drop out, suppose that the data for the cost functions of the Adagio Piano Company are

TABLE 6.4

Costs and Revenues, Adagio Piano Company (in dollars)

Output per Week (pianos)	Price	Total Revenue	Total Fixed Cost	Total Variable Cost	Average Variable Cost	Total Cost	Total Profit
0	1,000	0	1,000	0	—	1,000	−1,000
1	1,000	1,000	1,000	1,200	1,200	2,200	−1,200
2	1,000	2,000	1,000	2,600	1,300	3,600	−1,600
3	1,000	3,000	1,000	4,200	1,400	5,200	−2,200
4	1,000	4,000	1,000	6,000	1,500	7,000	−3,000
5	1,000	5,000	1,000	8,000	1,600	9,000	−4,000
6	1,000	6,000	1,000	10,200	1,700	11,200	−5,200
7	1,000	7,000	1,000	12,600	1,800	13,600	−6,600
8	1,000	8,000	1,000	15,200	1,900	16,200	−8,200

as shown in Table 6.4. In this case, there is no output rate such that average variable cost is less than price, which, you will recall, is $1,000 per piano. According to the results of the preceding paragraphs, the Adagio Piano Company should discontinue production under these conditions. The wisdom of this course of action is shown by the last column of Table 6.4, which demonstrates that the profit-maximizing—or, what amounts to the same thing, the loss-minimizing—output rate is 0.

Sometimes, as in the present case, the best thing to produce is nothing. The situation is analogous to the common experience of leaving a movie after the first 10 minutes when you know that you are about to watch a turkey. You ignore the fixed cost (the nonrefundable admission price), and deciding that the variable cost (the pleasure gained from other activities that would be forgone by seeing the rest of the show) is going to exceed the benefits of staying, you leave.

The Market Supply Curve

In Chapters 2 and 4, we described some of the factors underlying a commodity's market supply curve, but we could not go into much detail. Now we can, because our golden rule of output determination is the basis of the **firm's supply curve**, which shows how much the firm will want to produce at each price.

Firm's supply curve

The Firm's Supply Curve

Because the firm takes the price of its product as given (and can sell all it wants at that price), we know from previous sections that the firm chooses the output level at which price equals marginal cost. Or, if the price is below the firm's average variable cost curve at every output level, the firm produces nothing. These results are all we need to determine the firm's supply curve.

Suppose that the firm's short-run cost curves are as shown in Figure 6.3. The marginal cost curve must intersect the average variable cost curve at the latter's minimum point U. If the price of the product is less than P_3, the firm produces nothing, because there is no output level where price exceeds average variable cost. If the price of the product exceeds P_3, the firm sets its output rate at the point where price equals marginal cost. If the price is P_1, the firm produces Q_1; if the price is P_2, the firm produces Q_2; and so forth. Consequently, the firm's supply curve is exactly the same as the firm's marginal cost curve for prices above the minimum value of average variable cost (P_3). For prices at or below the minimum value of average variable cost, the firm's supply curve corresponds to the price axis, where the desire to supply at these prices is uniformly zero. Hence, the firm's supply curve is P_3UM.

Deriving the Market Supply Curve

Market supply curve

Our next step is to derive the market supply curve from the supply curves of the individual firms. If one assumption (which we consider shortly) holds, the **market supply curve** can be regarded as the horizontal summation of the supply curves of all the firms producing the product. If three firms are in the industry and their supply curves are as shown in Figure 6.4, the market supply curve is the horizontal summation of their three supply curves. Since these three supply curves show that firm 1 supplies 25 units of output at a price of $2 per unit, firm 2 supplies 40 units at this price, and firm 3 supplies 55 units at this price, the market supply curve shows that 120 units of output are supplied if the price is $2 per unit. Why? Because the market supply curve shows the *total* amount of the product that all the firms together supply at this price: 25 + 40 + 55 = 120. If there are only three firms, the market is not perfectly competitive, but we can ignore this inconsistency. Figure 6.4 is designed to illustrate that the market supply curve is the horizontal summation of the firms' supply curves, at least under one important assumption.

The assumption underlying this construction of the short-run market supply curve is that increases or decreases in output by all firms simultaneously do not affect input prices. This is a convenient simplification, but it is not always true. Although changes in the output of one firm alone often cannot affect input prices, the simultaneous expansion or contraction of output by all firms may well alter input prices, so that the individual firm's cost curves—and supply curve—shift. For instance, an expansion of the whole industry may bid up the price of certain inputs, with the result that the cost curves of the individual firms are pushed upward. A sudden expansion of the aerospace industry, for instance, might well increase the price of such inputs as the services of aerospace scientists and engineers.

FIGURE 6.4

Horizontal Summation of Short-Run Supply Curves of Firms

If the three firms' supply curves are as shown here (and if each firm supplies nothing if the price is below *H*), the market supply curve is the horizontal summation of the firms' supply curves, assuming that input prices are not influenced by the output of the industry.

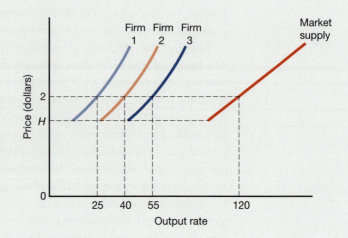

If, contrary to the assumption underlying Figure 6.4, input prices *are* increased by the expansion of the industry, we can still derive the short-run market supply curve by seeing how much the industry supplies in the short run at each price of the product. But it is then incorrect to assume that the market supply curve is the horizontal summation of the firms' supply curves.

Price and Output: The Short Run

How much of a particular product will be produced if the market is perfectly competitive, and what will the price be? The answers depend on the length of the time period being considered. To begin with, we consider the short run, the period during which each firm's plant and equipment are fixed. What determines the price and output of a good in a perfectly competitive market in the short run? The answer is the market demand and market supply curves. As we know from Chapter 2, the equilibrium price and output are at the point where the demand and supply curves intersect. Therefore, in panel B of Figure 6.5, the equilibrium price and output in the short run are *P* and *Q*.

Panel A of Figure 6.5 shows the behavior of an individual firm in short-run equilibrium. Since *P* is the price, the demand curve facing the firm is a horizontal line at *P*, as shown in panel A. To maximize profit, the firm produces an output of *q*, because price equals marginal cost at this output. In short-run equilibrium, firms may be making either profits or losses. In the particular case described in panel A, the firm earns a profit equal to the shaded area. Since the profit per unit of output equals *P* – *C*, total profit equals *P* – *C* multiplied by *q*, which is this shaded area.

FIGURE 6.5

Short-Run Competitive Equilibrium

In the short run, the equilibrium price is *P* and the equilibrium output of the industry is *Q*, since (as shown in panel *B*) the industry demand and supply curves intersect at this price and output.

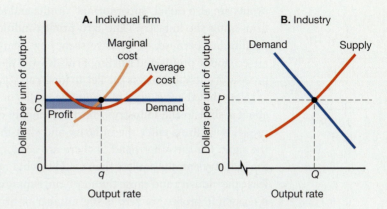

Taken together, the two panels of Figure 6.5 bring out the following important point. To the individual firm, the price of the product is taken as a given. If the price is *P*, then the firm in panel A reacts to this price by setting an output rate of *q* units. It cannot alter the price; it can only react to it. But the reactions of the firms *as a group* are a major determinant of the price of the product. The supply curve in panel B shows the total amount supplied by the entire group of firms at each price. It summarizes the reactions of the firms to various levels of the price. Put briefly, the equilibrium price is viewed by the individual firm as beyond its control; yet the supply decisions of all firms taken as a group are a basic determinant of the equilibrium price.

Price and Output: The Long Run

In the long run, what determines the output and price of a good in a perfectly competitive market? In the long run, a firm can change its plant size, which means that established firms may *leave* an industry if it has below-average profits or new firms may *enter* an industry with above-average profits. Suppose that textile firms can earn up to a 15 percent rate of return by investing their resources in other industries. If they can earn only 12 percent by keeping these resources invested in the textile industry, they will leave the textile industry. On the other hand, if a rate of return of 18 percent can be earned by investing in the textile industry, firms in other industries, attracted by this relatively high return, will enter the textile industry.

Equilibrium: Zero Economic Profit

Economic profits

Equilibrium is achieved in the long run when enough firms—no more, no less—are in the industry so that **economic profits** (defined as the excess of a firm's profits over what it could make in other industries) are zero. (Economic profits are also called "supernormal" profits and are usually eroded when new firms enter the industry.) The zero-profit condition is necessary for long-run equilibrium because, as we have seen, new firms enter the industry if there are economic profits and existing firms leave if there are economic losses. This process of entry and exit is the key to long-run equilibrium.

Note that the existence of economic profits or losses in an industry brings about a shift in the industry's short-run supply curve. If there are economic profits, new firms enter the industry and shift the short-run supply curve to the right. On the other hand, if there are economic losses in the industry (if the industry's profits are less than could be obtained elsewhere), existing firms leave the industry and cause the short-run supply curve to shift to the left. Only if economic profits are zero is the number of firms in the industry—and the industry's short-run supply curve—stable. Putting this equilibrium condition another way, the long-run equilibrium position of the firm is at the point at which its long-run average cost equals price. If price exceeds average total cost, economic profits are earned; if price is less than average total cost, economic losses are incurred.

Equilibrium: Maximum Economic Profit

Going a step further, long-run equilibrium requires that price equal the lowest value of long-run average total cost. In other words, firms must produce at the *minimum point* on their long-run average cost curves, because to maximize their profits, as we have seen, they must operate where price equals long-run marginal cost; at the same time, they have to operate where price equals long-run average cost. But if both these conditions are satisfied, long-run marginal cost must equal long-run average cost, since both equal price. And we know from Chapter 4 that long-run marginal cost equals long-run average cost only at the point at which long-run average cost is at a minimum.[2] Consequently, if long-run marginal cost equals long-run average cost, the firm must be producing at the minimum point on the long-run average cost curve.

This equilibrium position is illustrated in Figure 6.6. When all adjustments are made, price equals P. The equilibrium output of the firm is q, and the cost structure of its plant corresponds to the short-run average and marginal cost curves in Figure 6.6. At this output and with this plant, long-run marginal cost equals short-run marginal cost equals price. This ensures that the firm maximizes profit. Also, the long-run average cost equals short-run average cost equals price. This ensures that economic profits are zero. Since the long-run marginal cost and long-run average cost must be equal, the firm produces at the minimum point on its long-run average cost curve.

---

[2] The previous discussion of this point concerned short-run cost functions, but the argument applies just as well to long-run cost functions.

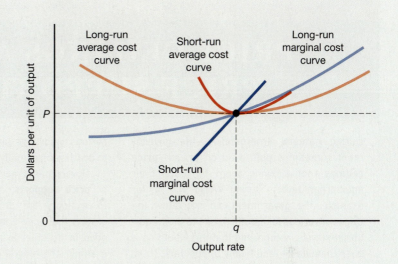

FIGURE 6.6

Long-Run Equilibrium of a Perfectly Competitive Firm

In long-run equilibrium, output is *q* and the firm's plant corresponds to the short-run average and marginal cost curves shown here.

To illustrate the process of entry and exit in an industry that has approximated perfect competition, consider the pre-World War II bituminous coal industry. Entry into this industry was relatively easy, but exit was relatively difficult for at least two reasons. First, it is costly to shut down a mine and reopen it later. Second, because of corrosion and water damage, it is hard to shut down a mine for longer than two years unless it is to be abandoned entirely. For these reasons, mines tended to stay open and produce even though short-term losses were incurred. In the period before World War II, the demand for coal fell substantially, but although the industry suffered substantial losses, mines were slow to close down. Nonetheless, the competitive process had its way. Slowly but surely, the number of mines fell markedly in response to these losses. Therefore, despite the barriers to rapid exit, firms eventually left the industry, just as the model would predict.

The Allocation of Resources under Perfect Competition: A More Detailed View

At this point, it is instructive to describe the process by which a perfectly competitive economy—one composed of perfectly competitive industries—allocates resources. In earlier chapters, we stressed that the allocation of resources among alternative uses is a major function of any economic system. Equipped with the concepts we have now learned, we can go much further in describing how a perfectly competitive economy shifts resources in accord with changes in tastes, technology, and other factors.

CASE STUDY 6.1

PRICE CEILINGS AND PRICE SUPPORTS

During national emergencies, the government sometimes puts a lid on prices—**price ceilings**—not allowing them to reach their equilibrium levels. During World War II, for example, the government did not allow the prices of various foodstuffs to rise to their equilibrium levels, recognizing that this would have been inequitable (and highly unpopular). Thus, the quantity demanded of a product exceeds the quantity supplied.

Since the price system is not allowed to perform its rationing function, some formal system of rationing or allocating the available supply of the product may be required. In World War II, families were issued ration coupons that determined how much they could buy of various commodities. And in 1979, when the Organization of Petroleum Exporting Countries (OPEC) cut back oil production and reduced exports of oil to the United States, there was serious talk that gasoline and oil might be rationed in a similar way. Such rationing schemes may be justified in emergencies (of reasonably short duration), but they can eventually result in serious distortions, since prices are not allowed to do the job normally expected of them.

Governments may also impose **price floors**, or **price supports**, as they are often called. Price floors are generally defended on the ground that they enable the producers of the good in question to make a better living. For example, the federal government has imposed price supports on a wide range of agricultural commodities to increase farm incomes. The result is that the quantity supplied exceeds the quantity demanded at the support price. There is a surplus of the commodity, and in the case of agricultural commodities, the government has to buy up and store these surpluses. As in the case of a price ceiling, the result is that the price system is not allowed to do the job expected of it.

Whether price ceilings or price floors are socially desirable depends on whether the loss in social efficiency resulting from them is exceeded by the gain in equity they achieve. Their purpose is to help or protect parts of the population that would be treated inequitably by the unfettered price system.

Consumers Turn from Corn to Wheat

Suppose that a change occurs in tastes: consumers become more favorably disposed toward wheat and less favorably disposed toward corn than in the past.[3] In the short run, the increase in the demand for wheat increases the price of wheat and results in some increase in the output of wheat. However, the output cannot be increased very substantially because the industry's capacity cannot be expanded in the short run. Similarly, the fall in the demand for corn reduces the price of corn and results in some reduction in output.

[3] Since we assume here that the markets for wheat and corn are perfectly competitive, it is also assumed that there is no government intervention in these markets.

But the output is not curtailed greatly because firms continue to produce as long as they can cover variable costs.

Prices Signal the Need for Resource Reallocation

The change in the relative prices of wheat and corn tells producers that a reallocation of resources is called for. Because of the increase in the price of wheat and the decrease in the price of corn, wheat producers are earning economic profits and corn producers are showing economic losses. This triggers a new deployment of resources. If some variable inputs in corn production can be used as effectively in the production of wheat, they may be switched from corn production to wheat production. Even if no variable inputs are used in both wheat and corn production, adjustments can be made in various interrelated markets, with the result that wheat production gains resources and corn production loses resources. (For example, some resources may move from corn production to manufacturing, and others may move from manufacturing to wheat production.) When short-run equilibrium is attained in both the wheat and corn industries, the reallocation of resources is not yet complete, since there has not been enough time for producers to build new capacity or liquidate old capacity. In particular, neither industry is operating at minimum average cost. The wheat producers are operating at greater than the output level where average cost is at a minimum, and the corn producers are operating at less than this level.

Effects in the Long Run

What happens in the long run? The shift in consumer demand from corn to wheat results in greater adjustments in production and smaller adjustments in price than in the short run. In the long run, existing firms can leave corn production and new firms can enter wheat production. Because of short-run economic losses in corn production, some corn land and related equipment are allowed to run down, and some firms engaged in corn production are liquidated. As firms leave corn production, the supply curve shifts to the left and causes the price to rise above its short-run level. The transfer of resources out of corn production stops when price has increased and costs have decreased to the point where losses are avoided.

While corn production loses resources, wheat production gains them. The prospect of positive economic profits in wheat production causes new firms to enter the industry. The increased demand for inputs raises input prices and costs of wheat production, while the price of wheat is depressed by the movement to the right of the supply curve because of the entry of new firms. Entry ceases when economic profits are no longer being earned. At this point, when long-run equilibrium is achieved, more resources are used in the industry than in the short run. (Note that if corn land and equipment

CASE STUDY 6.2

STARTING FROM SCRATCH: THE TRANSITION FROM COMMUNISM TO CAPITALISM

The political revolutions that swept Eastern Europe in 1989 and 1990 were the easy part. Much more difficult was the task of transforming these centrally planned economies into market economies. The microeconomic problems facing these countries were the result of (1) centralized decision making, (2) rigid price structure, (3) lack of private ownership, and (4) lack of currency convertibility. Not only were the vast and entrenched bureaucracies in the centrally planned economies highly inefficient, but they also saw reform as a threat and tried to slow it down in every way possible. Therefore, an essential first step in microeconomic reform was the dismantling, or at least the neutralization, of the central planning apparatus.

Price reform was also essential, given the distortions caused by price controls and subsidies. For example, many of these countries deliberately kept the price of bread low to appease consumers. The predictable result was an excess demand for bread—and long lines of consumers at stores. When price reforms were enacted in Poland and Hungary, the long lines disappeared and goods were again in plentiful supply; however, consumer budgets were also squeezed. In addition, while ideologically a giant stumbling block for countries that until recently espoused communism, private ownership of assets is an essential element of a market economy. The challenge facing these economies in the early 1990s was to sell off (privatize) state-owned assets without turning public monopolies into private monopolies.

Finally, full currency convertibility (the ability to exchange the domestic currency for any other country's currency at prevailing market rates) is also a sine qua non of a market economy. Without it, the centrally planned economies could not become integrated into the world economy and reap the benefits of international trade.

The political dilemma facing many of the embryonic democracies in Eastern Europe in the early 1990s was that the initial impact of all these reforms was quite painful. The payoff would come much later. It was inevitable, therefore, that many were tempted to delay the pain as long as possible.

In the two decades after the collapse of communism, those economies that adopted market-based reforms rapidly grew considerably faster than those that dragged their feet. Fast reformers—such as the Czech Republic, Hungary, and Poland—enjoyed cumulative economic growth of 45 to 220 percent between 1990 and 2011. On the other hand, slow reformers—such as Moldova and Ukraine—that tried to cling to the bad old ways for as long as possible saw their economies contract between 30 and 35 percent.

One of the single biggest factors that determined whether a country became a fast or slow reformer was the size of its bureaucracy at the beginning of the transition. In countries with large state-owned enterprises and large government bureaucracies, managers and government officials used their power to subvert the reform process by preserving lucrative subsidies, import restrictions, and export controls. This prevented the elimination of many price distortions in the economy and helped prolong the lives of many unprofitable state-owned enterprises, which, in turn, made the transition more difficult.

can be converted to the production of wheat, some of the entry may occur through existing farmers' shifting their crop mix toward wheat and away from corn.)

Finally, long-run equilibrium is established in both industries, and the reallocation of resources is complete. It is important to note that this reallocation can affect industries other than wheat and corn. If corn land and equipment can be easily adapted to the production of wheat, corn producers can simply change to wheat production. If not, the resources used in corn production are converted to some use other than wheat, and the resources that enter wheat production come from some use other than corn production.

REVIEW AND PRACTICE

Summary

1   Economists generally classify markets into four types: perfect competition, monopolistic competition, oligopoly, and monopoly. Perfect competition requires that the product of any seller be the same as the product of any other seller, that no buyer or seller be able to influence the price of the product, and that resources be able to switch readily from one use to another.

2   If it maximizes profit, a perfectly competitive firm should set its output rate in the short run at the level where marginal cost equals price, so long as price exceeds average variable cost. If there is no output rate at which price exceeds average variable cost, the firm should discontinue production.

3   The firm's supply curve coincides with its marginal cost curve for prices exceeding the minimum value of average variable cost. For prices less than or equal to the minimum value of average variable cost, the firm's supply curve coincides with the price axis.

4   As a first approximation, the market supply curve can be viewed as the horizontal summation of the supply curves of all the firms producing the product.

This assumes that increases or decreases in output by all firms simultaneously do not affect input prices.

5 Price and output under perfect competition are determined by the intersection of the market supply and demand curves.

6 In the long run, equilibrium is achieved under perfect competition when enough firms—no more, no less—are in the industry so that economic profits are eliminated. In other words, the long-run equilibrium position of the firm is at the point where its long-run average cost equals price. But since price must also equal marginal cost (to maximize profit), it follows that the firm must be operating at the minimum point on the long-run average cost curve.

7 In a perfectly competitive economy, prices are the signals used to guide the reallocation of resources in response to changes in consumer tastes, technology, and other factors.

Problems and Questions

1 Suppose that the total costs of a perfectly competitive firm are as follows:

Output Rate	Total Cost (dollars)
0	40
1	60
2	90
3	130
4	180
5	240

If the price of the product is $50, what output rate should the firm choose?

2 Suppose that the firm in question 1 experiences an increase of $30 in its fixed costs. Plot its new total cost function. What effect does this increase in its fixed costs have on the output it chooses?

3 After the increase in fixed costs described in question 2, what does the firm's marginal cost curve look like? Plot it on a graph. Does it differ from what it was before the increase in fixed costs? Why or why not?

4 After the increase in fixed costs described in question 2, what output rate does the firm choose if the price of its product is $40? $50? $60?

Key Terms

perfect competition
barriers to entry
firm's supply curve
market supply curve
economic profits
price ceilings
price floors
price supports

Viewpoint for Analysis

In an attempt to understand the failings of communism and the success of free-market economies, Mikhail Gorbachev, the last leader of the Soviet Union, sent high-ranking officials to Europe and the United States in the late-1980s to study how those economies were able to produce and distribute such a large variety of goods and services so easily and efficiently. When visiting a London food market, one of these officials reportedly asked, "Who is in charge of the price of bread?" The answer? "No one and everyone."[4]

(a) What do you think is the structure of the bread market in London? Why?

(b) Is the bread market characterized by many buyers and sellers or a few?

(c) What would happen if the government set the price of food above the free market price? What if the government set a price ceiling that was below the market price?

[4] Paul Seabright, *The Company of Strangers: A Natural History of Economic Life* (Princeton, NJ: Princeton University Press, 2004), 15.

Monopoly and Its Regulation

LEARNING OBJECTIVES

➤ To identify the conditions that define a monopolistic market structure and specify their causes

➤ To explain the golden rule of output determination for a monopolistic firm

➤ To compare the prices and outputs set under monopoly with those set under perfect competition

➤ To understand the case against monopolies and explain how monopolies can be regulated

➤ *(Exploring Further)* To understand the position defending monopoly power

At the opposite extreme from perfect competition is monopoly, which may well characterize the market for electricity, gas, or water in your area. Under a monopolistic market structure, what types of behavior can we expect? How much of the product will be produced, and at what level will its price be set? What are the social disadvantages of monopoly? In what ways have government commissions attempted to regulate industries whose market structures approximate monopoly? These are some of the major questions dealt with in this chapter.

Monopoly

To begin with, recall what is meant by **monopoly**: a market where there exists one, and only one, seller. Monopoly, like perfect competition, seldom corresponds more than approximately to conditions in real industries, but it is a very useful model. In several respects, monopoly and perfect competition stand as polar opposites. The firm in a perfectly competitive market has so many rivals that competition becomes entirely impersonal. The firm is a price taker, an inconspicuous seller in a sea of inconspicuous sellers. Under monopoly, on the other hand, the firm has no direct competitors at all; it is the sole supplier.

However, even the monopolist is affected by certain indirect and potential forms of competition. Suppose a firm manages to obtain a monopoly on wheat production. It will have to worry about competition from corn and other agricultural commodities that can be substituted for wheat. Moreover, the wheat monopolist will have to take into account the possibility that new firms might arise to challenge its monopoly if it attempts to extract conspicuously high profits. Thus, even the monopolist is subject to some restraint imposed by competitive forces.

Causes of Monopoly

There are many reasons why monopolies, or market structures that closely approximate monopoly, may arise.

Patents

Patents

A firm may acquire a monopoly over the production of a good by having **patents** on the product or on certain basic processes used in its production. The patent laws of the United States give an inventor the exclusive right to make a certain product or to use a certain process for 20 years (from initial filing). The purpose of the patent system is to encourage invention and innovation and discourage industrial secrecy. Many firms with monopoly power achieved it in considerable part through patents. For example, pharmaceutical companies can become sole suppliers of critical drugs (for example, to control cholesterol or combat HIV/AIDS) for many years through the control of basic patents.

Control of Inputs

A firm may become a monopolist by obtaining control over the entire supply of a basic input required to manufacture a product. The International Nickel Company of Canada (now a wholly owned subsidiary of the Brazilian mining company Vale) used to control about 90 percent of the proven nickel reserves in the world—obviously, a strong monopoly position. Similarly, the Aluminum Company of America (Alcoa) kept its dominant position for a long time by controlling practically all the sources of bauxite, the ore used to make aluminum. However, Alcoa's monopoly was broken in 1945 when the Supreme Court decided that Alcoa's control of practically all the industry's output violated the antitrust laws.

Government Action

A firm may become a monopolist if it is awarded a market franchise by a government agency. The government may give a particular firm the franchise to sell a particular product in a public facility. Or it may give a particular company the right to provide a service, such as electrification, to people in a particular area. In exchange for this right, the firm agrees to allow the government to regulate certain aspects of its operations. The form of regulation does not matter here; the important point is that the monopoly is created by the government.

Declining Cost of Production

A firm may become a monopolist if the average costs of producing the product reach a minimum at an output rate that is large enough to satisfy the entire market (at a price that is profitable). In a case like this, a firm obviously has an incentive to expand until it produces all the market wants of the good. (Its costs fall as it continues to expand.) Therefore, competition cannot be maintained in this case. If a number of firms are in the industry, the result is likely to be economic warfare and the survival of a single victor, the monopolist.

Natural monopolies

Cases where costs behave like this are called **natural monopolies**. When an industry is a natural monopoly, the public often insists that its behavior be regulated by the government. For example, electric power is an industry that is characterized by great economies of scale and decreasing average costs. Fuel consumed per kilowatt-hour is lower in larger power generating units, and there are economies in combining generating units at a single site. Because of these factors, little attempt has been made to force competition in the industry, since it has been regarded as wasteful. Instead, the market for electric power in a particular area has been a regulated monopoly.[1]

Network Effects

Network externality Network effect

A firm may become a monopolist as a result of network effects. For many information technologies, consumers benefit from using a common format or operating system. When the value of a product to one user increases with the number of other users, this is called a **network externality** or **network effect**. Telephone service, e-mail, Internet access, and social networks such as Facebook are all products with strong network externalities. Technologies subject to strong network effects tend to exhibit long lead times followed by explosive growth. As the installed base of users grows, more and more users find adoption worthwhile. Companies whose standards or systems are adopted can become monopolists.

Demand Curve and Marginal Revenue under Monopoly

Before we can make any statements about the behavior of a monopolistic market, we must point out certain important characteristics of the demand curve facing the monopolist. Since the monopolist is the only seller of the

---

[1] But technological change, deregulation, and other factors are changing the economics of electric power production, and competition is likely to become more important in the future.

TABLE 7.1

Demand and Revenue of a Monopoly Producer of Wind Turbines (in dollars)

Quantity	Price	Total Revenue (millions)	Marginal Revenue (millions)
1,000	100,000	100	
			80
2,000	90,000	180	
			60
3,000	80,000	240	
			40
4,000	70,000	280	
			20
5,000	60,000	300	
			0
6,000	50,000	300	
			−20
7,000	40,000	280	
			−40
8,000	30,000	240	

commodity, the demand curve it faces is the market demand curve for the product. And since the market demand curve almost always slopes downward to the right, the monopolist's demand curve must also slope downward to the right. This is quite different from perfect competition, where the firm's demand curve is horizontal. To illustrate the situation faced by a monopolist, consider the hypothetical case in Table 7.1 for a monopoly producer of specialty wind turbines. The price at which different quantities of wind turbines (shown in column 1) can be sold by the monopolist is shown in column 2. The firm's **total revenue** (its total dollar sales volume) is shown in column 3. Obviously, column 3 is the product of the first two columns. Column 4 contains the firm's **marginal revenue**, defined as the addition to total revenue attributable to the addition of 1,000 units to sales. If $R(q)$ is total revenue when q units are sold and $R(q - 1,000)$ is total revenue when $q - 1,000$ units are sold, the marginal revenue between q units and $q - 1,000$ units is $R(q) - R(q - 1,000)$.

Total revenue

Marginal revenue

Marginal revenue is very important to the monopolist. We can estimate it from the figures in the first three columns of Table 7.1. The marginal revenue from selling between 1,000 and 2,000 units of output per day is

$180 million – $100 million, or $80 million; the marginal revenue from selling between 2,000 and 3,000 wind turbines per day is $240 million – $180 million, or $60 million; the marginal revenue from selling between 3,000 and 4,000 turbines per day is $280 million - $240 million, or $40 milion; and so on. The results are shown in column 4 of the table (and plotted in Figure 7.1). Note that marginal revenue is analogous to marginal cost (and marginal utility and marginal product, for that matter). Recall that marginal cost is the extra cost resulting from an extra unit of production. Substitute *revenue* for *cost* and *sales* for *production* in the previous sentence, and what do you get? A perfectly acceptable definition of marginal revenue.

Marginal revenue is always less than price if the firm's demand curve slopes downward (as it does under monopoly and other market structures not perfectly competitive). In Table 7.1, the extra revenue from the second thousand units of turbines produced is $80 million, whereas the total price of these extra 1,000 units is $90 million (or $90,000 times 1,000 units). The basic reason is that the firm must reduce the price of all units of output, not just the extra units, to sell the extra units. In Table 7.1, the extra revenue from the second thousand units of turbines is $80 million because, while the price of the second thousand units is $90,000 each, the price of the first thousand units must be reduced by $10,000 each to sell each of the second thousand units. Hence, the extra revenue (marginal revenue) from selling each of the second thousand

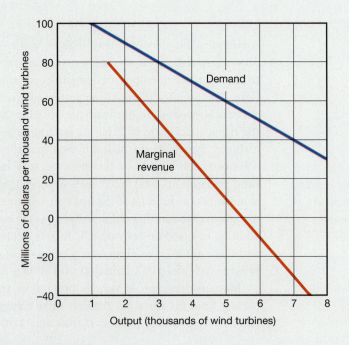

FIGURE 7.1

Marginal Revenue and Demand Curve

The demand curve comes from Table 7.1. Each value of marginal revenue is plotted at the midpoint of the range of output to which it pertains. Since the demand curve slopes downward, marginal revenue is always less than price, for the reasons discussed in the text.

turbines is \$90,000 – \$10,000, or \$80,000, which is less than the price of each of the second thousand units.

Similarly, the marginal revenue from selling each of the third set of 1,000 turbines (\$60,000, according to Table 7.1) is less than the price at which each of the third set of turbines can be sold (\$80,000, according to Table 7.1). Why? Because to sell each of the third batch of 1,000 turbines, the price of the turbines in each of the first two batches must be reduced by \$10,000 each (from \$90,000 to \$80,000). Therefore, the extra revenue (marginal revenue) from selling each of the turbines from the third batch is not \$80,000, but \$80,000 less the \$20,000 reduction in the amount received for each of the turbines from the first two batches.

Price and Output: The Short Run

We are now in a position to determine how output and price behave under monopoly. If the monopolist is free to maximize its profits, it will choose the price and output rate at which the difference between total revenue and total cost is greatest. Suppose that the firm's costs are as shown in Table 7.2 and that the demand curve it faces is shown by the data in Table 7.1. On the basis of the data in these two tables, the firm can calculate the profit that it makes at each output rate. To do so, it subtracts its total cost from its total revenue, as shown in Table 7.3. What output rate maximizes the firm's profit? According to Table 7.3, profit *rises* as its output rate increases from 1,000 to 3,000 turbines, and profit *falls* as its output rate increases from 4,000 to 8,000 turbines. Therefore, the *maximum* profit is achieved at an output rate between 3,000 and 4,000 units.[2] (Without more detailed data, we cannot tell precisely where the maximum occurs, but this is close enough for present purposes.) Figure 7.2 shows the same thing graphically.

What price does the monopolist charge? To maximize its profit, it must charge the price that results in its selling the profit-maximizing output, which in this case is between 3,000 and 4,000 units. According to Table 7.1, it must charge between \$70,000 and \$80,000 per unit. Why? Because if it charges \$70,000, it will sell 4,000 units, and if it charges \$80,000, it will sell 3,000 units. Consequently, to sell the profit-maximizing output of between 3,000 and units, it must charge a price of between \$70,000 and \$80,000 per unit.

The Golden Rule of Output Determination

In Chapter 6, we set forth the golden rule of output determination for a perfectly competitive firm. We can now formulate a golden rule of output determination for a monopolist: *Set the output rate at the point where marginal revenue*

---

[2] This assumes that the output rate can vary continuously and that there is a single maximum. These are innocuous assumptions.

TABLE 7.2

Costs of a Monopoly Producer of Wind Turbines (in dollars)

Quantity	Total Variable Cost (millions)	Total Fixed Cost (millions)	Total Costs (millions)	Marginal Cost (millions)
0	0	100	100	
				40
1,000	40	100	140	
				30
2,000	70	100	170	
				40
3,000	110	100	210	
				40
4,000	150	100	250	
				50
5,000	200	100	300	
				60
6,000	260	100	360	
				90
7,000	350	100	450	
				100
8,000	450	100	550	

TABLE 7.3

Profit of a Monopoly Producer of Wind Turbines (in dollars)

Quantity	Total Revenue (millions)	Total Cost (millions)	Total Profit (millions)
1,000	100	140	−40
2,000	180	170	10
3,000	240	210	30
4,000	280	250	30
5,000	300	300	0
6,000	300	360	−60
7,000	280	450	−170
8,000	240	550	−310

FIGURE 7.2

Total Revenue, Cost, and Profit of a Monopoly Producer of Wind Turbines

The output rate that maximizes the firm's profit is between 3,000 and 4,000 units. At this output rate, profit (which equals the vertical distance between the total revenue and total cost curves) is over $30 million. On the basis of the demand curve for its product (indicated in Table 7.1), the firm must set a price between $70,000 and $80,000 per unit to sell between 3,000 and 4,000 units.

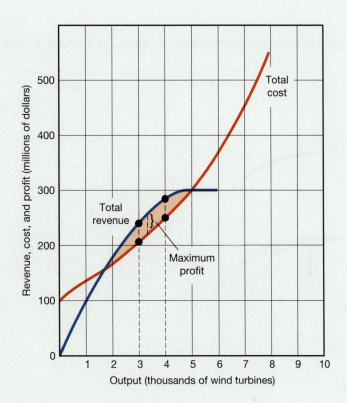

equals marginal cost. Table 7.4 and Figure 7.3 show that this rule results in a maximum profit in this example. It is evident from Table 7.4 that marginal revenue equals marginal cost at the profit-maximizing output of between 3,000 and 4,000 units. Figure 7.3 shows the same thing graphically.

Why is this rule generally a necessary condition for profit maximization? At any output rate at which marginal revenue *exceeds* marginal cost, profit can be increased by *increasing* output, since the extra revenue exceeds the extra cost. At any output rate at which marginal revenue is *less* than marginal cost, profit can be increased by *reducing* output, since the decrease in cost exceeds the decrease in revenue. Therefore, since profit is *not* at a maximum when marginal revenue exceeds marginal cost or falls short of marginal cost, it must be at a maximum only when marginal revenue equals marginal cost.

The Monopolist's Equilibrium Position

Figure 7.4 shows the equilibrium position of a monopolist in the short run. Short-run equilibrium occurs at the output *Q*, where the marginal cost curve

TABLE 7.4

Marginal Cost and Marginal Revenue of a Monopoly Producer of Wind Turbines (in dollars)

Quantity	Total Profit (millions)	Marginal Cost (millions)	Marginal Revenue (millions)
1,000	−40		
		30	80
2,000	10		
		40	60
3,000	30		
		40	40
4,000	30		
		50	20
5,000	0		
		60	0
6,000	−60		
		90	−20
7,000	−170		
		100	−40
8,000	−310		

FIGURE 7.3

Marginal Cost and Marginal Revenue of a Monopoly Producer of Wind Turbines

At the profit-maximizing output rate of between 3,000 and 4,000 units, marginal cost (which is $40 million at an output rate of between 3,000 and 4,000 units) equals marginal revenue (which also is $40 million at an output rate of between 3,000 and 4,000 units). Both marginal cost and marginal revenue are plotted at the midpoints of the ranges of output to which they pertain.

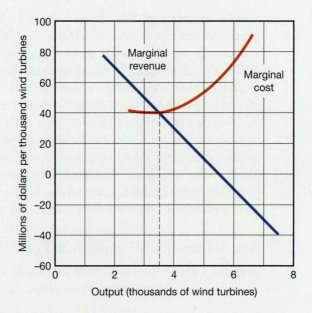

FIGURE 7.4

Equilibrium Position of a Monopolist

A monopolist sets its output rate at *Q*, where the marginal revenue curve intersects the marginal cost curve. At this output, price must be *P*. And profit per unit of output equals *P* – *C*, since average cost equals *C*.

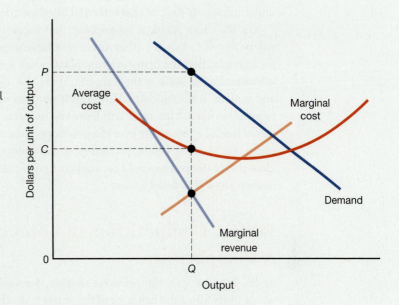

intersects the marginal revenue curve (the curve that shows the firm's marginal revenue at each output level). And if the monopolist is to sell *Q* units per period of time, the demand curve shows that it must set a price of *P*. Therefore, the equilibrium output and price are *Q* and *P*, respectively.

It is interesting to compare the golden rule of output determination for a monopolist (set the output rate at the point where marginal revenue equals marginal cost) with that for a perfectly competitive firm (set the output rate at the point where price equals marginal cost). The latter is really the same as the former because for a perfectly competitive firm, price equals marginal revenue. Since the perfectly competitive firm can sell all it wants at the market price, each additional unit sold increases the firm's total revenue by the amount of the price. Hence, for both the monopolist and the perfectly competitive firm, profits are maximized by setting the output rate at the point where marginal revenue equals marginal cost.

Price and Output: The Long Run

In contrast to the situation under perfect competition, the long-run equilibrium of a monopolistic industry may not be marked by the absence of economic profits. If a monopolist earns a short-run economic profit, it will not be confronted in the long run with competitors unless the industry ceases to be a monopoly. The entrance of additional firms into the industry is incompatible with the existence of monopoly. So the long-run equilibrium of an industry under monopoly may be characterized by economic profits.

On the other hand, a monopolist that incurs a short-run economic loss will be forced to look for other, more profitable uses for its resources. Suppose, for example, that the firm's existing plant is not optimal. If the firm can make alterations to its scale in the long run, it may be able to earn economic profits and remain in the industry. However, if no scale of plant will enable the firm to avoid economic losses, it will leave the industry in the long run. The mere fact of having a monopoly over the production of a certain commodity does not mean that the firm will be profitable. A monopoly over the production of cut-glass sherry decanters would be unlikely to catapult a firm into financial glory or even allow it to avoid losses.

Perfect Competition and Monopoly: A Comparison

At the beginning of the previous chapter, we said that a market's structure would likely affect the behavior of the market; in other words, a market's structure would influence how much was produced and the price that was set. If we could perform an experiment in which an industry was operated first under conditions of perfect competition and then under conditions of monopoly (assuming that the demand for the industry's product and the industry's cost functions were the same in either case[3]), we would find that the equilibrium price and output differ under the two sets of conditions.

Higher Price and Less Output under Monopoly

Specifically, if the product demand curve and the industry's cost functions are the same, the output of a perfectly competitive industry tends to be greater and the price tends to be lower than under monopoly. We see this in Figure 7.5, which shows the industry's demand and supply curves if it is perfectly competitive. Because price and output under perfect competition are given by the intersection of the demand and supply curves, Q_C is the industry output and P_C is the price. But what if all the competitive firms are bought by a single firm, which operates as a pure monopolist? Under these conditions, what formerly was the industry's supply curve is now the monopolist's marginal cost curve.[4] And what

---

[3] However, the cost and demand curves need not be the same. For example, the monopolist may spend money on advertising and thus shift the demand curve. The assumption that they are the same is more significant than it appears at first glance.

[4] The monopolist operates the various plants that would be independent under perfect competition as branches of a single firm. The marginal cost curve of a multiplant monopolist is the horizontal sum of the marginal cost curves of the individual plants. (To see why, suppose that a monopolist has two plants, *A* and *B*. The total amount that the monopolist can produce at a particular marginal cost is the sum of (1) the amount plant *A* can produce at this marginal cost and (2) the amount plant *B* can produce at this marginal cost.) This is also the supply curve of the industry if the plants are operated as separate firms under perfect competition.

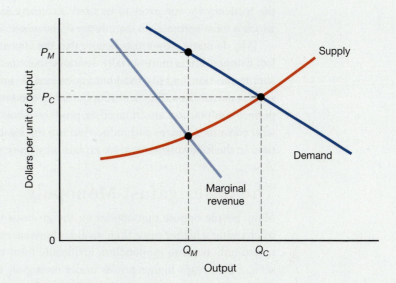

FIGURE 7.5

Comparison of Long-Run Equilibria: Perfect Competition and Monopoly

Under perfect competition, Q_c is the industry output and P_c is the price. Under monopoly, Q_M is the industry output and P_M is the price. Clearly, output is higher and price is lower under perfect competition than under monopoly.

formerly was the industry's demand curve is now the monopolist's demand curve. Since the monopolist chooses the output where marginal cost equals marginal revenue, the industry output is Q_M and the price will be P_M. Clearly, Q_M is less than Q_c, and P_M is greater than P_c, which is what we set out to prove.

Of course, all this is theory. But there is plenty of evidence that monopolists restrict output and charge higher prices than firms under competition. Take the case of tungsten carbide, which sold for $50 per pound until a monopoly was established in 1927 by General Electric. Then the price jumped to between $225 and $453 per pound, until the monopoly was broken by the antitrust laws in 1945. The price then dropped back to between $27 and $45 per pound.[5] This case was extreme but by no means unique. Indeed, for centuries people have observed that when monopolies are formed, output tends to be restricted and price tends to be driven up.

Monopoly and Resource Allocation

It has long been felt that the allocation of resources under perfect competition is socially more desirable than under monopoly. Society might be better off if more resources were devoted to producing the monopolized good in Figure 7.5 and if the competitive, not the monopolistic, output were produced. For example, in *The Wealth of Nations*, published more than two centuries ago, Adam Smith stressed

[5] W. Adams, *The Structure of American Industry*, 5th ed. (New York: Macmillan, 1977), p. 485.

that when competitive forces are thwarted by "the great engine . . . of monopoly," the tendency for resources to be used "as nearly as possible in the proportion which is most agreeable to the interest of the whole society" is thwarted as well.

Why do many economists believe that the allocation of resources under perfect competition is more socially desirable than under monopoly? This is not a simple question, and like most hard questions, it can be answered at various levels of sophistication. Put most simply, many economists believe that firms under perfect competition are induced to produce quantities of goods more in line with consumer desires and induced to use the least costly methods of production. In the following section, we explain why economists believe this to be true.

The Case against Monopoly

Many people oppose monopolies on the grounds that they gouge consumers by charging a higher price than would otherwise exist, a price that can be sustained only because monopolists artificially limit the supply. As we have just seen, a firm reaps higher profits under monopoly than under perfect competition and consumers pay higher prices under monopoly than under perfect competition. But is this bad?

To the extent that the monopolist is rich and the consumers are poor, we are likely to answer yes. And to the extent that the monopolist is less deserving than the consumers, we are also likely to answer yes. But suppose the monopolist is a selfless philanthropist who gives to the poor. Is monopoly still socially undesirable? The answer remains yes, because monopoly imposes a burden on society by misallocating resources. In the presence of monopoly, the price system cannot be relied on to direct the allocation of resources to their most efficient use.

The Misallocation of Resources

To see more precisely how monopoly interferes with the proper functioning of the price system, suppose that all industries other than the shoe industry are perfectly competitive. The shoe industry, however, has been monopolized. How does this cause a misallocation of resources? Under fairly general circumstances, a good's price can be taken as a measure of the social value of an extra unit of the good. If the price of a pair of socks is $5, the value to the consumer of an extra pair of socks can be taken to be $5. Moreover, under fairly general circumstances, a good's marginal cost can be taken as a measure of the cost to society of an extra unit of the good. If the marginal cost of a pair of shoes is $100, the cost to society of producing an extra pair of shoes can be taken to be $100.

In perfectly competitive industries, price is set equal to marginal cost, as we saw in Chapter 6. Each of the competitive industries produces up to the point where the social value of an extra unit of the good (which equals price) is set equal to the cost to society of producing an extra unit of the good (which equals

JOHN D. ROCKEFELLER AND STANDARD OIL OF OHIO

The offices of Standard Oil in the 1880s

In the mid-nineteenth century, the nascent oil industry was characterized by competition. With thousands of small-scale prospectors, drillers, and refiners competing, the supply of oil was plentiful. Prices were low, but so were profits. This was the oil industry John D. Rockefeller saw after the Civil War. He was doing well as a produce wholesaler, but he thought he could do better in oil. Not searching for it or drilling for it but refining it.

By 1865, Rockefeller had built two refineries. He borrowed all he could, paid any interest, and invested the rest in expanding his refineries' capacity. By 1869, he had the largest refinery in the country, and a year later Standard Oil

of Ohio was born. A firestorm of competition in oil refining during the 1870s made prices erratic and squeezed profit margins. Rockefeller responded by squeezing the competition. Willing competitors were bought. Unwilling competitors were liable to find railroads and pipelines closed to their oil shipments or their credit cut off. The more completely Rockefeller dominated the industry, the higher his profits and the more pressure he could bring to bear on would-be competitors.

By 1879, Rockefeller and Standard Oil controlled, directly and indirectly, 90 to 95 percent of the nation's crude oil supplies, refining capacity, and oil product sales.

Under Rockefeller's "guidance," the industry quickly became less crowded. As competition dropped and then disappeared, Rockefeller set prices where he thought they should be, for the good of Standard and, in his opinion, the good of the industry and the nation. He became a price maker. More than 20 years and four presidents were to pass before Standard Oil was broken up under the Sherman Antitrust Act of 1890.

marginal cost). This is the amount each of these industries should produce—the output rate that results in an optimal allocation of resources.

Why Is the Competitive Output Optimal? To see that the competitive output rate is the optimal one, consider what happens when an industry produces up to the point where the social value of an extra unit of the good is *more* than the cost to society of producing an extra unit. This is not the socially optimal output rate because a 1-unit increase in the output rate increases the social value of output by more than the social cost of production; this means that it increases social welfare. Since a 1-unit increase in the output rate increases social welfare, the existing output rate cannot be optimal.

Next, consider what happens when an industry produces up to the point where the social value of an extra unit of the good is *less* than the cost to society of producing the extra unit. This is not the socially optimal output rate because a 1-unit decrease in the output rate decreases the social value of output by less than the social cost of production; this means that it increases social welfare. Since a 1-unit decrease in the output rate increases social welfare, the existing output rate cannot be optimal.

Putting together the results of the previous two paragraphs, it follows that the socially optimal output rate must be at the point where the social value of an extra unit of the good *equals* the social cost of producing an extra unit of the good. Why? Because if the output rate is not optimal when the social value of an extra unit of the good exceeds or falls short of the cost to society of producing the extra unit, it must be optimal only when the two are equal.

The Monopolist Produces Too Little Let us return to the monopolistic shoe industry. Is the shoe industry producing the optimal amount of shoes? The answer is no. Like any monopolist, it produces at the point where marginal revenue equals marginal cost. And since marginal revenue is *less* than price (as was proved), the monopolist produces at a point where price is *greater* than marginal cost. Consequently, the monopolistic industry produces at a point where the social value of an extra unit of the good (which equals price) is greater than the cost to society of producing the extra unit (which equals marginal cost). As we saw, this means that the monopolist's output rate is too small. A 1-unit increase in the output of shoes increases the social value of output by more than the social cost of production.

Here lies the economist's principal complaint against monopoly: it results in a misallocation of resources. Too little is produced of the monopolized good. Society is less well off, in terms of its own tastes and potentialities, than it could be. The price system, which would not lead to or tolerate such waste if all industries were perfectly competitive, is not allowed to perform as it should.

Income Distribution

Misallocation of resources is only part of the economist's case against monopoly. As we have already pointed out, monopoly redistributes income in favor of the monopolists. In other words, monopolists can fatten their own purse by restricting their output and raising their prices. Admittedly, there is no scientific way to prove that monopolists are less deserving than the rest of the population, but it is also pretty difficult to see why they are more deserving.

Efficiency

Because monopolists do not have to face direct competition, they are likely to be less diligent in controlling costs and in using resources efficiently. As Nobel laureate Sir John Hicks put it, "The best of all monopoly profits is a quiet life." Certainly, we all dream at times of being able to take it easy. It would be strange if monopolists, having succeeded in insulating themselves from direct competition, did not take advantage of the opportunity to relax a bit and worry less about pinching pennies. For this reason, many economists believe that, to use Adam Smith's pungent statement, "Monopoly . . . is a great enemy to good management."

Technological Change

Further, it is often claimed that monopolists are slow to innovate and adopt new techniques and products. This lethargy stems from the monopolist's freedom from direct competition. Innovation tends to be disruptive, whereas old ways, like old shoes, tend to be comfortable. The monopolist may be inclined, therefore, to stick with "time-honored" practices. Without question, competition is an important spur to innovation and the rapid diffusion of innovations. But there are well-known arguments on the other side as well. Some economists argue (see Exploring Further in this chapter) that substantial monopoly power promotes innovation and technological change. In fact, some of the key technological breakthroughs in computers and telecommunications occurred in the research labs of IBM and AT&T.

Public Regulation of Monopoly

Public regulation

One way that society attempts to reduce the harmful effects of monopoly is through **public regulation**. Suppose that the long-run cost curve in a particular industry is such that competition is not feasible. In such a case, society may permit a monopoly to be established, but a commission or some other public body is also established to regulate the monopolist's behavior. Among the many such regulatory commissions in the United States are the Federal Energy Regulatory Commission, the Federal Communications Commission, and the Interstate Commerce Commission, which regulate the behavior of firms with monopoly power in the electric power, transportation, and other industries. These industries are key players in the economy, accounting for about 10 percent of the national output. Therefore, it is important to understand how these commissions operate and make decisions on prices and other matters.

Regulatory commissions often set the price—or the maximum price—at the level at which it equals average total cost, including a "fair" rate of return on the firm's investment. In Figure 7.6, the price would be established by the commission at P, where the demand curve intersects the average total cost curve, which includes what the commission regards as a fair profit per unit of output. Needless to say, there has been considerable controversy over what constitutes a fair rate of return. Frequently, commissions have settled on 8 to 10 percent. In addition, there has been a good deal of controversy over what should be included in the company's investment on which the fair rate of return is to be based. A company's assets can be valued at **historical cost** or **reproduction cost**: at what the company paid for them or at what it would cost to replace them. If the price level does not change much, these two approaches yield much the same answer. But if prices are rising, as they have been during most of the past 70 years, replacement cost is greater than historical cost, with the result that the company is allowed higher profits and rates if replacement cost is used. Most commissions now use historical cost.

Historical cost
Reproduction cost

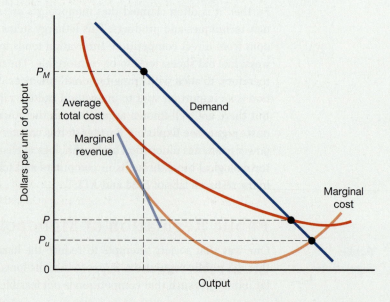

FIGURE 7.6

Regulation of Monopoly

The price established by a commission might be P, where the demand curve intersects the average total cost curve. (Costs here include what the commission regards as a fair profit per unit of output.) In the absence of regulation, the monopolist would set a price of P_M. For price to equal marginal cost, price per unit must equal P_u.

Does Regulation Affect Prices?

The regulatory commissions and the principles they use have become extremely controversial. Many observers feel that the commissions are lax and tend to be "captured" or co-opted by the industries they are supposed to regulate. Regulated industries, recognizing the power of such commissions, invest considerable time and money in attempts to influence them. The public, on the other hand, often has only a foggy idea of what the commissions do and whether they act in the public interest. According to some critics like Ralph Nader, "Nobody seriously challenges the fact that the regulatory agencies have made an accommodation with the businesses they are supposed to regulate—and they've done so at the expense of the public."[6] For these and other reasons, some economists believe that regulation has little effect on prices.

Deregulation

In a 1998 article, Clifford Winston, of the Brookings Institution, tried to quantify the effect on prices of this "regulatory capture."[7] He looked at the effect of **deregulation** on the prices of four industries: airlines, natural gas, railroads, and trucking. Based on his empirical analysis, he concluded that regulated prices were typically 30 to 50 percent higher than deregulated prices.

As we have stressed, competitive markets provide considerable incentives for a firm to increase its efficiency. Firms able to push their costs below those of their competitors reap higher profits than their competitors. As a simple illustration, suppose that both firms A and B have contracts to produce 100 airplanes, and the price they will get for each airplane is $25 million. Firm A's management, which is diligent, imaginative, and innovative, gets the cost per airplane down to $24 million and makes a healthy profit of $100 million. Firm B's management, which is lazy, unimaginative, and dull, lets the cost per airplane rise to $26 million and loses $100 million. Clearly, firm A is rewarded for its good performance, while firm B is penalized for its poor performance.

No Incentive for Efficiency

A primary purpose of regulators is to prevent a monopoly from earning excessive profits. The firm is allowed only a "fair" rate of return on its investment. One problem with this arrangement is that the firm is guaranteed this rate of return regardless of how well it performs. If the regulators decide that the Sleepy Hollow Electric and Gas Company should receive a 10 percent rate of return on its investment, this is the rate of return it will receive regardless of whether the Sleepy Hollow Electric and Gas Company is managed well or poorly. Why is this a problem? Because, unlike the competitive firms discussed in the previous paragraph, there is no incentive for the firm to increase its efficiency.

---

[6] Interview with Ralph Nader, *Playboy Magazine*, October 1968, 76.
[7] Clifford Winston, "U.S. Industry Adjustment to Economic Deregulation," *Journal of Economic Perspectives*, 12(summer 1998): 89–110.

NETWORK EFFECTS AND THE CASE AGAINST MICROSOFT

Bill Gates, Microsoft founder

In late 1997, the U.S. Department of Justice began an antitrust suit against Microsoft. The government's goal was to stop alleged anti-competitive practices involving Microsoft's tie-in of its Internet browser with Windows 95. Behind the suit was a widespread concern that because of so-called network effects, Microsoft could squeeze out other competitors' browsers and Internet applications.

A network effect, or externality, is an early standard, such as a computer operating system (for example, Windows 95) that greatly influences future standards because of the need for compatibility. There are at least three reasons for being concerned about network externalities. First, the product that becomes a network standard is not necessarily the most capable, most efficient, or highest-quality product on the market. For example, economists and technology experts have been debating for some time whether the QWERTY keyboard and the VHS (versus the now little used Betamax) video format are the most efficient.

Second, high switching costs can raise the barriers to entry for competitors, especially if new products cannot interconnect with those already in the market. This can make network monopolies quite stable and reduces the dominant firm's incentives to introduce innovative products and services.

Third, a network monopolist may have advantages in selling complementary goods that allow it to extend its dominance from one market to another. This was the essence of the case against Microsoft—that it was using its dominant position as the supplier of operating systems to become the dominant supplier of Internet browsers and applications.

As compelling as these concerns are, an impressive array of legal and economic minds disagreed with the government's position. A recurring theme of their counterarguments was that technology almost always undermines network externalities. The monopoly by IBM of computer mainframes was wiped out by the advent of the PC. Government-regulated telephone monopolies found themselves scrambling for market share with the widespread use of cellular phones and fiber-optic wires. Therefore, these experts argued, Microsoft's monopoly in operating systems was bound to be short-lived.

Moreover, some prominent economists hired by Microsoft argued that even though its Windows operating system was used by over 90 percent of the market, this did not represent a monopoly. In fact, they estimated that the monopoly price for Windows 98 would be between $900 and $2,000, instead of the much lower market price. Why could Microsoft not charge the monopoly price? Because users might have chosen to stay with the earlier Windows 95 version.

Finally, pro-Microsoft advocates argued that even if the company enjoyed a network monopoly, this did not violate the Sherman Antitrust Act (see Chapter 8). Under this act, technological monopolies are legal. Rather, actions to defend or extend the monopoly break the law.

In the end, the presiding judge, Thomas Penfield Jackson, ruled against Microsoft in a decision released on November 5, 1999. Judge Jackson conceded that the network effect was probably not that strong in this case. On the contrary, precisely because Microsoft feared that it might lose its commanding lead in the market, it engaged in anticompetitive practices. The final paragraph of the 207-page ruling summarizes this view:

> Most harmful of all is the message that Microsoft's actions have conveyed to every enterprise with the potential to innovate in the computer industry. Through its conduct towards Netscape, IBM, Compaq, Intel and others, Microsoft has demonstrated that it will use its prodigious market power and immense profits to harm any firm that insists on pursuing initiatives that could intensify competition against one of Microsoft's core products. Microsoft's past success in hurting such companies and stifling innovation

deters investment in technologies and businesses that exhibit the potential to threaten Microsoft. The ultimate result is that some business innovations that would truly benefit consumers never occur for the sole reason that they do not coincide with Microsoft's self-interest.

In June 2000, Microsoft was ordered to split up into two companies. However, in 2001, the company reached a settlement with the Department of Justice by agreeing to unbundle some of its software and curb some of its anticompetitive practices.

In the meantime, some competitors, such as AOL Time Warner (owner of Netscape) and Sun Micro Systems, launched separate private suits against Microsoft. European antitrust authorities also geared up to curtail the anticompetitive behavior of the software giant, accusing the company of using the dominance of Windows to monopolize the market for media-player software and the operating systems of bigger (server) computers.

In the end, the U.S. government's case against Microsoft will be seen as the opening salvo in a broad-based attempt to curb the software maker's monopolistic practices. One goal of the government's antitrust case was to prevent Microsoft and other high-tech firms from either suppressing the development of new technologies or denying access to these new technologies to competitors. Ironically, the biggest check on Microsoft's monopolistic behavior could well be the rapid pace of technological change in the information technology markets. Already Microsoft has had to transform itself many times to keep pace with the sea changes in the computer software and online industries. Recently, its biggest challenge has come from the proliferation of smartphones and tablets, which do not use Microsoft operating systems. While the company remains highly profitable, it has struggled to play catch-up in this most dynamic part of the high-tech market.

The available evidence indicates that if a firm is guaranteed a fixed amount of profit for a job (regardless of how efficiently it does this job), the firm tends to be less efficient than if the amount of profit it receives is directly related to its efficiency. The Department of Defense has found that when it bought goods or services on a cost-plus-fixed-fee basis, these goods and services were not produced as cheaply as when it bought them in a competitive market. This is reasonable. It takes time, energy, and lots of trouble to make a firm more efficient. Why should a firm's managers bother to induce added efficiency if the firm's profits are the same regardless of how efficient it is?

The Deregulation Movement

In the late 1970s and early 1980s, there was a dramatic movement toward deregulation in the United States. A variety of industries, including airlines, railroads, trucking, and financial institutions, were affected. In the case of the airlines, the seeds for deregulation were sown in the 1970s with the appointment of the late Alfred Kahn, a Cornell economist, as head of the Civil Aeronautics Board. During the late 1970s, airlines were allowed to institute discount fares, and entry restrictions were relaxed. Eventually, Congress passed legislation that phased out the board's powers. The power to regulate routes terminated at the end of 1981, and the power to regulate rates terminated at the end of 1982 (see Case Study 8.3). Possibly the best case for the deregulation was made by Kahn in his 2004 book *Lessons from Deregulation*:

> Deregulation shifts the major burden of consumer protection to the competitive market, and therefore, in important measure, to the enforcement of antitrust laws. But the experience with essentially unmanaged deregulation in airlines and pervasively managed deregulation in telecommunications also demonstrates that the focus of policy should be, first and foremost, on liberating competition from direct government restraint—not dictating market structures or outcomes. In particular, while in no way counseling indulgent antitrust treatment of predatory or unfairly exclusionary competitive *conduct*, they underline the need for humility in attempting to make industries more competitive by interfering with their achievement and exploitation of economies of scope and diluting their incentives for innovation—the most powerful competition of all.[8]

---

[8] Alfred Kahn, *Lessons from Deregulation: Telecommunications and Airlines after the Crunch* (Washington, DC: AEI-Brookings Joint Center for Regulatory Studies, 2004).

EXPLORING FURTHER

The Defense of Monopoly Power

Not all economists agree that monopoly power is a bad thing. On the contrary, some respected voices in the economics profession have been raised to praise monopoly power. In discussing the social problems due to monopoly earlier in this chapter, we assumed that the rate of technological change is independent of an industry's market structure. Some economists, like the late Joseph Schumpeter, of Harvard University, challenged this assumption. They assert that the rate of technological change is likely to be higher in an imperfectly competitive industry (monopoly, oligopoly, and so on) than in a perfectly competitive industry. Because the rate of technological change affects productivity and living standards, in their view a perfectly competitive economy is likely to be inferior in a dynamic sense to an economy containing many imperfectly competitive industries.

But is this assertion true? This question has been debated at great length. On the one hand, Schumpeter argues that firms under perfect competition have fewer resources to devote to research and experimentation than firms under imperfect competition. Because profits are at a relatively low level, it is difficult for firms under perfect competition to support large expenditures on research and development. Moreover, he argues, unless a firm has sufficient control over the market to reap the rewards from an innovation, introducing the innovation may not be worthwhile. If competitors can imitate the innovation very quickly, the innovator may be unable to make any money from it.

Defenders of perfect competition retort that there is likely to be less pressure for firms in imperfect markets to introduce new techniques and products, since such firms have fewer competitors. Moreover, established firms in imperfect markets are better able to drive out new entrants uncommitted to present techniques and likely to be relatively quick to adopt new ones. (New entrants, unlike established producers, have no vested interest in maintaining the demand for existing products and the profitability of existing equipment.) Also, there are advantages in having a large number of independent decision-making units. There is less chance that an important technological advance will be blocked by the faulty judgment of a few people.

It is very difficult to obtain evidence to help settle the question if it is posed in this way, since perfect competition is a hypothetical construct that does not exist in the real world. However, it does seem unlikely that a perfectly competitive industry (if such an industry could be constructed) would be able, in many areas of the economy, to carry out the research and development required to promote a high rate of technological change. Moreover, if entry is free and rapid, firms in a perfectly competitive industry have little motivation to innovate. Although the evidence is not at all clear-cut, at least this much can be granted the critics of perfect competition.

THE SAGA OF AT&T

For decades, AT&T (formerly the American Telephone and Telegraph Company) operated as a regulated monopoly, based on the logic that a telephone system was a natural monopoly. However, in 1982, AT&T was forced to divest its local phone networks, partly because of the wave of deregulation that swept the United States in the late 1970s and early 1980s and partly because of technology changes that were beginning to have a large impact on the telecommunications industry. AT&T was allowed to keep its long-distance business, but the local networks were spun off into companies that came to be known as the Baby Bells (AT&T was originally known as Bell Telephone, named after the inventor of the telephone, Alexander Graham Bell).

In an attempt to increase competition, the federal government allowed other companies to compete with AT&T in the provision of long-distance phone service. Two companies, MCI (later acquired by WorldCom) and Sprint, became serious competitors to AT&T in this market. Meanwhile, the seven Baby Bells were allowed to consolidate, and soon the local telephone business became dominated by three companies, Bell South, SBC (formerly Southwestern Bell Company), and Verizon.

To complicate matters, the 1996 Telecommunications Act allowed the Baby Bells to compete in the long-distance market and AT&T and others to compete in the local market. In the meantime, massive technological changes were shaking up the industry and allowing new competitors to enter the telecommunications market. First, the rapid rise in the use of cell phones allowed other

companies, such as Cingular, Nextel, and T-Mobile, to give AT&T and the Baby Bells a run for their money. Moreover, the advent of the Internet and the demand for broadband service also allowed cable companies to offer telephone service.

If things were not tough enough for AT&T and the other phone companies, during the high-tech boom of the late 1990s, they were forced to make massive investments in new technologies, including fiber-optic networks. Much of this investment was debt financed. When the high-tech bubble burst in 2000 and high-tech stock prices collapsed (falling an average of 60 percent from peak to trough), the telecom companies were badly hurt. WorldCom (later to be renamed MCI) went bankrupt, both because of its massive debt load and as a result of fraudulent claims about its profits (see Case Study 3.2). AT&T survived the ordeal but emerged financially much weaker.

The Saga of AT&T was not over yet. In 2002, it chose to divest once again. This time it sold off its wireless and cable operations and focused its efforts on the business market, where it was the most competitive. Ironically, a leaner and meaner AT&T became a target for acquisition. In 2003, both Bell South and SBC expressed interest in buying their former parent company. This turn of events would have been unthinkable two decades earlier. However, rapid changes in technology have so radically transformed the structure of the telecommunications industry that such a linkup can be contemplated without raising concerns about antitrust.

In the end, SBC did acquire AT&T in 2005 and rebranded itself AT&T Inc. In 2006, the new company bought Bell South. In the next four years, the new AT&T went on to purchase Cellular One, Centennial Communications, Wayport, and other assets that would solidify its strong position in the telecommunications industry. However, AT&T's buying "binge" came to an abrupt end (or pause?) in 2011 when the Obama administration filed suit to block the company's attempt to merge with T-Mobile. AT&T eventually withdrew its merger bid. Given the rapid changes in the telecommunications industry, it seems unlikely that the saga of AT&T will end here.

Monopoly Power, Big Business, and Technological Change

Some economists go much further than asserting that a certain amount of market imperfection promotes a more rapid rate of technological change. They say that an industry composed of or dominated by a few large companies is the best market structure for promoting rapid technological change. The late John Kenneth Galbraith said that the "modern industry of a few large firms [is] an almost perfect instrument for inducing technical change."[9] And in some circles, it is accepted as an obvious fact that giant firms, with their financial strength and well-equipped laboratories, are absolutely necessary to maintain a rapid rate of technological change.

Suppose, for a market of given size, we could replace the largest firms by a larger number of somewhat smaller firms, thus reducing the extent to which the industry is dominated by the largest firms. Is there any evidence that this would decrease the rate of technological change, as is sometimes asserted? The evidence currently available does not indicate that such a decrease in industrial concentration would reduce the rate of technological change in most industries. Specifically, the available studies do not show that total research and development expenditures in most industries would decrease if the largest firms were replaced by somewhat smaller ones. Nor do they indicate that the research and development expenditures carried out by the largest firms are generally more productive (or more ambitious or more risky) than those carried out by somewhat smaller firms. Moreover, they do not suggest that greater concentration of an industry results in a faster diffusion of innovations. However, these studies do suggest that if innovations require a large amount of capital, then the substitution of a larger number of smaller firms for a few large ones may lead to slower commercial introduction of the innovations.

Therefore, contrary to the allegations of Galbraith and others, there is little evidence that industrial giants are needed in most industries to ensure rapid technological change and rapid utilization of new techniques. This does

[9] John Kenneth Galbraith, *American Capitalism* (Boston: Houghton Mifflin, 1952), 91.

not mean, however, that industries composed only of small firms would necessarily be optimal for the promotion and diffusion of new techniques. On the contrary, there seem to be considerable advantages in a diversity of firm sizes. Complementarities and interdependencies exist among large and small firms. There is often a division of labor. Smaller firms may focus on areas requiring sophistication and flexibility and may cater to specialized needs, whereas bigger firms may concentrate on areas requiring large production, marketing, or technical resources. However, in most industries there is little evidence that firms considerably smaller than the biggest firms are not big enough for these purposes. The experience during the high-tech boom of the 1990s and 2000s in Silicon Valley and around Boston's Route 128 confirms these general conclusions. Small companies carried out a lot of the entrepreneurial activity and innovation during that boom. Some of these companies went on to become bigger and quite famous (see Case Study 11.3); others failed. However, smallness did not seem to get in the way of innovation. Quite the contrary, it seemed to help.

How Much Monopoly Power Is Optimal?

The discussion in previous sections makes it clear that the case against monopoly power is not open and shut. A certain amount of monopoly power is inevitable in practically all real-life situations, since perfect competition is a model that can be only approximated in real life. Moreover, a certain amount of monopoly power may be needed to promote desirable technological change. The difficult problem is to determine how much monopoly power is optimal under various circumstances (and how this power is to be measured). Some economists (like Galbraith) are convinced that a great deal of monopoly power is both inevitable and desirable. Others believe the opposite. And the economic arguments are not strong enough to resolve the differences of opinion. Much more is said on this score in Chapter 8.

REVIEW AND PRACTICE

Summary

1 A monopoly is a market with only one seller. Monopolies may occur because of patents, control over basic inputs, or government action, among other reasons.

2 If average costs reach their minimum at an output rate large enough to satisfy the entire market, perfect competition cannot be maintained; the public often insists that the industry (a natural monopoly) be regulated by the government.

3   Since the monopolist is the only seller of the product, the demand curve facing the monopolist is the market demand curve, which slopes downward (rather than being horizontal as in perfect competition).

4   The unregulated monopolist maximizes profit by choosing the output where marginal cost equals marginal revenue, where marginal revenue is defined as the addition to total revenue attributable to the addition of 1 unit to sales.

5   If monopolists cannot prevent losses from exceeding fixed costs, they, like perfect competitors, discontinue production. In contrast to the case in perfect competition, the long-run equilibrium of a monopolistic industry may not be marked by the absence of economic profits.

6   The output under monopoly tends to be smaller and the price tends to be higher than under perfect competition. Economists tend to believe that society would be better off if more resources were devoted to the production of the good than under monopoly. The competitive output often is regarded as best.

7   One way that society attempts to reduce the harmful effects of monopoly is through public regulation. Commissions often set price at the level at which it equals average total cost, including a "fair" rate of return on the firm's investment. In some industries (for example, airlines, trucking, and railroads), the late 1970s and early 1980s saw a strong movement toward deregulation.

8   Because regulated firms may be guaranteed a particular rate of return (regardless of how well or poorly they perform), there may be little incentive for them to increase their efficiency.

*9[10] In defense of monopoly power, some economists, including Joseph Schumpeter, assert that the rate of technological change is likely to be greater in an imperfectly competitive industry than under perfect competition.

*10 Contrary to the allegations of John Kenneth Galbraith and others, there is little evidence that giant firms are needed to ensure rapid technological change in a great many sectors of the economy. In fact, the contributions of smaller firms are much greater than is commonly recognized.

Problems and Questions

1   If you are the president of a firm that has a monopoly on a certain product, would you choose an output level where demand for the product is price inelastic? Explain.

[10] Starred (*) items refer to material covered in Exploring Further.

2   Suppose that the amount demanded for a monopolist's product at a variety
    of prices is as follows:

Quantity Demanded (per year)	Price (dollars)
8	1,000
7	2,000
6	3,000
5	4,000
4	5,000
3	6,000
2	7,000
1	8,000

Plot the firm's marginal revenue curve.

3   Suppose that the monopolist in question 2 has fixed costs of $10,000 and
    an average variable cost of $4,000. The average variable cost is the same
    for outputs of 1 to 10 units per year. What output rate will the firm choose?
    What price will it set?

4   Plot the marginal cost curve of the firm in question 3, using the same grid
    used in your response to question 2. Where does this curve intersect the
    marginal revenue curve you drew in question 2?

5   Suppose that the firm in question 3 experiences a 50 percent increase in
    both its fixed and average variable costs. If the demand curve represented
    by the table in question 2 remains valid, what effect does this cost increase
    have on the output rate and price that the firm chooses?

Key Terms

monopoly
patents
natural monopolies
network externality
network effect
total revenue
marginal revenue
public regulation
historical cost
reproduction cost
deregulation

Viewpoint for Analysis

On April 6, 1998, Gary S. Becker, professor at the University of Chicago and the 1992 Nobel laureate in economics, wrote in his regular column for *Business Week*: "Competitors that develop superior technologies are far better protectors of consumers than government officials and bureaucrats who march to the beat of political popularity."[11]

(a) Can you think of technologies that have destroyed monopolies?

(b) Can monopolies prevent new technologies from coming to market? How?

(c) What role can the government play in making sure that an existing monopoly does not prevent consumers from enjoying the benefits of a new technology?

Monopolistic Competition, Oligopoly, and Antitrust Policy

LEARNING OBJECTIVES

➤ To identify the conditions that define monopolistic competition and those that define oligopoly

➤ To compare prices and outputs under monopolistic competition with those under perfect competition and monopoly

➤ To explain how oligopolies are organized

➤ To compare prices and outputs under oligopoly with those under perfect competition and monopoly

➤ To describe the major antitrust laws and their effectiveness

The aircraft industry is dominated by two firms: Boeing and Airbus. The beer industry is dominated by a few firms, such as Anheuser-Busch, Miller, and Coors. The retail drug industry is composed of many firms, but it is not a perfectly competitive industry. How are price and output determined in these industries? One purpose of this chapter is to answer this question.

The industries encountered in the real world are seldom perfectly competitive or monopolistic. Although perfect competition and monopoly are very useful models that shed valuable light on the behavior of markets, they are polar cases. Economists have developed other models that portray more realistically the behavior of many modern industries. The model of monopolistic competition helps explain market behavior in industries like retail drugstores, whereas the model of oligopoly pertains to industries like aircraft and beer.

In this chapter, we will examine how resources are allocated and prices are set under monopolistic competition and oligopoly. The results are of considerable significance, because they give us a better understanding of how a variety of markets work and they provide valuable information on the social desirability of monopolistic competition and oligopoly.

Monopolistic Competition and Oligopoly: Their Major Characteristics

Monopolistic
competition

To begin with, we must recall what monopolistic competition and oligopoly are. **Monopolistic competition** occurs where there are many sellers (as in perfect competition) but there is product differentiation. In other words, the firms' products are not the same. It does not matter whether the differences between products are real or imagined. What is important is that the consumer regards the products as different.

Oligopoly

Oligopoly occurs in markets where there are few sellers. There are two types of oligopolies, one where all sellers produce an identical product and one where the sellers produce somewhat different products. Examples of the first

Pure oligopoly
Differentiated
oligopoly

type, **pure oligopoly**, are the markets for steel, cement, tin cans, and petro leum. Examples of the second type, **differentiated oligopoly**, are the markets for automobiles and machinery, where there are differences in car models and types of machinery

In contrast to the extremes of perfect competition and monopoly, monopolistic competition and oligopoly are intermediate cases that include elements of competition and monopoly and so are more realistic than the two extremes.

Monopolistic Competition

Product
differentiation

The key feature of monopolistic competition is **product differentiation**. In contrast to perfect competition, where all firms sell an identical product, firms under monopolistic competition sell somewhat different products. Each producer differentiates its product from that of other producers. This is the case in many U.S. markets. In many parts of retail trade, producers can differentiate their product by altering the product's physical makeup, the services they offer, and other such variables. Other differences, which may be spurious, are based on brand name, image making, advertising claims, and so on. In this way, the producers gain some monopoly power, but usually it is small, because the products of other firms are very similar.

Product group

In perfect competition, the firms included in an industry are easy to identify because they all produce the same product. But if product differentiation exists, it is no longer easy to define an industry, since each firm produces a somewhat different product. Nevertheless, it is useful to group together firms that produce similar products and call them a **product group**. We can formulate a product group called "toothpaste," "soap," or "chocolate bars." The process by which we combine firms into product groups is bound to be somewhat arbitrary, since there is no way to decide how close a pair of substitutes must be to belong to the same product group. But it is assumed that meaningful product groups can be established.

In addition to product differentiation, other conditions must be met for an industry to qualify as a case of monopolistic competition. First, there must be a large number of firms in the product group. In other words, the product must be produced by perhaps 50 to 100 or more firms, and each firm's product must be a fairly close substitute for the products of the other firms in the product group. Second, the number of firms in the product group must be large enough that each firm expects its actions to go unheeded by its rivals and is unimpeded by possible retaliatory moves on their part. If there is a large number of firms, this condition normally is met. Third, entry into the product group must be relatively easy, and there must be no collusion, such as price fixing or market sharing, among firms in the product group. With a large number of firms, collusion generally is difficult, if not impossible.

Price and Output under Monopolistic Competition

Under monopolistic competition, what determines how much output a firm produces and what price it charges? If each firm produces a somewhat different product, it follows that the demand curve facing each firm slopes downward to the right. That is, if the firm raises its price slightly, it will lose some but by no means all of its customers to other firms. And if it lowers its price slightly, it will gain some but by no means all of its competitors' customers. This is in contrast to perfect competition, where the demand curve facing each firm is horizontal.

Figure 8.1 shows the short-run equilibrium of a monopolistically competitive firm. The firm in the short run sets its price at P_0 and its output rate at Q_0, since this combination of price and output maximizes its profits. We can be sure that this combination of price and output maximizes profit, because marginal cost equals marginal revenue at this output rate. In the situation shown in Figure 8.1, economic profits are earned because price P_0 exceeds average total cost C_0 at this output rate.

What are the equilibrium price and output in the long run? One condition for long-run equilibrium is that each firm makes no long-run economic profits or losses, since entry or exit of firms occur otherwise, and entry and exit are incompatible with long-run equilibrium. Another condition for long-run equilibrium is that each firm maximizes its profits. At what price and output are both these conditions fulfilled? Figure 8.2 shows that long-run equilibrium is at a price of P_1 and an output of Q_1. The zero economic profit condition is met at this combination of price and output, since the firm's average cost at this output equals the price P_1. And the profit maximization condition is met, since the marginal revenue curve intersects the marginal cost curve at this output rate.

FIGURE 8.1

Short-Run Equilibrium: Monopolistic Competition

The firm sets its price at P_0 and its output rate at Q_0, since marginal cost equals marginal revenue at this output. It earns a profit of $P_0 - C_0$ per unit of output.

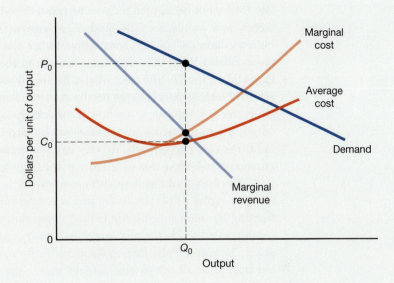

Comparisons with Perfect Competition and Monopoly

Market structure is important because it influences market behavior. We need to know how the behavior of a monopolistically competitive industry differs from that of a perfectly competitive industry or a monopoly. Suppose a magician can transform an industry's structure by a wave of a wand. (John D. Rockefeller

FIGURE 8.2

Long-Run Equilibrium: Monopolistic Competition

The long-run equilibrium is at a price of P_1 and an output of Q_1. There are zero profits, since long-run average cost equals price. Profits are maximized, since marginal cost equals marginal revenue at this output.

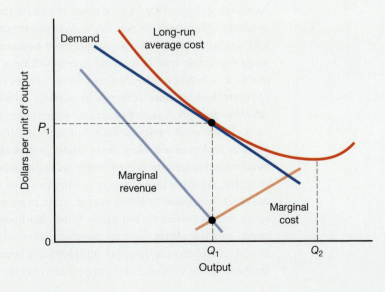

was a real-life magician who transformed the structure of the oil industry in the late 1800s, but he seemed to favor mergers, mixed with some ungentlemanly tactics, over wands; see Case Study 7.1.) Suppose that the magician makes an industry monopolistically competitive rather than perfectly competitive or monopolistic. What difference does it make in the behavior of the industry? Or, to take a less fanciful case, what difference does it make when government action or technological change results in such a change in an industry's market structure? It is difficult to say how the industry's behavior is affected, because output is heterogeneous in one case and homogeneous in the other and the industry's cost curves probably vary with its organization. But many economists seem to believe that differences of the following kind can be expected.

1. *The firm under monopolistic competition is likely to produce less and charge a higher price than under perfect competition.* The demand curve confronting the monopolistic competitor slopes downward to the right. Consequently, as we saw in the previous chapter, marginal revenue must be less than price. Therefore, under monopolistic competition, marginal cost must also be less than price, since marginal revenue must equal marginal cost at the firm's profit-maximizing output rate. But if marginal cost is less than price, the firm's output rate must be smaller—and the price higher—than if marginal cost equals price, as is the case under perfect competition. On the other hand, *relative to monopoly, monopolistically competitive firms are likely to have lower profits, greater output, and lower price.* The firms in a product group might obtain positive economic profits if they were to collude and behave as a monopolist. Such an increase in profits resulting from the monopoly would benefit the producers. Consumers would be worse off because of the higher prices and smaller output of goods.

2. *A firm under monopolistic competition may be somewhat inefficient.* As shown in Figure 8.2, it produces a smaller-than-minimum-cost output. (It produces Q_1 units of output; the output where average cost is at a minimum is Q_2 units of output.) Consequently, more firms exist than if average costs are minimized; this results in some overcrowding of the industry. Inefficiencies of this sort would not be expected under perfect competition. However, these apparent inefficiencies may not be socially undesirable if consumers highly value the product diversity occurring under monopolistic competition.

3. *Firms under monopolistic competition offer a wider variety of styles, brands, and qualities than firms under perfect competition, and they spend much more on advertising and other selling expenses than a perfectly competitive firm.* Whether this diversity is worth its cost is hard to say. Some economists are impressed by the apparent waste in monopolistic competition. They argue that it results in too many firms, too many brands, too much selling effort, and too much spurious product differentiation. But if the differences between products are real and understood by consumers, the greater variety available under monopolistic competition may be very valuable to consumers.

The proper evaluation of the social advantages and disadvantages of product differentiation is harder than may appear at first sight.

Oligopoly

Oligopoly (domination by a few firms) is a common and important market structure in the United States; many industries, including steel, automobiles, oil, airlines, and electrical equipment, are oligopolistic. General Motors, for example, is an oligopolist. The key characteristic of oligopoly is interdependence, actual and perceived, among firms. Each oligopolist formulates its policies with an eye to their effect on its rivals. Since an oligopoly contains a small number of firms, any change in one firm's price or output influences the sales and profits of its competitors. Moreover, since there are only a few firms, each must recognize that changes in its own policies are likely to result in changes in the policies of its rivals as well.

What factors are responsible for oligopoly? First, in some industries, low production costs cannot be achieved unless a firm produces an output equal to a substantial portion of the total available market, with the consequence that the number of firms tends to be rather small. Second, there may be economies of scale in sales promotion in certain industries; this, too, may promote oligopoly. Third, entry into some industries may be blocked by the requirement that a firm build and maintain a large, complicated, and expensive plant or have access to patents or scarce raw materials. Only a few firms may be in a position to obtain all these prerequisites for membership in the club.

Oligopoly Models

Unlike perfect competition, monopoly, and monopolistic competition, there is no single, unified model of oligopoly behavior. Instead, there are a number of models, each based on a somewhat different set of assumptions concerning the relationships between the firms that make up the oligopoly. Basically, no single model exists because economists have not yet been able to devise one that covers all the relevant cases adequately.

The Theory of Games

The rivalry among oligopolists has many of the characteristics of a game. In oligopoly, each firm must take into account its rivals' reactions to its own actions. For this reason, an oligopolistic firm cannot tell what effect a change in its output will have on the price of its product and its profits unless it can guess how its rivals will respond to the change. To understand game theory, you have to know what a game is. A **game** is a competitive situation where two or more persons pursue their own interests and no person can dictate the outcome. Poker is a game, and so is a situation in which two firms are engaged in competitive

Game

advertising campaigns. A game is described in terms of its players, rules, payoffs, and information conditions. These elements are common to all conflict situations.

More specifically, a player, whether a single person or an organization, is a decision-making unit. Each player has a certain amount of resources, and the rules of the game describe how these resources can be used. The rules of poker indicate how bets can be made and which hands are better than others. A strategy is a complete specification of what a player would do under each contingency in the playing of the game. For example, a corporation president may tell subordinates how an advertising campaign should start and what should be done at subsequent times in response to various actions of competing firms. The game's outcome clearly depends on each player's strategies. A player's payoff varies from game to game. It is win, lose, or draw in checkers and various sums of money in poker.

A Simple Two-Person Game

For simplicity, we restrict our attention to a two-person game: one with only two players. The relevant features of a two-person game can be shown by con **Payoff matrix** structing a **payoff matrix**. To illustrate, consider the case of two big soap producers, Procter & Gamble and Unilever. Suppose these two firms are about to stage rival advertising campaigns and each firm has a choice of strategies. Procter & Gamble can choose to concentrate on either television ads or magazine ads; Unilever has the same choice. Figure 8.3 shows what can happen to the profits of each firm when each combination of strategies is chosen. If both firms concentrate on TV ads, Procter & Gamble gains $30 million and Unilever gains $20 million. If Procter & Gamble concentrates on TV ads and Unilever

FIGURE 8.3

Payoff Matrix: Procter & Gamble and Unilever

		Possible Strategies for Unilever	
		Concentrate on TV	**Concentrate on magazines**
Possible Strategies for Procter & Gamble	**Concentrate on TV**	P&G's profit: $30 million Unilever's profit: $20 million	P&G's profit: $40 million Unilever's profit: $30 million
	Concentrate on magazines	P&G's profit: $20 million Unilever's profit: $30 million	P&G's profit: $30 million Unilever's profit: $40 million

concentrates on magazine ads, Procter & Gamble gains $40 million and Unilever gains $30 million. And so on.

Procter and Gamble's Viewpoint   Given the payoff matrix in Figure 8.3, there is a definite optimal choice (called a dominant strategy) for each firm. To see that this is the case, begin by looking at the situation from Procter & Gamble's point of view. If Unilever concentrates on TV ads, Procter & Gamble makes more money ($30 million rather than $20 million) if it concentrates on TV rather than magazines. If Unilever concentrates on magazines, Procter & Gamble makes more money ($40 million rather than $30 million) if it concentrates on TV rather than magazines. Therefore, regardless of the strategy chosen by Unilever, Procter & Gamble does best to concentrate on TV.

Unilever's Viewpoint   Now, look at the situation from the point of view of Unilever. If Procter & Gamble concentrates on TV ads, Unilever makes more money ($30 million rather than $20 million) if it concentrates on magazines rather than TV. If Procter & Gamble concentrates on magazines, Unilever makes more money ($40 million rather than $30 million) if it concentrates on magazines rather than TV. Therefore, regardless of the strategy chosen by Procter & Gamble, Unilever does best to concentrate on magazines.

The Solution of the Game   At this point, the solution of this game is clear. Procter & Gamble will concentrate on TV ads and Unilever will concentrate on magazine ads. This is the best either firm can do.

Collusion and Cartels

How Firms Collude

Collusion

Collusion occurs when firms get together and agree on price and output. Up to this point, we have assumed that oligopolists do not collude, but conditions in oligopolistic industries tend to promote collusion, since the number of firms is small and the firms recognize their interdependence. The advantages of collusion to the firms seem obvious: increased profits, decreased uncertainty, and a better opportunity to prevent entry.

Cartel

Not all collusion is disguised from the public or secret. In contrast to illicit collusion, a **cartel** is an open, formal collusive arrangement among firms. In many European countries, cartels have been common and legally acceptable. In the United States, most collusive arrangements, whether secret or open, were declared illegal by the Sherman Antitrust Act, which was passed in 1890.

However, this does not mean that such arrangements do not exist. Widespread collusion to fix prices occurred among U.S. electrical equipment manufacturers during the 1950s, and when the collusion was uncovered, a number of high executives were tried, convicted, and sent to jail (see Case Study 8.1).

FIGURE 8.4

Price and Output of a Cartel

The marginal cost curve shows the marginal cost for the cartel as a whole. On the basis of the demand curve for the industry's product, the cartel can derive the marginal revenue curve. The output that maximizes the total profit of the cartel members is Q. The corresponding price is P.

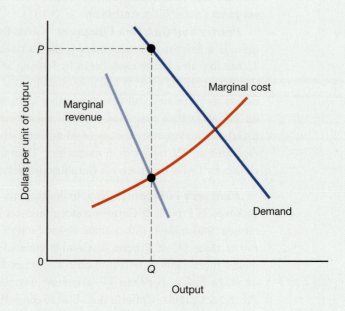

Moreover, collusion of this sort is not limited to a single industry or a single country. Some cartels are international in scope. A particularly famous international cartel is the Organization of Petroleum Exporting Countries (OPEC), which consists of 12 oil-producing countries, including Saudi Arabia and Iran.

Price and Output of a Cartel

If a cartel is established to set a uniform price for a particular product, what price does it charge? As a first step, the cartel must estimate the marginal cost curve for the cartel as a whole. Then it must find the output where its marginal cost equals its marginal revenue, since this output maximizes the total profit of the cartel members. In Figure 8.4, this output is Q. If it maximizes cartel profits, the cartel chooses a price of P, which is the monopoly price. In short, the cartel acts like a monopolist with a number of plants or divisions, each of which is a member firm.

How does the cartel allocate sales among the member firms? If its aim is to maximize cartel profits, it allocates sales to firms in such a way that the sum of the firms' costs is minimized. But this allocation is unlikely to occur in reality. The allocation process is a bargaining process, and firms with the most influence and the shrewdest negotiators are likely to receive the largest sales quotas, even though this decreases the total profits of the cartel.

Moreover, high-cost firms are likely to receive larger sales quotas than if total cartel profits were maximized, since they would be unwilling otherwise to stay in the cartel. In practice, it appears that cartels often divide markets geographically or in accord with a firm's level of sales in the past.

Barriers to Collusion

The idea that oligopoly can lead to collusion is not new. Back in 1776, Adam Smith warned that "people of the same trade seldom meet together even for merriment and diversion, but the conversation ends in a conspiracy against the public, or in some contrivance to raise prices."[1] However, we must bear in mind that collusive arrangements are often difficult to accomplish and to maintain for long. In particular, there are several important barriers to collusion.

Legal Problems

The antitrust laws, discussed in detail later in this chapter, forbid outright collusion and price fixing. This does not mean that firms do not break those laws; witness the electrical equipment manufacturers described in Case Study 8.1. But the antitrust laws are an important obstacle to collusion.

Technical Problems

Collusion is often difficult to achieve and maintain because an oligopoly contains an unwieldy number of firms, the product is quite heterogeneous, or the cost structures of the firms differ considerably. Clearly, a collusive agreement is more difficult to achieve and maintain if there are a dozen oligopolists than if there are three or four. Moreover, if the products sold by the oligopolists differ substantially, it probably is more difficult for them to find a common price strategy acceptable to all. Similarly, if the firms' cost structures differ, it will be more difficult to get agreement, since the low-cost firms will be more inclined to cut price. In the airline industry, for example, there are periodic "price wars" initiated by low-cost airlines.

Cheating

Oligopolists are constantly tempted to cheat on any collusive agreement. If other firms stick to the agreement, any firm that cheats—by cutting its price below that agreed to under the collusive arrangement—can take a lot of business away from the other firms and increase its profits substantially, at least in

[1] Adam Smith, *An Inquiry into the Nature and Causes of the Wealth of Nations* (London: W. Strahan and T. Cadell, 1776), Book 1, Chapter 10.

THE ELECTRICAL CONSPIRACY

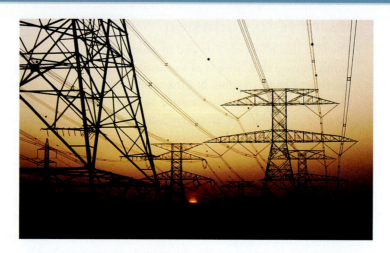

To illustrate how firms collude, we can consider the case of electrical equipment manufacturers. During the 1950s, there was widespread collusion among about 30 firms selling turbine generators, switchgear, transformers, and other products with total sales of about $1.5 billion per year. Representatives of these firms got together and agreed on prices for many products. The available evidence indicates that both prices and profits tended to be increased by the collusive agreements, at least until the firms were prosecuted under the antitrust laws by the Department of Justice. The following statement by F. M. Scherer, of Harvard University, is a good description of some of the procedures used by these firms:

> Some of the most elaborate procedures were devised to handle switchgear pricing. Each seller agreed to quote book prices in sales to private buyers, and meetings were held regularly to compare calculations for forthcoming job quotations. Sealed-bid competitions sponsored by government agencies posed a different set of problems, and new methods were worked out to handle them. Through protracted negotiation, each seller was assigned a specific share of all sealed-bid business; for example, General Electric's share of the high-voltage switchgear field was set at 40.3 percent in late 1958 and Allis-Chalmers' at 8.8 percent. Participants then coordinated their bidding so that each firm was lowest bidder in just enough transactions to gain its predetermined share of the market. In the power switching equipment line, this was achieved for a while by dividing the United States into four quadrants, assigning four sellers to each quadrant, and letting the sellers in a quadrant rotate their bids. A "phases of the moon" system was used to allocate low-bidding privileges in the high-voltage switchgear field, with a new seller assuming low-bidding priority every two weeks. The designated bidder subtracted a specified percentage margin

from the book price to capture orders during its phase, while others added various margins to the book price. The result was an ostensibly random pattern of quotations, conveying the impression of independent pricing behavior.*

General Electric, Westinghouse, and the other conspirators were found guilty of violating the antitrust laws. Some of the

executives were sentenced to jail on criminal charges, and the firms had to pay large amounts to customers to make up for the overcharges. In particular, 1,800 triple-damage suits against the firms resulted in payments estimated at between $400 million and $600 million.

* F.M. Scherer, *Industrial Market Structure and Economic Performance* (Boston: Houghton Mifflin, 1980), 160.

the short run. This temptation is particularly great when an industry's sales are depressed and its profits are low; every firm is hungry for business, and the temptation is difficult to resist. Moreover, one firm may be driven to cheat because it hears that another firm is doing so, with the eventual result that the collusive agreement is torn apart.

To illustrate the problems of maintaining a collusive agreement, we return to the electrical equipment manufacturers described in Case Study 8.1. As the *Wall Street Journal* summed it up:

> One of the great ironies of the conspiracies was that no matter how hard the participants schemed, no matter how friendly their meetings and communications might be, there was an innate tendency to compete. Someone was always violating the agreements to get more business and this continually called for new illegal plans. For example, price-cutting in sales of power switching equipment to government agencies was getting out of hand in late 1958. This led to the "quadrant" system of dividing markets.[2]

As one executive of General Electric complained, "No one was living up to the agreement and we . . . were being made suckers. On every job someone would cut our throat; we lost confidence in the group." Given that these agreements were illegal, it is remarkable that such a complaint was uttered with a straight face.

A more recent example of cheating involved members of OPEC, the oil cartel. Each member country is given a quota, or a maximum amount of oil it can produce. When the oil market is tight and everyone is producing as much oil as they possibly can, OPEC is able to maintain discipline with regard to production quotas. However, when there is a lot of excess capacity in world oil markets and country quotas are below maximum production potential,

[2] "Collusion Among Electrical Equipment Manufacturers," *Wall Street Journal*, Jan. 10 & 12, 1962, reprinted in E. Mansfield, *Monopoly Power and Economic Performance: The Problem of Industrial Concentration* 89 (1968).

then the incentives to cheat are substantial. This was the case in 1985, 1999, and 2009. Low prices encouraged cheating (and more supply), which in turn lowered prices further.

Price Leadership

Price leader

Dominant firm

Barometric firm

To coordinate their behavior without outright collusion, some industries have a **price leader**. It is quite common in oligopolistic industries for one or a few firms to set the price and for the rest to follow their lead. Two types of price leadership are the dominant firm model and the barometric firm model. In the **dominant firm** model, the industry has a single large dominant firm and a number of small firms. The dominant firm sets the price for the industry, but it lets the small firms sell all they want at that price. In the **barometric firm** model, one firm usually is the first to make changes in price that are generally accepted by other firms in the industry. The barometric firm may not be the largest or most powerful firm. Instead, it is a reasonably accurate interpreter of changes in basic cost and demand conditions in the industry as a whole. According to some authorities, barometric price leadership often occurs as a response to a period of violent price fluctuation in an industry, during which many firms suffer and greater stability is widely sought.

In the past, the steel industry was a good example of the dominant firm model of price leadership. The largest firm in the industry, U.S. Steel, was formed in 1901 by the merger of a number of companies. Judge Elbert Gary, the first chairperson of the board of U.S. Steel, sought the cooperation of the smaller firms in the industry. He inaugurated a series of so-called Gary dinners, attended by all the major steel producers, from which were made declarations of industry policy on pricing and other matters. Since any formal pricing agreements would have been illegal, they made no such agreements. But generally speaking, U.S. Steel set the pricing pattern and other firms followed. Moreover, this relationship continued long after Judge Gary had gone to his final reward. According to Walter Adams, of Michigan State University, U.S. Steel typically set the pace, "and the other companies follow in lockstep—both in their sales to private customers and in their secret bids on government contracts."

Illustrating the attitude of other firms was the statement by the president of Bethlehem Steel to a congressional committee in 1939 that "in the main we . . . await the (price) schedules of the [U.S.] Steel Corporation." However, there was some secret price cutting, particularly during depressions. On at least one occasion, U.S. Steel responded to such price cutting by announcing publicly that it would meet any price reduction it heard of. In this way, it attempted to discourage under-the-counter price cutting. In more recent times, U.S. Steel no longer seemed to be the price leader it once was. In 1962, it drew a great deal of criticism from President Kennedy for being the first steel firm to raise prices. Subsequently, smaller steel firms often took the lead. Indeed, in 1968, the world was treated to the amusing spectacle of Bethlehem Steel announcing a price cut to counter some secret price cutting by the former price leader, U.S. Steel. As a footnote, in 2001, Bethlehem Steel declared bankruptcy. Its assets were eventually acquired by ArcelorMittal, the world's largest steel company. U.S. Steel still exists. It is the largest American-owned steel manufacturer, but the tenth largest in the world.

Nonprice Competition

Oligopolists tend to compete more aggressively through advertising and product differentiation than through direct price reductions. In other words, when we observe the behavior of major oligopolies, we find that firms try hard to get business away from their rivals by outdoing them with better advertising campaigns and improvements in the product; but it is less common for oligopolists to slug it out, toe to toe, with price reductions. This is an important characteristic of oligopoly. In contrast to the case of perfect competition, nonprice competition plays a central role in oligopoly. It is therefore worth noting a few salient points about the advertising and product development strategies of oligopolists.

Advertising

Advertising is a very big business. Tens of billions of dollars per year are spent on it in the United States. One important purpose of advertising is to convince the consumer that one firm's product is better than another's. Advertising expenditures often are larger in industries where there is less physical differentiation of the product than in industries where the product varies more. Therefore, the cigarette, liquor, and soap industries spend over 10 percent of their gross revenues (excluding excise taxes) on advertising, whereas the automobile industry spends less than 1 percent of its gross revenue on advertising.

The social desirability of much of this advertising is debatable and much debated. While advertising can serve an important purpose by keeping the consumer better informed, some advertising is more misleading than informative. Unfortunately, it is difficult to make reliable estimates of the extent to which oligopolists may be overinvesting, from society's point of view, in advertising.

Product Development

The development of new and improved products is also a very big business in the United States. In 2002, industry spent over $190 billion on research and development. In many industries, R&D is a central part of oligopolistic competition. For example, a spectacular case in the telecommunications industry was the introduction of the iPhone in 2007 by Apple Inc., which had never sold phones before. By the first quarter of 2012, its sales were a stunning 37 million units.

HOW FORD BECAME NUMBER TWO AND GENERAL MOTORS BECAME NUMBER ONE

Henry Ford did not invent the car or the assembly line. But he brought the two together and gave the United States its first mass-produced car. Ford was an inventor and mechanic by trade, and no effort was spared to improve the car and the process by which it was built. The Tin Lizzie looked the same year after year, but Ford's mechanical genius made it run better each year than the last. His industrial genius made it cheaper to build and buy. He paid the highest wages in industry, $5 a day; and he made a car his workers could afford to buy. It seemed as though he had devised the perfect competitive product: it never wore out, it kept getting cheaper, and it was never out of style.

The Model T was not the only car on the road. Americans were driving Pierce Arrows, Stutz Bearcats, and Duesenbergs, as well as the Chevrolets, Buicks, Oldsmobiles, and Cadillacs made by Ford's number one competitor, General Motors, headed by Alfred P. Sloan. Sloan once said, "The primary object of the corporation is to make money, not just to make motor cars. The core of the GM product policy lies in the concept of mass producing a full line of cars graded upward in quality and price."

Sloan saw that even if GM could produce for less than Ford, it could not increase profits by decreasing prices. So, to do battle with Ford's black Model Ts, GM's massive research and development effort produced a brand for every pocketbook—Chevrolets, Pontiacs, Buicks, and Cadillacs—a color for every taste, and a wish list of options. Every year brought a new edition. GMs were old not when they wore out but when they went out of style.

Any business decision is a kind of gamble. Henry Ford bet that the United States wanted a car that would last forever, was cheap and easy to fix, and never went out of style. Alfred Sloan bet that there was something more attractive to U.S. drivers than a low price, that they were ready to have some fun with their cars, and that GM advertising could join their desires and GM's cars, at a profit to GM. Henry Ford knew cars, but Alfred Sloan knew the consumer; and he knew the 1920s. By the time the Great Depression started in 1929, Henry Ford had yielded to reality and started varying his cars. But he had lost the 50 percent share of the market he had commanded and had to settle for second place.

At that point, Apple's revenues from smartphone sales were higher than those of Nokia, the industry leader until then. By 2013, Nokia had agreed to be acquired by Microsoft, and Samsung was selling more phones worldwide than either Apple or Nokia.

Perhaps the main reason why oligopolists would rather compete through advertising and product differentiation than through price is that a firm's rivals can easily and quickly match a price reduction, whereas they may find it difficult to match a clever advertising campaign or an attractive product improvement. Therefore, oligopolists tend to feel that they have a better chance of improving their long-run profits at the expense of their rivals through non-price competition.

Comparing Oligopoly with Perfect Competition

We have seen that economists have constructed a number of models of oligopoly behavior: game theory models, cartel models, price leadership models, and others. But there is no agreement that any of these models is an adequate representation of oligopoly behavior. For this reason, it is difficult to estimate the effects of an oligopolistic market structure on price, output, and profits. Nonetheless, if a perfectly competitive industry is turned overnight into an oligopoly, it seems likely that certain changes will occur.

1. *Price is probably higher under oligopoly than under perfect competition.* The difference between the oligopoly price and the perfectly competitive price depends on the number of firms in the industry and the ease of entry. The larger the number of firms and the easier it is to enter the industry, the closer the oligopoly price will be to the perfectly competitive level.

2. *If the demand curve under oligopoly is the same as under perfect competition, it follows that output is less under oligopoly than under perfect competition.* However, it is not always reasonable to assume that the demand curve is the same in both cases, since the large expenditures for advertising and product differentiation incurred by some oligopolists may tend to shift the demand curve to the right. Consequently, in some cases, both price and output may tend to be higher under oligopoly than under perfect competition.

3. *Oligopolistic industries tend to spend more on advertising, product differentiation, and style changes than perfectly competitive industries.* The use of some resources for these purposes is certainly worthwhile, since advertising provides buyers with information and product differentiation allows greater freedom of choice. Whether oligopolists spend too much for these purposes is an open question. However, there is a widespread feeling among economists, based largely on empirical studies (and hunch), that in some oligopolistic industries, such expenditures have been expanded beyond socially optimal levels.

4. *From the models presented in this chapter, profits earned by oligopolists tend to be higher, on average, than profits earned by perfectly competitive firms.* This conclusion is supported by some statistical evidence. Joe Bain, of the University of California, found that firms in industries in which the biggest few firms had a large proportion of total sales tended to have higher rates of return than firms in industries in which the biggest few firms had a small proportion of

total sales. However, there has been much disagreement on this score. According to more recent evidence, a firm is likely to have higher than average profits if it has a relatively big share of the market, regardless of whether or not the industry as a whole is highly concentrated.[3]

The Antitrust Laws

National policies are too ambiguous and rich in contradictions to be summarized neatly and concisely. Consequently, it would be misleading to say that the United States has adopted a policy of promoting competition and controlling monopoly. To a large extent, it certainly is true that "competition is our fundamental national policy," as the Supreme Court said in 1963. But it is also true that we have adopted many measures to promote monopoly and limit competition. On balance, however, we have probably gone further in promoting competition than other major industrialized countries, and the principal pieces of legislation designed to further this objective are the **antitrust laws**.

Antitrust laws

The Sherman Act

In 1890, the first antitrust law, the Sherman Act, was passed by Congress. Although the common law had long outlawed monopolistic practices, it appeared to many Americans in the closing years of the nineteenth century that legislation was required to discourage monopoly and preserve and encourage competition. The formation of trusts (monopolistic combines that colluded to raise prices and restrict output) brought the matter to a head. The heart of the Sherman Act lies in the following two sections:

> Section 1. Every contract, combination in the form of trust or otherwise, or conspiracy, in restraint of trade or commerce among the several States or with foreign nations, is hereby declared to be illegal. Every person who shall make any such contract or engage in any such combination or conspiracy, shall be deemed guilty of a misdemeanor.

> Section 2. Every person who shall monopolize, or attempt to monopolize or combine or conspire with any other person or persons to monopolize, any part of the trade or commerce among the several States, or with foreign nations shall be deemed guilty of a misdemeanor.

---

[3] For some relevant discussion, see L. Weiss, "The Concentration-Profits Relationship and Antitrust," in *Industrial Concentration, The New Learning,* ed. H. Goldschmid, H. J. Mann, and J. F. Weston (Boston: Little Brown, 1974); and H. Demsetz, "Industry Structure, Market Rivalry, and Public Policy," *Journal of Law and Economics,* 16 (April 1973): 1–9.

AIRLINE DEREGULATION: SUCCESS OR FAILURE?

Until the late 1970s, airlines were heavily regulated. The Civil Aeronautics Board (CAB) had the responsibility of approving routes and airfares for the entire U.S. airline system. During the presidency of Jimmy Carter, at the recommendation of Alfred Kahn, chairman of the CAB at the time, the airline industry was deregulated and the CAB itself was abolished.

In the years that followed, two major changes took place. First, airlines adopted a hub-and-spoke system of operations, which was more efficient than the prior point-to-point system but created congestion in the hub airports (like Chicago's O'Hare Airport, which serves as the hub for both United Airlines and American Airlines). Second, the industry went through a period of consolidation, especially during the 1980s. Both immediately after deregulation and during the intervening years, many worried about potential negative effects, including a potential deterioration in airline safety and an increase in market concentration (which would result in higher ticket prices than under the CAB).

In the end, these fears have been unfounded, and by many measures, airline deregulation has been a huge success. Compared with 30 years ago, airfares are down by a third in nominal terms and by more than a half in real terms. This, combined with the greater availability of one-stop services to hundreds of cities (thanks to the hub-and-spoke system), has meant savings of around $20 billion dollars a year for U.S. travelers. The success of deregulation can also be measured in other ways. Three times as many passengers are flying now than in the early 1980s, and the airline industry employs twice as many people.

Many of the concerns voiced in the early days of deregulation have not materialized. Setting aside the risk of terrorism, airline safety has actually improved, not deteriorated, as many had feared. Moreover, while a number of airlines have gone out of business, the industry has not become dominated by a few large carriers. Quite the contrary, the smaller upstart airlines such as JetBlue and AirTran are doing well, while the large airlines such as American (which filed for bankruptcy in 2011) are in trouble. In fact, during the past 20 years, the share of air travelers being carried by these low-cost, no-frills airlines has risen from 10 percent to 30 percent.

Probably the single biggest complaint about flying these days is congestion. Flying on an airplane these days feels no better than a glorified bus ride. The average load factor (which measures how full airplanes are) has risen from 53 percent to 80 percent in the past 30 years. However, packed airplanes and overcrowded airports are not symptoms of the failure of deregulation; rather, they are the consequences of its success. The problem is that the federal, state, and local governments in the United States have not upgraded and expanded airports and air traffic control systems to meet the spectacular increase in demand triggered by deregulation.

The Clayton Act

The first 20 years of experience with the Sherman Act were not very satisfying to its supporters. The ineffectiveness of the Sherman Act led in 1914 to passage by Congress of two additional laws: the Clayton Act and the Federal Trade Commission Act. The Clayton Act was designed to be more specific than the Sherman Act in identifying certain practices that are illegal because they would "substantially lessen competition or tend to create a monopoly." In particular, the Clayton Act outlawed unjustified price discrimination, a practice whereby one buyer is charged more than another buyer for the same product. It also outlawed the use of a *tying contract*, which makes the buyers purchase other items to get the product they want. Further, it outlawed mergers that substantially lessen competition; but since it did not prohibit one firm's purchase of a competitor's plant and equipment, it really could not stop mergers. In 1950, this loophole was closed by the Celler-Kefauver Antimerger Act.

The Federal Trade Commission Act

The Federal Trade Commission Act was designed to prevent undesirable and unfair competitive practices. Specifically, it created a Federal Trade Commission to investigate unfair and predatory practices and issue cease and desist orders. The act states that "unfair methods of competition in commerce are hereby declared unlawful." However, the commission (composed of five commissioners, each appointed by the president for a term of seven years) was given the unenviable task of defining exactly what is "unfair." Eventually, the courts took away much of the commission's power; but in 1938, the commission acquired the function of outlawing untrue and deceptive advertising. Also, the commission has authority to carry out economic investigations of the structure and conduct of U.S. business.

The Role of the Courts

The antitrust laws, like any laws, are enforced in the courts. Typically, charges are brought against a firm or group of firms by the Antitrust Division of the Department of Justice, a trial is held, and a decision is reached by the judge. In key cases, appeals are made that eventually reach the Supreme Court. The real impact of the antitrust laws depends on how the courts interpret them. And the judicial interpretation of these laws has changed considerably over time.

Rule of reason

The first major set of antitrust cases took place in 1911, when the Standard Oil Company and the American Tobacco Company were forced to give up large shares of their holdings of other companies. In these cases, the Supreme Court put forth and used the famous **rule of reason**, which holds that only unreasonable combinations in restraint of trade, not all trusts, require conviction under the Sherman Act. In 1920, the rule of reason was used by the Supreme Court in its finding that

U.S. Steel had not violated the antitrust laws even though it had tried to monopolize the industry, since, according to the Court, it had not succeeded. Moreover, U.S. Steel's large size and its potential monopoly power were ruled beside the point, since "the law does not make mere size an offense. It ... requires overt acts."

During the 1920s and 1930s, the courts, including the Supreme Court, interpreted the antitrust laws in such a way that they became as toothless as a newborn babe. Although Eastman Kodak and International Harvester controlled very substantial shares of their markets, the Court, using the rule of reason, found them innocent on the grounds that they had not built up their near-monopoly position through overt coercion or predatory practices. Moreover, the Court reiterated that mere size was not an offense, no matter how great the unexerted monopoly power might be.

In the late 1930s, this situation changed greatly with the prosecution of the Aluminum Company of America (Alcoa). This case, decided in 1945 (but begun in 1937), resulted in a decision that ran counter to the decisions handed down in the *U.S. Steel* and *International Harvester* cases. Alcoa had achieved its 90 percent share of the market by means that would have been considered "reasonable" in the earlier cases: keeping its price low enough to discourage entry, building capacity to take care of increases in the market, and so forth. Nonetheless, the Court decided that Alcoa, because it controlled practically all the industry's output, violated the antitrust laws. To a considerable extent, the Court used market structure rather than market conduct as a test of legality.

The Role of the Justice Department

The impact of the antitrust laws is determined by the vigor with which the Antitrust Division of the Justice Department prosecutes cases. If the Antitrust Division prosecutes fewer cases, the laws are likely to have less effect. Like the judicial interpretation of the laws, the extent to which the Justice Department has prosecuted cases has varied from one period to another. Needless to say, the attitude of the political party in power had been an important determinant of how vigorously antitrust cases have been prosecuted. When the Sherman Act was first passed, it was of singularly little value. President Grover Cleveland's attorney general did not agree with the law and would not prosecute under it. "Trust busting" was truly a neglected art until President Theodore Roosevelt devoted his formidable energies to it. In 1903, he established the Antitrust Division of the Justice Department. Moreover, his administration started the major cases that led to the *Standard Oil, American Tobacco,* and *U.S. Steel* decisions.

Subsequently, there was a long hiatus in the prosecution of antitrust cases, reflecting the Supreme Court's rule of reason doctrine and a strong conservative tide in the nation. The lull continued for about 25 years, until 1937, when there was a significant upsurge in activity on the antitrust front. Led by Thurman Arnold, the Antitrust Division entered one of the most vigorous periods of antitrust enforcement to date. Arnold went after the glass, cigarette, cement, and other industries; the most important case was that against Alcoa. The Antitrust Division attempted in this period to reopen cases that were hopeless under the rule of reason doctrine. With the change in the composition of the Supreme Court, Arnold's activism turned out to be effective.

The Effectiveness of Antitrust Policy

How effective have the antitrust laws been? Obviously, it is difficult to tell with any accuracy, since there is no way to carry out an experiment in which U.S. history is rewritten to show what would have happened if the antitrust laws had not been on the books. Many experts seem to feel that the antitrust laws have not been as effective as they might—or should—have been, largely because they lack sufficient public support and no politically powerful pressure group pushes for their enforcement.

But this does not mean that the antitrust laws have had no effect. As Edward Mason, of Harvard University, points out, their effectiveness is due "not so much to the contribution that particular judgments have made to the restoring of competition as it is to the fact that the consideration of whether or not a particular course of action may or may not be in violation of the antitrust acts is a persistent factor affecting business judgment, at least in large firms."[4] This idea is summed up by the old saying that the ghost of Senator Sherman sits as an ex officio member of every firm's board of directors.

In 1982, two of the biggest antitrust cases in history were decided. As a result of one decision, American Telephone and Telegraph Company divested itself of 22 companies that provided most of the nation's local telephone service and kept its Long Lines Division, Western Electric, and Bell Laboratories (see Case Study 7.3). According to the other decision, a huge antitrust case against IBM Corporation, begun in 1969, was dropped by the government because it was "without merit." Despite considerable skepticism in some quarters concerning the beneficial effects of the antitrust laws, these two cases show that they continue to play an important role in U.S. economic life.

In 1997, the U.S. Justice Department began another landmark antitrust case, this time against Microsoft (see Case Study 7.2). The government was concerned that Microsoft had used its prodigious market power and immense profits to stifle innovation and harm both consumers and competitors, especially in the market for Internet browsers and applications. In November 1999, the presiding judge ruled against Microsoft. While the software giant eventually settled with the Department of Justice in 2002, the case had major reverberations in the information technology sectors of the U.S. economy, much like the IBM case two decades earlier.

---

[4] Edward Mason, Preface to Carl Kaysen and Donald Turner, *Antitrust Policy* (Cambridge, MA: Harvard University Press, 1959).

REVIEW AND PRACTICE

Summary

1   Monopolistic competition occurs where there are many sellers whose products are somewhat different. The demand curve facing each firm slopes downward to the right. The conditions for long-run equilibrium are that each firm maximizes profits and economic profits are zero.

2   The firm under monopolistic competition is likely to produce less and charge a higher price than the firm under perfect competition. Relative to pure monopoly, monopolistically competitive firms are likely to have lower profits, greater output, and lower prices. Firms under monopolistic competition offer a wider variety of styles, brands, and qualities than firms under perfect competition.

3   Oligopoly is characterized by a small number of firms and a great deal of interdependency, actual and perceived. Oligopoly is a common market structure in the United States.

4   A game is a competitive situation where two or more persons (or organizations) pursue their own interests and none of them can dictate the outcome. Game theory is used to analyze oligopolistic markets.

5   Conditions in oligopolistic industries tend to promote collusion. A cartel is an open, formal, collusive arrangement. A profit-maximizing cartel acts like a monopolist with a number of plants or divisions, each of which is a member firm.

6   Price leadership is quite common in oligopolistic industries; one or a few firms apparently set the price and the rest follow their lead.

7   Relative to perfect competition, it seems likely that both price and profits are higher under oligopoly. Moreover, oligopolistic industries tend to spend more on advertising, product differentiation, and style changes than perfectly competitive industries.

8   In 1890, the Sherman Act was passed. It outlawed any contract, combination, or conspiracy in restraint of trade and made it illegal to monopolize or attempt to monopolize. In 1914, Congress passed the Clayton Act, and the Federal Trade Commission was created. The Celler-Kefauver Antimerger Act of 1950 was another antitrust development.

9   The real impact of the antitrust laws depends on the interpretation placed on these laws by the courts. Many observers feel that the antitrust laws have not been as effective as they might—or should—have been, largely because they do not have sufficient public support. At the same time, many feel that the evidence, although incomplete and unclear, suggests that they have had a noteworthy effect on business behavior and markets. Three important recent cases involved AT&T, IBM, and Microsoft.

Problems and Questions

1 Suppose a cartel consists of four firms, each of which has a horizontal marginal cost curve. For each firm, marginal cost equals $4. Suppose that the marginal revenue curve for the cartel is $MR = 10 - 2Q$, where MR is marginal revenue (in dollars) and Q is the cartel's output per year (in thousands of units). What output rate will the cartel choose?

2 According to the Senate Subcommittee on Antitrust and Monopoly, "Some system of marketing quotas, whether overt or carefully hidden, must underlie any price-fixing agreement." Comment and evaluate.

3 "Perfect competition results in optimal efficiency and an optimal distribution of income. This is why the United States opts for a perfectly competitive economy." Comment and evaluate.

4 "The real impact of the antitrust laws depends on judicial interpretation." Comment and evaluate.

Key Terms

monopolistic competition	collusion
oligopoly	cartel
pure oligopoly	price leader
differentiated oligopoly	dominant firm
product differentiation	barometric firm
product group	antitrust laws
game	rule of reason
payoff matrix	

Viewpoint for Analysis

In Chapter 7, we presented the following quote by Alfred Kahn. Read this passage again; then answer the questions that follow.

Deregulation shifts the major burden of consumer protection to the competitive market, and therefore, in important measure, to the enforcement of antitrust laws. But the experience with essentially unmanaged deregulation in airlines and pervasively managed deregulation in telecommunications also demonstrates that the focus of policy should be, first and foremost, on liberating competition from direct government restraint—not dictating market structures or outcomes. In particular, while in no way counseling indulgent antitrust treatment of predatory or unfairly exclusionary competitive *conduct*, they underline the need for humility in attempting to make industries more competitive by interfering with their achievement and exploitation of economies of scope and diluting their incentives for innovation— the most powerful competition of all.[5]

(a) How has the role of government been different in airline and telephone deregulation (see Case Studies 7.3 and 8.3)?

(b) Can partial deregulation be worse than total deregulation? How?

(c) What is the role of technology in keeping the playing field level in an industry, especially one like telecommunications?

---

[5] Alfred Kahn, *Lessons from Deregulation: Telecommunications and Airlines after the Crunch* (Washington, DC: AEI-Brookings Joint Center for Regulatory Studies, 2004).

Pollution and the Environment

LEARNING OBJECTIVES

➤ To define external diseconomies and explain how they clarify the economic problem of pollution

➤ To distinguish between private costs and social costs

➤ To recognize how pollution is related to economic growth

➤ To understand the goals and methods of public policy toward environmental quality

Climate change and global warming have become major environmental issues in recent decades. Many scientists and others contend that burning fossil fuels increases the concentration of carbon dioxide and other "greenhouse" gases in the atmosphere, thus warming the earth's surface. What are the effects of global warming, and how should we respond to this threat? One purpose of this chapter is to answer this question.

According to many scientists and social observers, one of the costs of economic growth is environmental pollution. For many years, people in the United States paid relatively little attention to the environment and what they were doing to it. But this attitude has changed markedly over the last 50 years. The public has become genuinely concerned about environmental problems. However, in the effort to clean up the environment, choices are not always clear nor solutions easy.

Our Environmental Problems

Water Pollution

To see what we mean by environmental pollution, we begin with one of the most important parts of the environment: our water supplies. A broad range of human activities results in the discharge of large amounts of pollutants into streams, lakes, and the sea. Chemical wastes are released by industrial plants and mines, as well as by farms and homes when fertilizers, pesticides, and detergents run off into waterways. Oil is discharged into the waters by tankers, sewage systems, oil wells, and other sources. Organic compounds enter waterways from industrial plants and farms, as well as from municipal sewage plants; and animal wastes, as well as human wastes, contribute substantially to pollution.

Obviously, we cannot continue to increase the rate at which we dump wastes into our streams, rivers, and oceans. A river or ocean, like everything else, can bear only so much. In recent years, people in Pennsylvania, New York, and Wyoming have begun to worry about another potential threat to their water supplies. New technologies are allowing the extraction of natural gas from the massive shale deposits in these and other states. On the one hand, this is good news because it assures Americans of a plentiful supply of relatively cheap and relatively clean energy. On the other hand, the hydraulic fracturing ("fracking") used to release the natural gas from the shale rocks can potentially pollute both water and air. As with so many environmental issues, there is a tradeoff—in this case between cheap energy and the potential for more pollution.

Air Pollution

If clean water is vital to our survival, so, too, is clean air. Yet the battle being waged against air pollution in most of our major cities has not been won. Particles of various kinds are spewed into the air by factories that utilize combustion processes, grind materials, or produce dust. Motor vehicles release lead compounds from gasoline and rubber particles worn from tires and so help to create that unheavenly condition known as smog. Citizens of Los Angeles are particularly familiar with smog, but few major cities have escaped at least periodic air pollution. No precise measures have been developed to gauge the effects of air pollution on public health and enjoyment, but some rough estimates have suggested that perhaps 25 percent of all deaths from respiratory disease could be avoided by a 50 percent reduction in air pollution.

The Important Role of External Diseconomies

External diseconomy

The reason why our economic system has tolerated pollution of the environment lies largely in the concept of external diseconomies. An **external diseconomy** occurs when one person's (or firm's) use of a resource damages

RESERVE MINING: THE PRICE OF CLEANER WATER

Shortly after World War II, some far-sighted entrepreneurs decided there was money to be made in a rock called taconite, found in abundance beside the famous Mesabi iron range in Minnesota. Taconite contains iron—not a lot of iron but enough to make a profit if you know how to crush it into sand-sized particles and separate the grains of iron from the rest of the rock. And that is what the Reserve Mining Company set out to do in the early 1950s. Since the refining process requires vast amounts of water, Reserve decided to mine the rock near Babbit, Minnesota, and transport it on its own railway to a processing plant 40 miles away, on the shores of the largest freshwater lake in the Americas, Lake Superior. The costs of the operation are the same as for most industries—rents, wages, capital costs, debt service— but in Reserve's case, there is a hidden cost as well.

For every ton of iron pellets Reserve manufactured, it also produced 2 tons of waste, taconite tailings; and for 15 years, Reserve was able to dump these tailings into Lake Superior at no cost to itself. Reserve's original idea was that the tailings could be dumped into a deep trough in the lake and that they would settle to a depth of 400 feet or more, where they couldn't harm anybody or do any damage to the lake. But in fact, no one really knew what was happening to those tailings or whether they posed any real hazard to the lake or humans living around it. It was only a matter of time before Reserve's dumping practices came under fire. Environmentalists charged that Reserve was ruining Lake Superior. Reserve denied the charges but by late 1969 found itself involved in a court battle that would take seven years to resolve. One of the most hotly debated issues in the case was the discovery of asbestos-like fibers in the water supply of Duluth, Minnesota.

The court battle was resolved in 1977. Reserve was granted the necessary permits to begin construction of a new dumping facility. The cost of this new facility, by Reserve's calculations, was some $387 million. The costs of the new dumping site were absorbed in a number of ways: tax breaks, lower profits, higher prices. Today, there is little doubt that Lake Superior is a cleaner lake than it was before. Scientific analysis indicates that the asbestos levels have dropped by 90 percent.

other people who cannot obtain proper compensation. When this occurs, a market economy is unlikely to function properly. The price system is based on the supposition that the full cost of using each resource is borne by the person or firm that uses it. If this is not the case and the user bears only part of the full costs, then the resource is not likely to be directed by the price system into the socially optimal use.

To understand why this is so, we begin by briefly reviewing how resources are allocated in a market economy. Resources are used in their socially most valuable way because they are allocated to the people and firms who find it worthwhile to bid the most for them, assuming that prices reflect true social costs. Under these circumstances, a firm that maximizes its profits produces the socially desirable output and uses the socially desirable amounts of labor, capital, and other resources. Under these circumstances, there is no problem.

Private Cost Does Not Equal Social Cost

Private costs
Social costs

Suppose, however, that because of the presence of external diseconomies, people and firms do not pay the true social costs for resources. For example, suppose that some firms or people can use water and air for nothing but other firms or people incur costs as a consequence of this use. In this case, the **private costs** of using air and water differ from the **social costs**: the price paid by the user of water and air is less than the true cost to society. In a case like this, users of water and air are guided in their decisions by the private cost of water and air—the prices they pay. Since they pay less than the true social costs, water and air are artificially cheap to them, so they use too much of these resources, at least from society's point of view.

Note that the divergence between private and social costs occurs if, and only if, the use of water or air by one firm or person imposes costs on other firms or persons. If a paper mill uses water and then treats it to restore its quality, there is no divergence between private and social costs. But when the paper mill dumps harmful wastes into streams and rivers (the cheap way to get rid of its by-products), the towns downstream that use the water must incur costs to restore its quality. The same is true of air pollution. If an electric power plant uses the atmosphere as a cheap and convenient place to dispose of wastes, people living and working nearby may incur costs as a result, since the incidence of respiratory and other diseases may increase. In such cases, there may be a divergence between private and social costs.

We said previously that pollution-causing activities that result in external diseconomies represent a malfunctioning of the market system. At this point, the nature of this malfunctioning should be clear. Firms and people dump too much waste material into the water and the atmosphere. The price system does not provide the proper signals because the polluters are induced to use our streams and atmosphere in this socially undesirable way by the artificially low price of disposing of wastes in this manner. Moreover, because the polluters do not pay the true cost of waste disposal, their products are artificially cheap, so that too much of them is produced.

Economic Growth and Environmental Pollution

According to many authorities, economic growth (defined as increases in total economic output per capita) has been associated with increases in the level of environmental pollution. This is not very surprising, since practically all the things produced must eventually be thrown away in one form or another. Therefore, as output per capita goes up, the level of pollution is likely to go up as well. For example, as we grow more affluent and increase the number of automobiles per capita, we also increase the amount of such air pollutants as nitrogen oxide and tetraethyl lead, both of which are emitted by automobiles.

But it is important to recognize that pollution is not tied inextricably to national output. Although increases in national output in the past have been associated with increases in pollution, there is no reason why this correlation must continue in the future. We can produce things that are heavy polluters of the environment, like electric power and automobiles, or we can produce things that do not pollute the environment nearly so much, like pianos and bicycles.

Many environmentalists remain concerned that as people become richer, they do more damage to the environment—in other words, their "ecological footprint" becomes bigger. While there is some basis for this concern, there is room for optimism here as well.

Research shows that the relationship between many types of pollution and economic development (as measured by per capita income) looks like an upside-down U. As countries begin to grow rapidly, their per capita levels of pollution rise. However, once these countries reach an annual per capita income of between $5,000 and $8,000, the amount of pollution levels off and begins to fall. This relationship is called the environmental Kuznets curve, in honor of Nobel laureate Simon Kuznets.

Recent history shows that most people care more about pollution abatement when they are rich, not when they are poor and struggling to make ends meet. Societies as a whole follow the same pattern. There is a strong positive correlation between levels of prosperity and the number of environmental regulations enacted. Richer societies value environmental protection more and therefore put a higher priority on environmental policies.

Nevertheless, it is important to point out that not all types of pollution fall as incomes rise. There is, indeed, ample evidence that rich countries have successfully reduced levels of air and water pollution and improved sanitation; in most large U.S. cities, particulate air pollution is down by one-third or more over the past 20 years. But so far, there is less evidence of significant progress with regard to other types of environmental problems, including greenhouse gases, acid rain, and solid waste. The right kinds of policies can produce the desired results in these areas as well. The good news is that some European countries have made advances in controlling the levels of carbon emissions and amounts of solid waste being generated.

One of the biggest worries in the early years of the twenty-first century is that China—already the world's worst polluter—is on the rising part of the environmental Kuznets curve. In other words, if nothing is done, pollution will get a lot worse before it gets better. While China has numerous environmental laws on the books, it does not enforce them very rigorously, in part because lifting hundreds of millions of people out of poverty is a higher priority than the quality of air or water. This is one reason why China, India, and many other emerging markets did not sign the Kyoto Protocol, which set out to limit global carbon emissions. In fact, many of these countries encourage the wasteful use of fossil fuels by providing generous fuel subsidies (as part of broader programs to help the poor). Here again, though, there is hope. Policies can be changed, and the greener technologies of the developed world can be made more readily available to the developing world.

Public Policy toward Pollution

Pollution is caused as much by defects in our institutions as by malicious intent, greed, or corruption. In cases where waste disposal causes significant external diseconomies, economists generally agree that government intervention may be justifiable. But how can the government intervene? Perhaps the simplest way is through **direct regulation**: the issuance of certain enforceable rules for waste disposal. For example, the government can prohibit burning trash in furnaces or incinerators or dumping certain materials into the ocean, and it can make any person or firm that violates these restrictions subject to a fine or perhaps even imprisonment. Also, the government can ban the use of chemicals like the harmful pesticide DDT and require that all automobiles meet certain regulations for the emission of air pollutants. Further, the government can establish quality standards for air and water.

Another way the government can intervene is by establishing effluent fees. An **effluent fee** is a fee a polluter must pay to the government for discharging waste. In other words, a price is imposed on the disposal of waste into the environment; the more firms or individuals pollute, the more they must pay. The idea behind the imposition of effluent fees is that they can bring the private costs of waste disposal closer to the true social costs. Faced with a closer approximation to the true social costs of their activities, polluters reduce the extent to which they pollute the environment. Needless to say, many practical difficulties are involved in carrying out this seemingly simple scheme, but many economists believe that this can be a good way to deal with the pollution problem.

The government can also issue **transferable emissions permits**, which allow the holders of the permits to generate a certain amount of pollution. These permits,

Direct regulation

Effluent fee

Transferable emissions permits

THE UPHILL BATTLE TO RATIFY THE KYOTO CLIMATE TREATY AND CAP-AND-TRADE LEGISLATION IN THE UNITED STATES

In December 1997 at the environmental summit in Kyoto, Japan, the world's 24 most-developed countries pledged to cut their greenhouse gas emissions by 2010. The reduction targets, which also gave credit for planting trees that remove carbon dioxide from the atmosphere, were 7 percent below 1990 levels for the United States and 8 and 6 percent, respectively, below 1990 levels for Europe and Japan. These were aggressive targets, given that, in the United States before the Kyoto agreement, carbon emissions were projected to rise between 15 and 20 percent.

Proponents of the Kyoto Accord pointed to three reasons why they believed it provided the formula for success. First, the agreement adopted differentiated targets, recognizing that each country must address climate change on the basis of its own national energy profile and circumstances. Second, the accord let countries pursue their own paths to lower emissions. Third, the Kyoto agreement embraced market-based international mechanisms, including emissions trading. Many economists believe that tradable emissions permits are an economically efficient way of reducing carbon emissions. For example, if one firm is able to reduce emissions cheaply while another finds it difficult to do so, the first can sell permits to the second, thereby reducing the overall cost of achieving the environmental objective.

However, some economists believed that the Kyoto Accord was not a formula for success. First and foremost, the treaty was unacceptable to developing countries, which would be responsible for an increasing share of global emissions, about 45 percent, by 2010. Because of different resource endowments and levels of industrialization, there was unlikely to be any generally acceptable principle for allocating emissions rights and targets between rich and poor countries. And second, many economists felt that the Kyoto Accord should have included concrete government actions, especially a carbon tax. Without such actions, it was argued, not enough would be done to implement the Kyoto plan.

In 2000, the Kyoto negotiations collapsed over details of implementation, and the United States withdrew from the talks in 2001. The European Union and Japan ratified the protocol in 2002. However, by early 2004, with the United States not part of the treaty and Russia reluctant to sign, the accord was still in limbo.

In 2009, the administration of Barack Obama encouraged the drafting of legislation that would implement a cap-and-trade system (emissions trading) in the United States.

The goal was to bring the U.S. economy into closer compliance with the spirit, if not the letter, of the Kyoto Accord. The legislation was authored by Massachusetts congressman Edward J. Markey and California congressman Henry A. Waxman. In an attempt to get the Waxman-Markey bill passed in the U.S. House of Representatives, it was watered down considerably. Supporters were dismayed at how weak it had become, and opponents claimed that the proposed cap-and-trade system would raise taxes on U.S. households, with no offsetting tax cuts elsewhere. In the end, the bill narrowly passed the House but was defeated in the Senate. The troubled economic environment in the immediate aftermath of the financial crisis of 2008–2009 turned out to be a particularly inopportune time to tackle climate change.

limited in number, are sold by the government to the highest bidders. The price of a permit is set by supply and demand. One advantage of transferable emissions permits is that the authorities can predict how much pollution there will be. After all, the total amount of pollution cannot exceed the amount authorized by the total number of permits issued. In contrast, if an effluent fee is adopted, it is difficult to predict how much pollution will result, since this depends on how polluters respond to the particular level of the effluent fee that is chosen. For this reason, transferable emissions permits are often preferred over effluent fees.

Tax credits   Still another way for the government to intervene is to establish **tax credits** for firms that introduce pollution control equipment. There are, of course, many types of equipment that a plant can introduce to cut down on pollution—for example, scrubbers for catching poisonous gases and electrostatic precipitators for decreasing dust and smoke. But pollution control equipment is costly, and firms are naturally reluctant to spend money when the private rate of return is so low. To reduce the burden, the government can allow firms to reduce their tax bill by a certain percentage of the amount they spend on pollution control equipment. Tax incentives of this sort have been discussed widely in recent years, and some have been adopted. (For further discussion of policies to reduce greenhouse gases, see Cross Chapter Case: Part 2, at the end of this chapter.)

Pollution Control Programs in the United States

In recent decades, government programs designed to control pollution have grown considerably. For example, in 1974, the U.S. Environmental Protections Agency (EPA) had a budget of $518 million and employed about 9,700 people. In 2010, its budget was over $10 billion, and the number of employees had risen to over 17,000. The EPA works with state and local governments to achieve its environmental goals by setting standards for water and air quality and devising rules to reach these standards.

To curb water pollution, the federal government has for years operated a system of grants-in-aid to state, municipal, and regional agencies to help construct treatment plants; and grants are made for research on new treatment methods. Moreover, many state governments have provided matching grants to help municipalities construct treatment plants. In addition, the 1970 Water Quality Improvement Act authorized grants to demonstrate new methods and techniques and to establish programs to train people in water control management. The federal government has also regulated the production and use of pesticides. Both the federal government and the states have played an important role in water pollution control, setting standards for allowable pollution levels.

The 1970 Clean Air Act (subsequently updated by amendments in 1977 and 1990) directed the EPA to establish minimum ambient standards for air quality; and it set limits on the emission of carbon monoxide, hydrocarbons, and nitrous oxides from automobiles. But after a number of clashes between the EPA and the automakers, the EPA relaxed the deadlines by which these limits were supposed to be met. In 1972, amendments to the Pollution Control Act authorized the EPA to set up effluent standards for both privately and publicly owned plants. A stated goal of the amendments was to eliminate the discharge of pollutants into water by 1985, but for reasons discussed in the next section, this goal was unrealistically stringent. In general, recent legislation has emphasized direct regulation, although there has been some use of transferable emissions permits. For example, in 1991, the Chicago Board of Trade voted to create a private market for rights to emit sulfur dioxide. The rights are issued to electric power companies by the EPA as part of the nation's program to reduce acid rain.

Some people believe that public policy is moving too rapidly in this area; others believe that it is moving too slowly. It is not easy to determine how fast or how far we should go in attempting to reduce pollution. Those who bear the costs of reducing pollution have an understandable tendency to emphasize (and perhaps inflate) the costs and discount the benefits of such projects. Those particularly interested in enjoying nature and outdoor recreation (like the Sierra Club) are understandably inclined to emphasize (and perhaps inflate) the benefits and discount the costs of such projects. Politics inevitably plays a major role in the outcome of such cases. The citizens of the United States must indicate, through the ballot box as well as the marketplace, how much they are willing to pay to reduce pollution.

How Clean Should the Environment Be?

One of the most fundamental questions about pollution control is this: How clean do we want our environment to be? At first glance, it may seem that we should restore and maintain a pristine environment, but this is not a very realistic goal, since the costs of achieving it would be enormous. The EPA has estimated that it would cost over $100 billion to remove 85 to 90 percent of

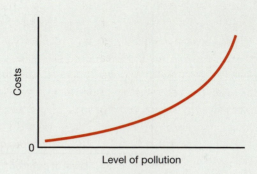

FIGURE 9.1

Costs to Society of Pollution

The costs to society of pollution increase with the level of pollution.

water pollutants from industrial and municipal sources. This is hardly a trivial amount, but it is far less than the cost of achieving zero discharge of pollutants, which would be a truly staggering sum.

Fortunately, however, there is no reason to aim at so stringent a goal. It seems obvious that as pollution increases, various costs to society increase as well. Some of these costs were described at the beginning of this chapter. For example, increases in air pollution result in increased deaths, and increases in water pollution reduce the recreational value of rivers and streams. Suppose we could get accurate data on the cost to society of various levels of pollution. Of course, it is extremely difficult to get such data, but if we could, we could determine the relationship between the amount of these costs and the level of pollution. It would look like the hypothetical curve in Figure 9.1; the greater the level of pollution, the higher these costs will be.

But these costs are not the only ones that must be considered. We must also take into account the costs of controlling pollution. In other words, we must look at the costs to society of maintaining a certain level of environmental quality. These costs are not trivial, as we saw at the beginning of this section. To maintain a very low level of pollution, it is necessary to invest heavily in pollution control equipment and make other economic sacrifices.[1] If we could get accurate data on the cost to society of controlling pollution, we could find the relationship between the amount of these costs and the level of pollution. It would look like the hypothetical curve in Figure 9.2; the lower the level of pollution, the higher these costs will be.

[1] It is important to recognize that the costs of pollution control extend far beyond the expense of constructing plants to treat water or control gas emissions. A serious pollution control program can put firms out of business, put people out of work, and bring economic trouble to entire communities. Further, a pollution control system can result in a redistribution of income. For example, automobiles, electric power, and other goods and services involving considerable pollution are likely to increase in price relative to other goods and services involving little pollution. To the extent that polluting goods and services play a bigger role in the budgets of the poor than of the rich, pollution controls hurt the poor and help the rich.

FIGURE 9.2

Costs to Society of Pollution Control

The more pollution is reduced, the higher the costs to society of pollution control.

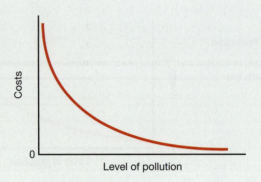

A Goal of Zero Pollution?

At this point, it should be obvious why we should not try to achieve a zero level of pollution. The sensible goal for our society is to minimize the sum of the costs of pollution and the costs of controlling pollution. In other words, we should construct a graph, as shown in Figure 9.3, to indicate the relationship between the sum of these two types of costs and the level of pollution. Then we should choose the level of pollution at which the sum of these two types of costs is at a minimum. In Figure 9.3, we should aim for a pollution level of *A*. There is no point in trying for a lower level; such a reduction would cost more than it would be worth. For example, the cost of achieving a zero pollution level would be much more than it would be worth. And if the pollution level were to exceed *A*, the extra cost to society of the additional pollution would be greater than the

FIGURE 9.3

Determining the Optimal Level of Pollution

The optimal level of pollution is at point *A*, since this is where the total costs are at a minimum. Below point *A*, the costs to society of more pollution are less than the costs of preventing it. Above point *A*, the costs to society of more pollution are greater than the costs of preventing it.

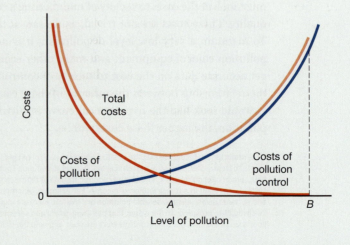

cost of preventing it. For example, the cost of allowing pollution to increase from *A* to *B* would be much greater than the cost of prevention.

It is easy to draw hypothetical curves but not so easy to actually measure these curves. Unfortunately, no one has a very clear idea of what the curves in Figure 9.3 really look like, although we can be sure that their general shapes are like those shown here. Therefore, no one really knows just how clean we should try to make the environment. Under these circumstances, expert opinion differs on the nature and extent of the programs that should be carried out. Moreover, as pointed out earlier, political considerations and pressures enter in. But one thing is certain: We will continue to live with some pollution and that, for the reasons just given, will be the rational thing to do.

Recent Directions of Environmental Policy

In the late 1970s and early 1980s, policy makers became increasingly concerned that regulatory agencies like the EPA had been paying too little attention to the costs involved in reducing pollution. For example, a government study found that a relaxation of the EPA's 1977 standard for water pollution control in the steel industry *with no change in its more stringent 1983 standard* would allow the industry savings in capital costs of $200 million. As President Carter's Council of Economic Advisers pointed out, "In making regulatory decisions on the speed of attaining standards, we should explicitly make a qualitative judgment about whether the gains from earlier attainment are worth the costs."[2]

Going a step further, some experts, like Lester Lave and Gilbert Omenn, of the Brookings Institution, concluded from their studies that the Clean Air Act had not been very effective. In their view, "the application of pollution controls to existing plants and older cars has been limited, and costs have been excessive, largely because Congress has failed to confront [many of] the difficult issues."[3]

During the 1980s, environmentalists and others charged that the Reagan administration was dismantling or at least emasculating the EPA. Anne Gorsuch resigned in 1983 as head of the EPA as criticism of the agency continued to build. James Watt, former secretary of the Interior, also angered environmentalists. Administration officials responded by claiming that they were trying to promote and restore balance between environmental objectives and economic growth.

The George H. W. Bush administration seemed more interested in new environmental initiatives than the Reagan administration. In late 1990, major changes were made in the Clean Air Act. For example, the law called for tighter restrictions on the pollutants causing urban smog and on automobile exhausts (beginning in the 1994 model year), as well as new limits on coal-burning power plants aimed at reducing emissions of sulfur dioxide and nitrogen oxide, both regarded as causes of acid rain. Some economists estimated that compliance

[2] *Economic Report of the President*, 1978, 211.
[3] *Clearing the Air: Reforming the Clean Air Act*, published in 1981 by the Brookings Institution Press, Washington, DC.

CASE STUDY 9.3

DOLPHIN-SAFE TUNA

Sometimes U.S. environmental laws can unintentionally violate international treaties signed by the United States. This happened in the early 1990s when, under pressure from environmental groups, the United States passed the Marine Mammals Act. The act banned the import of tuna from Mexico because the methods used to catch tuna in the eastern Pacific by Mexicans engaged in fishing as an occupation were killing an estimated 130,000 dolphins a year. Mexico challenged the U.S. ban under the terms of the World Trade Organization (WTO). The United States helped found the WTO and has been a strong advocate of free trade. Thus, the Mexican challenge was an embarrassment for the United States. It also had the unfortunate result of pitting U.S. environmental groups against the WTO and poor commercial fishing Mexican people.

Free trade and environmental protection can sometimes seem to conflict when countries have different living standards and environmental priorities. When countries with stricter environmental standards try to impose them on countries with looser standards, they can run afoul of the multilateral trade agreements. The WTO and the agreements that form the foundation of the multilateral trading system do not permit discrimination against imports based on the methods of production, even if it means hurting the environment.

The basic reasoning is as follows: Since each country's circumstances and priorities differ from those of other countries, every country will find something objectionable in other countries' production processes, and international trade will become more restrictive. Free trade principles aside, the Mexicans also questioned the fairness of threatening the jobs of 25,000 Mexicans engaged in commercial fishing to save marine mammals that were not endangered.

In the end, an agreement was worked out between the United States and Mexico, as well as with other countries that fished for tuna in the eastern Pacific. The number of dolphins killed in the process of catching tuna would be limited to 5,000, using a new type of net that would allow the dolphins to escape.

The tuna catches would be monitored to be sure that they were "dolphin safe." The agreement satisfied U.S. environmental groups, saved Mexican jobs, and avoided a major trade confrontation between the United States and Mexico.

with the tougher standards could cost about $30 billion per year. Whether the benefits exceed the costs will not be known for many years.

The Clinton administration was more inclined to take action to reduce greenhouse gases than was the George H. W. Bush administration, which, in the words of President Clinton's Council of Economic Advisers, "adopted what was called a 'no regrets' policy; it was willing to take steps to reduce emissions only if those actions would be beneficial for other reasons. . . . In contrast, this administration sees cost-effective policies to reduce greenhouse gas emissions as appropriate 'insurance' against the threat of climate change."[4] During the Kyoto

[4] *Economic Report of the President*, 1994, 184.

environmental summit in December 1997, the Clinton administration was able to incorporate some of its ideas about market-based solutions to reduce greenhouse gas emissions into the agreement that was signed (see Case Study 9.2).

George W. Bush received more mixed reviews than his predecessor. Environmental groups were more critical of his pro-business stance and felt that he did not do enough to improve air and water quality. They were especially upset by his decision to pull out of the Kyoto protocol and a number of decisions allowing private corporations to exploit resources on public lands.

The administration of Barak Obama was more activist on the environmental front. The EPA's role was beefed up, and it led the way in drafting legislation for a cap-and-trade system to limit greenhouse gases in the United States (see Case Study 9.2 and Cross Chapter Case: Part 2 at the end of this chapter). The EPA was also instrumental in developing the first set of regulations to limit air and water pollution from the hydraulic fracturing process (fracking) used to extract natural gas from shale.

REVIEW AND PRACTICE

Summary

1   A major social issue of the twenty-first century is environmental pollution. To a considerable extent, environmental pollution is an economic problem. Waste disposal and other pollution-causing activities result in external diseconomies.

2   Firms and individuals that pollute the water and air (and other facets of the environment) often pay less than the true social costs of disposing of their wastes in this way. Part of the true social costs is borne by other firms and individuals, who must pay to clean up the water or air or live with the consequences.

3   Because of the divergence of private from social costs, the market system does not result in an optimal allocation of resources. Firms and individuals create too much waste and dispose of it in excessively harmful ways. Because the polluters do not pay the full costs of waste disposal, their products are artificially cheap, with the result that they produce too much of these products.

4   The government can intervene in several ways to help remedy the breakdown of the market system in this area. One way is to issue regulations for waste disposal and other activities influencing the environment. Another is to establish effluent fees, charges a polluter must pay to the government for discharging wastes. Still another way is to issue transferable emissions permits.

5   It is extremely difficult to determine how clean the environment should be. The sensible goal for society is to permit the level of pollution that minimizes the sum of the costs of pollution and the costs of controlling pollution. However, no one has a very clear idea of what these costs are, and to a large extent, the choices must be made through the political process.

Problems and Questions

1   Suppose that the paper industry emits wastes into rivers and streams, and municipalities or firms downstream must treat the water to make it usable. Do the paper industry's private costs equal the social costs of producing paper? Why or why not?

2   Suppose that each ton of paper output results in pollution that costs municipalities and firms downstream $1 and that a law is passed that requires the paper industry to reimburse the municipalities and firms downstream for these costs. Prior to this law, the quantity of paper supplied at each price was as follows:

Price of Paper (dollars per ton)	Quantity Supplied (million tons)
1.00	10.0
2.00	15.0
2.50	17.5
3.00	20.0
4.00	25.0

After the law takes effect, what will be the quantity supplied at each price?

3   In question 2, which output—the one prevailing before the industry has to reimburse others or the one prevailing after—is socially more desirable? Why?

4   If the quantity of paper demanded at each price is as follows, what is the equilibrium output of paper before and after the paper industry has to reimburse the municipalities and firms downstream (as indicated in question 2)?

Price of Paper (dollars per ton)	Quantity Demanded (million tons)
1.00	30.0
2.00	25.0
3.00	20.0
3.50	17.5
4.00	15.0

Key Terms

external diseconomy
private costs
social costs
direct regulation
effluent fee
transferable emissions permits
tax credits

Viewpoint for Analysis

In an editorial in the *Financial Times* on December 1, 2003, Paula Dobriansky, Under Secretary of State for Democracy and Global Affairs in the George W. Bush administration, wrote:

> There are only two paths towards achieving big reductions in greenhouse emissions. One is to use existing technologies, at the expense of economic growth. The other is to use breakthrough technologies that transform how we produce and consume energy and allow us to reduce emissions, while continuing to grow and to improve the world living standards. The second course is the only acceptable, cost-effective option. It underpins the U.S.'s climate change policy.
>
> This approach is in stark contrast to the Kyoto protocol, an unrealistic and ever-tightening regulatory straightjacket, curtailing energy consumption. The protocol does not consider the impact of new technologies under development. Neither does it offer a path forward for developing countries, which will soon be the largest emitters of greenhouse gases and must contribute to the global effort in a way that allows them to grow and prosper.[5]

(a) Is there an inherent conflict between the strict guidelines of the Kyoto Protocol (which are end goals in confronting climate change) and the emphasis on technological solutions (which are a means to achieve those goals)?

(b) How can technology help developing countries achieve the types of goals outlined in the Kyoto Protocol (see Case Study 9.2)?

(c) What is the risk of relying exclusively on the free market to develop new technologies to clean up the atmosphere?

[5] Paula Dobriansky, "Only New Technology Can Halt Climate Change," *Financial Times*, December 1, 2003.

WHAT SHOULD BE DONE ABOUT GLOBAL WARMING?

Global warming has become one of the pressing environmental issues of the last few decades. The main source of concern is the possibility that increasing concentrations of carbon dioxide and other greenhouse gases in the atmosphere, resulting from the burning of fossil fuels, will act like a blanket to insulate the planet and warm its surface.

The current debate on climate change has shifted away from the causes of the problem toward assessing the relative effectiveness of various environmental policies. As is often the case, the most politically expedient policies are often the least effective or the most costly.

- The Least Effective Ways of Reducing Greenhouse Gases

Time and again, the most ineffective ways of reducing pollution have turned out to be the ones in which governments have engaged in the greatest amount of intervention.

- *Subsidies to Encourage "Green" Fuels*
  U.S. and European governments have recently jumped on the biofuels bandwagon, providing all types of incentives for the development and production of these alternative sources of energy. First, governments should not be in the business of picking which types of fuels (and which new technologies) the markets will eventually select as the most efficient means of reducing carbon emissions. Second,

biofuels are not necessarily the most energy-efficient sources of energy available or those with the lowest carbon content, given today's technologies—let alone tomorrow's. Biofuel subsidies effectively "lock in" inferior solutions to the problem of reducing greenhouse gases. Finally, special interest groups (especially agricultural lobbies) and the politicians who cave in to their wishes have hijacked the search for the best solutions to climate change.

- *Command and Control Regulations*
  While regulations that improve energy efficiency seem like a good way to cut carbon emissions, they can provide perverse incentives and produce unintended and undesirable consequences. A case in point is the U.S. corporate average fuel economy (CAFE) standards. Originally enacted in 1975, CAFE is one of the last remnants of the 1970s federally imposed price and allocation controls on gasoline that were a major factor behind the long lines at gasoline stations during the oil shocks of 1973 and 1979. Recently, the U.S. Congress passed legislation to raise the CAFE standards (for the first time since 1985) to 35 miles per gallon (mpg) in 2020, from 27.5 mpg for cars and 22.2 mpg for light trucks (minivans and SUVs) today. While well intentioned,

fuel economy standards have some serious drawbacks. To begin with, they don't necessarily reduce total fuel consumption. In fact, more fuel-efficient cars can, perversely, encourage more driving. Similarly, while in the United States the mpg per ton of cars has improved around 20 percent in the last two decades, average car weight has risen (heavier vans and SUVs now account for half of all light-vehicle sales, compared with 20 percent in the 1980s), so the mpg per vehicle has actually fallen about 10 percent. Equally problematic aspects of command and control solutions are their inflexibility (it took Congress nearly a quarter century to increase the CAFE standards) and their susceptibility to political manipulation by the affected industries. Moreover, mandatory standards provide no incentives to exceed those standards, even when feasible and cost-effective. Finally, raising CAFE standards addresses the fuel efficiency of new cars only—not older cars or other sources of carbon emissions.

One reason that politicians (and special interests) like both subsidies and command and control solutions is that the costs to the consumer are hidden. Biofuels subsidies for corn and oil seeds raise food prices, and CAFE standards increase car prices. Consumers are rarely made aware of the direct links between such policies and the prices they pay.

- Better Ways of Reducing Carbon Emissions

Economists prefer market-based solutions for cutting greenhouse gases because they are typically more efficient and more transparent.

Two such solutions, which have been discussed and implemented in recent years, are cap-and-trade systems and carbon taxes (including gasoline taxes).

- *Cap-and-Trade Systems* In 1990, the U.S. Environmental Protection Agency set a goal of cutting sulfur dioxide emissions in half by 2012. This has been done using a cap-and-trade system whereby power companies can buy and sell permits to emit sulfur dioxide. Each year, the total amount (cap) on these emissions is lowered. By allowing the market to set the price of these permits by trading them in the open market, the reduction in emissions has been accomplished 25 to 35 percent more efficiently than a command and control system, saving U.S. consumers as much as $ 1 billion a year. The success of cap-and-trade in the United States and elsewhere was a key factor behind this type of policy framework being incorporated into the Kyoto Protocol on global warming. In Europe, where cap-and-trade has become a centerpiece in the fight against global warming, the size of the carbon-trading market blossomed from $15 billion in 2005 to over $150 billion in 2011, and it is set to keep growing rapidly.

  Ideally, when permits are first allocated, they should be auctioned off, allowing the market to determine their value. Unfortunately, the European Union's Emissions Trading Scheme (ETS) essentially gave away permits, partly in response to heavy lobbying by industry groups. The results were predictable: the implied price of carbon plummeted, greatly reducing the incentives for companies to put in place emissions reduction programs. The European experience points to one of the big problems with cap-and-trade systems—they can be "gamed" by special interest groups. Another problem is that the implied price of the pollutant can be very volatile, since a fixed number of permits does not take into account the rise and fall of industrial activity and pollution levels during business cycles. Even the successful U.S. sulfur dioxide cap-and-trade program has seen yearly price fluctuations of as much as 40 percent. This type of volatility can make it very difficult for businesses to plan for the optimum levels of emissions reduction. In practice, volatility can be limited by setting price ceilings and floors; however, these types of administrative controls can also complicate matters. Companies can also protect themselves against volatility using financial instruments such as forward contracts. Last but not least, cap-and-trade systems are complicated and opaque. This suits politicians and special interest groups, but does not serve the public at large, which is kept in the dark about the true cost of such schemes.

- *Carbon Taxes* Carbon taxes (including gasoline taxes) are the most efficient way of reducing greenhouse gases. They are simple and transparent—the cost of cutting emissions is clear to everyone. Such taxes can be set to achieve specific levels of carbon emissions and can also be adjusted to reflect business cycle conditions. They can be phased in to reduce

big disruptions to businesses and burdens to households. Likewise, their economic impacts can be offset via cuts in payroll, income, and corporate taxes. Taxes of this sort also do not create the type of price volatility inherent in cap-and-trade systems. The more certain (less volatile) the markets for carbon are, the more likely that the emissions targets can be met. Finally and most important, carbon taxes allow companies to determine how best to cut their emissions and provide very strong incentives to reduce their levels of pollution as much as possible to minimize their tax burden.

The biggest drawback to carbon taxes is political. Politicians are loath to raise taxes because they are the most transparent policy option when it comes to showing the voting public how much reducing emissions (or any other social goal) will cost. A generation of politicians—especially in the United States—has convinced themselves and the public that raising taxes is a bad thing. In fact, during the 2008 presidential primaries—with gasoline prices at record levels—some of the candidates proposed a temporary suspension of gasoline taxes. This suggestion was criticized by a large number of economists because it would have encouraged more gasoline consumption and raised prices further. In the end, the public would likely be more sympathetic to carbon taxes (or higher gasoline taxes) if they were offset by other tax cuts.

The United States has had considerable success using excise taxes to cut the emissions of chlorofluorocarbons

(CFCs), which have been shown to be a big factor in the depletion of the world's ozone layer. The EPA imposed an excise tax of $1.37 per pound on CFCs in 1989, which was then raised gradually to $7.15 per pound by 1999. By 1997, CFC production had been cut to around 10 percent of its 1988 levels.

Reducing carbon (or any other) emission means that the price of any product or service using carbon (including most sources of energy) will rise. There is no escaping this hard reality. However, a recent study by the nonpartisan Congressional Budget Office showed that taxes are a much more cost-effective way of cutting emissions than command and control systems; specifically, a 10 percent reduction in gasoline consumption would cost consumers 27 percent (or $9 billion per year) less if done by increasing gasoline taxes rather than raising the CAFE standards. Moreover, carbon taxes are less distortionary than income taxes. So replacing the latter with the former would be a good policy shift.

Questions

1   In 1990, President George H. W. Bush's Council of Economic Advisers said that the use of transferable emissions permits would "provide a least-cost reduction in [greenhouse gas] emissions."[1] Is this true? Why?

2   President Bush's Council of Economic Advisers also said that any strategy to limit aggregate emissions without worldwide participation would likely fail. Do you agree? If so, why?

3   Further, President Bush's Council of Economic Advisers said that any effective strategy must cover all greenhouse gases. Do you agree? Why?

4   In 1995, President Clinton's Council of Economic Advisers said that "cost-effective greenhouse gas control policies must rely as much as possible on economic incentives, to motivate the response of the literally billions of people responsible for greenhouse gas-emitting activities."[2] Why are economic incentives so important?

[1] *Economic Report of the President*, 1990, 218.
[2] *Economic Report of the President*, 1995, 156.

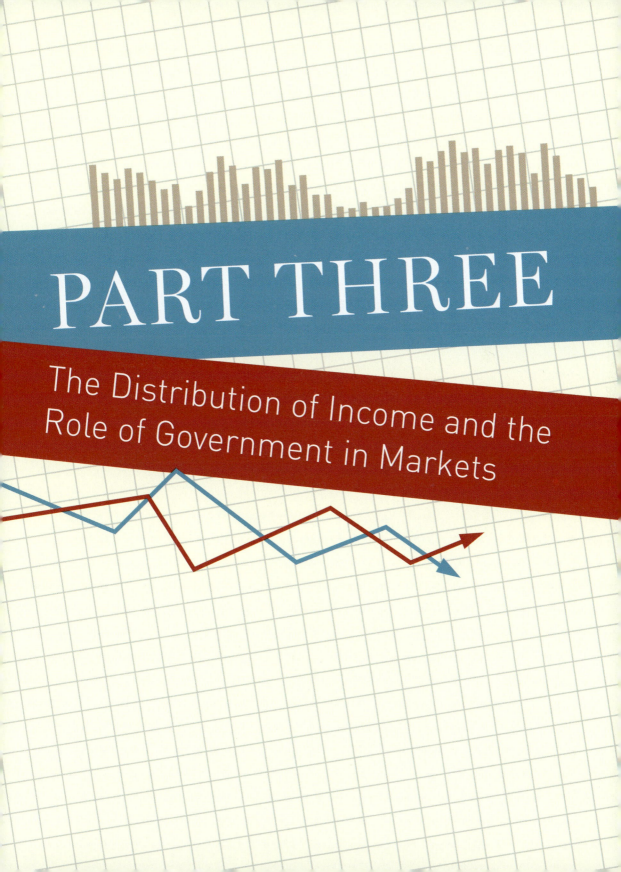

PART THREE

The Distribution of Income and the Role of Government in Markets

The Supply and Demand for Labor

LEARNING OBJECTIVES

➤ To derive the firm's demand curve for labor

➤ To describe the market demand curve for labor

➤ To explain how the equilibrium wage and quantity of labor are determined

➤ To understand the role of labor unions in the U.S. economy

➤ To explore how unions affect wages

In the early 1990s, the port of Philadelphia fought hard against other ports, like Wilmington, Delaware, and Miami, Florida, to maintain its dominant position as a destination for Chilean fruit. But union rules made this fight very difficult. How are unions organized, and what determines their behavior? One purpose of this chapter is to answer these questions.

Economists frequently classify inputs into three categories: labor, capital, and land. The disadvantage of this simple classification is that each category contains an enormous variety of inputs. Consider the services of labor, which include the work of a football star like Tom Brady, a salesman like Willy Loman (the protagonist in Arthur Miller's *Death of a Salesman*), and a knight like Don Quixote (the unforgettable hero of Miguel de Cervantes's novel). But this classification has the important advantage of distinguishing among the three main types of inputs. In this chapter, we are concerned with the determinants of the price of labor. The next chapter deals with the determinants of the price of capital and land as well as profits.

The Labor Force and the Price of Labor

At the outset, it is important to note that to the economist, labor includes a great deal more than the organized labor that belongs to trade unions. The secretary who works at General Motors, the young loan officer at Wells Fargo, the auto mechanic at your local garage, the professor who teaches molecular biology, the tech support person at Apple all put forth labor. Moreover, as shown in Table 10.1, many more people work in the service industry and retail trade than in manufacturing. About 85 percent of the people employed are white-collar workers (such as salespeople, doctors, secretaries, and managers) and service workers (such as servers, bartenders, and cooks), whereas only about 15 percent are blue-collar workers (such as carpenters, mine workers, and laborers) and farm workers.

It is also worthwhile to preface our discussion with some data concerning how much people get paid. As shown in Table 10.2, average weekly earnings vary considerably from one industry to another. For example, in 2010, workers in manufacturing averaged about $765 a week, while construction workers averaged $892 a week, workers in services averaged $606 a week, and employees in the information businesses averaged $940 a week. Also, average weekly earnings have varied considerably from one period to another. Table 10.2 shows that average weekly earnings in manufacturing in 1970 were only $129, as contrasted with $765 in 2010. In subsequent sections, we investigate the

TABLE 10.1

Employment: Nonagricultural Payrolls, by Major Industry, 2011

Industry	Employment (millions)
Mining	1
Construction	6
Manufacturing	12
Wholesale trade, transportation, and utilities	25
Information	3
Financial activities	8
Professional and business services	17
Educational and health services	20
Leisure and hospitality	13
Other services	5
Federal government	3
State and local government	19
Total	132

Source: Economic Report of the President, 2012.

TABLE 10.2

Average Weekly Earnings, Selected Industries, 1970–2010 (dollars)

Year	Manufacturing	Construction	Services	Information
1970	129	179	118	195
1975	186	250	157	253
1980	284	351	214	344
1985	381	449	269	430
1990	436	513	316	479
1995	509	571	364	564
2000	591	686	445	700
2005	673	750	509	805
2010	765	892	606	940

Source: Bureau of Labor Statistics.

reasons for these differences in wages, both between industries and over periods of time.

More broadly, we are concerned with the price of labor, which includes a great many forms of remuneration other than what we commonly regard as wages. As noted, economists include as labor the services performed by professional people (such as lawyers, doctors, and professors) and self-employed individuals (such as electricians, mechanics, and barbers). Therefore, the amount such people receive per unit of time is included here as a particular sort of price of labor, even though these amounts are often called fees or salaries rather than wages.

Finally, it is important to distinguish between *money* wages and *real* wages. Whereas the money wage is the amount of money received per unit of time, the real wage is the amount of real goods and services that can be bought with the money wage. The real wage depends on the price level for goods and services as well as on the magnitude of the money wage. The inflation we have experienced in recent years—albeit modest—has meant that real wages have increased less than money wages; hence, the year-to-year increases in earnings in Table 10.2 exaggerate the increase in real wages. In subsequent sections, since we assume that product prices are held constant, our discussion is in terms of real wages.

TABLE 10.3

The Firm's Demand for Labor under Perfect Competition

Number of Workers per Day	Total Output per Day	Marginal Product of Labor	Value of Marginal Product (dollars)
0	0		
		7	70
1	7		
		6	60
2	13		
		5	50
3	18		
		4	40
4	22		
		3	30
5	25		

Wage and Employment Determination under Perfect Competition

The Firm's Demand Curve for Labor

We begin by discussing the determinants of the price of labor under perfect competition. We assume that firms take the prices of their products, as well as the prices of all inputs, as given; and we assume that owners of inputs take input prices as given. Under these circumstances, what determines how much labor an individual firm hires (at a specified wage rate)? Once we answer this question, we can derive a firm's demand curve for labor. A **firm's demand curve for labor** is the relationship between the price of labor and the amount of labor utilized by the firm. That is, it shows, for each price, the amount of labor that the firm uses.

Firm's demand curve for labor

The Profit-Maximizing Quantity of Labor

Assume that we know the firm's production function and labor is the only variable input. Given the production function, we can determine the marginal product of labor when various quantities are used. (Recall that the marginal product of labor is the additional output resulting from an extra unit of labor.) The results of such a calculation are shown in Table 10.3. If the price of the firm's product is $10, let us determine the value to the firm of each additional worker it hires per day.[1] According to Table 10.3,

[1] For simplicity, we assume that the number of workers that the firm hires per day must be an integer, not a fraction. This assumption is innocuous and can easily be relaxed.

the firm achieves a daily output of 7 units when it hires the first worker, and since each unit is worth $10, this brings the firm's daily revenue up to $70. By hiring the second worker, the firm increases its daily output by 6 units, and since each unit is worth $10, the resulting increase in the firm's daily revenue is $60. Similarly, the increase in the firm's daily revenue from hiring the third worker is $50, the increase from hiring the fourth worker is $40, and so on.

How many workers should the firm hire per day if it wants to maximize profit? It should hire more workers as long as the extra workers result in at least as great an addition to revenue as they do to costs. If the price of a worker is $50 per day, it is profitable for the firm to hire the first worker, since this adds $70 to the firm's daily revenue but only $50 to its daily costs. Also, it is profitable to hire the second worker, since this adds $60 to the firm's daily revenue but only $50 to its daily costs. The addition of the third worker does not reduce the firm's profits. But beyond three workers per day, it does not pay for the firm to hire more labor. (The addition of a fourth worker adds $50 to the firm's daily costs but only $40 to its daily revenue.)

The Value of the Marginal Product of Labor

Value of the marginal product of labor

The optimal number of workers per day for this firm is three. Table 10.3 shows that this is the number of workers at which the value of the marginal product of labor is equal to the price of labor. What is the **value of the marginal product of labor**? It is the marginal product of labor multiplied by the product's price. In Table 10.3, the value of the marginal product of labor is $70 when between no worker and one worker is used per day. Why? Because the marginal product of labor is 7 units of output, and the price of a unit of output is $10. Therefore, this product, 7 times $10, equals $70.

To maximize profit, the value of the marginal product of labor must be set equal to the price of labor, because if the value of the marginal product is greater than labor's price, the firm can increase its profit by increasing the quantity of labor used, while if the value of the marginal product is less than labor's price, the firm can increase its profit by reducing the quantity of labor used. Hence, profits must be at a maximum when the value of the marginal product is equal to the price of labor.

Given these results, it is a simple matter to derive the firm's demand curve for labor. Specifically, its demand curve must be the value of marginal product schedule in the last column of Table 10.3. If the daily wage of a worker is between $51 and $60, the firm demands two workers per day; if the daily wage of a worker is between $41 and $50, the firm demands three workers per day; and so forth. The firm's demand curve for labor is its value of marginal product curve, which shows the value of labor's marginal product at each quantity of labor used. This curve is shown in Figure 10.1.

FIGURE 10.1

The Firm's Demand Curve for Labor under Perfect Competition

The firm's demand curve for labor is the firm's value-of-marginal-product curve, which shows the value of labor's marginal product at each quantity of labor used. The data for this figure come from Table 10.3.

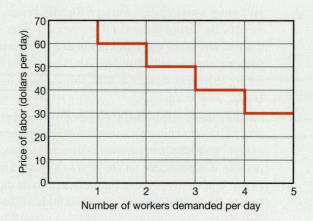

The Market Demand Curve for Labor

Market demand curve for labor

In previous sections, we were concerned with the demand curve of a single firm for labor. But many firms, not just one, are part of the labor market, and the price of labor depends on the demands of all of these firms. The situation is analogous to the price of a product, which depends on the demands of all consumers. The **market demand curve for labor** shows the relationship between the price of labor and the total amount of labor demanded in the market. That is, it shows, for each price, the amount of labor demanded in the entire market. The market demand curve for labor, like any other input, is quite analogous to the market demand curve for a consumer good, which we discussed in detail in Chapter 5.

Derived demand

But there is at least one important difference. The demand for labor and other inputs is a **derived demand**, since inputs are demanded to produce other things, not as an end in themselves. This helps explain why the price elasticity of demand is higher for some inputs than for others. In particular, the higher the price elasticity of demand for the product the input helps produce, the higher the price elasticity of demand for the input.

The Market Supply Curve for Labor

Market supply curve for labor

We already saw that a product's price depends on its market supply curve as well as its market demand curve. This is equally true for labor. The **market supply curve for labor** is the relationship between the price of labor and the total amount of labor supplied in the market. When individuals supply labor, they supply something they themselves can use, since the time that they do not work can be used for leisure activities. Because of this, the market supply curve for labor, unlike the supply curve for inputs supplied by business firms, may be a backward-bending supply curve, particularly for the economy as a whole. That is, beyond some point, increases in price may result in smaller amounts of labor's being supplied.

Backward-bending supply curve for labor

An example of a **backward-bending supply curve for labor** is provided in Figure 10.2. What factors account for a curve like this? Basically, as the price of labor increases, individuals supplying the labor become richer. And when they become richer, they want to increase their amount of leisure time, which means that they want to work less. Even though the amount of money per hour they give up by not working is greater than when the price of labor is lower, they nonetheless choose to increase their leisure time. This tendency has been particularly apparent in the last century. As wage rates increased and living standards rose, the average workweek tended to decline.

Note that there is no contradiction between the assumption that the supply curve of labor or other inputs to an individual firm is horizontal under perfect competition and the fact that the market supply curve for the input may not be horizontal. For example, unskilled labor may be available to any firm in a particular area at a given wage rate in as great an amount as it could possibly use. But the total amount of unskilled labor supplied in this area may increase relatively little with increases in the wage rate. The situation is similar to the sale of products. As we saw in Chapter 6, any firm under perfect competition believes that it can sell all it wants at the existing price. Yet the total amount of the product sold in the entire market ordinarily can be increased only by lowering the price.

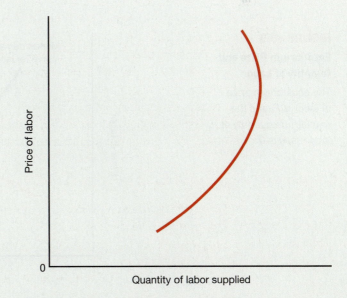

FIGURE 10.2

Backward-Bending Supply Curve for Labor

Beyond some point, increases in the price of labor may result in smaller amounts of labor being supplied. The reason for a supply curve of this sort is that as the price of labor increases, the individuals supplying the labor become richer and want to increase their amount of leisure time.

Equilibrium Price and Quantity of Labor

Labor's price (or wage rate) is determined under perfect competition in essentially the same way that a product's price is determined: by supply and demand.

The price of labor tends toward equilibrium at the level where the quantity of labor demanded equals the quantity of labor supplied. In Figure 10.3, the equilibrium price of labor is P. If the price were higher than P, the quantity supplied would exceed the quantity demanded, putting downward pressure on the price. If the price were lower than P, the quantity supplied would fall short of the quantity demanded, putting upward pressure on the price. By the same token, the equilibrium amount of labor utilized is also given by the intersection of the market supply and demand curves. In Figure 10.3, Q units of labor are utilized in equilibrium in the entire market.

Graphs such as Figure 10.3 are useful, but it is important to look behind the geometry and recognize the factors that lie behind the demand and supply curves for labor. Consider the markets for surgeons and unskilled labor. As shown in Figure 10.4, the demand curve for the services of surgeons is to the right of the demand curve for unskilled labor (particularly at high wage rates). Why is this so? Because an hour of a surgeon's services is worth more to people than an hour of an unskilled laborer's services. In this sense, surgeons are more productive than unskilled laborers. Also, as shown in Figure 10.4, the supply curve for the services of surgeons is far to the left of the supply curve for unskilled labor. Why is this so? Because very few people are licensed surgeons, whereas practically everyone can do unskilled labor. In other words, surgeons are much more scarce than unskilled laborers.

FIGURE 10.3

Equilibrium Price and Quantity of Labor

The equilibrium price of labor is P, and the equilibrium quantity of labor used is Q.

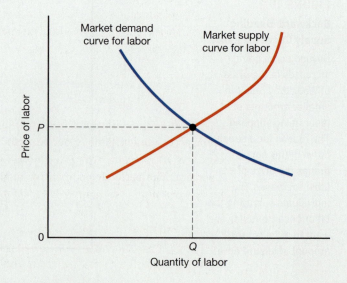

FIGURE 10.4

The Labor Market for Surgeons and Unskilled Labor

The wage for surgeons is higher than the wage for unskilled labor because the demand curve for surgeons is farther to the right and the supply curve for surgeons is farther to the left than the corresponding curves for unskilled labor.

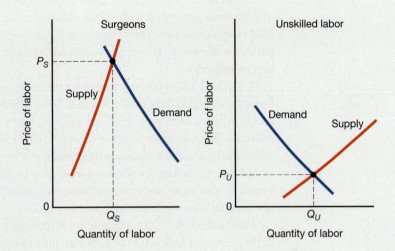

For these reasons, surgeons receive a much higher wage rate than unskilled laborers. As shown in Figure 10.4, the equilibrium price of labor for surgeons is much higher than that for unskilled labor. If unskilled laborers could quickly and easily turn themselves into competent surgeons, this difference in wage rates would be eliminated by competition, since unskilled workers would find it profitable to become surgeons. But unskilled workers lack the training and often the ability to become surgeons. Thus, surgeons and unskilled labor are examples of *noncompeting groups*. Wage differentials can be expected to persist between noncompeting groups because people cannot move from the low-paid to the high-paid jobs.

Labor Unions

In 2011, just under 12 percent of the nonfarm workers in the United States belonged to a union. Among public sector workers, the rate of union membership was 37 percent, whereas among private sector workers, it was only 7 percent. The perfectly competitive model does not apply to these workers. The biggest union, with approximately 3.2 million members, is the National Education Association. Next come the Teamsters, the Food and Commercial Workers, and the American Association of Federal, County, and Municipal Employees, each with about 1.4 million members. Among the large unions, the United Auto Workers is the smallest, with about 600,000 members.

The *national unions* are of great importance in the U.S. labor movement.[2] The supreme governing body of the national union is the convention, which is held every year or two. The delegates to the convention have the authority to set policy for the union. However, considerable power is exercised by the national union's officers.

A national union is composed of *local unions*, each in a given area or plant. Some local unions have only a few members; others have thousands. The local union, with its own president and officers, often plays an important role in collective bargaining (which we discuss later in this chapter). The extent to which the local unions maintain their autonomy varies from one national union to another. In industries where markets are localized (like construction and printing), the locals are more autonomous than in industries where markets are national (like steel, automobiles, and coal).

Finally, the AFL-CIO is a federation of national unions created by the merger of the American Federation of Labor and the Congress of Industrial Organizations in 1955. The AFL-CIO does not include all national unions. The United Mine Workers refused to join the AFL-CIO, and the Auto Workers left it in 1968. (The Teamsters were kicked out in the mid-1950s because of corruption, but in 1987 they were allowed to rejoin.) In 2005, the Teamsters, the Service Employees International Union, the United Farm Workers, and the United Food and Commercial Workers formed a new coalition called the Change to Win Federation. The AFL-CIO continues to play an important role in the U.S. labor movement, but because the national unions in the AFL-CIO have given up relatively little of their power to the federation, its authority is limited.

The U.S. Labor Movement

Early History of U.S. Labor Unions

To understand the nature and behavior of labor unions, we look briefly at the history of the U.S. labor movement. Unions arose because workers recognized that acting together gave them more bargaining power than acting separately. They frequently felt that they were at the mercy of their employers, and they formed fraternal societies and unions to promote economic and social benefits for the members. However, until the 1930s, unions in the United States were not very strong, partly because of employers' efforts to break them up and partly because the courts held that the unions' attempts to increase wages and influence working conditions were conspiracies in restraint of trade.

During the early 1930s, the tide began to turn. To a great extent, this was because of government encouragement of unions, beginning with the Norris–La Guardia Act of 1932. This act made it much more difficult for the courts to issue

[2] Sometimes national unions are called *international unions* because some locals are outside the United States—for example, in Canada.

injunctions prohibiting striking or picketing by unions, and it made *yellow-dog contracts*—agreements in which workers promise their employers not to join a union—unenforceable in federal courts. The next important step occurred in 1935, when Congress passed the Wagner Act, which made it an unfair labor practice for employers to refuse to bargain collectively with unions representing a majority of their workers or to interfere with their workers' right to organize. In addition, this act established the National Labor Relations Board to investigate unfair labor practices, issue orders enforceable in federal courts, and hold elections to determine which, if any, union would represent various groups of employees. The Wagner Act was a very important factor in encouraging the growth of labor unions in the United States—so important, in fact, that it has often been called U.S. labor's Magna Carta.

The 1930s were years of spectacular union growth. Aided by the pro-union attitude of the Roosevelt administration, new legislation, and the energy of its leaders, total union membership rose from less than 3 million in 1933 to more than 10 million in 1941. World War II witnessed further growth in total union membership. Stimulated by the increase in total employment and the government's favorable attitude toward their growth, unions increased their membership to almost 15 million (about 36 percent of all nonfarm workers) by 1945. The government helped unions gain recognition in exchange for union cooperation in promoting war production. By the end of World War II, labor unions were conspicuous and powerful features of the economic landscape.

The Structure of the AFL-CIO

The AFL-CIO is organized along the lines indicated in Figure 10.5. The constitution of the AFL-CIO puts supreme governing power in the hands of a biennial convention. The national unions are represented at these conventions on the basis of their dues-paying membership. Between conventions, the AFL-CIO's business is directed by its president (Richard Trumka in 2012) and secretary-treasurer, as well as by various committees and councils composed of representatives of various national unions or people elected at the convention. The AFL-CIO contains seven trade and industrial departments—for example, building trades, food and beverage trades, and maritime trades. Also, a few local unions are not affiliated with a national union but are directly affiliated with the AFL-CIO.

Internal Problems in Labor Unions

As unions have grown older and more secure and powerful, there has been more and more concern about the nature of their internal practices and leadership. After all, they are no longer the underdogs they were 80 years ago. They are huge organizations with immense power. Both in this country and in Europe, observers have charged that unions are often far from democratic.

FIGURE 10.5

Structure of the AFL-CIO

The AFL-CIO is organized with the governing power in the hands of a biennial convention.

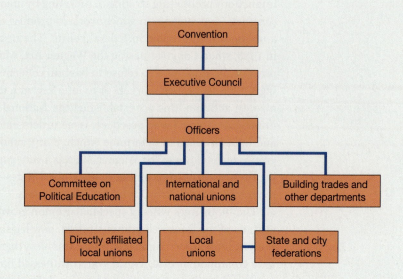

Members are frequently apathetic, for there is less interest in union affairs now than in the early days when unions were fighting for survival, and the leadership of some unions has become entrenched and bureaucratic. Moreover, there are frequent charges that unions engage in racial and other forms of discrimination.

Another problem is corruption within labor unions. In the 1950s, a Senate committee (the McClellan Committee) conducted lengthy and revealing investigations that showed that the leaders of the Teamsters Union had misused union funds, had questionable relations with the underworld, and had "shamefully betrayed their own members." Other unions were also accused of corrupt practices. It is important, however, to avoid smearing the entire labor movement. Although racketeering and fraud unquestionably are problems, they tend to be localized in relatively few industries, particularly the building trades, trucking, longshoring, laundries, and hotels. Many responsible and honest leaders of the labor movement have tried hard to rid the labor movement of these unsavory practices.

Postwar Labor Legislation

After World War II, public sentiment turned somewhat against unions. Strikes and higher prices got under the skin of the consumer as well as the employer, and there began to be a lot of talk in Congress and elsewhere about the prewar Wagner Act having been too one-sided, giving too many advantages to labor in its disputes with employers. In 1947, despite bitter labor opposition, the

THE BATTLE BETWEEN WALMART AND LABOR UNIONS

In recent years, Walmart has become a battleground for unions. Over the past 30 years, the company has become the largest retailer and largest employer in the United States (with more than a million workers in North America and 2 million worldwide). For years, unions have tried to organize Walmart's workforce. So far, they have not succeeded.

So who is hurt and who benefits when unions are kept out of a large company in the retail industry? The power of U.S. labor unions in the private sector has been diminishing in the past few decades. The share of unionized workers in the total workforce has fallen from 20 percent in 1980 to around 12 percent. Moreover, the retail industry is one of the few places where unskilled workers can find a job. Unionizing workers with few skills is always tough—

mostly because there are so many of them in the world.

Unions often succeed in getting higher wages and better benefits for their members. But in a fiercely competitive world, this can have unintended consequences, as companies have a greater incentive to automate (substitute machines for people) or offshore (substitute cheap foreign labor for expensive U.S. labor).

So keeping unions out of the retail industry can mean that wages and benefits are less generous. On the flip side, employers have less of an incentive to cut their workforce. By far the biggest beneficiaries of low-cost retailers are consumers—especially poor ones—who, by some estimates, save over $2,000 a year on average by shopping at low-cost retailers.

Taft-Hartley Act was passed with the purpose of redressing the balance between labor and employers. The act established standards of conduct for unions as well as employers, defined unfair union practices, and stated that unions could be sued for acts of their agents. Also, the act outlawed the closed shop, which requires that firms hire only workers who are already union members, and stipulated that unless the workers agree in writing, the checkoff is illegal.

Checkoff

(The **checkoff** is a system in which the employer deducts union dues from each worker's pay and hands them over to the union.)

In addition, the act tried to increase protection against strikes in which the public's safety and health are involved. If the president decides that an actual or impending strike imperils the national health or safety, the president can appoint a fact-finding committee to investigate the situation. After receiving the committee's report, the president can tell the attorney general to obtain an injunction forbidding a strike for 80 days, during which the parties can continue to negotiate. A Federal Mediation Service was established to help the parties settle such negotiations. The act does not forbid a strike at the end of the 80 days if no agreement has been reached.

In response to the evidence of union corruption presented by the McClellan Committee, Congress passed the Landrum-Griffin Act in 1959. This act attempts to protect the rights of individual union members from abuse by union leaders. It contains a "bill of rights" for labor, guaranteeing that each member can participate in union elections, that elections be held by secret ballot, and that other steps be taken to protect the rights of the members. It also requires unions to file financial reports, forbids payments (beyond wages) by employers to union representatives, and prohibits loans exceeding $2,000 by unions to union officials.

How Unions Increase Wages

Unions wield considerable power, and economists must take this into account if they want their models of the labor market to be accurate. Suppose, for example, that a union wants to increase the wage rate paid to its members. How can it accomplish this objective? In other words, how can it alter the market supply curve for labor or the market demand curve for labor so that the price of labor—its wage—increases?

1. *The union may try to shift the supply curve of labor to the left.* It may try to shift the supply curve, as shown in Figure 10.6, with the result that the price of labor will increase from P to P_1. How can the union cause this shift in the supply curve? Craft unions have frequently forced employers to hire only union members, then restricted union membership by high initiation fees, limits on new membership, and other devices. In addition, unions have favored legislation to reduce immigration, shorten working hours, and limit the labor supply in other ways.

FIGURE 10.6

Shift of Supply Curve for Labor

A union may try to shift the supply curve to the left by getting employers to hire only union members, then restricting union membership, or by other methods.

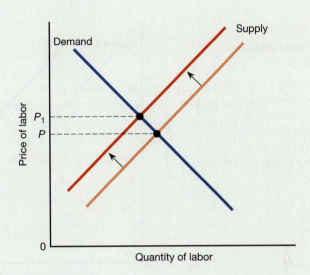

2. *The union may try to get employers to pay a higher wage, while allowing some of the supply of labor forthcoming at this higher wage to find no opportunity for work.* As shown in Figure 10.7, the union may try to exert pressure on the employers to raise the price of labor from P to P_1. At P_1, not all of the available supply of labor can find jobs. The quantity of labor supplied is Q_2, while the amount of labor demanded is Q_1. The effect is the same as in Figure 10.6,

FIGURE 10.7

Direct Increase in Price of Labor

A union may try to get the employer to raise the wage from P to P_1 and let the higher wage reduce the opportunity for work. This is commonly done by strong industrial unions.

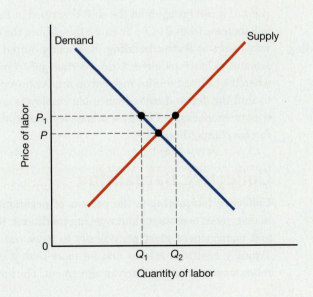

FIGURE 10.8

Shift in Demand Curve for Labor

A union may try to shift the demand curve for labor to the right by featherbedding or other practices and thus increase the wage from P to P_2.

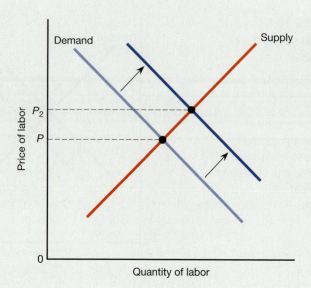

but in this case the union does not limit the supply directly. It lets the higher wage reduce the opportunity for work. Strong industrial unions often behave in this fashion. Having organized practically all the relevant workers and controlling the labor supply, the union raises the wage to P_1. This is a common and important case.

3. *The union may try to shift the demand curve for labor upward and to the right.* If it can bring about the shift described in Figure 10.8, the price of labor will increase from P to P_2. To cause this shift in the demand for labor, the union **Featherbedding** may resort to **featherbedding**: restricting output per worker to increase the amount of labor required to do a certain job. (For example, there was a time when the railroad unions insisted on much unnecessary labor.) Unions also try to shift the demand curve by helping employers compete against other industries or encouraging Congress to pass legislation that protects employers from foreign competition.

Collective Bargaining

Collective bargaining

Collective bargaining is the process of negotiation between the union and management over wages and working conditions. Representatives of the union and management meet periodically to work out an agreement or contract. Typically, each side asks at first for more than it expects to get, and compromises must be made to reach an agreement. The union representatives take the

THE CLOSING OF THE *HERALD TRIBUNE*

In 1965, New York City newspapers and their union employees were feeling the bite of computer technology. It took a linotype operator an hour to set 200 lines of newspaper type. A new machine, the teletypesetter, could do the same work in as little as half an hour, and computerized typesetting equipment on the drawing board would be able to do it in 17 seconds. The new technology would increase productivity and save labor—and displace printers.

The International Typographical Union's Local Six ("Big Six") had the bargaining power to keep the new technology out or let it in. The union did not seek to stand in the way of progress; although automated and computerized typesetting machinery could cost the jobs of union printers, higher wages without the increased productivity of automation could force less profitable papers to merge or even close—and that would cost jobs, too. Big Six wanted only to ensure that the new equipment would be operated by union members, so that the technology would not be used for union busting and its members and apprentices would be protected.

Six months of complicated maneuvering resulted in a contract without a strike. In addition to a pay raise, Big Six got what was in effect a veto over the introduction of automated equipment. The contract allowed the papers to use punched tape printing equipment, but set up a fund equal to 100 percent of the direct labor savings from the introduction of the new technology—a fund under the union's control and to be used to protect printers put out of work by the new equipment. The union had opened the door to automation, but it took most of what was saved and required the same wages and benefits from the unprofitable papers as from the big, profitable papers.

In less than a year, the new contract and the competitive New York newspaper business claimed their first victims. Profitable papers like the *New York Times* and the *Daily News* could afford to pay the price because they would save so much from automating. But three unprofitable papers, the *Herald Tribune*, the *Journal American*, and the *World Telegram*, merged into a new corporation, the World Journal Tribune Inc. Almost half the three papers' 4,700 employees lost their jobs, and about 400 Big Six printers were laid off.

April 25, 1966, was to have seen the first edition of the new *Herald Tribune* but was instead the first day of another strike. However, this strike was different. When Big Six had struck some papers in 1963, the others had shut down in solidarity. This time, the *Times*, the *News*, and the *Post* were on the stands as usual. And although Big Six had signed a contract with the World Journal Tribune by the end of May, the other unions had not, and the printers followed union tradition and refused to cross the picket lines. For 113 days, the *Herald Tribune* presses were silent, and on August 16, John Hay Whitney, publisher of the *Herald Tribune*, announced its closing.

agreement to their members, who must vote to accept or reject it. If they reject it, they may vote to strike or to continue to negotiate.

Collective bargaining agreements vary greatly. Some pertain to only a single plant, whereas others apply to an entire industry. However, an agreement generally contains the following elements: it specifies the extent and kind of recognition that management gives the union, the level of wage rates for particular jobs, the length of the workweek, the rate of overtime pay, the extent to which seniority determines which workers are first to be laid off, the nature and extent of management's prerogatives, and how grievances between workers and the employer are handled.

Closed shop
Union shop

Open shop

Historically, industries and firms have extended recognition to unions by accepting one of three arrangements: the closed shop, the union shop, or the open shop. In a **closed shop**, workers must be union members before they can be hired. This gives the union more power than if there is a **union shop**, in which the employer can hire nonunion workers who must then become union members in a certain length of time after being hired. In an **open shop**, the employer can hire union or nonunion labor, and once employed, nonunion workers need not join the union. As we have seen, the closed shop was banned by the Taft-Hartley Act. The Taft-Hartley Act also says that the union shop is legal unless outlawed by state laws, and about 20 states have right-to-work laws that make the union shop illegal. Right-to-work laws are opposed by organized labor, which regards them as a threat to its security and effectiveness.

Basic Forces at Work

Collective bargaining is a power struggle. At each point in their negotiations, both the union and the employer must compare the costs (or benefits) of agreeing with the other party with the costs (or benefits) of continuing to disagree. The costs of disagreement are the costs of a strike, whereas the costs of agreement are the costs of settling on less than optimal terms. These costs are determined by basic market forces. For example, during periods when demand is great, employers are more likely to grant large wage increases because the costs of disagreement (a strike) seem higher than the costs of settlement. The outcome of the negotiations depends on the relative strength of the parties. The strength of the employers depends on their ability to withstand a strike. The strength of the unions depends on their ability to keep out nonunion workers and enlist the support of other unions, as well as on the size of their financial reserves.

Recent Trends

The past four decades have not been easy for organized labor. In the 1980s, many important unions cut back on their wage requests. In the automobile industry, U.S. firms found it difficult to compete with their Japanese rivals,

WHY WAS EUROPE'S UNEMPLOYMENT RATE HIGHER THAN AMERICA'S IN THE 1990S?

In 1999, the U.S. unemployment rate was at a 30-year low—just over 4 percent. The picture in Western Europe was considerably less rosy—1 in 10 workers did not have a job. Unfortunately, the underlying causes of this high unemployment were (and still are) mostly structural. In other words, high growth alone does not reduce the ranks of those without jobs. In fact, unemployment rates in most European countries rose for the better part of two decades.

Why was the experience of the United States and Europe so different? A somewhat simplistic answer might be that European workers had been pricing themselves out of jobs. From 1970 to 1998, real (inflation-adjusted) labor costs in Europe rose by about 70 percent. In the United States, the rise was only 25 percent. However, during that same period, the U.S. economy created 70 percent more jobs, while employment in Europe increased by only 10 percent. European workers and politicians seemed to be less concerned about rising unemployment than with ensuring that those with jobs continued to receive large wage increases. Also, because of Europe's generous social welfare system, unemployed workers typically received larger unemployment benefits for longer than their U.S. counterparts.

European labor laws, de facto, seem to be designed to protect "prime-age" workers (mostly men) in the 25 to 54 age bracket. In 1998, the proportion of men aged 25 to 54 employed (the employment ratio) in the United States was 89 percent. The equivalent share in Europe was only a little lower at 86 percent. For all other demographic groups, the European employment shares were lower in Europe than in the United States. For women aged 25 to 54, the employment ratio in Europe was 54 percent compared with 63 percent in the United States. For young workers, aged 15 to 24, the European ratio was 37 percent, against a U.S. ratio of 59 percent. For older workers, in the 55 to 64 age range, the difference was equally large: 37 percent in Europe versus 58 percent in the United States. Similarly, the proportion of the European unemployed who were without a job for over 12 months in 1998 was 49 percent, compared with a mere 9 percent in the United States.

Politically, the European tradeoff between higher unemployment and preserving the higher wages of the prime-age workers did not seem to have created a political backlash. However, the economic cost was heavy, with generous social welfare benefits being financed with increasingly onerous tax burdens. Taxes in Europe are about 50 percent of GDP compared with 30 percent in the United States.

The financial crisis of 2008–2009 and the ensuing deep recession "equalized" the labor market conditions in the United States and Europe—in a bad way. Between 2000 and 2010, the U.S. youth unemployment rate rose from 9.3 percent to 18.4 percent, and the share of unemployed workers out of work for 12 months or more rose from 6 percent to 29 percent. These numbers were uncomfortably close to European levels, although some of the worsening employment conditions in the American economy was due to cyclical rather than structural reasons (for example, the depth of the recession and the sluggish recovery from 2009 on).

and many experts attributed this partly to the very high wages in the U.S. auto industry. In the trucking industry, unionized firms found it increasingly difficult to compete with nonunion firms. More and more union members in industries like autos, trucking, steel, rubber, and the airlines began to worry about the effects of hefty wage increases on whether they would have jobs. The climate for collective bargaining was quite different than in earlier decades.

Labor negotiations in the auto industry in 1987 are a good illustration. An important issue in these negotiations was the reform of work rules. After seeing productivity increases of 20 percent or more at some plants that adopted Japanese-style manufacturing systems (which organized workers in teams), auto executives pressed for the reduction of rigid union job classifications and work rules. Some union officials agreed, but because work rules are set in local, not national, negotiations and some union members strongly resisted such changes, reform was not easy. In the wake of the near collapse of the U.S. auto industry during the recession of 2008–2009 and the bailout of GM and Chrysler by the U.S. government, the industry was forced to go through a major restructuring. As a result, efficiency and productivity improved further.

We define a *union concession* as a wage reduction (or no wage increase), a reduction in cost-of-living adjustments in pay, a relaxation of work rules, the adoption of a "two-tier" wage structure (where newly hired workers are paid at a lower rate than existing workers), or the substitution of profit sharing (and related) plans for a wage increase. Since the late 1980s, a majority of workers in unions like the United Auto Workers, Steelworkers, Carpenters, Electrical Workers, and Food and Commercial Workers have accepted concessions in their new contracts, especially on issues such as health and retirement benefits. In the 1970s and 1980s, such concessions were rare.

When the Clinton administration took office, organized labor hoped that it would have easier sledding. But in late 1993, Bill Clinton pushed through the North American Free Trade Agreement, which was anathema to many unions because they felt it would encourage U.S. firms to move factories (and jobs) to Mexico. Clearly, the unions have continued to find themselves under pressure. The AFL-CIO and other unions actively supported former vice president Al Gore in his bid for the presidency. His narrow loss to George W. Bush put the U.S. labor movement on the defensive in the early 2000s. However, since 2009, under the presidency of Barack Obama, the tides have turned in favor of unions once again.

REVIEW AND PRACTICE

Summary

1. Assuming perfect competition, a firm employs each type of labor in an amount such that its marginal product times the product's price equals its wage. In other words, the firm employs enough labor that the value of the marginal product of labor equals labor's price.

2. The firm's demand curve for labor, which for each price of labor shows the amount of labor the firm uses, is the firm's value of marginal product curve (if labor is the only variable input). The market demand curve for labor shows the relationship between its price and the total amount of labor demanded in the market.

3. Labor's price depends on its market supply curve as well as on its market demand curve. Labor's market supply curve is the relationship between the price of labor and the total amount of labor supplied in the market. (Labor's market supply curve may be backward bending.)

4. An input's price is determined under perfect competition in essentially the same way that a product's price is determined: by supply and demand. The price of labor tends in equilibrium to the level at which the quantity of labor demanded equals the quantity of labor supplied. By the same token, the

equilibrium amount of labor utilized is also given by the intersection of the market supply and demand curves.

5 The AFL-CIO is a federation of national unions created by the merger in 1955 of the American Federation of Labor and the Congress of Industrial Organizations. It plays an important role in the U.S. labor movement, but because the national unions in the AFL-CIO have given up relatively little of their power to the federation, its authority is limited.

6 Unions can increase wages by shifting the supply curve for labor to the left, shifting the demand curve for labor to the right, or influencing the wage directly. Collective bargaining is the process of negotiation between union and management over wages and working conditions.

Problems and Questions

1 Suppose that a perfectly competitive firm's production function is as follows:

Quantity of Labor (years)	Output per Year (thousands of units)
0	0
1	3.0
2	5.0
3	6.8
4	8.0
5	9.0

The firm is a profit maximizer and the labor market is competitive. Labor must be hired in integer numbers and each person for one year (no more, no less). If the firm hires 4 years of labor (four workers each working one year), and if the price of a unit of the firm's product is $3, we can establish a range for what the annual wage prevailing in the labor market must be. What is the maximum amount it can be? What is the minimum amount? Why? Do these numbers seem realistic? Why or why not?

2 On the basis of the data in question 1, plot the marginal product of labor at various utilization rates of labor. Also, plot the value of labor's marginal product at each quantity of labor used.

3 "The unions should not be exempt from the antitrust laws." Comment and evaluate.

4 Describe the various ways that labor unions can influence the wage rate. Do you think that they attempt to maximize the wage rate? If not, what do you think their objectives are?

5 Suppose that you were the president of a small firm that hired nonunion labor. How would you go about estimating the marginal product of a certain worker or certain types of workers? Would it be easy? If not, does this mean that the theory of wage determination is incorrect or useless?

Key Terms

firm's demand curve for labor
value of the marginal product of labor
market demand curve for labor
derived demand
market supply curve for labor
backward-bending supply curve for labor
checkoff
featherbedding
collective bargaining
closed shop
union shop
open shop

Viewpoint for Analysis

According to the *Philadelphia Inquirer*, June 26, 1993: "Ports as near as Chester and Wilmington and as far away as Miami and New Orleans are working like crazy to undermine Philadelphia's dominant position as the destination for Chilean fruit. . . . Antiquated union pacts still in force [in Philadelphia] require that up to five members of [the longshoremen's] union must be present on a gang unloading fruit, although only two (at most) are needed. . . . [If] things continue as they are on the Philadelphia docks, very soon the longshoremen here will have a lot of time off—without pay."[3]

(a) How could rival ports try to undermine Philadelphia's dominant position in this regard?

(b) Were these union contracts intended to shift the demand curve for longshoremen in Philadelphia? If so, why would the employers agree to such contracts?

(c) If you had been president of the longshoremen's union in Philadelphia, would you have supported changes in these union contracts? If so, what sorts of changes would you have supported and why?

---

[3] *Philadelphia Inquirer*, June 26, 1993, p. A6.

Interest, Rent, and Profit

LEARNING OBJECTIVES

➤ To explain how the interest rate is determined and describe the economic functions it performs

➤ To consider the nature and importance of the present value of future income

➤ To define rent

➤ To explore the nature of profit and its function in a capitalistic economic system

The computer industry has had more than its share of heroic entrepreneurs, such as William Hewlett and David Packard. But no firm has had a more colorful history than Apple Computer, which was founded by the late Steve Jobs and Steve Wozniak. What incentives did the price system dangle before these two entrepreneurs? One purpose of this chapter is to answer this question.

Not all income is received in the form of wages. The schoolteacher who has a savings account at Bank of America receives income in the form of *interest*. The widow who rents out 100 acres of rich Iowa land to a farmer receives income in the form of *rent*. And people like Jobs and Wozniak, who founded and owned a firm that developed a new type of computer, receive income in the form of *profit*. All these types of income—interest, rent, and profit—are forms of property income. That is, they are incomes received by owners of property. In this chapter, we will explore the determinants of interest, rent, and profit. And we will try to explain the social functions of each of these types of property income.

The Nature of Interest

The English essayist Charles Lamb once wrote, "The human species, according to the best theory I can form of it, is composed of two distinct races, the men who borrow and the men who lend."[1] Whether or not such a division exists, most of the human species, at one time or another, are borrowers or lenders of money. Therefore, you almost certainly know that **interest** is a payment for the use of money, and the **interest rate** is the amount of money you must pay for the use of a dollar for a year. If the interest rate is 8 percent, you must pay 8 cents for the use of a dollar for a year.

Interest
Interest rate

Everyone who borrows money pays interest. Consumers pay interest on personal loans taken out to buy appliances, on mortgages taken out to buy houses, and on many other types of loans. Firms pay interest on bonds issued to purchase equipment and on short-term bank loans taken out to finance inventories. And governments pay interest on bonds issued to finance schools, highways, and other public projects.

Interest rates vary, depending on the nature of the borrower and the type of loan. One of the most important determinants of the rate of interest borrowers are charged is the *riskiness* of the loan. Lenders who have doubts about the chances of getting their money back charge a higher interest rate than they would if they were sure of being repaid. Small, financially rickety firms have to pay higher interest rates than large blue-chip firms; and large, well-known firms have to pay higher interest rates than the federal government. Another factor that influences the interest rate is the cost of bookkeeping and collection. If a firm makes many small loans and must hound the borrowers to pay up, these costs are a great deal larger than if it makes one large loan. Consequently, the interest rate that must be charged for such small loans is often considerably higher than for bigger loans.

Pure rate of interest

Despite the diversity of interest rates encountered at any point in time in the real world, it is analytically useful to speak of the **pure rate of interest**, which is the interest rate on a riskless loan. The rate of interest on U.S. government bonds, which are about as safe as one can get in this world, comes close to being a pure rate of interest. Actual interest rates vary from the pure rate, depending on the riskiness of the loan together with other factors, but the configuration of actual interest rates tends to move up and down with the pure interest rate.

Determining the Interest Rate

The Demand for Loanable Funds

Demand curve for loanable funds

Because the interest rate is the price paid for the use of loanable funds, it, like any price, is determined by demand and supply. The **demand curve for loanable funds** shows the quantity of loanable funds demanded at each interest rate.

---

[1] Charles Lamb, "The Two Races of Man," in *Essays of Elia* (London: Edward Moxon, 1823).

FIGURE 11.1

Determination of the Equilibrium Rate of Interest

The interest rate is determined by the demand and supply of loanable funds, where the equilibrium level of the interest rate is *i*.

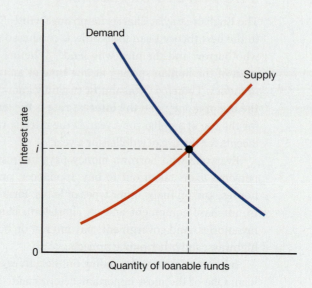

The demand for loanable funds is a demand for what these funds buy. Money is not wanted for its own sake, since it cannot build factories or equipment. Instead, it can provide command over resources (labor, equipment, and materials) to do things like build factories or purchase equipment.

As shown in Figure 11.1, the demand curve slopes downward to the right; this indicates that more loanable funds are demanded at a lower rate of interest than at a higher rate of interest. A very large demand for loanable funds stems from firms that want to borrow money to invest in capital goods like machine tools, buildings, and so forth. At a particular point in time, a firm has available a variety of possible investments, each of which bears a certain rate of return, which indicates the investment's profitability or net productivity. At higher interest rates, a firm finds it profitable to borrow money for fewer of these projects than at lower interest rates.

Rate of return   To be more specific, an asset's **rate of return** is the interest rate earned on the investment in the asset. Suppose that a piece of equipment costs $10,000 and yields a permanent return to its owner of $1,500 per year.[2] (This return allows for the costs of maintaining the machine.) The rate of return on this piece of capital is 15 percent. Why? Because if an investment of $10,000 yields an indefinite annual return of $1,500, the interest rate earned on this investment is 15 percent.

---

[2] It is unrealistic to assume that the yield continues indefinitely, but it makes it easier to understand the principle involved.

ANTI-USURY LAWS AND MORTGAGE ACTIVITY

Anti-usury laws can be traced back to biblical times. They place limits on the nominal interest rate. For example, a state anti-usury law may hold that the interest rate cannot exceed 15 percent per year. The idea behind such laws is to prevent the unregulated free market from allowing exorbitant interest rates. Needless to say, believers in free markets generally oppose such laws.

During the inflationary 1970s, interest rates on mortgages (loans to house buyers) rose, and savings accounts were deregulated. Banks and thrifts began an active competition for deposits. Rates started to approach the ceilings established by the anti-usury laws. As a consequence, less money was available for mortgages in states with anti-usury laws than in those without such laws.

Interest rates are particular types of prices. They balance the supply and demand of loanable funds. But limiting the interest rate will not affect the forces that lie behind the supply and demand curves. If an interest rate is legally kept too low, the underlying forces will circumvent the law by moving funds to uncontrolled markets; money flows to wherever it will get the highest return. In the 1970s, money either went out of state or was channeled by banks and savings and loan associations directly into other forms of investment. The banks and thrift institutions avoided placing mortgages (that is, lending money to house buyers) at artificially low interest rates.

If a firm maximizes profit, it borrows to carry out investments where the rate of return, adjusted for risk, exceeds the interest rate. For example, it is profitable for a firm to pay 10 percent interest to carry out a project with a 12 percent rate of return, but it is not profitable to pay 15 percent interest for this purpose. (More is said on this score in a subsequent section.) Consequently, the higher the interest rate, the smaller the amount that firms are willing to borrow.

Large demands for loanable funds are also made by consumers and the government. Consumers borrow money to buy houses, cars, and many other items. The government borrows money to finance the building of schools, highways, housing, and many other types of public projects. As in the case of firms, the higher the interest rate, the smaller the amount that consumers and governments are willing to borrow. Adding together the demands of firms, consumers, and government, we find the aggregate relationship at a given point in time between the pure interest rate and the amount of funds demanded, which is the demand curve for loanable funds. For the reasons given, this demand curve looks the way a demand curve should: it slopes downward to the right.

The Supply of Loanable Funds

**Supply curve
for loanable
funds**

The **supply curve for loanable funds** is the relationship between the quantity of loanable funds supplied and the pure interest rate. The supply of loanable funds comes from households and firms that find the available rate of interest sufficiently attractive to get them to save. In addition, the banks play an extremely important role in influencing the supply of loanable funds. Indeed, banks can create or destroy loanable funds (but, as we will see in Chapters 20 and 21, only within the limits set by the Federal Reserve, our central bank).

The equilibrium value of the pure interest rate is given by the intersection of the demand and supply curves. In Figure 11.1, the equilibrium rate of interest is *i*. Factors that shift the demand curve or supply curve for loanable funds tend to alter the interest rate. If people become more willing to postpone consumption to future time periods, the supply curve for loanable funds shifts to the right and the interest rate declines. Or if inventions result in very profitable new investment possibilities, the demand curve shifts to the right and the interest rate increases (see Figure 11.2).

However, this is only part of the story. Because of the government's influence on both the demand and supply sides of the market for loanable funds, the interest rate at any point in time is to a considerable extent a matter of public policy. A country's monetary policy can have a significant effect on the level of the interest rate. More specifically, when the Federal Reserve pursues a policy of easy money, interest rates tend to fall in the short run, because the Fed pushes the supply curve for loanable funds to the right. On the other hand,

FIGURE 11.2

How Shifts in the Demand and Supply Curves of Loanable Funds Affect the Equilibrium Interest Rate

If people become more willing to postpone consumption to future time periods, the supply curve shifts to the right and the equilibrium interest rate falls from *i* to i_0. If very profitable new investment opportunities open up, the demand curve shifts to the right and the equilibrium interest rate rises from *i* to i_0.

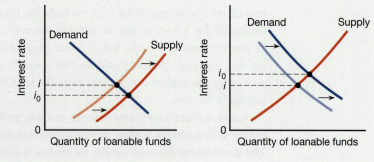

FIGURE 11.3

How Federal Reserve Policies Influencing the Supply Curve for Loanable Funds Affect the Equilibrium Interest Rate

When the Federal Reserve pushes the supply curve to the right (from S to S_2), the equilibrium interest rate falls from i to i_2. When the Federal Reserve pushes the supply curve to the left (from S to S_1), the equilibrium interest rate increases from i to i_1.

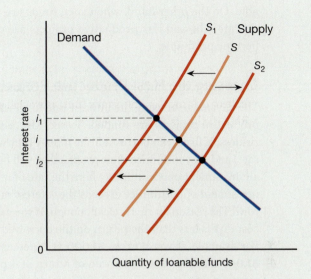

when the Federal Reserve pursues a policy of tight money, interest rates tend to rise in the short run, because the Fed pushes the supply curve for loanable funds to the left (see Figure 11.3).

The government is also an important factor on the demand side of the market for loanable funds because it is a big borrower. Between 1941 and 1945, it borrowed almost $200 billion to help finance World War II. During the past three decades, it has borrowed huge amounts to finance the mammoth federal deficits. In 2011, total federal debt (excluding the debt of state and local governments) held by the public was about $10.5 trillion.

Functions of the Interest Rate

Interest has often been a relatively unpopular and somewhat suspect form of income. Even the Greek philosopher Aristotle, who was hardly noted for muddleheadedness, felt that money was "barren" and that it was improper to charge interest. In real life and fiction, the moneylender is often the villain, almost never the hero. Yet, interest rates serve a very important function: they allocate the supply of loanable funds.

At a given point in time, funds that can be used to construct new capital goods are scarce, and society faces the problem of allocating these scarce funds among alternative possible uses. One way to allocate the loanable funds is through freely fluctuating interest rates. When such funds are relatively scarce, the interest rate rises, with the result that only projects with relatively high rates of return are carried out, since the others are not profitable. On the other hand, when such funds are relatively plentiful, the interest rate falls and less productive projects are carried out because they now become profitable.

Choosing the Most Productive Projects

The advantage of using the interest rate to allocate funds is that only the most productive projects are funded. To see why, assume that all investments are riskless. If firms can borrow all the money they want (at the prevailing interest rate) and they maximize their profits, they will buy all capital goods and accept all investment opportunities where the rate of return on these capital goods or investment opportunities exceeds the interest rate at which the firms can borrow.[3] The reason for this is clear enough. If you can borrow money at an interest cost that is less than the return on the borrowed money, you can make money. For example, if you borrow $1,000 at 3 percent per year interest and buy a $1,000 machine that has a rate of return of 4 percent per year, you receive a return of $40 per year and incur a cost of $30 per year. Since you make a profit of $10 per year, it pays to buy this machine.

At a particular point in time, many possible capital goods can be produced and investment projects carried out. Their rates of return vary a great deal; some goods or projects have much higher rates of return than others. Suppose we rank the capital goods or projects according to their rates of return, from highest to lowest. If only a few of the goods or projects can be accepted, only those at the top of the list are chosen. But as more and more can be accepted, society and private investors can go further and further down the list, with the consequence that projects with lower and lower rates of return are chosen. How many of these capital goods and investment projects are carried out? As noted, firms continue to invest as long as the rate of return on these goods or projects exceeds the interest rate at which they can borrow. So it follows that the most productive projects—all those with rates of return exceeding the interest rate— are carried out.

Capitalization of Assets

In a free market, or capitalist, economy, each asset has a market value. How can we determine what this value is? How much money is a particular asset worth? To keep things reasonably simple, suppose that you can get 5 percent on various investments open to you; for example, you can get 5 percent by investing your money in the stock of a local firm. That is, for every $1,000 you invest, you receive a permanent return of $50 a year, and this is the highest

---

[3] We assume here that the investment opportunities are independent in the sense that the rate of return from each opportunity is not influenced by whether some other opportunity is taken.

return available. Now suppose you have an opportunity to buy a piece of equipment that will yield you a permanent return of $1,000 per year. This piece of equipment is worth $1,000/0.05 = $20,000 to you. Why? Because this is the amount you would have to pay for any other investment open to you that yields an equivalent amount, $1,000, per year. (If you must invest $1,000 for every $50 of annual yield, $20,000 must be invested to obtain an annual yield of $1,000.)

In general, if a particular asset yields a permanent amount, X dollars, each year, how much is this asset worth? In other words, how much should you be willing to pay for it? If you can get a return of $100 \times r$ percent per year from alternative investments, you would have to invest X/r dollars to get the same return as this particular asset yields. Consequently, this asset is worth

$$\frac{\$X}{r}$$

If the rate of return on alternative investments had been 3 percent rather than 5 percent in this example, the worth of the piece of equipment would have been $1,000/0.03 = $33,333 (since $X = \$1,000$ and $r = 0.03$). This is the amount you would have to pay for any other investment open to you that yields an equivalent amount, $1,000, per year. To see this, note that if you must invest $1,000 for every $30 (not $50, as before) of annual yield, $33,333 (not $20,000, as before) must be invested to obtain an annual yield of $1,000.

Capitalization   This process of computing an asset's worth is called **capitalization**. Note one important point about an asset's capitalized value: holding constant an asset's annual returns, the asset's worth is higher the lower the rate of return available on other investments. For example, the piece of equipment discussed previously was worth $33,333 when you could get a 3 percent return on alternative investments but worth only $20,000 when you could get a 5 percent return on alternative investments. This makes sense. After all, the lower the rate of return on alternative investments, the more you must invest in them to obtain annual earnings equivalent to those of the asset in question. Therefore, the more valuable is the asset in question.

This principle helps explain why, in securities markets, bond prices fall when interest rates rise, and they rise when interest rates fall. A *bond* is a piece of paper that states that the borrower will pay the lender a fixed amount of interest each year (and the principal when the bond comes due). Suppose that this annual interest is $100 and that the interest rate equals $100 \times r$ percent per year. Then applying the results of the previous paragraphs, this bond will be worth $100/r$ dollars if the bond is due a great many years hence. Suppose that the interest rate is 5 percent. Then it is worth $2,000. But if the interest rate rises to 10 percent, it will be worth only $1,000, and if the interest rate falls to 4 percent, it will be worth $2,500. Securities dealers make these sorts of calculations all the time, for they recognize that the value of the bond falls when interest rates rise and rises when interest rates fall.

The Present Value of Future Income

In the previous section, we determined the value of an asset that yields a perpetual stream of earnings. Now we consider a case where an asset provides you with a single lump sum at a certain time in the future. Suppose you are the heir to an estate of $100,000, which you will receive in two years. How much is that estate worth now?

To answer this question, we must recognize the basic fact that a dollar now is worth more than a dollar later. Why? Because you can always invest money that is available now and obtain interest on it. If the interest rate is 6 percent, a dollar received now is equivalent to $1.06 received a year hence. Why? Because if you invest the dollar now, you get $1.06 in a year. Similarly, a dollar received now is equivalent to $(1.06)^2$ dollars two years hence. Why? Because if you invest the dollar now, you get $1.06 in a year, and if you reinvest this amount for another year at 6 percent, you get $(1.06)^2$ dollars.

Consequently, if the interest rate is 6 percent, the estate is worth $100,000/(1.06)^2$ dollars now. Since $(1.06)^2 = 1.1236$, the estate is worth

$$\frac{\$100,000}{1.1236} = \$89,000$$

In general, if the interest rate is $100 \times r$ percent per year, a dollar received now is worth $1/(1 + r)^2$ dollars two years from now. So whatever the value of the interest rate may be, the estate is worth

$$\frac{\$100,000}{(1 + r)^2}$$

The principle that a dollar now is worth more than a dollar later is of fundamental importance. If you do not understand it, you do not understand a basic precept of the world of finance. Although the example considered in the previous paragraphs pertains only to a two-year period, this principle remains valid no matter how long the period of time we consider. Table 11.1 shows the **present value** of a dollar received at various dates in the future. Its present value declines with the length of time before the dollar is received (so long as the interest rate remains constant).

Present value

TABLE 11.1		Interest Rate (Percent)			
Present Value of a Future Dollar (in cents)	**Number of Years Hence That Dollar Is Received**	**4**	**6**	**8**	**10**
	1	96.2	94.3	92.6	90.9
	2	92.5	89.0	85.7	82.6
	3	89.0	83.9	79.4	75.1
	4	85.5	79.2	73.5	68.3
	5	82.3	74.7	68.1	62.0
	10	67.6	55.8	46.3	38.5
	15	55.5	41.7	31.5	23.9
	20	45.6	31.1	21.5	14.8

Rent: Nature and Significance

Land

In addition to interest, another type of property income is rent. To understand rent, we must understand what economists mean by land. **Land** is defined by economists as any input that is fixed in supply, its limits established by nature. Since certain types of minerals and natural resources are in relatively fixed supply, they are included in the economist's definition of land. Suppose the supply of an input is completely fixed. Increases in its price do not increase its supply, and decreases in its price do not decrease its supply. Following the terminology of the classical economists of the nineteenth century, the price of such an input

Rent

is **rent**. Note that rent means something quite different to an economist than to the person in the street, who considers rent the price of using an apartment, a car, or some other object owned by someone else.

If the supply of an input is fixed, its supply curve is a vertical line, as shown in Figure 11.4. Thus, the price of this input, its rent, is determined entirely by the demand curve for the input. If the demand curve is D_0, the rent is P_0; if the demand curve is D_1, the rent is P_1. Since the supply of the input is fixed, the price of the input can be lowered without influencing the amount supplied. Therefore, a rent is a payment above the minimum necessary to attract this amount of the input.[4]

---

[4] In recent years, there has been a tendency among economists to extend the use of the word *rent* to encompass all payments for inputs above the minimum required to make these inputs available to the industry or the economy. To a great extent these payments are costs to individual firms; the firms must make such payments to attract and keep these inputs, which are useful to other firms in the industry. But if the inputs have no use in other industries, these payments are not costs to the industry as a whole (or the economy as a whole) because the inputs would be available to the industry whether or not these payments were made.

FIGURE 11.4

Rent

Rent is the price of an input in fixed supply. Since its supply curve is vertical, the price of such an input is determined entirely by the demand curve for the input. If the demand curve is D_0, the rent is P_0; if the demand curve is D_1, the rent is P_1.

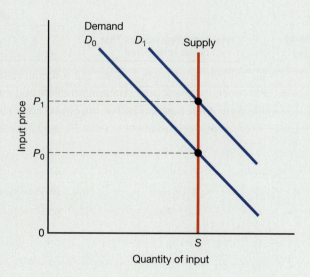

It is important to know whether a certain payment for inputs is a rent. If the payment is a rent, a reduction of the payment does not influence the availability and use of the inputs; but if the payment is not a rent, a reduction of the payment is likely to change the allocation of resources. If the government imposes a tax on rents, there is no effect on the supply of resources to the economy.

The Views of Henry George

In 1879, Henry George (1839–1897) wrote *Progress and Poverty*, a book in which he argued that rents should be taxed away by the government. In his view, owners of land receive substantial rents simply because their land happens to be well situated, not because they are doing anything productive. Since this rent is unearned income and the supply of land would not be influenced by such a tax, George felt that it is justifiable to tax away such rent. Indeed, he argued that a tax of this sort should be the only tax imposed by the government.

Critics of George's views pointed out that land can be improved, with the result that the supply is not completely price inelastic. Moreover, they argued that if land rents are unearned, so are many other kinds of income. In addition, they pointed out that it is unrealistic to expect such a tax to raise the needed revenue. George's single-tax movement gained a number of adherents in the last decades of the nineteenth century, and he even made an unsuccessful bid to become mayor of New York City. Arguments in favor of a single tax continue to surface from time to time.

Profit

In addition to interest and rent, another important type of property income is **profit**. The economist's concept of profit varies from the accountant's concept. According to accountants, profit is the amount of money the owner of a firm has left over after paying wages, interest, and rent and after providing proper allowance for the depreciation of buildings and equipment. Economists reject this view; their position is that the opportunity costs of the labor, capital, and land contributed by the owner should also be deducted.

Profit Statistics

Available statistics concerning profits are based on the accountant's concept, not the economist's. Before taxes, corporation profits have averaged about 5 to 10 percent of gross domestic product. Profits, expressed as a percentage of either net worth or sales, vary considerably from industry to industry and from firm to firm. (For example, the drug industry's profits in the postwar period have frequently been about 15 to 20 percent of net worth, considerably higher than in most other manufacturing industries—see Case Study 11.2.) Also, profits vary greatly from year to year and are much more erratic than wages. They fall more heavily in recessions and rise more rapidly in recoveries than wages do. Table 11.2 shows profit as a percentage of stockholders' equity in manufacturing in the United States during 2000–2010.

TABLE 11.2 **Annual Profit (after Taxes) as a Percentage of Stockholders' Equity, United States, 2000–2010**	Year	All Manufacturing Corporations	Durable Goods Industries	Nondurable Goods Industries
	2000	15.1	12.5	18.7
	2001	2.0	−7.0	14.7
	2002	7.5	2.1	14.5
	2003	12.1	8.5	16.3
	2004	15.8	12.9	19.3
	2005	16.7	12.4	21.7
	2006	17.6	13.9	21.4
	2007	15.2	10.7	19.8
	2008	8.9	2.9	14.9
	2009	10.3	4.1	16.1
	2010	15.0	14.9	15.2

Source: Economic Report of the President, 2012.

CASE STUDY 11.2

ARE DRUG COMPANY PROFITS TOO HIGH?

There is a popular perception that pharmaceutical companies charge "outrageously" high prices for new drugs and earn "obscenely" high profits. This view ignores the huge challenges, costs, and risks associated with the development of new drugs, which can take as long as a decade to create, test, and get approved by the U.S. Food and Drug Administration. The development costs can run into the hundreds of millions of dollars. If the drug succeeds, then the company that has created it can reap big profits. But the chances of success are only 10 to 20 percent—and competitor companies can bring their products to market first. So the

risks associated with drug development are very high indeed. Last but not least, the high profits of drug companies last only as long as the new drugs are covered by the relevant patents.

So are the high profits of drug companies justified? Without those profits to encourage the investments and risk taking associated with new drug development, we would likely not have seen the creation of new medicines to combat heart disease, cancer, and HIV-AIDS. Who ultimately would pay the price without those drugs? We all would, because we are the ones who benefit the most from these news cures.

Innovation, Uncertainty, and Monopoly Power

Why do profits, as economists define them, exist? Three important factors are innovation, uncertainty, and monopoly power. Suppose an economy were composed of perfectly competitive industries, entry completely free, and no changes in technology (no new processes, no new products, or other innovations) permitted. Moreover, suppose everyone could predict the future with perfect accuracy. Under these conditions, there would be no profits or losses, because people would enter industries where profits exist, reducing these profits eventually to zero, and leave industries where losses exist, reducing these negative profits eventually to zero. This sort of no-profit equilibrium has already been discussed in Chapter 6.

In the real world, innovations of various kinds are made. For example, DuPont introduces a new product like nylon, Henry Ford introduces the assembly line, or Marconi introduces the radio. The people who carry out these bold schemes are the **innovators**, those with vision and the daring to back it up. The innovators are not necessarily the inventors of new techniques or products, although sometimes the innovator and the inventor are one and the same. Often the innovator takes another's invention, adapts it, and introduces it to the market. According to economists like the late Joseph Schumpeter,

Innovators

of Harvard, profits are the rewards earned by innovators. The profits derived from any single innovation eventually erode with competition and imitation, but other innovations replace them, with the result that profits from innovation continue to be made.

Risk

In the real world, uncertainty also exists. Indeed, one of the real hazards in attempting to be an innovator is the **risk** involved. According to a theory set forth decades ago by the late Frank Knight, of the University of Chicago, all economic profit is due to uncertainty. Profit is the reward for bearing risk. Assuming that people would like to avoid risk, they prefer relatively stable, sure earnings to relatively unstable, uncertain earnings if the average level of earnings is the same. Consequently, to induce people to take the risks involved in owning businesses in various industries, a profit (a premium for risk) must be paid to them.

Still another reason for the existence of profits is that markets are not perfectly competitive. Under perfect competition, there is a tendency in the long run for profits to disappear. But as we have seen, this is not the case if an industry is a monopoly or oligopoly. Instead, profits may well exist in the long run in such imperfectly competitive industries. Much of our economy is composed of imperfectly competitive industries. Monopoly profits are fundamentally the result of "contrived scarcities." Because a firm's demand curve slopes downward if competition is imperfect, it pays the firm to take note of the fact that the more it produces, the smaller the price it receives. That is, the firm realizes that it spoils the market if it produces too much. Therefore, it pays firms to limit their output, and this contrived scarcity is responsible for the profits they make as a consequence.

The Functions of Profit

To many people, profit seems to be "something for nothing." They do not recognize the innovative or risk-bearing functions of the owners of the firm and consequently see no reason for the existence of profits. Other people, aware that profits arise because of imperfect competition, ignore the other functions of profit and regard it as entirely the ill-gotten gain of fat monopolists who smoke big cigars and sport a rapacious leer. But no group is more hostile to profits than the disciples of Karl Marx. According to Marx, the difference between the amount the employers receive for their products and the amount they pay the laborers that produce them is "surplus value." And, according to Marx, this "surplus value," which includes what we would call profit, is a measure of, and a consequence of, the exploitation of labor by the owners of firms.

Marx's views and those of others who look on profits with suspicion are rejected by most economists, who believe that profits play a legitimate and very important role in a capitalist system. In such a system, consumers, suppliers of inputs, and firms try to advance their own interests. Workers try to maximize

EBAY: THE STORY OF A SUCCESSFUL INTERNET COMPANY

In the late 1990s, there was a remarkable boom in the creation of Internet-based companies. Literally thousands of ".com" companies were started up in a matter of a few years. During the high-tech bust, in 2000 and 2001, most of these companies went bankrupt, giving rise to snide comments about ".gone" and ".bomb" companies. But some companies survived to become huge successes. Among these were Amazon.com, Yahoo, and Google. One of the most successful of the Internet companies is eBay, the online auction house.

Started in 1995, eBay has a very simple business model. It operates a website, leases no retail space, and never handles any of the merchandise sold on its site. Its revenues are derived from a listing fee and cut on every item sold. The company has a very strict set of rules for buyers and sellers, which it enforces vigorously. This includes a system that rates both buyers and sellers. These ratings are posted as personal profiles that can be examined by anyone and provide a means for traders to establish their credibility and good faith.

By the end of 2011, eBay had hundreds of millions of registered users worldwide and generated about $12 billion in revenues and $3.2 billion in profits, which makes the company one of the top 25 retailers in the world. Its success has generated an "eBay community" and an "eBay economy." It has been estimated that several million part-time businesses are run on eBay and that tens of thousands of people have given up their jobs to make a full-time living selling on the company's site. eBay has recently moved into the used-car business, handling the sales of close to half a million vehicles a year. This means that it is one of the biggest used-car markets in the world.

eBay's success has tempted other online companies to enter its market space, including Amazon.com, Yahoo, and Microsoft. However, eBay has fended off most of these challenges, ceding only a few niche markets to other companies. eBay's biggest competitive advantage (and some would say the source of its monopoly power) is its size and the networking effect it creates (see Case Study 7.2). For a seller, it is a place with the most buyers. For a buyer, it is the place with the most complete price information. In this respect, eBay's business model is ideally suited to the Internet.

their earnings, owners of capital look for the highest interest returns, landlords try to get the highest rents, and firm owners seek to maximize their profits. At first glance, this looks like a chaotic, dog-eat-dog situation, but as we have seen, it actually turns out to be an orderly and efficient system if competition is present.

Profits and Losses: Mainsprings of a Capitalist System

Profits and losses are principal movers of this system for several reasons.

1. *Profits and losses signal where resources are needed and where they are too abundant.* When an industry has economic profits, this is the signal for resources to flow into it; when an industry has economic losses, this is the signal for resources to leave it.

2. *Profits are important incentives for innovation and betting on the future.* For entrepreneurs like Joseph Wilson, of Xerox, profits are the bait society dangles before them to get them to take the risks involved in marketing a new product, like xerography. If their judgment turns out to be faulty, losses (negative profits) are the penalties society imposes on them.

3. *Profits are society's reward for efficiency.* Firms that use inefficient techniques or produce an inappropriate amount or type of product are penalized by losses. Firms that are particularly alert, efficient, and adaptive receive profits. Further, profits enable firms to embark on new projects. The profits that Xerox earned on xerography were used to support new ventures into other types of business machines.

The importance of profits in a free enterprise economy is clear enough. However, this does not mean that all profits are socially justified or that the system as a whole cannot be improved. Monopoly profits may not be socially justified; and a competitive system, despite its advantages, may produce some socially undesirable effects, such as an unfair income distribution.

REVIEW AND PRACTICE

Summary

1 Interest is a payment for the use of money. Interest rates vary a great deal, depending on the nature of the borrower and the type and riskiness of the loan. One very important function of interest rates is to allocate the supply of loanable funds.

2 The pure interest rate—the interest rate on riskless loans—is, like any price, determined by the interaction of supply and demand. However, because of the influence of the government on both the demand and supply sides of the market, it is clear that the pure interest rate is to a considerable extent a matter of public policy.

3 In a capitalist system, each asset has a market value that can be determined by capitalizing its earnings. Holding constant an asset's annual return, the asset's worth is higher the lower the rate of return available on other investments.

4 Any asset has a rate of return, which indicates its net productivity. An asset's rate of return is the interest rate earned on the investment in the asset. If firms maximize profits, they must carry out all projects where the rate of return exceeds the interest rate at which they can borrow.[5]

5 Rent is the price obtained for inputs that are fixed in supply. Since the supply of the input is fixed, its price can be lowered without influencing the amount supplied. Therefore, if the government imposes taxes on rents, there is no effect on the supply of resources to the economy.

6 Another important type of property income is profit. Available statistics on profits are based on the accountant's concept, not the economist's, with the result that they do not exclude the opportunity costs of the labor, capital, and land contributed by the owners of the firm. Profits play a very important and legitimate role in a free enterprise system.

7 Two important factors responsible for the existence of profits are innovation and uncertainty. Profits are the rewards earned by innovators and a

[5] In practice, firms often base their decisions on discounted cash flow rather than rates of return. The present discussion is necessarily simplified. For a more complete discussion, see Edwin Mansfield, *Microeconomics: Theory and Applications*, 11th ed. (New York: W. W. Norton, 2004).

payment for bearing risk. Still another reason for the existence of profits is monopoly power; because of contrived scarcity, profits are made by firms in imperfectly competitive markets.

Problems and Questions

1   Suppose that the quantity of loanable funds demanded at each interest rate is as follows:

Quantity Demanded (billions of dollars)	Interest Rate (percent)
50	4
40	6
30	8
20	10

Plot the demand curve for loanable funds on a graph. Describe the various kinds of borrowers on the demand side of the market for loanable funds.

Suppose that the quantity of loanable funds supplied at each interest rate is as follows:

Quantity Supplied (billions of dollars)	Interest Rate (percent)
20	4
25	6
30	8
35	10

Plot the supply curve for loanable funds on the same graph you used to plot the demand curve. What is the equilibrium rate of interest? If anti-usury laws do not permit interest rates to exceed 6 percent, what do you think will happen in this market?

2   Describe the social functions of the interest rate. Do you agree with Aristotle that it is improper to charge interest?

3   Assume that you inherit $1,000, which will be paid to you in two years. If the interest rate is 8 percent, how much is this inheritance worth now? Why?

4   "The supply curve for iron ore is horizontal, so its price is a rent." Comment.

5   According to Table 11.2, profits in 2008 were lower than in previous and subsequent years. Why? Also, profits during 2008 were lower in durable goods industries than in nondurable goods industries. Why?

Key Terms

interest
interest rate
pure rate of interest
demand curve for loanable funds
rate of return
supply curve for loanable funds
capitalization
present value
land
rent
profit
innovators
risk

Viewpoint for Analysis

In a *Wall Street Journal* editorial on December 27, 2011, Scott Gottlieb, of the American Enterprise Institute (and former Food and Drug Administration deputy commissioner), said: "Lipitor, the hugely successful cholesterol-lowering drug went off patent at the end of November, and generics are now on the market. The event is a turning point not only for Lipitor's maker, Pfizer, but also for the entire pharmaceutical industry. Big drug makers aren't chasing drugs like Lipitor anymore. . . ."[6]

(a) What impact does the termination of a drug patent have on the price of the drug and the profits of the drug maker?

(b) How might this affect the research and development efforts of the drug maker?

(c) What can drug companies do to compensate for the loss of profits that comes with the termination of patents?

[6] Scott Gottlieb, "Big Pharma's New Business Model," *Wall Street Journal*, December 27, 2011.

12 Poverty, Income Inequality, and Discrimination

LEARNING OBJECTIVES

➤ To explore the extent of income inequality in the United States

➤ To explain how the tax structure affects the distribution of income in the United States

➤ To describe the Social Security program

➤ To examine the nature and limitations of the major antipoverty programs

➤ To consider the economic effects of discrimination

Political leaders, both Democrats and Republicans, have expressed concern over the nation's welfare programs. Many have suggested that more emphasis should be put on training programs to help people get out of poverty. Recently, many economists have expressed concern about rising income inequality in the United States. What causes poverty and income inequality in a rich country like the United States, and what can be done about it? One purpose of this chapter is to examine these questions.

How Much Inequality of Income?

Income inequality

We do not need to be perceptive social observers to recognize that there is great **income inequality** in the United States. But our idea of what the distribution of income looks like depends on the sort of family and community we come from. A child brought up in Lake Forest, a wealthy suburb of Chicago, is unlikely to be as aware of the incidence of poverty as a child brought up on Chicago's poor South Side. For a preliminary glimpse of the extent of income inequality in the United States, scan Table 12.1, which shows the percentage of all U.S.

TABLE 12.1

Percentage Distribution of U.S. Household Income, 2012

Money Income (dollars)	Percentage of All Households
Under $15,000	13.0
$15,000–$24,999	11.7
$25,000–$34,999	10.7
$35,000–$49,999	13.6
$50,000–$74,999	17.5
$75,000–$99,999	11.7
$100,000–$149,999	12.5
$150,000–$199,999	5.0
$200,000 and over	4.5

Source: Income, Poverty, and Health Insurance Coverage in the United States: 2012, September 2013, U.S. Census Bureau.

households (including families and unrelated individuals living together) in various income classes in 2012. According to the table, the bottom 24.7 percent of the nation's households received an income of less than $24,999 in 2012. On the other hand, 9.5 percent of the nation's households received an income of $150,000 or more in 2012.

It may come as a surprise to some that so large a percentage of the nation's households made less than $30,000. The image of the affluent society projected in the Sunday supplements and on some television programs is strangely out of tune with these facts. Yet, to put these figures in perspective, it should be recognized that Americans are very rich relative to many other nationalities. This is shown clearly in Table 12.2, which gives for various countries the level of income per person, which is the total income of each nation divided by its population. The United States is among the leaders in this table with a per capita income of around $48,000 in 2011.

Some Causes of Inequality?

Although our poor may be better off than the bulk of the population in many other countries, the fact remains that there is substantial income inequality in this country. Why is this so? From our discussion of labor and property income in previous chapters, this question is not hard to answer. One reason is that some people possess greater ability than others. Since Alex Rodriguez and Vernon Wells have extraordinary skill as baseball players, it is easy to understand why they make a lot of money. Another reason is differences in the amount of education and training people receive. Physicians and lawyers must

TABLE 12.2

Selected Countries Grouped by Approximate Level of Per Capita Income (in 2012 dollars)

I. Countries with per capita income exceeding $25,000

United States	France	Japan
Australia	Germany	Spain
Canada	Greece	Sweden
Denmark	Hong Kong	Switzerland

II. Countries with per capita income between $10,000 and 25,000

Brazil	Mexico	Turkey
Malaysia	Russia	Venezuela

III. Countries with per capita income less than $10,000

El Salvador	India	Iran
Haiti	Indonesia	Thailand

Source: IHS Global Insight, Comparative World Overview Tables, May 2012.

receive a higher income than people in occupations requiring little or no training; otherwise, it would not pay for people to go through the rigors of medical or legal training. Still another reason is that some people own large amounts of property. Because of a shrewd choice of ancestry, current members of the Ford, Rockefeller, and Mellon families get high incomes from inherited wealth. Still other reasons are that some people have managed to obtain monopoly power, and others have had an extraordinary string of good luck. Racial, gender, and age discrimination can also result in income inequality.

How the Tax Structure Affects Income Inequality

Progressive

Regressive

So far we have looked at the distribution of before-tax income. But we must also consider the effect of the tax system on income inequality. A tax is **progressive** if the rich pay a higher proportion of their income for the tax than the poor. A tax is **regressive** if the rich pay a smaller proportion of their income for the tax than the poor.

Needless to say, people who feel that the tax system should promote a redistribution of income from rich to poor favor progressive, not regressive, taxes. In addition to the personal income tax, other progressive taxes are inheritance and estate taxes. (The federal government levies a gift tax to prevent wealthy people from circumventing the estate tax by giving their money away before death.) State governments also levy inheritance taxes (on persons who inherit money) and estate taxes (on the deceased's estate). All this is applauded by reformers who oppose accumulation and preservation of inherited wealth. But as in the case of the personal income tax, the portion of an estate subject to taxes can be reduced through clever use of various loopholes, all quite legal. Therefore, the estate tax is not as progressive as it looks.

Not all taxes are progressive; examples of regressive taxes are not hard to find. General sales taxes of the sort used by most states and some cities are regressive, since high-income people pay a smaller percentage of their income in sales taxes than low-income people. The Social Security and payroll tax is also regressive. It is difficult to tell whether the corporation income tax is progressive or regressive. At first glance, it seems progressive because the owners of corporations (the stockholders) tend to be wealthy people, and to the extent that the corporate income tax is paid from earnings that might otherwise be paid to the stockholders, we might conclude that it is progressive. But this ignores the possibility that the corporation may pass the tax on to the consumer by charging a higher price; in this case, the tax may not be progressive.

Factors Behind the Recent Rise in Inequality

By most measures, income inequality in the United States has risen in the past couple of decades. Why is this?

Technology, the Primary Culprit

The rapid changes in technology have increased the productivity of high-skilled workers much more than that of low-skilled workers and significantly increased the demand for the former. In this way, rapid innovation increases the "education premium" and consequently the salaries of workers with advanced degrees. For example, in 1980, people with a college degree earned around 40 percent more than those with only a high school education. But by 2000, this education premium had widened to around 80 percent. The gap has become even more pronounced in recent years. Between 2000 and 2005, the inflation-adjusted incomes of people with doctorates and those with degrees from business, medical, or law schools rose, while workers with less education saw their inflation-adjusted incomes fall. Ironically, skill-based technological change may hurt people in the middle of the income distribution more than those at the bottom. Recent studies have shown that information technology complements the skills of high-wage earners (for example, investment advisors), substitutes for the routine tasks found in many middle-wage jobs (for example, accountants and sales clerks), and has little impact on the nonroutine manual work done by low-wage earners (for example, cleaners and construction workers). What this means is that getting just a college degree is no longer enough.

The Winner-Take-All Structure of Some Markets

Technology alone cannot explain the huge increase in the pay scales of "superstar" athletes, actors, investment bankers, lawyers, and CEOs, to name a few. The combination of globalization (a much bigger market for talent), the ever-growing need for specialized skills, and the limited supply of people with those skills has greatly increased the rewards to the lucky few. The winner-take-all structure of some markets makes *relative performance* (being ranked number 1 rather than number 10 or lower) much more important than *absolute performance*. Consequently, the top 1 percent of Americans now earn about 15 percent of all income, compared with around 8 percent 40 years ago. More specifically, in 1967, the premium for young, "hot shot" lawyers on Wall Street versus the "run-of-the-mill" lawyers was around 14 percent. By 2005, the premium had risen to 120 percent. The high (and ever-rising) pay of these superstars has created both envy and outrage—especially vis-à-vis the pay of CEOs.

Globalization: A Convenient Scapegoat, but Not Entirely Blameless

Globalization

Many Americans are distrustful of **globalization** (trade, offshoring, and immigration), blaming it for many of today's economic ills, including the increase in income inequality that has occurred over the last three decades. While globalization has played a much smaller role than either technology or the rise of the "winner-take-all" culture, it has been a contributing factor. At the top end of the income distribution, music and movie stars, as well as CEOs of multinationals, operate in global markets. This greatly increases the demand for their "brand" and pushes up their earnings. In the middle of the income distribution, offshoring of manufacturing and, more recently, service sector jobs has put a damper on the rise in wages, especially for low-skilled jobs. At the low end of the wage scale, imports from China and other low-cost countries, as well as low-skilled immigrants, have kept earnings in check. That said, back-of-the-envelope calculations suggest that no more than about 5 to 10 percent of the American workforce is affected by globalization in a major way.

Unions and the Minimum Wage: Part of the Solution or Part of the Problem?

The share of unionized workers as a percent of the total workforce has been falling in the United States and other developed economies. The U.S. share fell from 20 percent in 1980 to around 12 percent in 2008. The fall in private sector unionization has been even faster, and nearly half of all union members now work for the government. Many factors have contributed to this: the shift from manufacturing to services, deregulation, globalization, and better worker protection by the government (for example, workplace safety and antidiscrimination laws), which reduces the need for union activism. Some have suggested that the demise of unions is a key factor behind rising income inequality in the United States. But there are many reasons to be skeptical. First, unions were fairly weak even before the recent rise in income inequality. Second, since 1990, the share of unionized workers has fallen even faster in Germany, with little apparent impact on income inequality. Third, while union-ized workers do enjoy higher wages than nonunionized workers in equivalent jobs, some have argued that these higher wage costs have contributed to declin-ing employment in some of the industries where unions still have a strong presence, including airlines, autos, and steel. Finally, in recent years, union membership has been falling at a slower pace. All this suggests that the demise of unions has played only a small role in the distribution of income becoming less equal. Similarly, it is unlikely that the flat (rather than declining) pattern of the inflation-adjusted minimum wage since the early 1980s has been a major contributor to rising income inequality.

Changes in American Family Structure

Two trends in the structure of families in the United States may have also contributed to rising income inequality. First, the number of single-parent households has risen substantially, especially at the bottom of the income distribution. Second, in many high-income households, both spouses work, often because they want to (not because they have to). These trends have also skewed the distribution income.

Income Inequality: The Pros and Cons

The Case against Income Inequality

Many distinguished social philosophers have debated the merits and demer-its of making the income distribution more equal. We cannot consider all the subtler points, but those who favor greater equality make four main arguments.

1. *Inequality of income lessens total consumer satisfaction, because an extra dollar given to a poor person provides that individual with more extra satisfac-tion than the loss of a dollar takes away from a rich person.* According to the British economist A. C. Pigou, "It is evident that any transference of income from a relatively rich man to a relatively poor man of similar temperament, since it enables more intense wants to be satisfied at the expense of less intense wants, must increase the aggregate sum of satisfactions."[1] A problem in this very appealing argument is its assumption that the rich man and the poor man have the same capacities to gain enjoyment from income. Most economists believe that there is no scientific way to make such comparisons. They deny that the

[1] Arthur Cecil Pigou, *The Economics of Welfare* (London: Macmillan, 1920).

satisfaction one person derives from an extra dollar of income can be measured against the satisfaction another person derives from an extra dollar. Although such comparisons may be drawn, they rest on ethical, not scientific, grounds.

2. *Income inequality is likely to result in unequal opportunities for young people to gain advanced education and training.* The children of the rich can get an education, while the children of the poor often cannot. The result is that some able and productive people may be denied an education simply because their parents are poor. This is a waste of resources.

3. *Income inequality is likely to lead to political inequality.* The rich may well influence legislation and political decisions more strongly than the poor, and there is likely to be one kind of justice for the rich and another kind for the poor.

4. *If people were framing a constitution for society without knowing what their class position would be, they would opt for equality.* This is the argument advanced by John Rawls, the late Harvard philosopher. He argued that "all social values . . . are to be distributed equally unless an unequal distribution . . . is to everyone's advantage"[2]; that is, unless an unequal distribution is to the advantage of society's least privileged group. Although Rawls's book, *A Theory of Justice,* has had considerable impact, many economists have pointed out that his prescription for society might not appeal to people who are willing to take risks. Suppose that you could establish a society that guaranteed every family $30,000 a year (no more, no less) or one where 99 percent of all families would receive $40,000 and 1 percent would receive $12,000. You might choose the latter kind of society because, although there is a small chance that you would do worse than in the egalitarian case, the chance of doing better seems worth this risk.

The Case for Income Inequality

In general, people who favor income inequality make five arguments.

1. *Income inequality is needed to give people an incentive to work and create.* After all, if everyone receives the same income, why bother to increase your production, try to invent a new process, or work overtime? Whatever you do, your income is the same. This is an important point, although it overlooks the fact that nonmonetary incentives like pride in a job well done can be as important as monetary incentives.

2. *It permits greater savings and thus greater capital formation.* Although this seems reasonable, it is not hard to cite cases where countries with greater inequality of income invest less, not more, than countries with less inequality of income. Some Middle Eastern countries with great income inequality have not had relatively high investment rates.

3. *The rich have been important patrons of new and high-quality products that benefit the entire society.* According to this argument, there are social

[2] John Rawls, *A Theory of Justice* (Cambridge, MA: Belknap Press of Harvard University Press, 1971).

advantages in having certain people with the wherewithal to pioneer new trends in consumption and support art and culture. In this view, a completely egalitarian society would be rather dull.

4. *Even if everyone received the same income, the poor would not be helped a great deal, because the wealthy are relatively few.* If the riches of the rich were transferred to the poor, each poor person would get only a little, because there are so many poor and so few rich.

5. *We must look at the justice of the process leading to the distribution of income and wealth to determine whether a certain degree of income inequality is unfair.* This argument has been made by the late Robert Nozick, another Harvard philosopher, and others. For example, suppose that an entertainer carries out a series of shows that are very successful and makes a lot of money. The process by which the entertainer makes this money is entirely legitimate. (People voluntarily pay for the tickets to the shows—and enjoy every minute of them.) According to this view, the resulting inequality of income is not unfair.

The Tradeoff between Equality and Efficiency

In trying to decide how much income inequality we favor, it is important to recognize that measures taken to reduce inequality are likely to decrease economic efficiency. In other words, if we reduce inequality, we may well cut society's total output. Why? Because, as pointed out in the previous section, people are likely to have less incentive to produce if their incomes are much the same regardless of how much they produce. This does not mean that all measures designed to reduce income inequality are bad. What it does mean is that if we want to reduce income inequality, we should be sensitive to the effects on output. In particular, we should try to find policies that attain a given reduction in inequality at a minimum cost in terms of reduced output.

In view of the strong feelings of many advocates and opponents of reduced income inequality, it is not surprising that they sometimes make extreme statements about the nature of the tradeoff between equality and efficiency. Some egalitarians deny that there is any tradeoff at all. They claim that inequality can be reduced without any cut in output. Some opponents of reductions in income inequality assert that there will be a catastrophic fall in output if the existing income distribution is tampered with. Although far too little is known about the quantitative character of this tradeoff, there seems to be general agreement among economists that the truth lies somewhere between these two extremes.

People vary considerably in their evaluation of how much society should pay (in terms of decreased total output) for a particular reduction in income inequality. The late Arthur Okun, of the Brookings Institution, suggested that to characterize your own feelings on this score, it is useful to view money as a liquid and visualize a bucket that carries money from the rich to the poor. The bucket is leaky, so only part of what is taken from the rich can be given to the poor.

If the leak is very small, a dollar taken from the rich may result in 99 cents going to the poor. Many people would accept a loss of this magnitude. If the leak is very large, a dollar taken from the rich may result in only 5 cents going to the poor. Few people would accept this big a loss. How big a loss would you accept? The larger the leak that you would find acceptable, the more willing you are to accept output losses to attain decreases in income inequality.

The argument between the advocates and opponents of reduced income inequality involves much more than economics. Whether you favor greater or less income inequality depends on your ethical and political beliefs. It is not a matter that economics alone can settle. What economists can do is assess the degree of income inequality in a country and suggest ways to alter the gap between the haves and have-nots in accord with the dictates of the people or their leaders. In recent decades, economists in and out of government have devoted much effort to designing programs aimed at reducing poverty. To understand these programs, we must discuss what poverty is and who the poor are.

What Is Poverty?

There is a popular saying that everything is relative. Certainly, this is true of poverty. Moreover, poverty is subjective. Consider the average young executive making $120,000 a year. After a bad day at the office or a particularly expensive family shopping spree, the executive is likely to claim, to anyone who will listen, to be as poor as a church mouse.

There is no well-defined income level that can be used in all times and places as a touchstone to define poverty. Poverty is partly a matter of how one person's income stacks up against that of others. What most people in the United States today regard as stark poverty would have seemed like luxury to many Americans of 200 years ago—and would seem like luxury in parts of Latin America and Africa today. Consequently, we must be careful not to define poverty in such a way that it cannot be eliminated—and then try to eliminate it. If poverty is defined as being in the bottom 10 percent of the income distribution, how can a war against poverty ever be won? Regardless of what measures are taken, there will always be a bottom 10 percent of the income distribution unless all income inequality is eliminated (which is highly unlikely).

Poverty

Perhaps the most widely accepted definition of **poverty** in the United States today is the one developed by the Social Security Administration, which began by determining the cost of a *minimal* nutritional food plan (given by the Department of Agriculture). Then, since low-income families spend about one-third of their incomes on food, this food cost was multiplied by 3 to obtain an income level that was used as a criterion for poverty. Families with less income were regarded as "living below the poverty level."

On the basis of such computations, a family of four needed an income of about $22,350 to make it barely over the Social Security Administration's poverty line in 2011. (Since farm families typically have lower food costs, the estimates for them are somewhat lower.) Although one could quarrel with this figure on various counts, most people probably would agree that families with income below this level are poor.[3]

Naturally, the poor are not confined to any particular demographic group, but some types of families are much more likely than others to be below the poverty line. In particular, African Americans are much more likely to be poor than whites. In 2010, over 27 percent of African Americans were poor, whereas 13 percent of whites were poor. Also, families headed by women are much more likely to be poor than families headed by men. In addition, very large families (seven persons and over) are much more likely to be poor than others.

Long-Term Decline in the Incidence of Poverty

According to estimates made by the federal government, about 15 percent of the total population in the United States were below the Social Security Administration's poverty line in 2011. In absolute terms, this means that around 46 million people were poor enough to fall below the criterion just described.

Fortunately, the incidence of poverty (measured by this criterion) generally has been declining in the United States. In 1947, about 30 percent; in 1960, about 20 percent; in 1992, about 14 percent; and in 2011, about 15 percent of the people were poor by this definition. This is what we would expect. As the average level of income rises, the proportion of the population falling below the poverty line (which is defined by a relatively fixed dollar amount of income) tends to decrease. Nonetheless, the fact that poverty is being eliminated in the United States does not mean that this process is going on as fast as it should. Many observers feel, as we shall see in subsequent sections, that poverty could and should be eradicated more rapidly.

Causes of Poverty

To a considerable extent, the reasons why families are poor lie beyond the control of the families themselves. About one-third of poor adults suffered a disability of some sort, the premature death of the family breadwinner, or family dissolution. Some have had to face a smaller demand for their occupation (because of technological or other change) or the decline of their industry or geographical area. Some have simply lived "too long": their savings gave out before their minds and bodies did. Another instrumental factor in making some families

---

[3] The basic figures come from the Department of Commerce's *Current Population Reports*, which explain in detail the way in which these figures are derived. The method described in the text is crude, but it provides results that are quite close to those of more complicated methods. Since 1969, the poverty line has been calculated on the basis of the consumer price index, not the price of food.

poor is discrimination of various kinds. The most obvious type is racial, but discrimination may also be based on sex, religion, age, residence, education, or seniority. In addition, some people are poor because they have very limited ability or little or no motivation. These factors should not be overlooked.

Important barriers tend to separate the poor from the rest of society. As the late Robert Lampman, of the University of Wisconsin, pointed out:

> Barriers, once established, tend to be reinforced from the poverty side by the alienated themselves. The poor tend to be cut off from not only opportunity but even from information about opportunity. A poverty subculture develops which sustains attitudes and values that are hostile to escape from poverty. These barriers combine to make events nonrandom; e.g., unemployment is slanted away from those inside the feudalistic walls of collective bargaining, disability more commonly occurs in jobs reserved for those outside the barriers, the subculture of poverty invites or is prone to self-realizing forecasts of disaster.[4]
>
> Judging from the available evidence, poverty often is self-perpetuating. Some families tend to be poor year after year, and their children tend to be poor. Because the families are poor, the children are poorly educated, poorly fed, and poorly cared for, and poverty is transmitted from one generation to the next. It is a vicious cycle.

Social Insurance

Old-Age Insurance

Until about 80 years ago, the federal government played little or no role in helping the poor. Private charity was available in limited amounts, and state and local governments provided some help, but the general attitude was "sink or swim." Self-reliance and self-support were the watchwords. The Great Depression of the 1930s, which changed so many attitudes, also made a marked change in this area. In 1935, with the passage of the **Social Security** Act, the federal government established a social insurance system providing compulsory old-age insurance for both workers and self-employed people, as well as unemployment insurance. By 2012, about 62 million Americans were receiving about $60 billion per month in benefits from the resulting system of old-age and survivors' insurance.

Social Security

Every wage earner covered under the Social Security Act pays a tax; the employer also pays a tax, which is equal to that paid by the employee. The amount that you can expect to receive each month in **old-age insurance**

Old-age insurance

[4] Robert J. Lampman, "Approaches to the Reduction of Poverty," *The American Economic Review*, March 1, 1965, 525.

benefits depends on your average monthly earnings. Also, the size of the benefits depends on the number of years you have worked. If you retire at 65 or 70, the monthly benefits are greater than if you retire at 62. These benefits are a retirement annuity. In other words, they are paid to the wage earner from the date of retirement to the time he or she dies. In addition, when a wage earner dies, Social Security provides payments to his or her spouse, dependent parents, and children until they are about 18 years of age (21 if they are in school). Further, payments are made to a wage earner (and dependents) if he or she is totally disabled and unable to work.

Controversies over Social Security

There are a number of controversial aspects of the Social Security program.

1. *The Social Security tax is regressive: those with very high annual earnings pay a smaller proportion of their income in Social Security taxes than those with low annual earnings.* For this and other reasons, many observers believe that the system is not as generous to the poor as it should be.

2. *Some people are disturbed that the Social Security system is not really an ordinary insurance system at all.* An ordinary insurance program must have assets sufficient to finance all the benefits promised the people in the program. This is not the case for Social Security. But this does not mean that you will not receive your Social Security. What it means is that the Social Security system is a means of transferring income each year from the working young and middle-aged to retired older people. It is up to future Congresses to determine what these benefits will be. Only time will tell how much you will receive.

3. *Some people are disturbed that Social Security is mandatory.* According to the late economist Milton Friedman, the government interferes with an individual's freedom to plan for the future by forcing him or her to be a member of the Social Security system. (Workers might be able to obtain larger pensions by investing the money that they contribute to Social Security in investments of their own choosing.) Other observers retort that without a mandatory system, some workers would make inadequate provision for their old age and might become public charges.

4. *Some people are concerned that Social Security is an impediment to saving and capital formation.* Martin Feldstein, Harvard professor and former chairman of President Reagan's Council of Economic Advisers, contends that Americans save relatively little because they depend on Social Security to take care of their old age. This, he believes, tends to depress capital formation in the United States, since savings can be used to build factories, expand old plants, and add in various ways to the nation's stock of capital. He favors a slowdown in the rate of growth of Social Security and more reliance on private pensions and personal savings.

JOB TRAINING PROGRAMS AND THE WAR ON POVERTY

The Affluent Society, the best-selling book by President Kennedy's friend, economist John Kenneth Galbraith, focused the president's attention on one of the United States's most serious problems: poverty. Galbraith pointed out that although everybody recognized the need for investing in factories and equipment, society was neglecting the need for investing in people—in education and training. The concept of structural unemployment was discussed widely during the Kennedy administration. (Structural unemployment occurs when new goods and new technologies call for new skills, and workers with old skills cannot find jobs.) Although the tax cut of 1964, as well as other federal measures that helped to lower unemployment to 3.8 percent in 1966, weakened some of the arguments regarding the importance of structural unemployment, plans were made for job training programs. These programs would be unlike those of the 1930s, when unemployment reflected a cyclical downturn

rather than the poor job skills of the participants; and unlike Social Security and other programs designed to reduce the symptoms of poverty, these would be designed to reduce its causes. President Johnson picked up the war on poverty that Kennedy had begun. Defense Secretary McNamara had observed high illiteracy rates among low-income military recruits and draftees and advocated training through the military as the answer. In 1967, the McNamara idea was developed into a program called the Job Corps, which was the key training program in the War on Poverty bill. Under the program, teenagers, mostly high school dropouts, would receive education and vocational training at Job Corps camps around the country. The effectiveness of the Job Corps proved controversial, although its supporters could point to many success stories. Decades later, conservatives, in particular, argued that any benefits of the Job Corps were not worth the cost.

Medicare, Unemployment Insurance, and Other Programs

Medicare

In 1965, Congress extended the Social Security program to include **Medicare,** a compulsory hospitalization insurance plan plus a voluntary insurance plan covering doctors' fees for people over 65. The hospitalization insurance pays for practically all the hospital costs of the first 90 days of each bout of illness, as well as some additional costs. The plan covers about 80 percent of doctors' fees after a deductible of around $1,100. This program is also an important factor in preventing and alleviating poverty. The incidence of illness is relatively high among the elderly; with the rapid rise in medical costs, it has become more difficult for them to afford decent care.

In addition to instituting old-age, survivors', and medical insurance, the Social Security Act also encouraged the states to set up systems of unemployment insurance. Such systems now exist in all states and are financed by taxes on employers. Insured workers who lose their jobs can obtain benefits after a short waiting period, generally a week. In most states, there is a 26-week ceiling on the duration of benefits. Clearly, unemployment insurance is another important device to keep people from falling below the poverty line.

Antipoverty Programs

According to the eighteenth-century English poet and essayist Samuel Johnson, "A decent provision for the poor is the true test of civilization."[5] There is general agreement that our social insurance programs, although useful in preventing and alleviating poverty, are not an adequate antipoverty program. For one thing, they focus largely on the elderly, which means that they do not aid many poor people. They do not help the working poor; and even for the unemployed, they provide only limited help for a limited period of time.

Consequently, the government started a number of additional programs specifically designed to help the poor, although many of them are aimed more at the symptoms of poverty than at its basic causes. There are programs that provide goods and services to the poor. The biggest of these programs is **Medicaid**, which pays for the health care of the poor. The **food programs**, which distribute food to needy families, are also of major significance in this regard. The federal government gives stamps that can be used to buy food to local agencies, which sell them (at less than the equivalent of market prices) or give them to low-income families (see Case Study 2.2).

Medicaid
Food
programs

In 1996, a major change was enacted in the nation's welfare programs, which have provided the poor with cash payments. The most important single program of cash payments was the Aid to Families with Dependent Children. (In 1990, this program paid out more than $20 billion.) In 1996, this program was replaced by a system of block grants and much greater authority for the states. The states have considerable latitude in how they use their grants. Also, work requirements are established for most people seeking welfare or other benefits. States that do not meet these requirements may lose some of their federal grants (see Case Study 12.2).

The Negative Income Tax

There has been widespread dissatisfaction with antipoverty, or welfare, programs. One suggestion that has received serious consideration is the negative income tax, an idea proposed by two Nobel laureates (both now deceased): Stanford University's Milton Friedman (an adviser to presidential candidate

---

[5] James Boswell, *The Life of Samuel Johnson, L.L.D.* (London: Printed by H. Baldwin for C. Dilly, 1791).

IS WELFARE REFORM WORKING?

President Clinton signs the 1996 welfare reform bill

August 1996, the U.S. Congress passed a landmark welfare reform bill whose goals were to end 60 years of federally guaranteed payments to low-income families and encourage welfare recipients to enter the workforce. Specifically, the Aid to Families with Dependent Children (AFDC) program was replaced by the Temporary Assistance for Needy Families. AFDC was launched in the 1930s primarily to help widows. However, with the increase in divorce rates and teen pregnancies, the program became a benefit for single mothers. Well before the passage of the welfare reform bill, there was growing concern that the AFDC program had created a large disincentive to work and produced a sizable "permanent welfare underclass."

The Temporary Assistance for Needy Families offers payments in return for work. In the context of this program, work includes everything from remedial classes to job training to subsidized jobs in the private sector to workfare-style community jobs paid for by state and local governments. The new welfare law also forces welfare recipients to find a job within two years and mandates that no one receives welfare payments for more than five years cumulatively over a lifetime. Welfare reform has also given state and local governments much more discretion over how to create job opportunities for former welfare recipients and how to train these entrants into the labor force.

Has welfare reform worked? Based on the initial drop in welfare rolls, the answer was a resounding yes. After peaking at 14 million in 1993, welfare rolls were down 50 percent by the end of 1999. More than 80 percent of this drop occurred after the passage of the welfare reform bill in 1996. In addition, the share of unwed mothers who were employed rose from less than 50 percent in the mid-1990s to over 60 percent by the end of the 1990s.

However, it would be premature to conclude that the entire decline in welfare rolls was due to welfare reform. Strong economic growth in the late 1990s and the fall in the unemployment rate to a 30-year low were also major contributing factors. During the same decade, the minimum wage was increased and the Earned Income Tax Credit

was made more generous. These made it easier for former welfare recipients to earn a living wage. However, there is little doubt that the reforms passed in 1996 provided a strong incentive for welfare recipients to participate in the economic boom.

Unfortunately, the true success of welfare reform could not be tested until the economy went into recession, which it did in 2001 and again in 2008. Predictably, poverty rates rose again but did not rise above the level they had reached in the 1990–1991 recession, even though the 2008–2009 recession was the deepest since the 1930s. This suggests that welfare reform can be given some of the credit for the improvement seen in the 1990s.

Barry Goldwater in 1964 and President Nixon) and James Tobin (professor at Yale University and an adviser to President Kennedy).

Negative income tax

A **negative income tax** would work as follows. Just as families with reasonably high incomes *pay* taxes, families with low incomes would *receive* a payment. In other words, the poor would pay a *negative* income tax. Figure 12.1 illustrates how a negative income tax might work; it shows the amount a family of four would pay, or receive, in taxes for incomes at various levels. According to Figure 12.1, $6,000 is the *break-even income*: the income at which a family of four neither pays nor receives income taxes. Above $6,000, a family pays taxes. A family with an income of $9,000 pays $750 in taxes. Below $6,000, a family receives a payment. A family with an income of $1,500 is paid $2,250.

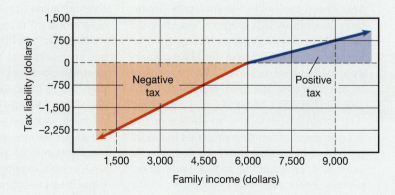

FIGURE 12.1

Example of Negative Income Tax

A family with more than $6,000 in income pays taxes. A family with an income of $9,000 pays $750 in taxes. A family with an income less than $6,000 receives a payment. A family with an income of $1,500 is paid $2,250.

However, many citizens remain skeptical about the negative income tax. For one thing, they are antagonistic to the idea of giving people an income without requiring any work in return. They also are unwilling to transfer large amounts from rich to poor. This amount would depend on how high the break-even income was set and the negative tax rates. In the late 1960s, it was estimated that a negative income tax would have meant that those above the break-even income level would transfer about $25 billion to those below the break-even level. Despite the attractive features of a negative income tax, a transfer of this magnitude has proved unacceptable in many quarters.

Also, the experiments with a negative income tax in Seattle and Denver have proved disappointing. These experiments, carried out with a sample of households, seem to indicate that under a generous negative income tax, people work significantly less, apparently because they are more willing to quit work and less willing to search hard for a new job.

In the end, however, some elements of a negative income tax have been incorporated into the U.S. federal tax code in the form of the Earned Income Tax Credit. The EITC is, in effect, a wage subsidy that supplements the incomes of low-wage workers.

The Problem of Discrimination

Racial Discrimination

Discrimination

Poverty, **discrimination**, and race are closely intertwined. Despite recent improvements, the sad fact is that racial discrimination occurs in many walks of life in many areas of the United States. Table 12.3 shows certain aspects of the relative position of the white and African American populations in the United States. The average income of African Americans is less than two-thirds that of whites. Almost one-quarter of the African American population is below the poverty line, compared with only about one-tenth of the white population. The unemployment rate is much higher among African Americans than among whites. Also, on the average, whites complete more years of schooling than African Americans, and a larger percentage of whites than African Americans are college graduates.

There is considerable agreement that at least part of these economic differences is the result of discrimination. Nonwhites are often prevented from reaching certain occupational or managerial levels. For example, it is rare to find an African American in the higher reaches of management in many corporations. To a considerable extent, they are cut off from job opportunities at higher levels by lack of education. But even at much lower levels, they are kept out of certain occupations by union policy (the building trades are a good example), and even when they do essentially the same kind of work as whites, there is sometimes a tendency to pay them less.

TABLE 12.3		**Whites**	**African Americans**
Economic	Median family income (dollars)	63,146	38,500
Characteristics of	Percent of persons in poverty	13.0	27.4
Whites and African	Percent unemployed (men)	9.6	18.4
Americans, United	Percent unemployed (women)	7.7	13.8
States, 2010	Percent unemployed (male teenagers)	26.3	45.4

Source: Economic Report of the President, 2012.

Effects of Discrimination

Some important effects of racial discrimination can be demonstrated by using the theory of wages. (The general point of this discussion holds true whether discrimination is on racial or other grounds.) The important thing to recognize at the outset is that nonwhite labor is not allowed to compete with white labor. This results in two different labor markets, one for whites and one for nonwhites. As shown in Figure 12.2, the demand curve for nonwhite labor is quite different from the demand curve for white labor; this reflects the fact that nonwhites are not allowed to enter many of the more productive occupations. Because of the difference in the demand (and supply) curves, the equilibrium wage for nonwhites, P_N, is lower than for whites, P_W.

FIGURE 12.2

Racial Discrimination

Under discrimination, the demand curve for white labor is quite different from the demand curve for nonwhite labor, and the supply curve for white labor is quite different from the supply curve for nonwhite labor, so the equilibrium wage for nonwhites (P_N) is lower than for whites (P_W). If there were no discrimination, the wage for all labor, nonwhite and white, would be P_T.

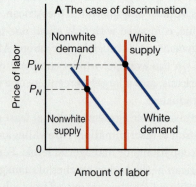

A The case of discrimination

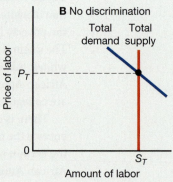

B No discrimination

How does this equilibrium differ from a situation of no discrimination? If nonwhites and whites competed in the same labor market, the total demand for labor, regardless of color, and the total supply of labor, regardless of color, would be as shown in panel B of Figure 12.2; the wage for all labor, regardless of color, would be P_T. A comparison of P_T with P_N shows that the wage rate of nonwhites would increase considerably. A comparison of P_T with P_W shows that the wage rates of whites would decrease slightly. The slight cut in white wages would be much smaller than the considerable increase in nonwhite wages because the nation's total production (and income) would increase once nonwhites had access to more productive employment.

Therefore, the effect of racial discrimination is to exploit nonwhites by reducing their wages relative to whites and to lower the nation's total output. Fortunately, there is evidence that racial discrimination is lessening. In part because of changing attitudes among whites, the growing restiveness of nonwhites, and the coming of age of new leadership, the old patterns of segregation and discrimination are breaking down. For example, African Americans are now being recruited actively by many prestigious colleges, and they are being hired and promoted to responsible positions in firms where formerly they remained at a relatively menial level. Progress is slow, but it unquestionably exists.

Discrimination against Women

Needless to say, discrimination is not limited to nonwhites—African Americans, Hispanics, Asians, and Native Americans. There is some discrimination against older workers. Even more widespread is discrimination against women. Holding age and education constant, women earn much less than men. To some extent, this difference in earnings arises because women work shorter hours and often have less experience in their jobs than men. But even after adjusting for factors such as education, work experience during the year, and lifetime work experience, there remains a substantial differential between the earnings of men and women. To a considerable extent, this differential is probably the result of discrimination, the nature of which has been described by the Council of Economic Advisers:

> There is clearly prejudice against women engaging in particular activities. Some patients reject women doctors, some clients reject women lawyers, some customers reject automobile saleswomen, and some workers reject women bosses. Employers also may have formulated discriminatory attitudes about women, exaggerating the risk of job instability or client acceptance and therefore excluding women from on-the-job training which would advance their careers. In fact, even if employers do estimate correctly the average job turnover of women, women who are strongly committed

CASE STUDY 12.3

INEQUALITY OF OUTCOMES VERSUS INEQUALITY OF OPPORTUNITIES

There continues to be a significant and potentially damaging misunderstanding about the causes of and solutions to the unequal distribution of income and wealth. There is a big difference between the inequality of *opportunity* and the inequality of *outcome*. Few would debate the reality that some people are much smarter than average or have greater talent in sports, music, business management, and so forth. Reducing the rewards that the market provides to such talented people would damage their incentives to innovate or perform to their maximum ability. Nevertheless, governments must ensure that everyone with these talents (regardless of race, gender, social status, economic background, and so on) has equal access to the market's rewards (also see Case Study 12.4).

The negative effects of forcing the equality of outcomes rather than the equality of opportunities were most evident in the former Communist states, where innovation and productivity stagnated for decades. It is also evident—but to a lesser extent—in Europe, where the instincts for egalitarianism are stronger than in the United States. One result of this relative egalitarianism is that income inequality is lower in Western European than in most regions of the world. At the same time, however, productivity growth in Western Europe has also been relatively poor compared with the United States and other dynamic regions, such as Asia.

At the other extreme are a majority of the countries in Latin America and Africa. Highly unequal distributions of income in these regions are symptomatic of poor access to education, health care, credit, and job opportunities.

Such inequality of opportunities can be highly counterproductive, especially in emerging markets, leading to corruption, the politics of envy, and social unrest. If people are excluded from access to the "good life" and blocked by the elite from upward mobility, then they will look for other, possibly more violent, ways of getting their share of the economic pie. For example, highly unequal distributions of income are part of the explanation for high crime rates in countries such as South Africa, Colombia, and Venezuela.

How does the United States fit into this picture? Income is distributed less equally than in Europe and Japan, slightly less equally than in Australia, Britain, Canada, and New Zealand, a little more equally than in China and other Asian countries, and much more equally than in Latin America and Africa.

In the United States, there has long been a sense that the American Dream—success for those who work hard—is potentially within reach of everyone. One of the biggest worries about the recent rise in inequality is that after decades of progress toward creating a true "land of opportunity," the United States may be running the risk of creating a stratified society. There currently seems to be a high correlation between the incomes of parents and their children. At the same time, some studies show that upward mobility has become less in the United States than in Europe.

Inequality is not inherently bad as long as (1) everyone has the opportunity to move up, (2) living standards are improving for the average person, and (3) there is help for those who cannot make it or who suffer temporary setbacks.

to their jobs may suffer from "statistical discrimination" by being treated as though their own behavior resembled the average. The extent to which this type of discrimination occurs depends on how costly it is for employers to distinguish women who will have a strong job commitment from those who will not. Finally, because some occupations restrict the number of newcomers they take in and because women move in and out of the labor force more often, more women than men tend to fall into the newcomer category and to be thus excluded. For example, restrictive entry policies may have kept women out of the skilled crafts.

On the other hand, some component of the earnings differential and of the occupation differential stems from differences in role orientation which start with differences in education and continue through marriage, where women generally are expected to assume primary responsibility for the home and subordinate their own outside work to their household responsibilities. It is not now possible to distinguish in a quantitative way between the discrimination which bars women from jobs solely because of their sex, and the role differentiation whereby women, either through choice or necessity, restrict their careers because of the demands of their homes. Some may label the latter as a pervasive social discrimination which starts in the cradle; nonetheless, it is useful to draw the distinction.[6]

In various ways, the government has set out to discourage discrimination against women. The Equal Pay Act of 1963 requires employers to pay men and women equally for the same work, and Title VII of the Civil Rights Act of 1964 bars discrimination in hiring, firing, and other aspects of employment. In addition, a number of women have been appointed to high-ranking government jobs, including economists Juanita Kreps (who was secretary of Commerce), Marina Whitman (who served as a member of the President's Council of Economic Advisers), Alice Rivlin (a former member of the Federal Reserve Board and a former head of the Congressional Budget Office), Nancy Teeters (a former member of the Federal Reserve Board), Laura D'Andrea Tyson (a former director of National Economic Council), and Janet Yellen (a former chairperson of the President's Council of Economic Advisers, a former vice-chair of the Federal Reserve Board, and currently chair of the Federal Reserve Board). The various antidiscriminatory measures undoubtedly have had a beneficial effect, but it must be recognized that eliminating discrimination of this kind will require basic changes in the attitudes of both males and females. The problem of discrimination against women is likely to be with us for a long time.

[6] Economic Problems of Women Hearings before the Joint Economic Committee, Congress of the United States, Ninety-third Congress, first session–second session (Washington, D.C.: U.S. Govt. Print. Off., 1973).

EQUAL PAY FOR WORK OF "COMPARABLE WORTH"

Women's earnings tend to be considerably lower than men's—roughly 20 percent lower in 2010. A striking fact about female employment is that although women can be found in virtually all occupations, they predominate overwhelmingly in a few like nursing and teaching. In 2010, women constituted 91 percent of registered nurses, 82 percent of elementary and middle school teachers, and 72 percent of medical and health services managers in the United States.

Some believe that these jobs are underpaid because they tend to be filled by women, and to eliminate what they regard as a major inequity, they argue for "equal pay for work of comparable worth." The idea is to compare the worth of one occupation with that of another occupation and press for equal wage rates for them if they are judged to be of equal worth. For example, if a nurse does work that is of equal worth to that of an accountant, nurses should get the same wage as accountants.

To measure the worth of an occupation, many proponents of "comparable worth" propose the use of a job evaluation point system. In 1983, a federal court found the state of Washington guilty of discrimination because it paid male-dominated occupations more than "comparable" female-dominated occupations. To determine what occupations were comparable, every state job was evaluated in terms of "accountability," "knowledge and skills," "mental demands," and "working conditions." A committee decided how many points to give each occupation on each of these criteria, and two occupations were regarded of comparable worth if they got the same total number of points.

An enormous amount of controversy has engulfed this decision, which said that Washington State should raise women's wages and grant restitution for past injuries to them. Although higher courts reversed this decision, many politicians have supported the idea that an occupation's wage rate should be determined by "comparable worth." In 1989, a law was enacted in Ontario, Canada, that says that employers must assess jobs in which at least 60 percent of the employees are women and use such a job evaluation system to see how much women should be paid.

Many economists are opposed to the use of such job evaluation systems to set wage rates. In their view, the proper determinants of wage rates are the supply and demand curves discussed in Chapter 10, which together set wage rates in competitive markets. To ignore these supply and demand curves is to run the risk that some occupations will have shortages while others will have too many people. Certainly, job evaluation systems of this sort may reduce economic efficiency. However, proponents of these job evaluation systems emphasize equity, not efficiency; in their view, these systems promote equity.

REVIEW AND PRACTICE

Summary

1   Many factors are responsible for existing income differentials. Some people are abler, better educated, or luckier than others. Some people have more property or more monopoly power than others.

2   Critics of income inequality argue that it lessens total consumer satisfaction because an extra dollar given to the poor provides them more extra satisfaction than the loss of a dollar takes away from the rich. Also, they argue that income inequality leads to social and political inequality.

3   Defenders of income inequality point out that it is scientifically impossible to make interpersonal comparisons of utility, that income inequality is needed to provide incentives for people to work and create, and that it permits greater capital formation.

4   No well-defined income level can be used in all times and all places to determine poverty. Perhaps the most widely accepted definition of poverty in the United States today is the one developed by the Social Security Administration.

5   To a considerable extent, the reasons for their poverty lie beyond the control of poor people. Some poor adults have suffered a disability of some sort, the premature death of the family breadwinner, or family dissolution. Most heads of poor families have no job.

6   The government aids the poor by providing them with goods and services— food stamps, for instance. Other programs, like Aid to Families with Dependent Children, have given them cash. When these programs are taken into account, the percentage of the population falling below the poverty line has been reduced considerably.

7   There is widespread dissatisfaction with existing antipoverty, or welfare, programs. They are judged to be inefficient, their costs have increased at an alarming rate, and they have provided little incentive for people to get off welfare. In 1996, a major change was made in the nation's welfare programs.

8   Despite recent improvements, the sad fact is that racial discrimination occurs in many walks of life in many areas of the United States. Nonwhites may be cut off from educational and job opportunities, and even when nonwhites do essentially the same kind of work as whites, there is sometimes a tendency to pay them less.

9   There is also much discrimination against women, which makes them less likely than men to enter better-paying occupations. Even after adjusting for factors such as education and work experience, women earn substantially less than men.

Problems and Questions

1   In 1987, there seemed to be bipartisan agreement that Aid to Families with Dependent Children should be transformed into a vehicle for education, training, and work. In what sense is work the solution to dependency? Can training and job placement enable long-term welfare recipients to break out of poverty and dependency?

2   "The Social Security system is actuarially unsound. The amounts currently collected in Social Security taxes do not equal the amounts currently paid out in benefits. We cannot keep this up!" Comment and evaluate.

3   According to some economists, Social Security should be voluntary, not mandatory. Present the arguments on each side of this issue in as much detail as you can.

4   Do the official government statistics concerning poverty recognize that many people below the poverty line receive noncash benefits from the government? If not, does this mean that these statistics are useless? Explain.

5   People are classified as poor on the basis of their current money income. Should the following items also be taken into account?

   (a) The assets of the person or family

   (b) The existence of rich relatives of the person or family

   (c) The person's or family's income over a period of years, not a single year

Key Terms

income inequality   old-age insurance
progressive tax   Medicare
regressive tax   Medicaid
globalization   food programs
poverty   negative income tax
Social Security   discrimination

Viewpoint for Analysis

According to June O'Neill, former head of the Congressional Budget Office, the percent of African American families headed by a woman (no husband present) increased from 22 percent in 1959 to 59 percent in 1990. In her view, "Experts cannot agree on why the female-headed family has increased so dramatically, but there is a growing consensus that growing up in [such a single-parent] family, dependent on welfare, is detrimental for children's chances to do well in school, work, and marriage. . . ."[7]

(a)   Suppose that the welfare system is such that if a family has a father present, it is ineligible for welfare payments. Would you favor such a system? Why or why not?

(b)   Is the encouragement of the formation of such single-parent families the only criticism directed at existing government policies in this area? If not, what are other criticisms?

(c)   Would a negative income tax encourage the formation of such single-parent families?

---

[7] June O'Neill, "The Changing Economic Status of Black Americans," *Economic Times* (New York: Conference Board, February 1993), 5.

Economic Growth

LEARNING OBJECTIVES

➤ To define economic growth and explain how it is measured

➤ To discuss the role of diminishing marginal returns in economic growth

➤ To analyze the effects of investment on economic growth

➤ To explore the role of public policy in promoting economic growth

In 2011, Boeing launched its new 787 Dreamliner, a wide-bodied 210- to 290-passenger jet aircraft. To save time and money in the development process, Boeing used a computer-aided design system first developed for its 777 jet (see Case Study 13.2). To save fuel costs for its customers, the 787 was the first major airliner to use composite, lightweight materials. What are such innovations, and how do they relate to economic growth? One purpose of this chapter is to answer these questions.

Turning from the aircraft industry to the population at large, the human condition has changed considerably during the past two centuries, first in the industrialized countries of the world and more recently in the emerging markets. Rising living standards have brought a decline in poverty, although by no means its disappearance. How has this increase in per capita output been achieved? This question fascinated economists for a long time. Although we still are far from completely understanding the process of economic growth, our knowledge has increased considerably through the efforts of economic researchers, both here and abroad. In this chapter, we will discuss the process of economic growth in industrialized countries.

What Is Economic Growth?

Economic
growth

Real GDP

There are two common measures of the rate of **economic growth**. The first is the rate of growth of a country's real (inflation-adjusted) gross domestic product (**real GDP**), which tells us how rapidly the economy's total real output of goods and services is increasing (gross domestic product is discussed in greater detail in Chapter 15). The second is the rate of growth of *per capita* real gross domestic product (real GDP divided by population), which is a better measure of the rate of increase of a country's standard of living. We use the second measure unless we state otherwise. Two aspects of the rate of growth of per capita real gross domestic product should be noted from the start.

1. *This measure is only a very crude approximation of the rate of increase of economic welfare.* For one thing, gross domestic product does not include one good that people prize most highly: leisure. For another, gross domestic product does not value accurately new products and improvements in the quality of goods and services, nor does it allow properly for noneconomic changes in the quality of life or for the costs of environmental pollution. What's more, gross domestic product does not take into account how the available output is distributed. Clearly, it makes a difference whether the bulk of the population gets a reasonable share of the output or a favored few get most of it.

2. *Small differences in the annual rate of economic growth can make very substantial differences in living standards a few decades later.* For example, per capita real GDP in the United States was about $49,270 in 2012. If it grows at 2 percent per year, it will be about $60,110 (in 2012 dollars) in the year 2022, whereas if it grows at 3 percent per year, it will be about $66,022 (in 2012 dollars) in the year 2022. Thus, an increase of 1 percentage point in the growth rate means an additional $5,912 (roughly 10 percent) increase in per capita real GDP by the year 2022. Even an increase of one-quarter of 1 percentage point can make a considerable difference. If the growth rate increases from 1.75 to 2 percent per year, per capita real GDP in the year 2022 will increase from $59,809 to $60,110.

Economic Growth as a Policy Objective

Following World War II, governments throughout the world became much more involved in trying to stimulate economic growth. In the United States, the government was not much inclined to influence the growth rate before the war. Of course, the government was generally interested in promoting economic growth; but it was normally taken for granted that, left to its own devices, our economy would manage to grow at more or less the proper rate.

Whether the government should increase the rate of economic growth is a political decision, of course; and your opinion of such a government policy depends on many things, including your attitude toward present sacrifice for future material gain. As we will see in subsequent sections, a more rapid rate of growth can often be achieved only if consumers are willing to give up some consumption now so that they and their children can have more goods and services in the future. To the extent that you believe that private decisions place too little weight on the future and too much weight on the present, you may be inclined to support a government policy designed to increase the growth rate. Otherwise, you may not favor such a policy.

Thomas Malthus and Population Growth

A country's rate of economic growth depends, among other things, on how much the quantities of inputs of various kinds increase. To illuminate the nature of the growth process, we will discuss the effect on the rate of economic growth of increasing each kind of input, holding the others constant. We begin by look-ing at the effects of changes in the quantity of labor. Economists have devoted a great deal of attention to the effects of population growth on the rate of eco-nomic growth. The classic work was done by Thomas Malthus (1776–1834), a British parson who devoted his life to academic research. The first professional economist, he taught at a college established by the East India Company to train its administrators—and was called "Pop" by his students behind his back. Whether "Pop" stood for population or not, Malthus's fame is based on his theo-ries of **population growth**.

Population growth

Malthus believed that the population tends to grow at a geometric rate. In his *Essay on the Principle of Population*, published in 1798, he pointed out the implications of such a constant rate of growth:

> If any person will take the trouble to make the calculation, he will see that if the necessities of life could be obtained without limit, and the number of people could be doubled every twenty-five years,[1] the population which might have been produced from a single pair since the Christian era, would have been sufficient, not only to fill the earth quite full of people, so that four should stand in every square yard, but to fill all the planets of our solar system in the same way, and not only them but all the planets revolving around the stars which are visible to the naked eye, supposing each of them . . . to have as many planets belong to it as our sun has.

In contrast to the human population, which tends to increase at a geometric rate, the supply of land can increase slowly if at all. And land, particularly in Malthus's time, was the source of food. Consequently, it seemed to Malthus that the human population was in danger of outrunning its food supply: "Taking the

---

[1] Of course, it does not matter to Malthus's argument whether the population doubles every 25 years or every 40 years. The important thing is that it increases at a geometric rate.

whole earth," he wrote, ". . . and supposing the present population to be equal to a thousand millions, the human species would increase as the numbers 1, 2, 4, 8, 16, 32, 64, 128, 256, and subsistence as 1, 2, 3, 4, 5, 6, 7, 8, 9. In two centuries, the population would be to the means of subsistence as 256 to 9; in three centuries as 4,096 to 13; and in two thousand years the difference would be incalculable."

A Bleak Prospect

Certainly, Malthus's view of humanity's prospects was bleak; as he himself acknowledged, "the view has a melancholy hue." Gone is the optimism of Adam Smith. According to Malthus, the prospect for economic progress was very limited. Given the inexorable increase in human numbers, the standard of living would be kept at the minimum level required to keep body and soul together. If it exceeded this level, the population would increase and drive the standard of living back down. On the other hand, if the standard of living were less than this level, the population would decline because of starvation. Certainly, the long-term prospects were anything but bright. Thomas Carlyle, the famous historian and essayist, called economics "the dismal science." To a considerable extent, economics acquired this bad name through the efforts of Parson Malthus.

Malthus's theory can be interpreted in terms of the law of diminishing marginal returns (discussed in Chapter 3). Living in what was still largely an agricultural society, he emphasized the role of land and labor as resources and assumed a relatively fixed level of technology. Since land is fixed, increases in labor, due to population growth, eventually cause the marginal product of labor to get smaller and smaller because of the law of diminishing marginal returns. (Recall from Chapter 10 that the marginal product of labor is the additional output resulting from an extra unit of labor.) In other words, because of this law, the marginal product of labor behaves as shown in Figure 13.1, with the

FIGURE 13.1

Diminishing Marginal Returns and the Effect of Population Growth

According to Malthus, the labor force tends to equal *P* because if output per worker exceeds *A*, the population increases, and if output per worker is less than *A*, starvation reduces the population.

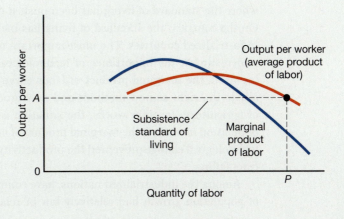

result that continued growth of the labor force ultimately brings economic decline, that is, a reduction in output per worker. This happens because as the marginal product of labor falls with increases in the labor force, the average product of labor eventually falls as well, and the average product of labor is another name for output per worker.

Of course, Malthus recognized that various devices could keep the population down: war, famine, and birth control measures, among others. In fact, he tried to describe and evaluate the importance of various checks on population growth. For example, suppose that population tends to grow to the point where output per worker is at a subsistence level, just sufficient to keep body and soul together. If this is the case and the subsistence level of output per worker is A, then the labor force tends to equal P in Figure 13.1. Why? Because, as noted, Malthus believed that if the standard of living rises appreciably above A, population increases, forcing it back toward A. On the other hand, if the standard of living falls below A, some of the population starves, pushing it back toward A.

Effects of Population Growth

Was Malthus right? Among some developing countries of the world, his analysis might seem relevant today. During the past 60 years, the population of the developing countries has grown very rapidly, in part because of the decrease in death rates, attributable to the transfer of medical advances from the industrialized countries to the developing countries. In recent years, the AIDS epidemic has slowed population growth in parts of the world; however, between 1940 and 1970, the total population of Asia, Africa, and Oceania almost doubled. There has been a tendency for growing populations to push hard against food supplies in some of the countries of Africa, Latin America, and Asia; the Malthusian model can explain important elements of the situation.

However, Malthus's theory seems far less relevant for the industrialized countries. In contrast to his model, population has not increased to the point where the standard of living has been pushed down to the subsistence level. On the contrary, the standard of living has increased dramatically in all the industrialized countries. The most important mistake Malthus made was to underestimate the importance of technological change. Instead of remaining fixed, the marginal product of labor curve in Figure 13.1 moved gradually to the right as new methods and new products increased the efficiency of agriculture. In other words, the situation is as shown in Figure 13.2. As population increased, the marginal product of labor did not go down. Instead, technological change prevented the productivity of extra agricultural workers from falling.

Among the industrialized nations, have countries with relatively high rates of population growth had relatively low or relatively high rates of economic

FIGURE 13.2

Shift over Time in the Marginal Product of Labor

Technological change has shifted the marginal product of labor curve to the right.

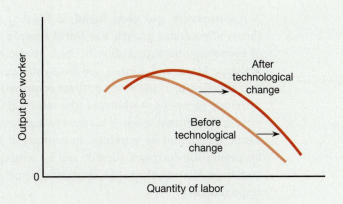

growth? In general, there seems to be little or no relationship between a nation's rate of population increase and its rate of economic growth. Figure 13.3 plots the rate of population increase against the rate of growth of output per person-year in 11 industrialized countries between 1913 and 1959. The results suggest little or no relation between the two measures, and the relationship that exists appears to be direct rather than inverse.

FIGURE 13.3

Relationship between Population Growth and Increases in National Product per Person-Year, 11 Industrialized Countries, 1913–1959

In industrialized countries, there is little or no relationship between a country's rate of population growth and its rate of economic growth.

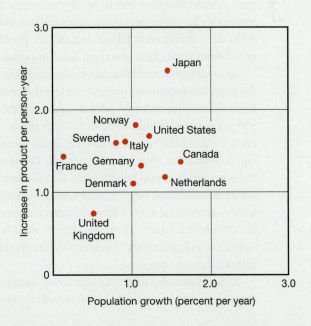

David Ricardo and Capital Formation

A contemporary and good friend of Malthus who also contributed to the theory of economic growth was David Ricardo (1772–1823). Of all the titans of economics, he is probably the least known to the general public. Smith, Malthus, Marx, and Keynes are frequently encountered names. Ricardo is not, although he made many brilliant contributions to economic thought. An extremely successful stockbroker who retired at the age of 42 with a very large fortune, he devoted much of his time to highly theoretical analyses of the economic system and its workings. In contrast to Malthus, who was reviled for his pessimistic doctrines, Ricardo and his writings were widely admired in his own time. He was elected to England's House of Commons and was highly respected there.

Ricardo on Income Distribution

Much of Ricardo's work is concerned with the distribution of income. Unlike Adam Smith, who paid much less attention to the conflict among classes, Ricardo emphasized the struggle between the industrialists (a relatively new and rising class in his time) and the landowners (the old aristocracy that resisted the rise of the industrial class). This clash was reflected in the struggle in Britain around 1800 over the so-called Corn Laws (*corn* being a general term covering all types of grain). Because of the increase in population, the demand for grain increased in Britain, causing the price of grain to rise greatly. This meant higher profits for the landowners. But the industrialists complained bitterly about the increase in the price of food, because higher food prices meant that they had to pay higher wages. As the price of grain increased, merchants began to import cheap grain from abroad. But the landowners, who dominated Parliament, passed legislation, the Corn Laws, to keep cheap grain out of Britain. In effect, the Corn Laws imposed a high tariff, or duty, on grain.

According to Ricardo's analysis, the landlords were bound to capture most of the benefits of economic progress unless their control of the price of grain could be weakened. As national output increased and population expanded, poorer and poorer land would have to be brought under cultivation to produce the extra food. As the cost of producing grain increased, its price would increase, and so would the rents of the landlords. The workers and the industrialists, on the other hand, would benefit little, if at all. As the price of grain increased, the workers would have to get higher wages, but only high enough to keep them at a subsistence level (since Ricardo agreed entirely with his friend Malthus on the population issue). Therefore, the workers would be no better off; neither would the industrialists, who would wind up with lower profits because of the increase in wage rates.

Ricardo believed that the Corn Laws should be repealed and that free trade in grain should be permitted. In a beautiful piece of theoretical analysis that is

CASE STUDY 13.1

THE CLUB OF ROME'S "LIMITS TO GROWTH" REPORT

In 1974, an MIT-based group produced a pessimistic analysis called the Club of Rome's "Limits to Growth" report. The report concluded that if the world's burgeoning population were to consume resources at the rate of the United States, many critical resources, minerals especially, would soon become very scarce, and with scarcity, prices would rise to unacceptable levels and economic and industrial growth would slow down.

The notion was not new. Thomas Malthus in 1798 had considered that population growth, and hence consumption, would soon undermine growth—indeed, civilization itself—in Europe. In 1908, President Theodore Roosevelt worried about a diminishing supply of raw materials and gathered a commission to ponder the future of a United States without minerals and metals. More resources were quickly found. In 1944, there was another review, and 21 commodities were placed on the endangered list. By now, those commodities should have been exhausted. None has been. What has repeatedly pulled us back from the pessimists' brink of doom?

Copper has often been listed as a mineral due for future scarcity. It is subject to fluctuating prices. In peak price years, there is a flurry of exploration, and new low-grade prophyries across the world are added to the tonnage in reserve. But in those peak price years, before new mines have time to develop, another factor comes into play: it becomes cost-effective for users to find substitutes for copper, like aluminum or plastics. And once substitutes are found, copper consumption does not return to its original levels. The telecommunications industry is a recent example where massive substitution has taken place, as fiber optics have come to the fore in intracity communications. So the Club of Rome doomsayers would seem to be discredited on two counts: increased prices generate greater supplies through improved exploration and mining technology, and increased prices encourage substitution of other materials (and the recycling of scrap) to satisfy demand.

But aren't the planet's mineral resources finite? They are, although the geochemical cycle that creates minerals is virtually infinite. Not much gets off the planet, and we have hardly scratched the surface in our search for greater supplies. The costs of extraction from deep within the earth's crust or the ocean floor might look excessively expensive today, but they looked astronomical a century ago, and the relative cost of minerals has remained roughly constant; it has hardly increased even with diminishing returns. Basic raw materials, then, will not run out for centuries. Our growth will continue, less dependent on supplies than on our technological ability and the wisdom of our investment.

In a similar vein, a few years ago the concept of "peak oil" and "peak energy" was quite the rage. The idea was that oil and gas production would "peak" and decline and that this would cause huge problems for continued economic growth. However, thanks to new technologies (and the more efficient use of existing technologies), vast new sources of oil and gas have been discovered in the United States. Current estimates suggest that U.S. oil and gas reserves could last another 200 years—at least.

FIGURE 13.4

Marginal Product of Capital

This curve shows the marginal product of capital under various assumptions concerning the total amount of capital. For example, if there is $100 billion of capital, the marginal product of capital is $A, whereas if there is $150 billion of capital, the marginal product of capital is $B.

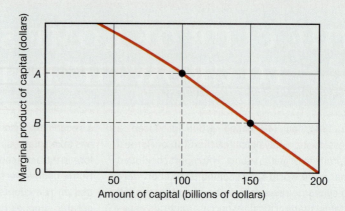

Ricardo's View of Capital Formation

**Capital
formation**

We turn to the effect on economic growth of increases in physical capital, holding other inputs and technology fixed. Ricardo constructed some interesting theories concerning the effects of **capital formation** (that is, investment in plant and equipment) on economic growth. Other things held constant, a nation's output depends on the amount of plant and equipment it has and operates. Moreover, we can draw a curve showing the marginal product of capital (the extra output that results from an extra dollar's worth of capital) under various assumptions about the total amount of capital in existence. This curve slopes downward to the right, as shown in Figure 13.4, because of the law of diminishing marginal returns. As more and more capital is accumulated, its marginal product eventually must decrease. For example, if $100 billion is the total investment in plant and equipment (or total capital), the extra output to

still reasonably fresh and convincing nearly 200 years after its publication,[2] he laid out the basic principles of international trade and pointed out the benefits to all countries that can be derived by specialization and free trade. For example, suppose England is relatively more efficient at producing textiles and France is relatively more efficient at producing wine. Then, on the basis of Ricardo's analysis, it can be shown that each country is likely to be better off by specializing in the product it is more efficient at producing—textiles in England, wine in France—and trading this product for the one the other country specializes in producing. (This concept is discussed at greater length in Chapter 27.)

[2] David Ricardo, *An Essay on the Influence of a Low Price of Corn on the Profits of Stock* (London: John Murray, 1815).

be derived from an extra dollar of investment is worth A; if the total investment is increased to $150 billion, however, the economy must resort to less productive investments, and the extra output to be derived from an extra dollar of investment is only worth B.

The curve in Figure 13.4 leads to the conclusion that investment in plant and equipment, although it increases the growth rate up to some point, eventually is unable to increase it further. As more and more is invested in new plant and equipment, less and less productive projects must be undertaken. Finally, when all the productive projects have been carried out, further investment in plant and equipment is useless. At this point—$200 billion of total capital in Figure 13.4—further investment in plant and equipment do not increase output at all.

This kind of analysis led Ricardo to the pessimistic conclusion that the economy would experience decreases in the profitability of investment in plant and equipment and the eventual termination of economic growth.

Was Ricardo Right?

Have we seen decreases in the profitability of investment in plant and equipment and the eventual termination of economic growth? No. Ricardo, like Malthus, was led astray by underestimating the extent and impact of future changes in technology. Suppose that, because of the development of major new products and processes, lots of new opportunities for profitable investment arise. Obviously, the effect on the curve in Figure 13.4 is to shift it to the right, because there are more investment opportunities than before above a certain level of productivity. But if this curve shifts to the right, as shown in Figure 13.5, we may be able to avoid Ricardo's pessimistic conclusions.

To see how this can occur, note that if X in Figure 13.5 is the relevant curve in a particular year and $100 billion is the total amount of capital, an extra

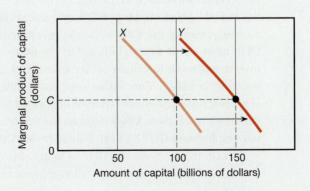

FIGURE 13.5

Effects of Technological Change on the Marginal Product of Capital

Technological change has shifted the marginal product of capital curve to the right. (Actually, Ricardo's variable input was a combined dose of capital and labor.)

dollar of investment in plant and equipment has a marginal product of C. A decade later, if Y is the relevant curve and the total amount of capital has grown to $150 billion, the marginal product of an extra dollar of investment in plant and equipment is still C. Hence, there is no reduction in the productivity of investment opportunities despite the 50 percent increase in the total amount of capital. Because of technological change and other factors, productive and profitable new investment opportunities are opened up as fast as old ones are invested in. The history of the United States is quite consistent with this sort of shift in investment opportunities over time. Even though we have poured an enormous amount of money into new plant and equipment, we have not exhausted or reduced the productivity or profitability of investment opportunities. The rate of return on investment in new plant and equipment has not fallen. Instead, it has fluctuated around a fairly constant level during the past century.

Capital Formation and Economic Growth

To see more clearly the role of investment in the process of economic growth, consider the following example. Suppose that the full-employment (full-capacity), noninflationary GDP this year is $1,000 billion and that investment this year is $100 billion (10 percent of GDP). Let us assume for the sake of simplicity that the remaining $900 billion is consumed. Next year's full-employment GDP will increase because this year's investment will raise the nation's productive capacity. In other words, this year's investment increases next year's full-employment GDP. The amount of the increase in full-employment GDP depends on the **capital-output ratio**, which is the number of dollars of investment (or extra capital goods) required to produce an extra dollar of output. For example, if the capital-output ratio is 2, $2 of investment is required to increase full-employment GDP by $1.

Capital-output ratio

Effect of Investment on Full-Employment GDP

Let us look more closely at the effect of investment on full-employment GDP. If the capital-output ratio is 2, full-employment GDP increases by $50 billion as a consequence of the $100 billion in investment. Therefore, full-employment GDP next year is $1,050 billion. On the other hand, suppose that this year's investment is $200 billion rather than $100 billion and that consumption spending is $800 billion rather than $900 billion (if GDP is $1,000 billion). What will full-employment GDP be next year? If the capital-output ratio is 2, it will be $1,100 billion. Why? Because the $200 billion in investment increases full-employment GDP by $100 billion, from $1,000 billion to $1,100 billion.

Hence, full-employment GDP is larger if investment is $200 billion than if it is $100 billion. Similarly, full-employment GDP is larger if investment

TABLE 13.1

Rate of Growth of
Output and Investment
as a Percentage of
Output (2001–2010)

Country	Output Growth (percent, average annual)	Percent of Output Invested (average annual)
Brazil	3.7	19.5
Canada	1.9	22.1
China	10.5	45.4
France	1.1	19.3
Germany	1.0	17.4
India	7.6	20.5
Japan	0.8	20.1
Russia	4.8	21.5

is $300 billion than if it is $200 billion. If the capital-output ratio is 2, full-employment GDP is $1,150 billion next year if investment is $300 billion. Why? Because the $300 billion in investment increases full-employment GDP by $150 billion, from $1,000 billion to $1,150 billion.

In general, the greater the percentage of GDP that the society devotes to investment this year, the greater the increase in its full-employment GDP. So long as the economy sustains noninflationary full employment and the capital-output ratio remains constant, the rate of growth of national output is directly related to the percentage of GDP devoted to investment.[3]

Some Evidence Concerning the Effects of Investment

Certainly, this result seems sensible enough. If a country wants to increase its growth rate, it should produce more blast furnaces, machine tools, and plows and fewer cosmetics, household furniture, and sports cars. But all this is theory. What do the facts suggest? Table 13.1 shows the rate of investment and the growth rate in six major industrialized nations and four emerging markets (Brazil, China, India, and Russia) in the 2000s. Among the industrialized economies, there is no strong relationship between rate of investment and output growth; in the emerging markets, there is a stronger link between investment and growth. There is growing evidence that the efficiency, or productivity, of capital is much higher in the United States, compared with other industrialized economies.

[3] It can be shown that the rate of growth of GDP equals s/b, where s is the proportion of GDP saved (and invested) and b is the capital-output ratio, assuming that both s and b are constant and full employment is maintained. For example, if $b = 2$ and $s = 0.10$, GDP grows at 5 percent per year, since $0.10/2 = 0.05$. This result is part of the so-called Harrod-Domar growth model developed by the late Sir Roy Harrod, of Oxford, and the late Evsey Domar, of MIT. Although useful, this result must be employed with caution, since it is based on highly simplified assumptions.

This suggests that the same amount of capital can deliver a lot more growth in the United States than, say, in Japan.

The Role of Human Capital

Human capital

A country's rate of economic growth is influenced by the rate at which it invests in **human capital** as well as physical capital. It may seem odd to speak of *human capital*, but every society builds up a certain amount of human capital through investments in formal education, on-the-job training, and health programs. You often hear people talk about investing in their children's future by putting them through college. For the economy as a whole, the expenditure on education and public health can also be viewed, at least partly, as an investment, because consumption is sacrificed in the present to make possible a higher level of per capita output in the future.

The United States invests in human capital on a massive scale. In 2011, U.S. spending on education was roughly $860 billion (or just under 6 percent of GDP). These enormous and rapidly growing investments in human capital have unquestionably increased the productivity, versatility, and adaptability of our labor force. They have certainly made a major contribution to economic growth.

Income tends to rise with a person's education. This is often referred to as the "education premium," and it has risen in recent decades. For example, in 1980, people with a college degree earned around 40 percent more than those with only a high school education. But by 2000, this education premium had widened to around 80 percent and has undoubtedly become even bigger in the past decade.

The Role of Technological Change

Technological change

A country's rate of economic growth depends on the rate of **technological change** as well as the extent to which quantities of inputs of various kinds increase. Indeed, the rate of technological change is perhaps the most important single determinant of a country's rate of economic growth. Recall from Chapter 1 that technology is knowledge concerning the industrial and agricultural arts (technology and technological change are also discussed in Chapter 23). Therefore, technological change often takes the form of new methods of producing existing products; new designs that make it possible to produce goods with important new characteristics; and new techniques of organization, marketing, and management. Two examples of technological change are new ways of producing power (for example, wind and solar power) and new ways of transmitting data (for example, fiber optics and wireless).

We already saw that technological change can shift the curves in both Figures 13.2 and 13.5, warding off the law of diminishing marginal returns.

COMPUTER-ASSISTED DESIGN AND MANUFACTURE AT BOEING AIRCRAFT

In the 1960s and 1970s, the design and manufacture of a Boeing 727 or 747 were far from smooth processes. Drawings were done by hand and passed from hand to hand with each requested improvement. When designs got to the shop floor, often they did not quite fit. Parts had to be rejigged, shaved, and modified here and there. The manufacturing process was full of fits and starts—beautiful and safe in the end, but inefficient and expensive getting there.

In 1978 and 1979, work began on the Boeing 767 and 757. Sophisticated interactive computer graphics were developed for drafting the designs. Each part, each point on every surface, was built into a mathematical program and stored on computer to be manipulated for any slight change. A set of drawings could now be changed in a day, rather than a week, and with more accuracy than before. *Computer-assisted design (CAD)* had arrived in the aircraft industry.

In the back rooms, productivity and growth increased.

The effect was felt on the assembly line, too. Fewer modifications had to be made on the shop floor. Costs were reduced because the designs could be applied more accurately. Airplane components fit together better. *Computer-assisted manufacturing (CAM)* controlled equipment precisely and so turned out wingskins, spare assemblies, and dozens of delicate rivets of high quality.

It all took some time to go through the learning process, but Boeing now experiences less overtime in rework and fewer delays in startup. For the newest generation of planes, such as the 777 and the 787 Dreamliner, productivity is enhanced even more as computers are more fully linked in design and manufacture. Technology continues to increase growth in output per hour of labor.

But note that new knowledge by itself has little impact. Unless knowledge is *applied*, it has little effect on the rate of economic growth. A change in technology, when applied for the first time, is called an *innovation*, and the firm that first applies it is called an *innovator*. Innovation is a key stage in the process leading to the full evaluation and utilization of a new process or product. The innovator must be willing to take the risks involved in introducing a new and untried process, good, or service; and in many cases, these risks are high. Once a change in technology has been applied for the first time, the **diffusion process** (the process by which the use of the innovation spreads from firm to firm and from use to use) begins. How rapidly an innovation spreads depends heavily on its economic advantages over older methods or products. The more profitable the innovation, the more rapidly it will spread.

Diffusion process

Joseph Schumpeter (1883–1950), Harvard's distinguished economist and social theorist, stressed the important role played by innovators in the process of economic growth. In Schumpeter's view, innovators are the mainspring of economic progress, the people with the foresight to see how new things can be brought into being and the courage and resourcefulness to surmount the obstacles to change. For this trouble, innovators receive profit, but this profit eventually is whittled down by competitors who imitate the innovators. The innovators push the curves in Figures 13.2 and 13.5 to the right, and once their innovations are assimilated by the economy, other innovators may shove these curves somewhat farther to the right. For example, one innovator introduces vacuum tubes, and a later innovator introduces semiconductors; one innovator introduces the steam locomotive, and a later innovator introduces the diesel locomotive. This process goes on and on and is a main source of economic growth.

Endogenous Technological Change

Recent economic theories stress that the rate and direction of technological change is influenced by economic factors, a fact long recognized by economists who study technology. In the jargon of economists, technological change is to some extent *endogenous*, which means that it is determined within (not outside) the overall economic system. While invention is an activity characterized by great uncertainty, it nonetheless shares most of the characteristics of other economic activities. In particular, the amount of resources devoted to inventing in a particular field depends heavily on how profitable the production of such inventions is.

Thus, the rate of technological change in a particular area is influenced by the same kinds of factors that determine the output of any good or service. On the one hand, demand factors influence the level of profits from particular types of technological change. For example, if a prospective change in technology will reduce the cost of a particular product, increases in the demand for the product are likely to increase the returns from effecting this technological change. Similarly, a growing shortage (and a rising price) of the inputs saved by the technological change are likely to increase the returns from implementing those technologies. As an illustration, consider the history of English textile inventions. During the eighteenth century, there was an increase in the demand for yarn due to decreases in the price of cloth and increased cloth output. This increase in demand, as well as shortages of spinners and increases in their wages, raised the returns to inventions that increased productivity in the spinning processes and directly stimulated the work leading to such major inventions as the water frame, the spinning jenny, and the spinning mule.

On the other hand, supply factors also influence the cost of making particular kinds of technological change. Obviously, whether people try to solve a given problem depends on whether they think it can be solved and how costly they think it is to solve, as well as on the expected payoff if they are successful. The cost of making science-based technological changes depends on the number of scientists and engineers in relevant fields and advances in basic science; for example, advances in physics clearly reduced the cost of effecting changes in technology in the field of atomic energy. In addition, the rate of technological change depends on the amount of effort devoted to making modest improvements that lean heavily on practical experience. Despite our tendency to focus on spectacular inventions, technological change in many industries may be due chiefly to a succession of minor improvements; for example, it has been shown that technological change in shipbuilding has been largely the result of small, gradual enhancements. In industries where this is a dominant source of technological change and where technological change is only loosely connected with scientific advance, we would expect the rate of technological change to depend on the number of people working in the industry, especially in positions to make improvements of this sort.

Entrepreneurship and the Social Environment

Still another set of factors influencing a country's level of potential output and its rate of economic growth is its economic, social, political, and religious climate. It is difficult, if not impossible, to measure the effect of these factors, but there can be no doubt of their importance. Some societies despise material goods and emphasize the glories of the next world. Some societies are subject to such violent political upheavals that it is risky, if not foolish, to invest in the future. Some societies are governed so corruptly that economic growth is frustrated. And some societies look down on people engaged in industry, trade, or commerce. Obviously, such societies are less likely to experience rapid economic growth than others with a more favorable climate and conditions.

The relatively rapid economic growth of the United States was undoubtedly stimulated in part by the attitude of its people toward material gain. It is commonplace to note that the United States is a materialistic society, a society that esteems business success, bestows prestige on the rich, accepts the Protestant ethic (which, crudely stated, is that work is good), and encourages individual initiative. The United States has been criticized over and over again for some of these traits, often by countries frantically trying to imitate its economic success. Somewhat less obvious is the fact that the United States is a young country whose people came from a variety of origins, so it did not inherit many feudal components in the structure of its society. This, too, was important in promoting economic growth.

The United States has also been characterized by great economic and political freedom, institutions flexible enough to adjust to change, and a government that encourages competition in the marketplace. This has meant fewer barriers to new ideas. Also, the United States has, for a long time, enjoyed internal peace, order, and general respect for property rights. There have been no violent revolutions since the Civil War, and for many years, we were protected from strife in other lands by two oceans, which then seemed much broader than they do now. All these factors undoubtedly contributed to rapid economic growth.

Entrepreneurs

The U.S. economy also seems to have been able to nurture a great many **entrepreneurs** and a vast horde of competent business executives. During the twentieth century, U.S. entrepreneurs were responsible for such basic innovations as the automobile assembly line, pioneered by Henry Ford (see Case Study 13.3). In many areas, the United States gained a technological lead over other countries, which it maintained for many years. But in the past four or five decades, according to many observers, our technological lead has been reduced considerably, and this is a major concern among U.S. government officials and business executives.

The Gap between Actual and Potential Output

Up to this point, our discussion of economic growth has centered on the factors that determine how rapidly a country's potential output grows—factors like technological change, increased education, investment in plant and equipment, and increases in the labor force. In other words, we have focused on the factors responsible for rightward shifts of the long-run supply curve for the whole economy. Although we have paid little attention in this chapter to the gap between actual and potential output, this does not mean that increases in per capita output cannot be achieved by reducing this gap. Obviously, they can be.

THE FORD ASSEMBLY LINE

Ford's Highland Park factory, 1913

By the beginning of the twentieth century, there were dozens of different models of automobiles. Made in tiny machine shops, all were designed and made differently, some gas driven, some steam driven, some electric. With car prices at around $5,000, the embryonic industry was supported by the New England wealthy. In Michigan machine shops, however, there was another idea: getting a car on the road for $1,000.

By 1908, the first Model T rolled off Henry Ford's plant in Highland Park, Detroit. That year, Ford led the industry in the number of cars sold and turned a $3 million profit. Yet, in a country of 89 million people, there were still fewer than 200,000 automobiles. To sell more cars, there had to be further reduction in price. Ford and his friends figured out that a $600 car

would tap this market. Between 1912 and 1914, the new Highland Park factory was completely reorganized. Before then, a worker spent half his day walking about to get small components for the assembly of the main component, which stayed in one place until assembly was complete. Ford's idea was to place the machine tools in such a way that the car parts could move past the equipment to complete subassembly, then these partially assembled parts would move past other lines of tools to final assembly. Stationary workers would help the line along.

To attain this goal, Ford first had to rationalize work tasks and routines by making them more efficient and using new technologies. He invested in labor; his stunning $5-a-day wage rate doubled the Michigan average overnight, and his workforce also stabilized overnight from a terrible 60 percent turnover rate per month. A second requirement was a standard design: cars must come off the line as alike as pins at a pin factory. But above all, Ford had to risk a heavy investment in machine tools and the moving assembly plant. In 1914, the Highland Park factory represented $3.6 million in new plant and $2.8 million in machine tool equipment. Although these tools were complicated, they were called *farmer's tools*, because they allowed even green farmhands to produce large quantities of high-quality work.

Output per worker shot up. Labor hours per engine dropped from 35 to 23; a person who formerly made 35 magnetos in a day could now produce 95; and most radical of all, the endless chain-driven conveyor for chassis production meant that a chassis was turned out in 1.5 labor-hours, compared with 12.5 labor-hours before. Each worker had more equipment to use, and although the wage had doubled, output increased even more.

Sales of the Model T rose from 78,000 units to 500,000 units, and the price came down to $600 per car and then to $360 per car in 1916.

However, only so much can be achieved by squeezing the slack out of the economy. For example, if there is a 7 percent unemployment rate, per capita output can be increased by perhaps 6 percent simply by reducing the unemployment rate to 5 percent. But this is a one-shot improvement. To get any further increase in per capita output, the country must increase its potential output. This does not mean that it is not important to maintain a high level of employment in the economy. Of course it is, for reasons we will discuss at length in Chapter 16. But once the economy gets to full employment, no further increase in per capita output can occur by this route. If a country wants further increases in per capita output over the long haul, it must influence the factors responsible for the rate of growth of potential output.

One of the most positive developments of the late 1990s and early 2000s was a significant increase in productivity growth in the United States. On the basis of this, economists estimated that instead of growing at 2.5 percent, potential real GDP increased at a rate of 3.5 percent. A 1 percentage point increase in trend growth over an extended period of time can have a huge impact on per capita income and standard of living. This "productivity miracle" was largely due to the ability of the United States to take advantage of the supply-side benefits of the twin technological revolutions of the PC and the Internet. Working in the United States's favor have been its flexible labor markets, relatively liberal immigration policies, vibrant venture capital markets, strong entrepreneurial culture, and open, competitive product markets. Unfortunately, productivity growth has slowed in recent years. The challenge now is to put in place policies that will once again bring about a resurgence of growth.

TECHNOLOGY AND THE RAPID RISE IN LIVING STANDARDS

Until around 1800, living standards were stagnant. Then came the Industrial Revolution, and ever since, they have increased 20- to 30-fold in countries such as the United States. Successive waves of new technologies have delivered not only greater productivity and higher levels of material well-being, but longer life spans, better health and education, lower levels of poverty, and greater time for leisure.

The Internet is simply the latest—though far from the last—wave of technological change. It has transformed the way we do business and the way we lead our personal lives. Businesses use the Internet to interact with suppliers and customers—in many instances reducing the need for intermediaries. The Internet has

allowed small companies and start-ups to compete with larger corporations and become large in the process—think Google and Yahoo! It has also fostered the creation of many new companies doing things that had never been done before—think YouTube, Facebook, Twitter, and Zipcar.

The Internet has also transformed the lives of ordinary people—allowing them, for example, to comparison-shop on line, to make travel arrangements without having to go through a travel agent, and to get college credits from home.

Technology has accounted for one-third to one-half of the rapid growth of the past two centuries. The Internet is no exception.

REVIEW AND PRACTICE

Summary

1 Economic growth is measured by the increase of per capita real gross domestic product, an index that does not measure accurately the growth of economic welfare but is often used as a first approximation.

2 One factor that may influence a country's rate of economic growth is the rate at which its population grows. In Malthus's view, population growth, unless checked in some way, ultimately means economic decline, since output cannot grow in proportion to the growth in population. The law of diminishing marginal returns ensures that beyond some point, holding the quantity of land constant, increases in labor result in smaller and smaller increments of output. However, Malthus underestimated the extent and importance of technological change, which offsets the law of diminishing marginal returns.

3 Another factor that determines whether per capita output grows rapidly or slowly is the rate of expenditure on new plants and equipment. Without

technological change, more and more of this sort of investment results in increases in the amount of capital per dollar of output and decreases in the profitability of investment in plant and equipment, as Ricardo pointed out. But because of technological change, none of these things has occurred. According to the available evidence, a country's rate of economic growth seems directly related to its rate of investment in plant and equipment.

4 A factor with an important effect on a country's rate of economic growth is the rate at which it invests in human capital. The United States invests in human capital on a massive scale, and these enormous and rapidly growing investments have unquestionably increased the productivity, versatility, and adaptability of our labor force.

5 To a considerable extent, economic growth here and abroad has resulted from technological change. A change in technology, when applied for the first time, is called an innovation, and the firm that first applies it is called an innovator. Innovation is a key stage in the process leading to the full evaluation and utilization of a new process or product. Unless knowledge is used, it has little effect on the rate of economic growth.

6 Still another set of factors influencing the rate of economic growth is the economic, social, religious, and political climate of the country. Some societies despise material goods, are subject to violent political upheavals, or are governed by corrupt groups. Such societies are unlikely to have a high rate of economic growth.

7 Finally, the rate of economic growth is also affected by the extent and behavior of the gap between actual and potential GDP. However, once a country gets to full employment, it cannot grow further by reducing this gap.

Problems and Questions

1 Suppose that a society produces only two goods, food and tractors, and in 2001 and 2002, the maximum quantity of food that it could produce when it produced various quantities of tractors was as follows:

Quantity of Food (millions of tons)	Quantity of Tractors (thousands of tractors)
0	9
1	8
2	7
3	5
4	3
5	0

If this society produced 4,000 tractors and 3 million tons of food in 2001 and 5,000 tractors and 3 million tons of food in 2002 (its population remaining constant), did any economic growth occur between 2001 and 2002? If so, to what was it due?

2   Suppose that the society in question 1 produced 6,000 tractors and 3 million tons of food in 2003 (its population remaining the same as in 2002). Did any economic growth occur between 2002 and 2003? If so, was it due entirely to a shift in the production possibilities curve? How can you tell?

3   Suppose a society produces only one commodity, wheat, and has the following aggregate production function:

Hours of Labor (millions)	Bushels of Wheat (billions)
0	0
1	2
2	4
3	6
4	7
5	7

What is the marginal product of labor when between 1 million and 2 million hours of labor are used? When between 2 million and 3 million hours of labor are used? When between 4 million and 5 million hours of labor are used? Do the results conform to the law of diminishing marginal returns? Why or why not?

4   Suppose that an advance in technology doubles the output that can be obtained from each amount of labor in question 3. Under these new conditions, what is the marginal product of labor when between 1 million and 2 million hours of labor are used? When between 4 million and 5 million hours of labor are used? Do the results conform to the law of diminishing marginal returns? Why or why not?

5   In question 3, suppose that the subsistence wage was 1,400 bushels of wheat. According to Malthus, what would have been the equilibrium labor force? What factors would push the labor force toward this level? What would be the effect of the technological advance in question 4 on the equilibrium labor force?

6   Some studies indicate that what matters most to people is their income relative to others around them rather than the absolute level of their income. Would this fact tend to reduce the importance of growth as a means of helping the poor? Explain.

7 "Ricardo's pessimistic view of the prospects for economic growth stemmed from his assumptions concerning the capital-output ratio. If he had recognized that it was not fixed, he would have been closer to correct." Comment and evaluate.

Key Terms

economic growth
real GDP
population growth
capital formation
capital-output ratio
human capital
technological change
diffusion process
entrepreneurs

Viewpoint for Analysis

In his 2005 book, Harvard economist Benjamin M. Friedman wrote, "Economic growth—meaning a rising standard of living for the clear majority of citizens—more often than not fosters greater opportunity, tolerance of diversity, social mobility, commitment to fairness, and dedication to democracy."[4]

(a) When living standards are rising, would you expect there to be more or less temptation for countries to go to war?

(b) Is it a coincidence that the American civil rights movement gained momentum during the 1960s, when economic growth was very strong?

[4] Benjamin M. Friedman, *The Moral Consequences of Economic Growth* (New York: Knopf, 2005).

Public Goods and the Role of the Government

LEARNING OBJECTIVES

➤ To consider the extent of the government's role in the economy

➤ To describe the characteristics of a public good

➤ To explore the nature and importance of externalities

➤ To understand the concept of tax incidence

➤ To explain the purposes of the tax system

During his first term as president, Bill Clinton talked about raising cigarette taxes by $2 a pack. What would be the effect of such a tax increase, and is the government justified in getting involved in this way in the nation's economy? One purpose of this chapter is to discuss these questions.

To state that the United States is a mixed capitalist system, in which both government decisions and the price system play important roles, is hardly to provoke a controversy. But going a step beyond takes us into areas where viewpoints often diverge. The proper functions of government and the desirable size and nature of government expenditures and taxes are not matters on which all agree. Indeed, the questions of how big government should be and what its proper functions should be are hotly debated by conservatives and liberals throughout the land. In Chapters 18 through 26, we will discuss the role of the government in stabilizing economic fluctuations. In this chapter, we will consider other roles for the government in the economy.

What Functions Should the Government Perform?

In Chapter 2, we discussed the limitations of the price system. Although it is generally agreed that there is a role for the government to redistribute income in favor of the poor, provide public goods, and offset the effects of external economies and diseconomies, considerable disagreement remains over how far the government should go in these areas and what additional areas the government should be responsible for. Some people feel that "big government" is already a problem, that government is doing too much. Others believe that the public sector of the economy is being undernourished and that government should be allowed to do more. This is a fundamental question, one that involves a great deal more than economics.

The Conservative View

Conservatives, such as the late Nobel laureate Milton Friedman, believe that the government's role should be limited severely. They believe that economic and political freedom is likely to be undermined by excessive reliance on the state. Moreover, they tend to be skeptical about the government's ability to solve the social and economic problems at hand. They feel that the prevailing faith in the government's power to make a substantial dent in these problems is unreasonable, and they call for more and better information concerning the sorts of tasks government can reasonably be expected to do—and do well. They point to the slowness of the government bureaucracy, the difficulty in controlling huge government organizations, the inefficiencies political considerations can breed, and the difficulties in telling whether government programs are successful or not. On the basis of these considerations, they argue that the government's role should be carefully circumscribed.

The flavor of the conservative position on this question is evident in the remarks of the late George Stigler, another Nobel laureate at the University of Chicago:

> I consider myself courageous, or at least obtuse, in arguing for a reduction in governmental controls over economic life. You are surely desirous of improving this world, and it assuredly needs an immense amount of improvement. No method of displaying one's public-spiritedness is more popular than to notice a problem and pass a law. It combines ease, the warmth of benevolence, and a suitable disrespect for a less enlightened era. What I propose is, for most people, much less attractive: close study of the comparative performance of public and private economy, and the dispassionate appraisal of special remedies that is involved in compassion for the community at large.[1]

[1] George J. Stigler and Paul A. Samuelson, "A Dialogue on the Proper Economic Role of the State," *Selected Papers*, No. 7, Graduate School of Business, University of Chicago, 1968.

The Liberal View

To such remarks, liberals respond with very telling salvos of their own. Just as conservatives tend to be skeptical of the government's ability to solve important social and economic problems, so liberals tend to be skeptical about the price system's ability to solve these problems. They point to the important limitations of the price system and assert that the government can do a great deal to overcome these limitations by regulating private activity and subsidizing and providing goods and services of which the private sector produces too little.

According to some distinguished liberals, like the late John Kenneth Galbraith, of Harvard, the public sector of the economy has been starved of needed resources, while the private sector has catered to relatively unimportant wants. In his best-selling book, *The Affluent Society*, Galbraith argues that consumers are led by advertising and other promotional efforts to purchase more and more goods of marginal significance to them. On the other hand, in his opinion, the nation is suffering because too little is spent on government services like education, transportation, and urban renewal.[2]

Liberals tend to be less concerned than conservatives about the effects on personal freedom of greater government intervention in the economy. They point out that the price system also involves a form of coercion by awarding the available goods and services to those who can pay their equilibrium price. In their view, people who are awarded only a pittance by the price system are coerced into discomfort and malnutrition.

Establishing the "Rules of The Game"

Rules of the game

Although there is considerable disagreement over the proper role of the government, both conservatives and liberals agree that it must do certain things. The first of these is to establish the **rules of the game**, a legal, social, and competitive framework enabling the price system to function as it should.

Maintaining a Legal and Social Framework

Specifically, the government must see to it that contracts are enforced, private ownership is protected, and fraud is prevented. Clearly, these matters must be tended to if the price system is to work properly. Also, the government must maintain order (through the establishment of police and other forces), establish a monetary system (so that money can be used to facilitate trade and exchange), and provide standards for the weight and quality of products.

As an example of this sort of government intervention, consider the Pure Food and Drug Act. This act, originally passed in 1906 and subsequently amended in various ways, protects the consumer against improper and

---

[2] J. K. Galbraith, *The Affluent Society*, 3d rev. ed. (New York: New American Library, 1978). For a quite different viewpoint, see M. Friedman, *Capitalism and Freedom* (Chicago: University of Chicago Press, 1962).

fraudulent activities on the part of producers of foods and drugs. It prohibits the merchandising of impure or falsely labeled food or drugs, and it requires that producers specify the quantity and quality of the contents on labels. These requirements strengthen the price system. Without them, the typical consumer would be unable to tell whether food or drugs are pure or properly labeled. Unless consumers can be sure that they are getting what they pay for, the basic logic underlying the price system breaks down. Similar regulations and legislation have been instituted in fields other than food and drugs for similar reasons.

Maintaining a Competitive Framework

In addition to establishing a legal and social framework that enables the price system to do its job, the government must see to it that markets remain reasonably competitive. Only if markets are competitive will prices reflect consumer desires properly. If, on the other hand, markets are dominated by a few sellers (or a few buyers), prices may be rigged by these sellers (or buyers) to promote their own interests. For example, if a single firm is the sole producer of aluminum, it is a safe bet that this firm will establish a higher price than if there were many aluminum producers competing among themselves. In Chapters 7 and 8, we studied the social problems due to monopoly.

Redistribution of Income

We have already noted the general agreement that governments should redistribute income in favor of the poor. In other words, it is usually felt that help should be given to people who are ill, handicapped, old and infirm, disabled, or unable for other reasons to provide for themselves. To some extent, the nation has decided that income (or at least a certain minimum income) should be divorced from productive services. Of course, this does not mean that people who are too lazy to work should be given a handout. It does mean that people who cannot provide for themselves should be helped. To implement this prin-

Income redistribution

ciple of **income redistribution**, various payments are made by the government to needy people, including the aged, the handicapped, and the unemployed.

These welfare payments are to some extent a "depression baby," for they grew substantially during the Great Depression of the 1930s, when relief payments became a necessity. But they also represent a feeling shared by a large segment of the population that human beings should be assured that however the wheel of fortune spins and whatever number comes up, they will not starve and their children will not be deprived of a healthy environment and basic schooling. Of course, someone has to pay for this. Welfare payments allow the poor to take more from the nation's output than they produce. In general, the more affluent members of society contribute some of their claims on output to pay for these programs by paying taxes. By using its expenditures to help certain groups and by taxing other groups to pay for these programs, the government accomplishes each year, without revolt and without bayonets, a substantial redistribution of income. This is a crucial aspect of the government's role in our economy and was discussed in some length in Chapter 12.

Providing Public Goods

Public goods

As we have indicated, the government provides many **public goods**. In this section, we will consider the nature of public goods in more detail.

What Is a Public Good?

One hallmark of a public good is that it can be consumed by one person without diminishing the amount that other people consume of it. Public goods tend to be relatively indivisible; they often come in such large units that they cannot be broken into pieces that can be bought or sold in ordinary markets. Also, once such goods are produced, there is no way to bar certain citizens from consuming them. Whether or not citizens contribute toward their cost, they benefit from them. This means that the price system cannot be used to handle the production and distribution of such goods.

An oft-cited example of a public good is a lighthouse. There might be general agreement that the cost of building a particular lighthouse would be more than justified by the benefits (saving lives and fewer shipwrecks). Nonetheless, no private firm or person would build and operate such a lighthouse because they might not be able to charge the ships using the lighthouse for the service.[3] Nor would any single user gain enough from the lighthouse to warrant constructing and operating it. Moreover, voluntary contributions are very unlikely to support such a lighthouse, because individual users are likely to feel that their contribution does not affect whether it is built and they will be able to use the lighthouse whether or not they contribute. Consequently, the lighthouse might be established and operated only if the government intervenes.

National Defense: A Major Example

National defense is another example of a public good. The benefits of expenditure on national defense extend to the entire nation. Extension of the benefits of national defense to an additional citizen does not mean that any other citizen gets less of these benefits. Also, there is no way of preventing citizens from benefiting from them, whether they contribute to their cost or not. Hence, there is no way to use the price system to provide for national defense. Since it is a public good, national defense, if it is to reach an adequate level, must be provided by the government.

---

[3] Under some circumstances, lighthouses have been able to charge users. For example, English lighthouses sometimes assessed the shipowners at the docks. Ordinarily, only one ship was in sight of the lighthouse at a particular point in time. The light would not be shown if the ship (which was identified by its flag) had not paid.

THE CASE OF 9/11— WHY AIRPORTS CAN BE PRIVATIZED, BUT AIRPORT SECURITY CANNOT

The horrific events of September 11, 2001, and the policy mistakes that led up to them are replete with lessons in foreign policy, national security, antiterrorism, and yes, economics. One of the principal economic lessons has to do with the simple fact that airport security cannot be left to the private sector. It is a quintessential example of a public good.

Before 9/11, the U.S. government had pushed the responsibility and cost of airline security onto the airlines themselves (and in some cases to private and public terminal operators). These costs were largely passed on to passengers. So far, so good. However, airlines were under severe competitive pressures from low-cost carriers. The need to cut costs forced them to slash all kinds of expenditures, especially fixed costs such as airport security. The number and quality of the personnel at airport security points declined. In the process, the United States left itself vulnerable to terrorist attacks.

After 9/11, the administration of George W. Bush was initially reluctant to let airport security agents become government employees, once again failing to acknowledge the public goods nature of airport security. But in November 2001, the Transportation Security Administration (TSA) was created, and tens of thousands of Transportation Security Officers (TSOs) were hired as employees of the federal government. A few airports still have private security agents, but they work under the authority of the TSA.

The operations of the TSA have been fraught with problems, including a number of covert security test failures, in which explosives and weapons have cleared airport checkpoints. However, the problems associated with the government's provision of public security (and other public goods) are likely to be less detrimental than if left to the private sector.

Decision Making Regarding Public Goods

Essentially, deciding how much to produce of a public good is a political decision. The citizens of the United States elect officials who decide how much should be spent on national defense and how it should be spent. These elected representatives are responsive to special interest groups as well as to the people as a whole. Many special interest groups lobby hard for the production of certain public goods. For example, an alliance of military and industrial groups presses for increased defense expenditures.

The tax system is used to pay for the production of public goods. In effect, the government says to each citizen, "Contribute a certain amount of money to pay for the expenses incurred by the government." The amount particular citizens are assessed may depend on their income (as in the income tax), the value of all or specific types of their property (as in the property tax), the amount they spend on certain types of goods and services (as in the sales tax), or still other criteria. In the last few decades, the tax system has often been the object of enormous controversy. Much more will be said about the tax system, and the controversies swirling around it, in a later section of this chapter.

Externalities

It is generally agreed that the government should act in regard to **externalities**; it should encourage the production of goods and services that entail external economies and discourage the production of those that entail external diseconomies. Take the pollution of air and water, discussed in Chapter 9. When a firm or individual dumps wastes into the water or air, other firms or individuals often must pay all or part of the cost of putting the water or air back into a usable condition. Thus, the disposal of these wastes entails external diseconomies. Unless the government prohibits certain kinds of pollution, enforces air and water quality standards, charges polluters in accord with the amount of waste they dump into the environment, or issues transferable emissions permits, there will be socially undesirable levels of pollution.

Externalities

Effects of External Diseconomies

To see how diseconomies affect the social desirability of the output of a competitive industry, consider Figure 14.1, where the industry's demand and supply curves are contained in the top left-hand panel. As shown there, the equilibrium output of the industry is Q_0. If the industry results in no external economies or diseconomies, this is likely to be the socially optimal output. But what if the industry results in external diseconomies, such as the pollution just described? Then the industry's supply curve does not fully reflect the true social costs of producing the product. The supply curve that reflects these social costs is S_1, which, as shown in the top right-hand panel of Figure 14.1, lies to the left of the industry's supply curve. The optimal output of the good is Q_1, which is less than the competitive output Q_0.

What can the government do to correct this situation? It can intervene in many ways to reduce the industry's output from Q_0 to Q_1. For example, it can impose taxes on the industry. Taxes of the right type and amount result in the desired reduction of output.

FIGURE 14.1

Effect of External Economies and Diseconomies on the Optimal Output of a Competitive Industry

The optimal output is Q_0 if neither external economies nor external diseconomies are present. If there are external diseconomies, curve S_1 reflects the true social costs of producing the product and Q_1 is the optimal output. If there are external economies, curve D_1 reflects the true social benefits of producing the product and Q_2 is the optimal output.

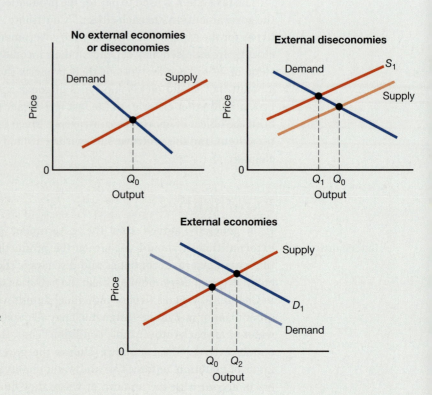

Effects of External Economies

What if the industry results in external economies? For example, what if the manufacture of one industrial product makes it cheaper to produce other products? A lot of industry R&D, with benefits to companies other than the developer, falls into this category. In such cases, the industry's demand curve underestimates the true social benefits of producing the product. The demand curve that reflects these social benefits correctly is D_1, which, as shown in the bottom panel of Figure 14.1, lies to the right of the industry's demand curve. The optimal output of the good is Q_2, which is greater than the competitive output Q_0.

As in the case where the industry results in external diseconomies, the government can intervene in various ways to change the industry's output. But in this case, the object is to increase, not decrease, its output. To accomplish this, the government can, among other things, grant subsidies to the industry. Subsidies of the right type and amount can be used to increase the industry's output from Q_0 to Q_2.

The Theory of Public Choice

According to many economists interested in the theory of public choice, many factors induce the government to make decisions that are not efficient from an economic point of view. Just as the price system suffers from certain limitations, the government also has shortcomings as a mechanism for promoting economic welfare. These factors, discussed next, often result in expanded government expenditures.

Special Interest Groups

It is no secret that politicians try to stay in office. In some cases, they must decide whether to adopt a policy that benefits a small number of people, each of whom gains a great deal, at the expense of a very large number of people, each of whom loses very little. The small group of gainers (the *special interest group*) is likely to be well organized, well financed, and vocal. The large group of losers is likely to be unaware of its losses and more indifferent to the outcome of this decision, since each member of this group has little at stake. In a case of this sort, a politician is inclined to adopt the policy favoring the special interest group. Why? Because the politician, by not adopting this policy, would lose the support of this group. On the other hand, by adopting this policy, the politician is unlikely to lose the support of the large group of people hurt by it, because they are much more interested in other issues where they have more at stake.

Politicians frequently adopt policies favoring special interest groups even though the total gains to the special interest groups are less than the total losses to other segments of society. Whereas such policies are unsound economics, they have been regarded as good politics. One example is the enactment of tariffs and quotas that reduce domestic competition and result in consumers paying higher prices. Also, government services that benefit special interest groups often are expanded to the detriment of society at large.

Bureaucratic Inefficiency

Many observers contend that government agencies are less efficient than private firms. As we have seen in previous chapters, the price system establishes strong incentives for firms to minimize their costs. Firms that can lower their costs can increase their profits, at least temporarily. Government officials, on the other hand, often have less incentive to reduce costs. Indeed, it is sometimes claimed that there is an incentive to increase costs, since an agency's power and influence are directly related to the size of its budget. Unfortunately, we have very little hard data concerning whatever differences may exist between the efficiency of government agencies and the efficiency of private firms, largely because of the difficulties in measuring the efficiency or inefficiency of government agencies. For example, how efficient is the Environmental Protection Agency? Because it

THE TENNESSEE VALLEY AUTHORITY

The TVA dam at Fort Loudoun

The Great Mississippi Flood of 1927 left 800,000 homeless and focused national attention on the federal government's responsibility for flood control. Such control had been considered for years on the Tennessee River. Senator George W. Norris, of Nebraska, campaigned for federal support for river control in the 1920s and early 1930s, but his attempts were unsuccessful, largely because local utilities feared that by building dams, the federal government would be providing not only flood control but electric power as well. The debate continued until 1933, when the Roosevelt administration created the Tennessee Valley Authority (TVA). The TVA was foremost a construction project that would create jobs in a depressed economy, but it was also created for regional development that would yield benefits for many

years to come. In addition to its responsibility for flood control and improving the navigability of the Tennessee's waters, the TVA built housing, worked on agricultural development, and provided electric power to the depressed area. And the local utilities challenged the TVA all the way.

By 1954, the TVA was well established and requested funds from Congress to build a steam-driven electric plant. Congress rejected the proposal because it did not feel that the TVA should be expanded into a federal power facility not exclusively hydroelectric or that it should be made into an even larger business.

Why is it proper for the government to provide for flood control, but not to build steam-driven electric power plants? The rationale for the government providing a service is a breakdown of the free market, that is, the failure of the private sector to provide the proper quantity of certain goods and services. Flood control and navigation are clearly public goods, and insofar as electrification is a by-product of flood control, it is reasonable for the government to provide this service, too. But the proposed steam-driven electric generators could have been as easily provided by the private sector as by the government.

is so difficult to measure the EPA's output and find a standard against which to measure its performance, this question is exceedingly difficult to answer.

One area where there has been evidence of inefficiency has been the development and production of new weapons by the Department of Defense and its contractors. Spectacular overruns have occurred in development and production costs. To some extent, such cost increases reflect the fact that new weapon systems tend to push the state of the art, so that problems must be expected. In addition, the firms that develop and produce these weapon systems often submit unrealistically low bids to get a contract, knowing that they are likely to get approval for cost increases later on. According to some observers, like Merton J. Peck, of Yale University, and F. M. Scherer, of Harvard University, these cost overruns have also been due to inadequate attention to the efficient utilization of technical, production, and administrative manpower—areas in which major cost reductions are possible.

Nonselectivity

Another point made by public choice theorists is that when citizens vote for their elected officials, they vote for a "bundle" of political programs. For example, in a particular election, the two candidates may be John Brown, who favors increased defense spending, reduced capital gains taxes, and a tougher policy against drug use, and Jane Smith, who opposes all these things. If you favor increased defense spending and a tougher policy against drug use but oppose reduced capital gains taxes, there is no way that you can elect a candidate who mirrors your preferences. All you can do is vote for the candidate whose bundle of programs is closest to your preferences.

In contrast, when citizens make choices in the marketplace, they are better able to pick a set of goods and services in accord with their preferences, since they need not buy items they do not want. If you want a shirt and a tie, you can buy them without having to buy a pair of socks as well. Because citizens cannot be so selective with regard to goods and services in the public sector, public choice theorists hold that the provision of such goods and services tends to be inefficient.

To conclude this brief section on the theory of public choice, it is important to recognize that no one accuses government officials of being stupid, lazy, or corrupt.

Some undoubtedly are, but this is true of business executives as well. The point is that the incentives faced by government officials and the nature of the political process result in decision making that can be suboptimal from an economic point of view. This helps explain why the government, like the price system, can bungle the job of organizing the nation's economic activities. Neither is a panacea.

Principles of Taxation

The government finances most of its expenditures through taxation. According to the English political philosopher Edmund Burke, "To tax and to please, no more than to love and to be wise, is not given to men." What constitutes a rational tax system? Do any generally accepted principles guide the nation in determining who should pay how much? The answer is that there are some principles most people accept, but they are so broad and general that they leave plenty of room for argument and compromise. Specifically, two general principles of taxation command widespread agreement.

Benefit Principle

Benefit principle

The first principle, the **benefit principle**, asserts that people who receive more from a certain government service should pay more in taxes to support it. Certainly, few people would argue with this idea. However, it is frequently difficult, if not impossible, to apply. For example, there is no good way to measure the amount of the benefits received by a particular taxpayer from many public services, such as police protection.

Ability-to-Pay Principle

Ability-to-pay principle

The second principle, the **ability-to-pay principle**, asserts that people should be taxed so as to result in a socially desirable redistribution of income. In practice, this has ordinarily meant that the wealthy have been asked to pay more than the poor. This idea, too, has generally commanded widespread support—although this, of course, has not prevented the wealthy from trying to avoid its being applied to them.

Applications of These Principles

It follows from these principles that if two people are in essentially the same circumstances (their income, purchases, utilization of public services are the same), then they should pay the same taxes. This is an important rule, innocuous though it may seem. It says that equals should be treated equally; whether one is a Republican and the other is a Democrat, or whether one is a friend of the president and the other is his enemy, or whether one has purely salary income and the other has property income, they should be treated equally. Certainly, this is a basic characteristic of an equitable tax system.

It is easy to relate most of the taxes in our tax structure to these principles. For example, the first principle, the benefit principle, is the basic rationale behind taxes on gasoline and license fees for vehicles and drivers. Those who use the roads are asked to pay for their construction and upkeep. Also, the property tax, levied primarily on real estate, is often supported on these grounds. It is argued that property owners receive important benefits (fire and police protection, for example) and that the extent of the benefits is related to the extent of their property.

The personal income tax is based squarely on the second principle, ability to pay. A person with a large income pays a higher proportion of income in personal income taxes than a person with a smaller income. In 2010 if a couple's income (after deductions and exemptions) was $10,000, their federal income tax rebate was $5,670, whereas if their income was $100,000, their federal income tax payment was $6,473. Also, estate and inheritance taxes hit the very rich much harder than the middle class.

These principles are useful and important, but they do not take us very far toward establishing a rational tax structure. They are too vague and leave too many questions unanswered. If I use about the same amount of public services as you do, but my income is twice yours, how much more should I pay in taxes? Twice as much? Three times as much? Half as much? These principles throw no real light on many of the detailed questions that must be answered by a real-life tax code.

The Personal Income Tax

Income tax

The federal personal **income tax** brings in hundreds of billions of dollars a year. Yet many people are unaware of just how much they contribute, because it is deducted from their wages each month or each week, so that they owe little extra when April 15 rolls around. (Indeed, they may even be due a refund.) This pay-as-you-go scheme reduces the pain but does not eliminate it; taxes are never painless.

The Tax Schedule

Obviously, how much a family has to pay in personal income taxes depends on the family's income. The tax schedule for the year 2010 is as shown in Table 14.1. The second column shows how much a couple would have to pay if their income were the amount shown in the first column. At an income of $40,000, their income tax rebate would be $2,531; at an income of $75,000, their income tax bill would be $3,398. Clearly, the percentage of income owed in income tax increases as income increases, but this percentage does not

TABLE 14.1

Federal Personal Income Tax, Married Couple with Two Dependents, 2010

Income after Deductions and Personal Exemptions (dollars)	Personal Income Tax (dollars)	Marginal Tax Rate (percent)	Average Tax Rate (percent)
10,000	−5,670	10	−56.7
40,000	−2,531	15	−6.3
75,000	3,398	25	4.5
100,000	6,473	25	6.5

Source: U.S. Census Bureau, *Statistical Abstract of the United States: 2012* (Washington, DC: Government Printing Office, 2012).

increase indefinitely. Even if the couple made $500,000 in 2010, the percentage of income owed in income tax would not have exceeded 35 percent.

The Marginal Tax Rate

Marginal tax rate

It is instructive to look further at how the "tax bite" increases with income. In particular, we ask ourselves what proportion of an *extra* dollar of income the couple will have to pay in personal income taxes. In other words, what is the **marginal tax rate**, the tax on an extra dollar of income? The third column of Table 14.1 shows that the marginal tax rate was 10 percent if the couple's income was $10,000, 25 percent if it was $75,000. The top marginal tax rate in 2010 was 35 percent. In January 2013, the marginal tax rate for couples filing jointly with incomes over $450,000 was raised to 39.6 percent.

The Property Tax and the Sales Tax

Property tax

The **property tax** is the fiscal bulwark of our local governments. The way it works is simple enough. Most towns and cities estimate the amount they will spend in the next year or two, then determine a property tax based on the assessed property values in the town or city. If there is $500 million in assessed property values in the town and the town needs to raise $5 million, the tax rate will be 1 percent of assessed property value. In other words, each property owner must pay 1 percent of the assessed value of his or her property. There are well-known problems in the administration of the property tax. First, assessed values of property often depart significantly from actual market values; the former are typically much lower than the latter. And the ratio of assessed to actual value is often lower among higher-priced pieces of property; so wealthier people tend to get off easier. Second, there is widespread evasion of taxes on

PROPOSITION 13

The combination of inflation and a housing shortage led to a rapid increase in land values in California in the late 1970s. This in turn resulted in steadily increasing property taxes.

Homes that sold for $600 after World War II were selling for $60,000 in the late 1970s, and it was not unusual for homeowners to be paying over $2,000 per year in property taxes. Many homeowners felt that the burden of local taxes was too much and that it was time to cut government expenditures. The taxpayers' revolt, led by Howard Jarvis, began with the collection of over a million signatures, more than enough to place Proposition 13 on the California state ballot. Proposition 13 would limit property taxes to 1 percent—a 60 percent rollback that would wipe out some $7 billion of local government funds. At the polls, Proposition 13 easily passed with 65 percent of the vote.

Subsequently, local government spending leveled out throughout the state, and local government services suffered. Public employees were laid off, and services such as summer school classes, library services, and garbage collection were curtailed. Some of the other consequences came as a surprise to voters. For example, of the $7 billion tax rollback, corporations got the lion's share. Jarvis was back in 1980 with a new initiative: Proposition 9, which would cut state income taxes by 50 percent. This time, however, Jarvis's opponents focused on equity issues. Amid widespread charges that Proposition 9 might simply let the rich get richer at the expense of the less well-to-do, Jarvis was defeated and the tax revolt fever began to cool down.

During the following three decades, spending in California rose by much more than taxes. This pushed the state and many local governments close to insolvency. In fact, in 2012, two cities, Stockton and San Bernardino, had to declare bankruptcy. This underlined one of the dilemmas of governments in democracies: the appetite of the public for government spending is big, but the appetite for taxes is small.

personal assets: securities, bank accounts, and so on. Many people simply do not pay up. Third, the property tax is not very flexible; assessments and rates tend to change rather slowly.

Sales tax

The **sales tax**, of course, is a bulwark of state taxation. It provides a high yield with relatively low collection costs. Most of the states have some form of general sales tax, the rate usually between 3 and 6 percent. If the rate is 4 percent, retailers add to the price of goods sold to consumers an amount equal to 4 percent of the consumer's bill. This extra amount is submitted to the state as the general sales tax. Some states exempt food purchases from this tax, and a few exempt medical supplies. Where they exist, these exemptions help reduce the impact of the sales tax on the poor, but in general, the sales tax imposes a greater burden relative to income on the poor than on the rich, for the simple reason that the rich save a larger percentage of their income. Practically all a poor family's income may be subject to sales taxes; a great deal of a rich family's income may not be, because it is not spent on consumer goods, but is saved.

Who really pays the property tax or the sales tax? To what extent can these taxes be shifted to other people? The answer is not as straightforward as you might expect. For the property tax, the owner of unrented residential property swallows the tax, since there is no one else to shift it to. But the owner of rented property may attempt to pass along some of the tax to the tenant. In the case of a general sales tax, it is generally concluded that the consumer pays the tax. But if the tax is imposed on only a single commodity, the extent to which it can be shifted to the consumer depends on the demand and supply curves for the taxed commodity. The following section explains in some detail why this is the case.

Tax Incidence

Tax incidence

Who pays the tax is the **tax incidence**. Suppose that a sales or excise tax is imposed on a particular good, say, beer. In Figure 14.2, we show the demand and supply curves for beer before the imposition of the tax. With no tax, the equilibrium price of a 6-pack of beer is $6, and the equilibrium quantity is 100 million 6-packs. If a tax of $1 is imposed on each 6-pack produced, what

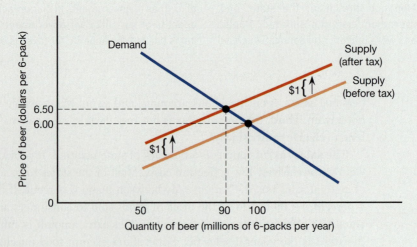

FIGURE 14.2

Effect of a $1 Tax on a 6-Pack of Beer

The tax shifts the supply curve upward by $1. Since the demand curve is unaffected, the equilibrium price of beer increases from $6.00 to $6.50 per 6-pack.

is the effect on the price of each 6-pack? Or, to see it from the beer drinker's perspective, how much of the tax is passed on to the consumer in the form of a higher price?

Since the tax is collected from the sellers, the supply curve is shifted upward by the amount of tax, as shown in Figure 14.2. For example, if the pretax price had to be $5 a 6-pack to induce sellers to supply 80 million 6-packs of beer, the post-tax price would have to be $1 higher, or $6 a 6-pack, to induce the same supply. Similarly, if the pretax price had to be $6 a 6-pack to induce sellers to supply 100 million 6-packs of beer, the post-tax price would have to be $1 higher, or $7 a 6-pack, to induce the same supply. The reason why the sellers require $1 more per 6-pack to supply the pretax amount is that they must pay the tax of $1 per 6-pack to the government. To wind up with the same amount of profit as before (after paying the tax), they require the extra $1 per 6-pack.

Who Pays the Tax?

Figure 14.2 shows that after the tax is imposed, the equilibrium price of beer is $6.50, an increase of $0.50 over its pretax level. Consequently, in this case, half the tax is passed on to consumers, who pay $0.50 per 6-pack more for beer. And half the tax is swallowed by the sellers, who receive (after they pay the tax) $0.50 per 6-pack less for beer. But it is not always true that sellers pass half the tax on to consumers and absorb the rest themselves. On the contrary, in some cases, consumers may bear almost all the tax (and sellers practically none of it), whereas in other cases consumers may bear almost none of the tax (and sellers practically all of it). The result depends on how sensitive the quantity demanded and the quantity supplied are to the price of the good.

Sensitivity of Demand to Price

In particular, holding the supply curve constant, the less sensitive the quantity demanded is to the price of the good, the bigger the portion of the tax shifted to consumers. To illustrate this, consider Figure 14.3, which shows the effect of a $1-per-6-pack tax on beer in two markets, one (panel B) where the quantity demanded is much more sensitive to price than in the other (panel A). As is evident, the price increase to consumers resulting from the tax is much greater in the market depicted in panel A than in the market depicted in panel B. And the amount of the tax absorbed by producers is much less in the market shown in panel A than in the market shown in panel B.

Sensitivity of Supply to Price

It can also be shown that if we hold the demand curve constant, the less sensitive the quantity supplied is to the price of the good, the bigger the portion of

FIGURE 14.3

Effect on Tax Incidence of the Sensitivity of the Quantity Demanded to Price

The supply curve is the same in panel A as in panel B. The quantity demanded is more sensitive to price in panel B than in panel A. Before the tax, the equilibrium price is P_0 in both panels. After the tax, the equilibrium price is P_1 in panel A and P_2 in panel B. The increase in price to the consumer is greater if the quantity demanded is less sensitive to price (panel A) rather than more sensitive to price (panel B).

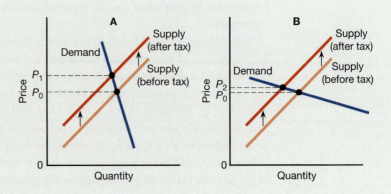

the tax absorbed by producers. To illustrate this, consider Figure 14.4, which shows the effect of a $1-per-6-pack tax on beer in two markets, one (panel A) where the quantity supplied is much more sensitive to price than in the other (panel B). As is evident, the price increase to consumers resulting from the tax is much greater in the market depicted in panel A than in the market depicted in panel B. And the amount of the tax absorbed by producers is much less in the market shown in panel A than in the market shown in panel B.

Effect of Tax on Quantity

Finally, note that the tax reduces the equilibrium quantity consumed of the taxed good, beer in this instance. One reason why governments impose taxes on goods like cigarettes and liquor is that these goods are regarded (in some circles at least) as socially undesirable. Clearly, the more sensitive the quantity demanded and supplied are to price, the larger the reduction in the equilibrium quantity. Therefore, if the government imposes a tax of this sort to reduce the quantity consumed of the good, the effect is greater if both the quantity demanded and the quantity supplied are relatively sensitive to price.

FIGURE 14.4

Effect on Tax Incidence of the Sensitivity of the Quantity Supplied to Price

The demand curve is the same in panel A as in panel B. The quantity supplied is more sensitive to price in panel A than in panel B. Before the tax, the equilibrium price is P_3 in both panels. After the tax, the equilibrium price is P_4 in panel A and P_5 in panel B. The increase in price to the consumer is greater if the quantity supplied is more sensitive to price (panel A) rather than less sensitive to price (panel B).

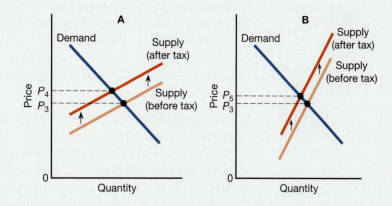

REVIEW AND PRACTICE

Summary

1 To a considerable extent, the government's role in the economy has developed in response to the limitations of the price system. There is considerable agreement that the government should redistribute income in favor of the poor, provide public goods, and offset the effects of external economies and diseconomies. Also, it is generally felt that the government should establish a proper legal, social, and competitive framework for the price system.

2 Beyond this, however, there are wide differences of opinion on the proper role of government in economic affairs. Conservatives tend to be suspicious of "big government," whereas liberals are inclined to believe that the government should do more.

3 Basically, the amount that the government spends on various activities and services must be decided through a country's political processes. Voting by ballots must be substituted for voting by dollars.

4   Just as the price system suffers from limitations, so does the government. Special interest groups sometimes gain at the expense of society as a whole. Government agencies sometimes have little incentive to increase efficiency. Citizens find it difficult to be selective in their choice of goods and services in the public sector. In recent years, economists seem to have put more emphasis on these (and other) limitations of the public sector.

5   It is generally agreed that people who receive more in benefits from a certain government service should pay more in taxes to support it. It is also generally agreed that people should be taxed so that the result is a socially desirable redistribution of income and that equals should be treated equally. But these general principles, although useful, cannot throw light on many of the detailed questions that a real-life tax code must answer.

6   The personal income tax is a very important source of federal revenue, the sales tax is an important source of state revenue, and the property tax is an important source of local revenue.

7   If a tax is imposed on a single commodity, the extent to which it can be shifted to the consumer depends on the demand and supply curves for the taxed commodity. If the quantity demanded is relatively insensitive to the price of the good or the quantity supplied is relatively sensitive to the price, a large portion of the tax is shifted to consumers.

Problems and Questions

1   "I believe the government should do only that which private citizens cannot do for themselves or cannot do so well for themselves." Interpret and comment. Indicate how we might determine in practice what the legitimate functions of government are, according to this proposition.

2   "The ideal public policy, from the viewpoint of the state, is one with identifiable beneficiaries, each of whom is helped appreciably, at the cost of many unidentifiable persons, none of whom is hurt much." Interpret and comment. Indicate how this proposition might be used to help predict government behavior.

3   Explain why national defense is a public good but a rifle is not a public good.

4   "I cannot get the amount of national defense I want and you, a different amount." Explain. Is this true of all public goods?

5 Suppose that the quantity of gin supplied at various prices is as given in this table:

Price of Gin (dollars per quart)	Quantity Supplied (millions of quarts)
4	5
5	6
6	7
7	8
8	9
9	10

Plot the supply curve on graph paper. Suppose that the government imposes a tax of $2 per quart on gin and the tax is collected from the sellers. Plot the posttax supply curve on graph paper.

6 Under the circumstances described in question 5, suppose that the quantity of gin demanded is 7 million quarts, regardless of the price (so long as it is between $4 and $9 per quart). What is the equilibrium price of gin before the tax and after it? How much of the tax is passed on to the consumer?

7 Under the circumstances described in question 5, suppose that the demand curve for gin is a horizontal line at $6 per quart. If this is the case, what is the equilibrium price of gin before the tax and after it? How much of the tax is passed on to the consumer?

Key Terms

rules of the game
income redistribution
public goods
externalities
benefit principle
ability-to-pay principle
income tax
marginal tax rate
property tax
sales tax
tax incidence

Viewpoint for Analysis

According to *Business Week*, March 22, 1993, "Raising cigarette taxes by $2 a pack would generate some $30 billion a year in federal revenue—even after allowing for a fall-off in consumption. . . . While $2 a pack may sound high, per-pack taxes total $3.68 in Denmark, $2.55 in Britain, and $2.11 in Germany. The knowledge of smoking's dangers has reduced consumption in the U.S., but every year the tobacco industry wins new customers—and the health industry some potential candidates for expensive and often fruitless care. Raising the financial disincentive could make Americans healthier. . . ."[4]

(a) Under what circumstances would a $2 increase in the cigarette tax raise the price per pack by $2? Under what circumstances would it have no effect on the price?

(b) If the supply curve for cigarettes is horizontal and the arc price elasticity of demand for cigarettes is 0.3 (which is a reasonable estimate, according to existing studies), what would be the effect on cigarette consumption of a tax that doubled the price of a pack of cigarettes?

(c) Should the government try to discourage smoking in this way? Who would be the gainers? Who would be the losers? What position would you take on this issue?

U.S. HEALTH CARE REFORM: THE TWIN CHALLENGES OF UNIVERSAL COVERAGE AND COST CONTROL

The health care market is the prototypical example of market failure. Unfortunately, few countries have come up with a satisfactory solution. At one extreme, the government-run health care systems of the United Kingdom and Canada provide a minimum level of care for everyone, but impose long waits for anything other than life-threatening conditions (except for people who can afford private care). At the other extreme, the mostly privately funded U.S. system provides some of the best health care for those who can afford it, is the most expensive in the world, and leaves tens of millions uninsured. The "optimal" solution is somewhere between these two systems, with both the public and the private sectors playing an important role.

Before we consider why the U.S. health care system is broken and some ways to fix it, a more detailed look at the data will reveal a few surprises.

- *U.S. spending on health care: more (and less) than in other rich countries.* In 2005, the United States spent more than 15 percent of GDP on health care. On average, rich countries spend only 9 percent of their GDP on health care. Nevertheless, only 45 percent of U.S. funding is provided by government (mostly for Medicare and Medicaid), compared with around 73 percent in most other developed nations. As a share of GDP, public funding for health care in most European countries and Japan is much higher than in the United States. Out-of-pocket spending by the typical household is also lower in the United States. Moreover, between 1995 and 2005, per capita health care spending in the United States grew by 3.6 percent (although it has risen more rapidly in the past few years, especially public spending), below the 4.0 percent average growth rate for all developed economies. Finally, these costs do not include the hidden costs of waiting that plague other health care systems, especially those in the United Kingdom and Canada. The cost of health care will continue to increase everywhere in the next couple of decades as populations age and as good health becomes ever more valuable to older and wealthier people. *The bottom line: American health care spending will continue to rise, but it has been growing at a slower pace than in many other rich countries, and the public burden is much less.*

- **Health care statistics:** *worse (and better) than those in other developed nations.* Pessimists about the U.S. health care system typically cite statistics about life expectancy at birth and infant mortality. The average American baby can expect to live 78 years (up from around 70 years in 1960), compared with a 79-year life expectancy for all rich countries. However, male life expectancy at age 65 is nearly a year higher for Americans than the average for all rich countries. The answer to this discrepancy lies in the much higher infant mortality rates in the United States, especially among the urban poor (partly because of high rates of teenage motherhood), along with higher U.S. death rates (especially among young males) as a result of auto accidents and homicides. These socioeconomic factors have little to do with how good or bad the U.S. health care system is. Optimists like to point out that other statistics show the U.S. system in a much better light. Mortality rates from cancer are about 10 percent lower than in other rich countries (203 per 100,000 compared with 235 in the United Kingdom, 244 in France, 270 in Italy, and 273 in Germany), while death rates from strokes are 40 percent lower. The percentage of Americans who have to wait more than four months for nonemergency surgery is less than 5 percent, compared with 24 to 36 percent in Australia, Canada, the United Kingdom, and New Zealand. U.S. patients are four to eight times more likely to receive the latest and most high-tech treatments than patients in Canada or Britain. *The bottom line: While the U.S. health care system is the most expensive in the world, Americans do have some things to show for it. In fact, one of the reasons U.S. health spending is so high is that it is more high-tech than most—and insured Americans insist on getting the very best care available, without delay.*

- **Health care coverage—and the lack thereof—defies simplification.** In the United States, around 47 million people (roughly 15 percent of the population) do not have health insurance. The United States is only one of a handful of rich countries that do not provide universal coverage. In most developed economies, health insurance for almost everyone is provided entirely by the government. Universal coverage has been adopted by some states, notably Massachusetts. It was one of the key themes of the 2008 U.S. presidential campaign and was the driving force behind the 2010 health care reforms (the Patient Protection and Affordable Care Act) enacted by President Barack Obama. Nevertheless, a closer look at the problem reveals a less bleak picture—and quite possibly a smaller problem in need of fixing. First, about 1 in 5 of the uninsured are not American citizens (including illegal aliens). Second, 1 in 4 uninsured persons have chosen not to take employer-provided insurance. Third, millions of people who are eligible for Medicaid (a program designed to provide medical insurance for the poor) have yet to apply for help. Finally, around 60 percent of the uninsured are less than 35 years old—in other words, young and healthy. *The bottom line: The number of Americans who want insurance but can't get it may be quite a* *bit smaller than the headline numbers suggest, which means that the problem is probably fairly manageable and may not require radical action.*

So why is the U.S. system so expensive and the results so mediocre? There are multiple problems that combine to fail to deliver the best care to consumers for the least cost.

- **Poor information.** Slow adoption of information technologies (for example, computerized records) by the medical profession means that there is still very limited information about which remedies work best, which hospitals and doctors have the best track records for treatment, and where the best health care deals can be found. *The bottom line: Information is crucial for consumers (especially poor ones) who are trying to make ends meet while trying to make the best health care choices.*
- **Lack of competition.** Much like public schools, hospitals and many local medical practices are local monopolies or oligopolies. The nonprofit nature of many of these institutions does not reduce or excuse the economic costs to consumers and the economy associated with this concentration of market power. Many local hospitals and regional or national hospital chains have vigorously resisted the establishment of smaller walk-in and specialty health care facilities. *The bottom line: The health care industry is perhaps unique in that rapid improvements in technology have not translated into lower prices. The absence of meaningful competition is a prime suspect.*

- **Few incentives to cut costs.** The fee-for-service system that exists in the United States today provides few incentives for either patients or health care providers to cut costs. The out-of-pocket spending by consumers as a share of total medical costs has fallen from around 33 percent in 1975 to 13 percent in 2005, at the same time that health care costs have risen; the two may be related. In other words, the incentive for consumers to save on health care has actually diminished in the past 30 years. At the same time, regional data show that there are huge variations in per capita health care spending across the United States that have no significant relationship to either income levels or health statistics. Similarly, there is no correlation between spending per beneficiary and the quality of medical care received. Finally, some studies have shown that administrative costs in the U.S. health care system are as high as $1,000 per person per year. *The bottom line: There is clearly a disconnect between the quality of services delivered and the true costs of delivering them, thus undermining market forces.*
- **A distorted and unfair tax structure, which reduces flexibility.** The current employer-sponsored health care system in the United States allows companies to write off the costs of providing health insurance. Likewise, these premiums are excluded from employees' taxable income—they are, in effect, a subsidy that is worth about 30 percent of the health care services covered. The federal revenue losses associated with these tax breaks have risen from around $40 billion in the

early 1990s to around $200 billion in the late 2000s. Unfortunately, the tax break for employers does not extend to uninsured individuals who would like to buy their own insurance. Nor does it extend to individuals who have lost a job (or are changing jobs) and would like to keep their old insurance plan. *The bottom line: The U.S. tax structure is both a disincentive for cost savings and a major factor behind the large number of people who find it too expensive to buy insurance on the private market. It also greatly increases the cost and anxiety associated with losing a job.*

What are the most effective solutions for fixing the U.S. health care mess? And are there lessons to be learned from other countries? The United States is not the only country that is struggling to fix its health care system. While most other developed countries provide universal health care coverage and are free of many of the problems facing the United States, every country faces the daunting task of containing runaway costs. Many countries that have lower costs than the United States achieve those savings through a combination of rationing (for example, longer waits and less access to high-tech cures) and much lower salaries for doctors and other health care professionals. Such government-imposed solutions are likely to be nonstarters in the United States. At the same time, dissatisfaction with health care systems in countries such as the United Kingdom and Canada are leading to both "medical tourism" for those who can afford it—including to the United States—and an exodus of doctors who are unhappy with the shortcomings of government-run systems. Meanwhile, some European countries, such as the Netherlands and Sweden, are experimenting with more competition in the provision of insurance and medical care.

There is no magic remedy for what ails the American health care system; instead, there are multiple solutions. These solutions have to tackle the problems on both the demand side of the market (lack of universal health insurance) and the supply side (high costs and lack of competition).

- *Remove tax distortions and increase the portability of health insurance.* Tax breaks should be extended to people who want to buy individual insurance and to workers who have lost their employer-provided insurance. The current tax system unfairly discriminates against those who are not covered by employer plans. Mandating universal health coverage (as in Massachusetts), especially for catastrophic illnesses, without providing tax breaks is just as unfair. Individual tax breaks can take the form of health savings accounts, refundable tax credits, or a much larger medical care tax deduction than is currently available. Each of these could be funded by capping or eliminating the current unlimited health care tax deduction for employers. Clearly, a principal advantage of individual tax breaks over the current system is that by making private insurance more affordable, they increase the portability of health insurance and reduce the costs of losing a job.
- *Improve the incentives to economize on health care.* The third-party payment system in the United States (including private insurance, Medicare, and Medicaid) seriously weakens the link between what consumers get and what

they pay for. This leads consumers to opt for the most expensive care, regardless. At the same time, there are no systematic incentives for providers to offer the most cost-effective treatments. One way around this would be to increase out-of-pocket payments by charging consumers higher copayments and deductible amounts, especially for expensive treatments and drugs for which there are cheaper alternatives. This would help contain costs, but it would also impose a proportionately larger burden on the poor. Nevertheless, this higher burden is something that could be offset through larger medical tax deductions, tax credits, and rebates.

- *Develop risk-pooling insurance alternatives.* One advantage of the employer-based insurance system (especially for large companies) is that it pools the risks of workers with costly medical problems with those who need little health care. Unfortunately, small companies and individuals do not have access to these risk-pooling systems and end up paying much higher premiums. This is an area where government can play a very beneficial role. Possible options include reinsurance by the government (that is, insuring the insurers) or developing a "premium rebate pool" to pay annual health care bills over a certain amount (say $50,000) for individuals and employees of small businesses. Such policies would reduce the problem of "adverse selection," whereby insurance companies discriminate against the people who need health insurance the most—namely, the very sick.

- *Increase the availability of the information needed to allow consumers to make cost-effective health care choices.* The government needs to mandate (and possibly be a clearinghouse for) the availability of information related to health insurance, provider performance, and overall quality and effectiveness— including "report cards" and "best practices." This will help increase value-based competition and improvements in quality. It will also make consumer choices much easier. Consumer-friendly information in the health care area lags that for most other types of consumer goods and services. Improved information flows are a critical ingredient for managing health care costs in the United States and other parts of the world.

- *Diminish the market power of insurers and providers.* There is too little competition among both medical insurance companies and health care providers. Most states do not allow people to buy medical insurance from out-of-state companies. This is clearly not in the interests of consumers. There are also state and local restrictions on the establishment of "convenient-care" facilities and small specialty hospitals (for example, ones that specialize in obstetrics and gynecology). In areas where these types of competitors have been allowed in, the cost of health care has decreased, in part because the overhead and administrative costs of such facilities are lower. Governments should also use the antitrust tools available to them to ensure that the trend toward monopolies among health care providers does not reduce competition and consumer choice. Some estimates suggest that the annual savings from greater competition and better information could be 30 percent of overall health care costs, or $300 billion to $400 billion a year. One way to foster greater competition is to encourage medical "tourism," in which patients travel to other parts of the world where the costs of medical procedures, such as hip replacements and heart surgery, are a fraction of the costs in the United States.

- *Reduce the scope of medical malpractice suits.* Malpractice insurance is a significant element of the American health care cost problem. Reducing the scope of malpractice suits and especially large punitive damages will lessen the practice of "defensive medicine" and help providers to increase the cost-effectiveness of treatments. This would probably be more politically acceptable if medical licensing boards were to take tougher action against inept doctors.

- *Provide incentives for healthier lifestyles.* Rising rates of obesity and a still high (though falling) percentage of people who smoke are important contributors to high health care costs. No solution would be complete without incentives to reduce the incidence of both.

During the last few years, much of the health care debate in the United States has focused on the problem of the uninsured. The pay-or-play plan in Massachusetts, which requires everyone to have medical insurance, has created a lot of interest, and some other states are considering similar schemes. The 2010 Patient Protection and Affordable Care Act (ACA for short) is, in effect, a national version of the Massachusetts plan. Despite some watering down by the 2012 Supreme Court ruling on the ACA, the good news is that progress is being made on the issue of universal coverage in the United States. The bad news is that such plans solve only part of the U.S. health care problem. Without more competition and incentives to reduce costs, pay-or-play systems could end up costing even more than current systems. In fact, during the first few years of implementation, the Massachusetts plan cost the state nearly twice as much as the original estimates. A less costly option would be to limit mandatory health care coverage to catastrophic illnesses and increase competition among health care providers.

So what are the elements of a cost-effective health care system? On the demand side, universal access to portable insurance and health care plans (via tax breaks, subsidies, and risk pooling), combined with better information and strong incentives to help consumers seek out the best deals. On the supply side, much more competition and much less litigation.

Questions

1 What do you think will happen to health care costs under the 2010 Affordable Care Act (ACA)? *Hint:* As coverage increases, what will happen to demand for health care services? Assuming that the supply of health care does not keep pace with demand (a plausible assumption), what will happen to prices?

2 What do you think might happen to U.S. health care statistics as the United States moves closer to universal health care?

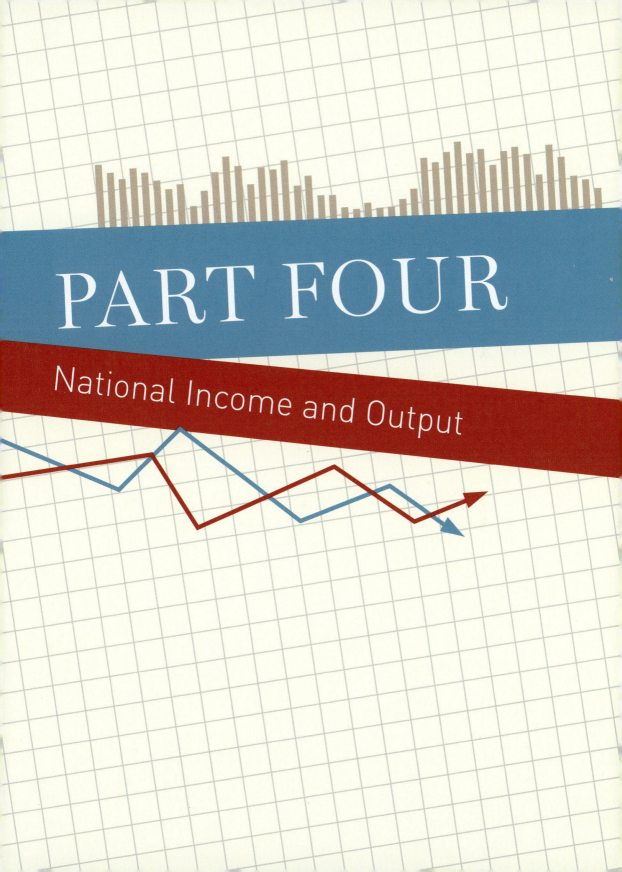

PART FOUR

National Income and Output

National Income and Product

LEARNING OBJECTIVES

➤ To explain what gross domestic product (GDP) measures and why it is important

➤ To understand the nature of a price index and how it can be used

➤ To describe two approaches for measuring GDP

Gross domestic product (GDP)

Economics is important in both war and peace. For example, in World War II, U.S. policy makers had to figure out how much our nation could produce to support the war effort. How did they make such estimates? One purpose of this chapter is to answer that question.

The U.S. **gross domestic product**, or **GDP** as it is often called, was about $16.2 trillion in 2012, as compared with about $6.5 trillion in 1992 and around $1.0 trillion in 1969. Put in the simplest terms, GDP is the value of the total amount of final goods and services produced by our economy during a particular period of time. This measure is important for its own sake and because it helps us understand both inflation and unemployment. The federal government and the business community watch GDP figures avidly. Government officials, from the president down, are interested because these figures indicate how prosperous we are and because they are useful in forecasting the future health of the economy. Business executives are also extremely interested in GDP figures because their sales are related to the level of GDP, and so the figures are useful in forecasting the future health of their businesses. All in all, it is no exaggeration to say that the gross domestic product is one of the most closely watched numbers in existence. In this chapter, we will discuss the measurement, uses, and limitations of gross domestic product.

Going back to the flow diagram introduced in Chapter 2, GDP can be measured in one of two ways: either as the sum of all the money income earned in a given period of time (with some adjustments, as we will see later in this chapter) or as the sum of all expenditures in the economy (subject to some qualifications, as we will also see later). In Figure 15.1, the upper part of the loop (income) and the lower part (expenditures) should each add up to GDP. In fact, the U.S. Department of Commerce, which collects and releases GDP numbers, refers to them in the national income and product accounts (NIPA). Later in the chapter, we will discuss both the income and expenditures measures of GDP. But first we need to understand what GDP actually measures.

FIGURE 15.1

The Circular Flow of Money and Products

Both the income flows and the expenditure flows in the economy can be used to calculate GDP.

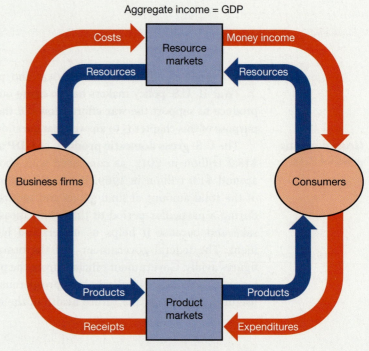

Aggregate income = GDP

Costs · Resource markets · Money income

Resources · Resources

Business firms

Consumers

Products · Product markets · Products

Receipts · Expenditures

Aggregate expenditures = GDP

GDP, GNP, AND OTHER MEASURES OF ECONOMIC ACTIVITY

Gross national product was designed as a measure of economic activity. It has been refined over the years to provide better estimates of the production of goods and services in the economy. For example, the switch from gross national product (GNP) to gross domestic product (GDP) some years ago gives a better idea of what is produced within the United States—rather than what is produced by Americans, whether in the United States or elsewhere.

GDP is far from perfect as a gauge of economic activity. For example, it does not measure the economic contribution of stay-at-home parents or output in the underground economy. It measures only those activities for which there is a measurable market price. Similarly, it does not take into account economic "bads," such as pollution.

Nor does GDP provide a complete picture of what is going on in an economy. For example, it does not measure how many people are employed (and how many people are not). Neither do the GDP statistics provide any gauge of the financial health of an economy. Fortunately, there are numerous other economic and financial statistics, which seen in conjunction with the GDP data, provide a more comprehensive view of the economy.

No, GDP is not a perfect measure of economic well-being. Nor can it measure things like happiness. That said, higher levels of GDP per person are closely correlated with improved living standards (including health, education, and leisure), which in turn have a positive influence on how people feel about their lives.

Economists will continue to search for better ways to measure economic output. In the meantime, despite all its flaws, GDP is a pretty good gauge of what is going on in the economy.

Measuring Gross Domestic Product

As noted, gross domestic product is a measure of how much the economy produces in a particular period of time. But the U.S. economy produces millions of types of goods and services. How can we add together everything from lemon meringue pies to helicopters, from books to houses? The only feasible answer is to use money as a common denominator and make the price of a good or service (the amount the buyer is willing to pay) the measure of value. In other words, we add the value in money terms of all the goods and services produced by the economy during a certain period, normally a year, and the result is gross domestic product during that period.

Although the measurement of gross domestic product may seem straight-forward (just "add the value in money terms of all the goods and services produced by the economy"), this is by no means the case. A number of pitfalls must be avoided and problems tackled.

Final goods and services

Intermediate good

> *Avoidance of double counting.* Gross domestic product does not include the value of *all* the goods and services produced; it includes only the values of the *final* goods and services produced. **Final goods and services** are goods and services destined for the ultimate user. For example, flour purchased for family consumption is a final good, but flour to be used in manufacturing bread is an **intermediate good**, not a final good. We would be double counting if we counted both the bread and the flour used to make the bread as output. Therefore, the output of intermediate goods (goods not destined for the ultimate user but used as inputs in producing final goods and services) must not be included in gross domestic product.

> *Valuation at cost.* Some final goods and services included in the gross domestic product are not bought and sold in the marketplace, so they are valued at what they cost. Consider the services performed by government: police protection, fire protection, the use of the courts, defense, and so forth. Such services are not bought and sold in any market (despite the old saying about the judge who was "the best that money could buy"). Yet, they are an important part of our economy's final output. Economists and statisticians have decided to value them at what they cost the taxpayers. This is not ideal, but it is the best practical solution advanced to date.

> *Nonmarket transactions.* For practical reasons it is necessary to omit certain types of final output from gross domestic product. In particular, some non-marketed goods and services, such as the services performed by homemakers, are excluded from gross domestic product. This is not because economists fail to appreciate these services, but because it is extremely difficult to get reasonably reliable estimates of the money value of a homemaker's services. At first glance, this may seem to be a very important weakness in our measure of total output, but so long as the value of these services does not change much (in relation to total output), the variation in gross domestic product provides a reasonably accurate picture of the variation in total output. And for our purposes, this is all that is required.

> *Nonproductive transactions.* Purely financial transactions are excluded from gross domestic product because they do not reflect current production. Such financial transactions include government transfer payments, private transfer payments, and the sale and purchase of securities. *Government transfer payments* are payments made by the government

to individuals who do not contribute to production in exchange for them. Payments to welfare recipients are a good example of government transfer payments. Because these payments are not for production, it would be incorrect to include them in GDP. *Private transfer payments* are gifts or other transfers of wealth from one person or private organization to another. Again, these are not payments for production, so there is no reason to include them in GDP. The sale and purchase of securities are not payments for production, so they, too, are excluded from GDP.

➤ *Secondhand goods.* Sales of secondhand goods are also excluded from gross domestic product. The reason for this is clear: When a good is produced, its value is included in GDP. If its value is also included when it is sold on the secondhand market, it will be counted twice, leading to an overstatement of the true GDP. Suppose that you buy a new bicycle and resell it a year later. The value of the new bicycle is included in GDP when the bicycle is produced. But the resale value of the bicycle is not included in GDP; to do so would be double counting.

Adjusting GDP for Price Changes

Current Dollars versus Constant Dollars

In the Prologue, we stressed that the general price level has changed over time. (Recall the rapid inflation of the 1970s and early 1980s.) Since gross domestic product values all goods and services at their current prices, it is bound to be affected by changes in the price level as well as by changes in total output. If all prices doubled tomorrow, this would produce a doubling of the gross domestic product. Clearly, if the gross domestic product is to be a reliable measure of changes in total output, we must correct it to eliminate the effects of such changes in the price level.

Base year

To make such a correction, economists choose some **base year** and express the value of all goods and services in terms of their prices during that year. If 2009 is taken as the base year and the price of beef was $8 per pound in 2009, beef is valued at $8 per pound in all other years. Therefore, if 100 million pounds of beef were produced in 2012, this total output is valued at $800 million even though the price of beef in 2012 was actually higher than $8 per pound. In this way, distortions caused by changes in the price level are eliminated.

Current dollars

Constant dollars

Gross domestic product is expressed either in current dollars or in constant dollars. Figures expressed in **current dollars** are actual dollar amounts, whereas those expressed in **constant dollars** are corrected for changes in the price level. Expressed in current dollars, gross domestic product is affected by changes in the price level. Expressed in constant dollars, gross domestic product is not affected by the price level because the prices of all goods are maintained at their base-year level. After being corrected for changes in the price level, GDP is called **real GDP**.

Real GDP

UNDERSTANDING THE NEW ESTIMATES OF GDP

The definition and measurement of GDP and its components are not static: they have changed over time to reflect the changing nature of the economy and to incorporate improved statistical techniques (Case Study 15.1 provides a good example of this). Roughly every four to five years, the Bureau of Economic Analysis (BEA) of the U.S. Department of Commerce publishes comprehensive revisions of the national income and product accounts (NIPA) to bring the GDP and national income estimates up to date. Some of these revisions are minor. However, in 1995, 1999, 2003, 2009, and 2013, the BEA made major benchmark revisions to the NIPA data, which made significant improvements in the calculation of the impact of computers on the U.S. economy. The BEA also corrected some of the biases that had crept into the estimates of GDP. In the 1995 revisions, the BEA shifted its emphasis from fixed-weighted measures to chain-weighted measures of real output and prices. What do these terms mean, and why did the government make the switch?

The government obtains its estimates of real output (the inflation-adjusted quantity of goods and services produced) in two steps. In the first step, the current market value of spending for each detailed component of GDP is calculated from the basic source data. This is called current-dollar or nominal output. In the second step, the effects of inflation are removed by dividing the nominal output of each type of good or service by its price index. These price indexes are normalized to equal 1 (or 100) in the base year, currently 2009. The govern-

ment calculates price indexes and real output for more than 1,000 categories of goods and services. At this most-detailed level, the real output data underlying fixed-weight and chain-weight measures are identical.

The crucial question is how real output for these subcomponents of GDP should be added together to obtain broader concepts, like real GDP or real consumption. Under the fixed-weight system, the subcomponents are added together using their relative prices in the base year. Thus, if an apple cost twice as much as an orange in 1996, apples would be given twice the weight of oranges in every year, no matter what their relative prices were in other years.

As long as relative prices do not change much, this weighting system functions reasonably well, as it did with few exceptions until the late 1980s. However, the growing importance of computers, coupled with the sharp decline in their relative price, introduced problems into this system. As a result, real fixed-weighted GDP became less reliable as a measure of the value of economic output and as an indicator of the amount of resources necessary to produce that output.

In the chain-weighted method of aggregation, these problems are avoided because the change in real output between successive years depends only on relative prices in those years, not on relative prices in the base year. For example, to calculate the growth in real chain-weighted GDP between 1992 and 1993, we would create two fixed-weight measures of real GDP for each year, one pair using 1992 prices as weights, the other pair using 1993 prices as weights. We can then calculate two different growth rates for real GDP in 1993, one using 1992 price weights, the other using 1993 price weights. The 1993 growth rate for real chain-weighted GDP then equals the average of these two growth rates.

To put things in perspective, the fixed-weight method of calculating real GDP produced an estimate of 4.3 percent for the average quarterly growth rate of the U.S. economy between the third quarter of 2001 and the second quarter of 2005. The chain-weight method calculated the growth rate to be only 2.7 percent. The 1.6-percentage-point difference is substantial, due mostly to the continued large declines in computer prices.

The new chain-weighted estimates of GDP have two disadvantages. First, they are more complex and harder to understand. Second, unlike fixed-weight estimates, chain-weighted estimates of the components of GDP (consumer spending, investments, exports, and so on) do not precisely add to total GDP. This nonadditivity introduces a distortion of its own, which, however, is much smaller on average than the bias of the fixed-weight estimates. On balance, therefore, the new approach provides a better estimate of GDP than the old approach.

In the 1999 revisions, the BEA made two major changes in the way it calculates the impact of software purchases and electronic transactions on the growth of productivity and real GDP. First, instead of treating software purchases as production inputs (in the same way that steel is a production input for a car), these purchases are now categorized as investments, recognizing that software is used over and over. Therefore, software purchases are now added directly to the computed value of GDP. Second, the 1999 revisions corrected a flaw in the measurement of banking productivity. Previously, banking productivity was assumed to be zero, so output rose at the same rate as the number of hours worked by bank employees. The new estimates now calculate the impact of ATM and other electronic transactions on banking productivity. As a result of these two revisions, nonfarm productivity is now estimated to have grown between 0.5 and 0.7 percentage point faster during the 1980s and 1990s than was previously estimated.

The 2013 benchmark revisions redefined fixed investment to include expenditures for research and development (R&D) and for entertainment, literary, and artistic originals, which provide long-lasting service to the businesses, nonprofit institutions, and government agencies that use them. This change makes the U.S. NIPA data more comparable with the data from other countries. Moreover, it is consistent with the way the BEA treats other intangible assets, such as software and mineral exploration. This new category of investment category is called "intellectual property products" and in 2013 accounted for about one-third of nonresidential fixed investment.

Figure 15.2 shows the behavior of both real GDP and GDP expressed in current dollars. GDP expressed in current dollars has increased more rapidly (due to inflation) than GDP in constant dollars (real GDP).

Price Indexes

It is often useful to have some measure of how much prices have changed over a certain period of time. One way to obtain such a measure is to divide the value of a set of goods and services expressed in current dollars by the value of the same

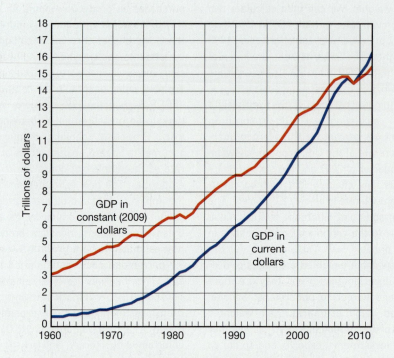

FIGURE 15.2

GDP Expressed in Current Dollars and 2009 Dollars, United States, 1960–2012

Because of inflation, GDP expressed in current dollars has increased more rapidly in recent years than GDP in constant (2009) dollars. This was particularly true in the 1970s and 1980s, reflecting the price surge then.

Source: U.S. Department of Commerce

set of goods and services expressed in constant (base-year) dollars. Suppose that a set of goods and services costs $100 when valued at 2012 prices, but $70 when valued at 2009 prices. Apparently, prices have risen an average of 43 percent for this set of goods between 2009 and 2012. How do we get 43 percent? The ratio of the cost in 2012 prices to the cost in 2009 prices is 100 ÷ 70 = 1.43; therefore, prices must have risen on the average by 43 percent for this set of goods.

The ratio of the value of a set of goods and services in current dollars to the value of the same set of goods and services in constant (base-year) dollars is a

Price index

Deflating

price index. Hence, 1.43 is the price index in the preceding example. An important function of a price index is to convert values expressed in current dollars into values expressed in constant dollars. This conversion, known as **deflating**, can be achieved simply by dividing values expressed in current dollars by the price index. In our example, values expressed in 2012 dollars can be converted into constant (2009) dollars by dividing by 1.43. This procedure is an important one, with applications in many fields other than the measurement of the gross domestic product. For example, firms use it to compare their output in various years. To correct for price changes, they deflate their sales by a price index for their products.

Price indexes are often multiplied by 100; that is, they are expressed as percentage changes. In the case described, the price index might be expressed as 1.43 × 100, or 143, which would indicate that 2012 prices on the average were 143 percent of their 2009 level. In Chapter 19, we will say more about price indexes expressed in this way. For now, we assume that the price index is not multiplied by 100.

To illustrate how a price index can be used to deflate some figures, suppose that we want to measure how much the output of bread rose in *real terms*—that is, in constant dollars—between 2007 and 2011. Suppose that the value of the output of bread in current dollars during each year is as shown in column 1 of Table 15.1 and that the price of bread is as shown in column 2. To determine the value of the output of bread in 2007 dollars, we form a price index with 2007 as the base year, as shown in column 3 (the index has a value of 1.00 in the base year). Then, dividing the figures in column 1 by this price index, we get the value of the output of bread during each year in 2007 dollars, shown in column 4. Thus, column 4 shows how much the output of bread has grown in real terms. The real output of bread has risen by 19 percent—(1,900 − 1,600) ÷ 1,600—between 2007 and 2011.

TABLE 15.1

Use of the Price Index to Convert from Current to Constant Dollars

Year	(1) Output of Bread (current dollars)	(2) Price of Bread (dollars)	(3) Price Index (price × 2007 price)	(4) Output of Bread (2007 dollars)*
2007	1,600 million	0.50	1.00	1,600 million
2008	1,768 million	0.52	1.04	1,700 million
2009	1,980 million	0.55	1.10	1,800 million
2010	2,090 million	0.55	1.10	1,900 million
2011	2,204 million	0.58	1.16	1,900 million

*This column was derived by dividing column 1 by column 3.

TABLE 15.2

Calculations for Real Gross Domestic Product

Year	(1) GDP (current dollars, billions)	(2) Price Index (2009 = 1.00)	(3) Real GDP (2009 dollars, billions)
1990	5,980	0.6685	8,945 (=5,980/0.6685)
2000	10,290	0.8189	12,565 (=10,290/0.8189)
2009	14,418	1.0	14,418 (=14,418/1.0)
2012	16,245	1.0500	15,471 (=16,245/1.0500)

Source: U.S. Department of Commerce.

Next, we take an actual case. Column 1 in Table 15.2 shows gross domestic product in selected years. Column 2 shows the relevant price index for GDP for each of these years. (The base year is 2009.) What was real GDP in 1990? To answer this question, we must divide GDP in current dollars in 1990 by the price index for 1990. The answer is $5,980 billion ÷ 0.6685, or $8,945 billion. In other words, when expressed in constant 2009 dollars, GDP in 1990 was $8,945 billion. What was real GDP in 2012? Applying the same principles, the answer is $16,245 billion ÷ 1.0500, or $15,471 billion. In other words, when expressed in constant 2009 dollars, GDP in 2012 was $15,471 billion. To test your understanding, see if you can figure out the value of real GDP in 2000. (To check your answer, consult footnote 1.)[1]

The preceding calculations use a relatively simple type of price index. In reality, the Bureau of Economic Analysis of the U.S. Department of Commerce uses a more complicated (and more accurate) type of index called a *chain-weighted index*, described in Case Study 15.2.

Using Value Added to Calculate GDP

We pointed out that gross domestic product includes the value of only the final goods and services produced. Obviously, however, the output of final goods and services is not due solely to the efforts of the producers of the final goods and services. The total value of an automobile when it leaves the plant, for example, represents the work of many industries in addition to the automobile manufacturers. The steel, tires, glass, and many other components of the automobile are not produced by the automobile manufacturers. In reality, the automobile manufacturers added only a certain amount of value to the value of the intermediate goods—steel, tires, glass, and so forth—they purchased. This point is basic to an understanding of how the gross domestic product is calculated.

---

[1] Real GDP in 2000 equaled $10,290 billion ÷ 0.8189, or $12,565 billion in 2009 dollars.

To measure the contribution of a firm or industry to final output, we use the concept of value added. **Value added** means just what it says: the amount of value added by a firm or industry to the total worth of the product. It is a measure in money terms of the extent of production taking place in a particular firm or industry. Suppose that $160 million worth of bread was produced in the United States in 2012. To produce it, farmers harvested $50 million worth of wheat, which was used as an intermediate product by flour mills, which turned out $80 million worth of flour. This flour was used as an intermediate product by the bakers who produced the $160 million worth of bread. What is the value added at each stage of the process? For simplicity, assume that the farmers did not have to purchase any materials from other firms to produce the wheat. Then the value added by the wheat farmers is $50 million; the value added by the flour mills is $30 million ($80 million – $50 million); and the value added by the bakers is $80 million ($160 million – $80 million). The total of the value added at all stages of the process ($50 million + $30 million + $80 million) must equal the value of the output of the final product ($160 million) because each stage's value added is its contribution to this value.

The Limitations of GDP

Although very useful, gross domestic product is by no means an ideal measure of economic well-being, and we need to understand its limitations. At least five limitations of GDP must always be kept in mind:

1. *Population.* GDP is not very meaningful unless we know the size of the population of the country in question. For example, the fact that a particular country's GDP equals $50 billion means one thing if the country has 10 million inhabitants and quite another thing if it has 500 million inhabitants. To correct for the size of the population, per capita GDP (GDP divided by the population) is often used as a rough measure of output per person in a particular country.

2. *Leisure.* GDP does not take into account one of our most prized activities: leisure. During the past century, the average workweek in the United States has decreased substantially, from almost 70 hours in 1850 to about 40 hours today. As people have become more affluent, they have chosen to substitute leisure for increased production. Yet this increase in leisure time, which surely contributes to our well-being, does not show up in GDP. Neither does the personal satisfaction (or displeasure and alienation) people get from their jobs.

3. *Quality changes.* GDP does not take adequate account of changes in the quality of goods. An improvement in a product is not reflected accurately in GDP unless its price reflects the improvement. For example, if a new type of drug is put on the market at the same price as an old drug and the output and cost of the new drug are the same as those of the old drug, GDP does not increase, even though the new drug is twice as effective as the old one.

4. *Value and distribution.* GDP says nothing about the social desirability of the composition and distribution of the country's output. Each good and service produced is valued at its price. If the price of a Bible is $10 and the price of a pornographic novel is $10, both are valued at $10, whatever you or I may think about their respective worth. Moreover, GDP measures only the total quantity of goods and services produced. It tells us nothing about how this output is distributed among the people. If a country's GDP is $500 billion, this is its GDP whether 90 percent of the output is consumed by a relatively few rich families or the output is distributed relatively equally among the citizens.

Social costs

5. *Social costs.* GDP does not reflect some of the **social costs** arising from the production of goods and services. In particular, it does not reflect the environmental damage resulting from the operation of our nation's factories, offices, and farms. It is common knowledge that the atmosphere and water supplies are being polluted in various ways by firms, consumers, and governments. Yet these costs are not deducted from GDP, even though the failure to do so results in an overestimate of our true economic welfare.

Two Approaches to GDP

Suppose we want to measure the market value of an automobile. One way to do this is to look at how much the consumer pays for the automobile. Although this is the most straightforward way to measure the car's market value, it is not the only way it can be done. Another equally valid way is to add all the wage, interest, rental, and profit incomes generated in the car's production. As pointed out in the circular flow model in Figure 15.1, the amount that the car's producer receives for this car is equal to its profit (or loss) on the car plus the amount it pays the workers and other resource owners who contributed their resources to its production. Therefore, if we add all the wage, interest, rental, and profit incomes resulting from the production of the automobile, the result is the same as if we determine how much the consumer pays for the automobile.

Expenditures approach

Income approach

By the same token, there are two ways to measure the market value of the output of the economy as a whole. Or, put differently, there are two ways of looking at GDP. One is the **expenditures approach**, which regards GDP as the sum of all the expenditures on the final goods and services produced this year. The other is the **income approach**, which regards GDP as the sum of all the incomes derived from the production of this year's total output.

Because both approaches are valid, it follows that GDP can be viewed as either the total expenditure on this year's total output or the total income stemming from the production of this year's total output:

Total expenditure on this year's total output
= GDP
= total income from the production of this year's total output

USING GDP ESTIMATES IN WORLD WAR II

During the Great Depression, policy makers had little idea of what was happening to the economy. In contrast, economists during World War II had a reasonably accurate picture of the economy's total output thanks to the new estimates of GDP, first published by the U.S. Department of Commerce in 1934. (Actually, estimates of GNP, not GDP, were published in those days, but the differences between them tend to be small.) At the Commerce Department, economists were being pushed by events to come up with predictions of what the U.S. economy could produce. At home, the first mobilization committees were set up under the Victory program. And economists at the Commerce Department went to work to see what kind of arsenal the United States could become and how quickly.

As the war intensified in Europe, the planners went to work. Experts were dispatched to London to find out what the Allies needed to survive. Specifically, the war planners began asking questions like these:

- Could the United States produce enough steel (for ships, guns, and tanks), aluminum (airplanes), and copper (ammunition)?
- How much of the entire economy could be diverted to the war effort without jeopardizing the basic needs of the U.S. people for food, clothing, housing, and transportation?
- How much money would the U.S. public be able to pay in taxes to support the war?

The effort that went into answering these questions helped to refine the national income and product accounts, and after the end of the war, the Commerce Department began to regularly produce estimates of GDP and related measurements.

This is an *identity*; the left-hand side of this equation must equal the right-hand side. (More precisely, the right-hand side should also include depreciation and indirect business taxes, as we will see later. But this refinement can be ignored at this point.)

It is important to understand both the expenditures approach and the income approach to GDP. In the following sections, we describe both approaches in more detail.

The Expenditures Approach to GDP

To use the expenditures approach to determine GDP, we must add all the expenditures on final goods and services. Economists distinguish among four broad categories of spending: personal consumption, gross private domestic investment, net exports, and government purchases of goods and services.

TABLE 15.3

Expenditures on Final Good and Services, United States, 2012

Type of Expenditure	Amount (billions of dollars)	
Personal consumption expenditures		11,150
Durable goods	1,203	
Nondurable goods	2,567	
Services	7,380	
Gross private domestic investment		2,495
Structures	437	
Equipment	908	
Intellectual property products	625	
Residential structures	439	
Change in inventories	86	
Net exports		–547
Exports	2,196	
Imports	2,743	
Government purchases of goods and services		3,167
Federal	1,296	
State and local	1,871	
Gross Domestic Product		*16,245*

Source: U.S. Department of Commerce.

Personal Consumption Expenditures

Personal consumption expenditures include spending by households on durable goods, nondurable goods, and services. This category of spending includes your expenditures on items like food and drink, which are nondurable goods. It also includes your family's expenditures on a car or an electric washer or dryer, which are durable goods. Further, it includes your payments to a dentist, who is providing a service (painful though it sometimes may be). Table 15.3 shows that in 2012, personal consumption accounted for about two-thirds of the total amount spent on final goods and services in the United States. Expenditures on consumer durable goods are clearly much less than expenditures on consumer nondurable goods, whereas expenditures on services are now larger than expenditures on either durable or nondurable goods.

Gross Private Domestic Investment

Gross private domestic investment consists of all investment spending by U.S. firms. As shown in Table 15.3, three broad types of expenditures are included in this category. First, all final purchases of tools, equipment, and machinery are included. Second, all construction expenditures, including expenditures on residential housing, are included. (One reason why houses are treated as investment goods is that they can be rented out.) Third, the change in total inventories is included. An increase in inventories is a positive investment; a decrease in inventories is a negative investment. The change in inventories must be included because GDP measures the value of all final goods and services produced, even if they are not sold this year. Therefore, GDP must include the value of any increases in inventories that occur during the year. On the other hand, if a decrease occurs during the year in the value of inventories, the value of this decrease must be subtracted in calculating GDP because these goods and services were produced prior to the beginning of the year. In other words, a decline in inventories means that society has purchased more than it has produced during the year.

Gross private domestic investment is "gross" in the sense that it includes all additions to a country's stock of investment goods, whether or not they are replacements for equipment or plant used up in producing the current year's output. Net private domestic investment includes only the addition to the country's stock of investment goods after allowing for the replacement of used-up plant and equipment. To illustrate the distinction between gross and net private domestic investment, consider the situation in 2012. In that year, the nation produced $2,475 billion worth of investment goods; hence, gross private domestic investment equaled $2,475 billion. But in producing the 2012 GDP, $2,543 billion worth of investment goods were used up (this is often referred to as capital consumption or depreciation). Hence, net private domestic investment equaled $2,475 billion −$2,543 billion, or −$68 billion. This was the net subtraction from the nation's stock of investment goods. Often in the aftermath of a deep recession (as we had in 2009), net private domestic private investment can be negative. More often than not, in any given year, net private domestic investment is positive.

Net private domestic investment indicates the change in a country's stock of capital goods. If it is positive, the country's productive capacity, as gauged by its capital stock, is growing. If it is negative, the country's productive capacity, as gauged by its capital stock, is declining. As pointed out in Chapter 1, the amount of goods and services that the country can produce is influenced by the size of its stock of capital goods. (Why? Because these capital goods are one important type of resource.) Therefore, this year's net private domestic investment is a determinant of how much the country can produce in the future.

In 2013, the Bureau of Economic Analysis of the U.S, Department of Commerce expanded the definition of gross private domestic investment to include investment in intellectual property (see Case Study 15.2).

Net Exports

Net exports equal the amount spent by other countries on our goods and services less the amount we spent on other countries' goods and services. This factor must be included, since some of our national output is destined for foreign markets, and we import some of the goods and services we consume. There is no reason why this component of spending cannot be negative, since imports can exceed exports. The quantity of net exports tends to be quite small. Table 15.3 shows that net exports in 2012 were equal (in absolute terms) to about 4 percent of the total amount spent on final goods and services in the United States.

Government Purchases of Goods and Services

This category of spending includes the expenditures of the federal, state, and local governments for the multitude of functions they perform: defense, education, police protection, and so forth. It does not include transfer payments, since they are not payments for current production. Table 15.3 shows that government spending in 2012 accounted for about one-fifth of the total amount spent on final goods and services in the United States. State and local expenditures are bigger than federal expenditures. Many of the expenditures of the federal government are on items like national defense, health, and education, whereas at the state and local levels, the biggest expenditures are for items like education and highways.

Putting Together the Spending Components

Finally, because these four categories of expenditures include all possible types of spending on final goods and services, their sum equals the gross domestic product. In other words,

> *GDP = personal consumption expenditures*
> *+ gross private domestic investment*
> *+ net exports*
> *+ government purchases of goods and services*

As shown in Table 15.3, gross domestic product in 2012 equaled $11,150 + $2,475 − $547 + $3,167, or $16,245 billion.

The Income Approach to GDP

To use the income approach to determine GDP, we must add all the incomes from the production of the year's output. These incomes are of various types: compensation of employees, rents, interest, proprietors' income, and corporate profits. In addition, we must also include indirect business taxes and depreciation.

Compensation of Employees

This is the largest of the income categories. It includes the wages and salaries paid by firms and government agencies to suppliers of labor. In addition, it contains a variety of supplementary payments by employers for the benefit of their employees, such as payments into public and private pension and welfare funds. These supplementary payments are part of the employers' costs and are included in the total compensation of employees.

Rental Income

In the present context, *rent* is defined as a payment to households for the supply of property resources. It includes house rents received by landlords. Quite different definitions of *rent* are used by economists in other contexts.

Net Interest

Interest includes payments of money by private businesses to suppliers of money capital. If you buy a bond issued by General Motors, the interest payments you receive are included. Interest payments made by the government on Treasury bills, savings bonds, and other securities are excluded on the grounds that they are not payments for current goods and services. They are regarded as transfer payments.

Proprietors' Income

What we refer to as *profits* are split into two parts in the national income accounts: proprietors' income and corporate profits. Proprietors' income consists of the net income of unincorporated businesses. In other words, it consists of the net income of proprietorships and partnerships (as well as cooperatives).

Corporate Profits

Corporate profits consist of the income of corporations. In the national income and product accounts, this item contains three parts: (1) dividends paid by companies to stockholders, (2) retained earnings (kept by companies), and (3) the amount paid by corporations as income taxes. In other words, NIPA profits are measured as corporate profits before the payment of corporate income taxes.

Indirect Business Taxes and Miscellaneous

All the items we have discussed here—compensation of employees, rents, interest, proprietors' income, and corporate profits—are forms of income. In addition, there are two non-income items, indirect business taxes and depreciation (along with a few other miscellaneous items, a statistical discrepancy adjustment, and net income from the rest of the world), that must be added to the sum of the income items to obtain GDP. The government imposes certain taxes, such as general sales taxes, excise taxes, and customs duties, which

TABLE 15.4	Type of Claim on Output	Amount of Claim (billions of dollars)*	
Claims on Output, United States, 2012	Compensation of employees	8,612	
	Rental income	541	
	Net interest	440	
	Proprietors' income	1,225	
	Corporate profits	2,010	
	Indirect business taxes and miscellaneous†	1,145	
	National Income		*13,972*
	Depreciation and statistical discrepancy	2,543	
	Gross National Product		*16,497*
	Net income from rest of world	−253	
	Gross Domestic Product		*16,245*

*Numbers may not add up due to rounding.

†Includes business transfer payments and the current surplus of government enterprises.

Source: U.S. Department of Commerce.

firms treat as costs of production. These taxes are called indirect business taxes because they are not imposed directly on the business itself, but on its products or services. A good example of an indirect business tax is the tax on cigarettes; another is the general sales tax. Before a firm can pay income to its workers, suppliers, or stockholders, it must pay these indirect business taxes to the government.

Depreciation

Depreciation is the value of a country's plant, equipment, and structures that are worn out this year. In the national income accounts, depreciation is often called a capital consumption allowance because it measures the value of the capital consumed during the year.

Putting Together the Income Components (Plus Indirect Business Taxes and Depreciation)

As we state repeatedly, the sum of the five types of income described here—plus indirect business taxes, depreciation, net income from the rest of the world (see Case Study 15.1), and a few other minor items—equals gross domestic product. In other words,

$GDP = compensation\ of\ employees$

$+ rents$

$+ interest$

$+ proprietors'\ income$

$+ corporate\ profits$

$+ indirect\ business\ taxes\ and\ miscellaneous$

$+ depreciation\ and\ statistical\ discrepency$

$+ net\ income\ from\ the\ rest\ of\ the\ world$

Table 15.4 shows the total amounts of various types of income paid out (or owed) during 2012. It also shows indirect business taxes, depreciation, and net income from the rest of the world. You can see for yourself that the total of these items equals gross domestic product. Also note that the difference between gross national product (GNP) and gross domestic product (GDP) is income receipts from the rest of the world less income payments to the rest of the world (see Case Study 15.1).

REVIEW AND PRACTICE

Summary

1   A key indicator of the health of any country's economy is the gross domestic product (GDP), which measures the total value of the final goods and services the country produces in a particular period. Since gross domestic product is affected by the price level, it must be deflated by a price index to correct for price-level changes. When deflated in this way, GDP is called real GDP or GDP in constant dollars.

2   There are many pitfalls in calculating the gross domestic product. We must avoid counting the same output more than once. Purely financial transactions that do not reflect current production must be excluded. Also, some final goods and services that must be included in GDP are not bought and sold in the marketplace, so they are valued at what they cost.

3   GDP is not an ideal measure of total economic output, let alone a satisfactory measure of economic well-being. It takes no account of a country's population, the amount of leisure time, or the distribution of income. It does not reflect many changes in the quality of goods and many social costs, like pollution.

4   One approach to GDP is the expenditures approach, which regards GDP as the sum of all the expenditures involved in taking the total output of final goods and services off the market. To determine GDP in this way, we

must add all the expenditures on final goods and services. Economists distinguish among four broad categories of spending: personal consumption, gross private domestic investment, government purchases, and net exports. GDP equals the sum of these four items.

5 Another approach to GDP is the income approach, which regards GDP as the sum of all the incomes derived from the production of the year's output (plus depreciation and indirect business taxes). To determine GDP in this way, we must add all the income from the production of the year's total output (plus depreciation and indirect business taxes). Economists identify five broad categories of income: compensation of employees, rent, interest, proprietors' income, and corporate profits. GDP equals the sum of these five items (plus depreciation and indirect business taxes).

Problems and Questions

1 The following table shows the value of GDP in the nation of Puritania. The figures shown are in millions of 1980 dollars and current dollars. Fill in the blanks.

Year	GDP (millions of 1980 dollars)	GDP (millions of current dollars)	Current Price Level / 1980 Price Level
1980	1,000	—	1.00
1984	—	—	1.20
1988	1,300	1,440	1.40
1992	1,500	—	1.60
1996	—	—	1.70
2000	1,700	2,720	1.80

2 If former president George W. Bush wins $100,000 from former president Bill Clinton in a poker game, will this increase, decrease, or have no effect on GDP? Explain.

3 If a paper mill produces $1 million worth of paper this year but adds considerably to the pollutants in a nearby river, are the social costs arising from this pollution reflected in the gross domestic product? If so, how? Should these costs be reflected in GDP? If so, why?

4 A small country contains only 10 firms. William Moran, the country's top statistician, calculates the country's GDP by totaling the sales of these 10 firms. Do you agree with this procedure? Why or why not?

Key Terms

gross domestic product (GDP)

final goods and services

intermediate goods

base year

current dollars

constant dollars

real GDP

price index

deflating

value added

social costs

expenditures approach

income approach

Viewpoint for Analysis

In 1993, the late Robert Eisner, professor of economics at Northwestern University and a former president of the American Economic Association, wrote: "Our GDP is running some $400 billion a year below normal. We are losing $100 billion a year of gross private domestic investment. We are losing countless billions more in public investment as states and localities across the country . . . are forced to curtail even necessary services."[2]

(a) Why should we care whether GDP is $400 billion a year below normal? What are the arguments in favor of increasing GDP? What are arguments against doing so?

(b) Based on Eisner's estimates, if net exports are equal to normal, can consumption expenditure be $300 billion a year below normal? Why or why not?

(c) How can anyone estimate the level of GDP that would be "normal" in a particular year? Do you think that Democrats and Republicans would agree on this score? Why or why not?

---

[2] R. Eisner, "Clinton, Deficits, and the Economy," *Challenge*, May–June 1993, 49.

Business Fluctuations and Unemployment

LEARNING OBJECTIVES

➤ To describe the four phases of business fluctuations

➤ To explain what aggregate demand and aggregate supply curves show

➤ To explore the types of unemployment and the costs they impose on society

➤ *(Exploring Further)* To describe the effects of shifts in the aggregate demand and aggregate supply curves

John Maynard Keynes, unquestionably one of the most influential economists of the last century, changed the way that people thought about cures for economic depression. At present, some of his ideas are widely accepted; others have been rejected. What exactly did he say? One purpose of this chapter is to answer this question; in subsequent chapters, we consider the views of his followers and critics.

First, however, we must recognize that while the U.S. economy has grown considerably over the past century, the ascent has not been a smooth one. The U.S. economy can be compared to a roller coaster that keeps moving higher and higher. In later chapters, we will discuss some of the reasons behind economic fluctuations and some of the proposed remedies. In this chapter, we need to define what we mean by a business cycle. Given the economic tools that we developed so far, we can describe in simple terms some of the fundamental forces that bring about business cycles. We also need to consider the consequences of these fluctuations for individuals and the economy as a whole. In particular, we must discuss unemployment.

Business Fluctuations

To illustrate what we mean by business fluctuations (or the business cycle), we look at how national output has grown in the United States. Figure 16.1 shows the behavior of real GDP (in constant dollars) in the United States since 1949. It is clear that output has grown considerably during this period. Indeed, GDP is more than six times what it was 60 years ago. It is also clear that this growth has not been steady. On the contrary, although the long-term trend has been upward, there have been periods (1969–1970, 1973–1975, January–July 1980, 1981–1982, 1990–1991, 2001, and 2008–2009) when national output has declined.

Potential gross domestic product   **Potential gross domestic product** is the total amount of goods and services that can be produced if the economy is operating at full capacity, or full employment. Figure 16.1 shows that national output tends to rise and approach its potential level (that is, its full-employment level) for a while, then falters and falls below this level, then rises to approach it once more, then falls below it again,

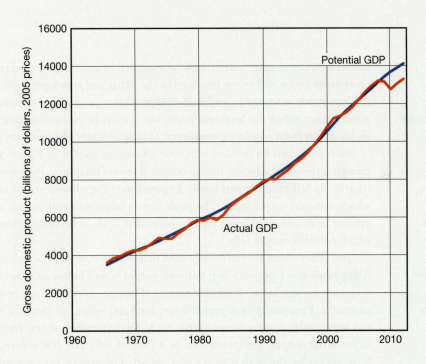

FIGURE 16.1

Gross Domestic Product (in 2005 dollars), United States, 1965–2011

Real GDP has not grown steadily. Instead, it approaches its potential level (that is, its full-employment level), then falters and falls below this level, then rises once more, and so on. Please note: at the time of publication a consistent set of potential GDP data with the 2009 base year was not available. Instead the 2005-base-year data were used. The newer data (when they are available) will show essentially the same pattern.

FIGURE 16.2

Four Phases of the Business Cycle

Each cycle can be divided into four phases: trough, expansion, peak, and recession.

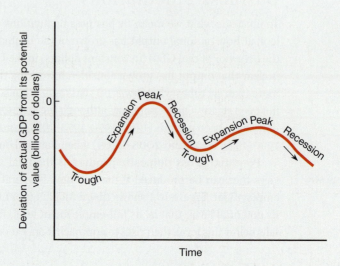

and so on. For example, output, having remained close to its potential level in the prosperous 1960s, fell below this level in the 1970s and rose again to this level in the late 1980s, late 1990s, and mid-2000s. This movement of national output is sometimes called the **business cycle**, but it must be recognized that business cycles are far from regular or consistent. On the contrary, they are very irregular.

Each cycle can be divided into four phases, as shown in Figure 16.2. The **trough** is the point where national output is lowest relative to its potential level (that is, its full-employment level). **Expansion** is the subsequent phase during which national output rises. The **peak** occurs when national output is highest relative to its potential level. Finally, **recession** is the subsequent phase during which national output falls.[1]

Two other terms are frequently used to describe stages of the business cycle. A **depression** is a period when national output is well below its potential level; it is a severe recession. Depressions are, of course, periods of excessive unemployment. **Prosperity** is a period when national output is close to its potential level (indeed, sometimes above it). If total spending is too high relative to potential output, prosperity can be a time of inflation. (Of course, in some business cycles, the peak may not be a period of prosperity because output may be below its potential level, and the trough may not be a period of depression because the output may not be far below its potential level.)

Business cycle

Trough
Expansion
Peak
Recession

Depression

Prosperity

[1] More precisely, the peak and trough are generally defined in terms of deviations from the long-term trend of national output, rather than in terms of deviations from the potential (full-employment) level of national output. Also, according to some people, a rough definition of a recession is at least two consecutive quarters of falling real GDP; it is not sufficient for output just to fall.

From 1949 to 2011, peaks occurred in 1953, 1957, 1960, 1969, 1973, 1980 (January), 1981, early 1990, 2000, and 2007; troughs occurred in 1949, 1954, 1958, 1961, 1970, 1975, 1980 (July), 1982 (November), 1991, 2001, and 2009. Relative to the Great Depression, none of these recessions was very long or very deep (although the 1974–1975, 1981–1982, and 2008–2009 recessions resulted in substantial unemployment).

Although business cycles have certain things in common, they are highly individualistic (see Figure 16.3). For some phenomena, it may be true that "if

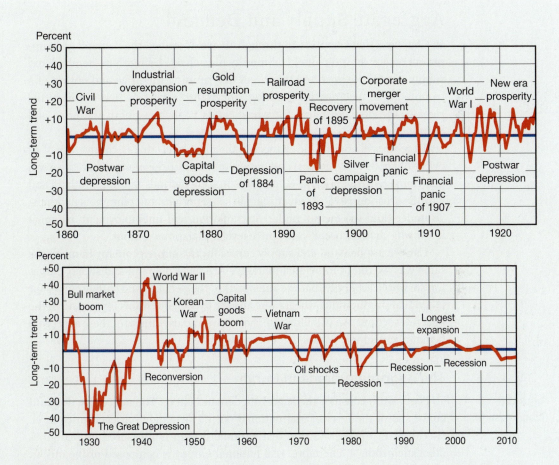

FIGURE 16.3

Business Fluctuations in the United States, 1860–2011

To construct this chart, a single index of economic activity was used. After fitting a trend line to it, the deviations of this index from its trend value were plotted. The results show the fluctuations in economic activity in the United States.

Source: Ameritrust Company and IHS Global Insight.

you've seen one, you've seen them all," but not for business cycles. They vary too much in length and nature. Moreover, the basic set of factors responsible for the recession and the expansion differs from cycle to cycle. This means that any theory designed to explain them must be broad enough to accommodate their idiosyncrasies. In subsequent chapters, much will be said about the causes of business fluctuations; however, using aggregate demand and supply curves, we can begin to understand how some of these fluctuations come about.

Aggregate Supply and Demand

In Chapter 2 and Chapters 16 through 18, we described the demand and supply curves for an individual commodity like wheat. Using these demand and supply curves, we analyzed the forces determining the price and output of a commodity in a competitive market. For example, we saw that a shift to the right in the demand curve for wheat tends to increase both the price and output of wheat.

Here we will analyze the changes in the price level (that is, the average of all prices of goods and services) and output of the entire economy. That is, we will determine why the price level increases in some periods but not in others and why the gross domestic product soars in some periods and plummets in others. To understand the factors underlying inflation and unemployment, we must know why changes occur in the price level and national output.

Can we use demand and supply curves for the entire economy in much the same way we did in individual markets? Are there demand and supply curves for the whole economy that are analogous to the demand and supply curves for individual products like wheat? The answer to both questions is yes. And in the next few sections, we will illustrate the nature and usefulness of these aggregate demand and supply curves.

The Aggregate Demand Curve

Aggregate demand curve

To begin with, consider the aggregate demand curve. The **aggregate demand curve** shows the level of real national output demanded at each price level. (Recall from Chapter 15 that real national output is measured by real gross domestic product. Therefore, real national output is composed of the output of food, automobiles, machine tools, ships, and a host of other final goods and services produced.) As can be seen in Figure 16.4, the aggregate demand curve slopes downward and to the right. In other words, when other things are held equal, the higher the price level, the smaller the total output demanded; and the lower the price level, the higher the total output demanded. This might be expected, since the demand curve for an individual product also slopes downward and to the right, as we saw in Chapter 2.

FIGURE 16.4

Aggregate Demand Curve

The aggregate demand curve shows the level of total real output demanded at each price level. If the price level is 100 (this is an aggregate price index with no specific units), a total real output of $220 billion is demanded. If the price level is 103, a total real output of $200 billion is demanded.

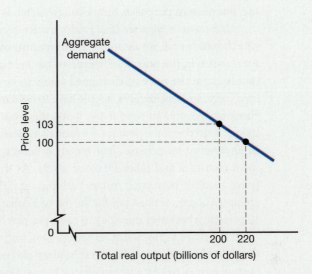

There are two fundamental reasons why the demand curve for an individual commodity like wheat slopes downward and to the right: (1) As the price of the commodity falls, consumers buy more of it because it is less expensive relative to other commodities, and (2) as the commodity's price falls, each consumer's money income (which is held constant) can buy a larger total amount of goods and services, so it is likely that more of this commodity will be bought.

Neither of these reasons can be used to explain the shape of the aggregate demand curve, which relates the economy's total real output to the price level. When the price level falls, the average price of all goods and services falls.[2] Unlike the demand curve for an individual commodity, it is not just a single price that falls, with the result that consumers find the relevant commodity relatively cheap and buy more of it. Because the aggregate demand curve is concerned with the economy's price level and total real output, not the price and output of a single commodity, the reasons for the downward slope of a demand curve for an individual commodity are not applicable to the aggregate demand curve.

Reasons for the Aggregate Demand Curve's Shape

Why, then, does the aggregate demand curve slope downward and to the right? The basic reasoning can be described in two steps. (In later chapters, we fill in many of the details regarding the demand for money and the effects of the

---

[2] Of course, this does not mean that the price of each good and service falls when the price level falls; only the average falls.

supply of money on interest rates and the effects of interest rates on total spending. For present purposes, only a rough sketch is needed.)

1. *Increases in the price level push up interest rates.* In constructing the aggregate demand curve, we assume that the quantity of money in the economy is fixed. An increase in the price level increases the average money cost of each transaction because the price of each good tends to be higher. Therefore, if the price level increases considerably, people have to hold more money in their wallets and checking accounts to pay for the items they want to buy. Since the quantity of money is fixed and the demand for money increases, there is a shortage of money. In an attempt to increase their money holdings, people borrow or sell government securities and other financial assets. As this happens, interest rates (the

Interest rate

prices paid for borrowing money) are bid up. (The **interest rate** is the annual amount a borrower must pay for the use of a dollar for a year. If the interest rate is 10 percent, a borrower must pay 10 cents per year for the use of a dollar for a year.)

2. *Increases in interest rates reduce total output.* When interest rates go up, firms that borrow money to invest in plant and equipment and consumers who borrow money to buy automobiles or houses tend to cut down on their spending on these items. With the higher interest rates, the cost of borrowing money is greater; hence, some of these investment projects and purchases no longer seem profitable or worthwhile. Because of the reduced spending on these items, the country's total real output declines.[3]

The Aggregate Supply Curve

Aggregate supply curve

Just as the aggregate demand curve is analogous to the demand curve for an individual product, so the aggregate supply curve is analogous to the supply curve for an individual product. The **aggregate supply curve** shows the level of real national output supplied at each price level. Aggregate supply curves can pertain to either the short run or the long run. In the short run, the prices of all inputs are assumed to be fixed; in the long run, they are permitted to adjust fully to eliminate the underemployment or shortage of inputs (like labor).[4]

Short-run aggregate supply curve

As can be seen in Figure 16.5, the **short-run aggregate supply curve** slopes upward and to the right. In other words, when other things are held equal, the higher the price level, the larger the total output supplied; and the lower the price level, the smaller the total output supplied. This might be expected, since the supply curve for an individual product also slopes upward and to the right, as we saw in Chapter 2.

---

[3] There are other reasons for the shape of the aggregate demand curve. For one thing, an increase in the price level reduces the real value of the currency and government bonds held by the public. (If you have $500 in cash, it represents less purchasing power if a hamburger costs $5 than if it costs $0.50.) A reduction in the real value of people's wealth lessens their demand for goods and services. Also, increases in the price level tend to lower net exports, because foreigners tend to respond to our price increases by cutting back their purchases from us.

[4] These definitions of the short run and long run are different from those in Chapter 3, but there is little danger of confusion, since the contexts in which the terms are used are quite different.

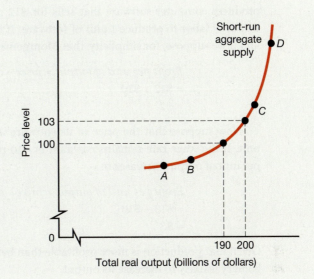

FIGURE 16.5

Short-Run Aggregate Supply Curve

The short-run aggregate supply curve shows the level of total real output supplied at each price level, given that the prices of all inputs are fixed. If the price level is 100, a total real output of $190 billion is supplied. If the price level is 103, a total real output of $200 billion is supplied.

But just as we could not derive the aggregate demand curve simply by adding the demand curves for all the individual commodities in the economy, so we cannot derive the aggregate supply curve by adding the supply curves for all the individual commodities. If we did this, we would commit a grave error because the factors held constant in constructing an individual supply curve are not held constant in constructing an aggregate supply curve. In particular, in constructing an individual supply curve, the price of only one commodity is allowed to vary, whereas in constructing an aggregate supply curve, the price level (and therefore every price) is allowed to vary.

Why the Short-Run Aggregate Supply Curve Slopes Upward and to the Right

To see why most economists believe that the short-run aggregate supply curve slopes upward and to the right, we begin by noting the obvious fact that firms are motivated to make profits. Because the profits earned by producing a unit of output equal the product's price minus the cost of producing it, increases in the product's price tend to increase the firm's profits. (Why? Because the wages of workers and the prices of raw materials are fixed in the short run.) Hence, since increases in product prices tend to increase the profit per unit resulting from the production of the product, they tend to induce firms to produce more output.

As an illustration, consider the Montgomery Software Corporation, which produces computer software that sells for $12 per unit. Suppose that it uses 1 hour of labor to produce 1 unit of software. If the wage rate is $10 per hour, and if we suppose, for simplicity, that Montgomery has no other costs, then

Profit per unit of output = price − cost per unit of output
= $12 − $10
= $2

Now suppose that the price of its software increases from $12 to $13 per unit. If the wage rate remains constant at $10 per hour, Montgomery's profit per unit of output increases to

Profit per unit of output = price − cost per unit of output
= $13 − $10
= $3

Given that production is more profitable than before the price increase, Montgomery is likely to increase its output.

Why the Short-Run Aggregate Supply Curve Gets Steeper

According to many economists, the short-run aggregate supply curve tends to be close to horizontal at relatively low levels of output and gets steeper and steeper as output increases. To see why it tends to be close to horizontal at relatively low output levels, note that there is likely to be considerable unutilized productive capacity under these conditions. If business picks up, firms are likely to increase their output by bringing this unutilized capacity back into operation. Since their costs per unit of output do not increase appreciably as their production rises, they will not raise prices substantially. Therefore, the short-run aggregate supply curve is close to horizontal.

On the other hand, at relatively high levels of output, production is pushing hard against capacity constraints, and it becomes increasingly difficult and costly for firms to increase their output further. Therefore, the short-run aggregate supply curve becomes steeper as output rises. Why? Because bigger and bigger increases in the price level are required to elicit a given additional amount of output. Moving from point *B* to point *C* to point *D* in Figure 16.5, the price level must go up by increasing amounts to elicit an additional billion dollars of real output. Eventually, the short-run aggregate supply curve may become close to vertical.

Not all economists agree that the short-run aggregate supply curve has the shape indicated in Figure 16.5. The new classical macroeconomists say that the short-run aggregate supply curve may be vertical. A discussion of their views is postponed to Chapter 26. All you should note at this point is that the shape of the short-run aggregate supply curve is a matter of controversy.

National Output and the Price Level

In the short run, the equilibrium level of real national output and the equilibrium price level are given by the intersection of the aggregate demand curve and the short-run aggregate supply curve. In Figure 16.6, the equilibrium level of real national output is $200 billion, and the equilibrium price level is 103. The price level is expressed as an aggregate index with no specific units. The reasoning here is essentially the same as in Chapter 2, where we showed that the equilibrium price and output of a commodity are given by the intersection of the commodity's demand and supply curves. In the present case, an equilibrium can occur only at a price level and level of real national output where aggregate demand equals aggregate supply.

Using aggregate demand and aggregate supply curves, we can begin to understand what has caused some of the swings in the U.S. economy. To illustrate, we consider how aggregate demand changed during the Great Depression and World War II.

The Great Depression

We begin with the late 1920s. During 1928 and 1929, the U.S. economy was in the midst of prosperity, and the gross domestic product was approximately equal to its potential value. Unemployment was low. Among the reasons for this prosperity was a relatively strong demand for machinery and equipment to produce new products (like the automobile, radio, telephone, and electric power) and replace old machinery and equipment that had been worn out or outmoded during World War I and its aftermath.

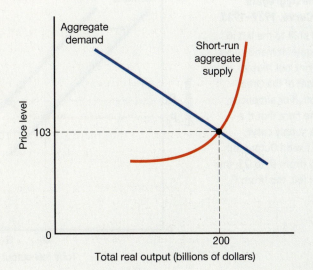

FIGURE 16.6

Equilibrium Price Level and Total Real Output

The equilibrium level of total real output and the equilibrium price level are given by the intersection of the aggregate demand curve and the short-run aggregate supply curve. Here, the equilibrium price level is 103 and the equilibrium level of total real output is $200 billion.

The picture changed dramatically in 1929. After the stock market plummeted in October of that year, the economy headed down at a staggering pace. Real GDP fell by almost one-third between 1929 and 1933. By 1933, unemployment had risen to an enormous 25 percent of the labor force. One important reason was the severe contraction of gross private domestic investment. (Recall from Chapter 15 that gross private domestic investment is spending on tools, equipment, machinery, construction, and additional inventories.) Whereas gross private domestic investment was about $16 billion in 1929, it fell to about $1 billion in 1933. (The reasons for this decrease are discussed in later chapters.) Another important factor was the decrease in the supply of money between 1929 and 1933. For the reasons we will discuss in Chapters 21 and 25, this, too, tended to depress spending and output.

Put in terms of the aggregate demand and supply curves, the situation was as shown in Figure 16.7. For the reasons given in the previous paragraph, the aggregate demand curve shifted markedly to the left; and as would be expected on the basis of Figure 16.7, total real output and the price level fell between 1929 and 1933.

World War II

The United States remained mired in the Great Depression until World War II (and the mobilization period that preceded the war). To carry out the war effort, the government spent huge amounts on military personnel and equipment. One result of this increase in spending was a substantial increase in real GDP,

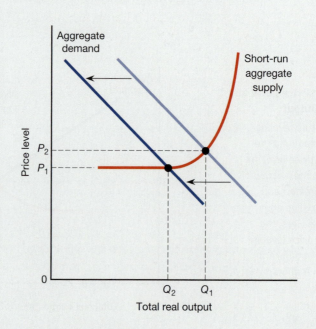

FIGURE 16.7

Shift of the Aggregate Demand Curve, 1929–1933

A marked shift to the left in the aggregate demand curve was the principal reason for the onset of the Great Depression. (For simplicity, we assume here that the aggregate supply curve remained fixed.) Output fell drastically (from Q_1 to Q_2); the price level fell, too (from P_2 to P_1).

FIGURE 16.8

Shifts of the Aggregate Demand Curve during World War II

When we entered World War II, the aggregate demand curve shifted to the right as military expenditures mushroomed. Output increased (from Q_0 to Q_1 to Q_2), and inflationary pressures mounted. (For simplicity, we assume that the aggregate supply curve remained fixed.)

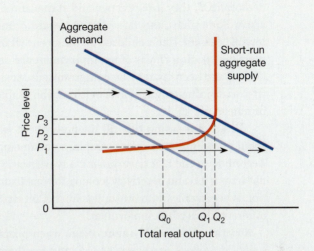

which rose by about 90 percent between 1939 and 1945. Another result was a marked reduction in unemployment, as the armed forces expanded and jobs opened up in defense plants and elsewhere. Still another result was the appearance of serious inflationary pressures. As the aggregate demand curve shifted to the right, there was severe upward pressure on the price level as increases in spending pushed national output to its maximum (see Figure 16.8). To counter this pressure, the government instituted price controls (which mandated that firms charge no more than particular amounts) and other measures that kept a temporary lid on prices; but when these controls were lifted after the termination of the war, the price level increased dramatically. Between 1945 and 1948, prices to consumers rose by about 34 percent.

Unemployment

One of the principal reasons why economists and policy makers are so interested in business fluctuations is that the unemployment rate tends to go up during recessions and depressions. As stressed in the Prologue, unemployment is an economic and social problem that concerns us all. The balance of this chapter is devoted to the definition, measurement, and effects of unemployment.

Over a century ago, Pope Leo XIII said, "Among the purposes of a society should be to arrange for a continuous supply of work at all times and seasons."[5] The word *unemployment* may be one of the most frightening in

[5] Pope Leo XIII, "Encyclical Letter on the Conditions of Labor," May 15, 1891.

the English language—and for good reason. Unemployed people become demoralized; they lose prestige and status and often see their families break apart. Sometimes, they are pushed toward crime and drugs; often they feel terrible despair. Their children are innocent victims, too. Indeed, perhaps the most devastating effects of unemployment are on children, whose education, health, and security may be compromised. Most people would agree that in this or any other country, every citizen who is able and willing to work should be able to get a job.

We are not saying that all unemployment, whatever its cause or nature, should be eliminated. (For example, some unemployment may be voluntary.) According to the U.S. government, any person 16 years old or older who does not have a job and is actively looking for one is unemployed. Since this definition is necessarily quite broad, it is important that we distinguish among three different kinds of unemployment.

Frictional unemployment occurs when people quit their jobs, when high school or college graduates are looking for their first job, or when seasonal workers experience down time. **Structural unemployment** occurs when new goods and new technologies call for new skills, and workers with older skills cannot find jobs. **Cyclical unemployment** occurs because of business fluctuations of the sort shown in Figure 16.3.

Frictional unemployment

Structural unemployment

Cyclical unemployment

The Unemployment Rate

Each month, the federal government conducts a scientific survey, asking the individuals in a carefully selected sample of the U.S. population whether they have a job and, if not, whether they are looking for one. According to most experts, the resulting figures are quite reliable but subject to a number of qualifications. For example, the figures do not indicate the extent to which people are underemployed. Some people work only part-time or at jobs well below their level of education or skill, but the government figures count them as fully employed. Also, some people have given up looking for a job and are no longer listed among the unemployed, even though they would be glad to get work if any was offered. To be counted as unemployed in the government figures, a person must be actively seeking employment.

To obtain the unemployment rate, the Bureau of Labor Statistics (the government agency responsible for producing the unemployment data) divides the estimated number of people who are unemployed by the estimated number of people in the labor force. To be in the labor force, a person must be either employed or unemployed. Note that the unemployment rate can rise either because people who formerly were employed are thrown out of work or because people who formerly were not in the labor force decide to look for jobs. For example, an increase in the number of homemakers who return to the labor force may raise the unemployment rate.

UNEMPLOYMENT: THE CLASSICAL VIEW

In early 1914, it was obvious that something was wrong with the U.S. economy. Unemployment was climbing, prices were falling, and factories were closing. While many were quick to blame the Wilson administration for the slump, few thought that the government should intervene to promote higher employment. The prevailing view among classical economists was that by purchasing more goods and services to take up the slack in business investment, the government might do more harm than good.

Economists of the time saw business cycle fluctuations as temporary aberrations that the price system, left to its own devices, would automatically correct. Classical economic thought held that there could be no such thing as general overproduction. Depressions would cure themselves. If labor was unemployed, workers had only to accept lower wages, whereupon business would gladly rehire them and prosperity would return.

Underlying this assumption was a doctrine called *Say's law*, after the nineteenth-century French economist J.-B. Say. According to this law, the production of a certain amount of goods and services results in the generation of an amount of income that, if spent, is precisely sufficient to buy that output. In other words, supply creates its own demand. The total amount paid out by the producers of the goods and services to resource owners must equal the value of the goods and services. So, if this amount is spent, it must be sufficient to purchase all the goods and services produced.

But what if resource owners do not spend all their income but save some of it instead? How, then, will the necessary spending arise to take all the output off the market? The answer

the classical economists offered is that each dollar saved is invested. Therefore, investment (expenditures by business firms on plant, equipment, and other productive assets) restores to the spending stream what resource owners take out through the saving process. The classical economists believed that the amount invested would automatically equal the amount saved because the interest rate (the price paid for borrowing money) would fluctuate in such a way as to maintain equality between them.

Further, the classical economists claimed that the amount of goods and services firms can sell depends on the prices they charge as well as on total spending. For example, $1 million in spending takes 100 cars off the market if the price is $10,000 per car and 50 cars off the market if the price is $20,000 per car. Recognizing this, the classical economists argued that firms would cut prices to sell their output. Competition among firms would prod them to reduce their prices in this way, with the result that the high-employment level of output would be taken off the market, with no surplus output or labor left over.

The prices of resources must also be reduced under such circumstances. Otherwise, firms would incur losses because they would be getting less for their product but paying no less for the resources. The classical economists believed that it was realistic to expect the prices of resources to decline in such a situation. Indeed, they were quite willing to assume that the wage rate (the price of labor) would be flexible in this way. Through the processes of competition among laborers, they felt that wage rates would be bid down to the level where everyone who really wanted to work could get a job.

KARL MARX ON UNEMPLOYMENT

Karl Marx

World War I had been good for the U.S. labor movement. But with the armistice, the economy slowed down, the demand for labor shrank, and support for unions almost vanished. Unemployment, virtually nonexistent during the war, jumped to 14 percent in 1921. To some workers, angry at unemployment, the views of Karl Marx were appealing. While the classical economists held that depressions were temporary and self-correcting aberrations, Marx argued that economic crises were not accidents but a built-in feature of the capitalist system. A meticulous German scholar who spent much of his life in poverty-ridden circumstances in Britain, Marx (1818–1883) wrote a huge, four-volume work on

economics, *Das Kapital*.* Eighteen years in the making, it remains one of the most influential books ever written.

To understand Marx, we need to know something about the times in which he lived. The period was characterized by revolutionary pressures against the ruling classes. In most of the countries of Europe, there was little democracy as we know it. The masses participated little, if at all, in the world of political affairs and very fully in the world of drudgery. For example, at one factory in Manchester, England, in 1862, people worked an average of about 80 hours per week. For these long hours of toil, the workers generally received small wages. They often could do little more than feed and clothe themselves. Given these circumstances, it is little wonder that revolutionary pressures were manifest.

Marx, viewing the economic system of his day, believed that capitalism was doomed to collapse. He believed that the workers were exploited by the capitalists—the owners of factories, mines, and other types of capital. And he believed that the capitalists, by introducing new labor-saving technology, would throw more and more workers into unemployment. This army of unemployed workers, by competing for jobs, would keep wages at a subsistence level. Marx felt that as machinery was substituted for labor, profits would fall. Unemployment would become more severe. Big firms would absorb small ones. Eventually, the capitalistic system was bound to collapse.

According to Marx, the inevitable successor to capitalism would be socialism, an economic system with no private property.

Instead, property would be owned by society as a whole. Socialism, constituting a "dictatorship of the proletariat," would be only a transitional step to the promised land of communism. Marx did not spell out the characteristics of communism in detail. He was sure that it would be a classless society where everyone worked and no one owned capital, and he was sure that the state would "wither away," but he did not attempt to go much

beyond this in his blueprint for communism. For the present purposes, it is not necessary to detail the many places where Marx's theories went astray. The important point here is that although the classical view of unemployment (discussed in Case Study 16.1) was the dominant one, it did not go unchallenged, even in the nineteenth century.

*Karl Marx, Das Kapital (New York: Modern Library, 1906).

How Much Unemployment Is There?

To get some idea of the extent of unemployment, we can consult Figure 16.9, which shows the percentage of the labor force unemployed during each year from 1930 to 2012. Note the wide fluctuations in the unemployment rate and the very high unemployment rates during the 1930s. Fortunately, unemployment since World War II has never approached the tragically high levels of the Great Depression of the 1930s. In 1981 and 1982, it rose to about 9.5 percent, after which it fell to about 5.2 percent in 1989. It rose again from 1990 to 1992, then declined to about 3.8 percent in 2000, before rising to 6.4 percent in 2003 and 10.1 percent in 2009. By the end of 2013 it fell back down below 7.5 percent. Although many of these variations in the unemployment rate may seem small, they are by no means unimportant. With a civilian labor force of over 150 million in the United States, a 1-percentage-point increase in the unemployment

FIGURE 16.9

Unemployment Rate, United States, 1930–2012

The unemployment rate has varied substantially. Fortunately, since World War II it has not approached the very high levels of the Great Depression of the 1930s. But the recessions of 1981 and 2008–2009 showed that the nation is not immune to severe bouts of unemployment.

rate means that over 1.5 million more people are unemployed. Any administration, Democratic or Republican, watches these figures closely and tries to avoid significant increases in unemployment.

The Costs of Unemployment

High levels of unemployment impose great costs on society. In this section, we describe these costs, both economic and noneconomic.

Economic Costs

The economic costs of unemployment include the goods and services that could have been produced by the unemployed. Because these people were unemployed, society had to forgo the production of the goods and services they might have produced, with the result that human wants were less effectively fulfilled than would otherwise have been the case. To determine how much society loses in this way by tolerating an unemployment rate above the minimum level resulting from frictional (and some structural) unemployment, economists estimate potential GDP, which is the level of gross domestic product that could be achieved with full employment. (We first introduced the concept of potential GDP in Figure 16.1.) Therefore, if **full employment** is defined as a 5 percent unemployment rate, potential GDP can be estimated by multiplying 95 percent of the labor force times the normal hours of work per year times the average output per hour of work at the relevant time.

Full employment

The gap between actual and potential GDP is a measure of what society loses by tolerating less than full employment. Figure 16.1 shows the estimated size of this gap from 1960 to 2011. Clearly, the economic costs of unemployment have been very substantial. Consider 1975, a recession year when unemployment was about 8.5 percent. As shown in Figure 16.1, society lost about $100 billion in that year alone. Although this estimate is very rough, it is accurate enough to suggest the social waste that accompanies large-scale unemployment.

One important problem in estimating this gap stems from the difficulty in defining full employment. For many years, a common definition of full employment was a 4 percent unemployment rate, since it was felt that frictional and structural unemployment could not be reduced below this level. During the 1970s, some argued that an unemployment rate of about 5 percent was a more realistic measure of full employment, because more young people, women, and minority workers were in the labor force. All these groups find it relatively hard to find jobs. In the 1980s, many economists felt that 6 percent (or higher) was a more appropriate figure, but in the late 1990s, some argued it was much lower, closer to the 4 percent of the 1960s (see Case Study 19.2). In the aftermath of the Great Recession of 2008–2009, the consensus swung back to believing that the full-employment unemployment rate was closer to 6 percent.

JOHN MAYNARD KEYNES AND THE GREAT DEPRESSION

John Maynard Keynes

The son of a British economist who was famous in his own right, John Maynard Keynes (1883–1946) was enormously successful in a variety of fields. He wrote a brilliant book on the theory of probability while still a relatively young man. Working for a half-hour in bed each morning, he made millions of dollars as a stock market speculator. He was a distinguished patron of the arts and a member of the Bloomsbury set, a group of intellectual pacesetters for British society. He was a faculty member at Cambridge University and a key figure in the British Treasury.

Keynes was born in the year that Marx died. His world was quite different from Marx's, and Keynes himself—polished, successful, a member of the elite—was quite different from

the poverty-stricken, revolutionary Marx. But the two great economists were linked in at least one important respect. Both were preoccupied with unemployment and the future of the capitalist system. As we saw in Case Study 16.2, Marx predicted that unemployment would get worse and worse, until at last the capitalist system would collapse. In the 1930s, when Keynes was at the height of his influence, the Great Depression seemed to many people to be proving Marx right.

In 1936, while the world was still in the throes of this economic disaster, Keynes's book *The General Theory of Employment, Interest, and Money** was published. His purpose in this book was to explain how the capitalist economic system could get stalled in the sort of depressed state of equilibrium that existed in the 1930s. He also tried to explain how governments might help to solve the problem.

Contrary to the classical economists, Keynes concluded that no automatic mechanism in a capitalist society would generate a high level of employment—or, at least, would generate it quickly enough to be relied on in practice. Instead, the equilibrium level of national output might for a long time be below the level required to achieve high employment. To push the economy toward a higher level of employment, Keynes advocated the conscious, forceful use of the government's power to spend and tax.

*John Maynard Keynes, *The General Theory of Employment, Interest, and Money* (New York: Harcourt, Brace, 1936).

A NEW (AND OLD) WAY OF LOOKING AT BOOMS AND BUSTS

In the words of the late economic historian Charles P. Kindleberger, financial crises are a "hardy perennial"; in other words, they keep happening with rather distressing frequency.

Recently, the International Monetary Fund cataloged 42 crises in 37 countries—since 1970 alone. In fact, booms and busts of this kind have been regular events in the global economy for centuries. Early examples include tulip mania in the 1630s, the South Sea bubble in the 1720s, and the U.S. railroad bubble in the 1860s and 1870s, which was followed by the longest U.S. recession ever—one that lasted five and a half years.

According to the late economist Hyman P. Minsky, financial booms and busts follow a very predictable pattern: easy credit, euphoria, speculation, and rising debt levels followed by financial stress, bankruptcies, panic, and a rush for the exits. Invariably, the "bust" part of such a financial cycle includes a recession.

While it may be tempting to place all the blame for the 2007–2009 subprime crisis and other financial convulsions of the last couple of centuries on free market capitalism and financial deregulation, we should resist that temptation. Two of the worst financial crises of the last three decades occurred in Japan and South Korea. These were heavily regulated economies that nevertheless ran into serious trouble. The "animal spirits" that drive booms and busts may be very hard to control. The best we may be able to do is limit the economic damage.

Noneconomic Costs

Unemployment strikes at the social fabric of families and societies; it is not only an economic phenomenon. There is a wide variety of responses to unemployment. Some people weather it pretty well, while others sink into despair; some people have substantial savings they can draw on, while others are hard-pressed; some people manage to shield their family from the blow, while others allow their misfortunes to spread to the rest of the family. But despite these variations, being without work generally deals a heavy blow to a person's feelings of worth. It hits hard at a person's self-image, suggesting that he or she is not needed, cannot support a family, and is not really a full and valuable member of society. The impact of widespread and persistent unemployment is most clearly visible at present among blacks and other racial minorities, where unemployment rates (around 40 percent among black teenagers in 2012) are much higher than among the white population. Unquestionably, the prevalence of unemployment among blacks and other racial minorities greatly influences how they view themselves and how they interact with the rest of the community.

EXPLORING FURTHER

Effects of Shifts in the Aggregate Demand and Short-Run Aggregate Supply Curves

Shifts in the Aggregate Demand Curve

In Chapter 2, we saw that shifts in the demand curve for an individual commodity result in changes in the price and output of this commodity. We now see that shifts in the aggregate demand curve result in changes in the price level and total real output.

Effect of a Rightward Shift Suppose consumers or investors decide to *increase* their spending, perhaps because of a change in their expectations. (They anticipate a marked improvement in economic conditions.) Since the level of total real output demanded at each price level increases, the aggregate demand curve shifts outward and the right, as shown in Figure 16.10. What is the effect on the price level and total output? The answer depends on where the aggregate demand curve intersects the short-run aggregate supply curve before the shift in the aggregate demand curve.

If the intersection occurs in the horizontal range of the short-run aggregate supply curve, the rightward shift of the aggregate demand curve increases the total real output but does not affect the price level (see panel A of Figure 16.10). As noted, many economists argue that this is so because of considerable underemployment of resources. More output does not entail increased prices.

If the intersection occurs in the vertical range of the short-run aggregate supply curve, the rightward shift of the aggregate demand curve increases the price level but has no impact on the total real output (see panel B of Figure 16.10). As pointed out, this is because the economy has no unutilized productive capacity. More spending bids up prices but cannot augment total real output, which is at its maximum level.

If the intersection occurs in the positively sloped range of the short-run aggregate supply curve, the rightward shift of the aggregate demand curve increases both the price level and total real output (see panel C of Figure 16.10). This is because increases in output can be attained in this range only if the price level increases, as we saw in a previous section.

Effect of a Leftward Shift In contrast to the previous situation, suppose that consumers or investors decide to *decrease* their spending. Since the level of

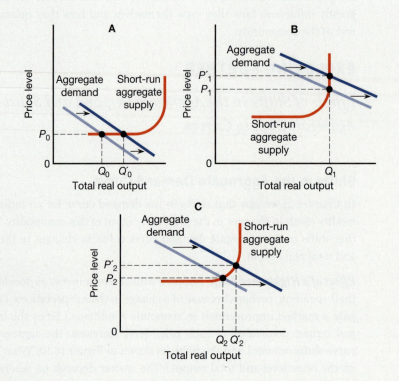

FIGURE 16.10

Effect of a Shift to the Right in the Aggregate Demand Curve

Panel A shows that in the horizontal range of the short-run aggregate supply curve, a rightward shift of the aggregate demand curve increases output but not the price level. Panel B shows that in the vertical range of the short-run aggregate supply curve, a rightward shift of the aggregate demand curve increases the price level but not output. Panel C shows that in the positively sloped range of the short-run aggregate supply curve, a rightward shift of the aggregate demand curve increases both output and the price level.

total real output demanded at each price level falls, the aggregate demand curve shifts inward to the left, as shown in Figure 16.11. The effect of this shift depends on where the aggregate demand curve intersects the short-run aggregate supply curve before the shift occurs.

If the intersection occurs in the horizontal range of the short-run aggregate supply curve, the leftward shift of the aggregate demand curve reduces total real output but has no effect on the price level (see panel A of Figure 16.11). If the intersection occurs in the vertical range of the short-run aggregate supply curve, this shift reduces the price level but has no effect on total real output (see panel B of Figure 16.11). If the intersection occurs in the positively sloped range

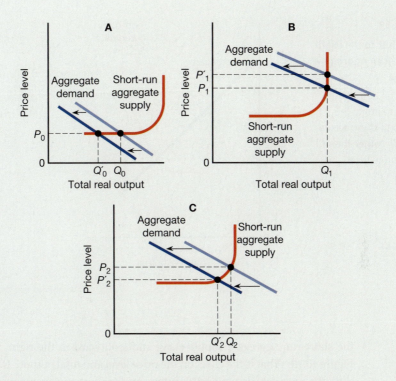

FIGURE 16.11

Effect of a Shift to the Left in the Aggregate Demand Curve

Panel A shows that in the horizontal range of the short-run aggregate supply curve, a leftward shift of the aggregate demand curve reduces output but not the price level. Panel B shows that in the vertical range of the short-run aggregate supply curve, a leftward shift of the aggregate demand curve reduces the price level but not output. Panel C shows that in the positively sloped range of the short-run aggregate supply curve, a leftward shift of the aggregate demand curve reduces both output and price level.

of the short-run aggregate supply curve, this shift reduces both the price level and the total real output (see panel C of Figure 16.11).

Shifts in the Short-Run Aggregate Supply Curve

Shifts in the short-run aggregate supply curve, like those in the aggregate demand curve, result in changes in the price level and total real output, as indicated next.

Effect of a Rightward Shift Suppose that because of increases in productive capacity or changes in technology, firms are willing and able to supply *more* goods and services (at any given price level) than in the past. Under these circumstances,

FIGURE 16.12

Effect of a Shift to the Right in the Short-Run Aggregate Supply Curve

If the short-run aggregate supply curve shifts to the right, the result is increased real output (*Q'* rather than *Q*) and a lower price level (*P'* rather than *P*).

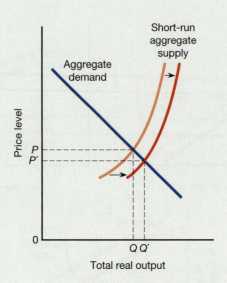

the short-run aggregate supply curve shifts outward to the right, as shown in Figure 16.12. What is the effect on the price level and total output? If, prior to this shift, the aggregate demand curve intersects the short-run aggregate supply curve at a point where the latter is positively sloped, the result is an increase in total real output and a reduction in the price level, as can readily be seen in Figure 16.12.

Effect of a Leftward Shift On the other hand, suppose that firms are willing and able to supply *less* goods and services (at any given price level) than in the past. For example, suppose that there is a worldwide shortage of important raw materials like oil or iron ore that results in increases in their prices. In this case, a given level of total real output can be produced only at a higher price level than previously. That is, the short-run aggregate supply curve shifts to the left, as shown in Figure 16.13. The effect is a reduction in total real output and an increase in the price level, as shown in Figure 16.13.

The Long-Run Aggregate Supply Curve

As pointed out at the beginning of this chapter, whereas input prices are fixed in the short run, in the long run they can adjust fully to eliminate the underemployment or shortage of inputs (like labor). Therefore, once these adjustments are made, full employment occurs and real national output is at its potential level. If the potential output of a particular economy is $100 billion, this is the amount of output supplied regardless of the price level.

FIGURE 16.13

Effect of a Shift to the Left in the Short-Run Aggregate Supply Curve

If the short-run aggregate supply curve shifts to the left, the result is a reduced real output (Q' rather than Q) and a higher price level (P' rather than P).

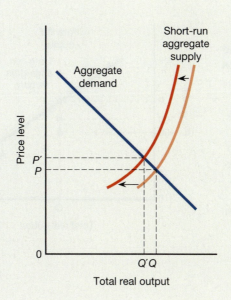

In other words, the aggregate supply curve is vertical in the long run. Why? Because, in the long run, wages and the prices of nonlabor inputs adjust. For example, there is time for old labor contracts to expire and new ones to be negotiated. Shortages of raw materials are resolved. Unemployed workers find jobs. In the long run, input prices change by the same proportion as product prices, with the result that there is no incentive for firms to alter their output levels. When the price of everything changes by the same proportion, the real value of everything is unchanged.

To see this, consider a firm that experiences a 10 percent increase in the price of its product. If this is due to a 10 percent increase in the general price level, this firm in the long run pays 10 percent more for its inputs. Consequently, its profit per dollar of sales is no different in the long run than it was before the 10 percent increase in the price level. Thus, it has no incentive to produce more than it did before the increase in the price level.

Long-run aggregate supply curve

Figure 16.14 shows the **long-run aggregate supply curve** for an economy with potential real GDP equal to Q. It is a vertical line because the total quantity of goods and services produced when all inputs are efficiently and fully utilized does not depend on the price level. If the price level (measured as an aggregate index with no specific units) were to increase from 100 to 120 (and if wages and the prices of nonlabor inputs were to increase by the same proportion), the total quantity of goods and services produced would remain equal to Q.

FIGURE 16.14

Equilibrium Price Level and Total Real Output: Long Run

In the long run, the aggregate supply curve is vertical. The equilibrium level of total real output and the equilibrium price level are given by the intersection of the aggregate demand and supply curves. Here, the equilibrium price level is *P* and the equilibrium level of total real output is *Q*.

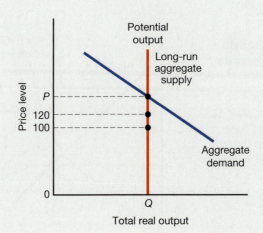

In the long run, the equilibrium level of real national output and the equilibrium price level are given by the intersection of the aggregate demand curve and the long-run aggregate supply curve. In Figure 16.14, the equilibrium value of real GDP is *Q*, and the equilibrium value of the price level is *P*. Note that the aggregate demand curve affects only the price level, not the level of real output, in the long run. The level of output equals its potential level regardless of the price level. In Chapter 13, we studied the factors determining the level of potential output, or what amounts to the same thing, the factors determining the location of the long-run aggregate supply curve.

REVIEW AND PRACTICE

Summary

1   National output tends to rise and approach its potential (full-employment) level for a while, then to falter and fall below this level, then to rise and approach it once more, and so on. These ups and downs are called business fluctuations or business cycles.

2   Each cycle can be divided into four phases: trough, expansion, peak, recession. Business cycles are very irregular and highly variable in length and amplitude.

3   Until the 1930s, most economists (classical economists) were convinced that the price system, left to its own devices, would ensure the maintenance of full employment. They thought it unlikely that total spending would be

too small to purchase the full-employment level of output and argued that prices would be cut if any problem of this sort developed.

4 In the 1930s, John Maynard Keynes developed a theory to explain how the capitalist economic system remained mired in the Great Depression, with its high levels of unemployment. Contrary to the classical economists, he concluded that there is no automatic mechanism in a capitalist system to generate and maintain full employment, or at least to generate it quickly enough to be relied on in practice.

5 The aggregate demand curve shows the level of real national output demanded at each price level. It slopes downward and to the right.

6 The short-run aggregate supply curve shows the level of real national output supplied at each price level if the prices of all inputs are fixed. Since increases in the price level tend to raise the profitability of firms' increasing output, the short-run aggregate supply curve tends to slope upward and to the right.

7 The equilibrium level of real national output and the equilibrium price level are given by the intersection of the aggregate demand and supply curves.

8 Unemployment is of various types: frictional, structural, and cyclical. The overall unemployment rate conceals considerable differences in unemployment among different types of people.

9 High levels of unemployment impose great costs on society. The economic costs of unemployment include the goods and services that could have been produced (but were not) by the unemployed. Potential GDP is the level of GDP that could have been achieved if full employment had been reached.

*10 [6]Whereas input prices are fixed in the short run, in the long run they can adjust fully to eliminate the underemployment or shortage of inputs (like labor). Once these adjustments have been made, full employment occurs and real national output is at its potential level. Therefore, the long-run aggregate supply curve is vertical.

Problems and Questions

1 What sorts of shifts in either the aggregate demand curve or the short-run aggregate supply curve (or both) would result in an increase in the price level but constant real output?

2 "One principal reason why the short-run aggregate supply curve slopes upward and to the right is that as total real output increases, the quantity of money must increase as well; this means that the price level must rise, at least beyond some point." Do you agree? Why or why not?

[6] Starred (*) item refers to material covered in Exploring Further.

3　Suppose that the aggregate demand curve is $P = 120 - Q$, where P is the price level and Q is real output (in billions of dollars). If the short-run aggregate supply curve (which is a horizontal line in the relevant range) shifts upward from $P = 102$ to $P = 104$, what happens to real output?

4　The aggregate demand curve in country X shifts to the right, with the result that the price level rises. Do you think that this will affect country X's short-run aggregate supply curve? Why or why not?

5　Suppose that the Organization of Petroleum Exporting Countries raises oil prices by 50 percent What effect will this have on the U.S. aggregate demand curve? On the U.S. short-run aggregate supply curve?

Key Terms

potential gross domestic product	**interest rate**
business cycle	**aggregate supply curve**
trough	**short-run aggregate supply curve**
expansion	**frictional unemployment**
peak	**structural unemployment**
recession	**cyclical unemployment**
depression	**full employment**
prosperity	**long-run aggregate supply curve**
aggregate demand curve	

Viewpoint for Analysis

According to testimony by Nobel Laureate Robert Solow, of the Massachusetts Institute of Technology, before the Joint Economic Committee of Congress on February 11, 1993, "If actual GDP grows by $2\frac{1}{4}$ percent during the four quarters of 1993, the gap between actual and potential [GDP] will still be 4 percent early in 1994 and the unemployment rate will remain near 7.1 percent. It would take faster growth of GDP to narrow the gap and reduce unemployment."[7]

(a)　In dollar terms, about how great would have been the amount of forgone output in 1993 if this gap had been 4 percent?

(b)　Would a rightward shift of the aggregate demand curve have increased the rate of growth of GDP and narrowed this gap? Why or why not?

(c)　What factors might have shifted the aggregate demand curve to the right?

(d)　What might have been the disadvantage of a rightward shift of the aggregate demand curve?

[7] R. Solow, "Statement to Joint Economic Committee, U.S. Congress," February 11, 1993, 4.

The Determination of National Output and the Keynesian Multiplier

LEARNING OBJECTIVES

➤ To explain the consumption function and the marginal propensity to consume

➤ To explain the saving function and the marginal propensity to save

➤ To understand what determines the level of gross investment

➤ To understand the significance of equilibrium GDP and why it must equal total intended spending

➤ To describe how equilibrium GDP can change and how the multiplier affects these changes

➤ *(Exploring Further)* To explore the causes and effects of shifts in the consumption and saving functions

How much firms spend on plant, equipment, and other forms of investment can vary greatly from year to year. Spending of this sort depends on the expectations of industrial managers concerning the size of prospective markets, among other things. How much effect do changes in investment spending have on GDP? One purpose of this chapter is to answer this question.

In the previous chapter, we presented an introductory sketch of business fluctuations and explained how aggregate demand and supply curves can be used to analyze these fluctuations. In this chapter, we go a step further. Rather than simply taking the position of the aggregate demand curve as a given, we will explore why the equilibrium level of national output is what it is. Why is the aggregate demand curve positioned to intersect the aggregate supply curve at this (rather than some other) output? We will also discuss how the economy can move from one equilibrium to another.

Simplifying Assumptions

Essentially, the model presented in this chapter is the simple model put forth by John Maynard Keynes in the 1930s (recall Case Study 16.3). The Keynesian model assumes that the price level is constant; in other words, the short-run aggregate supply curve is assumed to be horizontal. In subsequent chapters, this assumption is relaxed.

In addition, we make three other simplifying assumptions:

1. We assume that there are no government expenditures and that the economy is closed (no exports or imports). Therefore, total spending on final output (that is, on gross domestic product) in this simple case equals consumption expenditure plus gross investment.[1] (Why? Because the other two components of total spending—government expenditures and net exports—are zero.)

2. We assume that there are no taxes, no transfer payments, and no undistributed corporate profits. So, if we define *disposable income* as the total amount of income that people get to keep after paying personal taxes, GDP equals disposable income in this simple case. In later chapters, we relax this and the first assumption.

3. We assume that the total amount of intended investment (that is, the total amount that firms and individuals intend to invest) is *independent* of the level of gross domestic product. This, of course, is only a rough simplification, since the amount firms invest is affected by the level of national output. But this simplification is very convenient, and it is relatively easy to extend the model to eliminate this assumption.

The Consumption Function

Consumption function

An important part of the simple Keynesian theory of determining national output is the **consumption function**, which is the relationship between consumption spending and disposable income. It seems clear that consumption expenditures, whether those of a single household or the total consumption expenditures in the entire economy, are influenced heavily by income. Families with higher incomes tend to spend more on consumption than families with lower incomes. Of course, individual families vary a good deal in their behavior; some spend more than others even if their incomes are the same. But on the average, a family's consumption expenditure is tied very closely to its income.

---

[1] Since *personal consumption expenditure* and *gross private domestic investment* are cumbersome terms, we sometimes use *consumption expenditure* and *gross investment* instead in this and subsequent chapters.

FIGURE 17.1

Relationship between Personal Consumption Expenditures and Disposable Income, United States, 1929–1999 (Excluding World War II)

There is a very close relationship between personal consumption expenditure and disposable income in the United States.

What is true for individual families also holds for the entire economy: total personal consumption expenditures are closely related to disposable income. This is shown in Figure 17.1, where personal consumption expenditure in each year from 1929 to 1999 is plotted against disposable income in the same year. The points fall very near the straight line drawn in Figure 17.1 but not right on it. For practical purposes, we can regard the line drawn in Figure 17.1 as representing the relationship between personal consumption expenditure and disposable income. In other words, we can regard this line as the consumption function.

The Marginal Propensity to Consume

Suppose that we know what the consumption function for a given society looks like in a particular time period. For example, suppose that it is given by the figures for disposable income and personal consumption expenditure in the first two columns of Table 17.1. On the basis of our knowledge of the consumption function, we can determine the *extra* amount that families will spend on consumption if they receive an *extra* dollar of disposable income. This amount (the fraction of an extra dollar of income spent on consumption) is called the **marginal propensity to consume**.

Marginal propensity to consume

To make sure that you understand exactly what we mean by the marginal propensity to consume, consult Table 17.1. What is the marginal propensity to consume when disposable income increases from $1,000 billion to $1,050 billion? The second column shows that when income rises from $1,000 billion to $1,050 billion, consumption expenditure rises from $950 billion to $980 billion. Consequently, the fraction of the extra $50 billion of income consumed is $30 billion ÷ $50 billion, or 0.60. Therefore, the marginal propensity to consume is 0.60. On the basis of similar calculations, the marginal propensity to consume when disposable income rises from $1,050 billion to $1,100 billion is 0.60, the marginal propensity to consume when disposable income rises from $1,100 billion to $1,150 billion is also 0.60, and so forth.

The marginal propensity to consume can be interpreted geometrically as the slope of the consumption function. The slope of any line is the ratio of the

TABLE 17.1

The Consumption Function

Disposable Income (billions of dollars)	Personal Consumption Expenditure (billions of dollars)	Marginal Propensity to Consume	Average Propensity to Consume
1,000	950	$\frac{30}{50} = 0.60$	0.95
1,050	980	$\frac{30}{50} = 0.60$	0.93
1,100	1,010	$\frac{30}{50} = 0.60$	0.92
1,150	1,040	$\frac{30}{50} = 0.60$	0.90
1,200	1,070	$\frac{30}{50} = 0.60$	0.89
1,250	1,100	$\frac{30}{50} = 0.60$	0.88
1,300	1,130	$\frac{30}{50} = 0.60$	0.87

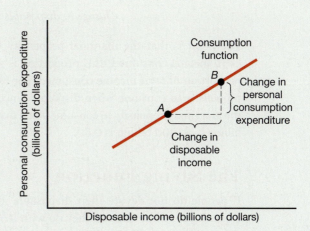

FIGURE 17.2

The Marginal Propensity to Consume Equals the Slope of the Consumption Function

The slope of the consumption function between points *A* and *B* equals the vertical change (which is the change in personal consumption expenditure) divided by the horizontal change (which is the change in disposable income).

vertical change to the horizontal change when a small movement occurs along the line. As shown in Figure 17.2, the vertical change is the change in personal consumption expenditure, and the horizontal change is the change in disposable income. Hence, the ratio of the vertical change to the horizontal change must equal the marginal propensity to consume.

In general, the marginal propensity to consume can differ, depending on the level of disposable income. For example, the marginal propensity to consume may be higher at lower levels than at higher levels of disposable income. Only if the consumption function is a straight line, as in Figure 17.1 (and Table 17.1), will the marginal propensity to consume be the same at all levels of income. For simplicity, we assume in much of the subsequent analysis that the consumption function is a straight line, but this assumption can easily be relaxed without affecting the essential aspects of our conclusions.

The Average Propensity to Consume

Average propensity to consume

It is important to distinguish between the marginal propensity to consume and the average propensity to consume. The **average propensity to consume** equals the proportion of disposable income consumed. In other words, it equals

$$\frac{Personal\ consumption\ expenditure}{Disposable\ income}$$

Clearly, this is not the same thing as the marginal propensity to consume, which is

$$\frac{\text{Change in personal consumption expenditure}}{\text{Change in disposable income}}$$

The point is that the marginal propensity to consume is the proportion of *extra* income consumed; this proportion is generally quite different from the proportion of *total* income consumed. For example, in Table 17.1, the average propensity to consume when disposable income is $1,100 billion is 0.92, but the marginal propensity to consume when disposable income rises from $1,050 billion to $1,100 billion is 0.60.

The Saving Function

Saving function

If people do not devote their disposable income to personal consumption expenditure, what else can they do with it? They can save it. When families refrain from spending their income on consumption goods and services (that is, when they forgo present consumption to provide for larger consumption in the future), they save. Therefore, we can derive from the consumption function the total amount people save at each level of disposable income. All we have to do is subtract the total personal consumption expenditure from disposable income at each level of disposable income. The difference is the total amount of saving at each level of disposable income. This difference is shown in the third column of Table 17.2. We can plot the total amount of saving against disposable income, as in Figure 17.3. The resulting rela tionship between total saving and disposable income is the **saving function**. Like the consumption function, it plays a major role in determining national output.

TABLE 17.2 The Saving Function	Disposable Income (billions of dollars)	Personal Consumption Expenditure (billions of dollars)	Savings (billions of dollars)	Marginal Propensity to Save
	1,000	950	50	
	1,050	980	70	$\frac{20}{50} = 0.40$
	1,100	1,010	90	$\frac{20}{50} = 0.40$
	1,150	1,040	110	$\frac{20}{50} = 0.40$
	1,200	1,070	130	$\frac{20}{50} = 0.40$
	1,250	1,100	150	$\frac{20}{50} = 0.40$
	1,300	1,130	170	$\frac{20}{50} = 0.40$

FIGURE 17.3

The Saving Function

The saving function describes the total amount of saving at each level of disposable income. The slope of the saving function equals the change in saving divided by the change in disposable income. The slope of the saving function equals the marginal propensity to save.

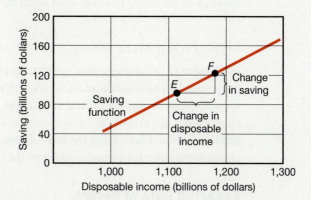

The Marginal Propensity to Save

Marginal propensity to save

If we know the saving function, we can calculate the marginal propensity to save at any level of disposable income. The **marginal propensity to save** is the proportion of an extra dollar of disposable income saved. To see how to calculate it, consult Table 17.2. The third column shows that when income rises from $1,000 billion to $1,050 billion, savings rise from $50 billion to $70 billion. Consequently, the fraction of the extra $50 billion of income that is saved is $20 billion ÷ $50 billion, or 0.40. Therefore, the marginal propensity to save is 0.40. Similar calculations show that the marginal propensity to save when disposable income rises from $1,050 billion to $1,100 billion is 0.40, the marginal propensity to save when disposable income rises from $1,100 billion to $1,150 billion is also 0.40, and so forth.

Note that at any particular level of disposable income, the marginal propensity to save plus the marginal propensity to consume must equal 1. By definition, the marginal propensity to save equals the proportion of an extra dollar of disposable income saved, and the marginal propensity to consume equals the proportion of an extra dollar of income consumed. The sum of these two proportions must equal 1 because the only thing that people can do with an extra dollar of disposable income is consume it or save it. Table 17.1 and Table 17.2 show this fact clearly.

Finally, it is worth noting that the marginal propensity to save equals the slope of the saving function, just as the marginal propensity to consume equals the slope of the consumption function. As pointed out, the slope of a line equals the vertical distance between any two points on the line divided by the horizontal distance between them. Since (as shown in Figure 17.3) the vertical distance is the change in saving and the horizontal distance is the change in disposable income, the slope of the saving function must equal the marginal propensity to save.

Determinants of Investment

In Chapter 15, we stressed that investment consists largely of the amount that firms spend on new buildings, factories, and equipment and increases in inventory. Investment plays a central role in the Keynesian theory of output and employment. To understand this theory, it is essential to understand the two primary factors determining the level of gross private domestic investment: the expected rate of return from capital and the interest rate.

Expected Rate of Return

Expected rate of return

The **expected rate of return** from capital is the perceived rate of return that businesses believe they can obtain if they put up new buildings or factories, add new equipment, or increase their inventories. Each of these forms of investment requires the expenditure of money. The rate of return measures the profitability of such an expenditure; it shows the annual profits to be obtained per dollar invested. Therefore, a rate of return of 10 percent means that for every dollar invested, an annual profit of 10 cents is obtained. Clearly, the higher is the expected rate of return from a particular investment, the more profitable the investment is expected to be.

Interest Rate

Interest rate

The **interest rate** is the cost of borrowing money. As pointed out in Chapter 16, it is the annual amount that a borrower must pay for the use of a dollar for a year. If the interest rate is 8 percent, a borrower must pay 8 cents per year for the use of a dollar. And if the interest rate is 12 percent, a borrower must pay 12 cents per year for the use of a dollar. Anyone with a savings account knows what it is to earn interest; anyone who has borrowed money from a bank knows what it is to pay interest.

The Investment Decision

To determine whether to invest in a particular project (a new building, piece of equipment, or other form of investment), a firm must compare the project's expected rate of return with the interest rate. If the expected rate of return is less than the interest rate, the firm loses money if it borrows money to carry out the project. For example, if the firm invests in a project with a 10 percent rate of return and borrows the money to finance the project at 12 percent interest, it receives profits of 10 cents per dollar invested and pays out interest of 12 cents per dollar invested. So it loses 2 cents (12 cents – 10 cents) per dollar invested.

Even if the firm does not borrow money to finance the project, it will be unlikely to invest in a project where the expected rate of return is less than the interest rate. Why? Because if the firm can lend money to others at the prevailing interest rate, it can obtain a greater return from its money by doing this than by investing in the project. Hence, if the interest rate is 12 percent and an investment project has an expected rate of return of 10 percent, a firm does better, if it has a certain amount of money, to lend it out at 12 percent than to earn 10 percent from the investment project.

Since firms are likely to invest only in projects where the expected rate of return exceeds the interest rate, the level of gross private domestic investment depends on the total volume of investment projects where the expected rate of return exceeds the interest rate. For example, if the interest rate is 10 percent, the level of gross investment depends on the total volume of investment projects where the expected rate of return exceeds 10 percent. The more such projects there are, the higher is the level of gross investment. Also, the higher the interest rate, the lower is the level of gross investment.

The Equilibrium Level of Gross Domestic Product

If a situation is in equilibrium, there is no tendency for change; the situation that exists can persist. In Chapter 2, we studied the equilibrium value of a product's price. Here we are interested in the equilibrium value of gross domestic product. In Chapter 2, we saw that price is at its equilibrium value when the quantity demanded equals the quantity supplied. Here we see that GDP is at its equilibrium value when the flow of income (generated by this value of GDP) results in a level of spending just sufficient (not too high, not too low) to take this level of output off the market. To understand this equilibrium condition, it is essential to keep three points in mind:

1. *The production of goods and services results in a flow of income to the workers, resource owners, and managers that help produce them.* Each level of GDP results in a certain flow of income. More specifically, under the assumptions made here, GDP equals disposable income. Whatever the level of GDP may be, we can be sure that the level of disposable income is equivalent to it.

2. *The level of spending on final goods and services depends on the level of disposable income.* As we saw earlier in this chapter, consumption expenditure depends on the level of disposable income. (For the moment, we assume that investment is independent of the level of output in the economy.) If we know the level of disposable income, we can predict what level of spending is forthcoming.

3.   *The level of production depends mainly on the level of spending.* If producers find that they sell goods faster than they produce them, their inventories decline. If they find that they sell goods slower than they produce them, their inventories rise. If GDP is at its equilibrium value, the intended level of spending must be just equal to GDP. Why? Because otherwise there is an unintended increase or decrease in producers' inventories, a situation that cannot persist. Much more is said on this score in the sections that follow.

Aggregate Flows of Income and Expenditure

Output Determines Income

We look in more detail at the process whereby national output (that is, GDP) determines the level of income, which in turn determines the level of spending. Suppose that the first column of Table 17.3 shows the various possible output levels (that is, the various possible values of GDP) the economy might produce this year. This column shows the various output levels that may be produced if producers expect enough spending to take this much output off the market at the existing price level. And, as stressed, disposable income equals GDP.

Income Determines Spending

Because disposable income equals GDP (under our current assumptions), the first column of Table 17.3 also shows the level of disposable income corresponding to each possible level of GDP. From this, it should be possible to determine

TABLE 17.3

Determination of Equilibrium Level of Gross Domestic Product (Billions of Dollars)

(1) Gross Domestic Product (= Disposable Income)	(2) Intended Consumption Expenditure	(3) Intended Saving	(4) Intended Investment	(5) Total Intended Spending (2) + (4)	(6) Tendency of National Output
1,000	950	50	90	1,040	Upward
1,050	980	70	90	1,070	Upward
1,100	1,010	90	90	1,100	No change
1,150	1,040	110	90	1,130	Downward
1,200	1,070	130	90	1,160	Downward
1,250	1,100	150	90	1,190	Downward

the level of spending corresponding to each level of GDP. Specifically, suppose that the consumption function is as indicated in Table 17.1. In this case, intended consumption expenditure at each level of GDP is as shown in column 2 of Table 17.3. For example, if GDP equals $1,000 billion, intended consumption expenditure equals $950 billion.

But the consumption expenditure is not the only type of spending. What about investment? Suppose that firms want to invest $90 billion regardless of the level of GDP. Under these circumstances, total spending at each level of GDP is as shown in column 5 of Table 17.3. (Since total intended spending equals intended consumption expenditure plus intended investment, column 5 equals column 2 + column 4.)

Output Must Equal Spending

Column 5 of Table 17.3 shows the level of total intended spending at each level of national output (and income). If GDP is at its equilibrium value, total intended spending must equal total output. In other words, if GDP is at its equilibrium value, total intended spending must equal GDP. The easiest way to show this is to show that if intended spending is not equal to GDP, GDP is not at its equilibrium value. The following discussion provides such a proof. First, we show that if intended spending is greater than GDP, GDP is not at its equilibrium level. Then we show that if intended spending is less than GDP, GDP is not at its equilibrium level.

If intended spending is greater than GDP, what happens? Since the total amount that is spent on final goods and services exceeds the total amount of final goods and services produced (the latter being, by definition, GDP), firms' inventories are reduced. Consequently, firms increase their output rate to avoid continued depletion of their inventories and to bring their output into balance with the rate of aggregate demand. Since an increase in the output rate means an increase in GDP, it follows that GDP tends to increase if intended spending is greater than GDP. GDP therefore is not at its equilibrium level.

On the other hand, what happens if intended spending is less than GDP? Since the total amount that is spent on final goods and services falls short of the total amount of final goods and services produced (the latter being, by definition, GDP), firms' inventories increase. As inventories pile up unexpectedly, firms cut back their output to bring it into better balance with aggregate demand. Since a reduction in output means a reduction in GDP, it follows that GDP tends to fall if intended spending is less than GDP. Once again, GDP is not at its equilibrium level.

Since GDP is not at its equilibrium value when it exceeds or falls short of intended spending, it must be at its equilibrium value only when it equals intended spending.

Why GDP Must Equal Intended Spending: Three Cases

To get a better idea of why GDP is at its equilibrium value only if it equals intended spending, consider three possible values of GDP ($1,050 billion, $1,150 billion, and $1,100 billion) to see what would happen in our simple economy (in Table 17.3) if these values of GDP prevail.

Case 1. GDP = $1,050 Billion What happens if firms produce $1,050 billion worth of final goods and services? Given our assumptions, disposable income also equals $1,050 billion (since disposable income equals GDP), so consumers would spend $980 billion on consumption goods and services. (This follows from the nature of the consumption function: see column 2 of Table 17.3.) Since firms want to invest $90 billion, total intended spending would be $1,070 billion ($980 billion + $90 billion, as shown in column 5). But the total amount spent on final goods and services under these circumstances exceeds the total value of final goods and services produced by $20 billion ($1,070 billion − $1,050 billion), so firms' inventories are drawn down by $20 billion. Clearly, this situation cannot persist for long. As firms see their inventories becoming depleted, they step up their production rates, so that the value of output of final goods and services (GDP) increases.

Case 2. GDP = $1,150 Billion What happens if firms produce $1,150 billion worth of final goods and services? Given our assumptions, disposable income also equals $1,150 billion (since disposable income equals GDP), with the result that consumers would spend $1,040 billion on consumption goods and services. (Again, this follows from the consumption function: see column 2 of Table 17.3.) Since firms want to invest $90 billion, total spending would be $1,130 billion ($1,040 billion + $90 billion, as shown in column 5). But the total amount spent on final goods and services under these circumstances falls short of the total value of final goods and services produced by $20 billion ($1,150 billion − $1,130 billion), so firms' inventories increase by $20 billion. Clearly, this situation, like the previous one, cannot continue for long. When firms see their inventories increasing, they reduce their production rates, causing the value of output of final goods and services (GDP) to decrease.

Case 3. GDP = $1,100 billion What happens if firms produce $1,100 billion worth of final goods and services? Disposable income also equals $1,100 billion (since disposable income equals GDP), so consumers would spend $1,010 billion on consumption goods and services. (Once again, this follows from the consumption function: see column 2 of Table 17.3.) Since firms want to invest $90 billion, total spending would be $1,100 billion ($1,010 billion + $90 billion, as shown in column 5). Therefore, the total amount spent on final goods and services under these circumstances exactly equals the total value of final goods and services produced. Consequently, there is no reason for firms to alter their production rates. This is an equilibrium situation, a set of circumstances where there is no tendency for GDP to change, and the equilibrium level of GDP in this situation is $1,100 billion.

These three cases illustrate the process that pushes GDP toward its equilibrium value (and maintains it there). So long as GDP is below its equilibrium value, the situation is like that described in case 1. So long as GDP is above its equilibrium value, the situation is like that described in case 2. Whether GDP is below or above its equilibrium value, there is a tendency for production rates to be altered so that GDP moves toward its equilibrium value. Eventually, GDP reaches its equilibrium value and the situation is like that described in case 3. The important aspect of this case (the equilibrium situation) is that for it to occur, intended spending must equal GDP.

Using a Graph to Determine Equilibrium GDP

We can represent the same argument in a diagrammatic, rather than tabular, analysis. Once again we will show that the equilibrium level of GDP is at the point where intended spending equals GDP, but now using a graph. Since disposable income equals gross domestic product in this simple case, we can plot consumption expenditure (on the vertical axis) versus gross domestic product (on the horizontal axis), as shown in Figure 17.4. This is the consumption function. We can also plot the sum of consumption expenditure and investment expenditure against GDP, as shown in Figure 17.4. This relationship, shown by the $C + I$ line, indicates the level of total intended

FIGURE 17.4

Determining the Equilibrium Value of Gross Domestic Product

The consumption function is C, and the sum of consumption and investment expenditure is $C + I$. The equilibrium value of GDP is at the point where the $C + I$ line intersects the 45-degree line, here $1,100 billion.

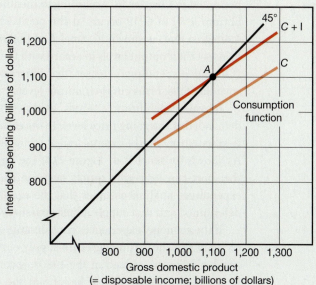

spending on final goods and services for various amounts of GDP. Finally, we can plot a 45-degree line, as shown in Figure 17.4. This line contains all points where the amount on the horizontal axis equals the amount on the vertical axis. Since GDP is on the horizontal axis and intended spending is on the vertical axis, it contains all points where total intended spending equals gross domestic product.

The equilibrium level of gross domestic product is at the point where total intended spending equals GDP. Consequently, the equilibrium level of GDP is at the point on the horizontal axis where the $C + I$ line intersects the 45-degree line. In Figure 17.4, this occurs at $1,100 billion. Under the conditions assumed here, no other level of GDP can be maintained for any considerable period of time.

Why can we be sure that the point where the $C + I$ line intersects the 45-degree line is the point where intended spending equals GDP? Because a **45-degree line** is, by construction, a line that includes all points where the amount on the vertical axis equals the amount on the horizontal axis. In this case, as noted, intended spending is on the vertical axis and GDP is on the horizontal axis. At point A, the point where the C + I line intersects the 45-degree line, intended spending must equal GDP.

45-degree line

Reconciling Aggregate Demand and Supply Curves with Income-Expenditure Analysis

Income-expenditure analysis

At this point, we must reconcile and integrate the income-expenditure analysis presented here with the aggregate demand–aggregate supply analysis presented in Chapter 16. According to **income-expenditure analysis**, the equilibrium level of GDP occurs at the point where the $C + I$ line intersects the 45-degree line, as shown in panel A of Figure 17.5. This analysis assumes that firms set their output levels in accord with the level of demand at current prices. If intended spending increases, firms increase their output levels; if intended spending falls, firms cut their output levels.

Income-expenditure analysis assumes that firms produce whatever is demanded at the going price level. In other words, it assumes that the economy is situated on the horizontal range of its short-run aggregate supply curve. As shown in panel B of Figure 17.5, the aggregate demand curve intersects the short-run aggregate supply curve in this range. Put differently, income-expenditure analysis assumes that the equilibrium level of output is demand determined and that supply adjusts passively to that demand.

If the economy experiences considerable unemployment and the horizontal range of the short-run aggregate supply curve is the relevant one, as Keynes and his followers argued in the 1930s, income-expenditure analysis tends to be a more revealing way of looking at the determinants of national output

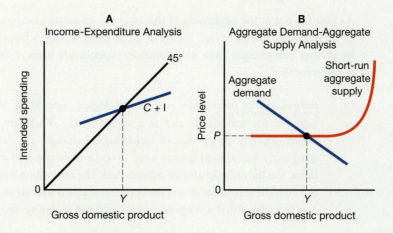

FIGURE 17.5

Relationship between the Income-Expenditure Analysis and the Aggregate Demand–Aggregate Supply Analysis

Income-expenditure analysis uses the intersection of the *C + I* line and the 45-degree line to find the equilibrium level of GDP. Aggregate demand–aggregate supply analysis uses the intersection of the aggregate demand and supply curves to find the equilibrium level of GDP. Both types of analysis yield the same result: that the equilibrium value of GDP is *Y*.

than aggregate demand–aggregate supply analysis. It shows the nature of the changes in spending, which are the prime movers in the model.

But if the economy is operating at a point where the aggregate supply curve is upward sloping or vertical, the aggregate demand–aggregate supply analysis is more relevant than the income-expenditure analysis, because it focuses on changes in the price level, which are not included or shown in income-expenditure analysis.

Changes in Equilibrium Output

On the basis of the simple model constructed in the previous sections, we can see that equilibrium output can be altered by changes in investment or consumption that are not due to changes in income. We conclude this chapter by discussing the volatility of investment spending and how changes in such spending have an amplified (multiplier) effect on output. In Exploring Further, we will show that shifts in the consumption function have similar effects on national output.

The Volatility of Investment

As pointed out at the beginning of this chapter, investment expenditure tends to be relatively unstable (see Figure 17.6). That is, it varies from year to year by greater percentages than consumption expenditure does. There are many reasons for this.

➤ *Irregularity of innovation rate.* Technological innovation occurs irregularly—in fits and starts—not at a constant rate. Therefore, investment, which depends on the rate of technological change, also tends to occur irregularly. Investment booms seem to occur in response to major innovations, like the railroad and the automobile. The innovation wave that swept through the information and telecommunications industries in the 1990s also brought with it a surge in new investment spending (see Figure 17.6).

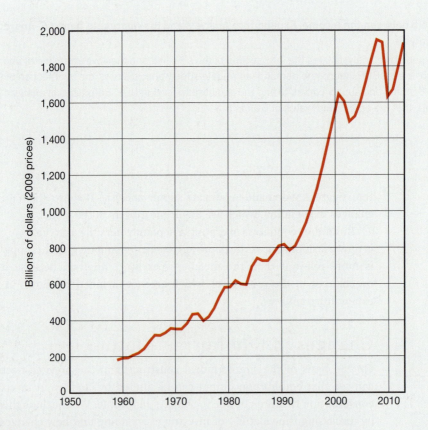

FIGURE 17.6

Gross Private Domestic Nonresidential Investment, United States, 1959–2012

Gross investment varies considerably from year to year.

However, the bursting of the high-tech bubble in 2000 brought with it a sharp retrenchment in spending on capital goods in 2001, which did not reverse until 2003.

➤ *Durability of capital goods.* Because capital goods tend to be quite durable, firms frequently can postpone investment decisions. For example, they can postpone the replacement of a piece of equipment by using it even though it is not as reliable as it once was. Or they can postpone the construction of a new building by tolerating crowded conditions in their existing buildings. Since many investment decisions are postponable, the exact time when projects are accepted may depend on the state of business expectations and the level of firms' profits, both of which are highly variable. Also, since the optimism or pessimism of business expectations tends to be contagious, firms often tend to invest at the same time.

➤ *Capacity utilization.* There are great differences from one year to the next in the extent to which existing productive capacity is utilized. In some years, sales are so great that firms work their plants at full capacity. In other years, sales are so slack that firms have plenty of excess capacity. In periods when the existing stock of capital goods is more than sufficient to meet current sales, the level of investment tends to be lower than in periods when the existing stock of capital goods is only barely sufficient to meet current sales. Because of the year-to-year variation in the extent to which sales levels press against productive capacity, there is considerable variation in the level of investment.

Effects of Changes in Intended Investment

Looking at the highly simplified model constructed in previous sections to explain the level of national output, what is the effect of a change in the amount of intended investment? Specifically, if firms increase their intended investment by $1 billion, what effect does this increase have on the equilibrium value of gross domestic product?

Autonomous change in spending

Induced change in spending

This is a very important question, and the answer sheds considerable light on the reasons for changes in national output in the simple Keynesian model. In answering this question, we assume that the change in investment is autonomous, not induced. An **autonomous change in spending** is one that *is not* due to a change in income or GDP. An **induced change in spending** is one that *is* due to a change in income or GDP.

The Spending Chain: One Stage after Another

The effects of intended investment can be divided into a number of stages. If intended investment increases by $1 billion, then firms spend an additional $1 billion on plant, equipment, or inventory in the first stage. This extra

KEYNES'S CRITICISMS OF THE CLASSICAL VIEW

As Keynes and his followers saw it, there are at least two basic flaws in the classical model. First, in their view, there is no assurance that total intended spending will equal GDP at a level ensuring high employment. The people and firms that save are often not the same people and firms that invest; they often have quite different motivations. In particular, a considerable amount of saving is done by families, who want to put something aside for a rainy day or for a car or appliance. On the other hand, a considerable amount of investment is done by firms interested in increasing their profits by expanding their plants or installing new equipment.

According to Keynes, we cannot be sure that changes in the interest rate will bring about the equality of saving and investment visualized by the classical economists. Total intended spending may equal GDP at a level corresponding to considerable unemployment (or to consider-

able inflation). Therefore, the Keynesian view is that a purely capitalist economic system, in the absence of appropriate government policies, has no dependable rudder to keep it clear of the shoals of serious unemployment or serious inflation.

Second, Keynes and his followers disputed the classical economists' assumption that prices and wages are flexible. In their view, the modern economy contains many departures from perfect competition that are barriers to the downward flexibility of prices and wages. In particular, many important industries are dominated by a few producers who try hard to avoid cutting prices. Even in the face of a considerable drop in demand, such industries have sometimes maintained extraordinarily stable prices. Moreover, the labor unions fight to avoid wage cuts. According to Keynes, it is unlikely that price and wage reductions can be depended on to maintain full employment.

$1 billion is received by workers and suppliers as extra income, which results in a second stage of extra spending on final goods and services. How much of their extra $1 billion in income do the workers and suppliers spend? If the marginal propensity to consume is 0.6, they spend 0.6 × $1 billion, or $0.6 billion. This extra expenditure of $0.6 billion is received by firms and disbursed to workers, suppliers, and owners as extra income. This brings about a third stage of extra spending on final goods and services. How much of this extra income of $0.6 billion do workers, suppliers, and owners spend? Since the marginal propensity to consume is 0.6, they spend 60 percent of this $0.6 billion, or $0.36 billion. This extra expenditure of $0.36 billion is received by firms and disbursed to workers, suppliers, and owners as extra income, which results in a fourth stage of spending, then a fifth stage, a sixth stage, and so on.

	Stage	Amount of Extra Spending (billions of dollars)
TABLE 17.4	1	1.00
The Multiplier Process	2	0.60
	3	0.36
	4	0.22
	5	0.13
	6	0.08
	7	0.05
	8	0.03
	9 and beyond	0.03
	Total	2.50

Table 17.4 shows the total increase in expenditure on final goods and services arising from the original $1 billion increase in intended investment. The total increase in expenditures is the increase in the first stage plus the increase in the second stage plus the increase in the third stage, and so on. Since there is an endless chain of stages, we cannot list all the increases. But because the successive increases in spending get smaller and smaller, we can determine their sum, which in this case is $2.5 billion. Thus, the $1 billion increase in intended investment results, after all stages of the spending and responding process have worked themselves out, in a $2.5 billion increase in total expenditures on final goods and services. In other words, it results in a $2.5 billion increase in GDP.

The Multiplier

In general, a $1 billion increase in intended investment results in an increase in equilibrium GDP of $1/MPS$ billion dollars, where MPS is the marginal propensity to save. This is a famous conclusion of the simple Keynesian model. To understand more clearly what it means, consider a couple of numerical examples involving values of the marginal propensity to save other than 0.4. For instance, if the marginal propensity to save is 0.33, a $1 billion increase in intended investment increases equilibrium GDP by $1 billion ÷ 0.33 that is, by $3 billion. Or take a case where the marginal propensity to consume equals 0.75. What is the effect of a $1 billion increase in intended investment? Since the marginal propensity to save must equal 1 − 0.75, or 0.25, the answer must be $1 billion ÷ 0.25. That is, equilibrium GDP increases by $4 billion.

INVESTMENT AND A GREAT CRASH

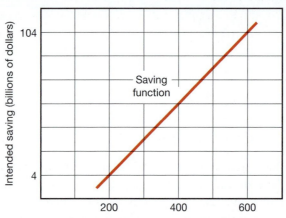

Between 1929 and 1933, annual investment spending in the United States fell by about $100 billion (in constant or inflation-adjusted terms). To get some idea of how a great crash, such as occurred then, can take place, consider a simple economy with no government or foreign trade. Suppose that intended investment in this economy falls from $104 billion to $4 billion and that the saving function is as follows:

According to the graph, intended saving equals $4 billion when GDP is $200 billion and it equals $104 billion when GDP is $600 billion. Since GDP equals disposable income under the assumed (highly simplified) conditions, the marginal propensity to save equals (104 – 4) ÷ (600 – 200) = 0.25. The multiplier equals the reciprocal of the marginal propensity to save, or 1/0.25 = 4 in this highly simplified case. The drop in investment ($100 billion) times the multiplier (4) is equal to the drop in GDP ($400 billion). So, in this example, GDP must have dropped by $400 billion. This is an illustration of how the multiplier can be used, presuming that the assumptions underlying the simple Keynesian model hold. Knowing the marginal propensity to save (0.25), we can calculate the multiplier (4), which enables us to determine the change in GDP ($400 billion).

Multiplier

Since a dollar of extra intended investment results in 1/*MPS* dollars of extra GDP, 1/*MPS* is called the **multiplier**. If you want to estimate the effect of a given increase in intended investment on GDP, multiply the increase in intended investment by 1/*MPS*. The result is the increase in GDP. Moreover, it is easy to show that the same multiplier holds for decreases in intended investment as well as for increases. That is, a dollar less of intended investment results in 1/*MPS* dollars less of GDP. Consequently, to estimate the effect of a given change in intended investment (positive or negative) on GDP, multiply the change in intended investment by 1/*MPS*.

It is important to note that, since *MPS* is less than 1, *the multiplier must be greater than 1*. In other words, an increase in intended investment of $1 results in an increase in GDP of more than $1. This means that GDP is relatively sensitive to changes in intended investment. Moreover, since the multiplier is the reciprocal of the marginal propensity to save, the smaller the marginal propensity to save, the bigger the multiplier—and the more sensitive GDP is to changes in intended investment.

EXPLORING FURTHER

Nonincome Determinants of Consumption

In previous sections, we were concerned with how changes in investment spending affect GDP. Now we will consider the effects of changes in consumption expenditure. It is important to recognize that many factors in addition to disposable income have an effect on personal consumption expenditure. Holding disposable income constant, personal consumption expenditure is likely to vary with the amount of wealth in the hands of the public, the ease and cheapness with which consumers can borrow money, consumers' expectations, the amount of durable goods on hand, the income distribution, and the size of the population. In this section, we will discuss the effects of these nonincome factors on consumption expenditure.

Shifts in the Consumption and Saving Functions

Suppose that a change occurs in one of these nonincome factors. For example, suppose that the amount of wealth in the hands of the public increases markedly. What effect does this have on the consumption function? It shifts the consumption function upward, as from position 1 to position 2 in Figure 17.7. Or suppose that it becomes more difficult and expensive for consumers to borrow money. What effect does this have on the consumption function? It shifts the consumption function downward, as from position 1 to position 3 in Figure 17.7.

Shifts in Functions versus Movements along Them

It is important to distinguish between a *shift* in the consumption function and a *movement along* a given consumption function. A shift in the consumption function means that the public wants to spend a different amount on consumption goods out of a given amount of disposable income than in the past. Therefore, if the consumption function shifts to position 2 in Figure 17.7,

FIGURE 17.7

A Shift versus a Movement along the Consumption Function

If the consumption function moves from position 1 to position 2 (or position 3), this is a shift in the consumption function. A movement from *A* to *B* (or from *C* to *D*) is a movement along a given consumption function.

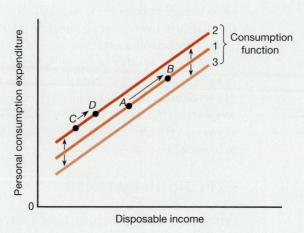

this means that the public wants to spend more on consumption goods out of a given amount of disposable income than when the consumption function was at position 1. And if the consumption function shifts to position 3 in Figure 17.7, this means that the public wants to spend less on consumption goods out of a given amount of disposable income than when the consumption function was at position 1.

In contrast, a movement along a given consumption function is a change in personal consumption expenditure induced by a change in disposable income, with no change in the relationship between personal consumption expenditure and disposable income. For example, the movement from point *A* to point *B* is a movement along a consumption function (in position 1). Similarly, the movement from point *C* to point *D* is a movement along a consumption function (in position 2).

How Shifts in the Consumption Function Are Related to Shifts in the Saving Function

Note that an *upward* shift in the consumption function must be accompanied by a *downward* shift in the saving function. If the public wants to spend *more* on consumption goods out of a given amount of disposable income, it must want to save *less* out of that amount of disposable income. (Why? Because personal consumption expenditure plus saving equals disposable income.) If the consumption function shifts upward from position 1 to position 2 in Figure 17.7, the saving function must shift downward from position 4 to position 5 in Figure 17.8.

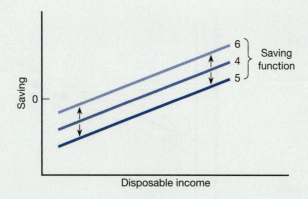

FIGURE 17.8

How Shifts in the Consumption Function Affect the Saving Function

An upward shift in the consumption function (as from position 1 to position 2 in Figure 17.7) is accompanied by a downward shift in the saving function (from position 4 to position 5 in the figure shown here). A downward shift in the consumption function (as from position 1 to position 3 in Figure 17.7) is accompanied by an upward shift in the saving function (from position 4 to position 6 in the figure shown here).

Also, a *downward* shift in the consumption function must be accompanied by an *upward* shift in the saving function. If the public wants to spend *less* on consumption goods out of a given amount of disposable income, it must want to save *more* out of that amount of disposable income. (Why? Because personal consumption expenditure plus saving equals disposable income.) If the consumption function shifts downward from position 1 to position 3 in Figure 17.7, the saving function must shift upward from position 4 to position 6 in Figure 17.8.

Effects of Shifts in the Consumption Function

Earlier in this chapter, we showed that in the simple Keynesian model, changes in intended investment have an amplified effect on the GDP, with the extent of the amplification measured by the multiplier. But it is important to note at this point that a shift in the consumption function also has such an amplified effect on GDP. For example, in Figure 17.9, if the consumption function shifts from C_1 to C_2, this means that at each level of disposable income, consumers intend to spend $1 billion more on consumption goods and services than they did before. This $1 billion upward shift in the consumption function has precisely the same effect on equilibrium GDP as a $1 billion increase in intended investment.

FIGURE 17.9

Shift in the Consumption Function

A shift in the consumption function from C_1 to C_2 means that at each level of disposable income, consumers intend to spend $1 billion more on consumption goods and services. Such a shift results in an increase of $1/MPS$ billion dollars in equilibrium GDP.

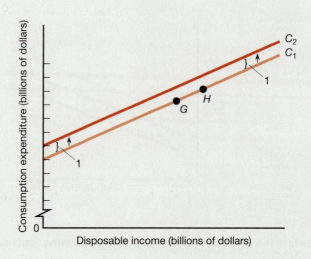

Moreover, a $1 billion downward shift in the consumption function has precisely the same effect on equilibrium GDP as a $1 billion decrease in intended investment. Hence, both upward and downward shifts in the consumption function (due to changes in tastes, assets, prices, population, and other things) has a magnified effect on GDP. GDP is sensitive to shifts in the consumption function in the same way that it is to changes in intended investment. This is an important point. Finally, to prevent misunderstanding, recall from the previous sections that a *shift* in the consumption function is quite different from a *movement along* a given consumption function. (An example of the latter would be the movement from point G to point H in Figure 17.9.) We are concerned here with shifts in the consumption function, not movements along a given consumption function.

REVIEW AND PRACTICE

Summary

1 The consumption function is the relation between personal consumption expenditure and disposable income. From the consumption function, one can determine the marginal propensity to consume, which is the proportion of an extra dollar of income spent on consumption. The marginal propensity to save is the proportion of an extra dollar of income saved.

2   The level of gross private domestic investment is determined by the expected rate of return from capital and the interest rate. The expected rate of return from capital is the rate of return that businesses expect to obtain if new buildings are put up, new equipment is added, or inventories are increased. The interest rate is the cost of borrowing money.

3   The equilibrium level of gross domestic product is the point where intended spending on final goods and services equals GDP. If intended spending exceeds GDP, GDP tends to increase. If intended spending falls short of GDP, GDP tends to fall.

4   If GDP is below its equilibrium level, the total amount spent on goods and services exceeds the total amount produced, so firms' inventories are reduced. Firms step up their output rates and thus increase GDP.

5   If GDP is above its equilibrium value, the total amount spent on goods and services falls short of the total amount produced, so firms' inventories increase. Firms cut their output rates and thus reduce GDP.

6   Investment expenditure tends to vary from year to year by greater percentages than consumption expenditure. This is due in part to the irregularity of innovation, the durability of capital goods, and the differences from year to year in the extent to which existing productive capacity is utilized.

7   A $1 billion change in intended investment results in a change in equilibrium GDP of 1/*MPS* billion dollars, where *MPS* is the marginal propensity to save. In other words, the multiplier is 1/*MPS*. The multiplier can be interpreted in terms of—and derived from—the successive stages of the spending process.

*8[2]   Holding disposable income constant, personal consumption expenditure is likely to depend on the amount of wealth in the hands of the public, the ease and cheapness with which consumers can borrow money, consumers' expectations, the amount of durable goods on hand, the income distribution, and the size of the population. Changes in these factors are likely to cause shifts in the consumption function.

*9   A shift in the consumption function has an amplified effect on GDP: a $1 billion shift in the consumption function results in a change in GDP of 1/*MPS* billion dollars.

Problems and Questions

1   Suppose that the consumption function in a particular economy is given by the following table:

[2] Starred (*) items relate to material covered in Exploring Further.

Disposable Income (billions of dollars)	Consumption Expenditure (billions of dollars)
400	300
500	360
600	410
700	440
800	470

If firms want to invest $140 billion, what is the equilibrium value of GDP? Can we be sure that this is the full-employment value of GDP? Why or why not? (The full-employment value of GDP is defined as the value of GDP that can be produced if there is full employment of all resources.)

2   Using the data in question 1, plot the consumption function and the $C + I$ line on a graph, and derive the equilibrium value of GDP graphically. Is the consumption function a straight line? If the consumption function is not a straight line, does this affect the validity of the analysis in any way?

3   Using the data in question 1, plot the saving function. Show that intended saving equals intended investment at the equilibrium level of GDP. Explain why this is true.

4   Suppose that the consumption function in a certain economy is $C = \$100$ billion $+ 0.8D$, where C is consumption expenditure and D is disposable income (both expressed in billions of dollars). If intended investment equals $10 billion, what is the equilibrium value of GDP?

Key Terms

consumption function

marginal propensity to consume

average propensity to consume

saving function

marginal propensity to save

expected rate of return

interest rate

45-degree line

income-expenditure analysis

autonomous change in spending

induced change in spending

multiplier

Viewpoint for Analysis

On February 11, 1993, Allan Meltzer, professor of economics at Carnegie-Mellon University, testified before the Joint Economic Committee of Congress. He said, "Public policy has discouraged investment in several ways. . . . The 1986 tax act shifted taxes from consumers to owners of capital. . . . Taxes should be shifted from earned income to consumed income. . . . This change would increase saving."[3]

(a)   What is the difference between earned income and consumed income? Would a shift in taxes from earned income to consumed income tend to increase the average propensity to save? Why or why not?

(b)   Why would a shift in taxes from consumers to owners of capital discourage investment? If investment falls, what is likely to happen to GDP in the short run? In the long run? Why?

(c)   Would you favor a policy of increasing investment? Why or why not? Can there be too much investment? Explain.

[3] A. Meltzer, "The Economy and Policy as 1993 Begins," statement prepared for the Joint Economic Committee, February 11, 1993.

Fiscal Policy and National Output

LEARNING OBJECTIVES

➤ To explore how government spending and taxation affect the level of GDP

➤ To explain the objectives and methods of fiscal policy

➤ To analyze the problems in formulating effective fiscal policy

➤ To describe the types of expenditures made and taxes collected by federal, state, and local governments

➤ *(Exploring Further)* To learn how to include net exports in the Keynesian model

Most governments change tax rates—sometimes up, sometimes down. What effect do these changes have on GDP? One purpose of this chapter is to answer this question. In the period after World War II, the idea that the government's power to spend and tax should be used to stabilize the economy (that is, to reduce unemployment and fight inflation) gained acceptance throughout the world. However, time has revealed that fiscal policy (the use of government spending and taxation for stabilization purposes) is far from a panacea. This chapter presents a first look at fiscal policy, beginning with the simplest Keynesian model, then using aggregate demand and aggregate supply curves. Chapters 24 and 26 present a more sophisticated analysis of fiscal policy.

Government Expenditure and Gross Domestic Product

In the previous chapters, we showed how the equilibrium level of gross domestic product was determined in a simplified economy without government spending or taxation. We now extend this theory to include both government spending and taxation. As we shall see, the results form the basis for some of our nation's past and present economic policy. In this section, we incorporate government spending into the simple Keynesian model for determining gross domestic product. In so doing, we assume that government spending does not affect the consumption function or the level of intended investment. In other words, we assume that government spending does not reduce or increase private desires to spend out of each level of income. (Government here includes federal, state, and local governments.)

Suppose that the government purchases $50 billion worth of goods and services and it purchases this amount whatever the level of GDP. (As pointed out in Chapter 15, only government purchases, not transfer payments, are included here.) Clearly, adding this public expenditure to the private expenditures on consumption and investment results in a higher total level of intended spending. In an economy with government spending (but no net exports), total intended spending on output equals consumption expenditure plus intended investment expenditure plus intended government expenditure. Since an increase in government expenditure (like increases in consumption or investment expenditure) results in an increase in total intended spending and the equilibrium value of gross domestic product is at the point where total intended spending equals GDP, it follows that an increase in government expenditure, as well as the induced increase in private spending, brings about an increase in the equilibrium value of GDP.

To see the effects of government expenditure on the equilibrium value of GDP, we use a graph similar to those in Chapter 17. We begin by plotting the consumption function, which shows intended consumption expenditure at each level of GDP (since GDP equals disposable income under our assumptions); the result is line C in Figure 18.1. Then we plot the sum of intended consumption expenditure and investment expenditure at each level of GDP; the result is line $C + I$. Next we plot the sum of intended consumption expenditure, investment expenditure, and government expenditure at each level of GDP to get line $C + I + G$. Since the $C + I + G$ line shows total intended spending and (as stressed in Chapter 17) the equilibrium value of GDP is the point where total intended spending equals GDP, it follows that the equilibrium value of GDP is the point where the $C + I + G$ line intersects the 45-degree line. This is at an output of $1,225 billion.

Effect of Increased Government Expenditure

What happens to the equilibrium level of GDP if government expenditure increases? Figure 18.2 shows the results of a $5 billion increase in government spending. The increased government expenditure (G_1) raises the $C + I + G$ line by $5 billion, as the figure shows. Since the $C + I + G_1$ line must intersect the 45-degree line at a higher level of GDP, increases in government expenditure result in increases in the equilibrium level of GDP. In Figure 18.2, the $5 billion increase in government expenditure raises the equilibrium value of GDP from $1,225 billion to $1,237.5 billion.

FIGURE 18.1

Determining Gross Domestic Product, Including Government Expenditure

The consumption function is C; the sum of consumption and investment expenditures is $C + I$; and the sum of consumption, investment, and government expenditures is $C + I + G$. The equilibrium value of GDP is at the point where the $C + I + G$ line intersects the 45-degree line, which here is $1,225 billion.

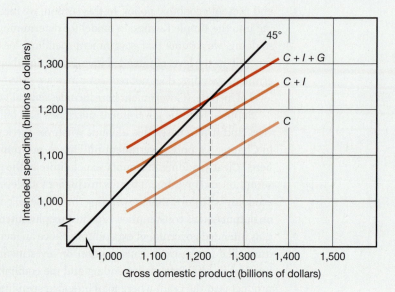

Effect of Decreased Government Expenditure

Figure 18.2 also shows what happens when government spending goes down by $5 billion (to G_2). The new $C + I + G_2$ line is $5 billion lower than the old $C + I + G$ line. Since the new $C + I + G_2$ line intersects the 45-degree line at a lower level of GDP, decreases in government expenditure result in decreases in

FIGURE 18.2

Effects on the Equilibrium Gross Domestic Product of a $5 Billion Increase and Decrease in Government Expenditure

A $5 billion increase raises the equilibrium value of GDP from $1,225 billion to $1,237.5 billion. A $5 billion decrease reduces the equilibrium value of GDP from $1,225 billion to $1,212.5 billion.

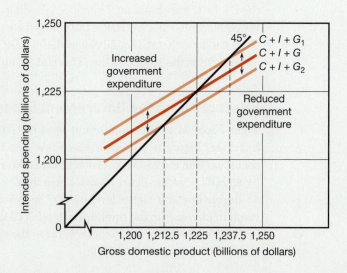

the equilibrium level of GDP. In Figure 18.2, the $5 billion decrease in government expenditure reduces the equilibrium value of GDP from $1,225 billion to $1,212.5 billion.

The Multiplier Effect for Government Expenditure

How sensitive is the equilibrium level of GDP to changes in government spending? In the previous chapter, we found that in the simple Keynesian model, a $1 billion change in intended investment—or a $1 billion shift in the consumption function—results in a change in equilibrium GDP of $1/MPS$ billion dollars, where MPS is the marginal propensity to save. The effect of a $1 billion change in government expenditure is exactly the same. It results in a change in equilibrium GDP of $1/MPS$ billion dollars. Therefore, a change in government expenditure has the same multiplier effect on GDP as a change in investment or a shift in the consumption function. For example, if the marginal propensity to consume is 0.6, an extra $1 billion in government expenditure increases equilibrium GDP by $2.5 billion.

Taxation and Gross Domestic Product

The previous section added government expenditure to the simple Keynesian model, but it did not include taxes. (Here we assume taxes to be net of transfer payments.) For simplicity, assume that all tax revenues stem from personal taxes. How do tax collections influence the equilibrium value of gross domestic product? For example, if consumers pay 16.67 percent of their income to the government in taxes, what effect does this have on GDP? Clearly, the imposition of this tax means that for each level of GDP, people have less disposable income than they would with no taxes. In particular, disposable income now equals 83.33 percent of GDP, whereas without taxes it equals GDP. The relationship between consumption expenditure and GDP is altered by the imposition of the tax. Before the tax is levied, the relationship is given by line C_0 in Figure 18.3; after the imposition of the tax, it is given by line C_1.

The relationship between consumption expenditure and national output changes in this way because consumption expenditure is determined by the level of disposable income. For instance, assume that consumption expenditure equals $350 billion plus 60 percent of disposable income. Therefore, since the tax reduces the amount of disposable income at each level of GDP, it also reduces the amount of consumption expenditure at each level of GDP. In other words, since people have less after-tax income to spend at each level of GDP, they spend less on consumption goods and services at each level of GDP. This seems reasonable. It is illustrated in Figure 18.3, where at each level of GDP, consumption expenditure after tax (given by line C_1) is less than before the tax (given by line C_0).

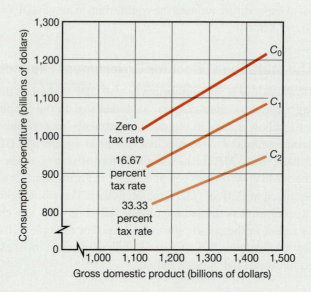

FIGURE 18.3

Relationship between Consumption Expenditure and the Gross Domestic Product, Given Three Tax Rates

If taxes are zero, C_0 is the relationship between consumption expenditure and GDP. If consumers pay 16.67 percent of their income in taxes, C_1 is the relationship; and if consumers pay 33.33 percent of their income in taxes, C_2 is the relationship. Clearly, the higher the tax rate, the less consumers spend on consumption from a given GDP.

Because the imposition of the tax influences the relationship between consumption expenditure and GDP, it also influences the equilibrium value of GDP. As stressed, the equilibrium value of GDP is the point where intended spending on output equals GDP. Lines C_0 and C_1 in Figure 18.3 show intended consumption expenditure at each level of GDP, before and after the tax. Adding intended investment and government expenditure to each of these lines, we get the total intended spending before and after the tax. Assume, in Figure 18.4, that the sum of intended investment and government spending equals $140 billion. The $C_0 + I + G$ line shows intended spending before the tax; the $C_1 + I + G$ line shows intended spending after the tax.

Effect of the Tax

The equilibrium level of GDP is appreciably lower after the imposition of the tax than before. Specifically, as shown in Figure 18.4, it is $980 billion after the imposition of the tax and $1,225 billion before. The tax reduces the equilibrium

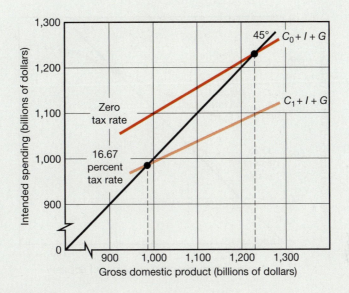

FIGURE 18.4

Determining the Equilibrium Value of Gross Domestic Product, with Zero and 16.67 Percent Tax Rates

The tax rate influences the relationship between consumption expenditure and GDP. (C_0 is the relationship with a zero tax rate, while C_1 is the relationship with a 16.67 percent tax rate; see Figure 18.3.) Consequently, the equilibrium value of the GDP is $1,225 billion if the tax rate is zero and $980 billion if it is 16.67 percent.

level of GDP because it lowers the $C + I + G$ line from $C_0 + I + G$ to $C_1 + I + G$. It does this because it reduces the amount people want to spend on consumption goods at each level of GDP. People still want to spend the same amount from each (after-tax) income level, but because of the tax, their spending decisions must be based on a reduced (after-tax) income, so they spend less on consumption goods and services at each level of GDP.

Effect of a Tax Increase

Going a step further, the higher the tax rate, the lower the equilibrium value of GDP; and the lower the tax rate, the higher the equilibrium value of GDP. This is a very important proposition, as we shall see in subsequent sections. To demonstrate it, let us see what happens to the equilibrium value of GDP when the tax rate is increased from 16.67 percent of GDP to 33.33 percent of GDP. If the tax rate is 33.33 percent, total intended spending at each level of GDP is given by line $C_2 + I + G$ in Figure 18.5.

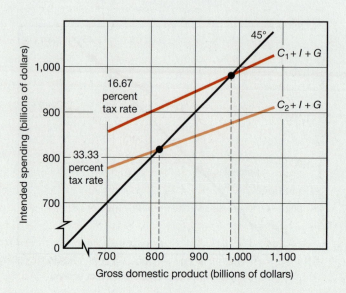

FIGURE 18.5

Determining the Equilibrium Value of Gross Domestic Product, with 16.67 percent and 33.33 Percent Tax Rates

The $C_1 + I + G$ line shows total intended spending at each level of GDP if the tax rate is 16.67 percent, and the $C_2 + I + G$ line shows total intended spending at each level of GDP if the tax rate is 33.33 percent. So the equilibrium value of GDP is $980 billion if the tax rate is 16.67 percent and $816.67 billion if it is 33.33 percent.

Since the equilibrium value of GDP is the point where the $C_2 + I + G$ line intersects the 45-degree line, the equilibrium value of GDP is $816.67 billion, rather than $980 billion (the equilibrium value when the tax rate is 16.67 percent). Therefore, the increase in the tax rate reduces the equilibrium value of GDP. By reducing the amount people want to spend on consumption at each level of GDP, the increase in the tax rate lowers the $C + I + G$ line from $C_1 + I + G$ to $C_2 + I + G$.

Fiscal Policy: Aggregate Demand and Supply Curves

So far we have described the effects of fiscal policy in the simple Keynesian model, where the price level is constant and the short-run aggregate supply curve is horizontal. But as pointed out in Chapter 17, these assumptions often are not applicable. Our purpose in this section is to analyze the effects of fiscal policy in the situation where the price level is not constant and the short-run aggregate supply curve is not horizontal. As in previous chapters, we make extensive use of aggregate supply and demand curves.

A Recessionary Gap

Recessionary gap

To begin with, suppose that the economy is suffering from excessive unemployment and output is well below its potential level. There is a **recessionary gap**, which means that equilibrium output is less than potential output. In particular, we assume that the situation is as shown in the top left-hand panel of Figure 18.6. As you can see, the equilibrium value of total real output is $200 billion, which is well below $250 billion, the economy's potential output. Given this situation, there are several ways in which output can be pushed up to its potential level so that full employment is restored. One way is to wait for wage rates and other input prices to fall in response to the high unemployment rate, shifting the short-run aggregate supply curve to the right, as shown in the top right-hand panel of Figure 18.6. Although some economists believe that such a strategy is feasible, most believe that it would take too long because, in their view, wages tend to be quite sticky (recall Chapter 16). In Chapter 26, we discuss more fully the controversies and evidence on this score.

Another way to deal with the recessionary gap in the top left-hand panel of Figure 18.6 is to wait for spending by the private sector to pick up, shifting the aggregate demand curve to the right, as shown in the bottom panel of Figure 18.6. Here, too, the problem is that it may take a painfully long time for such a shift in the aggregate demand curve to occur. As we saw in Chapter 16, some recessions go on for years.

Still another strategy is for the government to increase its spending, cut taxes, or both, shifting the aggregate demand curve to the right. As in the case described in the previous paragraph, such a shift in the aggregate demand curve can push output up to its potential level, as shown in the bottom panel of Figure 18.6. Governments eager to restore full employment often use fiscal policy in this way. One problem has been that the stimulus resulting from their actions sometimes is felt when spending by the private sector picks up, and the consequence has been inflationary pressure because the aggregate demand curve is pushed too far to the right.

An Inflationary Gap

Inflationary gap

Having described how fiscal policy can be used to deal with an economy suffering from excessive unemployment, we turn to a case where an economy is suffering from serious inflation. If the equilibrium value of real national output exceeds potential output, as shown in the top left-hand panel of Figure 18.7, economists say that there is an **inflationary gap**. In a situation of this sort,

FIGURE 18.6

Alternative Ways of Dealing with a Recessionary Gap

As shown in the top left-hand panel, equilibrium output is $200 billion, which is well below the potential output of $250 billion. Hence, there is a recessionary gap. One way to deal with this situation is to wait for wages and other input prices to fall, pushing the short-run aggregate supply curve to the right, as shown in the top right-hand panel. Another way is to wait for an increase in private sector spending to push the aggregate demand curve to the right, as shown in the bottom panel. Still another way is for the government to shift the aggregate demand curve to the right (as in the bottom panel) by increasing its own spending, cutting taxes, or both.

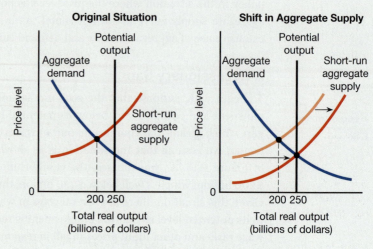

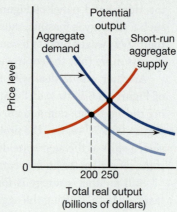

there are substantial inflationary pressures. Why? Because labor is in short supply, and wages are bid up, increasing firms' costs. There are several ways that the equilibrium value of real national output can be reduced so it no longer exceeds potential output and price stability is restored.

One way is to allow market forces to take their course. Since wages and other input prices are bid up, the short-run aggregate supply curve shifts to the left. The result is inflation, but when the price level increases to 115 (measured as an aggregate price index with no specific units) in the top right-hand panel of Figure 18.7, the inflation should stop.

FIGURE 18.7

Alternative Ways of Dealing with an Inflationary Gap

As shown in the top left-hand panel, equilibrium output is $300 billion, which is well above the potential output of $250 billion. Hence, there is an inflationary gap. One way to deal with this situation is to allow wages and other input prices to rise, pushing the short-run aggregate supply curve to the left, as shown in the top right-hand panel. Another way is to wait for a decrease in private sector spending to push the aggregate demand curve to the left, as shown in the bottom panel. Still another way is for the government to shift the aggregate demand curve to the left (as in the bottom panel) by cutting its own spending, raising taxes, or both.

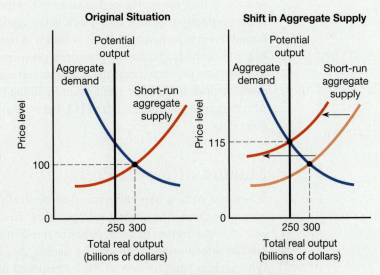

Original Situation

Shift in Aggregate Supply

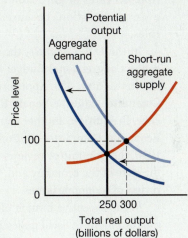

Shift in Aggregate Demand

Another way to deal with the inflationary gap in the top left-hand panel of Figure 18.7 is to wait for spending by the private sector to recede, shifting the aggregate demand curve to the left, as shown in the bottom panel of Figure 18.7. Unfortunately, however, such a reduction in aggregate demand may not occur in time to prevent the inflationary process in the top left-hand panel of Figure 18.7 from taking place.

Still another strategy is for the government to cut its spending, raise taxes, or both, shifting the aggregate demand curve to the left. As in the case described in the previous paragraph, such a shift in the aggregate demand curve can push output down to its potential level, as shown in the bottom panel of Figure 18.7. Eager to cut back inflationary pressures, governments often use fiscal policy in this way. One problem is that the economic restraint resulting from the government's actions sometimes is felt when spending by the private sector recedes, with the consequence that output falls below its potential level and unemployment rises.

Makers of Fiscal Policy

When you go to a baseball game, you generally get a program telling you who on each team is playing each position. To understand the formulation and implementation of fiscal policy in the United States, we need the same kind of information. Who are the people that establish our fiscal policy? Who decides that, in view of the current and prospective economic situation, tax rates or government expenditures should be changed? This is not a simple question, because many individuals and groups play important roles.

In the U.S. Congress, the House and Senate Budget Committees, as well as the Congressional Budget Office, are charged with important responsibilities in this area. The Appropriations Committees, the House Ways and Means Committee, and the Senate Finance Committee also have considerable influence. In addition, another congressional committee is of importance: the Joint Economic Committee of Congress. Established by the Employment Act of 1946, this committee reviews the annual *Economic Report of the President* on the state of the economy and, through its hearings, provides a major forum for review of economic issues.

In the executive branch of government, the most important person in the establishment of fiscal policy is, of course, the president. Although he (or she) must operate in the context of the tax and expenditure laws passed by Congress, he and his advisers are the country's principal analysts of the need for fiscal expansion or restraint and its leading spokespersons for legislative changes to meet these needs. Needless to say, he does not pore over the latest economic data and make the decisions all by himself. The Office of Management and Budget, which is part of the Executive Office of the President, is a very powerful adviser to the president on expenditure policy, as is the Treasury Department on tax policy. In addition, there is the Council of Economic Advisers, which is also part of the Executive Office of the President. Established by the Employment Act of 1946, its job is to help the president carry out the objectives of that act. During the past 56 years, the Council of Economic Advisers, headed by a series of distinguished economists who left academic and other posts to

THE EMPLOYMENT ACT OF 1946

President Harry S. Truman signing the Employment Act of 1946

The experiences of the Great Depression and World War II convinced many Americans that the government had both the duty and the power to guarantee jobs for all its citizens. And the theoretical basis for this belief came from John Maynard Keynes (see Case Study 16.3). Keynes argued that an industrial economy could stabilize at high levels of unemployment, and the length and depth of the Great Depression seemed to bear him out. He argued that massive government intervention could restore prosperity to a stalled economy, and the wartime experience seemed to prove him right. When prosperity was threatened at the end of the war, a Full Employment Bill was introduced in the U.S. Senate in January 1945.

The first shot had been fired in a year-long legislative battle. While everyone had been anxious to talk about full employment during the political campaigns of 1944, there was still plenty of resistance to the idea of this much government intervention in the economy. A year of compromises saw many changes in the language of the bill. The words "full employment" were replaced by the phrase "maximum employment, production and purchasing power." Gone were the original instructions to the president to initiate spending programs to guarantee employment. Conservatives rejoiced in a watered-down bill. Liberals denied that any retreat was involved.

The bill that President Truman signed into law on February 20, 1946, was called the Employment Act of 1946. It instructed the federal government "to promote maximum employment, production and purchasing power." The president was instructed to form a Council of Economic Advisers to assist him in preparing economic forecasts. The idea of a right to a job, and a spending program to guarantee that right, disappeared from the final bill. By the time the Employment Act became law, the war was over, but prosperity continued. Dire predictions of hard times and high unemployment vanished in the explosion of pent-up consumer demand. The end of the war marked the beginning of a long period of prosperity. And the Employment Act of 1946 marked the commitment of the government to use its considerable power to try to ensure a continuation of this prosperity.

contribute to public policy, has become an important actor on the national economic policy stage.

Automatic Stabilizers

Automatic
stabilizers

Now that we have met some of the major players, we must point out that in their efforts to fight serious unemployment or inflation, they get help from some **automatic stabilizers**—structural features of our economy that tend to stabilize national output. Although these economic stabilizers cannot do all that is required to keep the economy on an even keel, they help a lot. As soon as the economy turns down and unemployment mounts, they give the economy a helpful shot in the arm. As soon as the economy gets overheated and inflation escalates, they tend to restrain it. These stabilizers are automatic because they come into play without the need for new legislation or administrative decisions.

Tax Revenues

Changes in income tax revenues are an important automatic stabilizer. Our federal system relies heavily on the income tax. The amount of income tax collected by the federal government goes up with increases in GDP and goes down with decreases in GDP. This, of course, is just what we want to occur. When output falls off and unemployment mounts, tax collections fall off, too, so disposable income falls less than GDP. This means less of a fall in consumption expenditure, which tends to break the fall in GDP. When output rises too fast and the economy begins to suffer from serious inflation, tax collections rise, too; this tends to restrain the increase in GDP. Of course, corporate income taxes, as well as personal income taxes, play a significant role here.

Unemployment Compensation and Welfare Payments

Unemployment compensation is paid to workers who are laid off, adhering to a system that has evolved over the past 75 years. When unemployed workers go back to work, they stop receiving unemployment compensation. Therefore, when GDP falls off and unemployment mounts, the tax collections to finance unemployment compensation go down (because of lower employment), while the amount paid out to unemployed workers goes up. On the other hand, when GDP rises too fast and the economy begins to suffer from serious inflation, the tax collections to finance unemployment compensation go up, while the amount paid out to workers goes down as a result of less unemployment. Again, this is just what we want to see happen. The fall in spending is moderated when unemployment is high, and the increase in spending is curbed when there are serious inflationary pressures. Various welfare programs have the same kind of automatic stabilizing effect on the economy.

PRESIDENT EISENHOWER AND AUTOMATIC STABILIZERS

President Dwight D. Eisenhower

When Dwight Eisenhower took office in 1953, he inherited a prosperity that had been bubbling along since the postwar boom. But by August 1953, there were signs that the economy was headed for a recession. By 1954, the unemployment rate was 6 percent, the highest since the Great Depression. Although President Eisenhower remained outwardly confident, behind the scenes there was concern about the deepening recession and a debate about what the government should do. Because the recession reduced tax revenues, the government was running at a deficit, and some people felt that taxes should be raised.

But President Eisenhower was getting other advice. In 1954, the Committee for Economic Development (composed largely of top business executives) urged the president to forget about balancing the budget and leave the economy alone. As 1954 wore on and the Democrats and the labor unions demanded action, the economy stumbled, sputtered, then took off in an upward direction. The first Republican recession since 1929 had come and gone, and even dedicated Democrats had to admit that the nation had survived. But we survived by doing nothing. And in hindsight, nothing turns out to have been just the thing to do.

An important factor in promoting recovery was the existence of our economy's automatic stabilizers. The concept of automatic stabilizers had been brought to the Eisenhower administration by Arthur F. Burns, who chaired the Council of Economic Advisers. Ironically, in 1952 Congress had tried to kill the council by cutting off its funding. By the end of 1954, it was clear that the council, its chairperson, and its stabilizing budget policy had passed a major test with honors.

Discretionary Fiscal Policy

Discretionary fiscal policy

The federal government frequently changes tax rates—and to a lesser extent expenditures—in an attempt to cope with unemployment and inflation. The following kinds of measures, **discretionary fiscal policy**, can be adopted:

1. *The government can vary its expenditure for goods and services.* If increased unemployment seems to be in the wind, the government can step up outlays for roads, urban reconstruction, and other public programs. Of course, these programs must be well thought out and socially productive. There is no sense in pushing through wasteful and foolish spending programs merely to make jobs. Or if, as in 1969, the economy is plagued by inflation, the government can (as President Nixon did) stop new federal construction programs temporarily.

2. *The government can vary welfare payments and other types of transfer payments.* For example, a hike in Social Security benefits may provide a shot in the arm for an economy with too much unemployment. An increase in veterans' benefits or aid to dependent children may do the same thing. The federal government has sometimes helped the states extend the length of time that the unemployed can receive unemployment compensation; this, too, is expected to have the desired effect.

3. *The government can vary tax rates.* For example, if there is considerable unemployment, the government may cut tax rates, as it did in 1975 and more recently in 2001 and 2003. Or if inflation is the problem, the government may increase taxes, as it did in 1968, when after considerable political maneuvering and buck-passing, Congress was finally persuaded to put through a 10 percent tax surcharge to try to moderate the inflation caused by the Vietnam War. However, temporary tax changes may have less effect than permanent ones, since consumption expenditure may be influenced less by transitory changes in income than by permanent changes.

Problems in Formulating Effective Discretionary Fiscal Policies

Although governments frequently carry out discretionary fiscal policies, it is important to recognize the many types of problems that can interfere with the effectiveness of such policies. A big disadvantage of public works and similar spending programs is that they take so long to get started. Plans must be made, land must be acquired, and preliminary construction studies must be carried out. By the time the expenditures are finally made and have the desired effect, the dangers of excessive unemployment may have given way to the dangers of inflation, so that the spending, coming too late, may not be the right economic medicine at all.

In recent years, the feeling has been widespread that government expenditures should be set on the basis of their long-term desirability and productivity and not on the basis of short-term stabilization considerations. The optimal level of government expenditure is the point where the value of the extra benefits to be derived from an extra dollar of government expenditure is at least equal to the dollar of cost. This optimal level is unlikely to change much in the short run, and it would be wasteful to spend more—or less—than this amount for stabilization purposes when tax changes could be used instead. Therefore, many economists believe that tax cuts or tax increases should be the primary fiscal weapons to fight unemployment or inflation.

However, a big problem with tax changes is that it sometimes is difficult to get Congress to take speedy action. There is often considerable debate over a tax bill, and all too often it becomes a political football. Another difficulty with tax changes is that it generally is much easier to reduce taxes than to get them back up again. To politicians, lower taxes are attractive because they are popular, and higher taxes are dangerous because they may hurt an officeholder's chances of reelection. In discussing fiscal policy (or most other aspects of government operations, for that matter), to ignore politics is to risk losing touch with reality.

Further, economists warn that to the extent that discretionary fiscal policy involves reacting to short-term economic developments with little consideration of longer-term consequences, the result may be more harm than good. This problem is discussed at length in Chapter 26. The point is that changes in taxes and government spending aimed at stabilizing the economy in the short term may not be most effective in promoting the long-term health of the economy.

Nevertheless, there are still strong arguments for using fiscal policy to get the economy out of recession. Such arguments were used to pass the massive stimulus package proposed by the administration of Barack Obama in early 2009 to help the economy recover from its worst downturn since the Great Depression (see Case Study 18.4).

Size and Nature of Government Activities

How Big Is the Government?

Up to this point, we have been concerned primarily with fiscal policy and the role of the government in trying to stabilize the economy. We made no attempt to describe the size and nature of the functions of the U.S. government in quantitative terms. It is time to turn to some of the relevant facts.

To begin with, government expenditures are a much larger percentage of our national output than was true 75 or 100 years ago. There are many reasons why government expenditures grew so much faster than total output. Three of these are particularly important. First, the United States did not maintain anything like the kind of military force in pre–World War II days that

PRESIDENT KENNEDY AND THE TAX CUT OF 1964

President John F. Kennedy and Walter Heller

When the Kennedy administration took office in 1961, it was confronted with a relatively high unemployment rate, about 7 percent in mid-1961. By 1962, although unemployment was somewhat lower (about 6 percent), the president's advisers, led by Walter W. Heller, chairperson of the Council of Economic Advisers, pushed for a tax cut to reduce unemployment further. The president, after considerable discussion of the effects of such a tax cut, announced in June 1962 that he would propose such a measure to Congress; and in January 1963, the bill was finally sent to Congress.

The proposed tax bill was a victory for Heller and the Council of Economic Advisers. Even though it would mean a deliberately large deficit, the president had been persuaded to cut taxes to push the economy closer to full employment. But Congress was not so easily convinced. Many members of Congress labeled the proposal irresponsible and reckless. Others wanted to couple tax reform with tax reduction. It was not until 1964, after President Kennedy's death, that the tax bill was enacted. It took a year from the time the bill was sent to Congress for it to be passed, and during this interval, there was a continuous debate in the executive branch and in Congress. The secretary of the Treasury, Douglas Dillon; the chairperson of the Federal Reserve Board, William M. Martin; and numerous congressional representatives—all powerful and all initially cool to the proposal— eventually were won over. The result was a tax reduction of about $10 billion per year.

The effects of the tax cut are by no means easy to measure, in part because the rate of growth of the money supply increased at the same time, and this should also affect GDP. But in line with the theory presented in earlier sections, consumption expenditure did increase sharply during 1964. Moreover, the additional consumption expenditure undoubtedly induced additional investment. According to some estimates, the tax cut resulted in an increase in GDP of about $24 billion in 1965 and more in subsequent years. The unemployment rate, which had been about 5.5 to 6 percent during 1962 and 1963, fell to 5 percent during 1964 and to 4.7 percent in the spring of 1965. It is fair to say that most economists were extremely pleased with themselves in 1965. Fiscal policy based on their theories seemed to work very well indeed!

THE OBAMA FISCAL STIMULUS OF 2009

The decisions about fiscal policy were easier in the depths of the Great Recession than they were two years later when the recovery was under way. In early 2009, the new president, Barack Obama, and the U.S. Congress agreed quickly—some would say in record time—on a large fiscal stimulus package. While there is still some disagreement over the size of the stimulus (too big or too small?) and over its composition (more tax cuts or more spending increases?), there is some consensus that without it the state of the economy would have been much worse. By some estimates, the U.S. unemployment rate would have been 1½ to 2 percentage points higher without the stimulus—that's 2 to 3 million jobs.

The challenge in 2011 was entirely different. Given the fragility of the recovery and the large and rising debt of the U.S. government, the essence of the debate boiled down to two issues: first, should fiscal policy be tightened immediately or later, and second, should most of the adjustment occur on the spending side or the tax side? Few debated the need to cut the deficit and reduce the national debt. But there were big differences in opinion about when and how to tighten.

The debate over timing had to do with concerns about the durability of the recovery and its ability to withstand spending cuts or higher taxes versus concerns over the "crowding out" of private investment by large budget deficits. In the end, the president and Congress agreed to cut spending by only a little in the near term. The longer-term deficit reduction debate was—and is likely to remain—far more contentious. Republicans prefer to keep taxes low and to reduce the deficit by cutting spending, including politically sensitive entitlement programs such as Medicare. The Democrats would rather cut spending less and increase taxes, especially on the rich.

Political realities have forced compromise on both sides. Republicans have had to live with higher taxes than they would like, and Democrats have had to accept more spending cuts than they would like. This is, in fact, what happened in early 2013, when Congress raised Social Security taxes and the top marginal tax rate. At the same time, it let stand automatic the spending cuts that have come to be known as the "sequester."

it does now. In earlier days, when weapons were relatively simple and cheap and we viewed our military and political responsibilities much more narrowly than we do now, our military budget was relatively small. The cost of being a superpower in the days of nuclear weaponry is high by any standards. Second, there has been a long-term increase in the demand for the services provided by government, such as more and better schooling, more extensive highways, and more complete police and fire protection. As incomes rise, people want more of these services. Third, government **transfer payments**—payments in return

Transfer payments

for no products or services—have grown very substantially. For example, various types of welfare payments have risen, and Social Security payments have increased greatly.

How the Federal, State, and Local Governments Spend Money

There are three levels of government in the United States: federal, state, and local. The state governments spend the least, while the federal government spends the most. This was not always the case. Before World War I, local governments spent more than the federal government. In those days, the federal government did not maintain the large military establishment it does now, nor did it engage in the many programs in health, education, welfare, and other areas that it currently does.

Table 18.1 shows how the federal government spends its money. Over one-half goes for Social Security, Medicare, welfare (and other income security) programs, health, and education. About one-fifth goes for defense and other items connected with international relations and national security. The rest goes to support farm, transportation, housing, and other such programs, as well as to pay interest on the federal debt and to run Congress, the courts, and the executive branch of the federal government.

What about local and state governments? On what do they spend their money? Table 18.2 shows that the biggest expenditure of state and local governments is on schooling. Traditionally, schools in the United States have been a responsibility of local governments—cities and towns. State governments spend most of their money on education, on welfare, old age, and unemployment benefits, and on highways. (In addition to supporting education directly, they help localities cover the costs of schooling.) In addition, local and state governments support hospitals, redevelopment programs, courts, and police and fire departments.

What the Federal, State, and Local Governments Receive in Taxes

To get the money to cover most of the government expenditures, governments collect taxes from individuals and firms. As Table 18.3 shows, at the federal level, the personal income tax is the biggest single money raiser. It brings in almost one-half of the tax revenue collected by the federal government. The next most important taxes at the federal level are the Social Security, payroll, and employment taxes. Other important taxes are the corporation income taxes, excise taxes (levied on the sale of tobacco, liquor, imports, and certain other items), and death and gift taxes. (Even when the Grim Reaper shows up, the Tax Man is not far behind.)

TABLE 18.1

Federal Expenditures, Fiscal Year 2012

Purpose	Amount (billions of dollars)	Percent of Total
National defense	680	19
International affairs	47	1
Energy	15	*
Veterans benefits	125	4
General science, space, and technology	29	1
Agriculture	20	1
Education, training, employment, and social services	89	3
Health	348	10
Natural resources and environment	42	1
Commerce and housing credit	40	1
Transportation	91	3
Community and regional development	26	1
Interest	222	6
General government	23	1
Income security	542	15
Administration of justice	58	2
Medicare	472	13
Social Security	773	22
Offsetting receipts	−104	−3
Total†	*3,538*	*100*

*Less than one-half of 1 percent.

†The numbers in this table may not add up to totals because of rounding.

Source: Economic Report of the President, 2013 (Washington, DC: Government Printing Office).

TABLE 18.2

Expenditures of State and Local Governments, United States, 2009—2010

Type of Expenditure	Amount (billions of dollars)	Percent of Total
Education	860	34
Highways	156	6
Public welfare	461	18
Other	1,066	42
*Total**	*2,542*	*100*

*The numbers in this table may not add up to totals because of rounding.

Source: Economic Report of the President, 2013 (Washington, DC: Government Printing Office).

TABLE 18.3

Federal Receipts by Tax, Fiscal Year 2012

Type of Tax	Amount (billions of dollars)	Percent of Total
Personal income taxes	1,132	46
Corporation income taxes	242	10
Social insurance taxes	845	35
Excise taxes	79	3
Estate and gift taxes	14	1
Other revenues	136	6
Total†	*2,449*	*100*

*Less than one-half of 1 percent.

†The numbers in this table may not add up to totals because of rounding.

Source: Economic Report of the President, 2013 (Washington, DC: Government Printing Office).

As shown in Table 18.4, at the *local* level, the most important form of taxation and source of revenue is the property tax. This is a tax levied primarily on real estate. Other important local taxes, although dwarfed in importance by the property tax, are local sales taxes and local income taxes. Many cities levy a sales tax equal to a certain percent (nearly 9 percent in New York City) of the value of each retail sale. The tax is simply added on to the amount charged the customer. Also, many cities (for example, Philadelphia and Pittsburgh) levy an income (or wage) tax on their residents and even on people who work in the city but live outside it. At the *state* level, sales (and excise) taxes are the biggest money raiser, followed by income taxes and highway-user taxes. The

TABLE 18.4

State and Local Tax Revenues by Source, United States, 2009—2010

Tax Source	Amount (billions of dollars)	Percent of Total
General sales taxes	431	17
Property taxes	442	18
Personal income taxes	260	10
Corporate income taxes	43	2
Other taxes	702	28
Revenues from federal government	624	25
*Total**	*2,502*	*100*

*The numbers in this table may not add up to totals because of rounding.

Source: Economic Report of the President, 2013 (Washington, DC: Government Printing Office).

last includes taxes on gasoline and license fees for vehicles and drivers. Often they exceed the amount spent on roads, and the balance is used for a variety of nonhighway uses.

EXPLORING FURTHER

Including Net Exports in the Simple Keynesian Model

We began this chapter by describing the effects of government spending and taxation in the simple Keynesian model. To keep matters as simple as possible, we assumed that net exports are zero. Now we relax that assumption. Recall from Chapter 15 that gross domestic product equals consumption expenditure plus gross investment plus government spending plus net exports, where net exports equal exports minus imports. In other words, $Y = C + I + G + (X - M_I)$, where Y is GDP, C is consumption expenditure, I is investment, G is government spending, X is exports, and M_I is imports. Recall, too, that the equilibrium level of GDP is the point where intended spending on GDP equals GDP.

$C + I + G$
$+ (X - M_I)$ **line**

In Figure 18.8, the equilibrium level of GDP must be $500 billion, since this is the level at which the $C + I + G + (X - M_I)$ **line** intersects the 45-degree line. To see this, note that we are merely carrying out a straightforward extension of the analysis in Figure 18.1, where we assumed that net exports were zero.

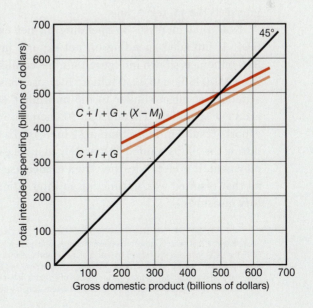

FIGURE 18.8

Effects of Foreign Trade on Gross Domestic Product

The equilibrium level of GDP is at the point where the $C + I + G + (X - M_I)$ line intersects the 45-degree line, in this case $500 billion.

FIGURE 18.9

Effect of Increase in Net Exports on Gross Domestic Product

If net exports increase from $20 billion to $40 billion, the equilibrium level of GDP increases from $500 billion to $550 billion.

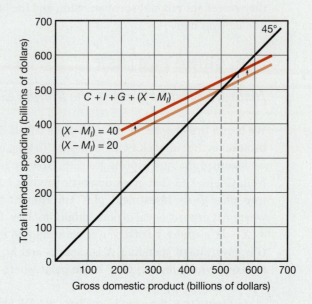

Once this assumption is relaxed, intended net exports must be added to the $C + I + G$ line to get total intended spending, and the equilibrium level of GDP is the point where the resulting total-intended-spending line, $C + I + G + (X - M_I)$, intersects the 45-degree line.

Note that increases in spending on net exports result in increases in GDP. If intended spending on net exports increases from $20 billion to $40 billion, as shown in Figure 18.9, the equilibrium level of GDP increases from $500 billion to $550 billion. Increases in spending on net exports have a multiplier effect similar to the multiplier effect for investment or government spending. Therefore, a $1 increase in intended spending on net exports results in more than a $1 increase in GDP.[1] Because governments during the 1930s wanted desperately to increase their GDP to reduce unemployment, it is clear why they tried to increase their net exports. (However, all that resulted was a reduction in international trade because of retaliatory measures.)

---

[1] If we assume that exports, government expenditures, and tax receipts are the same at all levels of GDP, then a $1 increase in intended spending on net exports results in an increase in equilibrium GDP of $1 ÷ ($MPS$ + MPI), where MPS is the marginal propensity to save and MPI is the marginal propensity to import. (The *marginal propensity to import* is the proportion of an extra dollar of income spent on imports.) Note that the multiplier is smaller now than in the case of a closed economy (where MPI equals zero).

REVIEW AND PRACTICE

Summary

1   Assuming that net exports are zero, the equilibrium level of gross domestic product is the level where intended consumption plus intended investment plus intended government spending equal gross domestic product.

2   An increase in the tax rate shifts the relationship between consumption expenditure and GDP downward, reducing the equilibrium value of GDP. A decrease in the tax rate shifts the relationship upward, increasing the equilibrium value of GDP.

3   If GDP is below its potential value, there is a recessionary gap. Under these circumstances, governments frequently try to push the aggregate demand curve to the right. Fiscal policy is often used for this purpose.

4   If GDP exceeds its potential value, there is an inflationary gap. Under these circumstances, the government is likely to try to use fiscal policy to induce a leftward shift of the aggregate demand curve, causing the price level to be lower than it otherwise would be.

5   Policy makers receive a lot of help in stabilizing the economy from automatic stabilizers—automatic changes in tax revenues, unemployment compensation, and welfare payments. However, the automatic stabilizers can only reduce variations in unemployment and inflation, not eliminate them.

6   Discretionary programs are often used to supplement the effects of automatic stabilizers. Such discretionary actions include changing tax rates, changing government expenditure on public works and other programs, and changing welfare payments and other such transfers.

7   In the past 75 to 100 years, government spending in the United States has increased considerably, both in absolute terms and as a proportion of total output. It is now about one-third of our total output.

8   To get the money to cover most of these expenditures, governments collect taxes from individuals and firms. At the federal level, the most important form of taxation is the personal income tax; at the local level, the property tax is very important; and at the state level, sales and excise taxes are the biggest money raisers.

*9   [2]If net exports are not zero, the equilibrium level of GDP is where intended spending on GDP, which equals intended consumption expenditure plus

---

[2] Starred (*) item refers to material covered in Exploring Further.

intended investment plus government spending plus intended net exports, equals GDP.

Problems and Questions

1 Suppose that the consumption function in a particular economy is given by the following table:

Disposable Income (billions of dollars)	Consumption Expenditure (billions of dollars)
400	350
500	425
600	500
700	575
800	650

Assuming that no taxes are imposed (and that net exports are zero), what is the equilibrium value of GDP if government expenditures are $50 billion and intended investment is $50 billion?

2 Based on the data in question 1, plot the *C* + *I* + *G* line in a graph. Using a graph of this sort, estimate the effect on the equilibrium level of GDP of a $10 billion increase in government spending.

3 Suppose that taxes are 20 percent of GDP. Using the data in question 1, fill in the blanks.

GDP (billions of dollars)	Consumption Expenditure (billions of dollars)
—	350
—	425
—	500
—	575
—	650

4 Using the data in question 3, what is the equilibrium value of GDP if government expenditures are $50 billion and intended investment is $50 billion? How does this result compare with the result in question 1? Explain the difference between these two results.

5 Using the data in question 3, is the government's budget balanced at the equilibrium level of GDP if government expenditures are $50 billion and intended investment is $50 billion? If not, how big is the surplus or deficit?

Key Terms

recessionary gap
inflationary gap
automatic stabilizers
discretionary fiscal policy
transfer payments
$C + I + G + (X - M_i)$ line

Viewpoint for Analysis

In his 2003 *Economic Report*, President George W. Bush said:

> An important goal of fiscal policy is to promote growth by limiting the share of output commanded by the government. In 2001 the Congress and the Administration made major progress along these lines with the passage of the Economic Growth and Tax Relief Reconciliation Act, which featured a broad-based cut in marginal tax rates.
>
> Rebate checks ($300 for most single tax payers, $600 for most married couples filing jointly) arrived in mail boxes in the summer of 2001. The timing of the resulting $36 billion infusion of spendable income into the economy could not have been more favorable. . . . As a result, without the checks, third quarter GDP would have declined at an annual rate of 1.5 percent rather than the 0.3 percent actually observed. In the fourth quarter, tax relief continued to add 1.2 percentage points to the annual rate of real GDP growth.[3]

(a) Would lower income tax rates in the form of tax rebates be expected to shift the consumption function? Would such a shift be likely to push the economy out of a recession? Why or why not?

(b) What would have happened if this tax cut had been temporary instead of permanent?

(c) Can there be too much fiscal stimulus? Under what circumstances can an expansionary fiscal policy be a mistake?

[3] *Economic Report of the President* (Washington, DC: U.S. Government Printing Office, 2003,), 52–53.

Inflation

LEARNING OBJECTIVES

➤ To explore the nature and effects of inflation

➤ To explain how inflation is measured

➤ To differentiate between demand-side inflation and supply-side inflation

➤ To consider the instability of the Phillips curve

In 2012, the rate of inflation in the United States was about 2 percent. How is inflation measured, and why are people so concerned about it? One purpose of this chapter is to answer these questions.

At the very beginning of this book, we stressed that unemployment and inflation are two major economic evils. Up to this point, we have devoted much more attention to unemployment than to inflation. According to most economists, inflation and unemployment are not unrelated. Unfortunately, the link between them is complex and consequently has been the subject of much debate among economists. Inflation, its costs, and its causes cannot be covered in one chapter alone. This chapter contains part of the relevant discussion; the rest is in Chapter 22.

What Is Inflation?

It is hard to find anyone these days who does not know the meaning of inflation firsthand. Try to think of goods you regularly purchase that cost less now than they did several years ago. Chances are that you can come up with precious few.

Inflation **Inflation** is a general upward movement of prices. In other words, goods and services that currently cost $10 may soon be priced at $11 or even $12, and wages and other input prices increase as well. It is essential to distinguish between the movements of individual prices and the movement of the entire price level. As we saw in Chapter 2, the price of an individual commodity can move up or down with the shifts in the commodity's demand or supply curve. If the price of a particular good (corn, say) goes up, this need not be a sign of inflation; if the prices of other goods are going down at the same time, the overall price level (the general average level of prices) remains much the same. Inflation occurs only if the prices for most goods and services in a society move upward—that is, if the average level of prices increases.

In periods of inflation, the value of money is reduced. A dollar is worth what it buys, and what it buys is determined by the price level. Therefore, a dollar was more valuable in 1940, when the price of a Hershey chocolate bar was 5 cents, than in 2012, when it was about 90 cents. But it is important to recognize that inflations may vary in severity. **Runaway inflation** wipes out the value of money quickly and thoroughly, while **creeping inflation** erodes its value gradually and slowly. The following examples illustrate the important differences between runaway inflation and creeping inflation.

Runaway inflation **Creeping inflation**

Runaway Inflation

The situation in Germany after World War I is a good example of runaway inflation. Germany was required to pay large reparations to the victorious Allies after the war. Rather than attempting to tax its people to pay these amounts, the German government merely printed additional quantities of paper money. This new money increased total spending in Germany, and this in turn resulted in higher prices because the war-devastated economy could not increase output substantially. As more and more money was printed, prices rose higher and higher, until they reached utterly fantastic levels. By 1923, it took a *trillion* marks (the unit of German currency) to buy what one mark would buy before the war began in 1914.

The effect of this runaway inflation was to disrupt the economy. Prices had to be adjusted from day to day. People rushed to the stores to spend the money they received as soon as possible, since very soon it would buy much less. Speculation was rampant. This inflation was a terrible blow to Germany. The middle class was wiped out; its savings became completely worthless. It is no wonder that Germany has in recent years been more sensitive than many other countries to the evils of inflation.

Creeping Inflation

For the past 50 years, the price level in the United States has tended to go one way only—up. Since 1950, there have been very few years when the price level has fallen (2009 was one such year). Certainly, this has not been a runaway inflation, but it has resulted in a very substantial erosion in the value of the dollar. Like a beach slowly worn away by ocean waves, the dollar has gradually lost a considerable portion of its value. Specifically, prices now tend to be around 10 times what they were about 60 years ago. The dollar now is worth about a tenth of what it was worth then. Although a creeping inflation of this sort is much less harmful than a runaway inflation, it has a number of unfortunate social consequences, described in detail in subsequent sections of this chapter.

Measuring Inflation

Consumer price index (CPI)

The most widely quoted measure of inflation in the United States is the **consumer price index (CPI)**, published monthly by the Bureau of Labor Statistics. Until 1978, the purpose of this index was to measure changes in the prices of goods and services purchased by urban wage earners and clerical workers and their families. In 1978, the index was expanded to include all urban consumers (although the narrower index was not discontinued). The first step in calculating the index is to find out how much it costs in a particular month to buy a market basket of goods and services that is representative of the buying patterns of these consumers. The amount is then expressed as a ratio of what it would have cost to buy the same market basket of goods and services in the base period (1982–1984), and this ratio is multiplied by 100. This (like most commonly used indexes) shows the *percentage,* not the proportional, change in the price level. For example, the consumer price index was 233.5 in October 2013; this means that it cost 233.5 percent more to buy this market basket in October 2013 than in 1982–1984. To obtain results based on Chapter 15's definition of a price index, all we have to do is divide this index by 100.

The market basket of goods and services that is included in the consumer price index is chosen with great care and is the result of an extensive survey of people's buying patterns. Among the items that are included are food, automobiles, clothing, homes, furniture, home supplies, drugs, fuel, doctors' fees, legal fees, rent, repairs, transportation fares, and recreational goods. Prices, as defined in the index, include sales and excise taxes. Also, real estate taxes, but not income or personal property taxes, are included in the index. In addition to the overall index, a separate price index is computed for various types of goods or services, such as food, rent, new cars, medical services, and a variety of other items. Also, a separate index is computed for each of 28 metropolitan areas, as well as for the entire urban population.

The consumer price index is widely used by industry and government. Labor agreements often stipulate that to offset inflation, wages must increase in accord with changes in the index. Similarly, pensions, welfare payments, royalties, and even alimony payments are sometimes related to the index. However, this does not mean that it is an ideal, all-purpose measure of inflation. For one

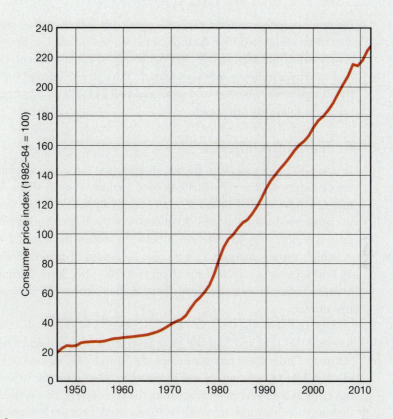

FIGURE 19.1

Consumer Price Index, 1946–2012

Inflation has been a continual problem in the United States, particularly in the late 1970s and early 1980s.

thing, it does not include the prices of industrial machinery or raw materials. For another thing, it is not confined to currently produced goods and services.

Figure 19.1 shows the behavior of the consumer price index since 1946. As pointed out in the previous section, the price level has increased considerably in the United States in the past six and a half decades. Substantial inflation followed World War II: the price level increased by about 24 percent between 1946 and 1948. Bursts of inflation recurred during the Korean War and then during the Vietnam War. The 1970s were a period of particularly high inflation; between 1969 and 1979, the price level doubled. The 1980s began with double-digit inflation, but there was a steady reduction in the inflation rate from 1982 to the early 2000s. Inflation has stayed low since then.

The Impact of Inflation

Citizens and policy makers generally agree that inflation, like unemployment, should be minimized. For example, in 1981, the Council of Economic Advisers identified inflation as the chief economic problem confronting the United States. Why is inflation so widely feared? What are its effects? Inflation affects the distribution of income and wealth as well as the level of output, as we will see in the following discussion.

Redistributive Effects

Because all money incomes do not go up at the same rate as prices, inflation results in an arbitrary redistribution of income. People with relatively fixed incomes, lenders, and savers tend to be hurt by it, and major inflations tend to cripple total output as well. To understand the redistributive effects of inflation, it is necessary to distinguish between money income and real income. A family's **money income** is its income measured in current dollars, whereas its **real income** is adjusted for changes in the price level. During periods of inflation, a family with a relatively fixed money income experiences a declining real income.

Money income
Real income

Suppose that the Murphy family earned $40,000 last year and earns $41,000 this year and that the price level is 10 percent higher this year than last year. Under these circumstances, the Murphy family's money income has increased by $1,000, but its real income has fallen (because its money income has risen by a smaller percentage than the price level). This is the sort of effect that inflation has on people with relatively fixed incomes, lenders, and savers—three groups that tend to be hit hard by inflation.

> ➤ *Those on fixed money incomes.* Inflation may seem no more than a petty annoyance; after all, most people care about relative, not absolute, prices. For example, if the Howe family's money income increases at the same rate as the price level, the Howe family may be no better or worse off under inflation than if its money income remained constant and no inflation occurred. But not all people are as fortunate as the Howes. Some people cannot increase their wages to compensate for price increases because they work under long-term contracts, among other reasons. These people take a considerable beating from inflation. One group that sometimes is particularly hard hit by inflation is the elderly, since old people often must live on pensions and other relatively fixed forms of income. Thus, inflation sometimes has a substantial, inequitable, and unwelcome impact on our older citizens.

> ➤ *Lenders.* Inflation hurts lenders and benefits borrowers, since it results in the depreciation of money. A dollar is worth what it buys, and what it buys is determined by the price level. If the price level increases, a dollar

is worth less than before. Consequently, if you lend Bill Dvorak $100 in 2012 and he pays you $100 in 2017, when a dollar buys less than in 2001, you lose on the deal. In terms of what the money buys, he is paying you less than what he borrowed. Of course, if you anticipate considerable inflation, you may be able to recoup by charging him a high enough interest rate to offset the depreciation of the dollar, but it is not so easy to forecast the rate of inflation and protect yourself.

➤ *Savers.* Inflation can have a devastating and inequitable effect on savers. The family that works hard and saves for retirement (and a rainy day) finds that its savings are worth far less, when it finally spends them, than the amount it saved. Consider the well-meaning souls who invested $1,000 of their savings in U.S. savings bonds in 1939. By 1949, these bonds were worth only about $800 in 1939 dollars, including the interest received in the 10-year period. These people had $200 taken away from them in just as real a sense as if someone picked their pockets.[1]

Effects of Anticipated and Unanticipated Inflation

Anticipated inflation

Unanticipated inflation

Economists are fond of pointing out that the effects of **anticipated inflation** tend to be less severe than those of **unanticipated inflation**. To see why this is the case, suppose that everyone anticipates (correctly) that the price level will be 6 percent higher next year than this year. In such a situation, everyone builds this amount of inflation into his or her decisions. Workers realize that their money wage rates must be 6 percent higher next year just to avoid a cut in their real wage rates. The Murphy family, which earns $41,000 this year, realizes that it must earn $1.06 \times \$41,000$, or $43,460, next year if it is to avoid a reduction in its real earnings. And people thinking of lending money for a year recognize that they must charge 6 percent interest just to break even. Why? Because when the money is repaid next year, $1.06 will be worth no more in real terms than $1.00 is now.

Because people build the anticipated rate of inflation into their calculations, the effects of anticipated inflation are likely to be less pronounced than those of unanticipated inflation. However, in the real world in which we all live, this frequently is of small comfort, since it is very difficult to anticipate the rate of inflation correctly. Even the most sophisticated econometric models have not had a very distinguished record in forecasting the rate of inflation. Therefore, it seems foolish to believe that the typical citizen (like those who invested in U.S. savings bonds in 1939) can anticipate inflation well enough to protect himself or herself against its consequences.

---

[1] However, it is important to recognize that the form of the savings matters. If someone can put his or her savings in a form where its monetary value increases as rapidly as the price level, the saver is not harmed by inflation. But this is not always easy to do.

An Arbitrary "Tax"

While inflation hurts some people, it benefits others. Those who are lucky enough to invest in goods, land, equipment, and other items that experience particularly rapid increases in price may make a killing. For this reason, speculation tends to be rampant during severe inflation. However, it is important to recognize that the rewards and penalties resulting from inflation are meted out with little or no regard for society's values or goals. As the late Arthur Okun, a former chair of the Council of Economic Advisers, put it, "Sharpies . . . make sophisticated choices and often reap gains on inflation which do not seem to reflect any real contribution to economic growth. On the other hand, the unsophisticated saver who is merely preparing for the proverbial rainy day becomes a sucker."[2] This is one of the most undesirable features of inflation, and it helps account for inflation's sometimes being called an arbitrary "tax."

Effects on Output

Creeping inflation, unlike unemployment, does not seem to reduce national output; in the short run, output may even increase, for reasons taken up in subsequent chapters. But although a mild upward creep of prices at the rate of a few percentage points per year is not likely to reduce output, a major inflation can have adverse effects on production. For one thing, it encourages speculation rather than the productive use of savings. People find it more profitable to invest in gold, diamonds, real estate, and art (all of which tend to rise in monetary value during inflation) than in many kinds of productive activity. Also, businesspeople tend to be discouraged from carrying out long-range projects because of the difficulty of forecasting future prices. If the rate of inflation reaches the catastrophic heights that prevailed in Germany after World War I, the monetary system may break down. People may be unwilling to accept money. They may insist on trading goods and services directly for other goods and services. The result is likely to be considerable inefficiency and substantially reduced output.

Demand-Side and Supply-Side Inflation

Inflation is often triggered by rightward shifts of the aggregate demand curve (see the left-hand panel of Figure 19.2). This kind of inflation stems from the demand, or spending behavior, of the country's consumers, firms, and government. We have had many inflations of this kind. The major inflations during the Revolutionary War and Civil War were basically caused by demand-side factors; and so was the inflation arising from the Vietnam War.

[2] Arthur Okun, *Inflation: The Problems It Creates and the Policies It Requires* (New York: New York University Press, 1970).

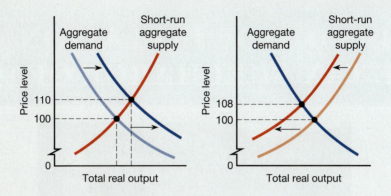

FIGURE 19.2

Demand-Side and Supply-Side Inflation

In the left-hand panel, the price level increases from 100 to 110 (expressed as an aggregate index with no specific units) because of a rightward shift of the aggregate demand curve. This is a case of demand-side inflation. In the right-hand panel, the price level increases from 100 to 108 because of a leftward shift of the aggregate supply curve. This is a case of supply-side inflation.

Demand-side inflation

In those extreme cases where resources are fully utilized, the rise in the price level that occurs in **demand-side inflation** can be viewed as a matter of arithmetic: since the national output is fixed, the rise in the price level must be proportional to the increase in total spending. For example, take the very simple case where a country produces only one good, corn. Suppose that the amount of money spent on this country's corn crop doubles while the size of the corn crop is fixed. What happens to the price of corn? It doubles.

Supply-side inflation

In addition to demand-side inflation, which is due to rightward shifts of the aggregate demand curve, is **supply-side inflation**, which results from leftward shifts of the aggregate supply curve (see the right-hand panel of Figure 19.2). For example, when the oil-producing countries increased the price of crude oil in 1974 and 1979, this resulted in price increases in a wide variety of products that are made (directly or indirectly) from petroleum. Because these price increases were not offset by price reductions elsewhere in the economy, the overall price level increased (and at a very rapid rate) in 1974 and 1979. Of course, the price hike for crude oil (and other materials) was not the sole reason for the inflation during the 1970s, but unquestionably it played a noteworthy role in shifting the aggregate supply curve upward and to the left, as shown in the right-hand panel of Figure 19.2. This was an example of supply-side inflation.

DEMAND-SIDE INFLATION AND THE TAX SURCHARGE OF 1968

President Lyndon B. Johnson with economic adviser Walter Heller

The economic policies carried out under Presidents Kennedy and Johnson seemed successful in stimulating growth in demand; business was thriving, plants were operating close to capacity, and there were plenty of jobs. But many felt that by mid-1965, the economy showed signs of overheating.

In addition to the boost to private demand, government spending was beginning to grow rapidly. President Johnson had succeeded in getting many of his programs passed to reduce domestic poverty. Moreover, military spending rose as dark war clouds began to gather in Southeast Asia. In late July 1965, President Johnson announced that the United States would send 50,000 more troops to Vietnam. From fiscal 1965 to fiscal 1966, defense expenditures rose from $50 billion to $60 billion, a large increase in government expenditure and one that took place at a time of relatively full employment. Such an increase in government expenditure could be expected to cause inflationary pressures. The Council of Economic Advisers recognized this danger and recommended in late 1965 that the president urge Congress to increase taxes. President Johnson was reluctant. Inflationary pressures mounted during 1966, and little was done by fiscal policy makers to quell them.

Even in 1967, Congress was unwilling to raise taxes. The case for fiscal restraint was, it felt, not clear enough. As for the president, he said, "It is not a popular thing for a president to do . . . to ask for a penny out of a dollar to pay for a war that is not popular either." Finally, in mid-1968, a 10 percent surcharge on income taxes, together with some restraint in government spending, was enacted. This increase in taxes was obviously the right medicine, but it was at least two years too late, and its effects were delayed and insufficient. In the meantime, the rate of inflation had risen from 2 percent in 1965 to 6 percent in 1969.

FIGURE 19.3

The Phillips Curve

If all inflation is demand-side inflation, we might expect the inflation rate to be inversely related to the unemployment rate. (Expected inflation is assumed to be constant.)

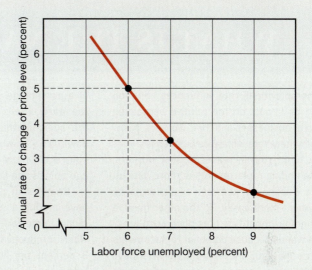

The Phillips Curve

Phillips curve

During the 1960s, economists placed a great deal of emphasis on the Phillips curve, named after the late A. W. Phillips, of the London School of Economics, who first called attention to it. The **Phillips curve** shows the relationship between the annual rate of change of the price level in an economy and the unemployment rate in that economy.[3] For example, if the relationship is like that plotted in Figure 19.3, the inflation rate is inversely related to the unemployment rate. If the unemployment rate is 6 percent, the inflation rate will be 5 percent per year. To reduce the inflation rate to 2 percent, the unemployment rate must be increased to 9 percent.

If the Phillips curve in Figure 19.3 remains fixed, the government is faced with a fundamental choice. It can reduce unemployment only if it is willing to accept a higher rate of inflation, and it can reduce the rate of inflation only if it is willing to accept a higher rate of unemployment. For example, in Figure 19.3, if the unemployment rate is 7 percent, the inflation rate is 3.5 percent. The government would like to reduce unemployment; but if it reduces it to 6 percent, the inflation rate will jump to 5 percent. The government would also like to reduce inflation; but if it cuts it to 2 percent, the unemployment rate will jump to 9 percent. This poses a problem for the government (and society as a whole), since it would be desirable to reduce both inflation and unemployment.

[3] Originally, Phillips plotted data showing the relationship between the unemployment rate and the rate of change of wages, not prices. Therefore, the Phillips curve sometimes is defined as the relationship between the rate of change of the wage level (not the price level) and the unemployment rate. But for the present purposes, it is more convenient to adopt the definition in the text, which is often used by economists.

WHAT IS THE NAIRU?

The unemployment rate influences inflation through its impact on the relative bargaining position of businesses and their workers. A low unemployment rate increases businesses' willingness to give pay increases to their workers, because finding replacements is more difficult and the existing workers can find alternative employment more easily. On the other hand, a high unemployment rate puts downward pressure on wages because potential replacements are more plentiful and existing workers have fewer viable alternatives. Because labor costs ultimately account for almost two-thirds of the cost of production, a low unemployment rate translates into rising price inflation, while a high unemployment rate reduces inflation.

Economists define the NAIRU (the nonaccelerating inflation rate of unemployment) as the unemployment rate at which the labor market is exerting no upward or downward pressure on inflation. Inflation accelerates if the unemployment rate remains below the NAIRU and decelerates if the unemployment rate remains above the NAIRU. The degree of acceleration or deceleration is proportional to the difference between the unemployment rate and the NAIRU. Economists often refer to the NAIRU as the natural rate of unemployment or the full-employment rate.

Although the unemployment rate primarily reflects the looseness or tightness of the labor market, it also reflects the age distribution of the labor force. In particular, unemployment rates fall as age increases, so the aggregate unemployment rate is higher when there is a greater percentage of teenagers and 20- to 24-year-olds in the working-age population. The entrance of the baby boomers into the labor force added more than one-half

of a percentage point to the NAIRU between the early 1960s and the late 1970s, while the aging of this generation and a gradual downtrend in women's unemployment rates subtracted more than one-half of a percentage point since then.

Changes in productivity growth, however, have produced much more dramatic movements in the NAIRU. During most of the 1960s, when productivity growth averaged almost 3 percent per year, the NAIRU was below 5 percent. As productivity growth slowed, the NAIRU rose to around 6 percent in the late 1960s and early 1970s, then surged to roughly 7.5 percent after the first OPEC shock, much higher than was realized at the time. As productivity growth picked up again in the late 1980s and 1990s, the NAIRU fell back to about 5 percent.

A surge in productivity is also part of the explanation for the remarkable performance of the U.S. economy in the late 1990s. During this period, the unemployment rate hovered just below 4 percent—a 30-year low—while inflation remained quiescent. Part of this was due to good luck. The emerging markets crisis in 1997 and 1998 triggered a collapse of commodity prices and a drop in world inflation. However, an improvement in productivity growth, thanks to high-tech investments and the Internet, also played a crucial role. Recent estimates suggest that productivity growth in the late 1990s was around 2.5 percent, compared with 1.5 percent in the 1980s. This led analysts to think that the NAIRU probably fell in the 1990s.

In 2001, the U.S. economy went into a mild recession, which was followed by a rather lackluster recovery. The unemployment rate peaked at 6.4 percent before coming-back down again. However, remarkably, productivity growth continued to surge, averaging about 4 to 5 percent during the recovery. The consensus during this period was that the NAIRU had probably moved back to around 5 percent.

Unfortunately, during the Great Recession of 2008 and 2009, the United States not only saw a rise in the actual unemployment rate to over 10 percent, but also an increase in the NAIRU to at least 6 percent.

Why should the Phillips curve slope downward to the right? In other words, why should the inflation rate be inversely related to the unemployment rate? If all inflation is demand-side inflation, some economists have explained such an inverse relationship in the following way. Suppose that the economy is in equilibrium at point A in Figure 19.4. If the aggregate demand curve shifts to the right from D_0 to D_1, total real output increases from $100 billion to $110 billion, and the price level increases from 100 to 105 (expressed as an aggregate index with no specific units). On the other hand, suppose that the aggregate demand curve shifts farther to the right, from D_0 to D_2. Then total real output increases

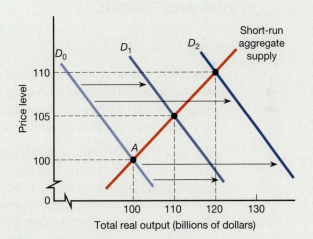

FIGURE 19.4

Effects of Rightward Shifts of the Aggregate Demand Curve (from D_0 to D_1 or D_2) on the Total Real Output and the Price Level

If the aggregate demand curve shifts from D_0 to D_2, there is a greater increase in total real output and the price level than if the aggregate demand curve shifts from D_0 to D_1. Specifically, total real output increases from $100 billion to $120 billion if the aggregate demand curve shifts from D_0 to D_2, but it increases only from $100 billion to $110 billion if the curve shifts from D_0 to D_1. The price level increases from 100 to 110 (expressed as an aggregate index with no specific units) if the aggregate demand curve shifts from D_0 to D_2, but it increases only from 100 to 105 if the curve shifts from D_0 to D_1.

from $100 billion to $120 billion (rather than $110 billion), and the price level increases from 100 to 110 (rather than 105).

Clearly, the greater rightward shift of the aggregate demand curve (to D_2 rather than D_1) results in a bigger increase in output (to $120 billion rather than $110 billion); this means that the unemployment rate is lower than if the aggregate demand curve shifted only to D_1. At the same time, the greater rightward shift of the aggregate demand curve results in a 10 percent inflation rate rather than a 5 percent inflation rate. (Recall that the price level increases from 100 to 110 if the aggregate demand curve shifts to D_2, whereas it increases from 100 to 105 if the aggregate demand curve shifts to D_1.) Hence, a lower unemployment rate is associated with a higher inflation rate.

As we will see in Chapter 22, the Phillips curve in Figure 19.3 has not remained fixed. Instead, during the 1970s and early 1980s, the curve in Figure 19.3 shifted upward and to the right. High unemployment coexisted with high inflation. In recent years, more and more economists seem to have become persuaded that the reductions in unemployment due to increased inflation are only transitory and that increases in inflation bring little or nothing in the way of reduced unemployment in the long run. Much more will be said on this score in Chapter 22.

REVIEW AND PRACTICE

Summary

1   Inflation is a general upward movement of prices. Runaway inflation occurs when the price level increases very rapidly, as in Germany after World War I. Creeping inflation occurs when the price level rises a few percentage points per year, as in the United States during the 1950s and 1960s.

2   High rates of inflation produce considerable redistributions of income and wealth. People with relatively fixed incomes, such as the elderly, tend to take a beating from inflation. Inflation hurts lenders and benefits borrowers, since it results in the depreciation of money. Inflation can also have a devastating effect on savers. The penalties (and rewards) resulting from inflation are meted out arbitrarily, with no regard for society's values or goals. Substantial rates of inflation may also reduce efficiency and total output.

3   Inflation caused by rightward shifts of the aggregate demand curve is called demand-side inflation. Inflation caused by leftward shifts of the aggregate supply curve is called supply-side inflation.

4   The Phillips curve shows the relationship between the rate of increase of the price level and the level of unemployment. If the Phillips curve remains fixed, it poses an awkward dilemma for policy makers. If they reduce unemployment, inflation increases; if they reduce inflation, unemployment increases.

5 During the 1970s and early 1980s, the Phillips curve shifted upward and to the right. High unemployment and high inflation occurred simultaneously.

Problems and Questions

1 "The Employment Act of 1946 should be amended to include the goal of stabilizing the purchasing power of the dollar as well as the goal of maintaining high-level employment." Comment and evaluate.

2 "Inflation is a necessary cost of economic progress." Comment and evaluate.

3 Suppose that a family's money income remains constant at $40,000 and that the price level increases 10 percent per year. How many years will it take for the family's real income to be cut in half?

4 If you believe that the United States is about to suffer severe inflation, would you be better off investing your money in land or in government bonds? Explain your answer.

5 "The inflations arising from the Revolutionary, Civil, and Vietnam Wars were largely supply side." Comment and evaluate.

6 Suppose that the relationship between the annual rate of increase of the price level and the percent of the labor force unemployed is as shown in the following table:

Rate of Increase of Price Level (percent per year)	Unemployment Rate (percent)
5	8
6	7
7	6
8	5

Plot the Phillips curve on a graph.

Key Terms

inflation
runaway inflation
creeping inflation
consumer price index (CPI)
money income
real income

anticipated inflation
unanticipated inflation
demand-side inflation
supply-side inflation
Phillips curve

Viewpoint for Analysis

On July 20, 1993, Alan Greenspan, then chair of the Board of Governors of the Federal Reserve System, said: "The role of expectations in the inflation process is crucial. Even expectations not validated by economic fundamentals can themselves add appreciably to wage and price pressures for a considerable period, potentially derailing the economy from its growth path."[4]

(a) If workers are convinced that inflation is about to increase greatly, what effect does this have on their wage demands? Do their wage demands fuel further inflation?

(b) If the managers of firms are convinced that inflation is about to increase greatly, what effect does this have on their pricing decisions? Do their pricing decisions fuel further inflation?

(c) How can inflation derail the economy from its growth path? Cite cases in the past where inflation derailed the U.S. economy from its growth path. Be specific.

[4] Alan Greenspan, testimony before the Committee on Banking, Finance, and Urban Affairs of the U.S. House of Representatives, July 20, 1993.

THE TREASURY LAUNCHES A NEW TYPE OF SECURITY

In late 1996, the U.S. Treasury announced that it would issue inflation-indexed bonds. The value of an inflation-indexed bond is protected from inflation because it is adjusted periodically in accord with changes in the consumer price index. As in the case of ordinary bonds, the investor lends the government a certain amount of money (say, $10,000), receives interest (say, 3.25 percent) on the loan, and is promised by the government that he or she will be repaid in a fixed amount of time (say, 10 years). The new wrinkle is that the government adjusts the size of the loan to keep pace with inflation. Therefore, if inflation during a particular year is 4 percent, the amount owed by the Treasury to a bondholder goes up by 4 percent.

In early 1997, the first U.S. inflation-indexed securities were issued. The United States was not the first country to issue such securities; for example, Australia, Canada, New Zealand, and Sweden had already done so. The country with the biggest amount of such debt in the 1980s and 1990s was the United Kingdom. When the bonds were first issued in 1981, inflation was considered a serious problem, and people were frightened. It seemed sensible to purchase protection from inflation. More recently, as inflation (both actual and expected) has fallen, higher returns on these bonds have been required to attract buyers.

Indexed securities are available in denominations as small as $1,000, to encourage demand from small savers. One early study concluded that investor concerns about inflation risk might add as much as 0.5 to 1 percentage point to the required yield on some Treasury securities. Thus, by issuing indexed securities, the Treasury may be able to reduce average borrowing costs.[1]

Ironically, soon after the inflation-indexed bonds were issued, the demand for them slackened. Low inflation in 1997 through 1999 was an important factor behind the lack of interest. Equally important was the surge in equity prices that occurred during those years. Most investors were more interested in the high returns offered by the stock market than in protecting their investments against inflation. The bursting of the high-tech bubble in 2000 brought in its wake a three-year bear market. However, this did little to boost the demand for inflation-indexed bonds, since the rate of inflation continued to fall during that period and, for a time, investors were worried about deflation (see Case Study 22.2). Inflation remained muted throughout the decade of the 2000s, especially in the wake of the Great Recession of 2008–2009. It kept falling in the early 2010s.

QUESTIONS

1 What do investors get from this new type of government bonds that they did not get from older types?

2 According to the Council of Economic Advisers, a shift from conventional government bonds to these new bonds should reduce the Treasury's average borrowing costs. Why?

3   An executive at a Chicago investment firm expressed some skepticism regarding these new bonds. He said, "In the 1970s, inflation-indexed bonds would have been a great investment, but I think we have learned our lesson very well. . . ."[2] In his view, high inflation is no longer a threat. Do you agree? Why or why not?

4   Some observers worry that if a large amount of such securities were issued, there might be less political pressure on the government to keep inflation low. Does this seem reasonable? Why or why not?

[1] *Economic Report of the President*, 1997, 62, 64.
[2] *Philadelphia Inquirer*, September 26, 1996.

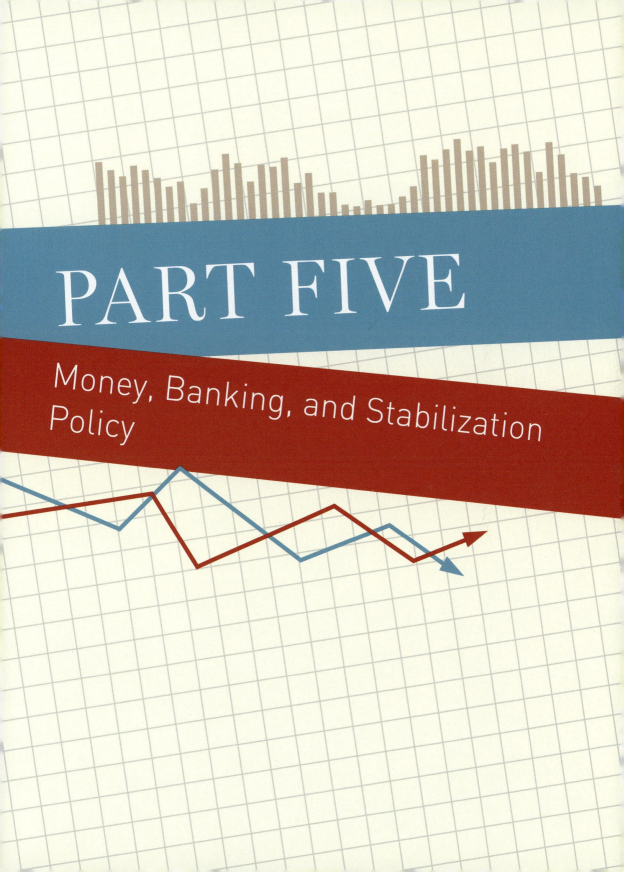

PART FIVE

Money, Banking, and Stabilization Policy

PART FIVE

Money and the Banking System

LEARNING OBJECTIVES

➤ To explore the nature and functions of money

➤ To explain how the money supply is measured

➤ To describe how commercial banks operate and explain the concept of fractional reserve banking

➤ To illustrate how banks can increase or decrease the money supply

Bank of America does not have enough cash to pay off all its depositors if they decide to withdraw all the funds in their accounts; neither does JPMorgan Chase, Citibank, or any other bank. Is this dangerous, and if not, why not? One purpose of this chapter is to answer this question.

In this chapter, we are concerned with the nature of money and the key economic role played by banks and the banking system. Banking is often viewed as a colorless, dull profession whose practitioners are knee-deep in deposit slips and canceled checks. Yet, despite these notions, most people recognize the importance of the banks in our economy, perhaps because banks deal in such an important and fascinating commodity—money—and also because of the role they played in precipitating the financial crisis of 2008–2009. One purpose of this chapter is to introduce you to the operations of the banking system, which is neither as colorless nor as mysterious as is sometimes assumed.

What Is Money?

Money

We begin by defining **money**. At first, it may seem natural to define it by its physical characteristics and to say that money consists of bills of a certain size and color with certain words and symbols printed on them, as well as coins of a certain type. But this definition would be too restrictive, since money in other societies has consisted of whale teeth, wampum, and a variety of other things. Therefore, it is better to define money by its functions rather than by its physical characteristics. Like beauty, money is as money does.

Medium of Exchange

Money acts as a *medium of exchange*. People exchange their goods and services for something called *money*, and then use this money to buy the goods and services they want. To see how important money is as a medium of exchange, suppose that it did not exist. To exchange the goods and services they produce for the goods and services they want to consume, people would resort to *barter*, or direct exchange. If you were a wheat farmer, you would have to contact the people who produce the meat, clothes, and other goods and services you want and swap some of your wheat for each of these goods and services. Of course, this would be a very cumbersome procedure, since it would take lots of time and effort to locate and make individual bargains with each of these people. To get some idea of the extent to which money greases the process of exchange in any highly developed economy, consider all the purchases your family made last year: cheese from Wisconsin and France, automobiles from Detroit or Japan, oil from Texas and the Middle East, books from New York, and thousands of other items from all over the world. Imagine how few of these exchanges would have been feasible without money.

Standard of Value, Store of Value

Money acts as a *standard of value*. It is the unit in which the prices of goods and services are measured. How do we express the price of coffee or tea or shirts or suits? In dollars and cents. Money prices tell us the rates at which goods and services can be exchanged. If the money price of a shirt is $40 and the money price of a tie is $20, a shirt exchanges for two ties. Put differently, a shirt is "worth" twice as much as a tie.

Money acts as a *store of value*. A person can hold onto money and use it to buy things later. You often hear stories about people who hoard a lot of money under their mattresses or bury it in their backyards. These people have an overdeveloped appreciation of the role of money as a store of value. But even those of us who are less miserly use this function of money when we carry some money with us or keep some in the bank to make future purchases.

Finally, it should be recognized that money is a social invention. It is easy to assume that money has always existed, but this is not the case. Someone had to get the idea, and people had to come to accept it. Nor has money always had the characteristics it has today. In ancient Greece and Rome, money consisted of gold and silver coins. By the end of the seventeenth century, paper money was established in England, but this paper currency, unlike today's currency, could be exchanged for a stipulated amount of gold. Only recently has the transition been made to money that is not convertible into a fixed amount of gold or silver. But regardless of its form or characteristics, anything that is a medium of exchange, a standard of value, and a store of value is money.

The Money Supply, Narrowly Defined

In practice, it is not easy to draw a hard-and-fast line between what is money and what is not money, for reasons discussed later. But everyone agrees that coins, currency, demand deposits (that is, checking accounts), and other checkable deposits are money. And the sum total of coins, currency, demand deposits, and other checkable deposits is called the *money supply*, narrowly defined.[1]

Coins and Currency

Coins are a small proportion of the total quantity of money in the United States. This is mainly because coins come in such small denominations. It takes a small mountain of pennies, nickels, dimes, quarters, and half-dollars to make a billion dollars. Of course, the metal in each of these coins is worth less than the face value of the coin; otherwise people would melt them down and make money by selling the metal. In the 1960s, when silver prices rose, the government stopped using silver in dimes and quarters to prevent coins from meeting this fate.

Currency

Currency—paper money like the $5 and $10 bills everyone likes to have on hand—constitutes a second and far larger share of the total money supply. Together, currency and coins outstanding totaled about $1,140 billion in September 2013, as shown in Table 20.1. The Federal Reserve System, described in detail in the next chapter, issues practically all our currency in the form of Federal Reserve notes. Before 1933, it was possible to exchange currency for a stipulated amount of gold, but this is no longer the case. (The price of gold on the free market varies; so the amount of gold we can buy for a dollar varies, too.) All U.S. currency (and coin) is presently *fiat* money: it is money because the government says so and the people accept it. There is no metallic backing of the currency anymore. But this does not mean that we should be suspicious

---

[1] In addition, traveler's checks are included in the money supply, narrowly defined, since we can pay for goods and services about as easily with traveler's checks as with cash. As indicated in Table 20.1, traveler's checks are only about 0.1 percent of the money supply narrowly defined. Since they are so small a percentage of the money supply, we ignore them in the following discussion.

TABLE 20.1

U.S. Money Supply, September 2013

	Amount (billions of dollars)
Demand deposits	955
Currency and coins*	1,140
Other checkable deposits†	457
Traveler's checks‡	4
Total	2,556

*Only currency and coins outside bank vaults (and the U.S. Treasury and Federal Reserve) are included.

†Includes ATS and NOW balances at all institutions and credit unions, share drafts, and other minor items.

‡See text footnote 1.

Source: Federal Reserve.

of the soundness of our currency, since gold backing is not what gives money its value. (In fact, to some extent, cause and effect work the other way. The use of gold to back currencies has in the past increased the value of gold.) Basically, the value of currency depends on its acceptability by people. And the government, to ensure its acceptability, must limit its quantity.

Demand Deposits and Other Checkable Deposits

Demand deposits

Demand deposits—bank deposits subject to payment on demand—are another part of the narrowly defined money supply. At first you may question whether these demand deposits—or checking accounts, as they are commonly called—are money at all. In everyday speech, they often are not considered money. But economists include demand deposits as part of the money supply, and for good reason. After all, you can pay for goods and services just as easily by check as with cash. Indeed, the public pays for more things by check than with cash. This means that checking accounts are just as much a medium of exchange, and just as much a standard of value and a store of value, as cash. Since they perform all the functions of money, they should be included as money.

Other checkable deposits include negotiable order of withdrawal (NOW) accounts and other accounts that are very close to being demand deposits. A *NOW account* is essentially an interest-bearing checking account available at banks, savings banks, and other thrift institutions. First created in 1972 by a Massachusetts savings bank, such accounts became available in more and more states, particularly in the Northeast. In 1980, Congress passed a financial reform act that permitted federally chartered thrift institutions to have NOW accounts. Banking innovations like NOW accounts have blurred the distinction between checking and savings accounts. Since many savings and loan associations, mutual savings banks, and credit unions are now providing accounts against which checks can be drawn, it would make no sense to include as money only demand deposits in commercial banks. Instead, all such checkable deposits are included.

Together, demand deposits and other checkable deposits are a larger part than currency and coins, as shown in Table 20.1.

In the past 60 years, the quantity of money has generally increased from one year to the next, and the increase has been at an average rate of about 5 to 10 percent per year. However, the rate of increase of the quantity of money has not been constant. In some years, like 2011, the quantity of money increased by nearly 15 percent; in other years, like 2010, it increased by less than 10 percent. A great deal will be said later about the importance and determinants of changes in the quantity of money.

The Money Supply, Broadly Defined

The narrowly defined money supply (which includes coins, currency, demand deposits, and other checkable deposits) is not the only definition of the money supply used by economists. There is also the broadly defined money supply, which includes savings and small time deposits (under $100,000), money market mutual fund balances and money market deposit accounts, as well as coins, currency, demand deposits, and other checkable deposits.

M1
M2

The money supply narrowly defined is often called **M1**, whereas the money supply broadly defined is often called **M2**. The traditional reason for excluding time and savings deposits from the narrow definition of money is that in most instances, you cannot pay for anything with them. For example, suppose that you have a savings account at a commercial bank. You cannot draw a check against it, as you can with a demand deposit. And to withdraw your money from the account, you might have to give the bank a certain amount of notice (although in practice this requirement might be waived for a penalty). Nonetheless, since this savings account can so readily be transformed into cash, it is almost like a checking account—not quite, but almost.

In addition to time and savings accounts, many other assets can be transformed into cash without much difficulty, though not quite as easily as time and savings deposits. There is no way to draw a hard-and-fast dividing line between money and nonmoney, since many assets have some of the characteristics of money. Consequently, still other definitions of the money supply are more inclusive than M2. Any dividing line between money and nonmoney must be arbitrary. In this book, we use the narrow definition, M1, when we refer to the money supply.

Commercial Banks in the United States

There are thousands of commercial banks in the United States. This testifies to the fact that in contrast to countries like England, where a few banks with many branches dominate the banking scene, the United States has promoted the growth of a great many local banks. In part, this has stemmed from a traditional suspicion in this country of "big bankers."

Commercial banks have two primary functions. First, banks hold demand deposits and permit checks to be drawn on these deposits. This function is familiar to practically everyone. Most people have a checking account in some commercial bank and draw checks on this account. Second, banks lend money to industrialists, merchants, homeowners, and other individuals and firms. At one time or another, you will probably apply for a loan to finance some project for business, home, or education.

Commercial banks are not the only kind of financial institution. Mutual savings banks, savings and loan associations, and credit unions hold savings and time deposits and various forms of checkable deposits; consumer finance companies lend money to individuals; insurance companies lend money to firms and governments. All these types of financial institutions play an important role in the U.S. economy. In general, they all act as intermediaries between savers and investors; that is, they all turn over to investors money that they receive from savers. This process of converting savings into investment is very important in determining gross domestic product.

How Banks Operate

Although it is difficult to generalize about the operation of commercial banks because they vary so much, certain principles and propositions generally hold.

1. *Banks generally make loans to both firms and individuals and invest in securities, including the bonds (which are essentially IOUs) of state and local governments as well as federal government bonds.* The relationship between a business firm and its bank is often a close and continuing one. The firm keeps a reasonably large deposit with the bank for long periods of time, and the bank provides the firm with needed and prudent loans. The relationship between individuals and their banks is much more casual, but banks like consumer loans because they tend to be relatively profitable. In addition to lending to firms and individuals, banks buy large quantities of government bonds.

2. *Banks, like other firms, operate to make a profit.* They do not do it by producing and selling a good, like automobiles or steel. Instead, they perform various services, including lending money, making investments, clearing checks, and keeping records. They manage to make a profit from these activities by lending money and making investments that yield a higher rate of interest than they must pay their depositors. For example, Bank of America, one of the nation's largest banks, may be able to get 6 percent interest on the loans it makes, whereas it

CASE STUDY 20.1

THE FAILURE OF THE KNICKERBOCKER TRUST IN 1907

The Knickerbocker Trust in New York City was a successful bank at the start of the twentieth century. The Knickerbocker Trust's main branch was at a fashionable Fifth Avenue address, where many well-to-do people (including the writer Mark Twain) kept their accounts. At its downtown office near Wall Street, the Knickerbocker Trust held some of the deposits of large corporations like General Electric and the Pennsylvania Railroad. In turn, the bank made loans to numerous growing businesses. Under its dynamic president, Charles T. Barney, the Knickerbocker held city bonds and invested in the development of the transit system, new hotels along Fifth Avenue, and elegant apartment buildings on the Upper West Side. Not all of the bank's loans paid off. But most did, and the bank prospered.

An opportunity then came along for Charles Barney to make a lot of money if he was willing to take some major risks. Barney had connections with a speculator named Charles Morse. Morse and his partner, Frederick Heinze, formulated a scheme to manipulate the price of copper stock on Wall Street in 1907. The extent of Barney's involvement is debatable, but many believed that he made behind-the-scenes arrangements for the Morse-Heinze combine, which, on October 15, 1907, tried and failed to squeeze the copper market, whereupon the syndicate went under. There was no evidence that Barney had overcommitted loans to Morse, but there were rumors to this effect; and Barney, like any banker of the day, realized

that gossip could lead to the death of his bank before any facts were proved. He knew that as the word spread that the Knickerbocker was in trouble, the depositors would start a run of withdrawals. Like any banker caught in that situation, Barney also knew that if he could temporarily pull enough cash together, he might be able to calm his customers. If they were made to believe that the bank could make its payouts, his bank might be saved.

On Sunday, October 20, Charles Barney left his home on Park Avenue to try to borrow the cash he needed. He went to appeal to the only person who could save him: J. P. Morgan. Morgan had helped tide over banks in trouble before, and he was one of the few men who had the reputation and resources to do it. Morgan had been friendly with Barney and owned some Knickerbocker stock. But Morgan refused even to see him. For Barney, disaster was inescapable. Trying to forestall the rumors, the bank's board of directors on Monday forced Barney's resignation. It did not help. The run on the Knickerbocker began. On Tuesday morning, bank officials announced they had $8 million cash in their vaults, but most of it was gone before the end of the day. The Knickerbocker closed its doors. Those customers who had not withdrawn their money were out of luck for an unforeseeable future. The failure of the Knickerbocker Trust led to doubts about other banks and snowballed into the Panic of 1907. Realizing that the ensuing bank failures could endanger the entire system, including his own holdings,

J. P. Morgan subsequently stepped in, and under his leadership, a large reserve fund was pooled together. But by the time the panic was over, 246 banks had closed, and a disgraced, distraught Charles Barney had killed himself. Ironically, the Knickerbocker Trust was not all that bad a bank; it reopened five months later, and depositors got most of their money back.

must pay only 3 percent interest to its depositors. (Commercial banks pay interest on some but not all deposits.) In this case, it receives the difference of 3 percent, which goes to meet its expenses—and to provide it with some profits.

3. *Banks must constantly balance their desire for high returns from their loans and investments against the requirement that these loans and investments be safe and easily turned into cash.* Since a bank's profits increase if it makes loans or investments that yield a high interest rate, it is clear why a bank favors high returns from its loans and investments. But those that yield a high interest rate often are relatively risky, which means that they may not be repaid in full. Because a bank lends out its depositors' money, it must be careful to limit the riskiness of the loans and investments it makes. Otherwise it may fail (see Case Study 20.1).

Until 80 years ago, banks used to fail in large numbers during recessions and cause depositors to lose their money. Even during the prosperous 1920s, over 500 banks failed per year. It is no wonder that the public viewed the banks with less than complete confidence. Since the mid-1930s, bank failures have been far fewer, in part because of tighter standards of regulation by federal and state authorities. For example, bank examiners audit the books and practices of the banks. In addition, confidence in the banks was strengthened by the creation in 1934 of the Federal Deposit Insurance Corporation (FDIC), which insures over 99 percent of all commercial bank depositors. At present, each depositor per bank is insured up to $250,000. Nonetheless, as we shall see, there was much more concern over the safety of the banks during the late 1980s and early 1990s and especially during the financial crisis of 2008–2009 than during the previous half century.

The Balance Sheet of an Individual Bank

A good way to understand how a bank operates is to look at its balance sheet. A firm's balance sheet shows the nature of its assets, tangible and intangible, at a certain point in time. Suppose that Table 20.2 shows the balance sheet of a particular bank at the end of 2011.

> ➤ *The left-hand side.* The left-hand side shows that the total assets of this bank were $187 billion and that these assets were made up as follows: $13 billion in cash, $32 billion in bonds and other securities, $123 billion in loans, and $19 billion in other assets. In particular, note that the loans

Assets		Liabilities and Net Worth	
TABLE 20.2			
Cash	13	Deposits	142
Securities	32	Other liabilities	28
Loans	123	Net worth	17
Other assets	19		
Total	187	Total	187

Balance Sheet, Hypothetical Bank, December 31, 2011 (billions of dollars)

included among the assets of this bank are the loans it made to firms and individuals. As we have emphasized, lending money is a major function of a commercial bank.

➤ *The right-hand side.* The right-hand side of the balance sheet says that the total liabilities (or debts) of this bank were $170 billion and that these liabilities were made up of $142 billion in deposits (both demand and time) and $28 billion in other liabilities. Note that the deposits at this bank are included among its liabilities, since this bank owes the depositors the amount of money in their deposits. You may recall from the previous sections that maintaining these deposits is a major function of a commercial bank. The difference between the bank's total assets and its total liabilities ($17 billion) is its net worth. (A firm's *net worth* is the value of its owners' claims against its assets.)

Cash Less Than Deposits

One noteworthy characteristic of any bank's balance sheet is the fact that a very large percentage of its liabilities must be paid on demand. For example, if all the depositors of the bank in Table 20.2 tried to withdraw their demand deposits, a substantial proportion of its liabilities would be due on demand. Of course, the chance of all depositors wanting to draw out their money at once is infinitesimally small. Instead, on any given day, some depositors withdraw some money while others make deposits, and most depositors neither withdraw nor deposit money. Consequently, any bank can get along with an amount of cash to cover withdrawals that is much smaller than the total amount of its deposits.[2]

Is it dangerous for a bank to hold an amount of cash much less than the amount it owes its depositors? The answer is no. All banks hold much less cash than the amount they owe their depositors. This is a perfectly sound banking practice, as we shall see.

[2] Note that "cash" here includes the bank's deposit with the Federal Reserve and its deposits with other banks, as well as cash in its vault. The Federal Reserve is our nation's central bank, described later and in subsequent chapters.

TABLE 20.3

Bank Balance Sheet: Case Where Reserves Equal Demand Deposits (millions of dollars)

Assets		Liabilities and Net Worth	
Reserves	2.0	Demand deposits	2.0
Loans and investments	0.5	Net worth	0.5
Total	*2.5*	*Total*	*2.5*

Fractional Reserve Banking

Fractional reserve banking

To understand the crucial significance of **fractional reserve banking**, as this practice is called, we compare two situations: one where a bank's reserves must equal the amount the bank owes its depositors, and another where its reserves need not match that amount. In the first case, the bank's balance sheet might be as shown in Table 20.3 if demand deposits equal $2 million and net worth equals $500,000. The bank's loans and investments in this case are made entirely with funds put up by the owners of the bank. To see this, note that loans and investments equal $500,000 and that the bank's net worth also equals $500,000. Therefore, if some of these loans are not repaid or some of these investments lose money, the losses are borne entirely by the bank's stockholders. The depositors are protected completely because every cent of their deposits is covered by the bank's reserves.

Now let's turn to the case of fractional reserve banking. In this case, the bank's balance sheet might be as shown in Table 20.4 if deposits equal $2 million and net worth equals $500,000. Some of the loans and investments made by the bank are made not with funds put up by the owners of the bank, but with funds deposited in the bank by depositors. Although depositors deposited $2 million in the bank, the reserves are only $400,000. What happened to the remaining $1.6 million? Since the bank (in this simple case) has only two kinds of assets, loans (and investments) and reserves, the bank must have lent out (or invested) the remaining $1.6 million.

Origins of Fractional Reserve Banking

The early history of banking is the story of an evolution from the first to the second situation. The earliest banks held reserves equal to the amounts they owed depositors and were simply places where people stored their gold. But

TABLE 20.4

Bank Balance Sheet: Fractional Reserves (millions of dollars)

Assets		Liabilities and Net Worth	
Reserves	0.4	Demand deposits	2.0
Loans and investments	2.1	Net worth	0.5
Total	*2.5*	*Total*	*2.5*

as time went on, banks began to practice fractional reserve banking. It is easy to see how this evolution could take place. Suppose that you owned a bank of the first type. You would almost certainly be struck by the fact that most of the gold entrusted to you was not demanded on any given day. Sooner or later, you might be tempted to lend out some of the gold and obtain some interest. Eventually, as experience indicated that this procedure did not inconvenience your depositors, you and other bankers might make this practice common knowledge.

You might use several arguments to defend this practice. First, you would probably point out that none of the depositors had lost any money. (To the depositors, this would be a rather important argument.) Second, you could show that the interest you earned on the loans made it possible for you to charge depositors less for storing their gold. Consequently, you would argue that it was to the depositors' advantage (because of the savings that accrued to them) for you to lend out some of the gold. Third, you would probably argue that putting the money to work benefited the community and the economy. After all, in many cases firms can make highly productive investments only if they can borrow the money, and by lending out your depositors' gold, you would enable such investments to be made.

Legal Reserve Requirements

Arguments of this sort led society to permit fractional reserve banking. In other words, banks are allowed to hold less in reserves than the amount they owe their depositors. But what determines how much banks hold in reserves? For example, the bank in Table 20.2 held cash equal to about 9 percent of its total deposits. It probably could have gotten away with holding much less in reserves, so long as there was no panic among depositors and it made sound loans and investments. But the Federal Reserve System requires every commercial bank (whether or not it is a member of the system) to hold a certain percentage of its deposits as reserves.

Federal Reserve System (Fed)   What is the **Federal Reserve System** (commonly called the **Fed**)? It is our nation's central bank, and its most important functions are to help control the quantity of money, provide facilities for the collection of checks, supply the public with currency, and supervise the operation of commercial banks.

According to the 1980 Financial Reform Act, the Fed can set the percentage of deposits that a bank must hold as reserves for checkable deposits (that is, deposits subject to direct or indirect transfer by check).[3] Also, on the affirmative action of five of the seven members of the Fed's Board of Governors, it can impose additional reserve requirements. And in

---

[3] The 1980 law also applies these reserve requirements to deposits in other thrift institutions (savings and loan associations, mutual savings banks, and credit unions), not just banks.

extraordinary circumstances, the Fed can, for 180 days, set the percentage at any level it deems necessary. These are **legal reserve requirements**; they also exist for time deposits (of businesses and nonprofit institutions), but are lower than for checkable deposits. In 2012, the reserve requirement for banks with deposits of more than $71 million was 10 percent. Banks with deposits between $11.5 million and $71 million had a reserve requirement of 3 percent. Banks with less than $11.5 million in deposits had no minimum reserve requirement.

Most of these reserves are held in the form of deposits by banks at the Federal Reserve. In addition, some of any bank's reserves are held in cash on the bank's premises. However, its legal reserves are less than the "cash" entry on its balance sheet, since its deposits with other banks do not count as legal reserves. The most obvious reason why the Fed imposes these legal reserve requirements would seem to be to keep the banks safe, but in this case the obvious answer is not the right one. Instead, the most important reason for legal reserve requirements is to control the money supply. It takes some more discussion before this becomes clear.

The Safety of the Banks

It can be argued that the reserve requirements imposed by the Federal Reserve System exceed what would be required under normal circumstances to ensure the safety of the banks. To support our argument, we might cite some authorities who claim that a bank would be quite safe if it had reserves equal only to about 2 percent of its deposits. Under these circumstances, it still would be able to meet its depositors' everyday demands for cash. Obviously, this level of reserves is much lower than the legally required level.

The Role of Bank Management

High reserve requirements by themselves do not ensure bank safety. For example, suppose that a bank lends money to every budding inventor with a scheme for producing perpetual-motion machines and it grants particularly large loans to those who propose to market these machines in the suburbs of Missoula, Montana. This bank is going to fail eventually, even if it holds reserves equal to 20 percent—or 50 percent, for that matter—of its demand deposits. It will fail simply because the loans it makes will not be repaid, and eventually these losses will accumulate to more than the bank's net worth. In other words, if the bank is sufficiently inept in making loans and investments, it will lose all the owners' money and some of the depositors' money as well.

The well-managed bank must make sensible loans and investments. In addition, it must protect itself against short-term withdrawals of large amounts of money. Although much larger than usual withdrawals are not very likely to occur, the bank must be prepared to meet a temporary upswing in withdrawals.

COMPARING THE U.S. SAVINGS AND LOAN CRISIS AND THE JAPANESE BANKING CRISIS

In the late 1980s, the United States suffered through one of its worst banking crises in the postwar period. At the epicenter of the crisis was the savings and loan (S&L) industry. What brought on this debacle? The responsibility for the crisis lay with many different institutions and resulted from a number of trends, some of which had little to do with the S&L industry. One of the foundations of the crisis was laid in the late 1970s and early 1980s, when the Federal Reserve drove up interest rates to rid the United States of double-digit inflation (see Case Study 26.2). This meant that the S&Ls had to pay higher interest rates on their deposits or risk losing them to other financial institutions.

At the same time, a wave of deregulation hit U.S. financial institutions. While the federal government led the way, state governments eagerly followed. The result was that S&Ls were allowed to make riskier (and higher-yielding) investments in real estate and junk bonds. This, combined with a rather lax attitude on the part of many regulators, provided a strong temptation for these thrift institutions to pursue high-risk strategies.

In the mid-1980s, the energy price collapse unmasked the bad investments of many Texas S&Ls. Likewise, the bursting of the real estate bubble in New England and California in the late 1980s exposed the shakiness of the S&Ls in those regions as well. Finally, partisan politics and the inability of Congress to quickly enact an S&L bailout plan compounded the problem and raised the price tag of the eventual rescue package.

By 1990, it was estimated that the problems of the S&L industry had cost U.S. taxpayers roughly $200 billion (or 3.5 percent of GDP). Hundreds of insolvent S&Ls were closed, and since the federal government insured their deposits, taxpayers were stuck with the bill.

In the late 1980s, the makings of a much larger banking crisis were brewing in Japan. Under pressure from the Japanese Ministry of Finance, the Bank of Japan held down interest rates to help boost domestic demand and imports and, in so doing, cut Japan's trade surplus with the United States. As a result, credit was cheap and financial liquidity was plentiful. This led to pervasive speculation in the property and stock markets, financed primarily with bank lending. Between 1986 and 1989, equity and land prices more than doubled. Meanwhile, companies and households borrowed heavily on the basis of the rise in asset values.

On Christmas day 1989, the Bank of Japan burst the Japanese asset bubble by raising interest rates. This led to a 60 percent drop in the Japanese stock market and a 70 percent drop in Japanese property prices over the next four years. Banks that had loaned money on the basis of inflated asset values saw this collateral wiped out and were left with a huge volume of nonperforming (dud) loans. By some estimates, the size of the bad-loan problem in Japan was 6 to 10 times greater than in the U.S. S&L crisis.

Unfortunately, the Bank of Japan and the Ministry of Finance exacerbated the problem. The central bank was too slow to ease monetary policy after the bubble burst. The Ministry of Finance badly mishandled the banking crisis by underestimating the magnitude of the problem and then moving very slowly to solve it. It was not until 1998, nine years after the crisis began, that Japan put in place a financial restructuring program that remotely resembled the one that finally cleaned up the S&L mess in the United States. In the meantime, Japan suffered through a "lost decade," which included a deep recession in 1998. Thus, not only was Japan's banking problem much more serious than the S&L crisis, but the Japanese government's poor response made things even worse.

One way is to invest in securities that can readily be turned into cash. For example, the bank may invest in short-term government securities that can readily be sold at a price that varies only moderately from day to day. Such securities are often referred to as *secondary reserves*.

The Role of the Government

Banks tend to be safer today than they were 100 years ago. The reason is that the government has put its power squarely behind the banking system. It used to be that runs were made on the banks: depositors, afraid that their banks would fail and that they would lose some of their money, would line up at the teller's windows and withdraw as much money as they could. Faced with runs of this sort, banks were sometimes forced to close because they could not satisfy all the demands for withdrawals. Needless to say, no fractional reserve banking system can satisfy demands for the total withdrawal of funds.

Runs on banks are rare now. For one thing, the government, including the Federal Deposit Insurance Corporation, the Federal Reserve, and other public agencies, has made it clear that it will not stand by and tolerate the panics that used to occur periodically in this country. The FDIC insures the accounts of depositors in practically all banks, so that even if a bank fails, depositors will get their money back—up to $250,000. What's more, the banks themselves tend to be better managed and regulated. For example, bank examiners are sent out to look over the bankers' shoulders and determine whether they are solvent.

Problems during the 1990s and 2000s

Despite the various safeguards, we cannot really say that bank regulation has been all that it might be or that the health of the banking industry has been particularly robust. On the contrary, in early 1991, there were persistent

FINANCIAL REREGULATION AFTER THE FINANCIAL CRISIS OF 2008–2009

At the risk of oversimplification, the root cause of financial crises is the tendency of banks and other financial institutions to make lots of bad loans. When economic times are good, a portfolio of bad loans is not a big problem. However, the moment growth falters or asset prices (including real estate prices) plunge, banks are left holding the bag.

The major point of financial regulation has been to save bankers from themselves! Well-designed financial regulation should be simple and easy to enforce, with the goals of protecting small depositors and reducing the risks of future crises without curtailing the ability of financial markets to innovate and to provide greater access to credit for everyone. Regulations should also reduce the incentives (and big financial rewards) for bankers to make huge risky bets that put their institutions (and, if they are big enough, the entire financial system) in jeopardy.

The problem during the 2008–2009 subprime crisis was not so much the lack of regulation as the lack of enforcement of existing regulations. Unfortunately, there is no guarantee that new financial regulation will be enforced any more effectively than past regulation.

The Dodd-Frank Wall Street Reform and Consumer Protection Act was passed in the summer of 2010 in the hopes of preventing another financial crisis. It was the most significant change in financial regulation since the Great Depression. Time will tell whether it succeeds in preventing another major banking crisis. It is certainly far more complex than the prior regulatory structure and, as a result, possibly harder to enforce. It has also encouraged the large banks to become even larger, potentially worsening the problem of "too big to fail"—banks that are so big that they have to be bailed out with taxpayer money, lest they take down the entire financial system.

rumors and reports that many huge New York banks, as well as a variety of smaller banks elsewhere, were in serious financial troubles because many of their real estate loans went sour when the real estate market did not live up to expectations (see Case Study 20.2). These banks were hurt when, beginning in the 1960s, they started to lose the business of many large firms that began to get funds from foreign banks or the securities markets because interest rates were lower. Also, some banks had made risky investments in high-yield bonds ("junk bonds") and risky loans to developing countries like Argentina and Brazil. While these problems did not mean that your bank deposit was not insured (up to $250,000), it did mean that your bank might fail, with attendant losses to its owners, among others. However, as it turned out, the banks dodged the bullet. Their earnings rose substantially, and by 1994, there was no longer talk of widespread financial problems among the banks.

U.S. banks got themselves into trouble again in the late 2000s because of what has come to be known as the "subprime crisis." During the housing bubble of the early and mid-2000s, U.S. financial institutions (including large commercial banks) began to ease borrowing conditions for mortgages. This included smaller down payment requirements and less stringent credit standards. As a result, the percentage of lower-quality (subprime) loans rose from around 8 percent of the total in 2000 to around 20 percent in 2006. When the housing bubble burst and house prices plunged, many of these subprime mortgages became "submerged"; that is, the value of the house was less than the value of the mortgage. As a result, many families foreclosed on their mortgage loans, leaving banks with a huge volume of bad (unrecoverable) debt. In the end, the Federal Reserve, the Federal Deposit Insurance Corporation, and the federal government all came to the rescue, and the banking system was saved. However, the regulations on banks were tightened considerably in response to the crisis (see Case Study 20.3).

How Banks Can Create Money

Genesis tells us that God created heaven and earth. Economists tell us that banks create money. To many people, the latter process is as mysterious as the former. To see how banks can create money, imagine the following scenario. First, suppose that someone deposits $10,000 of newly printed money in a particular bank, which we call bank A. Second, suppose that bank A lends Ms. Smith $8,333 and that Smith uses this money to purchase some equipment from Mr. Jones, who deposits Smith's check in his account at bank B. Third, suppose that bank B buys a bond for $6,944 from Ms. Stone, who uses the money to pay Mr. Green for some furniture. Green deposits the check to his account at bank C. We assume that the legal reserve requirements are that $1 in reserves must be held for every $6 in demand deposits.

Money Creation at Bank A

The first step in our drama occurs when someone deposits $10,000 in newly printed money in bank A. The effect of this deposit is shown in the first three rows of Table 20.5: bank A's demand deposits and its reserves both go up by $10,000. Now bank A can make a loan of $8,333, since this is the amount of its **Excess reserves** **excess reserves** (those in excess of legal requirements).

Because of the $10,000 increase in its deposits, its legally required reserves increase by $10,000 ÷ 6, or $1,667 (recall that $1 in reserves must be held for every $6 in deposits). Therefore, if it had no excess reserves before, it now has excess reserves of $10,000 – $1,667, or $8,333. When Smith asks one of the loan officers of the bank for a loan to purchase equipment, the loan officer approves a loan of $8,333. Smith is given a checking account of $8,333 at bank A.

How can bank A get away with this loan of $8,333 without winding up with less than the legally required reserves? The answer is given in the rest of Table 20.5. Rows 4 through 6 of this table show what happens to bank A's balance sheet when bank A makes the $8,333 loan and creates a new demand deposit of $8,333. Obviously, both demand deposits and loans go up by $8,333. Next, look at rows 7 through 9 of Table 20.5, which show what happens when Smith spends the $8,333 on equipment. As pointed out, she purchases this equipment from Jones. Jones deposits Smith's check in his account in bank B, which presents the check to bank A for payment. After bank A pays bank B (through the Federal Reserve System), the result, as shown in rows 7 through 9, is that bank A's deposits go down by $8,333, since Smith no longer has the deposit. Bank A's reserves also go down by $8,333, since bank A has to transfer these reserves to bank B to pay the amount of the check.

TABLE 20.5
Changes in Bank A's Balance Sheet (dollars)

	Assets		Liabilities and Net Worth	
Bank receives deposit	Reserves	+10,000	Demand deposits	+10,000
	Loans & investments	No change	Net worth	No change
	Total	+10,000	Total	+10,000
Bank makes loan	Reserves	No change	Deposit deposits	+8,333
	Loans & investments	+8,333	Net worth	No change
	Total	+8,333	Total	+8,333
Smith spends $8,333	Reserves	–8,333	Demand deposits	–8,333
	Loans & investments	No change	Net worth	No change
	Total	–8,333	Total	–8,333
Total effect	Reserves	+1,667	Demand deposits	+10,000
	Loans & investments	+8,333	Net worth	No change
	Total	+10,000	Total	+10,000

As shown in the last three rows of Table 20.5, the total effect on bank A is to increase its deposits by the $10,000 deposited originally and increase its reserves by $10,000 − $8,333, or $1,667. In other words, reserves have increased by one-sixth as much as demand deposits. This means that bank A meets its legal reserve requirements.

It is important to recognize that bank A has now created $8,333 in new money. To see this, note that Jones winds up with a demand deposit of this amount that he did not have before; this is a net addition to the money supply, since the person who originally deposited the $10,000 in currency still has his or her $10,000, although it is in the form of a demand deposit rather than currency.

Money Creation at Bank B

The effects of the $10,000 deposit at bank A are not limited to bank A. As we shall see, other banks also create new money as a consequence of the original $10,000 deposit at bank A. We begin with bank B. Recall from the previous section that the $8,333 check made out by Smith to Jones is deposited by Jones in his account at bank B. This is a new deposit of funds at bank B. As pointed out in the previous section, bank B gets $8,333 in reserves from bank A when bank A pays bank B to get back the check. Thus, the effect on bank B's balance sheet, as shown in Table 20.6, is to increase both demand deposits and reserves by $8,333.

Bank B is in much the same position as bank A was when the latter received the original deposit of $10,000. Bank B can make loans or investments equal to its excess reserves, which are $6,944.[4] Specifically, it decides to buy a bond for $6,944 from Stone and credits her checking account at bank B for this amount. As shown in Table 20.6, the effect of this transaction is to increase bank B's investments by $6,944 and its demand deposits by $6,944. Stone writes a check for $6,944 to Green to pay for some furniture. Green deposits the check in bank C. Bank B's demand deposits and its reserves are decreased by $6,944 when it transfers this amount of reserves to bank C to pay for the check. When the total effects of the transaction are summed up, bank B, like bank A, continues to meet its legal reserve requirements, since, as shown in Table 20.6, the increase in reserves ($1,389) equals one-sixth of its increase in demand deposits ($8,333).

Bank B has also created some money—$6,944, to be exact. Green has $6,944 in demand deposits that he did not have before; this is a net addition to the money supply, since the person who originally deposited the currency in bank A still has his or her $10,000, and Jones still has the $8,333 he deposited in bank B.

---

[4] Since bank B's deposits increase by $8,333, its legally required reserves increase by $8,333 ÷ 6, or $1,389. Therefore, $1,389 of its increase in reserves is legally required, and the rest ($8,333 − $1,389 = $6,944) is excess reserves.

TABLE 20.6
Changes in Bank B's Balance Sheet (dollars)

	Assets		Liabilities and Net Worth	
Bank receives deposit	Reserves	+8,333	Demand deposits	+8,333
	Loans & investments	No change	Net worth	No change
	Total	+8,333	Total	+8,333
Bank makes loan	Reserves	No change	Deposit deposits	+6,944
	Loans & investments	+6,944	Net worth	No change
	Total	+6,944	Total	+6,944
Smith spends $8,333	Reserves	−6,944	Demand deposits	−6,944
	Loans & investments	No change	Net worth	No change
	Total	−6,944	Total	−6,944
Total effect	Reserves	+1,389	Demand deposits	+8,333
	Loans & investments	+6,944	Net worth	No change
	Total	+8,333	Total	+8,333

The Total Effect of the Original $8,333 in Excess Reserves

How big an increase in the money supply can the entire banking system support as a consequence of the original $8,333 in excess reserves arising from the $10,000 deposit in bank A? Clearly, the effects of the original injection of excess reserves into the banking system spread from one bank to another, since each bank handed new reserves (and deposits) to another bank, which in turn handed them to another bank. For example, bank C now has $6,944 more in deposits and reserves and so can create $5,787 in new money by making a loan or investment of this amount.[5] This process goes on indefinitely, and it would be impossible to describe each of the multitude of steps involved. Fortunately, it is not necessary to do so. We can figure out the total amount of new money the entire banking system can support as a consequence of the original excess reserves at bank A without going through all these steps. When the process works itself out, the entire banking system can support $50,000 in new money as a consequence of the original injection of $8,333 in excess reserves.[6]

[5] Why $5,787? Because it must hold $6,944 ÷ 6 = $1,157 as reserves to support the new demand deposit of $6,944. Therefore, it has excess reserves of $5,787, and it can create another new demand deposit of this amount.

[6] The proof of this is as follows. The total amount of new money supported by the $8,333 in excess reserves is $8,333 + $6,944 + $5,787 + ..., which equals $8,333 + 5/6 × $8,333 + (5/6)^2 × $8,333 + (5/6)^3 × $8,333 +..., which equals $8,333 × [1 + 5/6 + (5/6)^2 + (5/6)^3 +...] = $8,333 × 1/(1 − 5/6) = $50,000, since 1 + 5/6 + (5/6)^2 + (5/6)^3 +... = 1/(1 − 5/6).

EXPLORING FURTHER

A General Proposition Concerning the Effect of Excess Reserves

The Effect of an Increase in Reserves

To obtain the total increase in the money supply that can be achieved from a certain amount of excess reserves, we multiply the amount of excess reserves by the reciprocal of the required ratio of reserves to deposits—or, what amounts to the same thing, divide the amount of excess reserves by the legally required ratio of reserves to deposits.

For example, suppose that the banking system gains excess reserves of $10,000 and the required ratio of reserves to deposits is 1/6. To determine how much the banking system can increase the money supply, we must divide the amount of the excess reserves, $10,000, by the required ratio of reserves to deposits, 1/6, to get the answer: $60,000. Now suppose that the required ratio of reserves to deposits is 1/10. By how much can the banking system increase the money supply? Dividing $10,000 by 1/10, we get the answer: $100,000. Note that the higher the required ratio of reserves to deposits, the smaller the amount by which the banking system can increase the money supply on the basis of a given amount of excess reserves.

Although it is useful to trace through the effect of an increase in the reserves of a single bank—bank A in our previous case—in reality, lots of banks experience an increase in reserves at about the same time. Thus, they all have excess reserves at about the same time, and they all make loans or investments at about the same time. The result is that when the people who borrow money spend it, each bank tends to both gain and lose reserves. On balance, each bank need not lose reserves. In real life, the amount of bank money often expands simultaneously throughout the banking system until the legally required ratio of deposits to reserves is approached.

The Effect of a Decrease in Reserves

Up to this point, we have been talking about the effect of an increase in reserves. What happens to the quantity of money if reserves decrease?

In general, if the banking system has a deficiency of reserves of a certain amount, the banking system as a whole reduces demand deposits by an amount equal to the deficiency in reserves multiplied by the reciprocal of the required ratio of reserves to deposits.

In other words, to obtain the total decrease in demand deposits resulting from a deficiency in reserves, we divide the deficiency by the legally required ratio of reserves to deposits. Although there is often a simultaneous contraction of money on the part of many banks (just as there is often a simultaneous expansion), this does not affect the result.

Suppose, for example, that the banking system experiences a deficiency in reserves of $8,333 and the required ratio of reserves to deposits is 1/6. We divide the deficiency in reserves, $8,333, by the required ratio of reserves to deposits, 1/6, to get the answer, which is a $50,000 reduction in demand deposits. Note that the effect of a $1 deficiency in reserves is equal in absolute terms to the effect of $1 in excess reserves.[7]

REVIEW AND PRACTICE

Summary

1 Money performs several basic functions. It serves as a medium of exchange, a standard of value, and a store of value. The money supply narrowly defined is composed of coins, currency, demand deposits, and other checkable deposits. Economists include demand (and other checkable) deposits as part of the money supply because you can pay for goods and services about as easily by check as with cash.

2 In addition to this narrow definition of money, broader definitions include savings and time deposits (and money market mutual fund shares and money market deposit accounts). It is not easy to draw a line between money and nonmoney, since many assets have some of the characteristics of money.

3 Commercial banks have two primary functions. First, they hold demand (and other checkable) deposits and permit checks to be drawn on them. Second, they lend money to firms and individuals. Most of our money supply is not coin and paper currency but bank money—demand (and other checkable) deposits. This money can be created by banks.

4 The Federal Reserve System requires every commercial bank (and other thrift institutions with checkable deposits) to hold a certain percentage of its deposits as reserves. The major purpose of these legal reserve requirements is to control the money supply.

5 Banks tend to be safer than they were 100 years ago because of better management and regulation as well as the government's stated willingness to insure and stand behind their deposits. However, bank failures still occur, and bank regulation has not been as stringent as it might be.

[7] The results set forth in this chapter are based on a number of simplifying assumptions. We assume that when excess reserves are made available to the banking system, there is no withdrawal of part of them in the form of currency and that when deficiencies in reserves occur, no currency is deposited in banks. If such changes in the amount of currency take place, the change in demand deposits equals the excess reserves left permanently with the banking system divided by the legally required ratio of reserves to deposits. Also, we assume that banks want to hold no excess reserves. Clearly, an injection of excess reserves or a deficiency of reserves will not have their full, or maximum, effect on demand deposits if the banks do not lend and invest as much as possible.

*6 [8]The banking system as a whole can increase its demand deposits by an amount equal to its excess reserves divided by the legally required ratio of reserves to deposits. Thus, if excess reserves in the banking system equal a certain amount, the banking system as a whole can increase demand deposits by the amount of the excess reserves divided by the legally required ratio of reserves to deposits.

*7 If there is a deficiency in reserves in the banking system, the system as a whole must decrease demand deposits by the amount of this deficiency divided by the legally required ratio of reserves to deposits.

Problems and Questions

1 "Banks do not create money. After all, they can only lend out money they receive from depositors." Comment and evaluate.

2 Suppose that the legally required ratio of reserves to deposits is 1/5 and that banks have no excess reserves. If the banking system's reserves shrink by $50 million, by how much does the money supply change?

3 "Demand deposits are increased by banks when they call in loans and sell investments." Comment and evaluate.

4 "Money, in and of itself, has no value whatsoever. It is valuable only because of what it can buy." Comment and evaluate.

5 Suppose that the legally required ratio of reserves to deposits is 1/10. If $100 million in excess reserves are made available to the banking system, by how much can the banking system increase the money supply? What is the answer if the legally required ratio of reserves to deposits is 1/6 rather than 1/10?

6 Explain in detail why the following items are not money:

(a) Government bonds

(b) General Motors stock

(c) Gold

(d) Uranium

7 Give some reasons why savings accounts should be regarded as money. Give some reasons why they should not. Which side of the argument do you find more convincing?

---

[8] Starred (*) items refer to material in Exploring Further.

Key Terms

money

currency

demand deposits

M1

M2

fractional reserve banking

Federal Reserve System (Fed)

legal reserve requirements

excess reserves

Viewpoint for Analysis

According to Sandy Weill, former chair of Citigroup, in a July 2012 interview on CNBC, "What we should probably do is go . . . and have banks do something that's not going to risk taxpayer dollars, that's not going to be too big to fail."

(a) What does the expression "too big to fail" mean?

(b) Is it really a choice of the government to let large banks fail, thus endangering the financial system?

(c) Should taxpayers foot the bill for poorly managed large banks, or should others (for example, executives, investors, and shareholders) bear the brunt of the loss?

The Federal Reserve and Monetary Policy

LEARNING OBJECTIVES

➤ To explore the aims and nature of monetary policy

➤ To survey the groups empowered to make monetary policy

➤ To describe the workings of the Federal Reserve System

➤ To consider the pros and cons of monetary policy

➤ *(Exploring Further)* To explore the effects of monetary policy on the aggregate demand curve

L ike fiscal policy, monetary policy is no panacea but a very important tool for stabilizing the economy. In recent years, monetary policy has been the subject of considerable controversy. During 2012, for example, some analysts claimed that the Federal Reserve's aggressive and unorthodox policies after the financial crisis of 2008–2009 would generate runaway inflation. Others maintained that the Fed needed to do even more—much more. Without doubt, such controversies will continue in the future, since one thing is certain: economists of all persuasions agree that monetary policy has a major impact on the economy.

The Aims of Monetary Policy

Monetary policy

Monetary policy is the exercise of the central bank's control over the quantity of money and interest rates to promote the objectives of national economic policy. (In the United States, the central bank is the Federal Reserve.) The money supply affects gross domestic product and the price level. Increases in the money supply tend to push up real GDP and the price level, whereas decreases in the money supply tend to push them down. The extent to which the effect is on the price level rather than real GDP depends on the steepness of the short-run aggregate supply curve. The steeper it is, the greater the effect on the price level and the smaller the effect on real GDP. In the long run, increases in the money supply raise only the price level, not real GDP, and decreases in the money supply lower the price level, not real GDP.

When a recession seems imminent and business is soft, the central bank often increases the money supply and pushes down interest rates. That is, it "eases credit," or "eases money," as the newspapers put it. On the other hand, when the economy is in danger of overheating and serious inflation threatens, the central bank often reins in the money supply and pushes up interest rates. That is, in newspaper terms, it "tightens credit," or "tightens money."

In formulating monetary policy, the government's objective generally is to attain or maintain reasonably full employment without excessive inflation. As we shall see, not all economists agree that the sorts of discretionary policies described in the previous paragraph are likely to achieve this objective, but we postpone a discussion of this controversy. Regardless of how you think the central bank should behave, it is important that you understand the ways in which it can increase or decrease the money supply.

A country's monetary authorities can influence the money supply by managing the reserves of the banking system. Suppose that the monetary authorities want to increase the money supply more rapidly. How can they realize this objective? By providing the banks with plenty of excess reserves. As we saw in the previous chapter, excess reserves enable the banks to increase the money supply. Indeed, we learned that the banks could increase the money supply by $6 for every $1 of excess reserves, assuming that the legal reserve requirement is 16.67 percent.[1] Thus, in our example in Chapter 20, the $8,333 of excess reserves at bank A enabled the banking system as a whole to increase the money supply by $50,000.

On the other hand, suppose that the Federal Reserve decides to cut back on the rate of increase of the money supply. To do so, it can slow down the rate of increase of bank reserves. As we saw in Exploring Further in the previous chapter, this forces the banks to curtail the rate of growth of their demand deposits by easing off on the rate of growth of their loans and investments. Indeed, if the Federal Reserve goes so far as to reduce the reserves of the banking system, this tends to reduce the money supply. Under the assumptions made in the previous chapter, the banks must cut back the money supply by $6 for every $1 deficiency in reserves.

---

[1] If the legal reserve requirement is 10 percent, a $10 increase in the money supply can be supported by $1 of excess reserves. As more advanced texts explain, a much smaller increase in the money supply may result from a dollar of reserves if banks want to hold excess reserves and currency is withdrawn.

Makers of Monetary Policy

Who establishes our monetary policy? Who decides that in view of the current and prospective economic conditions, the money supply should be increased (or decreased) at a certain rate? As in the case of fiscal policy, this is not a simple question to answer; many individuals and groups play important roles. Certainly, however, the leading role is played by the Federal Reserve Board and the Federal Open Market Committee, both of which are described in detail in subsequent sections. The chair of the Federal Reserve Board is the chief spokesperson for the Federal Reserve System. The recent chairs—Ben Bernanke, Alan Greenspan, Paul A. Volcker, G. William Miller, and Arthur F. Burns—undoubtedly had considerable influence over monetary policy.

Although the Federal Reserve is responsible to Congress, Congress has established no clear guidelines for its behavior. Therefore, the Federal Reserve has wide discretionary powers over monetary policy. But the Federal Reserve System is a huge organization, and it is not easy to figure out exactly who influences whom and who decides what. Formal actions can be taken by a majority of the board and the Federal Open Market Committee. However, this tells only part of the story.

To get a more complete picture, it is essential to note, too, that many agencies and groups other than the Fed have an effect on monetary policy, although it is difficult to measure their respective influences. The Treasury Department frequently has an important voice in the formulation of monetary policy. The Fed must take into account the fact that the Treasury is faced with the task of selling huge amounts of government securities (that is, government IOUs) each year. Also, congressional committees hold hearings and issue reports on monetary policy and the operations of the Federal Reserve. These hearings and reports cannot fail to have some effect on Fed policy. In addition, since 1975, Congress has stipulated that the Fed must publish its long-term targets for growth in the money supply. Finally, the president may attempt to influence the Federal Reserve Board. To keep the board as free as possible from political pressure, members are appointed for long terms (14 years), and a term expires every 2 years. But since members frequently do not serve out their full terms, a president may be able to name more than two members during each term in office.

The Federal Reserve System

In the previous chapter, we briefly discussed the Federal Reserve and stressed its importance. Now we must look in some detail at its organization and functions. After a severe financial panic in 1907, when many banks failed (recall Case Study 20.1), there was strong public pressure to strengthen our banking system. At the same time, many people feared the centralized domination of the nation's banks. The result, after six years of negotiation and discussion, was the establishment by Congress of the Federal Reserve System in 1913.

Commercial Banks

As shown in Figure 21.1, the organization of the Federal Reserve System can be viewed as a triangle. At the base are the commercial banks. In 1980, Congress gave the Federal Reserve very substantial powers over all banks and nonbank depository institutions, even those that did not belong to the Federal Reserve System.

Federal Reserve Banks

In the middle of the triangle in Figure 21.1 are the 12 Federal Reserve Banks, each located in its own Federal Reserve district. The entire nation is divided into 12 Federal Reserve districts, with Federal Reserve Banks in New York, Chicago, Philadelphia, San Francisco, Boston, Cleveland, St. Louis, Kansas City, Atlanta, Richmond, Minneapolis, and Dallas. Though each of these banks is a corporation owned by the commercial banks, the commercial banks do not in any sense act as owners of the Federal Reserve Bank in their district. Instead, each Federal Reserve Bank is a public agency. These Federal Reserve Banks act as bankers' banks; they perform much the same sorts of functions for commercial banks that commercial banks perform for the public. That is, they hold the deposits of banks and make loans to them. In addition, the Federal Reserve Banks perform a function no commercial bank can perform: they issue Federal Reserve notes, which are the nation's currency.

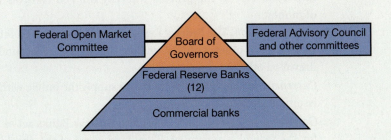

FIGURE 21.1

Organization of the Federal Reserve System

The Federal Reserve System contains commercial banks, the 12 regional Federal Reserve Banks, and the Board of Governors, as well as the Federal Open Market Committee and various advisory councils and committees.

The Board of Governors

Federal
Reserve Board

Federal
Open Market
Committee
(FOMC)

At the top of the triangle in Figure 21.1 is the Board of Governors of the Federal Reserve System. Located in Washington, D.C., this board, generally called the **Federal Reserve Board**, has seven members appointed by the president for 14-year terms. The board, which coordinates the activities of the Federal Reserve System, is supposed to be independent of partisan politics and to act to promote the nation's general economic welfare. It is responsible for supervising the operation of the money and banking system of the United States. The board is assisted by the **Federal Open Market Committee** (**FOMC**), which establishes policy concerning the purchase and sale of government securities. The Federal Open Market Committee is composed of the board plus the presidents of five Federal Reserve Banks. The board is also assisted by the Federal Advisory Council, a group of 12 commercial bankers that advises the board on banking policy.

Functions of the Federal Reserve

Central banks

The Federal Reserve Board, with the 12 Federal Reserve Banks, is the central bank of the United States. Every major country has a central bank. England has the Bank of England, and France has the Bank of France. **Central banks** are very important organizations, and their most important function is to help control the quantity of money. But this is not their only function. A central bank also handles the government's financial transactions and coordinates and controls the country's commercial banks. Specifically, the Federal Reserve System is charged with the following responsibilities:

> *Bank reserves.* The Federal Reserve Banks hold deposits, or reserves, of the commercial banks. As we have seen, these reserves play an important role in the process whereby the Fed controls the quantity of money.

> *Check collection.* The Federal Reserve System provides facilities for check collection. In other words, it enables a bank to collect funds for checks drawn on other banks.

> *Currency.* The Federal Reserve Banks supply the public with currency by issuing Federal Reserve notes.

> *Government fiscal agent.* The Federal Reserve Banks act as fiscal agents for the federal government. They hold some of the checking accounts of the U.S. Treasury and aid in the purchase and sale of government securities.

> *Bank supervision.* Federal Reserve Banks supervise the operation of the commercial banks. Recall our discussion of bank supervision and regulation in the previous chapter.

The Federal Reserve Banks: Their Consolidated Balance Sheet

We know that the Federal Reserve controls the money supply largely by controlling the quantity of bank reserves. To understand how the Federal Reserve can control the quantity of bank reserves, we must begin by examining the consolidated balance sheet of the 12 regional Federal Reserve Banks. Such a consolidated balance sheet is shown in Table 21.1. It pertains to August 22, 2012. As shown in Table 21.1, included among the assets of the Federal Reserve Banks are gold certificates, securities, and loans to commercial banks.

1. *Gold certificates* are warehouse receipts issued by the Treasury for gold bullion. For the present purposes, this item is less important than securities or loans to commercial banks.
2. The *securities* listed on the Federal Reserve Banks' balance sheet are U.S. government bonds, notes, and bills (bonds are long-term IOUs, notes are medium-term IOUs, and bills are short-term IOUs). By buying and selling these securities, the Federal Reserve exercises considerable leverage on the quantity of bank reserves.
3. The *loans to commercial banks* listed on the Federal Reserve Banks' balance sheet are loans of reserves that the Fed has made to commercial banks. The Fed can make such loans if it wants to. The interest rate charged for such loans (the discount rate) is discussed later.

According to Table 21.1, the liabilities of the Federal Reserve Banks are largely of three kinds: outstanding Federal Reserve notes, Treasury deposits, and reserves of banks.

TABLE 21.1

Consolidated Balance Sheet of the 12 Federal Reserve Banks November 20, 2013 (billions of dollars)

Assets	
Gold certificates	11
Securities	3,841
Loans to commercial banks and other assets	55
Total	*3,907*

Liabilities	
Outstanding Federal Reserve notes	1,177
Reserves of banks	2,559
Treasury deposits	48
Other liabilities and adjustments	123
Total	*3,907*

Source: Federal Reserve.

1. The *outstanding Federal Reserve notes* are the paper currency we use. Since these notes are debts of the Federal Reserve Banks, they are included among the banks' liabilities.

2. *Treasury deposits* are the deposits that the U.S. Treasury maintains at the Federal Reserve Banks. The Treasury draws checks on these deposits to pay its bills.

3. The *reserves of banks* were discussed in some detail in the previous chapter. Although these reserves are assets from the point of view of the commercial banks, they are liabilities from the point of view of the Federal Reserve Banks.

Open Market Operations

Table 21.1 shows that government securities constitute about 90 percent of the assets held by the Federal Reserve Banks. The market for government securities is huge and well developed. The Federal Reserve is part of this market. Sometimes it buys government securities; sometimes it sells them. Whether it is buying or selling—and how much—can have an impact on the quantity of bank reserves. Indeed, the most important means the Federal Reserve has to control the quantity of bank reserves (and thus the quantity of excess reserves) are **open market operations**, which is the name given to the purchase and sale by the Federal Reserve of U.S. government securities in the open market.

Open market operations

Buying Securities

Suppose that the Federal Reserve buys $1 million worth of government securities in the open market and the seller of these securities is General Motors.[2] To determine the effect of this transaction on the quantity of bank reserves, we look at the effect on the balance sheet of the Fed and the balance sheet of Bank of America, General Motors' bank.[3] In this transaction, the Fed receives $1 million in government securities and gives General Motors a check for $1 million. When General Motors deposits this check to its account at Bank of America, the bank's demand deposits and reserves increase by $1 million.

Hence, as shown in Table 21.2, the left-hand side of the Fed's balance sheet shows a $1 million increase in government securities, and the right-hand side shows a $1 million increase in bank reserves. The left-hand side of Bank of America's balance sheet shows a $1 million increase in reserves, and the right-hand side shows a $1 million increase in demand deposits. Clearly, the Fed has added $1 million to the banks' reserves. The situation is somewhat analogous to the $10,000 deposit at bank A in the previous chapter.

---

[2] Large corporations often hold quantities of government securities.
[3] For simplicity, we assume that General Motors has only one bank, Bank of America. This may not be the case, but it makes no difference to the point we make here. We make a similar assumption regarding JPMorgan Chase in the next section.

TABLE 21.2	Assets		Liabilities and Net Worth	
Effect of Fed's Purchasing $1 Million of Government Securities (millions of dollars)	A. Effect on Fed's balance sheet			
	Government securities	+ 1	Member bank reserves	+ 1
	B. Effect on balance sheet of Bank of America			
	Reserves	+ 1	Demand deposits	+ 1

Selling Securities

Suppose that the Federal Reserve sells $1 million worth of government securities in the open market. They are bought by JPMorgan Chase, a huge bank. What effect does this transaction have on the quantity of bank reserves? To find out, we look at the balance sheet of the Fed and the balance sheet of JPMorgan Chase. When JPMorgan Chase buys the government securities from the Fed, the Fed gives JPMorgan Chase the securities in exchange for JPMorgan Chase's check for $1 million. This means that JPMorgan Chase's demand deposits and reserves decrease by $1 million.

Hence, as shown in Table 21.3, the left-hand side of the Fed's balance sheet shows a $1 million decrease in government securities, and the right-hand side shows a $1 million decrease in reserves. The left-hand side of JPMorgan Chase's balance sheet shows a $1 million decrease in reserves, and the right-hand side shows a $1 million decrease in demand deposits. Clearly, the Fed has reduced the reserves of the banks by $1 million.

The Federal Open Market Committee

As indicated already, open market operations are the Fed's most important method for controlling the money supply. The Federal Reserve adds to bank reserves when it buys government securities and reduces bank reserves when it sells them. Obviously, the extent to which the Federal Reserve increases or reduces bank reserves depends in an important way on the amount of

TABLE 21.3	Assets		Liabilities and Net Worth	
Effect of Fed's Selling $1 Million of Government Securities (millions of dollars)	A. Effect on Fed's balance sheet			
	Government securities	− 1	Member bank reserves	− 1
	B. Effect on balance sheet of JPMorgan Chase			
	Reserves	− 1	Demand deposits	− 1

government securities it buys or sells. The greater the amount, the greater the increase or decrease in bank reserves.

The power to decide on the amount of government securities the Fed should buy or sell at any given moment rests with the Federal Open Market Committee. This group wields an extremely powerful influence over bank reserves and the nation's money supply. Every three or four weeks, the Federal Open Market Committee meets to discuss the current situation and trends and gives instructions to the manager of the Open Market Account at the Federal Reserve Bank of New York, who actually buys and sells the government securities.

Changes in the Legal Reserve Requirements

Legal reserve requirements

Open market operations are not the only means the Federal Reserve has to influence the money supply. Another way is to change the **legal reserve requirements**. In other words, the Federal Reserve Board can change the amount of reserves banks must hold for every dollar of demand deposits. As we saw in Chapter 20, in 1934, Congress gave the Federal Reserve Board the power to set, within certain broad limits, the legally required ratio of reserves to deposits for both demand and time deposits. From time to time, the Fed uses this power to change legal reserve requirements. For example, in 1958, it cut the legally required ratio of reserves to deposits in big city banks from 17.5 percent to 16.5 percent; the ratio remained at 16.5 percent until 1968, when it was raised to 17 percent. Table 21.4 shows the legal reserve requirements in 2012.

Effect of an Increase in the Reserve Requirements

The effect of an increase in the legally required ratio of reserves to deposits is that banks must hold larger reserves to support the existing amount of demand deposits. This, in turn, means that banks with little or no excess reserves have to sell securities, refuse to renew loans, and reduce their demand deposits to meet the new reserve requirements. For example, suppose that a bank has $1 million in reserves and $6 million in demand deposits. If the

TABLE 21.4

Legal Reserve Requirements of Depository Institutions, 2012

Type and Size of Deposits	Reserve Requirements (percent of deposits)
Net transaction accounts	
Up to $71 million	3
Over $71 million	10
Nonpersonal time deposits	0

Source: Federal Reserve.

TABLE 21.5

Consolidated Balance Sheet of All Banks, before and after an Increase (from 16 Percent to 20 Percent) in the Legal Reserve Requirement (billions of dollars)

Assets		Liabilities	
A. Before the increase in the legal reserve requirements			
Reserves	1.00	Demand deposits	6.25
Loans and investments	7.25	Net worth	2.00
Total	8.25	Total	8.25
B. After the increase in the legal reserve requirement			
Reserves	1.00	Demand deposits	5.00
Loans and investments	6.00	Net worth	2.00
Total	7.00	Total	7.00

legal reserve requirement is 16 percent, it has excess reserves of $1 million – $960,000 (0.16 × $6 million), or $40,000. It is in good shape. If the legal reserve requirement is increased to 20 percent, this bank now needs $1.2 million (0.20 × $6 million) in reserves. Since it only has $1 million in reserves, it must sell securities or refuse to renew loans.

Consider now what happens to the banking system as a whole. Clearly, an increase in the legally required ratio of reserves to deposits means that with a given amount of reserves, the banking system can maintain less demand deposits than before. For example, if the banking system has $1 billion in total reserves, it can support $1 billion ÷ 0.16, or $6.25 billion, in demand deposits when the legal reserve requirement is 16 percent. But it can support only $1 billion ÷ 0.20, or $5 billion, in demand deposits when the legal reserve requirement is 20 percent (see Table 21.5).[4] Therefore, increases in the legal reserve requirement tend to reduce the amount of demand deposits (bank money) the banking system can support.

Effect of a Decrease in the Reserve Requirements

What is the effect of a decrease in the legally required ratio of reserves to deposits? In this scenario, banks are able to hold smaller reserves to support the existing amount of demand deposits; this, in turn, means that banks suddenly find themselves with excess reserves. If the banking system has $1 billion in reserves and $5 billion in demand deposits, there are no excess reserves

[4] We assume arbitrarily in Table 21.5 that the total net worth of the banks is $2 billion. Obviously, this assumption makes no difference to the point we make here. Also, for simplicity, here and later, we ignore checkable deposits other than demand deposits.

THE INDEPENDENCE OF THE FEDERAL RESERVE

Janet Yellen with President Obama and Ben Bernanke

During World War II, the Federal Reserve was called on to buy up Treasury securities to aid the Treasury in financing the war. Buying bonds pumped lots of money into circulation; this could have caused inflation had not the high employment of the war effort, combined with wage and price controls, offset the inflationary pressure. When the war ended, the Treasury insisted on continuing this arrangement with the Fed. In effect, the Fed lost control of the money supply, and Marriner Eccles, Fed chair in the late 1940s, called the agreement an "engine of inflation."

In 1951, the Fed and the Treasury worked out an accord that gave the Fed a freer hand in conducting monetary policy: the Fed would temporarily support long-term government securities but would thereafter be free to

follow a more flexible policy consistent with noninflationary growth. Nevertheless, the independence of the Fed has been and will continue to be the subject of much debate.

Some say the Fed is responsible to Congress. Its enabling legislation was passed by Congress in 1913, and it presumably could be reorganized should it sufficiently rouse Congress' wrath. But Congress moves with nothing if not deliberate speed, and it seldom has sought to influence the Federal Reserve through major new legislation. The president fills vacancies on the Board of Governors, but since terms on the board run for 14 years, presidents may have to wait until their second term to appoint a majority of the board.

In fact, as knowledgeable observers often agree, there are two groups that, without appearing prominently on the organization chart, exercise considerable influence over the policies of the Fed. One is the business community—a group with a definite interest in preserving the value of a dollar. The other is the board's professional staff of senior economists. Administrations come and go, but staff economists remain, and their uniquely detailed knowledge of the workings of the Fed assure them a hearing at 20th and Constitution.

All chairs of the Fed—Janet Yellen, Ben Bernanke, Alan Greenspan, Paul Volcker, G. William Miller, and Arthur Burns in recent years—have been sensitive to the ultimate vulnerability of the Fed's independence and so have been reluctant to buck administration policy too dramatically. Whether the Federal Reserve's current procedures can survive a general call for more accountability is an open question. In early 1975, Congress passed a resolution that the Federal Reserve must publish its targets for growth in the money supply. But the extent to which this really has tied the Fed's hands is by no means clear.

when the legal reserve requirement is 20 percent. But suppose the Federal Reserve lowers the legal reserve requirement to 16 percent. Now the amount of legally required reserves is $800 million ($5 billion × 0.16), so the banks have $200 million in excess reserves; this means that they can increase the amount of their demand deposits. Therefore, decreases in the legal reserve requirements tend to increase the amount of demand deposits (bank money) the banking system can support.

Changes in legal reserve requirements are a rather drastic way to influence the money supply; they are to open market operations as a cleaver is to a scalpel and so are made infrequently. For example, for about 10 years (from April 1958 to January 1968), no change at all was made in legal reserve requirements for demand deposits in city banks. Nonetheless, the Fed can change legal reserve requirements if it wants to. And there can be no doubt about the potential impact of such changes. Large changes in reserve requirements can rapidly alter bank reserves and the money supply. When the Fed eased credit in December 1990, it eliminated the 3 percent reserve requirement on certificates of deposit held by corporations with maturities of less than 18 months—and quickly added billions of dollars to bank reserves.

Changes in the Discount Rate

Discount rate

Still another way that the Federal Reserve can influence the money supply is through changes in the discount rate. As shown by the balance sheet of the Federal Reserve Banks (in Table 21.1), commercial banks can borrow from the Federal Reserve when their reserves are low (if the Fed is willing). This is one function of the Federal Reserve. The interest rate the Fed charges the banks for loans is called the **discount rate**, and the Fed can increase or decrease the discount rate whenever it chooses. Increases in the discount rate discourage borrowing from the Fed, while decreases in the discount rate encourage it.

TABLE 21.6

Average Discount Rate, 1963–2013

Year	Discount Rate (percent)	Year	Discount Rate (percent)	Year	Discount Rate (percent)
1963	3.23	1980	11.77	1997	5.00
1964	3.55	1981	13.41	1998	4.92
1965	4.04	1982	11.02	1999	4.62
1966	4.50	1983	8.50	2000	5.73
1967	4.19	1984	8.80	2001	3.40
1968	5.17	1985	7.69	2002	2.50
1969	5.87	1986	6.33	2003	2.11
1970	5.95	1987	5.66	2004	2.34
1971	4.88	1988	6.20	2005	4.19
1972	4.50	1989	6.93	2006	5.96
1973	6.45	1990	6.98	2007	5.86
1974	7.83	1991	5.45	2008	2.39
1975	6.25	1992	3.25	2009	0.50
1976	5.50	1993	3.00	2010	0.72
1977	5.46	1994	3.60	2011	0.75
1978	7.46	1995	5.21	2012	0.75
1979	10.28	1996	5.02	2013	0.75

Source: Federal Reserve Board.

The discount rate can change substantially and fairly often (see Table 21.6). For instance, the discount rate was increased from 12 percent to 13 percent in early 1980, then reduced to 12 percent in May, 11 percent in June, and 10 percent in July, after which it was raised back to 13 percent by December 1980. When the Fed increases the discount rate (relative to other interest rates), it makes it more expensive for banks to augment their reserves by borrowing from the Fed; hence, it tightens up a bit on the money supply. On the other hand, when the Fed decreases the discount rate, it is cheaper for banks to augment their reserves in this way; hence, the money supply eases up a bit. Therefore, from 1990 to 1993, the Fed, trying to stimulate a weak economy, reduced the discount rate from 7 percent to 3 percent. Between 1994 and 1995, the Fed raised the discount rate to above 5 percent to cool down the economy. During the emerging markets crisis (1997–1998), the Fed reversed course and cut interest rates. In 1999 and 2000, as the crisis dissipated and the U.S. economy began to show signs of overheating, the Fed began raising rates once again. However, by 2001, the economy was in a recession and the Fed had to cut interest rates again. The subsequent recovery in 2002 and 2003 was so weak that the Fed lowered the discount rate to 2 percent by mid-2003. As the recovery gained momentum, the Fed raised the discount rate again, pushing it all the way to 6.25 percent by early 2007. However, during the financial crisis of 2008–2009 it, once again slashed the discount rate—this time all the way down to 0.50 percent.

The Fed is largely passive in these relations with the banks. It cannot make the banks borrow. It can only set the discount rate and see how many banks show up at the "discount window" to borrow. Also, the Fed does not allow banks to borrow on a permanent or long-term basis. They are expected to use this privilege only to tide themselves over for short periods, not to relend at a profit. To discourage banks from excessive use of the borrowing privilege, the discount rate is kept relatively close to short-term market interest rates.

Most economists agree that changes in the discount rate have relatively little direct impact, and the Fed's open market operations can and do offset easily the amount the banks borrow. Certainly, changes in the discount rate cannot have anything like the direct effect on bank reserves of open market operations or changes in legal reserve requirements. The principal importance of changes in the discount rate lies in their effects on people's expectations. When the Fed increases the discount rate, this is generally interpreted as a sign that the Fed will tighten credit and the money supply. A cut in the discount rate is generally interpreted as a sign of easier money and lower interest rates.

EXPLORING FURTHER

More on the Effects of Monetary Policy

In this section, we describe how monetary policy influences the aggregate demand curve. We will discuss the view that changes in the money supply were an important cause of the Great Depression, and we will present some evidence concerning the lags in the effects of monetary policy.

Monetary Policy and the Aggregate Demand Curve

Monetary policy has an important effect on the aggregate demand curve. As you may recall from Chapter 16, the aggregate demand curve is drawn on the assumption that the money supply is fixed. An increase in the money supply shifts the aggregate demand curve to the right. A decrease in the money supply shifts the aggregate demand curve to the left. Because an increase in the money supply lowers interest rates and increases investment, it raises aggregate demand (when the price level is held constant).

FIGURE 21.2

Effect of Increase in the Money Supply

If the Fed increases the money supply so that the aggregate demand curve shifts from AD_1 to AD_2, the price level increases from P_1 to P_2.

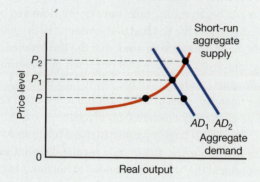

Suppose that the economy is experiencing inflationary pressures. Specifically, assume that the price level is P and the aggregate demand curve is AD_1, as shown in Figure 21.2. If the money supply remains fixed, the price level increases to P_1, at which point aggregate demand and short-run aggregate supply are equal.

Suppose that the Fed increases the money supply to such an extent that the aggregate demand curve shifts from AD_1 to AD_2. When the price level increases from P to P_1, inflationary pressures remain. The price level must increase from P_1 to P_2, at which point aggregate demand and short-run supply are equal. Therefore, inflation does not abate after the increase in the price level to P_1. (And so long as the Fed continues to increase the money supply at a relatively rapid rate, it will not abate.)

What Caused the Great Depression?

There has been much disagreement over what caused the Great Depression of the 1930s. According to Nobel laureate Milton Friedman and Anna J. Schwartz, the Great Depression was due in large measure to changes in the money supply, indicated here:

TABLE 21.7

Year	Money Supply (billions of dollars)	
	M1	**M2**
1929	26.6	46.6
1930	25.8	45.7
1931	24.1	42.7
1932	21.1	36.0
1933	19.9	32.2
1934	21.9	34.4

CRISIS MANAGEMENT BY THE FED

There is almost universal agreement that the Fed was at least partly to blame for the depth of the Great Depression, and some economists have given it a failing grade for crisis management in the 1930s (see "What Caused the Great Depression?" in this section). However, the Fed has received much higher grades for crisis management during the last couple of decades. In 1987, 1998, 2001, and most importantly in 2008 and 2009, the central bank moved quickly to prevent financial panics from turning into anything worse.

On Monday, October 19, 1987, since dubbed Black Monday, the Dow Jones Industrial Average plummeted over 500 points (a 35 percent drop in the market). The panic that ensued brought financial markets to a virtual standstill, and there was a serious threat of one or more large securities firms collapsing as investors fled the stock market. Concerned about a financial meltdown, the Fed moved quickly. Before markets opened on Tuesday, October 20, Fed chair Alan Greenspan announced the Fed's "readiness to serve as a source of liquidity to support the economic and financial system." In addition to this unprecedented announcement, the Fed made it clear that it would provide discount loans to any bank that would make loans to the securities industry. The stock market recovered and a recession was averted. However, later, some analysts blamed the Fed for being too generous and setting the stage for higher inflation in 1989 and 1990.

On August 17, 1998, a little more than a year after the beginning of the Asian financial crisis, Russia defaulted on its short-term domestic debt and devalued its currency, allowing the ruble to fall 35 percent in one day. Western investors had poured money into the Russian government bond markets believing (foolishly, in retrospect) that the Russian government would neither default on its obligations nor devalue. In the panic that followed, investors not only fled Russian markets but also other emerging markets, creating a severe liquidity crunch in global financial markets.

Many banks and mutual funds felt the squeeze, and one large hedge fund, Long-Term Capital Management (LTCM), almost went under. Hedge funds typically invest in high-risk, high-reward financial instruments (such as Russian government bonds) and, in so doing, provide liquidity in many markets. More often than not, their bets pay off and they make a lot of money for their investors. However, when such bets fail in the spectacular way they did in the summer of 1998, then highly leveraged funds, such as LTCM, can fail. It is no small irony that two of the principals of LTCM, Myron Scholes and Robert Merton, had won the Nobel Prize in economics a year earlier for their pioneering work in options pricing theory.

The near collapse of LTCM sent shock waves through the U.S. and global financial markets. The Dow Jones fell almost 20 percent from August to October. The Fed began to worry that the problems of LTCM would spill over into the banking sector. It engineered a swift rescue of the hedge fund by persuading a consortium of large banks to keep lending money to LTCM. It also pumped liquidity into the U.S. financial system and cut the federal funds rate by 75 basis points (0.75 percentage point). The liquidity crunch was eased and the financial panic dissipated.

In 2001, the Fed once again demonstrated its adeptness in reacting quickly to crises. The bursting of the high-tech bubble in early 2000 and its ripple effects throughout the economy set the stage for the recession that started in the first quarter of 2001. Since inflation had remained low in the boom that ended in the millennium (thanks to strong productivity growth; see Case Study 23.3), the Fed had the leeway to cut interest rates aggressively, and it did. Between January and August 2001, the federal funds rate was lowered from 6.5 percent to 3.5 percent.

The terrorist attacks of September 11, 2001, on New York and Washington closed down the U.S. stock market for four days and paralyzed the U.S. and world financial systems. Before the stock market reopened on Monday, September 17, the Fed announced that it would cut interest rates another 0.5 percent. Other central banks around the world followed suit. Global stock markets initially saw big drops in share prices. However, within a matter of days, these markets were stabilized and began growing again.

By the end of 2001, the Fed had cut interest rates another 1.25 percent, bringing the federal funds rate all the way down to 1.75 percent. Partly as a result, the 2001 recession ended up being one of the mildest in the postwar period.

The Fed was, arguably, put to its greatest test since the 1930s during the financial crisis of 2008–2009. The collapse of Lehman Brothers in September 2008 and the subsequent freezing up of global credit threatened to plunge the U.S. and world economies into another depression.

With Ben Bernanke (a scholar of the policy mistakes that led to the Great Depression) at the helm of the Fed, the U.S. central bank effectively pulled out all the stops. Not only did Bernanke and his colleagues push short-term interest rates all the way down to zero, but they also tried to push long-term interest rates down as well—something the Fed does not normally do. It also engaged in other unorthodox policies, such as purchases of mortgage-backed securities.

Did it work? Yes and no. The recession was officially declared over by June 2009, and by early 2011, the level of inflation-adjusted GDP was above where it was before the financial crisis. Unfortunately, employment was still about 7 million below where it was at the beginning of the Great Recession. Some of this was simply due to the fact that the recovery in employment always lags the recovery in GDP. Some of it reflects the reality that the Fed is not all-powerful.

Nevertheless, in the final analysis, there is little doubt that the Fed did a much better job of crisis management in the 1980s, 1990s, and 2000s than in the 1930s.

Following the substantial drop in GDP after 1929, the Fed, according to Friedman and Schwartz, did not undertake large-scale open market purchases until 1932. Friedman and Schwartz, among others, argue that this was an incorrect policy and that the Fed should have adopted a more expansionary policy in the early 1930s. The Friedman-Schwartz interpretation of the Great Depression has been challenged by MIT's Peter Temin, who argues that the decline in the money supply from 1929 to 1933 was due to a reduction in the demand for money. A drop in investment or a downward shift in the consumption function might have reduced GDP. The reduction in GDP would have reduced the demand for money. The result was a decrease in interest rates, which could reduce the money supply. For example, banks might have been induced to hold more excess reserves. However, Ben Bernanke, former chair of the Federal Reserve Board, also spent much of his academic career studying the policy mistakes that led up to the Great Depression. He generally agrees with the Friedman-Schwartz view that in the 1930s, the Fed effectively tightened monetary policy, turning a garden variety recession into something far, far worse (see Viewpoint for Analysis at the end of this chapter).

How Quickly Does Monetary Policy Work?

An enormous amount of statistical and econometric research has been carried out to determine how quickly an unanticipated recession can be combated by monetary policy. According to Robert Gordon of Northwestern University, the total lag between the occurrence of such an unanticipated slowdown in economic activity and the impact of monetary policy is about 14 months. In other words, it takes about 14 months for the Federal Reserve to become aware of the slowdown, to take the appropriate action, and to have these actions affect real GDP. According to Gordon, the lags are approximately as follows:

TABLE 21.8

Lag	Months
From slowdown to reflection in economic data	2
From reflection in economic data to change in money supply	3
From change in money supply to effect on real GDP	9
Total	*14*

By the time the effects of the expansionary monetary policy are felt, the economy may not need additional stimulus. Suppose you were driving a car in which the wheels responded to turns of the steering wheel with a substantial lag. The problems would be analogous to those confronting the Fed.

REVIEW AND PRACTICE

Summary

1 The Federal Reserve System is responsible for regulating and controlling the money supply. Established in 1913, the Federal Reserve System is composed of commercial banks, 12 regional Federal Reserve Banks, and the Federal Reserve Board, which coordinates the activities of the system. The Federal Reserve is the central bank of the United States.

2 Monetary policy is concerned with the money supply and interest rates. Its purpose is to attain and maintain full employment without inflation.

3 When a recession seems imminent, the monetary authorities are likely to increase the money supply and reduce interest rates. When the economy is in danger of overheating and inflation threatens, the monetary authorities are likely to rein in the money supply and push up interest rates.

4 Although monetary policy is influenced by Congress, the Treasury, and other segments of the government and the public at large, the chief responsibility for the formulation of monetary policy lies with the Federal Reserve Board and the Federal Open Market Committee. To a very large extent, monetary policy operates by changing the quantity of bank reserves.

5 The most important tool of monetary policy is open market operations, which involve buying and selling government securities in the open market by the Federal Reserve. When the Fed buys government securities, this increases bank reserves. When the Fed sells government securities, this reduces bank reserves.

6 The Fed can also tighten or ease the money supply by increasing or decreasing legal reserve requirements or the discount rate.

*7 [5]Monetary policy influences the aggregate demand curve. Increases in the money supply tend to push the aggregate demand curve to the right. Decreases in the money supply tend to push the aggregate demand curve to the left.

Problems and Questions

1 Suppose that the Federal Reserve buys $5 million worth of government securities from General Motors. Insert the effects in the blanks that follow.

Effects on Fed's balance sheet:

Securities _____ Member bank reserves _____

Effects on balance sheet of General Motors' bank:

Reserves _____ Demand deposits _____

2 Suppose that the Federal Reserve sells $5 million worth of government securities to General Motors. What is the effect on the quantity of bank reserves?

3 "When the Fed increases the legal reserve requirements, it loosens credit, because the banks have more reserves." Comment and evaluate.

[5] Starred (*) item refers to material covered in Exploring Further.

4 If the Federal Reserve buys $500 million worth of government securities, does this tend to shift the aggregate demand curve to the right? To the left? Explain.

5 Suppose you have $5,000 to invest. At a restaurant, you overhear someone saying that the Fed is almost certain to increase the discount rate dramatically. If this rumor is correct, do you think that you should invest now or wait until after the increase in the discount rate? Or doesn't it matter? Be sure to explain the reasons for your preference (or lack of it) in this regard.

Key Terms

monetary policy
Federal Reserve Board
Federal Open Market Committee (FOMC)
central banks
open market operations
legal reserve requirements
discount rate

Viewpoint for Analysis

In a lecture at George Washington University on March 20, 2012, former Fed chair Ben Bernanke said: "[In the 1930s] . . . the Federal Reserve failed in this first challenge in both parts of its mission. It did not use monetary policy aggressively to prevent deflation and the collapse of the economy, so it failed in the economic stability function. And it didn't adequately perform its function as lender of last resort, allowing many bank failures and a resulting contraction in credit and also with the money supply."[6]

(a) What is meant by the term *lender of last resort*? Why is such a role important?

(b) If there is no lender of last resort, where can banks get help when they run into trouble?

(c) What is the mechanism whereby a bank collapse leads to credit tightening?

---

[6] www.federalreserve.gov/newsevents/lectures/about.htm

Supply Shocks and Inflation

LEARNING OBJECTIVES

➤ To explain how supply shocks affect inflation

➤ To determine the relationship between supply-side inflation and demand-side inflation

➤ To explore the nature of stagflation

➤ To recognize the disadvantage of wage and price controls

➤ *(Exploring Further)* To consider how the Fed can accommodate supply-side inflation

Stagflation

Supply shocks—a spike in oil prices or a bumper crop that pushes down food prices—can push up or push down the rate of inflation. In the 1970s and early 1980s, successive oil shocks dramatically raised the rate of inflation in the United States and other industrialized economies. During the late 1990s, the emerging markets financial crisis triggered a collapse in commodity prices and lowered inflation in most of the world. Therefore, in the 1970s and 1980s, the United States had high unemployment and inflation (**stagflation**), and in the late 1990s, we had low unemployment and inflation. This contradicts the logic of the Phillips curve (introduced in Chapter 19) and means that the task of policy makers, especially the Fed, is far more complicated. In this chapter, we continue our discussion of inflation and anti-inflationary measures. (We explore the topic of supply shocks further in Chapter 26.)

During the supply shocks of the 1970s, and previously during wartime, the United States and other countries adopted price and wage controls to combat inflation. But few economists or policy makers believe that such controls are either effective in the long run or an appropriate anti-inflationary tool. This chapter also looks at the case for and against such controls.

Supply-Side Inflation

As we saw in Chapter 19, demand-side inflation is not the only kind of inflation. There is another kind: supply-side inflation. According to some observers, strong labor unions sometimes play a role in supply-side inflation. By pushing up wages, unions may increase firms' costs; then, in an attempt to protect their profit margins, firms push up the prices of their goods and services. These price increases affect the costs of other firms and the consumer's cost of living. As the cost of living goes up, labor feels entitled to, and obtains, higher wages to offset the higher living costs. Firms again pass on the cost increase to the consumer in the form of a price increase. This so-called **wage-price spiral** can be important in supply-side inflation.

Wage-price spiral

Also, increases in the price of materials may play a major role in supply-side inflation. When the oil-producing countries (like Saudi Arabia and Iraq) raised the price of crude oil in 1974 and 1979, this resulted in price increases in a host of products made directly or indirectly from petroleum and helped shift the aggregate supply curve upward and to the left, as shown in Figure 22.1. The result, as we know from Chapter 19, was substantial inflation in 1974 and 1979.

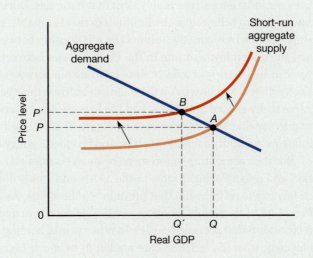

FIGURE 22.1

Increase in the Price Level Due to a Shift in the Short-Run Aggregate Supply Curve

According to many economists, the inflation of the middle and late 1970s was due in considerable part to shifts upward and to the left in the aggregate supply curve because of shortages and price increases in oil and other materials. Such a shift results in an increase in the price level from *P* to *P'*.

Difficulties in Distinguishing Supply-Side from Demand-Side Inflation

Generally, it is difficult, if not impossible, to sort out supply-side inflation from demand-side inflation. For example, an increase in aggregate demand may raise firms' demand for labor and cause workers to demand higher wages; this in turn may lead firms to raise their prices. In such a case, the inflation may occur from the demand side, in that the ultimate cause is an increase in aggregate demand, but also from the supply side, in that the proximate cause of the increase in the price level is an increase in wages.

It is also important to note that a supply-side inflation of the sort shown in Figure 22.1 is unlikely to continue for a long period of time unless the Fed "accommodates" or "validates" it by following with policies that shift the aggregate demand curve to the right. If the aggregate demand curve does not shift, the inflation dies out. In Figure 22.1, once the economy moves from point *A* to point *B*, the inflation is over. There are no further increases in the price level. (For further discussion, see Exploring Further.)

The Instability of the Phillips Curve

In Chapter 19, we introduced the Phillips curve and discussed the tradeoff between inflation and unemployment that it implies. During the 1960s, economists came to believe that the Phillips curve was a stable, predictable relationship. Panel A of Figure 22.2 shows the relationship between the inflation rate and the unemployment rate in the United States between 1955 and 1969. As you can see, there was a fairly close relationship between them in this period. Economists relied heavily on these data to buttress their belief that the Phillips curve really existed and that it had the hypothesized shape. It is no exaggeration to say that the Phillips curve in Figure 22.2 (the heavy line) had a major influence on both economic analysis and economic policy in the 1960s.

But then something unforeseen (by most economists) occurred. The inflation and unemployment rates in the 1970s and 1980s did not conform at all closely to the relationship that prevailed in the 1960s. As shown in panel B of Figure 22.2, the points for 1970 to 1990 lie far above and to the right of the relationship that prevailed earlier. In other words, holding constant the unemployment rate, the inflation rate tended to be much higher in the 1970s and 1980s than in the 1960s. Or, holding the inflation rate constant, the unemployment rate tended to be much higher in the 1970s and 1980s than in the 1960s. Whichever way you look at it, this departure from the earlier relationship between inflation and unemployment was bad news.

Why did this departure from the earlier relationship occur? In part, it occurred because the inflation of the 1970s was to a considerable extent of the

FIGURE 22.2

Relationship between the Inflation Rate and the Unemployment Rate, 1955–2012

Source: Economic Report of the President, 1979, 1991, 2000, and 2013.

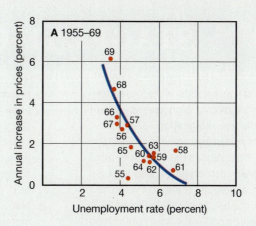

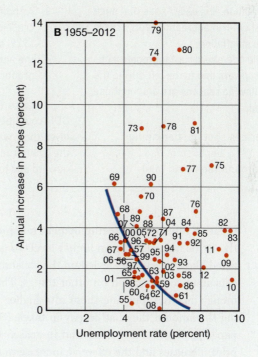

supply-side, not the demand-side, variety. When we explained in Chapter 19 why the Phillips curve might exist, we assumed that all inflation was demand-side inflation. Clearly, this was not true during the 1970s. On the contrary, there was a shift to the left in the aggregate supply curve due to price hikes in oil, agricultural products, and other raw materials. Because of this shift, both the

CASE STUDY 22.1

STAGFLATION

The 1970s and early 1980s were characterized by a combination of high unemployment and high inflation: stagflation. (The term *stagflation* was coined by combining *stagnation* and *inflation*.) What caused this turn of events? According to many economists, it was because the short-run aggregate supply curve shifted upward and to the left, as shown in Figure 22.1. Since a reduction in national output means high unemployment and an increase in the price level means inflation, it is easy to see that such a shift in the short-run aggregate supply curve might result in stagflation.

But why did the short-run aggregate supply curve shift upward and to the left during the 1970s? The following reasons are among those frequently cited:

1. Food prices shot up, beginning in late 1972, because of bad crops around the world (and the disappearance of Peruvian anchovies, which caused a drop in the fish catch off the South American coast). The drop in the fish catch meant the almost total elimination of fishmeal, a primary substance fed to beef cattle.

2. Many other raw-material prices increased rapidly because of worldwide shortages.

3. As pointed out in the text, the price of crude oil increased greatly in 1974, 1979, and other years because of the actions of Arab and other oil-producing countries.

Because of these factors, a given level of GDP could be produced only at a higher price level than was previously the case. That is, the short-run aggregate supply curve shifted upward and to the left.

inflation rate and the unemployment rate increased. And the rapid inflation of the 1970s helped bring on higher levels of unemployment. The oil price hikes acted like an excise tax levied on the consumer; they reduced the amount that consumers could spend on other things. The general inflation raised people's money incomes, pushing them into higher income tax brackets and increasing the amount they had to pay in taxes. (Similarly, the inflation swelled the paper profits of many firms and increased their tax bills.) Because of the oil price increases and the effective increase in taxes, as well as other factors, like the decline in the stock market, consumers cut back on their spending. Therefore, the equilibrium value of GDP fell.

In the middle to late 1990s, the Phillips curve shifted once again, this time to the left. The cluster of data points was again very reminiscent of the 1960s, with unemployment rates of 4 percent and inflation rates between 2 and 3 percent. There were at least two reasons for this fortuitous turn of events. First, the emerging markets crisis, which started in Asia in the summer of 1997 and subsequently spread to Russia and Latin America, brought about a sharp decline in commodity prices and a drop in the rate of inflation. This had the same effect as a tax cut and resulted in a boom in consumer spending in 1998 and 1999. The second trend that shifted the Phillips curve back was much stronger productivity growth in the late 1990s (see Chapter 23). Both these trends pushed the supply curve in Figure 22.1 down and to the right.

The decade of the 2000s also did not validate the notion of a stable Phillips curve. This was a decade of demand shocks (the Great Recession of 2008–2009) and huge swings in the prices of oil and other commodities. Thus, while the big increase in the unemployment rate from 2008 to 2010 would have suggested a large fall in the rate of inflation, the volatility in commodity prices pushed inflation up (in 2009 and 2011) as well as down (in 2008 and 2010).

The Transitory Nature of the Tradeoff Between Inflation and Unemployment

Another reason for the collapse of the Phillips curve is that policy makers (and some economists) misinterpreted this curve and attempted to establish combinations of inflation and unemployment that were unsustainable. As seen in earlier chapters, the economy, left to its own devices, tends to eliminate gaps between actual and potential output. By doing so, it makes certain points on the Phillips curve unsustainable. That is, if the government pushes the economy to any of these points, the economy will not stay there.

Leading economists like Milton Friedman and Edmund Phelps pointed out that the Phillips curve in Figure 19.3 is only a short-run relationship. They were not surprised that, holding constant the unemployment rate, the rate of inflation was higher in the 1970s than in the 1960s. In their view, expansionary monetary and fiscal policies that resulted in inflation reduce unemployment only temporarily, with the result that the rate of inflation tends to accelerate.

Their basic point was that the Phillips curve in the long run is vertical. That is, the unemployment rate in the long run is the same, regardless of the inflation rate. There is a certain natural (or full-employment) rate of unemployment, which is determined by how long workers search before taking a new job. The more reluctant they are to take unattractive or low-paying jobs, the higher the natural rate of unemployment. Economists who stress the importance of structural unemployment argue that the natural rate of unemployment depends, too, on the rates at which changes in technology and tastes occur and the speed with which workers in declining industries can be retrained for jobs in expanding industries.

HOW SERIOUS OF A THREAT IS DEFLATION?

After two bouts of double-digit inflation in the mid-1970s and early 1980s, the United States saw a trend decline in its inflation rate to the low single digits in the 2000s (4 percent or lower), a process sometimes referred to as disinflation. Much of the credit for this improvement goes to the Fed, which started taking a tougher stance against inflation in the early 1980s and has been vigilant ever since. The Fed's job has been made easier by a shift in popular opinion and political consensus against inflation. The absence of major supply shocks in the past couple of decades also helped.

In the mid-1990s, a small but vocal group of analysts began asserting that inflation was dead because of the structural changes in the U.S. and global economies. They based this conclusion on three trends: (1) labor-saving technologies that raise productivity and help keep down price pressures; (2) a decline in the membership and power of unions, which has kept a lid on wage growth; and (3) increased competition both in the United States (because of deregulation and privatization) and from abroad (because of fierce competition from low-wage countries).

While there is agreement among economists that technology and globalization have allowed the United States and other economies to grow somewhat faster than in the past before inflation takes off, this is a far cry from saying that inflation is dead. Moreover, the three trends cited as causes of inflation's demise have been a part of the American economic landscape for some time, and their influence may be overstated by those who believe that inflation is headed inexorably lower. The United States is still not a very open economy, with exports

Physician making a virtual house call using time-saving technology

and imports each accounting for only about 15 percent of GDP. Therefore, foreign competition only has a limited impact on the economy. Also, a majority of the service sectors of the economy, which account for over 75 percent of jobs, generally do not compete in the global marketplace. So while the structural changes in the global economy may have helped reduce inflationary pressures, they were not the principal cause of disinflation. The lower inflation we enjoy today is, in large measure, due to more sensible macroeconomic policies.

By the early 2000s, the steady drop in the inflation rate began to alarm many analysts, who were concerned that the United States would lapse into a period of outright deflation, much like Japan in the 1990s or the more virulent form that plagued the United States in the 1930s. Deflation is a situation in which prices fall and inflation turns negative.

Both earlier encounters with deflation were preceded by stock and property market bubbles, which, when they burst, triggered massive wealth destruction and serious banking crises. In each case, egregious policy mistakes exacerbated the downturn and worsened the deflationary problems. Some analysts worried that the bursting of the high-tech bubble (in 2000) and the housing bubble (in 2006–2009) in the United States increased the risk of deflation.

However, the circumstances in the United States during the 2000s were different from the Great Depression or Japan's "lost decade" of the 1990s. In the earlier episodes, deflation was a consequence of very weak or falling demand (a leftward shift in the aggregate demand curve), which in turn was the result of a collapse in bank lending and overly restrictive monetary and fiscal policies (not the case in the United States in the 2000s). The massive fiscal and monetary response, both in 2000–2001 and 2008–2009, prevented another Great Depression and a recurrence of deflation. Moreover, a large part of the decline in the rate of inflation during the late 1990s and early 2000s was due to a surge in productivity, which amounted to a "positive supply shock" (a rightward shift in the aggregate supply curve). This type of disinflation or even deflation is much less problematic than one triggered by falling demand. Nevertheless, deflation, if left unchecked, can become a serious challenge to policy makers. Throughout the lackluster recovery after the deep recession of 2008–2009, worries about deflation persisted in the United States, Europe, and Japan.

The Importance of Expectations

Expectations

Why do expansionary monetary and fiscal policies aimed at pushing the unemployment rate below its natural (full-employment) level produce only temporary reductions in unemployment (but accelerate inflation)? To answer this question, it is essential to recognize that the short-run Phillips curve reflects people's **expectations** concerning the future rate of inflation. If people expect a higher rate of inflation than in the past, this shifts the Phillips curve upward and to the right. To illustrate, we compare two situations; one where workers and firms expect that prices will increase by 10 percent per year in the immediate future, the other where they expect no inflation at all. In the former case, unions are not content to obtain less than a 10 percent increase in money wages, since a smaller increase would mean a cut in real wages. In the latter case, unions can afford to settle for a much more moderate increase in money wages, since none of the money wage increase is expected to be offset by inflation. Therefore, the rate of increase in wages is likely to be greater in the former case than in the latter case if the unemployment rate is the same.

In summary, the more inflation people expect, the further upward and out from the origin the short-run Phillips curve is likely to be. And the less inflation people expect, the further downward and close to the origin the short-run Phillips curve will be.

How the Phillips Curve Self-Destructs: An Example

Having stressed the importance of people's expectations concerning the inflation rate, we turn to the following example. Suppose that the natural rate of unemployment is 5.5 percent and the government, not realizing that it is this high, uses expansionary monetary and fiscal policies to reduce unemployment to 4 percent. Because of the resulting increase in aggregate demand, the price level rises, and if the level of money wages remains relatively constant, firms' profits go up. Higher profits lead to expanded output and more employment. Hence, the economy moves from point *C* (where it was before the government's expansionary policies) to point *D* in Figure 22.3. This movement is entirely in accord with the concept of the Phillips curve: a reduction in unemployment is gained at the expense of more inflation (6 percent rather than 4 percent).[1]

However, this movement is only temporary, because workers adjust their expectations concerning inflation. Before the government's expansionary monetary and fiscal policies were adopted, the inflation rate was 4 percent; and this was (more or less) what workers expected. The movement from point *C* to point *D* means an increase in the inflation rate to 6 percent, which the workers do not expect. Although they are fooled at first, people *adapt* their expectations; that is, the rate of inflation they expect is adjusted upward toward the new 6 percent rate. As pointed out in the previous section, this increase in the expected amount of inflation shifts the short-run Phillips curve upward and out from the origin. The short-run relationship between the unemployment rate and the inflation rate shifts from curve 1 to curve 2 in Figure 22.3, and unemployment returns to 5.5 percent, the natural rate. In other words, the economy moves from point *D* to point *E*. Faced with this new short-run curve, the government raises the inflation rate to 8 percent if it persists in trying to maintain the unemployment rate at 4 percent. That is, it must move to point *F* in Figure 22.3.

A Second Try

Suppose that the government continues to try to maintain a 4 percent unemployment rate. Since the inflation rate increases to 8 percent as a consequence, people once more begin to adapt their expectations to the new

[1] To prevent confusion, note that we are not assuming that the Phillips curve in Figure 22.3 is the same as in Figure 19.3. Figure 22.3 pertains to one situation; Figure 19.3 pertains to another situation (perhaps another country or time period).

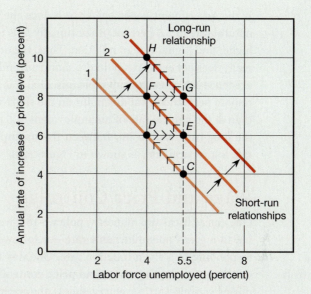

FIGURE 22.3

A Vertical Long-Run Phillips Curve

Expansionary monetary and fiscal policy results in a temporary reduction in the unemployment rate from 5.5 percent to 4 percent (a movement from point *C* to point *D*). But the increase in the inflation rate (from 4 percent to 6 percent) results in a higher expected rate of inflation, which shifts the short-run relationship from curve 1 to curve 2. If the government persists in trying to reduce the unemployment rate below the natural rate of 5.5 percent, all that it achieves is a higher and higher rate of inflation. In the long run, the unemployment rate returns to the natural rate (5.5 percent in this case). Hence, the long-run relationship between the unemployment rate and inflation rate is vertical.

inflation rate. Workers, trying to compensate for the higher inflation rate, ask for bigger wage increases, and firms are more willing to grant such increases because they recognize that the inflation rate has risen. Once again, the short-run Phillips curve shifts upward and outward from the origin. The short-run relationship between the unemployment rate and the inflation rate shifts from curve 2 to curve 3 in Figure 22.3, and unemployment returns to 5.5 percent, the natural rate. In other words, the economy moves from point *F* to point *G*. If the government persists in trying to keep the unemployment rate at 4 percent, the economy moves next to point *H*, where the inflation rate is 10 percent.

The Long-Run Relationship

If the government keeps trying to reduce the unemployment rate below the natural rate of 5.5 percent, it continually fails to do so. All that it achieves is a higher and higher rate of inflation. Thus, the downward-sloping Phillips curve really does not exist, except in the short run, and governments that believe in its existence can cause considerable mischief. It is not possible for the economy to remain permanently at any point on the short-run curves in Figure 22.3 other than at the natural rate of unemployment (5.5 percent in this case). Therefore, the long-run relationship between the unemployment rate and the inflation rate is a vertical line, as shown in Figure 22.3.

Wage and Price Controls

One aim of fiscal and monetary policy is to lower the inflation rate corresponding to a given unemployment rate—or to lower the unemployment rate corresponding to a given inflation rate. One way that the government can try to do this is by adopting **wage and price controls**. During 1971–1974 (as well as during various wartime emergencies), the government imposed controls of this sort. The government intervened directly in the marketplace to make sure that wages and prices did not increase by more than a certain amount. The economics profession has little enthusiasm for direct controls of wages and prices, for several reasons:

Wage and price controls

1. *Such controls are likely to result in a distorted allocation of resources.* Wage and price controls do not permit prices to perform their functions in allocating resources, and the result is inefficiency and waste.

2. *Such controls are likely to be expensive to administer.* For example, during the Korean War, the Economic Stabilization Agency had 16,000 employees; even so, it was difficult to prevent violation or evasion of the controls.

3. *There is widespread opposition to detailed government regulation and control of this sort on the grounds that it impairs our economic freedom.* The Council of Economic Advisers undoubtedly spoke for most of the economics profession when it said in 1968:

> The most obvious—and least desirable—way of attempting to stabilize prices is to impose mandatory controls on prices and wages. While such controls may be necessary under conditions of an all-out war, it would be folly to consider them as a solution to the inflationary pressures that accompany high employment under any other circumstance. . . . Although such controls may be unfortunately popular when they are not in effect, the appeal quickly disappears once people live under them.[2]

---

[2] *Economic Report of the President* (Washington, DC: U.S. Government Printing Office, 1968).

While wage and price controls are no longer in effect in the United States and most other developed nations, they are still widely used in many developing countries.

Incomes Policies

As already mentioned, the 1970s and early 1980s were a period of uncomfortably high inflation. For example, in 1980, the price level in the United States was increasing by more than 10 percent per year. Such high rates of inflation spurred considerable interest, both here and abroad, in using incomes policies to help curb inflation without cutting back on aggregate demand. According to one common definition, an **incomes policy** contains three elements:

Incomes policy

1. *Targets for wages (and other forms of income) and prices for the economy as a whole.* For example, the target may be to stabilize the price level, to permit the consumer price index to increase by less than 2 percent per year, or to allow wage increases not exceeding a certain percentage.

2. *More detailed guides to particular firms and industries for decision making on wages (and other forms of income and prices).* These guides are set to fulfill overall targets for the entire economy. For example, if the aim is price stability, these guides tell firms and unions what kinds of decisions are compatible with this target. To be useful, the guides must be specific and understandable enough to be applied in particular cases. There obviously is little point in telling firms and unions to avoid inflationary wage and price decisions if they do not know whether a particular decision is inflationary.

3. *Mechanisms to get firms and unions to follow its guidelines.* An incomes policy differs from wage and price controls in that it seeks to induce firms and unions to follow its guidelines voluntarily. But, if it is to have any effect, clearly the government must be prepared to use certain forms of persuasion beyond appeals to patriotism. In fact, governments sometimes have publicly condemned decisions by firms and unions regarded as violating the guidelines. Government stockpiles of materials and government purchasing policies have also been used to penalize or reward particular firms and industries. Other pressures, too, have been brought to bear in an attempt to induce firms to follow the established guidelines. Hence, the difference between an incomes policy and wage and price controls is one of degree and emphasis, not a clear-cut difference in kind.

An example of an incomes policy in the United States was the so-called Kennedy-Johnson guidelines. Although earlier administrations (for example, the Eisenhower and Truman administrations) had often appealed to business and labor to limit wage and price increases, the first systematic attempt at a fairly specific incomes policy in the United States occurred during the Kennedy administration. In 1961, President Kennedy's Council of Economic Advisers issued wage-price guidelines, which called for the rate of increase in wage rates (including fringe benefits) in each industry be equal to the trend rate of *overall productivity advance.* General acceptance of this guide would maintain stability of labor cost per unit of output for the economy as a whole—though not of course for individual industries. The general guide for noninflationary price behavior called for price reduction if the industry's rate of productivity increase exceeded the overall rate—for this would mean declining unit labor costs; it called for an appropriate increase in price if the opposite relationship prevailed; and it called for stable prices if the two rates of productivity increase were equal.

Productivity here means output per hour of labor. (*Labor productivity* is another term meaning the same thing.) To see what these guidelines mean, consider prices and wages in the auto industry. Suppose that labor productivity in the economy as a whole was increasing at 3.2 percent per year. Then according to the guidelines, wages in the automobile industry should increase by 3.2 percent per year. If labor productivity in the auto industry was increasing by 4.2 percent per year, then, if the automakers applied this guideline, the labor cost of producing a unit of output would decrease by 1 percent per year in the auto industry (since the 3.2 percent rate of increase in wages minus the 4.2 percent rate of increase of labor productivity equals –1 percent). Therefore, the guidelines specified that prices in the auto industry should decrease, perhaps by about 1 percent per year.

The Kennedy-Johnson Guidelines: Criticism and Experience

Soon after the Kennedy-Johnson wage-price guidelines were announced, critics began to point out the following problems:

> ➤ *Inefficiency.* Some observers feared that the guidelines would result in inefficiency and waste. In a free enterprise economy, we rely on price changes to direct resources into the most productive uses and signal shortages or surpluses in various markets. If the guidelines were accepted by industry and labor, prices would not be free to perform this function. Of course, the guidelines specified that modifications of the general rules could be made in the case of shortages, but critics of the guidelines felt that this escape hatch was too vague to be very useful.

> ➤ *Freedom.* Many observers were concerned about the reduction in economic freedom. Of course, the guidelines were presented in the hope that they would be observed voluntarily. But a time was sure to come when they would be in serious contradiction with the interests of firms and unions. In such a situation, what would happen if the firms or unions decided not to follow them? To the extent that the government applied

THE STEEL PRICE INCREASE: INCOMES POLICY IN ACTION

To conform to our definition of an incomes policy, the Kennedy-Johnson wage and price policy had to have an overall target, more detailed guidelines for wage and price decisions, and a mechanism to get firms and unions to observe these guidelines. The overall target was the stabilization of prices, and the more detailed guidelines for wage and price decisions are described in the text. But what about the mechanisms to induce acceptance of these guidelines? How did the government get industry and labor to go along?

The famous confrontation in 1962 between President Kennedy and the steel industry is an interesting case study of how pressure was brought to bear. Before the wage-price guidelines were issued, President Kennedy asked the major steel companies to avoid raising prices, and no price increases occurred. Then, after the issuance of the guidelines, he asked the steel union for restraint in the wage negotiations coming up in March 1962. Arthur Goldberg, Kennedy's secretary of labor, played an important role in persuading the union to accept a 2.5 percent increase in compensation, which was clearly noninflationary. At this point, government and the press felt quite optimistic about the apparent success of the president's program.

In the week following the wage agreement, however, the United States Steel Corporation (now USX Corporation) increased all its prices by 3.5 percent, and most of the major steel companies followed suit. The price increase was clearly a violation of the president's guidelines. It almost seemed as if the steel companies were trying to demonstrate once and for all that pricing was up to them and them alone. Their action elicited a wrathful speech by the president

publicly denouncing them. Roger M. Blough, chair of U.S. Steel, tried to rebut the president's arguments by claiming that U.S. Steel's profits were too low to attract new capital.

Three of the major steel producers—Armco, Inland, and Kaiser—did not follow U.S. Steel's lead in the day or so after its price increase. Government officials, noting this as well as prior public arguments against price increases by Inland officials, quickly began to apply pressure on these three producers to hold their prices constant. Government officials who knew executives of these firms called them and tried to persuade them to do so. The firms were also informed that government contracts would be directed to firms that held their prices constant. Apparently, the government's campaign succeeded. Inland and Kaiser made public statements that they would not raise prices. Faced with this fact, the other steel companies had no choice but to rescind the price increase.

This is an example of how presidential pressure can induce firms to go along with wage and price guidelines. Often Kennedy's Council of Economic Advisers tried to head off price increases before they were announced. The council would learn of an impending price increase, sometimes from the companies themselves, and then ask the firms to meet to discuss the situation. In these meetings, the council would explain the importance of price stability, and both parties would discuss the proposed increase. It is difficult, of course, to measure the impact of such discussions, but according to the council, they sometimes resulted in the postponement or reduction of planned price increases.

pressure on the firms or unions, there would certainly be a reduction in economic freedom, and to some observers, it seemed likely that the next step might well be direct government controls. Moreover, the non-legislated character of the guidelines and the government's freedom to choose whom to pursue raised important political questions.

➤ *Feasibility.* Many believed that the guidelines were not really workable. Even if the public went along with them, in many cases they would be impossible to apply, because accurate and relevant data on changes in labor productivity in particular industries were often unobtainable, and the situations where exceptions were allowed were so vaguely specified.

➤ *Symptoms.* Some economists felt that reliance on the guidelines was dangerous because it focused attention on the symptoms rather than the causes of inflation. In their view, inflation was largely the result of improper monetary and fiscal policies. In other words, the basic causes had to be laid at the government's door. But by setting up guidelines, the government seemed to be saying that the fault lay with industry and labor. Therefore, some critics felt that the guidelines tended to cloud the real issues and let the government escape responsibility for its actions.

From 1962 to 1964, the government claimed that the guidelines were work-ing well. Their success during this period may have resulted from the consider-able slack the economy still had and the noninflationary expectations of firms and individuals engendered by several years of relative price stability. By 1965, as labor markets tightened and prices rose in response to the Vietnam buildup, it became much more difficult to use the guidelines. Union leaders fought them tooth and nail, mainly because consumer prices were rising. In various impor-tant labor negotiations, unions demanded and got higher wage increases than the guidelines called for. The airline machinists, for example, got a 4.9 percent increase in 1966. By 1968, the guidelines were dead. No one paid any attention to them.

What effect did the guidelines have? Some economists claim that they had no real effect at all, whereas others claim that they reduced supply-side infla-tion in the early 1960s by a considerable amount. Since it is difficult to separate the effects of the guidelines from the effects of other factors, there is consider-able dispute over the question. Considering the level of unemployment in the early 1960s, wages increased less rapidly then than in earlier or later periods. Prices, too, increased less rapidly during that period—holding unemployment constant—than earlier or later. But whether these developments were due to the guidelines, noninflationary expectations, or some other factors is hard to say.

The guidelines broke down largely because they could not deal with the strong demand-side inflation of the late 1960s. Even the strongest defenders of the guidelines are quick to point out that they are no substitute for proper mon-etary and fiscal policy. If fiscal or monetary policy generates strong inflationary pressures, such as existed in the late 1960s, it is foolish to think that guidelines can save the situation. Perhaps they can cut down on the rate of inflation for a while, but in the long run, the dike is sure to burst. If the guidelines are voluntary, firms and unions ignore them, and the government finds it difficult, if not impossible, to do anything. Even wage and price controls will not contain the strong inflationary pressures generated by an overly expansive fiscal or monetary policy. Such controls may temporarily suppress the symptoms of inflation, but over the long haul, these inflationary pressures have their effect.

EXPLORING FURTHER

The Fed and Supply-Side Inflation

Suppose that labor unions suddenly demand that their wage rate (in money, not real terms) be doubled. Since firms must increase prices if they are to be willing to produce the same output as before, the short-run aggregate supply curve will shift upward and to the left, as shown in Figure 22.4.

If the Federal Reserve holds the money supply at its initial level, as shown in Figure 22.4, the economy moves from point A to point B. Hence, real output falls from Q_0 to Q_1 and the decrease in real output increases unemployment. Because the price level at point B is higher than at point A, although the money wage has doubled, the real wage has less than doubled.

By increasing the money supply, the Fed can push the aggregate demand curve to the right. If it pushes it far enough to the right, it can make it intersect the new aggregate supply curve at point C, where real GDP is at its original level Q_0. The price level rises considerably. As shown in the diagram, the price level at point C is much higher than at point A. The Fed, by enabling the action of the unions to increase the price level without resulting in additional unemployment, is said to have *accommodated* the supply-side inflation.

FIGURE 22.4

Accommodation of Supply-Side Inflation by the Fed

By increasing the money supply, the Fed can maintain real output at Q_0, but the price level will increase greatly.

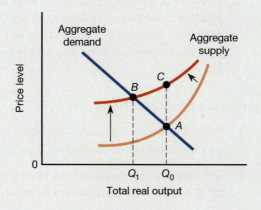

REVIEW AND PRACTICE

Summary

1   The Phillips curve shows the relationship between the rate of increase of the price level and the level of unemployment. If the Phillips curve remains fixed, it poses an awkward dilemma for policy makers. If they reduce unemployment, inflation increases; if they reduce inflation, unemployment increases.

2   From 1955 to 1969, the inflation rate and the unemployment rate were fairly closely related. Then something unforeseen by most economists occurred. The inflation and unemployment rates in the 1970s and 1980s did not conform at all closely to the relationship that prevailed in the 1960s. Both the unemployment rate and the inflation rate tended to be much higher in the 1970s and 1980s than in the 1960s. However, by the late 1990s, both the unemployment and the inflation rate had returned to their 1960s levels.

3   Some economists believe that the downward-sloping Phillips curve is only a short-run relationship. They believe that in the long run, it is vertical. In their view, expansionary policies that result in inflation reduce unemployment only temporarily, with the result that the government, if it sets out to reduce unemployment to below its natural level, must permit higher and higher rates of inflation.

4   To reduce the inflation rate (at a given unemployment rate), governments have tried wage and price controls. Although a few economists favor such controls during peacetime, most do not. Such controls are likely to distort the allocation of resources, be difficult to administer, and run counter to our desire for economic freedom.

5   Many countries experimented with various kinds of incomes policies. An incomes policy contains targets for wages and prices for the economy as a whole, more detailed guidelines for wage and price decisions in particular industries, and some mechanisms to get firms and unions to follow these guidelines. Although guidelines of this sort have a short-term effect on the price level, how much effect they have in the long run is hard to say.

Problems and Questions

1   Some economists say that it is far better that inflation be open than that it be suppressed by price guidelines. Do you agree? Why or why not?

2   The Kennedy-Johnson guidelines for noninflationary price behavior called for price reduction if an industry's rate of productivity increase exceeded the overall rate. Some economists believe that is unrealistic to expect price cuts of this sort. Do you agree? Why or why not?

3   Some believe that reliance on incomes policies is dangerous because it looks at symptoms, not the basic causes of our problems. Comment and evaluate.

Key Terms

stagflation
wage-price spiral
expectations
wage and price controls
incomes policy

Viewpoint for Analysis

According to the 1993 annual report to Congress of President George H. W. Bush's Council of Economic Advisers: "The costs of high and variable inflation are considerable but more subtle than the costs of recessions. In a market economy, prices provide essential information about the relative scarcity of goods and services. High and volatile inflation obscures this information and distorts the allocation of resources."[3]

(a)   Do you agree that inflation obscures this information and distorts the allocation of resources? If so, why does this occur?

(b)   Do both supply-side inflation and demand-side inflation have these effects? Or does neither have such effects?

(c)   A U.S. senator argues that if wage and price controls are adopted, these costs of inflation can be reduced greatly, if not eliminated. Do you agree? Why or why not?

(d)   A Treasury official claims that if the Phillips curve were stable, inflation would not have these effects. Do you agree? Why or why not?

---

[3] *Economic Report of the President* (Washington, DC: U.S. Government Printing Office, 1993), 79.

Productivity, Growth, and Technology Policy

LEARNING OBJECTIVES

➤ To consider the importance of productivity and what causes it to increase or decrease

➤ To describe the productivity slowdown in the United States in the 1970s and 1980s and its effects on the economy

➤ To explore the sorts of public policies that can be used to stimulate productivity

➤ *(Exploring Further)* To examine the effects of supply-side government policies

Between 2000 and 2012 labor productivity in the United States increased by 1.8 percent a year, on average. During the same period the labor productivity in the Eurozone only rose by 0.7 percent a year, on average.[1] Why do some economies trail behind others in productivity? One purpose of this chapter is to answer this question.

In the 1970s and 1980s, the rate of increase of output per hour in the United States declined dramatically, causing enormous concern in Washington and elsewhere. However, by the late 1990s and through much of the 2000s, productivity growth had picked up again and was almost at the rate of the 1960s. Another purpose of this chapter is to describe and analyze these productivity swings.

---

[1] OECD Economic Outlook, November 2013.

Growth of Per Capita Output in the United States

We begin by looking at the salient facts about the rate at which per capita output in the U.S. economy has grown in the past. Soon after its emergence as an independent nation, the United States achieved a relatively high level of economic development. By 1840, it ranked fourth in per capita output, behind England, France, and Germany. During the next 30 years, the United States experienced relatively rapid economic growth. By 1870, it ranked second only to England in per capita output. Over the next 40 years, the U.S. economy continued to grow rapidly. National product per person employed grew by about 2.2 percent per year between 1871 and 1913. This growth rate was higher than for practically any other major industrialized nation; and well before the turn of the century, output per capita was greater in the United States than in any other country in the world.

Between 1913 and 1959, the U.S. growth rate was somewhat lower than in previous years. National product per person employed grew by about 1.8 percent per year. Nonetheless, although we grew less rapidly than in earlier years, we pulled further ahead of most other industrialized countries, because we continued to grow faster than they did. Of course, our rate of economic growth varied from decade to decade (by rate of economic growth we mean the rate of growth of real GDP per capita). Economic growth does not proceed at a steady rate. In some decades (like the 1920s), our economy grew very rapidly, while in others (like the 1930s), it grew little if at all. During periods of recovery and prosperity, the growth rate was high; during depressions, it was low.

Table 23.1 shows average annual rates of growth of per capita real GDP in the United States and other major industrialized countries from 1870 to 1998. You can see that for the period as a whole, per capita real GDP in the United States grew at an average rate of about 2 percent per year. Compared with France,

TABLE 23.1 **Average Annual Growth Rates of Per Capita Real GDP, Selected Industrialized Countries**	COUNTRY	1870–1913 (percent)	1913–1950 (percent)	1950–1973 (percent)	1973–1998 (percent)
	United States	1.8	1.6	2.5	2.0
	France	1.4	1.1	4.1	1.6
	Germany	1.1	0.2	5.0	1.6
	Italy	1.3	0.9	5.0	2.1
	Japan	1.5	0.9	8.1	2.3
	United Kingdom	1.0	0.9	2.4	1.8

Source: Angus Maddison, *The World Economy: A Millennial Perspective,* Organization for Economic Cooperation and Development (Paris: 2001).

Germany, Italy, Japan, and the United Kingdom, our growth rate was impressive, especially from 1913 to 1950, during a period of two world wars and the Great Depression. However, in the two and a half decades after World War II, the per capita real GDP growth in Japan and Europe was much faster than in the United States. The growth in American living standards continued to lag those of other industrialized countries until the mid-1990s, when an acceleration in U.S. productivity growth helped the United States to pull ahead of the pack, once again.

Technological Change

Technological change

Technological change takes the form of new methods to produce existing products, new designs that make it possible to create new products, and new techniques for organization, marketing, and management. Economic growth in the United States has been due in very considerable part to technological change. Table 23.2 shows that according to Stephen Oliner and Daniel Sichel, formerly of the Federal Reserve Board, investment in information technology and the more efficient use of resources contributed almost half of the growth of the nonfarm business sector in the United States during the boom years of the late 1990s. This was almost double the contribution of these factors from 1974 to 1990. Such estimates are rough but useful. It is very difficult to separate the effects of technological change on economic growth from those of investment in physical capital, since to be used, new technology often must be embodied in physical capital, such as new machines and equipment. For example, to apply thin slab casting technology, Nucor built a new plant in Crawfordsville, Indiana. Nor can the effects of technological change easily be separated from those of education. After all, the returns from increased education are enhanced by technological change, and the rate of technological change is influenced by the extent and nature of a society's investment in education. Nonetheless, the estimates in Table 23.2 are useful.

TABLE 23.2

Estimated Sources of Growth in Real Nonfarm Business Output 1974–1999 (percent of total growth)

SOURCE	1974–1990	1991–1995	1996–1999
Information technology capital (computers, software, and telecommunication equipment)	16	21	23
Other capital	28	16	16
Labor hours	38	30	31
Labor quality (education and training)	7	16	24
Greater efficiency (total factor productivity)	11	17	24

Source: Stephen D. Oliner and Daniel E. Sichel, *The Resurgence of Growth in the Late 1990s: Is Information Technology the Story?*, Federal Reserve Board (Washington, DC: May 2000).

In interpreting U.S. economic growth, we must recognize that the United States has long been a technological leader. There is scattered evidence that even before 1850, the United States was ahead of other countries in many technological areas. And after 1850, productivity was higher in the United States than in Europe, the United States held a strong position in technically progressive industries, and Europeans tended to imitate U.S. techniques. Needless to say, the United States did not lead in all fields, but it appears to have held a technological lead in many important aspects of manufacturing. This was in contrast to pure science, where, until World War II, the United States was not a leader.

Research and development (R&D)

Recent decades have witnessed tremendous growth in the amount spent on **research and development (R&D)**. In the United States in 2009, R&D expenditures were over 11 times what they were in 1953 (after adjusting for inflation). Although the bulk of these expenditures go for rather minor improvements rather than major advances, this vast increase in research and development generated much economic growth. As shown in Table 23.3, the

TABLE 23.3

Estimated National Expenditures for Research and Development, by Performing Sector and Source of Funds, 2009 (billions of dollars)[1]

Performers	Total	SOURCE OF FUNDS			
		Industry	Federal Government	U&C	Other Nonprofit Institutions
Total	400	247	127	11	14
Industry	282	242	40		
Industry FFRDCs	6		6		
Federal Government	32		32		
U&C	54	3	36[2]	11	4
U&C FFRDCs	5	5			
Other Nonprofits	17	1	7		9
Nonprofit FFRDCs	4		4		

[1]Numbers may not add up due to rounding.

[2]Federal government funding of U&C includes a small amount of state funding.

Key: FFRDC = federally funded research development center; U&C = universities and colleges.

Source: National Science Foundation.

federal government is the source of over 30 percent of all R&D funds ($127 billion out of a total of $400 billion in 2009), which are heavily concentrated on defense and space technology. In the eyes of many economists, this vast investment in R&D would probably have had a bigger impact on the rate of economic growth if more of it had been directed at civilian rather than military and political objectives.

The Productivity Slowdown and Its Consequences

During the 1970s and 1980s, the decreasing rate of growth of output per hour of labor was a cause of concern among U.S. policy makers. According to the Bureau of Labor Statistics, output per hour of labor (in the business sector) decelerated considerably from the mid-1970s to the mid-1990s—it subsequently reaccelerated (see Table 23.4). Nevertheless, this slowdown

TABLE 23.4 Output per Hour of Nonfarm Labor, United States, Percent Change from Previous Year, 1962–2011	Year	Percent Change	Year	Percent Change	Year	Percent Change
	1962	4.5	1979	-0.4	1996	2.6
	1963	3.5	1980	-0.3	1997	1.5
	1964	2.9	1981	1.4	1998	2.9
	1965	3.1	1982	-1.1	1999	3.3
	1966	3.6	1983	4.4	2000	3.4
	1967	1.7	1984	2.0	2001	2.9
	1968	3.4	1985	1.6	2002	4.6
	1969	0.2	1986	3.1	2003	3.7
	1970	1.5	1987	0.3	2004	2.6
	1971	4.0	1988	1.6	2005	1.6
	1972	3.3	1989	0.8	2006	0.9
	1973	3.1	1990	1.8	2007	1.5
	1974	-1.6	1991	1.5	2008	0.6
	1975	2.8	1992	4.0	2009	2.9
	1976	3.3	1993	0.8	2010	3.1
	1977	1.6	1994	1.0	2011	0.7
	1978	1.3	1995	0.4		

Source: Economic Report of the President, 2013.

in the rate of productivity increase worried policy makers for at least two reasons. First, to the extent that it reflected a decrease in the rate of technological change, it spelled trouble for our rate of economic growth, since the latter is dependent on our rate of technological change. Second, since higher productivity can offset the effect of higher wages on average cost, the slowdown in productivity increase was likely to contribute to a higher rate of inflation.

Many observers were also concerned about the apparent reduction of the U.S. technological lead over other countries and the slow rate of productivity growth in the United States relative to other major countries. During 1960 to 1995, the percentage gain in output per worker was smaller in the United States than in France, Germany, Japan, or the United Kingdom. However, by the late 1990s and early 2000s, U.S. productivity was growing faster than in these countries.

Causes of Productivity Swings

What factors were responsible for this significant slackening of U.S. productivity growth in the 1970s and 1980s and the subsequent rebound in the 1990s and 2000s? To begin with, consider the following factors that have been frequently cited:

➤ *Changes in the composition of the labor force.* Output per hour of labor tends to be relatively low among women and new entrants into the labor force, in part because of their limited experience and training and the sort of work they get. During the late 1960s, women and new entrants increased as a proportion of the labor force. On the basis of calculations by the Bureau of Labor Statistics, this change in labor force composition may have been responsible for a 0.2- to 0.3-percentage-point difference between the average rate of productivity increase during 1947–1966 and that during 1966–1973. With the maturation of the baby boom generation, these trends have likely reversed somewhat.

➤ *The rate of growth of the capital-labor ratio.* During 1948–1973, relatively high rates of private investment resulted in a growth of the capital-labor ratio of almost 3 percent per year. After 1973, relatively low rates of investment resulted in the growth of the capital-labor ratio by only about 1.75 percent per year. According to the Council of Economic Advisers, this reduction in the rate of growth of the capital-labor ratio may have reduced the rate of productivity increase by up to 0.5 percentage point per year. An investment boom in the 1990s reversed this trend. Similarly, after the Great Recession of 2008–2009, businesses seemed eager to substitute capital (machinery, computers, and so on) for labor.

➤ *Government regulation.* A variety of new environmental, health, and safety regulations were adopted in the 1970s. Because reduced pollution, enhanced safety, and better health are generally not included in measured output, the use of more of society's resources to meet these regulations is likely to result in a reduction in measured productivity growth. Also, the litigation and uncertainty associated with new regulations may discourage investment and efficiency, and the form of the regulations sometimes may inhibit socially desirable adaptations by firms. According to the Council of Economic Advisers, the direct costs of compliance with environmental, health, and safety regulations may have reduced the growth of productivity by about 0.4 percentage point per year during the 1970s.

➤ *Shift of national output toward services and away from goods.* There has been considerable disagreement over whether the shift in the composition of national output toward services and away from goods is responsible for much of the productivity slowdown. For example, some economists argue that it is more difficult to increase productivity in service industries than in manufacturing industries. Others feel that this factor is of relatively little importance. However, recent revisions to the national income and product accounts show much higher productivity growth in some services over the past couple of decades (see Case Study 15.1).

Has There Been a Decline in the U.S. Innovation Rate?

Innovation

In recent years, some observers have asserted that the productivity slowdown was due in part to a decline in the rate of **innovation** in the United States. In their opinion, the rate of introduction of new products and processes has fallen. This hypothesis is difficult to test and should be viewed with caution. In many parts of the economy, such as microelectronics, the rate of innovation seems to be hale and hearty. Advances in microprocessors, microcomputers, wireless devices, and the Internet are regarded by experts as extremely important and have had widespread effects on many areas of the economy. Computers have become cheaper, smaller, and smarter. Another potentially important area is biotechnology, where many major advances are expected. For instance, new biological techniques may allow the development of new plants.

The Diminishing U.S. Technological Lead

It is important to distinguish between a reduction in the rate of technological change in the United States and a reduction in the U.S. technological lead over other countries. Obviously, the United States no longer has the commanding technological lead it enjoyed during the 1950s and 1960s. As countries like Japan and Germany completed their recovery from World War II and devoted much more attention to transferring, adapting, and extending technology, they narrowed the technological gap considerably and in some areas surpassed the United States. But this does not mean that the U.S. rate of innovation declined. Even in microelectronics, where there is little or no evidence of a decline in the U.S. rate of innovation, the gap between the United States, on the one hand, and Japan and China, on the other, has been reduced considerably, because, according to many experts, the Japanese and Chinese rates of advance (from lower levels) has exceeded our own.

Mechanisms for Federal Support of Civilian Technology

There are various means by which the federal government can encourage investment in civilian technology.

R&D Tax Credits

In 1981, Congress passed an incremental tax credit (and keeps extending it) to encourage industrial R&D. Such an R&D tax credit reduces the after-tax cost of R&D and thus encourages R&D. Perhaps the most important advantages of this mechanism are that it requires less direct government control than some of the other mechanisms and in some respects is relatively easy to administer. Its most important disadvantages are that it rewards firms for doing R&D they would have done anyhow and does not help firms that have no profits. Moreover, any program of this sort is likely to run into difficulties in defining R&D, since firms have an incentive to use as wide a definition as possible. Studies of such tax credits, both in the United States and in other countries (like Canada and Sweden), seem to indicate that they have only a modest effect on industrial R&D expenditures.

Federal Grants and Contracts

The federal government can also make grants and contracts in support of civilian technology. This, of course, is the route taken by the Department of Defense and the National Aeronautics and Space Administration in much of their work. It has the advantage of being direct and selective, but it can involve political problems in the choice of contractors as well as problems relative to the disposition of patents resulting from such contracts and grants. Still another, more fundamental difficulty with this mechanism for supporting private sector R&D is that it is so difficult to predict the social

CASE STUDY 23.1

POSITIVE EXTERNALITIES AND THE ROLE OF THE GOVERNMENT IN ENCOURAGING INNOVATION

Technological innovation has been a major factor in the growth of productivity in the United States. The development of new products and processes allows people to do what they were doing before—just using less time to do it—and to do what they never dreamed of doing before. There is a catch, however. Since the benefits of innovation do not accrue only to the person or company that develops the new technology, but are often enjoyed by society as a whole, there can be a disincentive to the developer. Specifically, others can use or exploit the innovation without compensating the innovator. Economists classify this type of technology spillover as a positive externality (or external economy; see Chapter 2).

Unfortunately, given the disincentives associated with such spillovers, the free market, left to its own devices, will encourage less innovation than is socially desirable. To remedy this problem, the government can "internalize the externality" in multiple ways: by sponsoring research and development at one of the many government-run labs, by giving subsidies for private sector R&D, and by strengthening patent protection.

There are lots of examples of government-sponsored technologies transforming our lives: the NASA moon program spurred the development of the all-pervasive microchip; the Department of Defense's DARPA Net was eventually transformed into the Internet; and the Global Positioning System (GPS), developed for the military, has made it easier for all of us to find our way around.

These success stories have led some economists to advocate for an even bigger government involvement in innovation. Other economists are more skeptical of this type of industrial policy. They worry that the government is not in the best position to pick technology winners and that the process can become highly politicized. They advocate, instead, greater use of the patent protection system, which gives inventors a temporary monopoly on new technologies.

costs and benefits of a proposed R&D project, and government agencies may not be very adept at making what are essentially commercial development decisions.

During the 1990s and 2000s, the United States spent a considerable amount in support of civilian technology. For example, the Advanced Technology Program awarded matching funds to industry to conduct research on processes and products.

Expanded Responsibility of Federal Laboratories

The federal government could support additional civilian R&D by initiating and expanding relevant work in its own laboratories. While this approach has the advantage of being direct and selective, problems arise when R&D is conducted by organizations not in close touch with the production and marketing of the product. It is very important to have an unimpeded flow of information and good coordination of R&D, on the one hand, and production and marketing, on the other.

Importance of Investment in Plant and Equipment

Since investment in plant and equipment accounts for a relatively large proportion of the cost of many innovations, measures that encourage investment are likely to encourage innovation. And since the profitability of R&D depends on the profitability of the entire business venture of which it is a part, measures that reduce the after-tax costs to the firm of plant and equipment are likely to increase the profitability of R&D.

Encouraging investment in plant and equipment also is likely to increase the rate of diffusion of new techniques and thus increase the rate of growth of productivity. Many new techniques cannot be employed unless new plant or equipment is constructed and utilized. Thus, public policies that encourage investment are likely to encourage both innovation and the diffusion of new technology.

Recent studies suggest that the amount a country invests in machinery has an important influence on its rate of growth of per capita output. During 1965–1995, countries (such as South Korea) that invested relatively heavily in equipment tended to expand per capita output more rapidly than countries (such as Argentina) that invested relatively little in equipment. Investments in structures seem to have had far less effect on a country's rate of productivity growth than investments in equipment. One reason why countries with high productivity growth rates tend to invest more in equipment than countries with low productivity growth rates is that the former countries have lower equipment prices than the latter countries. Some economists believe that one key to raising a country's productivity growth rate is to increase its investment in equipment.

Relative to countries like Japan and Germany, the United States has tended to devote a low percentage of its output to plant and equipment. For example, in the 1970s, the United States devoted about 15 percent of its output to plant and equipment, whereas Germany devoted about 20 percent and Japan devoted about 25 percent. This factor is often cited as a reason why the rate of growth of per capita output has been lower in the United States than

ASIAN GROWTH: MIRACULOUS OR NOT?

Malaysia's capital, Kuala Lumpur

In the years immediately preceding the Asian financial crisis in 1997 and 1998, a noisy argument erupted between a group of U.S. academic economists and a number of Asian policy makers. The subject of this vocal debate was the sustainability of the Asian "miracle." Key policy analysts in Asia, especially in Singapore and Malaysia, had been arguing that high Asian growth rates were not only sustainable but the logical result of a combination of thrift, educational emphasis, and cultural values. The U.S. challenge to this view was led in the 1990s by Professors Alwyn Young, (formerly of Boston University and now at the London School of Economics), and Paul Krugman, (formerly of MIT and now a Nobel Laureate at Princeton University). They pointed out that most of the growth in Asia was the result of factor accumu-lation (for example, high levels of investment in human and physical capital), not special cultural advantages. The analyses of Krugman, Young, and others showed that growth in Asian productivity was no higher than in the OECD countries or, for that matter, in Latin America and other developing regions.* Moreover, they asserted that as the returns to factor accumu-lation diminished, growth rates in Asia would also fall.

More specifically, the critique of the Asian "miracle" suggested that four key trends accounted for most of the growth in Asia.

1. Rising labor force participation rates, especially among women, accounted for as much as 1 to 1.5 percentage points of the growth rates in the region.

2. Rapid rises in educational attainment improved the quality of the labor force. In 1960, only one-quarter of the labor force in countries like Korea and Taiwan had a secondary or higher education. By the 1990s, this proportion had risen to almost 70 percent.
3. High and rising investment rates accounted for 40 to 70 percent of the high growth rates. In Singapore and Korea, the investment-GDP ratio quadrupled from 1960 to 1990.
4. The movement of workers from agriculture to manufacturing also played a critical role in success. Employment in manufacturing rose 1.5 to 2.5 times faster than population growth during the last 35 years.

Proponents of the Asian "miracle" pointed out that the large number of regional success stories suggested common attributes shared by these countries: high rates of investment in human and physical capital, macroeconomic stability, and relatively low levels of trade, price, and exchange rate distortions. Most important, they claimed that the outward orientation of these economies and their integration into the global economy had been the key to continued high rates of return on investment. In the open economies of Asia, returns from investment were likely to stay high longer because they were servicing worldwide demand.

Nevertheless, some of the more thoughtful proponents of Asian growth conceded that little of the growth in Singapore, Malaysia, and Indonesia was a result of innovation and that these countries faced an "innovation challenge." Still, they maintained that while growth was likely to slow down, in the worst-case scenario it would decelerate by only a couple of percentage points.

The Asian financial crisis resulted in deep recessions in many of the fast-growing East Asian economies, including Thailand, Malaysia, South Korea, Indonesia, and Hong Kong. Critics of the Asian "miracle" saw this as a vindication of their point of view. However, this may be unfair. The crisis was triggered by a combination of poor macroeconomic policies, volatile capital flows, poorly regulated banks, and crony capitalism that led to a surge in speculative investment during the early 1990s. It is true that the high rates of investment during the late stages of the "miracle" years were either wasted (on stock market or property speculation) or used inefficiently (to add capacity in industries where there was already a global capacity glut). Nevertheless, the other building blocks of Asia's success (higher educational attainment, greater labor force participation, and so on) were not causes of the crisis and in fact helped set the stage for a return to rapid growth in the early 2000s.

Asia's growth was not miraculous. However, the Asian economies did many of the things that economic theory suggests boosts growth. The challenge for Asia over the next few decades is to build on its successes and learn from its failures.

* Alwyn Young, "Lessons from the East Asian NICS: A Contrarian View," National Bureau of Economic Research, Working Paper No. 4482.

in Japan and Germany. However, recent evidence suggests that, at least in the 1990s, the United States used its plant and equipment more efficiently than Germany or Japan. In other words, the productivity of its capital was higher than that of any other country.

HOW WIDESPREAD WAS THE PRODUCTIVITY BOOM OF THE LATE 1990S?

Starting in 1990, there was an acceleration in the trend rate of growth of investment in equipment. From 1960 to 1990, spending on this type of investment grew at a steady 6 percent a year. In the 1990s, that growth rate doubled to 12 percent a year. Most of this faster growth was due to the spread of PCs and the Internet.

The impact of this acceleration in investment on productivity was felt with a lag. In the first half of the 1990s, productivity growth was 1.75 percent annually, unchanged from the rate in the 1970s and 1980s. However, in the second half of the 1990s, productivity growth accelerated to 2.3 percent, and the rate in 1998 and 1999 was an even higher 2.8 percent.

The pervasiveness and sustainability of this productivity boom became hotly debated topics. On the one hand were the proponents of the "new economy" and "new paradigms," who believed that the U.S. economy was in the midst of a technological revolution with far-reaching and long-lasting ramifications for productivity growth and living standards.

On the other hand were the skeptics. Chief among these was Robert Gordon, professor of economics at Northwestern University. In a study released in 1999, he showed that all of the surge in productivity was due to gains in the high-tech sectors: computer hardware and software manufacturers and related businesses had achieved productivity gains of more than 40 percent. However, in the rest of the economy, productivity growth was no higher than the rate in the 1970s and 1980s, 1.75 percent.

Most mainstream economists found themselves somewhere in between these two extreme views. While not disputing Gordon's methodology, they questioned the overall quality of the productivity data, especially in the service sector. Most economists believed that the acceleration of productivity was reasonably widespread among a large number of industries (in fact, research at the Federal Reserve confirmed this) but were quick to point out that there was no guarantee that the productivity boom would last. Some even raised an intriguing prospect. If Gordon's estimates were correct, then the potential for higher and more pervasive productivity gains throughout the U.S. economy were high and the productivity boom still had a long way to go before it ran out of steam.

During the recession of 2001 and the subsequent recovery, U.S. productivity growth remained strong. This suggested that the productivity boom of the 1990s was not cyclical (as suggested by Gordon) but structural and therefore more durable. In fact, during the early 2000s, the 4 to 5 percent growth in labor productivity was largely the result of "old economy" industries, such as consumer retail stores, and using computers and the Internet more effectively. In the end, even Gordon admitted that the surge in productivity was more widespread than he had originally believed.

Importance of the General Economic Climate

Broad economic policies can have a major impact on innovation. One of the strongest influences on technological innovation is the general economic climate; measures that encourage economic growth, saving and investment, and price stability are quite likely to enhance our technological position. Indeed, improvements in our general economic climate may have more impact on the state of U.S. technology than many of the specific measures proposed to stimulate technological change.

As an illustration, consider the effects of the high rate of inflation in the United States during the late 1970s and early 1980s. Inflation that is high, on average, tends to be very variable in its rate; this reduces the efficiency of the price system as a mechanism for coordinating economic activity. In particular, economists, both liberals and conservatives, worry about the negative effects of high rates of inflation on investment. In particular, high rates of inflation are often followed by a tightening of monetary policy (i.e. higher interest rates), which, in turn, can trigger recessions—all of which discourages investment.

Of course, very high unemployment rates, as well as very high inflation rates, tend to discourage innovation. When sales are depressed and the future looks grim, the climate for innovation is not bright. Neither severe and prolonged recession nor double-digit inflation constitutes a benign climate for industrial innovation. The long expansion, low inflation, and low unemployment rate of the 1990s helped boost investment and productivity.

EXPLORING FURTHER

Supply-Side Government Policies and the Aggregate Supply Curve

It is clear that rightward shifts of the aggregate supply curve are likely to result in more output and a quelling of inflationary pressures (see Figure 23.1). Since these are desirable goals, it is not surprising that government policies have often emphasized measures designed to push the aggregate supply curve outward and to the right. This emphasis on the aggregate supply curve is not new; in fact, in 1776, Adam Smith recognized the importance of such shifts in the aggregate supply curve, although he did not couch his discussion in those terms. But in the late 1970s and early 1980s, much more talk was heard about the supply side—that is, shifts in the short-run (and long-run) aggregate supply curve—than in previous decades (see Case Study 23.4).

FIGURE 23.1

Effect of a Shift to the Right in the Aggregate Supply Curve

If the short-run aggregate supply curve shifts to the right, the result is increased real output (Q' rather than Q) and a lower price level (P' rather than P). In the early 1980s, there was much discussion of supply-side policies to achieve such a shift in the aggregate supply curve. Of course, the emphasis was on shifting the long-run aggregate supply curve as well as the short-run aggregate supply curve.

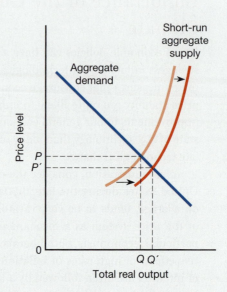

CASE STUDY 23.4

SUPPLY-SIDE ECONOMICS AND TAX CUTS

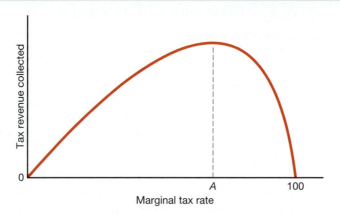

In the late 1970s and early 1980s, some economists advocated tax reductions to stimulate national output. Their views came to be known as **supply-side economics**, and they came to be known as supply-siders. Their views received considerable attention when some of them received high-level posts in the Reagan administration, and they played an important role in formulating and helping to push through the very large tax cut passed in August 1981.

The supply-siders advocated cuts in taxes on labor income on the grounds that people would then work longer and harder. Many economists are skeptical of this proposition. The available evidence seems to indicate that the hours worked by prime-age men would not be affected much by tax changes. But the amount of work done by married women seems more responsive to changes in tax rates. (If the marginal tax rate—the proportion of an extra dollar of income paid in taxes—is high, some women feel it is not worthwhile to work outside the home.)

The supply-siders also advocated reductions in taxes on capital income. For example, they called for cuts in taxes on dividends, interest income, and capital gains (capital gains are increases in the value of assets). In their view, such cuts would encourage additional saving. Although economists agree that saving and investment tend to promote the growth of an economy, there is considerable controversy over the extent to which saving is influenced by tax cuts. Early studies of consumption and saving found saving behavior to be relatively insensitive to changes in the rate of return that savers receive. (That is, if people can obtain a 10 percent annual return from their savings in banks and elsewhere, they may not save much more than if they can obtain only 5 percent.) More recent studies challenge this conclusion, but critics respond that the 1981 tax cut did not increase the percent of total income devoted to saving.

Some supply-siders argued that the tax burden had been so high that further increases in the marginal tax rate would result in lower, not higher, total tax revenue. To explain why they believed this to be true, they used the **Laffer curve**, which relates the amount of income tax revenue collected by the government to the marginal tax rate. According to Arthur Laffer (after whom the curve was named), tax revenues are zero if the tax rate is zero.

This is indisputable. Also, he points out that tax revenues are zero if the marginal tax rate is 100 percent. Why? Because if the government takes all the income in taxes, an individual has no incentive to earn taxable income.

According to the Laffer curve (shown on previous page), the maximum tax revenue is reached when the tax rate is at some intermediate level between 0 and 100 percent. This level is *A*. According to Laffer, U.S. tax rates already had reached or exceeded this level. Many other economists denied this. Although they admitted that a reduction in tax rates could reduce the incentive to cheat on taxes and find tax loopholes (as well as encourage people to work harder and save more), they felt that Laffer's evidence was too weak to support his conclusions. It seems fair to say that there is considerable uncertainty about the shape of the Laffer curve and where the United States is located on it. Even the existence and usefulness of such a curve is a matter of dispute.

Despite academic skepticism, supply-side tax cuts have continued to be a major part of the Republican Party's platform in recent presidential elections. In 1996, Republican nominee Bob Dole proposed a 15 percent across-the-board income tax cut. Unfortunately for Dole, the broader electorate did not share his enthusiasm for tax cuts. In 2000, all the leading Republican candidates (George W. Bush, John McCain, and Steve Forbes) proposed tax cuts of one type or another. Forbes put forth the most radical plan in which everyone would pay a flat tax rate of 17 percent. The closeness of the 2000 election suggested that the topic of tax cuts was still not resonating with voters. Nevertheless, the administration of George W. Bush proposed (and Congress approved) the enactment of two large tax cuts in 2001 and 2003. While these cuts had the beneficial effects of preventing the 2001 recession from being deeper and boosting growth during the subsequent recovery (by shifting the aggregate demand curve to the right), there is little evidence, in retrospect, that the impact on the supply-side of the economy was significant.

When the Reagan administration took office in 1981, it pushed through Congress a number of measures that it felt would help shift the aggregate supply curve to the right. In particular, the 25 percent cut in the personal income tax and the accelerated depreciation of plant and equipment (both included in the 1981 tax bill) were supposed to further this aim. According to the administration, the important thing was to encourage people and firms to work, invest, and take prudent risks. There has been considerable controversy inside and outside the economics profession as to the effectiveness and side effects of some of these tax changes. All we want to emphasize here is that the Reagan administration promoted measures to shift the aggregate supply curve.

REVIEW AND PRACTICE

Summary

1   Compared with other major industrialized countries, the U.S. rate of growth of per capita output generally has been impressive over the past century because of rapid technological change, increases in education and training, investment in plant and equipment, plentiful natural resources, and our social and entrepreneurial climate.

2   Since the late 1960s, the United States has experienced a notable slowdown in its rate of increase of output per hour of labor. Among the factors cited in the 1970s as being responsible for the slowdown were these:

- The increase in the proportion of youths and women in the labor force
- The reduction in the rate of growth of the capital-labor ratio
- Increased government regulation
- The reduction in the proportion of GDP devoted to research and development

The reversal of some of these trends in the 1990s helped boost productivity growth in the second half of the decade.

3   In recent years, some observers asserted that the productivity slowdown is due in part to a decline in the rate of innovation in the United States. The R&D tax credits, federal R&D grants and contracts, and expanded work by federal laboratories are among the measures that have been adopted or proposed to help deal with whatever underinvestment in R&D exists.

4   Investment in plant and equipment is an important factor that can raise productivity substantially. In the United States, investment in plant and equipment (as a percentage of output) has been considerably lower than in other major industrialized countries, such as Germany and Japan.

5   One of the strongest influences on the rate of innovation is the general economic climate. Measures that encourage economic growth, saving and investment, and price stability are likely to enhance our technological position.

*6 [2]The Reagan administration pushed through Congress some very large tax cuts in 1981; the intention was to shift the aggregate supply curve to the right, reflecting the emphasis at that time on supply-side economics.

Problems and Questions

1   According to the available evidence, Japanese firms devote a larger percentage of their R&D expenditures to new processes (rather than new products) than U.S. firms. What advantages accrue to firms that do considerable research into their own productive processes, rather than leave this work to equipment manufacturers and input suppliers?

2   Did the United States have a technological lead over many other industrialized countries in the nineteenth century? In the twentieth century? If so, what were some factors responsible?

3   One of the most important determinants of the extent of the economic impact of a new technique like the industrial robot is its rate of diffusion. Why is the rate of diffusion of a new technique so important? What influences the rate of diffusion?

4   Must increases in the rate of technological change result in increases in aggregate unemployment? Why or why not?

5   "There is a role for government policy in financing technological progress because the full benefits of research are rarely captured solely by the firm or individual undertaking the research. Rather, additional benefits accrue to society as a whole."[3] Why does this imply that the government should support research and development?

Key Terms

technological change
research and development (R&D)
innovation
supply-side economics
Laffer curve

---

[2] Starred (*) items refer to material covered in Exploring Further.
[3] *Economic Report of the President*, 1990, 112.

Viewpoint for Analysis

On January 4, 2004, Roger Ferguson, former vice-chair of the Federal Reserve Board, said:

> All of us as government economists, policymakers, and citizens have a stake in learning the lessons from the past productivity booms. As I have said, productivity improvements translate directly into improvements in the standard of living. Economists will continue to debate the relative importance of various factors underlying productivity growth. But our experience in the United States clearly suggests that periods of relatively rapid trend productivity growth are characterized by innovations in technology that are accompanied by changes in organizational structure and in business financing arrangements and by investments in human capital. Productivity booms in the United States have been of varying duration, but we have seen two of them last as long as 20 years. We do not know definitively what brings these booms to an end. In our experience, however, periods of elevated increases in trend productivity are best fostered in an environment of economic and personal freedom and by government policies that are focused on erecting sound and stable macroeconomic conditions that are most conducive to private-sector initiative.[4]

(a) How do you think changes in business organization, better access to finance, and better education can help new technologies boost productivity?

(b) What can the government do to enhance both the development of new technologies and their adoption by businesses?

(c) What is the role of the Federal Reserve, in particular, and macroeconomic policies, in general, in fostering better productivity growth?

---

[4] Speech by Roger W. Ferguson, Jr., vice-chair of the Board of Governors of the U.S. Federal Reserve System, at the meetings of the American Economic Association, San Diego, January 4, 2004.

Surpluses, Deficits, Public Debt, and the Federal Budget

LEARNING OBJECTIVES

➤ To explore the issues concerning a balanced federal budget

➤ To explain the significance of the structural deficit

➤ To analyze the nature and effects of the national debt

➤ To describe the fiscal policies employed in the United States in recent decades

R egardless of who occupies the White House, there are controversies over the federal budget. Every candidate, Democrat or Republican, seems to be concerned. A perennial question that arises is this: Should the federal government balance its budget? One purpose of this chapter is to answer this question.

Budget deficit

In the early 1990s, the **budget deficit** (that is, the difference between federal expenditures and federal revenue) was sizable. (In 1992, it was about $290 billion.) During the 1980s, there had been a sharp increase in both the deficit and the national debt (the amount owed by the federal government). The rise in both the deficit and the debt rekindled the controversy about how government spending should be financed and whether the federal budget should be balanced. In the late 1990s, with the economy booming, the deficits turned into surpluses.

Budget surplus

A **budget surplus** occurs when revenues are larger than expenditures. New arguments arose about what to do with these surpluses. By 2000, the budget surplus was around $236 billion. However, as a result of a recession in 2001 and two large tax cuts in the early 2000s, the red ink began to flow again. By 2004, the budget deficit was huge again ($413 billion). As the economy grew in the mid-2000s, the deficit fell again to about $161 billion in 2007. Unfortunately, with the Great

Recession of 2008–2009 and the large stimulus package (to the tune of about $830 billion) enacted in early 2009, the deficit skyrocketed to a record $1.4 trillion that year. In this chapter, we will consider under what circumstances the government's budget should or should not be balanced and how the deficit or surplus should be measured. We will also discuss how deficits can be financed, the impact of the national debt, and how surpluses should be used.

How Big Are U.S. Budget Surpluses or Deficits?

To begin with, it is important to be clear regarding the size of the surplus or deficit. Obviously, the size of the deficit or surplus must be related to the size of the economy. A $175 billion surplus or deficit means one thing if a country's GDP is $100 billion and quite another thing if its GDP is $10 trillion. Therefore, a surplus or deficit that would be huge for a tiny country like Monaco would be insignificant for a large country like the United States.

One way to relate the size of the deficit to GDP is to express the deficit as a percentage of GDP. Figure 24.1 shows that the deficit increased from

FIGURE 24.1

Federal Deficit and Surplus as a Percentage of GDP, 1960–2012

The federal deficit increased from about 1 percent of GDP in the 1960s to over 2 percent in the 1970s to between 3 and 6 percent in the 1980s and early 1990s. By the late 1990s, the budget was in surplus. However, by the early 2000s, the budget was back in deficit again. By 2009, the deficit was over 10 percent of GDP.

Source: Economic Report of the President, February 2013.

about 1 percent of GDP in the 1960s to over 2 percent in the 1970s to between 3 percent and 6 percent in the 1980s and early 1990s. Clearly, the deficit increased substantially relative to GDP.[1] By 2000, however, the budget had a surplus of about 2.4 percent of GDP. Unfortunately, by 2004, the budget balance had swung the other way again; the surplus had disappeared, and there was a deficit of about 3.5 percent of GDP. With the Great Recession and the big stimulus program of early 2009, the deficit rose to 10.1 percent of GDP. This was not a record, though. During World War II, the deficit was over 30 percent of GDP.

Controversies over Deficits

Are budget deficits really such a bad thing? This question has been raised repeatedly. In 1984, there was a public fracas within the Reagan administration over the need to reduce the deficit. According to Martin Feldstein, then chair of President Reagan's Council of Economic Advisers, the deficits of the early 1980s were very dangerous to the long-term health of the economy. If they were allowed to continue, they would push up interest rates and result in a crowding-out of private investment in plant and equipment. Also, U.S. exports would be hurt because high U.S. interest rates would push up the value of the dollar relative to other currencies, making our exports more expensive to foreign purchasers. For these and other reasons, Feldstein (and many other economists) were extremely worried about the deficit.

In contrast, Donald Regan, who in 1984 was secretary of the Treasury, played down the importance of the deficit. In his view, deficits do not push up interest rates and do not result in an overvaluation of the dollar relative to other currencies. In part, his arguments seemed to be based on studies carried out by some supply-side economists (see Case Study 23.4), including members of the Treasury staff. But most economists did not buy these arguments. If the government increases its demands for credit because of the very large deficits, the interest rate (which is the price of borrowing money) rises.

A similar controversy raged in the early 2010s, when growth was sluggish but the U.S. economy was saddled with record government deficits and debt. Some economists, such as Paul Krugman, of Princeton University, and Joseph Stiglitz, of Columbia University (both Nobel laureates), felt that much more stimulus was needed. Others, such as John Taylor, of Stanford University, questioned the efficacy of more stimulus and advocated instead for a long-term credible deficit reduction plan.

---

[1] However, not all economists believed that these measurements were correct. The late Robert Eisner, of Northwestern University, argued that when adjusted for inflation, the budget deficit was smaller than it appeared when stated in nominal terms. For these and other reasons, he believed that fiscal policy was not as effective as it could be. For example, in his view, the reported deficit in 1980 of $61 billion was actually an adjusted surplus of almost $8 billion. However, Eisner's views were controversial and failed to comfort the many people who were concerned about the size and persistence of recent federal budget deficits.

Are Budget Deficits Inflationary?

One reason why the public is concerned about deficits is that deficits are often thought to cause inflation. Whether this is the case depends on how the deficits are financed. One way the government can finance a deficit is to print new money. In other words, the Fed can increase the money supply, enabling the government to use the additional money to pay for the portion of its expenditures not covered by tax revenues. If deficits are financed in this way and the consequent increases in the money supply are substantial, the result may be inflation. This follows from the fact, stressed repeatedly in previous chapters, that substantial increases in the money supply may cause inflation.

But recent deficits in the United States have been financed largely by government borrowing. Every so often, the Treasury sells a few billion dollars worth of IOUs (bonds, notes, or bills). To sell its securities, the Treasury must offer potential buyers a high enough rate of return to make them an attractive investment. Suppose that the Treasury issues $1 billion worth of one-year securities today to cover a deficit of $1 billion. If the rate of interest is 10 percent, it must pay the $1 billion plus interest of $100 million at the end of one year. To pay this $1.1 billion to the holders of these securities, it must borrow $1.1 billion a year from now. If it again has to pay 10 percent interest, it will owe $1.21 billion (the principal of $1.1 billion plus $0.11 billion in interest) a year hence. Therefore, the amount that the government has to borrow to finance a $1 billion deficit today grows over time.

However, so long as the government does not create new money to finance the deficit, the result need not be inflationary. But what if the government sells its securities to the Federal Reserve rather than to households and firms? In this case, when the Fed purchases the securities from the government, it creates new money to buy them. (Recall from Chapter 21 that the Fed increases bank reserves when it buys government securities. But unlike the case considered there, the Fed purchases the securities from the government, not from General Motors.) This increase in the money supply results in an increase in aggregate demand, which eventually pushes up the price level.

Going a step further, Nobel laureate Thomas Sargent, of New York University, and Neil Wallace, of Pennsylvania State University, have pointed out that even if deficits are not financed right away by the creation of new money, they may have inflationary consequences. As previously illustrated, the interest payments resulting from a growing national debt can become very large indeed. Suppose that investors become convinced that at some point in the reasonably near future the level of government debt will become so big that the interest payments will constitute a disturbingly large proportion of the government's budget. If they think that the government will resort to the creation of new money at that time to finance all or part of the deficit, they are likely to fear substantial inflation at that time.

Faced with this prospect, investors may insist on a relatively high interest rate on government securities to compensate them for the anticipated inflation, and they may try to hold less money, since the value of money is expected to fall. At the same time, they may increase their demand for goods, thus pushing up the price level now. The result is that even though the deficit is not financed right away by the creation of new money, there may be inflation.

But if the deficit is kept within reasonable bounds, this situation need not occur. So long as the deficit is small enough that investors remain convinced that the government is willing and able to keep the money supply under proper control, inflation is avoidable. Even if the deficit is very large, inflation can be avoided if people believe that deficits of this magnitude are only temporary and that in a relatively short time, the budget will be brought into closer balance.

Do Budget Deficits Crowd Out Private Investment?

Another reason why people are concerned about large budget deficits is that they fear that the government's deficit spending may result in a substantial cut in investment spending by the private sector. In other words, they fear that government budget deficits may crowd out private investment. Why may this occur? Because large government borrowing may push up the interest rate, which in turn may cut private investment.

Crowding-out effect

To illustrate how the **crowding-out effect** can occur, consider panel A of Figure 24.2, which shows the private sector's demand and supply curves for loanable funds. The demand curve for loanable funds, D_1, shows the total quantity of loanable funds demanded by firms and households at each interest rate. (Recall from Chapter 17 that the interest rate is the price paid for the use of loanable funds.) The supply curve for loanable funds, S_1, shows the total quantity of loanable funds supplied by households, firms, and others at each interest rate. The equilibrium level of the interest rate, where the quantity of loanable funds demanded equals the quantity supplied, is 8 percent; and the equilibrium amount of funds borrowed for all purposes is $500 billion.

Now suppose that the government, which formerly did not have to borrow, increases its spending by $200 billion, and the spending increase is financed entirely by borrowing. The result, as shown in panel A of Figure 24.2, is that the demand curve for loanable funds shifts to the right (from D_1 to D_2); this reflects the government's demand for the additional $200 billion. Because of this shift of the demand curve, the equilibrium interest rate rises to 10 percent and the quantity of funds borrowed increases to $600 billion. But $200 billion of these funds go to the government, which means that the private sector borrows only $400 billion. Therefore, the private sector borrows, and hence invests, $100 billion less than it did before the government entered the market for loanable funds to finance its $200 billion deficit.

However, this analysis may be incomplete. If the extra $200 billion in government expenditure increases national output (and disposable income),

FIGURE 24.2

How Government Borrowing Can Crowd Out Private Investment

If the government enters the market for loanable funds to finance its $200 billion deficit, the demand curve for loanable funds shifts to the right from D_1 to D_2, with the result that the interest rate rises from 8 percent to 10 percent and the quantity of funds borrowed by the private sector drops from $500 billion to $400 billion, as shown in panel A. If the extra government expenditure increases national output (and disposable income), the amount of saving may increase, pushing the supply curve to the right from S_1 to S_2, as shown in panel B. The result is that the interest rate rises to only 9 percent and the quantity of funds borrowed by the private sector falls to only $450 billion, not $400 billion.

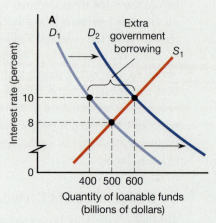

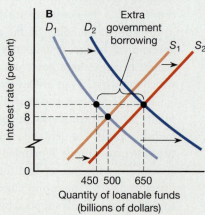

the amount of saving may increase (in accord with the discussion on the saving function in Chapter 17). Consequently, the supply curve for loanable funds may shift to the right (from S_1 to S_2), as shown in panel B of Figure 24.2, with the result that the interest rate rises to only 9 percent, and the private sector borrows, and hence invests, $450 billion (rather than the $400 billion in panel A). Therefore, the private sector invests $50 billion less than it did before the government set out to borrow $200 billion (rather than the $100 billion less in panel A). Under these circumstances, a smaller amount of private investment is crowded out than in panel A, where the increased government expenditure did not increase national output.

Why does it matter if some private investment is crowded out? The answer is that if private investment is crowded out, the total amount of capital in the economy is smaller than otherwise. (Recall from Chapter 15 that net investment equals the change in the total amount of capital.) And a smaller capital stock means that our population has fewer and poorer tools to work with—hence, less output. Consequently, large and persistent budget deficits really can harm future generations, because they may result in a smaller total amount of capital being passed on to our descendants.

In fact, however, private investment in the United States did not fall substantially in the face of the large deficits of the 1980s, because foreigners provided much of the funds. For example, the Japanese purchased large amounts of our government securities. What this means is that future generations of Americans, while they will have a capital stock that is not much reduced, will owe a substantial amount to foreigners. Obviously, when the government borrows from abroad, purchasing power is transferred from foreigners to us when the borrowing occurs but from us to foreigners when we pay interest on the debt and repay the principal.

Another effect of the high interest rates induced by large deficits was an increase in the value of the dollar relative to other currencies. This was because foreign investors had to buy dollars in the early 1980s to purchase U.S. securities, which (because of our high interest rates) were attractive to them. Due to the swollen demand for dollars, the value of a dollar (relative to the Japanese yen or German mark) rose. One consequence of this was that U.S. exports fell (because U.S. goods became more expensive relative to foreign goods) and U.S. imports rose (because foreign goods became cheaper relative to U.S. goods). Thus, large deficits tend to depress our net exports.

Crowding-in effect

Finally, some economists believe that under certain circumstances, deficits can increase, not decrease, investment. This is known as the **crowding-in effect**. The idea is that if the economy experiences considerable unemployment, the government's deficit spending may increase national output, which in turn may increase investment. Of course, the magnitude of this effect depends on how sensitive real GDP is to the extra government spending and how sensitive investment by the private sector is to whatever increase occurs in real GDP. If the economy is at or close to full employment, it is unlikely that this effect will occur, but if the economy is at the pit of a depression, this effect, according to some economists, may overwhelm the crowding-out effect.

The Structural Deficit

To see whether fiscal policy is *expansionary* (increasing aggregate demand) or *contractionary* (reducing aggregate demand), people often look at the size of the budget deficit. A large deficit often is viewed as more expansionary than a small one (or a surplus). However, this can be quite misleading, since budget deficits can occur because the economy is at less than full employment (that is,

Structural deficit

the lowest sustainable unemployment rate compatible with reasonable price stability). A better measure is the **structural deficit**, which shows the difference between government expenditures and tax revenues that would result if gross domestic product were at its potential, not its actual, level.

For example, consider the situation in 1958, when the Eisenhower administration ran a deficit of over $10 billion. Basically, the reason for this deficit was that with the unemployment rate at about 7 percent, there was a substantial gap between actual and potential output. The gross domestic product fell from 1957 to 1958, and as a result, incomes and federal tax collections fell and the government ran a deficit. But this $10 billion deficit was entirely due to the high level of unemployment in the country (see Case Study 18.2).

Had gross domestic product been at its potential level, there would have been a surplus of about $5 billion in 1958. Incomes and federal tax receipts would have been higher. Government spending and the tax rates in 1958 were not such as to produce a deficit if output had been at its potential level. On the contrary, if gross domestic product had been at its potential level, tax receipts would have increased so that federal revenues would have exceeded expenditure by about $5 billion.

It is important to distinguish between the structural deficit and the actual deficit. If the actual budget deficit is growing but the structural budget deficit is falling, most economists would feel that fiscal policy is not becoming more expansionary. As you can see in Figure 24.3, the structural deficit can differ substantially

FIGURE 24.3

Structural and Actual Budget Deficits as a Percent of GDP, 1980–2011

The structural deficit shows the difference between government expenditure and tax revenue that would result if the gross domestic product were at its potential level. (*Note*: The structural budget deficits have been adjusted for inflation.)

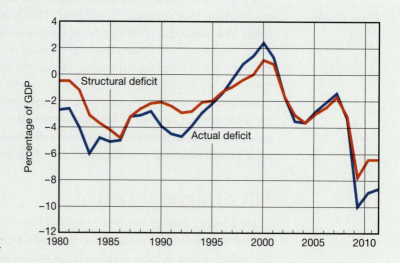

Source: Budget and Economic Outlook: Fiscal Years 2012 to 2022 (Washington, DC: Congressional Budget Office, January 2012).

from the actual deficit. To understand whether fiscal policy is becoming more expansionary or contractionary, you must understand the difference.

The National Debt: Size and Growth

National debt

As we have seen, when the federal government incurs a deficit, it generally borrows money to cover the difference. The **national debt** (composed of bonds, notes, and other government IOUs of various kinds) is the result of such borrowing. These IOUs are held by individuals, firms, banks, and public agencies. There is a large and very important market for government securities, which are relatively riskless and highly liquid. If you look at the *New York Times* or *Wall Street Journal*, for example, you can find the prices at which each of a large number of issues of these bonds, notes, and bills are quoted.

How large is the national debt? In 2012, as shown in Figure 24.4, it was about $16.2 trillion. Without question, this is a huge amount, but it is important to relate the size of the national debt to the size of our national output. After all, a $16.2 trillion debt means one thing if our annual output is $16 trillion and another thing if our annual output is $1 trillion. As a percent of output, the national debt was roughly twice as large in 2012 as in 1939. In 2012, the debt

FIGURE 24.4

Size of the National Debt, United States, 1940–2012

The national debt, about $16.2 trillion in 2012, grew rapidly in the 1980s, 1990s, and 2000s due to huge government deficits.

Source: Economic Report of the President, February 2013.

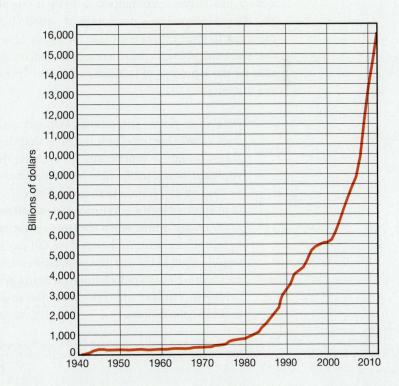

FIGURE 24.5

National Debt as a Percentage of National Output, United States, 1929–2012

As a percentage of national output, the national debt declined steadily from World War II to about 1980. During the 1980s and early 1990s, it increased. It fell in the late 1990s but has since risen sharply.

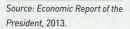

Source: Economic Report of the President, 2013.

was about 104 percent of output; in 1939, it was about 54 percent of output. The debt (expressed as a percentage of output) is shown in Figure 24.5. The rapid rise in recent years is a cause for alarm. Many economists have warned that there are problems in incurring large deficits of the kind that were responsible for the rapid rate of increase in the debt during the 1980s, 1990s, 2000s and 2010s:[2]

> ➤ *Burden on future generations.* Why are people so agitated about the debt's size? One important reason is that they see the debt as a burden thrust on future generations. To evaluate this idea, it is important to recognize that a public debt is not like your debt or mine, which must be paid off at a certain time in the future. In practice, new government debt is issued by the government to pay off maturing public debt. There never comes a time when we must collectively reach into our pockets to pay off the debt. And even if we did pay it off, the same generation would collect as the one that paid. However, as stressed, the deficits that create the debt can put a burden on future generations if they crowd out private investment and thus reduce the amount of capital turned over to future generations.

[2] Note that much of the public debt is in the hands of government agencies, not held by the public. For example, in 2012, about 70 percent was held by the public. Much of the rest was held by the Social Security trust fund.

➤ *Effects of externally held debt.* To the extent that the debt is held by foreigners, we must send goods and services overseas to pay the interest on it. This means that less goods and services are available for our citizens. Therefore, if we finance a particular government activity by borrowing from foreigners, the costs may be transferred to future generations, since they must pay the interest. But from the point of view of the world as a whole, the current generation sacrifices goods and services, since the lending country forgoes current goods and services. Even if the debt is incurred to purchase capital goods, they may produce enough extra output to cover the interest payments.

➤ *Redistribution of income and the effects on incentives.* Taxes must be collected from the public at large to pay interest to the holders of government bonds, notes, and other obligations. To the extent that the bondholders receiving the interest are wealthier than the public as a whole, there is some redistribution of income from the poor to the rich. To the extent that the taxes needed to obtain the money to pay interest on the debt reduce incentives, the result also may be a smaller national output.

A postscript should be added regarding the idea that the national debt imposes a burden on future generations. The principal way in which one generation can impose such a burden on another is by using up some of the country's productive capacity or failing to add a normal increment in this capacity. This, of course, is quite different from incurring debt. For example, World War II would have imposed a burden on subsequent generations whether or not the national debt was increased. However it was financed, the war would have meant that our resources had to be used for tanks and war planes rather than for keeping up and expanding our productive capacity during 1941–1945. And this imposed a real burden on Americans living after 1945—as well, of course, as those living during the war.

The Political Economy of Budget Deficits

One reason why it has been so difficult to reduce the government's large budget deficits is that politicians have been extremely reluctant to favor tax hikes, which seldom are popular with voters. Another reason is that Congress and the president have found it difficult to agree on the sorts of government expenditures that should be cut.

The Reagan administration was opposed to tax increases and in favor of spending reductions but not cuts in defense spending. In 1987 and 1988, Democrats tried to pin the responsibility for the huge deficit on President Reagan because of his unwillingness to raise taxes or cut defense spending. Republicans, in turn, tried to pin the responsibility on congressional Democrats who resisted cuts in spending on domestic programs.

In late 1990, President George H. W. Bush, abandoning his opposition to new taxes, engaged in a long series of negotiations with Congress to try to reduce the deficit. The result was an increase in the income tax rate for highest-income families from 28 percent to 31 percent, a hike in taxes on cigarettes, beer, and wine, and other tax increases, as well as statements that spending cuts would occur. However, government forecasts indicated that the budget deficit was likely to be over $300 billion in 1991, due in part to the recession.

When President Clinton took office in 1993, one of his first steps was to increase taxes. Income taxes on the well-to-do increased substantially, with the top income tax rate going up to about 40 percent. However, while this measure, which only narrowly passed in Congress, cut the deficit, it by no means eliminated it. In 1995, the deficit was still $164 billion. However, sustained strong economic growth in the late 1990s accomplished what the Reagan, Bush, and early Clinton administrations had failed to do—balance the budget.

President George W. Bush campaigned on a platform of tax cuts. Despite a close and contested election, he went on to enact two very large tax cuts in 2001 and 2003. These, along with the 2001 recession and the wars in Afghanistan and Iraq, put the budget back in deficit again.

With the deep recession of 2008–2009 (the worst since the Great Depression) and the large stimulus enacted in early 2009 by the Obama administration, the U.S. public debt skyrocketed.

Alternative Philosophies Regarding the Federal Budget

At least three philosophies concerning the government budget are worthy of examination.

Should the Budget Be Balanced Annually?

The first budgetary philosophy says that the government's budget should be balanced each year. This is the philosophy that generally prevailed, here and abroad, until a few decades ago. Superficially, it seems reasonable. After all, won't a family or firm go bankrupt if it continues to spend more than it takes in? Why should the government be any different? However, the truth is that the government has economic capabilities, powers, and responsibilities entirely different from those of any family or firm, and it is misleading—sometimes even pernicious—to assume that what is sensible for a family or firm is also sensible for the government.

If this policy of balancing the budget is accepted, the government cannot use fiscal policy as a tool to stabilize the economy. Indeed, if the government attempts to balance its budget each year, it may make unemployment or inflation worse rather than better. For example, suppose that severe unemployment occurs because of a drop in national output. When incomes drop, tax receipts drop as well. If the government attempts to balance its budget, it must cut its spending or increase tax rates, both of which may tend to lower, not raise, national output. On the other hand, suppose that inflation occurs because spending increases too rapidly. When incomes increase, tax receipts increase, too. For the government to balance its budget, it must increase its spending or decrease tax rates, either of which may tend to raise, not lower, spending.

Despite these considerations, a constitutional amendment to mandate a balanced federal budget has had a considerable amount of political support from time to time. No doubt, the federal government, through inappropriate fiscal or monetary policies, has frequently been responsible for excessive inflation or unemployment. Some economists go so far as to say that the real problem is how to prevent the government from creating disturbances, rather than how to use the government budget (and monetary policy) to offset disturbances arising from the private sector. But for the reasons discussed already, most economists would not go so far as to conclude that the government should balance its budget each year.

Should the Budget Be Balanced over the Business Cycle?

A second budgetary philosophy says that the government's budget should be balanced over the course of each business cycle. As we saw in previous chapters, the rate of growth of national output tends to behave cyclically. It tends to increase for a while, then drop, increase, then drop, and so on. Unemployment also tends to ebb and flow in a similar cyclical fashion. According to this second budgetary policy, the government is not expected to balance its budget each year but is expected to run a big enough surplus during periods of high employment to offset the deficit it runs during the ensuing period of excessive unemployment. This policy seems to give the government enough flexibility to run the deficits or surpluses that, according to many economists, may be needed to stabilize the economy, while at the same time allaying any public fear of a chronically unbalanced budget. It certainly seems to be a rational way to reconcile the government's use of fiscal policy to promote noninflationary full employment with the public's uneasiness over chronically unbalanced budgets.

Unfortunately, however, it does contain one fundamental flaw. There is no reason to believe that the size of the deficits required to eliminate excessive unemployment equals the size of the surpluses required to moderate the subsequent inflation. Suppose that national output falls sharply and causes severe and prolonged unemployment, then regains its full-employment level only briefly, and falls again. In such a case, the deficits incurred to get the economy back to full employment are likely to exceed by far the surpluses run during the brief period of full employment. Hence, there would be no way to stabilize the economy without running an unbalanced budget over the course of this business cycle. If the government attempted to balance the budget over the course of each business cycle, its actions might run counter to an effective fiscal policy designed to promote full employment with stable prices.

Should the Budget Be Balanced at All?

Finally, a third budgetary philosophy says that the government's budget should be set to promote whatever attainable combination of unemployment and inflation seems socially optimal, even if this means that the budget is unbalanced over considerable periods of time. Proponents of this policy argue that although it may mean a continual growth in the public debt, the problems caused by a moderate growth in the public debt are small when compared with the social costs of unemployment and inflation.

Changes in Public Attitudes

Certainly, the history of the past 50 years has been characterized by enormous changes in the nation's attitude toward the government budget. Fifty years ago, the prevailing attitude was that the government's budget should be balanced. The emergence of the Keynesian theory of the determination of national output and employment shook this attitude, at least to the point where it became respectable to advocate a balanced budget over the business cycle rather than in each year. In many circles, persistent deficits of moderate size were viewed with no alarm.

In the late 1970s and early 1980s, there was some movement back toward earlier views favoring balanced budgets. Conservatives emphasized the usefulness of the balanced budget as a device to limit government spending, which they regarded as excessive. The public tended to blame very high rates of inflation on large deficits. Although neither political party was prepared (even remotely) to renounce deficits, considerable lip service was paid to the desirability of a balanced budget. For example, in August 1982, the Senate approved a constitutional amendment requiring a balanced budget, while at the same time the government was running a deficit of over $100 billion. In the late 1990s, with the budget in surplus, the debate shifted, and the big fiscal policy question became what to do with the surplus: cut taxes, raise spending, or pay down the national debt (see Case Study 24.2). During the 2004 presidential campaign, the focus was back on ways to cut the large and

CAN WE AFFORD SOCIAL SECURITY AND MEDICARE?

George W. Bush

The simple (if scary) answer to this question is no—at least, not given current economic and demographic trends.

In 2012 the Social Security system had a surplus of about $55 billion. This surplus is expected to decline in the next decade as the baby boom generation starts to retire. Over the next 20 years, Social Security will come under pressure as a result of two adverse trends: declining birth rates and increasing longevity. This means that the dependency ratio (the ratio of people withdrawing money from the Social Security trust fund to those contributing to it) will rise from 20 percent to 40 percent by the middle of the century.

The problem is worse for Medicare and Medicaid because of the rapid rise in health care costs. As a share of the GDP, the cost of these two medical programs is expected to rise from 3.5 percent in 2012 to around 6 percent by 2050. In contrast, the share of Social Security

will rise "only" from 5 percent to 6 percent. As a result, over the next 40 to 50 years, these entitlement programs, as they are called, will generate cumulative deficits worth tens of trillions of dollars. The problem is actually bigger outside the United States, since the populations in Japan and most European countries are aging faster than in the United States.

What is to be done about this problem? There are two basic types of solutions: raise taxes and cut benefits. It seems inevitable that in the course of our lifetime, Social Security taxes will be raised. Just as likely will be cuts in benefits, which probably will show up as some combination of actual cuts in benefits paid to individual recipients, increases in the retirement age (the age at which you can collect benefits), and means testing (paying benefits only to people below a threshold income).

As a proposed solution to this looming problem, the administration of George W. Bush recommended the "privatization" of Social Security. Specifically, it recommended that contributors to Social Security be allowed to invest at least part of these funds for their own retirement, including in the stock market. While such an idea may have merits in its own right, the higher potential returns on the retirement contributions will not be anywhere near enough to close the big gap in Social Security. In the end, workers in the United States and elsewhere must save more for retirement. Either they will have to do this on their own, or it will be done for them via higher taxes.

growing budget deficits. President George W. Bush (supported by congressional Republicans) proposed spending cuts. Most of the Democratic contenders proposed various types of tax increases. While this discussion was put on hold during the 2008–2009 recession and subsequent anemic recovery, it was a source of contentious debate before, during and after the 2012 presidential election. Between 2011 and 2013, the debate over how to cut the federal budget deficit and stabilize the U.S. debt ratio were among the most bitter and divisive in decades.

CASE STUDY 24.2

WHAT HAPPENED TO THE FEDERAL BUDGET SURPLUS?

After years of wrangling over how to distribute the pain of deficit cutting (raising taxes or slashing spending), in the late 1990s, the president and Congress had to deal with an easier choice—at least in theory.

Three basic choices about the surplus could be made: (1) spend the money on education, health care, defense, and so on; (2) give the surplus back to the taxpayers in the form of tax cuts; or (3) pay down the national debt and, in effect, use the surplus to replenish the trust funds of the Social Security system.

In the summer of 1999, the *Wall Street Journal* conducted a survey that asked: "After setting aside two-thirds of the projected surpluses for Social Security and Medicare, what should be done with the rest?"* Approximately 33 percent of the respondents voted for a tax cut and 55 percent voted for spending increases. During the presidential primaries in early 2000, the debate focused primarily on the choice between cutting taxes and cutting the national debt, even though the support for the former was limited.

The case for giving the surplus back to taxpayers was argued by supply-siders (see Case Study 23.4). They used two types of reasoning. The first was the classic supply-side argument that tax rate reductions increase incentives to work and save, thereby increasing economic growth. The second was a taxpayer fairness argument that the revenue belongs to the taxpayer, and if the government has no need for it, the government should return it.

Those opposed to tax cuts countered that in light of the booming economy and stock market, it was hard to argue that tax rates in the United States were depressing economic growth. As for the taxpayer fairness argument, giving back the surplus now would only leave a large debt burden for future generations. Finally, opponents argued that cutting taxes during an economic boom ran the risk of triggering higher inflation. Why not save the option to cut taxes for when the economy really needs it, during the next recession?

The case for paying off the debt relied foremost on classical fiscal theory, which says that running surpluses and reducing debt adds to national saving, which in turn spurs investment and economic growth. Second, proponents of debt repayment reasoned that, given the uncertainties of the business cycle, the surpluses could turn into deficits again in the near future; therefore, why take chances with tax cuts or spending increases?

The opposition to the debt reduction plans came from both sides of the political spectrum.

Supply-siders argued that raising economic growth (using tax cuts) was a much better way of reducing the debt burden than saving the surplus. Liberal Democrats maintained that accumulating budget surpluses depresses growth and increases unemployment. In the end, the "great surplus of the millennium" disappeared and the red ink started to flow again for a complex set of reasons. First, the Bush administration, with the approval of Congress, put in place large multiyear tax cuts in both 2001 and 2003. Second, after the terrorist attacks of September 11, 2001, federal spending on homeland security and the war against terror increased dramatically. Third, the war in Iraq during the spring of 2003 and the subsequent reconstruction effort boosted defense spending. Last but not least, 2001 was a recession year, and recessions have a way of making surpluses evaporate. By 2003, the federal budget deficit was at record levels. It fell briefly in the mid-2000s and then shot up to record levels in 2008 and 2009, thanks to an even deeper recession and a huge stimulus program.

Wall Street Journal, July 29, 1999, p. 1.

The Federal Budgetary Process

Determining how much the federal government should spend is a mammoth undertaking, involving thousands of people and hundreds of thousands of hours of labor. Decisions on expenditures are part of the budgetary process. The **federal budget** is a statement of the government's anticipated expenditures and revenues. The federal budget is for a fiscal year, from October 1 to September 30.

Federal budget

About 15 months before the beginning of a particular fiscal year, the various agencies of the federal government begin to prepare their program proposals for that year. Then they make detailed budget requests, which the president, with his Office of Management and Budget, goes over. Since the agencies generally want more than the president wants to spend, he usually cuts down their requests.

In January (preceding the beginning of the fiscal year), the president submits his budget to Congress. Congress then spends many months in intensive deliberation and negotiation. Congressional committees concerned with particular areas like defense or education recommend changes in the president's budget. The Congressional Budget Office, headed in 2012 by Douglas Elmendorf, makes various economic analyses to help senators and representatives evaluate alternative programs.

The Federal Tax Legislative Process

It is one thing for the federal government to decide how much to spend and on what; it is another to raise the money to underwrite these programs. This section describes how the federal government decides how much to tax. Of course, this problem is not tackled from scratch every year. Instead, the government takes the existing tax structure and changes it from time to time as desirable. Frequently, the major initiative leading to a change in the tax laws comes from the president, who requests tax changes in his State of the Union message, his budget message, or a special tax message. Much of the groundwork underlying his proposals is carried out by the Treasury Department, which includes the Internal Revenue Service.

The proposal of a major tax change generally brings about considerable public debate. Representatives of labor, industry, agriculture, and other economic and social groups present their opinions. Newspaper articles, radio shows, and television commentators analyze the issues. By the time Congress begins to look seriously at the proposal, the battle lines between those who favor the change and those who oppose it generally are clearly drawn. The tax bill incorporating the change is first considered by the Ways and Means Committee of the House of Representatives, a powerful committee composed of members drawn from both political parties. After public hearings, the committee goes into executive session and reviews each proposed change with its staff and the Treasury staff. After careful study, the committee arrives at a bill it recommends, though this bill may or may not conform to what the president asked for. Then the bill is referred to the entire House of Representatives for approval. Only rarely is a major tax bill recommended by the committee turned down by the House.

Next, the bill is sent to the Senate. There it is referred to the Finance Committee, which is organized like the House Ways and Means Committee. The Finance Committee also holds hearings, discusses the bill at length, makes changes to it, and sends its version of the bill to the entire Senate, where there frequently is considerable debate. Ultimately, it is brought to a vote. If it does not pass, that ends the process. If it does pass (and if it differs from the House version of the bill, which is generally the case), then a conference committee must be formed to iron out the differences between the House and Senate versions.

Finally, when this compromise is worked out, the result must be passed by both houses and sent to the president. The president rarely vetoes a tax bill, although it has occasionally been done.

Recent U.S. Experience with Fiscal Policy and Deficits

It should be evident by now that more is known today about the impact of deficits—and fiscal policy generally—than when the economy was staggered by the Great Depression. But this does not mean that economists have all (or nearly all) the answers. Enough is known to keep the economy from careening off a bumpy road; avoiding the potholes (some of which are very large) is another matter. The hard choices faced by economists in the top councils of government can be demonstrated by a close inspection of attempts in the past 35 years to give the economy a smoother ride.

The Carter Years

We begin with the Carter years. When Jimmy Carter became president in 1977, the unemployment rate was 6.9 percent and the inflation rate was 6.7 percent. In the face of heightened inflation, fiscal policy did not attempt to rein in the economy very much. The deficit in 1978 was about $30 billion; the structural budget deficit was over $10 billion. Some observers were not sure that the inflation rate could be reduced substantially without a recession. In 1979, there was a continuing debate within the administration and in public over this question. In 1980, there was a very brief recession, but it did little to cool off inflation. As in previous years, the federal government ran a structural budget deficit.

The Reagan Years

When the Reagan administration took office in 1981, it was committed to cut both government expenditures and taxes. In August 1981, the administration pushed through Congress a huge tax cut for both individuals and businesses. At the same time, it reduced federal expenditures (relative to the level that former President Carter had proposed). However, the tax cuts were far in excess of the spending cuts, particularly since reductions in GDP in late 1981 also tended to reduce tax receipts. Therefore, the administration was faced with record deficits of over $100 billion in fiscal 1982 and $150 billion in fiscal 1983. In early 1982, President Reagan said he would try to cut spending further in an attempt to soak up some of the red ink. But the economy was in a recession (with an unemployment rate of 9 percent) and little sympathy could be found on Capitol Hill for further spending cuts. Since inflation had fallen to well under double digits, unemployment once again seemed to be public enemy number one.

In November 1982, the economy pulled out of the recession and the expansion began. Economists of all schools, but particularly supply-side economists (recall Chapter 23), gave the 1981 tax cut considerable credit for increasing real GDP and reducing unemployment. During 1983 and 1984, both years of healthy expansion, the federal government ran huge deficits of about $200 billion. President Reagan vowed that he would not raise taxes and proposed cuts in nonmilitary government expenditures. In 1986, Congress passed a major tax reform bill that lowered tax rates and broadened the tax base by reducing loopholes. In late 1987, after the sharp stock market decline, President Reagan and congressional leaders met to try to find a mutually agreeable way to cut the huge deficits, but limited progress was made.

The George H. W. Bush Years

In November 1988, George H. W. Bush, then vice president, was elected to the presidency on a platform of "no new taxes." Many critics, here and abroad, doubted that the federal deficit could be reduced without additional tax revenue. During 1989 and 1990, the deficit continued to be about $200 billion. In late 1990, Congress and President Bush agreed to a fiscal package that would reduce the deficit but by no means eliminate it. There were additional taxes, including increased tax rates for high-income families and bigger taxes on cigarettes, beer, and wine. After an expansion of record length, the U.S. economy entered a recession in late 1990, and some observers questioned whether it was a good time to raise taxes.

The Clinton Years

Bill Clinton, in his campaign for the presidency, promised a tax cut for the middle class and substantial tax increases for the wealthy. After his election, he abandoned the idea of a middle-class tax cut but pressed for an upper-income tax increase. After intricate negotiations with congressional Democrats, he managed to get his plan accepted in 1993 by the narrowest of margins. Also included in his plan was a reduction in government expenditures, but Republicans (none of whom voted for the Clinton plan) argued that these spending cuts were too small (and, in some cases, too uncertain). The effect of his plan was to reduce the deficit, which both Democrats and Republicans (as well as supporters of Ross Perot) seemed to favor. In Clinton's second term in office, thanks to the longest U.S. expansion, the budget deficit was eliminated and the United States had a budget surplus for the first time in over 25 years.

The George W. Bush Years

George W. Bush, having learned from his father not to raise taxes (especially after promising not to), campaigned on a pledge of large tax cuts. Even though he won by the narrowest of margins, he proceeded to enact (with the help

RISING NATIONAL DEBT LEVELS ARE UNSUSTAINABLE

Few countries have survived the steady rise of their government debt levels unscathed. Circumstances may differ, but most countries that have seen the ratio of their government debt to GDP rise to over 100 percent have suffered some kind of crisis of confidence. This usually means that investors flee the country, pushing up interest rates and pushing down the value of the currency.

It is hard to say when something like this could happen to the United States, which, after all, does have something of a unique role in the world economy. Nevertheless, even the United States cannot write IOUs indefinitely. In 2012, gross national debt was already over 100 percent of GDP. At some point, investors will begin to worry that the American government may have some trouble repaying its debt. These investors will then do one of two things: either sell U.S. government bonds or demand higher interest rates to hold those bonds. The resulting higher interest rates could do a lot of economic damage.

Fortunately, the U.S. problem is inherently more manageable than the problems facing many of the highly indebted countries in Europe (for example, Greece, Italy, Japan, and Spain) for several reasons: (1) The American population is aging more slowly than the populations of other rich countries, creating less pressure on pensions and health care programs; (2) tax rates are lower in the United States than in most other rich countries (leaving the option open for tax increases to be part of the solution); (3) productivity growth is higher in the United States than in most other rich countries (helping to bring in more tax revenues); and (4) private pension and health plans play a bigger role in the United States than in most other rich countries (helping to keep the debt burden from rising even further).

Nevertheless, it would be foolhardy to assume that the "debt bomb" will defuse itself, even in the United States. Going forward, political leaders will have to do some combination of the following: exercise spending restraint, something that has been woefully lacking in recent years; fix the entitlement programs so as not to put an increasing burden on future generations; and resist the temptation to make large permanent cuts in taxes without also enacting meaningful tax reform.

So, in the end, inaction is not an option when it comes to the large and growing U.S. national debt.

of Congress) massive tax cuts in 2001 and 2003. These cuts, along with the 2001 recession and higher spending on homeland security (after the terrorist attacks of September 11, 2001) and defense (because of the war in Iraq), wiped out the budget surpluses and generated massive deficits. During the presidential campaign in 2004, the deficit (and how to cut it) became a major topic of debate.

The Obama Years

Barack Obama became president of the United States in the middle of the worst recession since the 1930s. Early in his administration, the fiscal choice was relatively easy—to provide massive stimulus to help prevent another Great Depression. However, soon the discussion turned to how to reign in the runaway deficits and debt. The debate between the president and congressional Democrats, on the one hand, and congressional Republicans, on the other, proved to be highly contentious and damaging to confidence in the United States. Democrats wanted to cut the deficit mostly by raising taxes (especially on the rich). Republicans wanted to reduce the deficit primarily by cutting spending. During these standoffs (in particular during the summer of 2011 and the autumn of 2013), the risk that the US might default on its debt rose—so much that in 2011 Standard & Poor's lowered the credit rating on U.S. government debt. Also, in the fall of 2013 the deadlock over the budget meant that large parts of the U.S. government were shut down for 16 days. The good news is that despite this very poor way of conducting policy, Congress and the president were able to stabilize the U.S. debt ratio and stop it from rising.

REVIEW AND PRACTICE

Summary

1 The budget deficit or surplus is the difference between government expenditures and receipts. Many, but not all, economists are concerned about the size and persistence of the deficit.

2 One reason why the public is concerned about deficits is that deficits are thought to cause inflation. If the government finances the deficit by increasing the money supply, this may well be the case.

3 Many economists believe that the government's deficit spending may result in a significant cut in investment spending by the private sector. In other words, they fear that government budget deficits may crowd out private investment because government borrowing may push up the interest rate, and this in turn may reduce private investment.

4 A large deficit is often viewed as being more expansionary than a small one (or a surplus). But this can be misleading, because budget deficits may occur because the economy is at less than full employment. A better measure is the structural deficit, which is the difference between government expenditures and tax revenues that would result if gross domestic product were at its potential, not its actual, level.

5 The national debt is the result of the federal government's borrowing to finance deficits. To the extent that the debt is held by foreigners, we must send goods and services overseas to pay the interest on it (as well, of course, as the principal).

6 The spending decisions of the federal government take place in the context of the budgetary process. The president submits his budget, which is a statement of anticipated expenditures and revenues, to Congress, which votes appropriations.

Problems and Questions

1 Explain how large budget deficits can discourage investment and inhibit the growth of the nation's stock of capital.

2 "An important advantage of public works as a tool of fiscal policy is that they can be started quickly. An important advantage of tax rate changes is that they almost never get embroiled in partisan politics." Comment and evaluate.

3 "The structural deficit is just a lot of hocum to persuade the public that big deficits are smaller and less inflationary than they really are." Comment and evaluate.

4 According to the 1990 *Economic Report of the President*, "research and experience have demonstrated the great advantages of establishing a credible commitment to a policy plan. Improved credibility, which is enhanced by achieving stated policy goals and consistently following stated principles, can favorably affect expectations."[3] Does this mean that the federal government should have acted in accord with its professed desire to reduce the budget deficit?

5 In February 1994, President Clinton said, "On August 10, 1993, I signed the historic budget plan that passed several days earlier; it will reduce federal deficits by more than $500 billion."[4] What difference does it make whether the deficit was cut or not? What are the advantages in cutting it?

Key Terms

budget deficit
budget surplus
crowding-out effect
crowding-in effect

structural deficit
national debt
federal budget

[3] *Economic Report of the President*, 1990, 22.
[4] *Economic Report of the President*, 1994, 3.

Viewpoint for Analysis

In early 2004, the International Monetary Fund published a paper that expressed grave concern about the deteriorating fiscal picture in the United States. Among other things, this paper stated:

> Although fiscal policies have undoubtedly provided valuable support to the recovery so far, the return to large deficits raises two interrelated concerns. First, with budget projections showing large federal fiscal deficits over the next decade, the recent emphasis on cutting taxes, boosting defense and security outlays, and spurring an economic recovery may come at the eventual cost of upward pressure on interest rates, a crowding out of private investment, and an erosion of longer-term U.S. productivity growth.
>
> Second, the evaporation of fiscal surpluses has left the budget even less well prepared to cope with the retirement of the baby boom generation, which will begin later this decade and place massive pressure on the Social Security and Medicare systems. Without the cushion provided by earlier surpluses, there is less time to address the programs' underlying insolvency before government deficits and debt begin to increase unsustainability, making more urgent the need for reform.[5]

(a) How do large budget deficits crowd out private investment and hurt productivity?

(b) In the long term, which is likely to be the less harmful way of reducing the deficit: cutting spending or raising taxes?

(c) What are some ways the government could address the long-term insolvency of Social Security and Medicare?

---

[5] *U.S. Fiscal Policies and Priorities for Long-Run Sustainability* (Geneva, Switzerland: International Monetary Fund, January 7, 2004).

Monetary Policy, Interest Rates, and Economic Activity

LEARNING OBJECTIVES

➤ To explain how the quantity of money affects national output

➤ To describe the relationship between the interest rate and the quantity of money

➤ To recognize the importance and limitations of the crude quantity theory

➤ To assess the Fed's performance in managing the money supply

Just as physicians differ in their treatment of arthritis or cancer, so economists do not see eye to eye on many aspects of monetary policy. In early 2000, the Federal Reserve pushed interest rates up, to the consternation of some economists and the applause of others. Many now feel that the Fed kept interest rates "too low for too long" in 2003 and 2004, helping to fuel the housing bubble, which eventually burst in 2007 and triggered the worst economic downturn since the 1930s. Why should we care what the level of interest rates is? Why all the commotion in the press and on television? The answer may seem obvious, but one purpose of this chapter is to answer this question in some depth.

In previous chapters, we discussed in general terms the impact of money on the economy. In this chapter, we present a more detailed picture of how changes in the quantity of money affect interest rates and economic activity. We also consider how effective monetary policy has been in recent years. To begin with, we consider questions like these: What determines the value of money? What factors influence the demand for money, and what factors influence its quantity? What is the relationship between the quantity of money and the price level? What is the relationship between the quantity of money and the level of gross domestic product? To more fully understand the workings of our economy and the nature of our government's economic policies, we must be able to answer these questions.

The Value of Money

We go back to a very important point mentioned briefly in Chapter 20: there is no gold backing for our money. In other words, there is no way that you can exchange a $10 bill for so many ounces of gold. (If you look at a $10 bill, you will see that it says nothing about what the government gives you in exchange for it.) Currency and demand (and other checkable) deposits are really just debts or IOUs. Currency is the debt of the government, whereas demand deposits are the debts of the banks. Intrinsically, neither currency nor a deposit has any real value. A $10 bill is merely a small piece of paper, and a deposit is merely an entry in a bank's accounts. And as we have seen, even coins are worth far less as metal than their monetary value.

All this may make you feel a bit uncomfortable. After all, if our coins, currency, demand deposits, and other checkable deposits have little or no intrinsic value, doesn't this mean that they can easily become worthless? To answer this question, we must realize that, basically, money has value because people accept it in payment for goods and services. If your college accepts your check in payment for your tuition and your grocer accepts a $20 bill in payment for your groceries, your demand deposit and your currency have value. You can exchange them for the goods and services you want. And your college and grocer accept this money only because they have confidence that they can spend it for the goods and services they want.

Money's Value Depends on the Price Level

Therefore, money is valuable because it buys things. But how valuable is it? For example, how valuable is $1? Clearly, the value of a dollar is equivalent to what a dollar buys. And what a dollar buys depends on the price level. If all prices doubled, the value of a dollar would be cut in half, because a dollar would buy only half as many goods and services as it formerly could. On the other hand, if all prices were reduced by 50 percent, the value of a dollar would double, because a dollar would be able to buy twice as many goods and services as it formerly could. You often hear people say that today's dollar is worth only 50 cents. What they mean is that it will buy only half what a dollar could buy at some specified time in the past.

It is interesting to see how the value of the dollar, as measured by its purchasing power, has varied over time. Figure 25.1 shows how an index of the price level in the United States has changed since 1779. Over time, prices fluctuated sharply, and some of the greatest fluctuations resulted from wars. For example, the price level fell sharply after the Revolutionary War, and our next war—the War of 1812—sent prices skyrocketing, after which there was another postwar drop in prices. The period from about 1820 to about 1860 was marked by relative price stability, but the Civil War resulted in an upward burst followed by

FIGURE 25.1

**Index of Wholesale Prices,
United States, 1779–2012
(1910–1914 = 100)**

The price level has fluctuated
considerably, with sharp
increases generally occurring
during wartime. Since World
War II, however, the price
level has generally tended to
go only one way—up. In the
past 45 years, the price level
has risen more than sixfold.

Source: Economic Report of the
President, 2013.

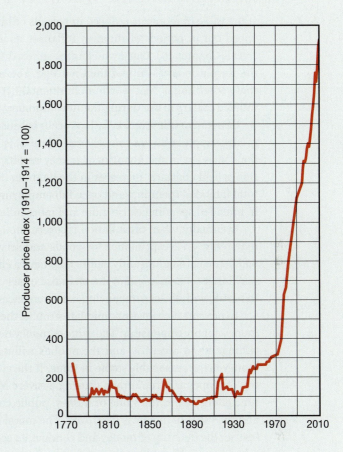

a postwar drop in prices. After a period of relative price stability from 1875 to
1915, there was a doubling of prices during World War I and the usual postwar
drop. World War II saw a price increase of about 40 percent, but there was no
postwar drop in prices. Instead, there has been continual inflation; during the
past 45 years, the price level has risen about fivefold.

The value of money is inversely related to the price level. In inflationary times,
the value of money decreases; the opposite is true when the price level falls (an
infrequent phenomenon in the past four decades). Therefore, the wartime periods, when the price level rose greatly, were periods when the value of the dollar
decreased greatly. The doubling of prices during World War I meant that the
value of the dollar was chopped in half. Similarly, the postwar periods, when the
price level fell greatly, were periods when the value of the dollar increased. The 50
percent decline in prices after the Civil War meant a doubling in the value of the
dollar. Given the extent of the variation in the price level shown in Figure 25.1,
it is clear that the value of the dollar has varied enormously during our history.

Inflation and the Quantity of Money

If the value of money is reduced in periods of inflation, its value can be largely wiped out in periods of runaway inflation, as in Germany after World War I (recall Chapter 19). Our own country suffered from runaway inflation during the Revolutionary War and the Civil War. You may have heard the expression that something is "not worth a continental." It comes from the fact that the inflated dollars in use during the Revolutionary War were called continentals.

Generally, such severe inflations occur because the government increases the money supply at an enormously rapid rate. It is not hard to see why a tremendous increase in the quantity of money results in a runaway inflation. Other things held constant, increases in the quantity of money results in increases in total intended spending, and once full employment is achieved, such increases in intended spending cause more and more inflation.

Eventually, when the inflation is severe enough, households and businesses may refuse to accept money for goods and services, because they fear that it will depreciate significantly before they have a chance to spend it. Instead, they may insist on being paid in merchandise or services. Thus, the economy turns to barter, with the accompanying inconveniences and inefficiency.

To prevent such an economic catastrophe, the government must manage the money supply responsibly. The value of money depends basically on the public's willingness to accept it, and the public's willingness to accept it depends on money being reasonably stable in value. If the government increases the quantity of money at a rapid rate, causing a severe inflation and an accompanying precipitous fall in the value of money, public confidence in money is shaken, and the value of money is destroyed. The moral is clear: the government must restrict the quantity of money and conduct its economic policies so as to maintain a reasonably stable value of money.

Unemployment and the Quantity of Money

In the previous section, we were concerned primarily with what happens when the quantity of money grows too rapidly. The result is inflation. But the quantity of money also can grow too slowly. When this happens, the result, according to most economists, is increased unemployment. If the money supply grows very slowly or decreases, there is a tendency for total intended spending to grow very slowly or decrease. This, in turn, causes national output to grow very slowly or decrease, causing unemployment to increase. (Of course, a cut in national output is particularly likely to push up unemployment.)

According to many economists, the recessions of 1974–1975 and 1980–1982 were due partly to an inadequate growth of the money supply. The Federal Reserve, trying to stem the inflationary tide in 1974 and 1979, cut back on the rate of increase of the money supply. Looking back over past business fluctuations, it appears that an inadequate rate of increase in the quantity of money was responsible, at least in part, for many recessions.

Determinants of the Quantity of Money

Judging from our discussion thus far, it is clear that if we are to avoid excessive unemployment or excessive inflation, the quantity of money must not grow too slowly or too quickly. But what determines the quantity of money? To a considerable extent, it is determined by the Federal Reserve, our nation's central bank. Within limits, the Federal Reserve can and does control the quantity of money. But to some extent, the private sector of the economy also determines the quantity of money. For example, the nation's commercial banks, through their lending (and other) decisions, can influence the money supply.[1] In the remainder of this chapter, we will make the simplifying assumption that the money supply is governed solely by the Federal Reserve.

The Demand for Money

We discussed in general terms how changes in the quantity of money affect the tempo of economic activity. Now we will take a closer look at how changes in the quantity of money affect gross domestic product. The first step in doing this is to discuss the demand for money. Why does a family or firm want to hold money? Certainly, a family can be wealthy without holding much money. We all know stories about very rich people who hold very little money, since virtually all their wealth is tied up in factories, farms, and other nonmonetary assets. Unlike assets that yield profits or interest, money produces no direct return. So why do people and firms want to hold money rather than other kinds of assets? Two of the most important reasons are the **transactions demand for money** and the **precautionary demand for money**.

Transactions demand for money

Precautionary demand for money

Transactions Demand for Money

To carry out most transactions, money is required. Therefore, people and firms have to keep some money on hand and in their checking accounts to buy things. The higher a person's income—in real terms—the more goods and services that person probably will want to purchase and hence the more money he or she will want to hold for transaction purposes. For example, a doctor currently earning $400,000 a year will probably keep more money on hand for transactions purposes than she did many years ago when she was making perhaps $10,000 a year. Because the quantity of money demanded by a household or firm increases with its income, it follows that the total quantity of money demanded

---

[1] Of course, banks do not create money all by themselves. The public's preferences and actions, as well as bank behavior, influence the amount of demand deposits.

for transactions purposes in the economy as a whole is directly related to real gross domestic product. That is, the higher (or lower) the level of real GDP, the greater (or less) the quantity of money demanded for transactions purposes.

In addition, the total quantity of money demanded for transactions purposes is directly related to the price level. That is, the higher (or lower) the price level, the greater (or less) the quantity of money demanded for transactions purposes. Obviously, if the price level were to double tomorrow, you would want to keep more money on hand for transactions purposes. To purchase the same goods and services as before, you would need more money.

Precautionary Demand for Money

In addition to the transactions motive, households and firms like to hold money because they are uncertain concerning the timing and size of future disbursements and receipts. Unpredictable events often require money. People get sick, and houses need repairs. Also, receipts frequently do not come in exactly when expected. To meet such contingencies, people and firms like to put a certain amount of their wealth into money and near-money. In the economy as a whole, the total quantity of money demanded for precautionary purposes (like the quantity demanded for transactions purposes) is likely to vary directly with real GDP and the price level. If GDP goes up, households and firms want to hold more money for precautionary purposes, because their incomes and sales are higher than before the increase in GDP. If the price level goes up, they want to hold more money to offset the reduced purchasing power of the dollar.[2]

The Interest Rate and the Demand Curve for Money

Up to this point, we have discussed why individuals and firms want to hold money. But there are disadvantages, as well as advantages, to holding money. One disadvantage is that the real value of money falls if inflation occurs. Another is that an important cost of holding money is the interest or profit we lose, since instead of holding money, we might have invested it in assets that yield interest or profit. For example, the annual cost of holding $5,000 in money if we can obtain 6 percent on existing investments is $300, the amount of interest or profit forgone.[3]

---

[2] Still another motive for holding money is speculation. People like to hold some of their assets in a form in which they can be sure of its monetary value and can take advantage of future price reductions. The amount of money individuals and firms keep on hand for speculative reasons varies with their expectations concerning future price movements. In particular, if people feel that the prices of bonds and stocks are about to drop soon, they are likely to demand a great deal of money for speculative reasons. By holding money, they can obtain such securities at lower prices than at present.

[3] For simplicity, we assume here that money yields no interest or profit. This is not true, because as we saw earlier, the money supply includes some interest-bearing checkable deposits. But this makes no real difference to our argument. Even if money yields some interest, it yields a much smaller return than alternative investments like bonds. Hence, there is a cost involved in holding money.

FIGURE 25.2

The Demand for Money

Holding the interest rate and price level constant, the quantity of money demanded is directly related to real GDP, as shown in panel A. Holding the interest rate and real GDP constant, the quantity of money demanded is directly related to the price level, as shown in panel B. Holding real GDP and price level constant, the quantity of money demanded is inversely related to the interest rate, as shown in panel C. This last relationship is known as the demand curve for money.

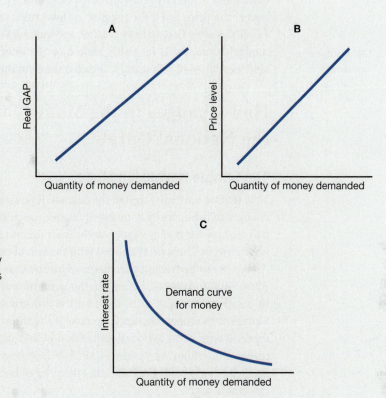

With GDP constant, the amount of money demanded by individuals and firms is inversely related to the interest rate. The higher the interest rate, the smaller the amount of money demanded. The lower the interest rate, the greater the amount of money demanded. This is because the cost of holding money increases as the interest rate or yield on existing investments increases. For example, if the interest rate were 7 percent rather than 6 percent, the cost of holding $5,000 in money for one year would be $350 rather than $300. So, as the interest rate or profit rate increases, people try harder to minimize the amount of money they hold. So do firms. Big corporations like IBM or General Motors are very conscious of the cost of holding cash balances.

Figure 25.2 summarizes three important conclusions of our discussion in this and the previous section. Panel A shows that holding the interest rate and price level constant, the quantity of money demanded is directly related to real GDP. As we explained in the previous section, the higher (or lower) the level of real GDP, the greater (or less) the quantity of money demanded. Panel B shows that with the interest rate and real GDP constant, the quantity of money demanded is directly related to the price level. In other words, the higher (or lower) the price level, the greater (or less) the quantity of money demanded. Panel C shows that with real GDP and price level constant, the quantity of money demanded is inversely related to the interest rate.[4] This last relation ship, described in this section, is called the **demand curve for money**.

Demand curve for money

How Changes in the Money Supply Affect the National Output

The Simple Keynesian Model

Now that we have investigated the demand for money, we are ready to show how changes in the quantity of money influence the value of GDP. To begin with, we will see how the money supply can be inserted into the simple Keynesian model (discussed in Chapters 17 and 18) with the aim of explaining the level of GDP.

We begin by tracing the effects of an increase in the money supply from $200 billion to $250 billion. If the demand curve for money is as shown in panel A of Figure 25.3, the result is a decrease in the interest rate from 8 percent to 6 percent. Why? Because if the interest rate is 8 percent, people demand only $200 billion, not the $250 billion supplied. Having more money on hand than they want, they will invest the excess in bonds, stocks, and other financial assets, with the result that the price of bonds, stocks, and other financial assets rise.[5]

Such a rise in the price of bonds is equivalent to a fall in the interest rate. (To see why, suppose that a very long-term bond pays interest of $300 per year. If the price of the bond is $3,000, the interest rate on the bond is 10 percent. If the price of the bond rises to $4,000, the interest rate on the bond falls to 7.5 percent. Thus, the increase in price amounts to a reduction in the interest rate.) When the interest rate falls to 6 percent, people are willing to hold the $250 billion in money. At this interest rate, the quantity of money demanded equals the quantity of money supplied.

The decrease in the interest rate from 8 percent to 6 percent affects the invest-ment function.[6] Recall from Chapter 5 that the level of investment is inversely related to the interest rate. Because it is less costly to invest—and because credit is more readily available—the investment function shifts upward, as shown

---

[4] However, the relationship between the quantity of money and the interest rate is only in the short run. In the long run, increases in the money supply, if they result in increased inflation, may raise interest rates, because lenders require a greater return to offset the greater rate of depreciation of the real value of the dollar. Still, the real rate of interest (the rate of interest adjusted for inflation) may decline.

[5] For simplicity, we assume that when people have excess money balances, they use the money to buy financial assets. (Also, we assume that when people have smaller money balances than they want, they sell financial assets to get more money.)

[6] Changes in the money supply, interest rates, and credit availability affect the consumption function, govern-ment spending, and net exports as well as the investment function. We focus attention on the investment function in Figure 25.3 merely because this simplifies the exposition.

FIGURE 25.3

Effect of an Increase in the Money Supply

If the money supply increases from $200 billion to $250 billion, the interest rate drops from 8 percent to 6 percent (panel A). Because of the decrease in the interest rate, the investment function shifts upward (panel B), and the equilibrium level of GDP increases from *D* to *E* (panel C).

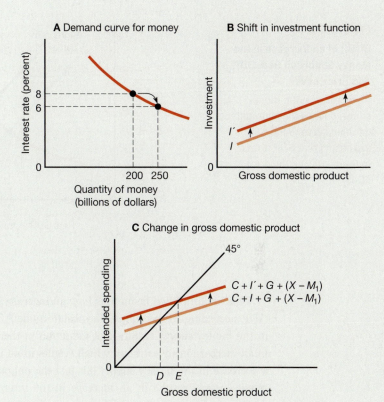

A Demand curve for money

B Shift in investment function

C Change in gross domestic product

in panel B of Figure 25.3.[7] This occurs because at each level of gross domestic product, firms want to invest more, since investment is more profitable (because of the cut in the interest rate) and funds are more readily available.[8]

This shift in the investment function then affects the equilibrium level of gross domestic product. As shown in panel C of Figure 25.3, the equilibrium level of gross domestic product increases from *D* to *E*, in accord with the principles discussed in Chapters 17 and 18; recall that the equilibrium value of GDP is at the point where the $C + I + G + (X - M_f)$ line intersects the 45-degree line. Therefore, the effect of the increase in the money supply is to increase gross domestic product.

[7] Note that it is not just a matter of interest rates. Availability of credit is also important. When money is tight, some potential borrowers may find that they cannot get a loan, regardless of what interest rate they are prepared to pay. When money is easy, people who otherwise might find it difficult to get a loan may be granted one by the banks. To repeat, both availability and interest rates are important.

[8] Many firms depend to a considerable extent on retained earnings to finance their investment projects. Since they do not borrow externally, the effect on their investment plans of changes in interest rates and credit availability may be reduced. However, since changes in the interest rate reflect changes in the opportunity cost of using funds to finance investment projects, they still may have an appreciable effect on the investment function.

FIGURE 25.4

Effect of an Increase in the Money Supply on Real GDP and Price Level

An increase in the money supply pushes the aggregate demand curve to the right, increasing real GDP from Q_0 to Q_1 and raising the price level from P_0 to P_1.

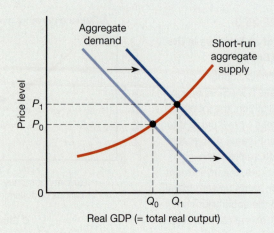

This, in simplified fashion, is how an increase in the money supply affects GDP, according to the simple Keynesian model.[9] To summarize, the increase in the money supply results in a reduction in the interest rate, which results in an increase in investment, which results in an increase in GDP. Of course, a decrease in the money supply has just the opposite effect: a decrease in the money supply results in an increase in the interest rate, which results in a decrease in investment, which results in a decrease in GDP.[10]

No Assumption of a Constant Price Level

The simple Keynesian model discussed in the previous section assumes that the price level is fixed. If we relax this assumption, we must use the aggregate supply and demand curves described in Chapter 16. As in the previous section, suppose that the money supply increases from $200 billion to $250 billion, with the result that the interest rate falls from 8 percent to 6 percent and the investment function shifts upward.[11] As indicated in Figure 25.4, the increase in investment spending pushes the aggregate demand curve to the right. This makes sense, since the quantity of total real output demanded (at the existing price level) goes up.

[9] The alert reader will recognize that the increase in GDP in panel C shifts the demand curve for money in panel A. For simplicity, we ignore this feedback.
[10] Harking back to Chapter 16, we now are in a better position to understand why the aggregate demand curve slopes downward and to the right. An increase in the price level increases the transactions demand for money because the average money cost of each transaction tends to go up. Therefore, the demand curve for money shifts to the right, with the result that the interest rate increases. As indicated in this section, the higher interest rate results in reduced spending on output. Hence, there is an inverse relationship between the price level and aggregate demand.
[11] Recall that for simplicity, we assume in this and the previous section that changes in the money supply, interest rates, and credit availability influence only the investment function, not consumption expenditure, government spending, or net exports. See footnote 6.

What is the effect of this increase in the money supply? The answer depends heavily on the shape of the short-run aggregate supply curve. If the economy is fully employed and the short-run aggregate supply curve is vertical (or close to it), increases in the money supply result in inflation but little or no extra real output. However, if the intersection of the aggregate demand and short-run aggregate supply curves prior to the increase in the money supply occurred in the upward-sloping range of the short-run aggregate supply curve, as in Figure 25.4, the effect is an increase in real GDP from Q_0 to Q_1 and an increase in the price level from P_0 to P_1. Thus, the increase in the money supply raises both total real output and price level. (Of course, if the intersection occurred in the horizontal range of the short-run aggregate supply curve, the situation would be like that discussed in the previous section, since the price level would be constant.)

Just as an increase in the money supply pushes the aggregate demand curve to the right, so a decrease in the money supply pushes it to the left. As pointed out in the previous section, a decrease in the money supply results in an increase in the interest rate, which results in a decrease in investment. Since the quantity of total real output demanded (at each price level) goes down, the aggregate demand curve shifts to the left. If the short-run aggregate supply curve is vertical (or close to it), the result is a reduction in the price level but little or no cut in real output. But if the economy is operating in the upward-sloping range of the short-run aggregate supply curve, the result is a reduction in both the price level and real output. And if the short-run aggregate supply curve is close to horizontal, the result is a reduction in real output but little or no fall in the price level.

Closing a Recessionary Gap

In recent decades, governments throughout the world have tried to manipulate the money supply to close (or at least reduce) recessionary and inflationary gaps. Suppose that the economy is in the short-run equilibrium position shown in Figure 25.5. There is a recessionary gap, as evidenced by the fact that the equilibrium level of real national output, Q_1, is less than its potential level, Q_0. (Recall that potential output is the amount of output that would be produced if there were full employment.) One way to deal with this situation is to leave things alone. As we know from previous chapters, a recessionary gap of this sort eventually cures itself. As wages and prices eventually fall, the short-run aggregate supply curve shifts to the right, and the equilibrium level of real output rises toward the potential level, Q_0. Eventually, the economy moves to point A, where the aggregate demand curve intersects the long-run aggregate supply curve, which is the vertical line at Q_0. (If you are somewhat hazy concerning this process, review the top right-hand panel of Figure 18.6.)

FIGURE 25.5

Increasing the Money Supply to Close a Recessionary Gap

Initially, there is a recessionary gap, since the equilibrium level of output, Q_1, is less than the potential level, Q_0. One way to close this gap may be to increase the money supply, shifting the aggregate demand curve from position D_1 to position D_0. Although this increases the output to its potential level, there are inflationary consequences: The price level increases from P_1 to P_0.

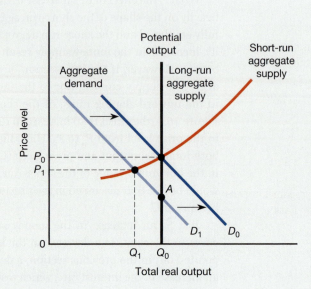

But as Keynes and his followers pointed out, this process may take a long time to work itself out, and the pain inflicted on the unemployed and others may be substantial. Therefore, many economists have recommended that governments increase the money supply to help close a recessionary gap. For example, in Figure 25.5, the government might increase the money supply to push the aggregate demand curve from its initial position (D_1) rightward to D_0, with the result that total real output is raised from Q_1 to its potential level, Q_0. In this way, the recessionary gap is closed.

However, one undesirable side effect is that the increase in the money supply raises the price level from P_1 to P_0. In other words, there are inflationary consequences. As pointed out in the previous section, the extent of the inflationary consequences depends on the steepness of the short-run aggregate supply curve. If the short-run aggregate supply curve is close to vertical, the inflationary consequences may be very great; but if the short-run aggregate supply curve is close to horizontal, they may be quite modest.

Closing an Inflationary Gap

Turning from a recessionary gap to an inflationary gap, suppose that the economy is in the short-run equilibrium position shown in Figure 25.6. There is an inflationary gap, as indicated by the fact that the equilibrium

FIGURE 25.6

Reducing the Money Supply to Close an Inflationary Gap

Initially, there is an inflationary gap, since the equilibrium level of output, Q_2, exceeds the potential level, Q_0. One way to close this gap is to reduce the money supply, shifting the aggregate demand curve from position D_2 to position D_0. This results in the price level equaling P_0, which is lower than P_3, which it would have equaled without the shift in the aggregate demand curve.

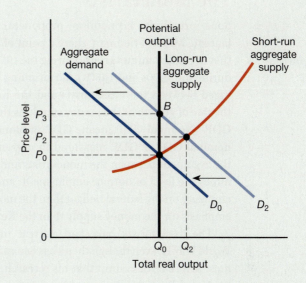

level of real national output, Q_2, is greater than the potential level, Q_0. Here, as in the case of a recessionary gap, one way to deal with the situation is to leave things alone. As we know from previous chapters, an inflationary gap of this sort eventually cures itself. As wages and prices are bid up, the short-run aggregate supply curve shifts to the left. Eventually, the economy moves to point B, where the aggregate demand curve intersects the long-run aggregate supply curve, and the equilibrium level of real national output equals the potential level, Q_0. (For a review of this process, see the top right-hand panel of Figure 18.7.)

However, this leftward shift of the short-run aggregate supply curve results in inflation until the price level rises to P_3 in Figure 25.6. Given the many undesirable consequences of such inflation (detailed in Chapter 19), many economists have recommended that governments cut back on the money supply to help close an inflationary gap. For example, in Figure 25.6, the government might reduce the money supply to push the aggregate demand curve from its initial position, D_2, leftward to D_0, with the result that the price level is P_0 rather than P_3. In this way, the government closes the inflationary gap.

Unfortunately, one side effect may be that unemployment increases. Although this increase in unemployment is likely to be temporary, many economists believe that it can be substantial and prolonged.

The Monetarists

Some prominent economists, proponents of the late economist and Nobel laureate Milton Friedman, share a point of view known as *monetarism*; hence, they are called **monetarists**. During the 1950s and 1960s (and to a lesser extent during the 1970s and 1980s), a continuing (and sometimes bitter) controversy raged between the monetarists and the Keynesians. The monetarists regard the rate of growth of the money supply as the principal determinant of nominal GDP. (Nominal GDP means GDP in money, not real terms. In other words, nominal GDP is GDP measured in current, not constant, dollars.) At heart, the argument between the monetarists and the Keynesians is over what determines the level of output, employment, and prices. The Keynesians put more emphasis on the federal budget than the monetarists; the monetarists put more emphasis on the money supply than the Keynesians.

Monetarists

The monetarists have had a great impact on economic thought since World War II, even though theirs has been a minority view. Professor Friedman's most severe critics admit that his research in this area (which helped win him the Nobel Prize) has been pathbreaking. According to his findings:

> The rate of change of the money supply shows well-marked cycles that match closely those in economic activity in general and precede the latter by a long interval. On the average, the rate of change of the money supply has reached its peak nearly 16 months before the peak in general business and has reached its trough over 12 months before the trough in general business.[12]

The Velocity of Circulation of Money

The monetarists revived interest in the so-called quantity theory of money, which was developed many years ago by such titans of economics as Alfred Marshall, of Cambridge University, and Irving Fisher, of Yale University. To understand this theory, it is useful to begin by defining a new term: the velocity of circulation of money. The **velocity of circulation of money**—or the more commonly used **velocity of money**—is the rate at which the money supply is used to make transactions for final goods and services. It equals the average number of times per year that a dollar is used to buy the final goods and services produced by the economy. In other words,

Velocity of circulation of money
Velocity of money

$$V = \text{GDP}/M \qquad (25.1)$$

where V is velocity, GDP is the nominal gross domestic product, and M is the money supply. For example, if our nominal gross domestic product is $1 trillion

---

[12] Milton Friedman, "The Relationship of Prices to Economic Stability and Growth," testimony before the Joint Economic Committee, 85th Congress, 2nd session.

and our money supply is $200 billion, the velocity of circulation of money is 5, which means that on the average, each dollar of our money generates $5 worth of purchases of gross domestic product.

Nominal gross domestic product can be expressed as the product of real gross domestic product and the price level. In other words,

$$GDP = P \times Q \qquad (25.2)$$

where P is the price level (the average price at which final goods and services are sold) and Q is gross domestic product in real terms. For example, suppose that national output in real terms consists of 200 tons of steel. If the price of a ton of steel is $100, then nominal GDP = $P \times Q$, or 100×200, or $20,000.[13]

If we substitute $P \times Q$ for GDP in equation (25.1), we have

$$V = (P \times Q)/M \qquad (25.3)$$

That is, velocity equals the price level (P) times real GDP (Q) divided by the money supply (M). This is another way to define the velocity of circulation of money, a way that proves very useful.

The Equation of Exchange

Equation of exchange

Now that we have a definition of the velocity of circulation of money, our next step is to present the so-called **equation of exchange**. The equation of exchange is nothing more than a restatement, in somewhat different form, of the definition of the velocity of circulation of money. To obtain the equation of exchange, we multiply both sides of equation 25.3 by M. The result is

$$MV = PQ \qquad (25.4)$$

To understand exactly what this equation means, we look more closely at each side. The right-hand side equals the amount received for final goods and services during the period, because Q is the output of final goods and services during the period and P is their average price. Therefore, the product of P and Q must equal the total amount received for final goods and services during the period: nominal GDP. For example, if national output in real terms equals 200 tons of steel and the price of a ton of steel is $100, then 100×200 must equal the total amount received for final goods and services during the period.

The left-hand side of equation 25.4 equals the total amount spent on final goods and services during the period. Why? Because the left-hand side equals the money supply M times the average number of times V during the period that

---

[13] Since real GDP is measured here in physical units (tons), P is the price level. If real GDP had been measured in constant dollars, P would have been a price index. In either event, our conclusions would be basically the same.

a dollar is spent on final goods and services. Consequently, $M \times V$ must equal the amount spent on final goods and services during the period. For example, if the money supply equals $10,000 and velocity equals 2, the total amount spent on final goods and services during the period must equal $10,000 × 2, or $20,000.

Thus, since the amount received for final goods and services during the period must equal the amount spent on final goods and services during the period, the left-hand side must equal the right-hand side.

The equation of exchange—equation 25.4—holds by definition. Yet it is not useless. On the contrary, economists regard the equation of exchange as very valuable, because it sets forth some of the fundamental factors that influence GDP and the price level. This equation has been used by economists for many years. It is the basis for the crude quantity theory of money used by the classical economists, as well as the theories put forth by the monetarists.

The Crude Quantity Theory of Money and Prices

Crude quantity theory of money and prices

The classical economists discussed in Chapter 16 assumed that both V and Q are constant. They believed that V is constant because it is determined by the population's stable habits of holding money, and they believed that Q remains constant at its full-employment value.[14] On the basis of these assumptions, they propounded the **crude quantity theory of money and prices**, a theory that received a great deal of attention and exerted considerable influence in its day.

If these assumptions hold, it follows from the equation of exchange ($MV = PQ$) that the price level (P) must be proportional to the money supply (M), because V and Q are assumed to be constant. [In the short run, the full-employment level of real gross domestic product (Q) does not change much.] Hence, we can rewrite equation 25.4 as

$$P = (V/Q)M \tag{25.5}$$

where V/Q is a constant. So P must be proportional to M if these assumptions hold.

The conclusion reached by the crude quantity theorists (that the price level is proportional to the money supply) is very important if true. To see how they came to this conclusion, we must recognize that they stressed the transactions motive for holding money. Recall that on the basis of this motive, we would expect the quantity of money demanded to be directly related to the level of nominal GDP. Further, the demand for money is assumed to be stable, and

---

[14] In some cases, they did not really assume continual full employment. Instead, they were concerned with the long-run changes in the economy and compared the peaks of the business cycle, where full employment frequently occurs.

little or no attention is paid to the effect of the interest rate on the demand for money. Indeed, the crude quantity theorists went so far as to assume that the quantity of money demanded is proportional to the level of nominal GDP. This amounts to assuming that velocity is constant.

Suppose there is a 10 percent increase in the quantity of money. Why would the crude quantity theorists predict a 10 percent increase in the price level? To begin with, they would assert that since the quantity of money increased relative to the value of nominal GDP, households and firms now hold more money than they want to hold. Further, they would argue that households and firms spend their excess money balances on commodities and services, and the resulting increase in total intended spending increases the nominal value but not the real value of GDP (since full employment is assumed). In other words, the increase in aggregate demand bids up prices. More specifically, they would argue that prices continue to be bid up until they have increased by 10 percent, since only then is the nominal value of GDP big enough that households and firms are content to hold the new quantity of money.

Evaluating the Crude Quantity Theory

The crude quantity theory is true to its name: it is only a crude approximation of reality. One important weakness is its assumption that velocity is constant. Another is its assumption that the economy is always at full employment, which we know from previous chapters to be far from true. (For a version of the quantity theory that relaxes this assumption, see Exploring Further in this chapter.) But despite its limitations, the crude quantity theory points to a very important truth. If the government finances its expenditures by an enormous increase in the money supply, the result is drastic inflation. For example, if the money supply is increased 10-fold, there is a marked increase in the price level. If we take the crude quantity theory at face value, we would expect a 10-fold increase in the price level; but that is a case of spurious accuracy. Perhaps the price level goes up only 8-fold. Perhaps it goes up 12-fold. The important thing is that it goes up a lot.

There is a great deal of evidence to show that the crude quantity theory is a useful predictor during periods of runaway inflation, such as in Germany after World War I. The German inflation occurred because the German government printed and spent large bundles of additional money. You sometimes hear people warn of the dangers in this country of the government "resorting to the printing presses" and flooding the country with a vast increase in the money supply. It is a danger in any country. And one great value of the crude quantity theory is that it predicts correctly what occurs as a consequence: rapid inflation.

There is also considerable evidence that the crude quantity theory works reasonably well in predicting long-term trends in the price level. For example, during the sixteenth and seventeenth centuries, gold and silver were imported

CASE STUDY 25.1

THE VELOCITY OF CIRCULATION OF MONEY AND THE FED'S 1975 DECISION

In view of the weakness of the economy at the end of 1974, the Federal Reserve and the Ford administration decided that stimulative measures were necessary. The administration asked for and quickly got a large retroactive tax cut in March 1975, and the Fed set a goal for a higher money growth rate. The inflation rate had been in the double digits in 1974 and was expected to be about 7 to 8 percent in 1975, but the Fed targeted money supply growth at only 5 to 7 percent. Why did the Fed set such a low target? How could a 5 to 7 percent growth in the money supply finance an expansion of 3 to 4 percent real growth with 7 to 8 percent inflation? Many economists agreed that the Fed embarked on a very restrictive policy and that the expansion would be choked off.

Federal Reserve chair Arthur Burns argued that a dollar typically finances more transactions (and therefore supports a higher nominal income) during a business recovery than during a recession. "We knew from a careful reading of history," he said, "that the turnover of money balances tends to rise rapidly in the early stages of economic upswing. Consequently, we resisted the advice of those who wanted to open the tap and let money flow out in greater abundance." It turned out that Burns was correct. From the second quarter of 1975 to the first quarter of 1976, the velocity of money increased even more rapidly than the Fed had predicted, and the relatively low rate of monetary growth was sufficient to accommodate a growth rate of more than 14 percent for nominal GDP—6 percent in real terms.

by the Spanish from the New World; this resulted in a great increase in Europe's money supply. The crude quantity theory would predict a great increase in the price level, and this is what occurred. Or consider the period during the nineteenth century when the discovery of gold in the United States, South Africa, and Canada brought about a large increase in the money supply. As the crude quantity theory would lead us to expect, the price level rose considerably as a consequence.

When Is Monetary Policy Tight or Easy?

In previous sections of this chapter, we focused on the ways in which the money supply affects economic activity. Now we will look in more detail at the difficulties faced by the Federal Reserve in conducting monetary policy in the United States. Given what we learned in previous sections, we can understand these difficulties more clearly.

Everyone daydreams about being powerful and important. It is a safe bet, however, that few people daydream about being members of the Federal Reserve Board or the Federal Open Market Committee (see Chapter 21). Yet, the truth is that the members of the board and the committee are among the most powerful people in the nation. Suppose you were appointed to the Federal Reserve Board. As a member, you would have to decide—month by month, year by year—exactly how many government securities the Fed should buy or sell, as well as whether and when changes should be made in the discount rate, legal reserve requirements, and other instruments of Federal Reserve policy. How would you go about making your choices?

Obviously, you would need lots of data. Fortunately, the Fed has a very large and able research staff to provide you with plenty of the latest information about what is going on in the economy. But what sorts of data should you look at? One thing you would want is some information on the extent to which monetary policy is inflationary or deflationary, that is, the extent to which monetary policy is *easy* or *tight*. This is not a simple thing to measure, but there is general agreement that the members of the Federal Reserve Board— and other members of the financial and academic communities—look closely at short-term interest rates and the rate of increase of the money supply.

The Level of Short-Term Interest Rates

As indicated earlier, Keynesians have tended to believe that changes in the quantity of money affect aggregate demand via their effects on the interest rate. High interest rates tend to reduce investment, and this in turn reduces GDP. Low interest rates tend to increase investment, and this in turn increases GDP. Because of their emphasis on these relationships, Keynesians tend to view monetary tightness or ease in terms of the behavior of interest rates. High interest rates are interpreted as meaning that monetary policy is tight. Low interest rates are interpreted as meaning that monetary policy is easy.

Real interest rate

According to many economists, the real interest rate, not the nominal interest rate, is what counts in this context. The **real interest rate** is the percentage increase in *real* purchasing power that the lender receives from the borrower in return for making the loan. The *nominal* interest rate is the percentage increase in *money* that the lender receives from the borrower in return for making the loan. The crucial difference between the real rate of interest and the nominal rate of interest is that the former is adjusted for inflation, whereas the latter is not.

Suppose that a firm borrows $1,000 for a year at 12 percent interest, and the rate of inflation is 9 percent. When the firm repays the lender $1,120 at the end of the year, this amount of money is worth only $1,120 ÷ 1.09, or about $1,030 when corrected for inflation. Hence, the real rate of interest on this loan is 3 percent, not 12 percent (the nominal rate). Why? Because the lender receives $30 in constant dollars (which is 3 percent of the amount loaned) in return for making the loan. The real rate of interest is of importance in investment decisions because it measures the real cost of borrowing money.[15]

The Rate of Increase of the Money Supply

As indicated earlier, monetarists tend to link changes in the quantity of money directly to changes in GDP. Consequently, they tend to view monetary tightness or ease in terms of the behavior of the money supply. When the money supply is growing at a relatively slow rate (much less than 4 or 5 percent per year), this is interpreted as meaning that monetary policy is tight. A relatively rapid rate of growth in the money supply (much more than 4 or 5 percent per year) is taken to mean that monetary policy is easy.

Monetary base   Another measure stressed by the monetarists is the **monetary base**, which by definition equals bank reserves plus currency outside banks. The monetary base is important because the total money supply depends on, and is made from, it. A relatively slow rate of growth in the monetary base (much less than 4 or 5 percent per year) is interpreted as a sign of tight monetary policy. A relatively rapid rate of growth (much more than 4 or 5 percent per year) is taken to mean that monetary policy is easy.

Should the Fed Pay More Attention to Interest Rates or to the Money Supply?

We have just seen that the level of interest rates and the rate of growth of the money supply are two principal indicators of monetary tightness or ease. Unfortunately, the Fed may not be able to control them both. To see this, suppose that the existing money supply equals $300 billion and the public's demand curve for money shifts upward and to the right, as shown in Figure 25.7. At each level of the rate of interest, the public demands a greater amount of money than before. If the interest rate remains at 12 percent, the quantity of money demanded by the public exceeds $300 billion, the existing quantity supplied. Therefore, the level of interest rates rises from 12 percent to 14 percent, as shown in Figure 25.7. Economists who favor the use of interest rates as an indicator are likely to warn that unless interest rates are reduced, a recession will ensue.

The Fed can push the level of interest rates back down by increasing the quantity of money. The equilibrium value of the interest rate is the one where the quantity of money demanded equals the quantity of money supplied. If the demand curve for money remains fixed at its new higher level, the Fed can push the interest rate back down to 12 percent by increasing the quantity of money to $330 billion. With this quantity of money, the equilibrium interest rate is

---

[15] Expressed as an equation, $i_r = i_n - p$, where i_r is the real rate of interest, i_n is the nominal rate of interest, and p is the rate of inflation. In the example in the text, $i_n = 12$ percent and $p = 9$ percent; therefore, $i_r = 3$ percent.

FIGURE 25.7

Effect of a Shift in the Demand Curve for Money

If the demand curve for money shifts upward and to the right, as shown here, the equilibrium value of the interest rate increases from 12 percent to 14 percent if the quantity of money supplied remains $300 billion. If the Fed wants to push the equilibrium level of the interest rate back to 12 percent, it must increase the quantity of money supplied to $330 billion.

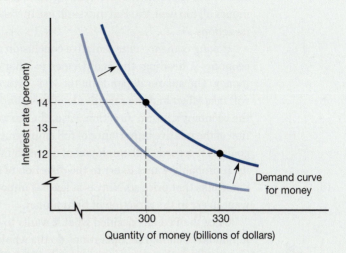

12 percent, as shown in Figure 25.7. However, by doing so, the Fed no longer is increasing the money supply in accord with its previous objectives. Economists who favor the use of the rate of growth of the money supply as an indicator are likely to warn that the Fed is increasing the money supply at too rapid a rate.

Therefore, the Fed is faced with a dilemma. If it does not push interest rates back down to their former level, some economists claim it is promoting recession. If it does do so, other economists claim it is promoting inflation. Unfortunately, it is very difficult for the Fed (or anyone else) to tell exactly how much weight should be attached to each of these indicators. In the 1950s and 1960s, the Fed paid much more attention to interest rates than to the rate of increase of the money supply. In the 1970s and early 1980s, because of the growing influence of the monetarists, the Fed put more emphasis on the rate of growth of the money supply, although it continued to pay close attention to interest rates. Subsequently, the Fed seemed more inclined to use nominal GDP as a target variable. Many central banks around the world have also adopted inflation targets (see Case Study 26.1).

Problems in Formulating Monetary Policy

The Fed maintains a constant watch on the economy; it checks for signs that the economy is sliding into a recession, being propelled into an inflationary boom, or growing satisfactorily. There is no foolproof way to forecast the economy's short-term movements. Recognizing the fallibility of existing forecasting techniques all too well, the Fed must still use these techniques as best it can to guide its actions.

Having come to some tentative conclusion about the direction in which the economy is heading, the Fed decides to what extent it should tighten or ease money. The answer depends on the Fed's estimates of when monetary changes will take effect and the magnitude of their impact, as well as on its forecasts of the economy's future direction. Also, the answer depends on the Fed's evaluation of the relative importance of full employment and price stability as national goals. If it regards full employment as much more important than price stability, it probably wants to err in the direction of easy money. On the other hand, if it thinks that price stability is at least as important as full employment, it may want to err in the direction of tight money.

Once the Fed has decided what it wants to do, it must figure out how to do it. Should open market operations do the whole job? If so, how big must be the purchase or sale of government securities? Should a change be made in the discount rate or in legal reserve requirements? How big a change? These are the operational questions the Fed must answer.

In answering these questions, the Fed must reckon with two very inconvenient facts, both of which make life difficult:

1. *Often there is a long lag between an action by the Fed and its effect on the economy.* Although the available evidence indicates that monetary policy affects some types of expenditures more rapidly than others, it is not uncommon for the bulk of the total effects to occur a year or more after the change in monetary policy.[16] Therefore, the Fed may act to head off an imminent recession but find that some of the consequences of its action are not felt until later, when inflation, not recession, is the problem. Conversely, the Fed may act to curb an imminent inflation but find that the consequences of its action are not felt until some time later, when recession, not inflation, has become the problem. In either case, the Fed can wind up doing more harm than good (recall Exploring Further in Chapter 21).

2. *Experts disagree about which of the available measures (such as interest rates, the rate of increase of the money supply, or the rate of increase of the monetary base) is the best measure of how tight or easy monetary policy is.* Fortunately, these measures often point in the same direction, but when they point in different directions, the Fed can be misled. During 1967–1968, the Fed wanted to tighten money. Using interest rates as the primary measure of the tightness of monetary policy, it increased interest rates. However, at the same time, it permitted a substantial rate of increase in the money supply and the monetary base. By doing so, the Fed, in the eyes of many experts, really eased rather than tightened money.

---

[16] Robert Gordon, of Northwestern University, estimated that it takes about nine months for a change in the money supply to affect real GDP.

HOW MUCH ATTENTION SHOULD THE FED PAY TO THE STOCK MARKET (AND HOUSE PRICES)?

Fed chair Alan Greenspan asked this question on December 5, 1996. At that time, the Dow Jones Industrial Average was around 6,500. It subsequently rose 75 percent over the next three years, reaching 11,500 in January 2000. The Fed was clearly worried about the stock market being overvalued in 1996. However, instead of trying to bring the market back down to earth by raising interest rates, the Fed tried to "talk" the market down. It did not work, and many analysts blamed the Fed for letting the market get out of control.

The Fed's mandate is to target goods inflation, not asset inflation. Nevertheless, the Fed and other central banks have many reasons to worry about bubbles in the stock and property markets.

- To begin with, asset price inflation can be a leading indicator of higher goods inflation, as measured by the consumer price index (CPI) or the GDP deflator. Rising asset prices increase household wealth, encouraging consumers to splurge. Similarly, a booming stock market can reduce the cost of capital for companies, leading to a surge in investment spending. Thus, an asset bubble can lead to excess demand and higher inflation.
- Ideally, an effective measure of inflation should include not only the prices of goods consumed today but also the prices of goods consumed tomorrow. For example, a rise in housing prices today increases the costs of repairs in future years. Therefore, some economists argued that the Fed should pay some attention to asset prices. Unfortunately, this is easier said than done, because asset prices are generally more volatile than goods prices.
- Surges in asset prices can distort price signals and create misallocation of resources. A booming stock market may tempt companies to overinvest. In fact, during the 1980s Japanese bubble, there was ample evidence that companies overindulged in capacity expansion and helped set the stage for the recession that followed. Similarly, some analysts were concerned that there was an investment bubble in the United States in the late 1990s.
- Finally, the bursting of an asset bubble is often followed by a recession or worse. The bursting of the U.S. bubble in 1929 and the Japanese bubble in 1989 led to protracted downturns. Rising asset prices encourage households and companies to borrow heavily, leaving them heavily exposed to a fall in asset prices. When the

markets do crash, borrowers often cannot repay their debts. In turn, this can lead to a banking crisis. This downward spiral has been labeled *debt deflation*.

As compelling as the arguments are for central banks to pay attention to asset prices, there are equally compelling arguments for proceeding with great caution.

- It is often very difficult to be sure that a rise in asset prices represents a speculative bubble. In the late 1990s, there was much talk of a significant improvement in fundamentals brought on by the new technologies of the PC and the Internet. Many analysts believed that the rise in the stock market was simply a reflection of this improvement.
- The Fed has only blunt instruments (interest rates) with which to deflate asset bubbles. Too small of a rise in interest rates and the bubble persists (the United States in the 1990s).

Too big of a rise in interest rates and the economy goes into a tailspin (Japan in the 1990s).

- Last but not least, the Fed and other central banks do not have the mandate to burst bubbles. Therefore, the unfortunate history of bubbles in the twentieth century has been one in which central banks have typically waited too long and done too much too late.

Greenspan revisited this topic in a speech in early 2004, when he said,

> It is far from obvious that bubbles, even if identified early, can be preempted at lower cost than a susbstantial economic contraction and possible financial desta- bilization—the very outcomes we would be seeking to avoid.

Unfortunately, the story did not end in 2004. The housing bubble of the 2000s continued to inflate until it burst a few years later (see Case Study 25.3).

Should the Fed Be Governed by a Rule?

Some monetarists, inspired by the late Milton Friedman, go so far as to say that the Fed's attempts to "lean against the wind"—by easing money when the economy begins to dip and tightening money when the economy begins to overheat—do more harm than good. (The new classical economists, discussed in Chapter 26, say much the same thing.) In their view, the Fed intensifies business fluctuations by changing the rate of growth of the money supply. Why? Partly because the Fed sometimes pays too much attention to measures other than the money supply. But more fundamentally, it is because the Fed tends to overreact to ephemeral changes, and the effects of changes in the money supply on the economy occur with a long, highly variable lag. In the view of these monetarists, this lag is so unpredictable that the Fed—no matter how laudatory its intent—tends to intensify business fluctuations.

According to Professor Friedman and his followers, the Fed should aban- don its attempts to lean against the wind. The Fed should conform to a rule that the money supply should increase at some fixed, agreed-on rate, such as 4 or

5 percent per year. The Fed's job would be simply to see that the money supply grows at approximately this rate. The monetarists do not claim that a rule of this sort would prevent all business fluctuations—only that it would work better than the existing system. In particular, they believe that it would prevent the sorts of major depressions and inflations we have experienced in the past. Without major decreases in the money supply (such as occurred during the crash of 1929–1933), major depressions could not occur. Without major increases in the money supply (such as occurred during World War II), major inflations could not occur. Of course, it would be nice if monetary policy could iron out minor business fluctuations as well, but in their view, this simply cannot be done at present.

This proposal has received considerable attention from both economists and politicians. A number of studies have been carried out to try to estimate what would have happened if Friedman's rule had been used in the past. The results, although by no means free of criticism, seem to indicate that such a rule might have done better than discretionary action in preventing the Great Depression of the 1930s and the inflation experienced during World War II. But in the period since World War II, the evidence in favor of such a rule is less persuasive. Most economists believe that it would be a mistake to handcuff the Fed to a simple rule of this sort.

The need for flexibility was apparent during the Great Recession of 2008–2009, when the worst financial crisis and economic contraction since the Great Depression forced the Fed to take aggressive and unorthodox measures (see Case Study 21.2). While most economists applauded the Fed's crisis management, a few criticized the central bank for not taking a more orthodox (and rule-based) course of action.

The debate over rules versus discretionary action goes on, and the issues are still very much alive.

Unorthodox Policies in a Time of Crisis

The debate about rules versus discretion became moot in the dark days of the financial crisis of 2008–09. In its attempt to prevent the "Great Recession" from turning into the "Great Depression 2.0," the Fed adopted highly unorthodox policies. Specifically, it embarked on an aggressive campaign to buy long-term government bonds and mortgage-backed securities. Its goal was to keep long-term interest rates (including mortgage rates) low in order to revive the economy, especially housing (see Case Study 21.2). This policy has come to be known as "quantitative easing" or QE. While quite controversial, it was also adopted by other central banks, including the Bank of England, the Bank of Japan and the European Central Bank. While some economists maintained that the gains from QE were small and the program ran the risk of re-igniting inflation, others felt just as strongly that the Fed and other central banks had no alternative, and that without QE the "Great Recession" would have lasted much longer.

EVALUATING THE FED'S PERFORMANCE BEFORE AND AFTER THE FINANCIAL CRISIS OF 2008–2009

Despite the sluggish recovery after the Great Recession, most economists give the Fed fairly high marks for its crisis management (see Case Study 21.2). It prevented the worst financial crisis since the 1930s from turning into another Great Depression. In particular, the Fed bought massive amounts of government bonds and mortgage-backed securities and in so doing pumped huge amounts of liquidity into the economy and brought long-term interest rates down to record lows.

There is a much less charitable view of the Fed's role in the period before the financial crisis of 2008–2009. Many economists believe that in 2003 and 2004, the Fed kept interest rates "too low for too long" and in the process contributed to the housing bubble that was a root cause of the financial meltdown. Some have even called the Fed a "serial bubble blower"—referring to the tech bubble of the 1990s and housing bubble of the 2000s.

There is some justification for this point of view. On October 19, 2004, then Fed Chair

Alan Greenspan said, "While local economies may experience significant price imbalances, a national severe price distortion seems most unlikely in the United States, given its size and diversity." Subsequently, Mr. Greenspan did express concern about the housing market and the Fed began to raise interest rates—though, arguably, not soon enough to prevent house prices from escalating to dangerous levels.

More thoughtful analysts worry that the response of central banks to asset bubbles has been dangerously asymmetrical: benign neglect when prices are rising and dramatic action when they are falling. While some of this criticism is justified, hindsight is 20/20, and operationally targeting asset prices can be difficult (see Case Study 25.2). Nevertheless, given the boom-bust cycle of both stock and house prices since the 1990s, central bankers will have to pay much more attention to them in the future than they have in the past.

EXPLORING FURTHER

More on the Velocity of Money

The crude quantity theory is based on two simplifying assumptions, both of which are questionable. One assumption is that real gross domestic product (Q) remains fixed at its full-employment level. The other is that the velocity of circulation of money (V) remains constant. A more sophisticated version of the quantity theory can be derived by relaxing the first assumption. This version of the quantity theory recognizes that the economy is often at less than full employment and that, consequently, real gross domestic product (Q) may vary a good deal.

So long as the velocity of money remains constant, the equation of exchange, $MV = PQ$, can be used to determine the relationship between gross domestic product in current dollars and M, even if Q is allowed to vary. On the basis of the equation of exchange, it is obvious that $P \times Q$ should be proportional to M if the velocity of circulation of money (V) remains constant. Since $P \times Q$ is nominal gross domestic product, it follows that if this assumption holds, nominal gross domestic product should be proportional to the money supply. In other words,

$$\text{GDP} = aM \qquad\qquad (25.6)$$

where GDP is nominal gross domestic product and V is assumed to equal the constant a. Hence, if the money supply increases by 10 percent, the nominal value of GDP should increase by 10 percent; if the money supply increases by 20 percent, the nominal value of GDP should increase by 20 percent; and so forth.

If the velocity of money is constant, this version of the quantity theory should enable us to predict nominal gross domestic product if we know the money supply. Also, if the velocity of money is constant, this version of the quantity theory should enable us to control nominal gross domestic product by controlling the money supply. Clearly, if the velocity of money is constant, equation 25.6 is an extremely important economic relationship, one that goes a long way toward helping to forecast and control GDP. But is the velocity of money constant? Since equation 25.6 is based on this assumption, we must find out.

Figure 25.8 shows how the velocity of circulation of money has behaved since 1920. Obviously, the velocity of money has not been constant. Excluding World War II, it has generally fluctuated between 2.5 and 11 in the United States. The velocity of money tends to decrease during depressions and increase during booms. We must conclude from Figure 25.8 that the velocity of money is not so stable that equation 25.6 alone can be used in any precise way to forecast or control gross domestic product.[17]

However, this does not mean that equation 25.6 is useless or that the more sophisticated quantity theory is without value. On the contrary, this version of the quantity theory points out a very important truth: the money supply has an important effect on gross domestic product (in money terms). Increases in the quantity of money are likely to increase nominal GDP; decreases in the quantity of money are likely to decrease nominal GDP. Because velocity is not constant, the relationship between the money supply and gross domestic product is not as neat and simple as that predicted by equation 25.6, but there is a relationship, as shown in Figure 25.9.

---

[17] It is important to note that the velocity of money figures in Figure 25.8 are based on the narrow definition of the money supply, M1. If M2 is used instead, the velocity of money has been more nearly constant. For example, between 1960 and 1976, the velocity of money based on M2 varied within a very narrow range.

FIGURE 25.8

Velocity of Circulation of Money, United States, 1920–2012

The velocity of the circulation of money has generally been between 2.5 and 15, except during World War II.

Source: Economic Report of the President, 2013.

FIGURE 25.9

Relationship between the Money Supply and Nominal GDP, United States, 1960–2012

There has been a reasonably close relationship between the money supply and the money value of national product. As one goes up, the other tends to go up, too.

Source: Economic Report of the President, 2013.

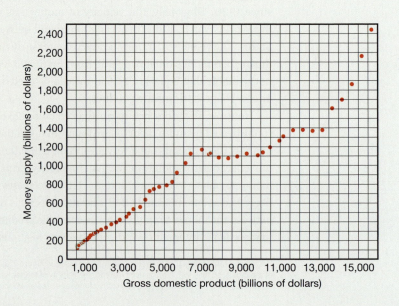

Going a step further, sophisticated monetarists often relax the assumption that V is constant and assert that it is possible to predict V as a function of other variables, like the frequency with which people are paid, the level of business confidence, and the cost of holding money (the interest rate). According to some economists, one of Friedman's major contributions was to replace the constancy of V with its predictability. Other economists feel that changes in V reflect, rather than cause, changes in GDP. In recent years, V seems to have become less predictable than in the past. This development has caused some consternation in the monetarist camp. Moreover, Federal Reserve officials have lamented that the relationship between the money supply and GDP has become less reliable because of financial deregulation and the recent tendency of people to move their money into mutual funds and other "near money" assets (that allow you to write checks), which are not considered part of the money supply. Obviously, this makes it more difficult for the Fed to devise an effective monetary policy.

REVIEW AND PRACTICE

Summary

1 The United States has seen many sharp fluctuations in the price level. Some of the greatest fluctuations resulted from wars.

2 According to the simple Keynesian model, increases in the quantity of money result in lower interest rates, which result in increased investment (and other types of spending), which results in a higher GDP. Conversely, decreases in the quantity of money result in a lower GDP.

3 An increase in the money supply tends to push the aggregate demand curve to the right; a decrease in the money supply tends to push it to the left. Governments often increase the money supply in an attempt to eliminate a recessionary gap and cut back on the money supply in an attempt to eliminate an inflationary gap.

4 The monetarists, led by Milton Friedman, emphasize the equation of exchange: $MV = PQ$, where M is the money supply, V is velocity, P is the price level, and Q is gross domestic product in real terms.

5 If the velocity of circulation of money remains constant and real gross domestic product is fixed at its full-employment level, the price level is proportional to the money supply. This is the crude quantity theory, which is a reasonably good approximation during periods of runaway inflation and works reasonably well in predicting long-term trends in the price level.

6   As indicators of how tight or easy monetary policy is, the Fed has looked at the level of short-term interest rates, the rate of growth of the money supply, and the rate of growth of the monetary base.

7   The job of the Federal Reserve is complicated by an often long and highly variable lag between an action by the Fed and its effect on the economy. Also, considerable disagreement ensues over the best way to measure how tight or easy monetary policy is.

8   Some monetarists, inspired by Milton Friedman, believe that monetary policy would be improved if discretionary policy were replaced by a rule that the Fed should increase the money supply at some fixed, agreed-on rate, such as 4 or 5 percent per year.

*9   [18] If the velocity of money remains constant, gross domestic product in money terms should be proportional to the money supply. In fact, however, the velocity of money has by no means remained constant over time. Nonetheless, nominal GDP has been fairly closely related to the money supply.

Problems and Questions

1   If the value of GDP (in money terms) increases 10 percent and the money supply remains fixed, does the velocity of money increase? Why or why not? What are some factors that might cause an increase in the velocity of money?

2   "The history of the United States is an account of one inflation after another. The currency is being debased further and further. Soon we may experience a runaway inflation." Comment and evaluate.

3   Describe how the quantity of money influences nominal and real GDP according to

     (a) the Keynesian model

     (b) the crude quantity theory

     (c) the analysis (based on aggregate demand and supply curves) in Figure 25.4.

4   Suppose that a bond pays annual interest of $100 forever. What is the interest rate if its price is

     (a) $1,000

     (b) $2,000

     (c) $3,000?

[18] Starred (*) items refer to material covered in Exploring Further.

5 Why is the interest rate regarded as the price of holding money? What factors shift the demand curve for money to the right? To the left?

Key Terms

transactions demand for money
precautionary demand for money
demand curve for money
monetarists
velocity of circulation of money (velocity of money)
equation of exchange
crude quantity theory of money and prices
real interest rate
monetary base

Viewpoint for Analysis

In a speech at the Federal Reserve Bank of Kansas City Economic Symposium in Jackson Hole, Wyoming, on August 31, 2012, former Fed Chair Ben Bernanke said:

> Early in my tenure as a member of the Board of Governors, I gave a speech that considered options for monetary policy when the short-term interest rate is close to the effective lower bound. I was reacting to common assertions at the time that monetary policymakers would be "out of ammunition" as the federal funds rate came closer to zero. I argued, to the contrary, policy could still be effective near the lower bound. Now, with several years of experience with nontraditional policies both in the United States and in other advanced economies, we know more about how such policies work. It seems clear, based on this experience, that such policies can be effective, and that, in their absence, the 2007–09 recession would have been deeper and the current recovery would have been slower than has actually occurred.[19]

(a) Why is monetary policy more of a challenge when interest rates are close to zero?

(b) What nontraditional policies was Mr. Bernanke referring to? (*Hint:* Look at Case Study 25.3.)

(c) What would have happened if the Fed had not enacted nontraditional policies?

---

[19] http://www.federalreserve.gov/newsevents/speech/bernanke20120831a.htm

Controversies over Stabilization Policy

LEARNING OBJECTIVES

➤ To recognize the disagreements between the new classical macroeconomists and new Keynesians (as well as between the monetarists, Keynesians, and supply-side economists) over business fluctuations, the stability of the economy, and the use of a monetary rule

➤ To discuss the pros and cons of policy activism

➤ To differentiate between rigid policy rules, feedback policy rules, and discretionary policy

No longer are the debates over monetary and fiscal policy dominated by the Keynesians and monetarists; there now are supply-side economists, new classical macroeconomists, and new Keynesians. How do their views differ? One purpose of this chapter is to answer this question.

During the past several decades, there have been many disagreements among economists over the effects of monetary and fiscal policies on output and employment as well as over the kinds of public policies that the government should adopt. These disputes have engaged the attention of many leading economists and have had a strong influence on the thinking of policy makers in both the public and private sectors of the economy. In previous chapters, we discussed particular aspects of these controversies. Now we will look at them in more detail.

Monetarists versus Keynesians: The Central Debate of the 1960s and 1970s

As stressed in the previous chapter, the principal debate of the 1960s and 1970s was between the monetarists and the Keynesians. This debate was not limited to the classroom and scholarly gatherings. It spilled over onto the pages of daily newspapers and aroused considerable interest in Congress and other parts of the government. At heart, the argument was over what determines the level of output, employment, and prices. The Keynesians put more emphasis on the federal budget than did the monetarists; the monetarists put more emphasis on the money supply than did the Keynesians. To understand this debate, we need to know something about the development of economic thought. Until the Great Depression of the 1930s, the prevailing theory was that GDP, expressed in real terms, would tend automatically to its full-employment level. (Recall from Chapter 16 the classical economists' reasons for clinging to this belief.) Moreover, the prevailing view was that the price level could be explained by the crude quantity theory of money. In other words, the price level (P) was assumed to be proportional to the quantity of money (M) because $MV = PQ$, and both Q (real GDP) and V (the velocity of money) were thought to be essentially constant.

During the Great Depression, this theory appeared inadequate to many economists. GDP seemed not to be tending automatically toward its full-employment level. And the crude quantity theory seemed to have little value. In contrast, Keynes's ideas appeared to offer the theoretical guidance and policy prescriptions needed. Keynesians did not neglect the use of monetary policy entirely, but they felt that it should play a subsidiary role. Particularly in depressions, monetary policy seems to be of relatively little value, since you cannot "push on a string." In other words, monetary policy can make money available but cannot ensure that it is spent. To Keynesians, fiscal policy was of central importance.

During the 1940s, 1950s, and early 1960s, the Keynesian view was predominant here and abroad. But by the mid-1960s, it was being challenged seriously by the monetarists, led by Milton Friedman and his supporters. The monetarist view harked back to the pre-Keynesian doctrine in many respects. In particular, it emphasized the importance of the equation of exchange as an analytical device and the importance of the quantity of money as a tool of economic policy. The monetarist view gained adherents in the late 1960s, partly because of the long delay in passing the federal tax increase of 1968. The reluctance of the Johnson administration to propose and the reluctance of Congress to enact this tax increase vividly illustrated some of the difficulties in using fiscal policy for stabilization. Even more important was that the tax increase, when finally enacted, failed to have the restrictive effect on GDP (in the face of expansionary monetary policy) that some Keynesians predicted.

During the 1970s, as more and more evidence accumulated, many of the differences between the monetarists and the Keynesians seemed to wane in importance. Most monetarists conceded that fiscal policy can affect output and the price level; most Keynesians conceded the same regarding monetary policy. Although it would be incorrect to say that no differences remained on this score, there seemed to be a growing recognition that the differences had narrowed considerably. The late Milton Friedman, a leading monetarist, was quoted as saying, "We are all Keynesians now." And the late Franco Modigliani, a leading Keynesian, responded in his 1976 presidential address to the American Economic Association by saying, "We are all monetarists now."

Supply-Side Economists

While the differences between the monetarists and the Keynesians were narrowing, a new group of economists, known as *supply-side economists*, entered the fray. Since we have already discussed supply-side economics at length in Chapter 23, there is no need for a long discussion here. As you will recall, supply-side economists, who rose to prominence in the late 1970s and 1980s, are concerned primarily with influencing aggregate supply, particularly through the use of various financial incentives, such as tax reductions. Supply-side economics is not really new. Major economists of the eighteenth and nineteenth (as well as twentieth) centuries were concerned with the stimulation of aggregate supply. In the early 1980s, supply-side economists were very influential in the Reagan administration (for further discussion, see Case Study 23.3).

The New Classical Macroeconomists

New classical macro-economists

Also emerging in the 1970s were the **new classical macroeconomists**, led by Nobel laureates Robert Lucas, of the University of Chicago, and Thomas Sargent, of New York University, together with Neil Wallace, of Pennsylvania State University. They formulated a theory of macroeconomics based on three assumptions. First, they assumed that markets clear; in other words, the prices of inputs and outputs vary so as to equate the quantity supplied to the quantity demanded. Second, they assumed that people and firms have imperfect information. And third, they assumed that the expectations of people and firms conform to the theory of rational expectations.

Rational Expectations

Rational expectations

The theory of **rational expectations**, formulated initially by Indiana University's John Muth, had a substantial impact on economic analysis and policy. Put briefly, people's expectations (or forecasts) of a particular economic

CASE STUDY 26.1

INFLATION TARGETING BY CENTRAL BANKS

Two of the strongest advocates for inflation targeting are Ben Bernanke and Fredric Mishkin, respectively a former chair and former governor of the Board of Governors of the Federal Reserve System. They and their academic colleagues have shown that central banks adopting formal inflation targeting have reduced both the level and the volatility of inflation in their economies. In the words of Ben Bernanke:

Inflation targeting, at least in its bestpractice form, consists of two parts: a policy framework of constrained discretion and a communication strategy that attempts to focus expectations and explain the policy framework to the public. Together, these two elements promote both price stability and well-anchored inflation expectations; the latter in turn facilitates more effective stabilization of output and employment. Thus, a well-conceived and well-executed strategy of inflation targeting can deliver good results with respect to output and employment as well as inflation.[1]

[1] Ben Bernanke, "A Perspective on Inflation Targeting: Why It Seems to Work," *Business Economics*, July 2003, pp. 7–15.

variable are rational if they make the best possible use of whatever information is available. This does not mean that the forecasts are necessarily very accurate; but it does mean that individuals do their homework and do not make stupid mistakes. For example, if information is available concerning the size of the wage increases granted by the auto industry and this information is relevant in making forecasts of what the inflation rate will be, people are assumed to obtain and take proper account of this information in making forecasts of the inflation rate. If they do not, their expectations are not rational, according to the economist's definition.

On the basis of the theory of rational expectations, individuals and firms do not make systematic errors in forecasting the future. For example, suppose that a person uses a model to forecast the inflation rate and experience indicates that this model always underestimates the actual inflation rate. If this person's expectations are rational, we would expect that individual to recognize this downward bias and compensate for it by adding an amount to forecasts based on this model. On the average, forecasts, if they are rational, are correct. To repeat, this does not mean that forecasters are always accurate. Instead, it means that if we look at the results of a very large number of forecasts, we find that the *average* forecasting error is zero. Unlike the forecasting model that always underestimates the inflation rate, there is no downward or upward bias. The forecasting errors are random.

Unemployment and Business Fluctuations

According to the new classical macroeconomists, high rates of unemployment are not evidence of a gap between actual and potential output that can be reduced; instead, output fluctuations result from random errors. Markets are assumed to work efficiently; and firms, acting to maximize their profits, are assumed to make the best possible decisions. According to Robert Lucas, since unemployed workers have the option of accepting pay cuts to get jobs, excess unemployment is essentially voluntary.

Fluctuations in aggregate demand are due principally to erratic and unpredictable government policy, in Lucas's view. Changes in the quantity of money induce cyclical fluctuations in the economy. But the power of policy changes to affect real GDP is limited. People come to learn the way in which policy is made, and only unanticipated government policy changes can have a substantial impact on output or employment. Once firms and individuals learn of any systematic rule for adjusting government policy to events, the rule will have no effect.

Can Stabilization Policies Work?

The new classical macroeconomists conclude that the government cannot use monetary and fiscal policies to close recessionary and inflationary gaps in the way described in Chapters 18, 24, and 25, because the models presented in those chapters do not recognize that the expectations of firms and individuals concerning their incomes, job prospects, sales, and other relevant variables are influenced by government policies. If firms and individuals formulate their expectations rationally, they tend to frustrate the government's attempts to use activist stabilization policies.

To illustrate what these economists are saying, suppose that the economy is in a recession and the government, trying to close the recessionary gap in the ways described in Chapters 18, 24, and 25, increases the amount it spends on goods and services and increases the money supply. Because prices tend to move up while wages do not, profits tend to rise and firms find it profitable to expand. But this model is based on the supposition that labor is not smart enough to foresee that prices are going to go up and its own real wage is going to diminish. If labor does foresee this (that is, if its expectations are rational), it will insist on an increase in its money wage, which will mean that firms will not find it profitable to expand, and the government's antirecession policy will not work as expected.

Reactions Pro and Con

These views have received considerable attention in academic and policy circles. For example, in one of its annual reports, the Federal Reserve Bank of Minneapolis stated:

> The [new classical] view conjectures that some amount of cyclical swing in production and employment is inherent in the micro-level processes of the economy that no government macro policies can, or should attempt to, smooth out. Expected additions to money growth certainly won't smooth out cycles, if the arguments in this paper are correct. Surprise additions to money growth have the potential to make matters worse. . . . One strategy that seems consistent with the significant, though largely negative, findings of [the new classical macroeconomists] would have monetary policy focus its attention on inflation and announce, and stick to, a policy that would bring the rate of increase in the general price level to some specified low figure.[1]

Given that the new classical macroeconomists have challenged the core of the theory underlying discretionary stabilization policies, it is not surprising that many economists, particularly liberals, have attacked their conclusions. Franco Modigliani, for instance, has claimed that their model is inconsistent "with the evidence; if it were valid, deviations of unemployment from the natural rate would be small and transitory—in which case [Keynes's] *General Theory* would not have been written."[2] In other words, if Lucas's theory were true—if excess unemployment were the result of purely unexpected events—then unemployment would fluctuate randomly around its equilibrium level. But critics point out that recessions sometimes last quite a long time.

Critics also claim that the new classical macroeconomics neglects the inertia in wages and prices. Contracts are written for long periods of time. Workers stick with firms for considerable periods. Consequently, wages and prices do not adjust as rapidly as is assumed by the new classical macroeconomists. According to the critics, most empirical analysis does not support the view that wages and prices adjust rapidly. On the contrary, wage and price movements show only slow and adaptive changes.

One of the most serious criticisms has centered on the new classical macroeconomists' contention that business fluctuations would be eliminated if firms and consumers had accurate current information about the aggregate price level.

---

[1] Federal Reserve Bank of Minneapolis, *Rational Expectations—Fresh Ideas That Challenge Some Established Views of Policy Making* (Minneapolis: Federal Reserve Bank, 1977), 12–13.
[2] F. Modigliani, "The Monetarist Controversy, or, Should We Forsake Stabilization Policies," *American Economic Review, 67* (March 1977), 6.

RECESSION AS A MEANS TO STOP INFLATION IN 1982

President Ronald Reagan presenting his tax package

When President Reagan came into office in 1981, the inflation rate was 11 percent. The combination of President Carter's efforts to stimulate the economy in 1977–1978 and the oil price shock of 1979 had apparently created an underlying inflation rate of about 8 percent. During his campaign, Reagan promised to reduce inflation by encouraging the Federal Reserve to reduce the rate of growth of the money supply and by creating greater incentives for the economy to produce more goods. He would therefore attack the traditional causes of inflation, "too much money chasing too few goods," from both sides.

By the 1980s, most economists believed that people's expectations about the possible effects of future government policies could affect how well the policies worked. For example, if the government tried to stimulate the economy by increasing the rate of growth of the money supply, its policy would fail if firms and labor unions simply raised prices and wages in expectation of higher inflation. The additional money supplied to the economy would go into higher prices rather than toward stimulating more production.

One group of economists felt that it would take a long time to get business and labor to reduce their expectations of future inflation. In addition, wage increases tended to be set in advance by multiyear contracts, so wage gains could not be easily reduced even if expectations of future inflation fell. Because of this, the only way to reduce price increases and wage demands quickly, this group argued, would be to create a large increase in unemployment.

In contrast, another group of economists felt that inflation could be reduced without a large increase in unemployment if the government's resolve to stick to inflation-fighting policies was credible. These economists argued that the problem with the government's anti-inflation efforts in the past was that they were not steady enough. At the first sign of a recession, the Fed would back off and rekindle inflation with an easy money policy.

In fact, the Fed did adhere to a tight money policy long after the recession of 1982 became quite severe. Fed chair Paul Volcker tightened up on the money supply in the summer of 1981. Interest rates rose, and the economy slid into recession. In early 1982, the unemployment rate was over 9 percent, but Volcker still maintained a tight policy. It was not until October 1982 that the Fed eased up.

By that time, the rate of inflation had fallen from the 11 percent level of early 1981 to 3.5 percent. But the cost of reducing inflation had been a severe downturn in business activity. According to many observers, the Fed had no choice but to take a strong stand against inflation. Nonetheless, the results suggest that once inflation becomes embedded, it is difficult to reduce it because expectations of continued inflation can be halted only by deep recession.

Given that the consumer price index is widely disseminated with a relatively short lag, this does not seem very plausible. As Northwestern's Robert Gordon put it, "With monthly and even weekly data on the money supply available, people could make expectational errors about monetary changes lasting for only a few weeks, not nearly enough to explain business cycles lasting an average of four and one-half years in the postwar era, and twelve years for the period of high unemployment between 1929 and 1941."[3]

Real Business Cycle Models

Real business cycle models

In contrast to the models described in the previous section, some new classical macroeconomists, such as Nobel laureate Edward Prescott, of Arizona State University, and the Federal Reserve Bank of Minneapolis, argue that business fluctuations are due predominantly to real rather than monetary factors. These economists, whose influence within the new classical camp has grown substantially in recent years, are proponents of **real business cycle models**. In their view, business fluctuations are the natural (indeed *efficient*) response of the economy to changes in technology and the availability of resources. Therefore, business fluctuations are due predominantly to shifts in the aggregate supply curve, not the aggregate demand curve.

To illustrate what they have in mind, consider Figure 26.1. Suppose that technological change shifts the long-run aggregate supply curve to the right,

[3] R. Gordon, *Macroeconomics*, 5th ed. (Glenview, IL: Scott Foresman, 1990), 202.

FIGURE 26.1

Favorable and Unfavorable Supply Shocks

In panel A, a favorable supply shock (technological advance) shifts the aggregate supply curve to the right and increases real GDP from Y_0 to Y_1. In panel B, an unfavorable supply shock (oil cutback) shifts the aggregate supply curve to the left and decreases real GDP from Y_1 to Y_2.

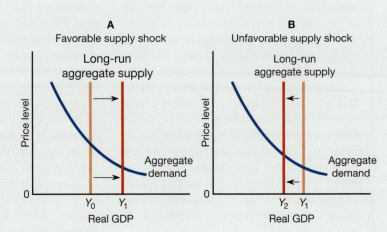

with the result that real GDP increases from Y_0 to Y_1 (in panel A). Then suppose that OPEC cuts back on the supply of oil, causing a shift of the aggregate supply curve to the left, with the result that real GDP falls from Y_1 to Y_2 (in panel B). These output fluctuations are due to shifts in the aggregate supply curve, not the aggregate demand curve. According to real business cycle models, this is the way that business fluctuations in the real world tend to occur.

What factors shift the aggregate supply curve, causing business fluctuations? Among the most important are new products, new methods of production, new sources of raw materials, changes in the price of raw materials, and good or bad weather (recall Chapter 16). These factors are sometimes called **Supply shocks** **supply shocks** (a concept first introduced in Chapter 22). The effects of a *favorable* supply shock (one that pushes the aggregate supply curve to the right) may persist for several years, after which an *unfavorable* supply shock (one that pushes the aggregate supply curve to the left) may be felt. For example, in Figure 26.1, the technological advance that increases real GDP from Y_0 to Y_1 is a favorable supply shock, which is succeeded by an unfavorable supply shock (the cutback of oil from OPEC), which reduces real GDP from Y_1 to Y_2.

As in the other new classical models discussed earlier in this chapter, real business cycle models assume that equilibrium is achieved in all markets. In other words, markets clear. Each firm produces the amount of output it desires and hires the quantity of labor it wants. Workers get as much work as they want; there is no involuntary unemployment. Prices and wages respond flexibly to changing economic conditions. This is in contrast to the new Keynesian models, taken up in succeeding sections, which assume that many factors prevent markets from clearing. It is also in contrast to the original Keynesian model, which assumes that wages are inflexible.

The Effect of a Supply Shock

To illustrate in more detail how supply shocks can cause business fluctuations, suppose there is a temporary decline in agricultural productivity due to bad weather and this productivity decline reduces real income in agriculture. As Chapter 17 would lead us to expect, this cut in real income leads farmers to decrease their consumption of goods and services, but they do not decrease their consumption levels all at once. Instead, they spread the reduction of consumption over time. Thus, a supply shock of this sort would be expected to spread from one sector of the economy to another. As farmers cut back their consumption levels, nonagricultural industries, like clothing and automobiles, may feel the pinch. And since farmers cut back their consumption spending gradually, the adverse effects on the sales of other industries, like clothing and automobiles, are likely to continue for some time.

An unfavorable supply shock, such as this decline in agricultural productivity, leads firms to want fewer workers at the prevailing wage. According to real business cycle models, real wages fall as the demand curves for labor shift to the left. Thus, these models predict that real wages tend to fall when real GDP falls—and real wages tend to rise when real GDP rises—which is in accord with past experience, according to some observers, but not according to others.[4]

Responses to the Models

According to proponents of real business cycle models, these models can explain the recent history of the U.S. economy reasonably well. If this is true, it is a remarkable achievement, given that so little attention is given to shifts in the aggregate demand curve. But many economists are skeptical, particularly because they are very uncomfortable with a theory that provides such a small role for monetary policy. As stressed in Chapter 25, there is a significant direct relationship between the money supply and real GDP. How do the proponents of real business cycle models explain this relationship? In their view, changes in real GDP cause changes in the money supply, rather than the other way around. As output goes up or down during a business cycle, the volume of transactions does the same; and the demand for money tends to go up or down, too.

Enthusiasm and Skepticism

Proponents of real business cycle models say that these models enable economists to take a more integrated approach to business fluctuations and economic growth. At present, business fluctuations (the relatively short-term

---

[4] Gordon, *Macroeconomics*; and C. Walsh, "New Views of the Business Cycle: Has the Past Emphasis on Money Been Misplaced?," *Business Review of the Federal Reserve Bank of Philadelphia,* January–February 1986.

ups and downs of the economy) are often studied separately from economic growth (the relatively long-term, generally upward movement of the economy). According to real business cycle models, both business fluctuations and economic growth stem from factors that shift the long-run aggregate supply curve. Because some factors have only temporary effects, they result in business fluctuations, whereas other factors leave more permanent effects, resulting in economic growth.

However, there is considerable skepticism that supply shocks of this sort are big enough to cause the business fluctuations we have experienced. As Robert Gordon, of Northwestern University, put it:

> Skeptics doubt that any conceivable supply shock could explain why output fell one-third in the Great Depression of the 1930s. Only the oil price shocks of the 1970s . . . qualify as a supply shock severe enough to explain the recessions that occurred in 1974–75 and 1980–82. Proponents of the real business cycle approach have failed to identify particular events in particular sectors that could be labeled supply shocks in earlier episodes like the Great Depression and postwar recessions before 1974. At an industry level, one would expect technology shocks to occur randomly. Highly distinctive technologies are used in different industries; for instance, an innovation that increases the speed of a laptop computer has little effect on the productivity of coal miners. Favorable shocks in some industries would cancel out adverse shocks in other industries, which deepens the skepticism that (except for the oil shocks of the 1970s) the *average* effect of all the separate industry shocks could be large enough to explain actual booms and recessions.[5]

The New Keynesians

Just as there is a new classical macroeconomics, so there is a new Keynesianism.

New Keynesians Like the original Keynesians, the **new Keynesians** do not believe that markets clear continuously; in other words, they do not believe that the quantity demanded of a good or input always equals the quantity supplied. Instead, they believe that if there is a sudden shift in the demand or supply curve, prices fail to adjust quickly enough to equate the quantity demanded to the quantity supplied. In their view, the economy can stay in a state of disequilibrium for years if prices adjust slowly enough.

As we know from previous sections, this is quite a different view from that held by the new classical macroeconomists, who assume that markets clear

[5] Gordon, *Macroeconomics*, 205–206.

continuously because prices adjust quickly. The new Keynesians, like the old Keynesians, say that their view is the more realistic one. They argue that it is unrealistic to assume that workers unemployed during recessions are voluntarily unemployed. Ask such a worker, they say, whether he or she would refuse a job offer at the prevailing wage. In their view, it is very unlikely that such a worker would refuse the offer, shedding doubt on whether the labor market actually clears. Turning to product markets, they ask whether a firm in a recession is selling all that it would like to sell. In their view, such a firm would likely say it was not, shedding doubt on whether the product market actually clears.

Like the new classical economists, the new Keynesians have adopted the theory of rational expectations. For example, Stanley Fisher (a former professor at MIT and a former governor of the Bank of Israel) showed that if the public has rational expectations, systematic monetary policy can stabilize the economy. But his theory assumes that wages are inflexible, whereas the new classical macroeconomists assume that they are flexible. This is a fundamental difference.

How Do New Keynesians Differ from Old Keynesians?

Both old and new Keynesians assume that prices or wages or both tend to adjust slowly in the short run, with the result that the quantity of output, more than price, tends to adjust to changes in aggregate demand. But whereas old Keynesians merely assumed that wages tend to be rigid and that prices are sticky, new Keynesians have developed theories that help to explain why such wage and price stability can be expected, given the rational behavior of individuals and firms. In other words, new Keynesians have tried to construct a microeconomic foundation for Keynesianism that old Keynesians failed to provide.

Menu Costs and Sticky Prices

To explain why prices adjust slowly, the new Keynesians assume that markets are not perfectly competitive. In other words, firms are assumed to have some control over the prices of their products. For many products, like computers, oil, or beer, this is a reasonable assumption. Going a step further, they also assume that a firm incurs costs when it changes its price. Such costs are called **Menu costs** **menu costs**. Why? Because they are the same sort of costs that a restaurant incurs when it changes its prices and must print new menus.

As an illustration, consider the Jefferson Company, a producer of a wide variety of hand tools. If it changes its price schedule, it must print new catalogs, spend a considerable amount to inform its customers of the price changes, change many aspects of its billing system, and so forth.

TABLE 26.1		Prices Are Raised	Prices Are Not Raised
Jefferson Company's Profit If It Raises or Does Not Raise Its Prices, Original Situation	Sales	$1,095,000	$1,070,000
	Costs	840,000	850,000
	Profit	$255,000	$220,000

Its accountants may figure that it costs Jefferson $40,000 every time it changes its price schedule.

Suppose that there is an upward shift in the demand curve for Jefferson's product. Given this increase in demand, Jefferson's president suspects that it may be wise to raise the firm's prices. According to the firm's accountants, the firm's sales, costs, and profits are as shown in Table 26.1 if it raises or does not raise its prices. Clearly, the president is right; Jefferson would make higher profits if it increased its prices. However, the figures in Table 26.1 do not take into account the $40,000 cost of changing prices. When these menu costs are taken into account, it is not profitable for Jefferson to increase its prices.

In the next few months, the upward shift in the demand curve for Jefferson's product continues, and its president wonders once again whether the firm should raise its prices. The firm's accountants estimate that its sales, costs, and profits are as shown in Table 26.2 if it now raises or does not raise its prices. At this point, is it profitable for Jefferson to change its price schedule? The answer is yes, because Table 26.2 shows that the increase in profit ($260,000 – $210,000 = $50,000) is more than sufficient to cover the menu costs of $40,000.

The point here is that according to the new Keynesians, prices can be sticky because of the existence of menu costs. This is one way they explain why prices adjust slowly and why markets do not clear continuously.

TABLE 26.2		Prices Are Raised	Prices Are Not Raised
Jefferson Company's Profit If It Raises or Does Not Raise Its Prices, Subsequent Situation	Sales	$1,120,000	$1,080,000
	Costs	860,000	870,000
	Profit	$260,000	$210,000

Long-Term Labor Contracts and Sticky Wages

Like prices, wages can be sticky, according to the new Keynesians, and this is due in part to long-term labor contracts. In the United States, formal labor contracts prevail in heavily unionized industries like steel, automobiles, rubber, and electrical machinery. Those contracts influence the level of wages in other industries, since they tend to be imitated elsewhere. Many contracts extend for three years; the contract calls for specified increases in wage rates each year plus (in some instances) extra wage increases that offset whatever changes occur in the consumer price index.

Not all contracts come up for renewal at the same time. Instead, as shown in Figure 26.2, some contracts come up for renewal each year. Assuming for simplicity that all contracts are negotiated at the beginning of the year and last for three years, the contracts negotiated in 2009 cover 2009, 2010, and 2011; those negotiated in 2010 cover 2010, 2011, and 2012; and so on. One important consequence of these multiyear labor contracts is that wages adjust slowly, with a substantial lag, to changes in aggregate demand.

Given that long-term contracts tend to slow the rate of adjustment of wages, it is interesting to ask why workers and firms prefer to enter into such agreements. One reason is that each wage negotiation costs both workers and firms a considerable amount of time and money, since each side must prepare its case thoroughly. Therefore, both sides are happy if these negotiations take place only every few years. Also, if labor and management do not come to an agreement, a strike may occur, with substantial potential losses to both sides. Neither side really wants a strike (except in very unusual circumstances), and if there are wide time intervals between negotiations, there also are likely to be wide time intervals between strikes. In reality only a small share of the labor force is covered in such multi-year contracts, so this theory only offers a partial answer to why wages are sticky.

FIGURE 26.2

Overlapping Three-Year Labor Contracts

Not all contracts come up for renewal at the same time; instead, they overlap. One consequence is that wages adjust slowly, with a substantial lag, to changes in aggregate demand.

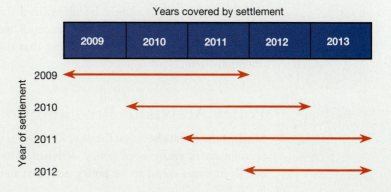

Implicit Contracts

Implicit
contracts

Another theory used by the new Keynesians to explain wage rigidity focuses on **implicit contracts**, which are agreements between workers and firms not found in any formal, written contracts. Rather, they are informal or implicit. Workers and firms have many understandings that are not formalized in any written agreement. Indeed, it would be impossible to write down all the understandings that grow up between labor and management.

According to this theory, workers are more inclined to shun risk than their employers; this seems reasonable given that the owners of firms have been willing to assume the risks of operating a business. In particular, workers are reluctant to assume the risks involved in allowing wage rates to adjust quickly to clear the labor markets, because this would mean that wage rates would vary considerably during business fluctuations.

Instead, according to implicit contract theory, wages are set on the basis of long-term considerations and do not go up and down during business fluctuations. Thus, wages do not behave so as to clear markets, and employment varies considerably. Firms in effect provide insurance for workers, who do not want their wages to vary over the business cycle. Responding to their workers' preferences, firms maintain relatively rigid wages but at a level that allows them to increase their profits.

In particular, firms often lay off workers with the least seniority when it is necessary to lay off anyone. This means that workers with considerable seniority have a relatively good "insurance policy" against being laid off. Most workers may prefer a system of this sort (whereby relatively few workers with little seniority are laid off when times get tough, but the wages of those that are not laid off are quite rigid) to a system where wages are permitted to vary enough over the business cycle so that labor markets clear continuously.

Critics note that if workers are not willing to be bound by the prevailing implicit contracts, they may refuse unemployment after being laid off by finding work elsewhere. Similarly, when the demand for labor grows, resulting in the rigid prevailing wages being lower than what other firms may be willing to pay for their services, workers may leave the firm and take jobs elsewhere. Further, it should be recognized that according to this theory, unemployment really is voluntary, since all workers enter freely into the relevant implicit contracts, recognizing that they are accepting the risk of unemployment.

Policy Activism: Pros and Cons

Much of the debate between the new Keynesians and the new classical macroeconomists is really over policy activism. The new Keynesians—like the old Keynesians—tend to be policy activists; they believe that discretionary monetary and fiscal policies are required to keep the economy on a reasonably even keel. The new classical macroeconomists tend to be very skeptical about how much stabilization policies of this sort can achieve. The debate over the pros and cons of policy activism has been going on for decades. While it is difficult to try to summarize the views of each side (since there is considerable disagreement within each camp), the disagreements tend to be along the following lines:

- ➤ *Stability of private spending.* Many opponents of policy activism tend to believe that if the government's economic policies did not destabilize the economy, private spending would be quite stable. Policy activists, on the other hand, believe that business and consumer spending represent a substantial source of economic instability that should be offset by monetary and fiscal policies.
- ➤ *Flexibility of prices.* Even if intended private spending is not entirely stable, flexible prices tend to stabilize it, according to the nonactivists. The policy activists reply that prices are relatively inflexible downward; in their view, the length of time required for the economy to get itself out of a severe recession would be intolerably long. Their opponents seem more inclined than policy activists to believe that high unemployment causes wages and input prices to fall, shifts the short-run aggregate supply curve to the right, and increases output in a reasonable period of time.
- ➤ *Rules versus activism.* Opponents of policy activism tend to believe that even if intended private spending is not entirely stable and prices are not entirely flexible, activist monetary and fiscal policies to stabilize the economy are likely to do more damage than good. As pointed out in Chapter 25, they sometimes favor a rule stipulating that the money supply grow steadily at a constant rate because of the difficulties in forecasting the future state of the economy and the long and variable time lags in the effects of changes in the quantity of money on output and prices. The policy activists, while admitting that monetary and fiscal policies have sometimes been destabilizing, are much more optimistic about the efficacy of such policies in the future.

Policy Rules and Time Inconsistency

The new classical macroeconomists stress repeatedly the importance of the public's expectations regarding future policy. For this reason, they think it is important to distinguish between rigid policy rules, feedback policy rules, and discretionary policy. A **rigid policy rule** specifies completely the behavior of the variable governed by the policy rule. For example, Milton Friedman's

Rigid policy rule

CASE STUDY 26.3

THE TROUBLED ASSET RELIEF PROGRAM (TARP)

On October 3, 2008 (in the depths of the financial crisis and the Great Recession), President George W. Bush signed the Troubled Asset Relief Program (TARP). It was a deeply unpopular move, and it took Congress two tries to pass it.

The TARP was originally authorized to use $700 billion of taxpayer money to bail out banks and other troubled companies. In 2010, this amount was reduced to $475 billion. Many of America's largest financial institutions (including Citigroup, Bank of America, American International Group, Wells Fargo, Goldman Sachs, and Morgan Stanley) used some of the TARP money. The bailout of General Motors and Chrysler was also financed with these funds.

To some people, TARP was—and still is—a four-letter word. To these people it represented all that is wrong with our financial system—especially the part about taxpayer money being used to bailout Wall Street "fat cats."

There are several myths about the TARP. One is that the program was designed to save financiers from their own follies. True enough, but it was also used to save two of the three large U.S. auto companies. Another myth is that the "fat cats" got all the money. They did not. The funds were disbursed as temporary loans, almost all of which were returned. In fact, TARP cost taxpayers a tiny fraction of the total amount (roughly $32 billion)—and the government may have actually made a profit on parts of the program.

In the end, the TARP was an emergency program that—along with the unorthodox and massive monetary stimulus provided by the Fed—prevented the implosion of the U.S. financial system and the decimation of large parts of the U.S. automotive industry. Without it, chances are good that things would have been a lot worse for the economy and the American people.

The TARP is a classic example of the need for maximum flexibility and activism in a crisis. The depths of a financial crisis and deep recession are not the times to be practicing "tough love" vis-à-vis large companies, whose demise could do serious damage to the economy. By the same token, these companies cannot be left with the impression that there are no consequences for them of their profligate behavior in good times.

suggestion that the money supply be set so that it grows at a fixed, agreed-on percentage rate is a rigid policy rule. Once the government establishes the percentage growth rate, the behavior of the money supply is completely specified. Regardless of what happens, the money supply must grow at this particular rate so long as this policy rule is in force.

Feedback policy rule

In contrast, a **feedback policy rule** allows the behavior of the variable governed by the policy rule to change, depending on future circumstances. For example, the government might specify that if the unemployment rate exceeds

7 percent, the rate of increase of the money supply will be set at 6 percent, whereas if the unemployment rate does not exceed 7 percent, it will be set at 5 percent. In this case, the government does not specify the behavior of the money supply completely, since it cannot predict whether at a given time in the future the unemployment rate will be above 7 percent. But it does issue a well-defined formula indicating how the money supply will behave, depending on future circumstances.

The new classical macroeconomists argue that feedback policy rules cannot affect real GDP. If the public knows the feedback rule in advance, any change in the money supply specified by the rule is anticipated by the public. Hence, Robert Lucas and his coworkers believe that such a rule will not be effective. Why? Because, according to Lucas, only unexpected changes in the price level result in changes in aggregate supply (recall page 622). Consequently, Lucas and his coworkers feel that a rigid policy rule of the sort proposed by monetarists like Milton Friedman is best. In their view, the adoption of such a rule would promote the credibility of monetary policy. In other words, the public would be convinced that the money supply really would grow in accord with this rigid policy rule.

Discretionary policy, as we know from previous discussions, is policy formulated at the discretion of the policy makers. According to the new classical macroeconomists, one of the big problems arising from discretionary policy is **time inconsistency**. Suppose, for example, the government is trying to reduce the rate of inflation. Once it convinces the public that the inflation rate is going to go down—once it makes its disinflationary policy credible—policy makers may feel that it is in their interest to depart from their announced policy. For example, suppose that an election is coming up. If they nudge the rate of increase of the money supply up a bit, the resulting unexpected increase in the price level is likely to raise real GDP and reduce the unemployment rate, increasing their chances of victory in the election. Of course, as people become more and more used to being double-crossed in this way, it becomes harder and harder for the government to convince them that any of its announced policies will really be carried out.[6]

[margin terms]
Discretionary policy

Time inconsistency

The New Keynesian Response

The new Keynesians take quite a different tack. They believe that changes in the attitudes and expectations of firms and consumers can cause substantial economic instability, which should be offset by government stabilization policy. In contrast to the new classical macroeconomists, they do not favor rigid policy rules. For example, they point out that the increase in the velocity of

---

[6] For some relevant discussion, see N. G. Mankiw, "A Quick Refresher Course in Macroeconomics," *Journal of Economic Literature*, 28 (December 1990), 1645–1660.

money in the United States since 1982 has been very erratic (recall page 614); this would seem to suggest that the growth rate of nominal GDP would have fluctuated considerably if a rigid rule calling for a constant growth of the money supply had been applied. As we have seen, the new Keynesians put a great deal of emphasis on the existence of long-term wage and price contracts. Consequently, they are less concerned than the new classical macroeconomists with the credibility of the government's policies. Because wages and prices tend to be sticky, total real output tends to be affected by the actual behavior of the money supply and price level, not just by unanticipated changes in the price level.

In recent years, activists have recognized more fully and more openly the many difficulties in formulating an effective economic stabilization policy. In the 1960s, there was considerable talk among activists about fine-tuning the economy; such optimism is long gone. Activists readily admit that there may be a long and variable lag between the time when a policy change occurs and when its effects are felt. Also, they recognize that it is very difficult to forecast the state of the economy when the effects of a policy change occur. Nonetheless, activists have not abandoned the attempt to formulate effective discretionary stabilization policies. On the contrary, they continue to press for changes in monetary and fiscal policies that, in their eyes, would keep the economy on a more even keel. But they also tend to be cautious, certainly more cautious than 50 years ago, in their claims for what discretionary stabilization policies can achieve. That said, the deep recession of 2008–09 and the big fiscal stimulus put in place by the Obama administration in early 2009 have revived this debate (see Cross Chapter Case: Part 5).

Divergent Political Beliefs

One final and very important point is that while economics is a science, not a mere reflection of the economist's political beliefs, it nonetheless is impossible to divorce an economist's views of the economy from his or her political feelings where policy issues are involved. To a considerable extent, the differences between the policy activists and their opponents stem from divergent political beliefs. The policy activists tend to be optimistic concerning the extent to which the government can be trusted to formulate and carry out a responsible set of monetary and fiscal policies. They recognize that some politicians are willing to win votes in the next election by destabilizing the economy, but they nonetheless believe that discretionary action by elected officials generally is more effective than automatic rules. Opponents of policy activism, on the other hand, are skeptical of the willingness of politicians to do what is required to stabilize the economy rather than what is politically expedient. Since this aspect of the debate is difficult to resolve (in any scientific way), a complete resolution of this controversy is not likely any time soon.

REVIEW AND PRACTICE

Summary

1   The principal debate of the 1960s and 1970s was between Keynesians and monetarists. The Keynesians put more emphasis than the monetarists on the federal budget; the monetarists put more emphasis than the Keynesians on the money supply.

2   In the late 1970s, supply-side economists came to prominence; their emphasis is on the aggregate supply curve. To stimulate rightward shifts in the aggregate supply curve, supply-siders favor the use of various financial incentives, particularly tax cuts.

3   The new classical macroeconomists, like Robert Lucas, also came to prominence in the 1970s. On the basis of their assumptions, the new classical macroeconomists conclude that the government cannot use monetary and fiscal policies to close recessionary and inflationary gaps in the ways described in Chapters 18, 24, and 25. One central assumption they make is that prices and wages are completely flexible.

4   According to real business cycle models, business fluctuations are due predominantly to shifts in the aggregate supply curve, not the aggregate demand curve. Among the most important factors shifting the aggregate supply curve are new products, new methods of production, new sources of raw materials, and good or bad weather.

5   The new Keynesians, like the old Keynesians, believe that prices and wages tend to be rigid in the short run, with the result that the quantity of output, more than the price, tends to adjust to changes in aggregate demand.

6   According to the new Keynesians, prices tend to be sticky because of menu costs (costs incurred by firms when they change prices), and wages tend to be sticky because of long-term labor contracts. On the basis of the theory of implicit contracts, they conclude that wages are set according to long-term considerations. (Responding to workers' aversion to risk, firms maintain relatively rigid wages.)

7   The debate over the pros and cons of policy activism continues. Opponents of policy activism tend to believe that activist monetary and fiscal policies to stabilize the economy are likely to do more damage than good.

Policy activists, while admitting that discretionary monetary and fiscal policies have sometimes been destabilizing, are much more optimistic about the efficacy of such policies in the future.

Problems and Questions

1 "New Keynesians are liberal activists who want to push our society in the direction of socialism. Their emphasis on policy activism is a reflection of their desire to have the government purchase more of the national output." Comment and evaluate.

2 "New classical macroeconomists are archconservatives with a strong laissez-faire orientation. They prefer monetary policy over fiscal policy because it involves less direct interference by government in the market-place." Comment and evaluate.

3 "The Keynesian model can easily be translated into monetarist terms, and the monetarist model can easily be translated into Keynesian terms. Hence, there really is no basic difference between the Keynesians and the monetarists." Do you agree? Why or why not?

4 After the cyclical trough of 1982, the velocity of money fell substantially below its postwar growth path. Does this mean that monetarism is useless? Explain.

5 What are rational expectations? Do you agree with the new classical macro-economists that much unemployment is voluntary? Explain.

6 **(a)** "Working hours are fixed by custom at about 40 hours per week. Cutting taxes will not affect them." Do you agree? Why or why not?

   (b) "Business executives work about as hard as they can to keep their heads above water. Cutting taxes will not affect how hard they work." Do you agree? Why or why not?

Key Terms

new classical macroeconomists
rational expectations
real business cycle models
supply shocks
new Keynesians
menu costs

implicit contracts
rigid policy rule
feedback policy rule
discretionary policy
time inconsistency

Viewpoint for Analysis

In a June 28, 2012, op-ed piece in the *Financial Times*, Paul Krugman (Princeton University) and Richard Layard (London School of Economics) said: "More than four years after the financial crisis began, the world's major advanced economies remain deeply depressed, in a scene all too reminiscent of the 1930s. The reason is simple: we are relying on the same ideas that governed policy during that decade. These ideas, long since disproved, involve profound errors both about the causes of the crisis, its nature and the appropriate policy response."[7]

(a) How similar was the situation in 2012 with that of the 1930s?

(b) What policy mistakes were Krugman and Layard referring to?

[7] Paul Krugman and Richard Layard, "A Manifesto for Economic Sense," *Financial Times*, June 28, 2012.

THE DEBATE OVER POST-CRISIS FISCAL AUSTERITY

The Keynesian-classical debate over policy activism and fiscal austerity or stimulus was played out in a very vocal and passionate way in the immediate aftermath of the financial crisis and Great Recession of 2007–2009.

In the early 2010s, despite evidence that the momentum of growth was slowing in advanced economies, and despite growing anxiety about a double-dip recession, many countries (especially in Europe) embarked on a course of fiscal tightening. The dilemma for these countries was that, partly as a result of the financial crisis and recession, the budget deficits and public debt of these countries ballooned. In some cases, the fiscal tightening was the result of explicit actions (tax hikes and spending cuts). In other cases, the expiration of stimulus (including incentive programs to encourage the purchases of homes and cars) amounted to a de facto tightening of fiscal conditions. The United States was an example of the latter.

The case for fiscal tightening now (rather than later when growth would be stronger) was articulated by current and former central bankers (Jean-Claude Trichet, of the European Central Bank, and Alan Greenspan, of the U.S. Federal Reserve) and some academics (including Alberto Alesina, of Harvard University). The essence of the argument was that fiscal austerity would restore confidence on the part of financial markets and help to lower risk premiums and interest rates. This would offset the impact of tightening and help to create a better environment for healthy long-term growth. There were a couple of associated arguments that were used to bolster the case. First, consumers and businesses worry about future tax hikes and spending cuts and are therefore "over" savings. Second, deficits are inflationary and "crowd out" private investment. Proponents of austerity usually point to countries such as Sweden, Canada, and Australia, which were able to both cut deficits and enjoy strong growth in the 1990s.

The case for austerity is weaker than advocates would like to believe. To begin with, drastic austerity measures did little to lower risk premiums for high-debt countries such as Greece, Italy, Portugal, and Spain. Second, crowding out and inflation are not serious threats when there is a lot of slack in the global economy (as there was in the early 2010s). Finally, the decade of the 1990s is not a useful guide for the latter period. Most of the global economy was booming in the earlier decade, so export-led growth was an option for countries that were going through severe fiscal adjustment. Also, interest rates for most affected countries were higher in the 1990s than in the 2010s, so (arguably) monetary stimulus (where it was available) was more effective in the earlier decade.

The Keynesian case (go growth now and tighten later) was articulated most vocally by Nobel laureate Paul Krugman, of Princeton University, in numerous *New York Times* op-ed pieces and by Martin Wolf, columnist for the *Financial Times*. The essence of their argument was that global growth was too fragile in the post-crisis world and that governments ran the risk of making the same mistake as the Roosevelt administration in the mid-1930s and the Japanese government in 1997. In both cases, nascent recoveries were aborted when fiscal policy was tightened. Moreover, the Keynesians argued that in advanced countries there was an "epidemic of thrift" on the part of consumers (as they tried to reduce their debt levels) and financial institutions (as they tried to repair their balance sheets). So, they argued, governments need to keep running deficits, especially when interest rates are close to zero (and monetary policy has largely run out of ammunition).

The Keynesian case was also based on weak evidence. First, the Great Recession was not a repeat of the Great Depression, as Krugman and others were suggesting. For example, the drop in GDP during the Great Depression was nearly 10 times greater than in the Great Recession, and the peak unemployment rate was nearly three times as high. Second, the fiscal tightening in the 1930s was around 5 percent of GDP—about three to four times bigger than the United States was facing in the early 2010s. Moreover, the parallels with Japan were also exaggerated. Part of the reason for the post-fiscal-tightening recession in 1998 in Japan was due to the Asian financial crisis (1997–1998) and its big negative impact on Japanese exports.

Few economists debated the need, in the 2010s, for most advanced countries to put in place credible deficit and debt reduction programs in the medium to long term.

The only question was when should the tightening begin? There is no universally applicable answer to this question. High debt countries, such as Greece, had no room to maneuver. Continued access to financial markets dictated that they tighten immediately. At the other extreme, Germany and the United States had the luxury of time. Markets were not pressuring them to put in place austerity measures immediately. One manifestation of this was that long-term interest rates in the United States were very low.

With no clear-cut answer, the debate rages on.

Questions

1 Some have suggested a quid pro quo of more monetary stimulus in return for fiscal tightening. Assuming that this is possible, is it a good idea?

2 In the long run, is it more effective to reduce deficits by cutting spending or raising taxes?

3 Some have suggested that cutting taxes will also lead to spending cuts and a smaller government. This argument is sometimes referred to as "starving the beast." Do you think it might work? Why or why not?

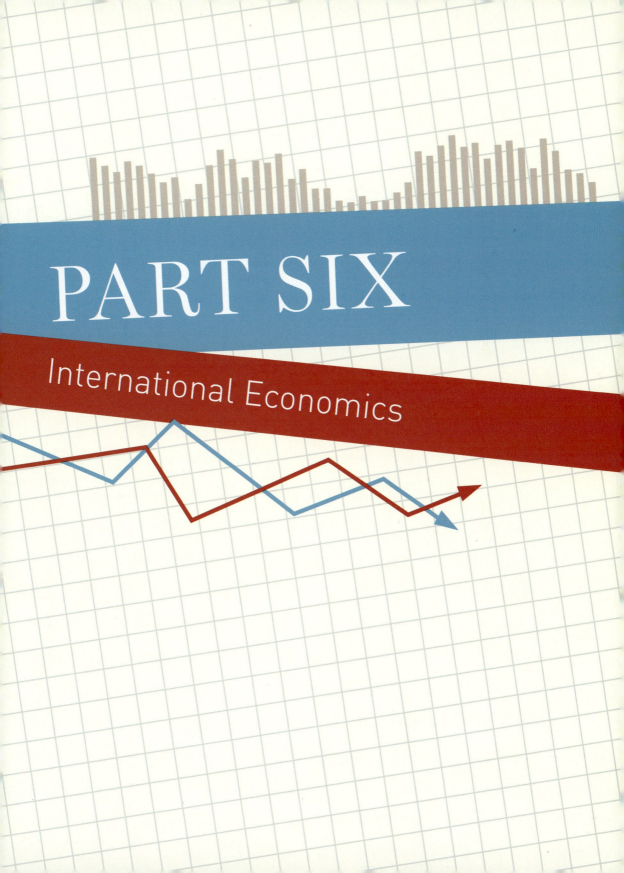

PART SIX

International Economics

International Trade

LEARNING OBJECTIVES

➤ To define comparative advantage and explain its relation to international trade

➤ To define tariffs and quotas

➤ To explore the impact of tariffs and quotas on international trade

➤ To state the arguments for and against tariffs and quotas

M ost economists believe that tariffs and other trade restrictions limit competition, which in turn reduces efficiency and productivity. What are these trade restrictions, and why do many observers urge that they be phased out? One purpose of this chapter is to answer these questions.

Practically all people realize that they are not islands unto themselves and that they benefit from living with, working with, and trading with other people. Exactly the same is true of countries. They, too, must interact with one another; and they, too, benefit from trade with one another. No country can be an island unto itself, not even the United States. To understand how the world economy functions, we need to grasp the basic economic principles of international trade.

Although small relative to our national product, U.S. foreign trade plays a very important role in our economic life. Many of our industries depend on other countries for markets or such raw materials as coffee, tea, or tin. Our **exports** (the things we sell to other countries) amount to about 13 percent of our gross domestic product. In absolute terms, our exports (and imports) are the second largest in the world (after China). Without question, our way of life would have to change considerably if we could not trade with other countries.

Exports

Specialization and Trade

Why do we trade with other countries? Do we (and do our trading partners) benefit from this trade? And if so, what determines the sorts of goods we should export and import? These are very important questions, among the most fundamental in economics. The answers are not new. They have been well understood for considerably more than a century, from the work of such great economists as David Hume, David Ricardo, Adam Smith, and John Stuart Mill.

Why Do Individuals Trade?

As a first step, it is useful to recognize that the benefits countries receive through trade are essentially the same as those individuals receive through trade. Consider the hypothetical case of John and Judy Abogado and their two children. The Abogado family, like practically all families, trades continually with other families and with business firms. John and Judy are lawyers, and they trade their legal services for money, which they use to buy the food, clothing, housing, and other goods and services their family wants. Why does the Abogado family do this? What advantages does it receive through trade? Why doesn't it attempt to be self-sufficient?

To see why the Abogado family is sensible indeed to opt for trade rather than self-sufficiency, let's consider what would happen if the Abogado family attempted to be self-sufficient. The Abogados would have to provide their own transportation, telephone service, foodstuffs, clothing, and a host of other things. John and Judy are lawyers—well-trained, valuable, productive members of the community. But if they were to try their hand at making automobiles—or even bicycles—it might be a total loss. If they attempted to be self-sufficient, they might be unable to provide many of the goods their family now enjoys.

Why Do Countries Trade?

Trade permits specialization, and specialization increases output. This is the advantage of trade, for both individuals and countries. In our hypothetical example, it is obvious that, because they can trade with other families and with firms, John and Judy can specialize in doing what they are good at—law. Consequently, they can be more productive than if they were forced to be jacks-of-all-trades, as they would have to be if they could not trade with others. The same principle holds for countries. Because the United States can trade with other countries, it can specialize in the goods and services it produces particularly well. Then it can trade them for goods that other countries are especially good at producing. Thus, both we and our trading partners benefit.

Some countries have more and better resources of certain types than others. Saudi Arabia has oil, Canada has timber, Japan has skilled labor, and so on.

International differences in resource endowments and the relative quantity of various types of human and nonhuman resources are important bases for specialization. Consider countries with lots of fertile soil, little capital, and much unskilled labor. They are likely to find it advantageous to produce agricultural goods, whereas countries with poor soil, much capital, and highly skilled labor probably do better to produce capital-intensive high-technology goods. We must recognize, however, that the bases for specialization do not remain fixed over time. Instead, as technology and the resource endowments of various countries change, the pattern of international specialization changes as well. For instance, the United States specialized more in raw materials and foodstuffs about a century ago than it does now.

Absolute Advantage

To clarify the benefits of trade, consider the following example. Suppose that the United States can produce two supercomputers or 5,000 cases of wine with 1 unit of resources. Suppose that France can produce one supercomputer or 10,000 cases of wine with 1 unit of resources. Given the production possibilities in each country, are there any advantages in trade between the countries? And if so, which commodity should each country export and which should each country import? Should France export wine and import computers, or should it import wine and export computers?

To answer these questions, assume that the United States produces a certain number of computers and a certain amount of wine and France produces a certain number of computers and a certain amount of wine. If the United States shifts 1 unit of its resources from producing wine to producing computers, it increases its production of computers by two computers and reduces its production of wine by 5,000 cases of wine. If France shifts 1 unit of resources from the production of computers to the production of wine, it increases its production of wine by 10,000 cases and reduces its production of computers by one computer.

The case just described is a very special one, since one country (France) has an absolute advantage over another (the United States) in the production of one good (wine), whereas the second country (the United States) has an absolute advantage over the first (France) in the production of another good (computers). What do we mean by absolute advantage? Country A has an **absolute advantage** over country B in the production of a good when country A can produce a unit of the good with fewer resources than can country B. Since the United States can produce a computer with fewer units of resources than France, it has an absolute advantage over France in the production of computers. Since France requires fewer resources than the United States to produce a given amount of wine, France has an absolute advantage over the United States in the production of wine.

Absolute advantage

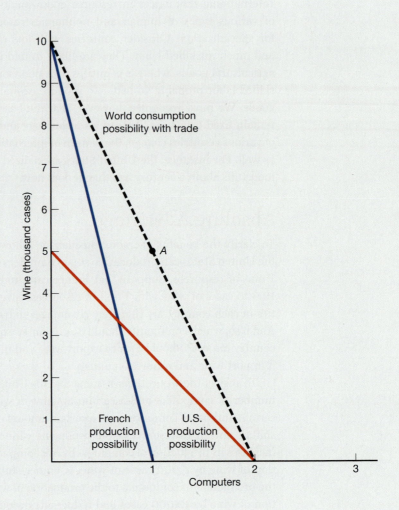

FIGURE 27.1

Absolute Advantage and Trade

Figure 27.1 illustrates the case of absolute advantage, using production possibilities curves for the United States and France.[1] As you can see from this graph, for any given unit of resources, the United States is more efficient (absolutely) at producing computers and France is more efficient (absolutely) at producing wine. As will become apparent, both countries are better off if they specialize in producing those goods for which they have an absolute advantage and then trade.

Table 27.1 shows the *net* effect of this shift in the utilization of resources on *world* output of computers and wine. World output of computers increases

[1] Production possibilities curves were introduced in Chapter 1. For the sake of simplicity, the lines are assumed to be straight rather than curved. This means that the trade off between wine and computer production is the same, regardless of how much is produced.

TABLE 27.1

Case of Absolute Advantage

	Increase or Decrease In Output of	
	Computers	Wine (thousands of cases)
Effect of United States shifting 1 unit of resources from wine to computers	+ 2	– 5
Effect of France shifting 1 unit of resources from computers to wine	– 1	+ 10
Net effect	+ 1	+ 5

(by one computer) and world output of wine increases (by 5,000 cases) as a result of the redeployment of resources in each country. Thus, specialization increases world output.

Moreover, if world output of each commodity is increased by shifting 1 unit of U.S. resources from wine to computers and shifting 1 unit of French resources from computers to wine, it follows that world output of each commodity is increased further if each country shifts *more* of its resources in the same direction. This is because the amount of resources required to produce a unit of each good is assumed to be constant, regardless of how much is produced.

In this situation, one country (the United States) should specialize in producing computers, and the other country (France) should specialize in producing wine. This maximizes world output of both wine and computers and permits a rise in both countries' standards of living. The gains from trade with absolute advantage can be seen in Figure 27.1. The dashed line shows the additional output available when both countries specialize and trade (this line is sometimes referred to as the *consumption possibilities curve*). If the United States produces two computers and trades one for 5,000 cases of wine (at point *A* in Figure 27.1), it is better off because on its own, it would have to sacrifice two computers for 5,000 cases of wine. France is also better off with trade, because it can get one computer for 5,000 cases of wine instead of sacrificing 10,000 cases of wine without trade.

Complete specialization of this sort is somewhat unrealistic, since countries often produce some of both commodities, but this simple example illustrates the basic principles involved.

Comparative Advantage

But what if one country is more efficient in producing both goods? If the United States is more efficient in producing both computers and wine, is there still any benefit to be derived from specialization and trade? At first glance, you are probably inclined to answer no. But if this is your inclination, you should reconsider, because you are wrong.

To see why specialization and trade have advantages even when one country is more efficient than another at producing both goods, consider the following example. Suppose the United States can produce two supercomputers or 5,000 cases of wine with 1 unit of resources, and France can produce one supercomputer or 4,000 cases of wine with 1 unit of resources. In this case, the United States is a more efficient producer of both computers and wine. Nonetheless, as we shall see, world output of both goods increases if the United States specializes in the production of computers and France specializes in the production of wine.

Table 27.2 demonstrates this conclusion. If 2 units of U.S. resources are shifted from wine to computer production, four additional computers and 10,000 fewer cases of wine are produced. If 3 units of French resources are shifted from computer to wine production, three fewer computers and 12,000 additional cases of wine are produced. The combined effect of this redeployment of resources in both countries is to increase world output of computers by one computer and world output of wine by 2,000 cases. Even though the United States is more efficient than France in the production of both computers and wine, the world output of both goods is maximized if the United States specializes in computers and France specializes in wine.

Basically, this is because although the United States is more efficient than France in the production of both goods, it has a greater advantage in computers than in wine. It is twice as efficient as France in producing computers, but only 25 percent more efficient than France in producing wine. To derive these numbers, recall that 1 unit of resources produces two computers in the United States but only one computer in France. Therefore, the United States is twice as efficient in producing computers. On the other hand, 1 unit of resources produces 5,000 cases of wine in the United States but only 4,000 cases in France. Therefore, the United States is 25 percent more efficient in producing wine.

TABLE 27.2		Increase or Decrease in Output of	
Case of Comparative Advantage		Computers	Wine (thousands of cases)
Effect of United States shifting 2 units of resources from wine to computers		+ 4	– 10
Effect of France shifting 3 units of resources from computers to wine		– 3	+ 12
Net effect		+ 1	+ 2

The gains from trade when countries have a comparative advantage in producing goods are also illustrated in Figure 27.2. In this example, the United States has an absolute advantage in producing both computers and wine. However, the United States has a comparative advantage (it is relatively more efficient) in producing computers. France has a comparative advantage in producing wine.

Even in this case, both countries are better off specializing and trading. If France specializes in the production of wine and trades 2,500 cases for one computer (point *B* in Figure 27.2), it is better off, since without trade, it would have to sacrifice 4,000 cases of wine for one computer. Similarly, if the United States specializes in computers and trades one computer for 4,000 cases of wine (point *C*), it is better off, since without trade, it would have to sacrifice one computer to get only 2,500 cases of wine. As long as these two countries trade computers for wine at a ratio between 1:2,500 and 1:4,000, both countries are better off with trade.

Trade Depends on Comparative Advantage

Comparative advantage

A country has a **comparative advantage** in those products where its efficiency relative to other nations is highest. In the preceding example, the United States has a comparative advantage in the production of computers and a comparative disadvantage in the production of wine. So long as a country

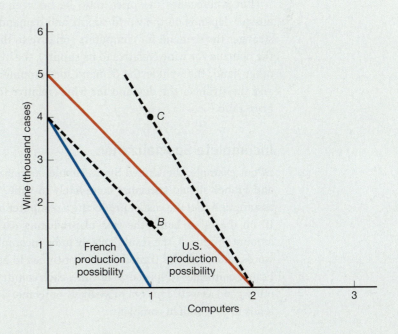

FIGURE 27.2

Comparative Advantage and Trade

has a comparative advantage in the production of some commodities and a comparative disadvantage in the production of others, it can benefit from specialization and trade. A country specializes in products in which it has a comparative advantage and imports those in which it has a comparative disadvantage. The point is that specialization and trade depend on comparative, not absolute, advantage. One of the first economists to understand the full significance of this fact was David Ricardo, a British economist of the early nineteenth century.

The Terms of Trade

Terms of trade   The **terms of trade** are the quantity of imported goods a country can obtain in exchange for a unit of exported goods. In the previous example, the terms of trade for the United States are measured by the ratio of the price of a computer to the price of a case of wine, since this ratio shows how many cases of French wine the United States can get in exchange for a U.S. computer. It is important to note that this ratio must be somewhere between 2,500:1 and 4,000:1. By diverting its own resources from wine production to computer production, the United States can exchange a computer for 2,500 cases of wine. Since this is possible, it will not pay the United States to trade a computer for less than 2,500 cases of wine. Similarly, since France can exchange a case of wine for 1/4,000 of a computer by diverting its own resources from computers to wine, it clearly will not be willing to trade a case of wine for less than 1/4,000 of a computer.

But where does the price ratio lie between 2,500:1 and 4,000:1? The answer depends on the world supply and demand for the two products. The stronger the demand for computers (relative to their supply) and the weaker the demand for wine (relative to its supply), the higher the price ratio. On the other hand, the weaker the demand for computers (relative to their supply) and the stronger the demand for wine (relative to its supply), the lower the price ratio.

Incomplete Specialization

In our example, the United States should specialize completely in computers and France should specialize completely in wine. This result stems from the assumption that the cost of producing a computer or a case of wine is constant. If, on the other hand, the cost of producing each good increases with the amount produced, the result is likely to be incomplete specialization. In other words, although the United States continues to specialize in computers and France continues to specialize in wine, each country also produces some of the other good as well. This is a more likely outcome, since specialization generally tends to be less than complete.

THE MAQUILADORA PROGRAM—HOW THE IMPACT OF INTERNATIONAL INVESTMENT IS VERY SIMILAR TO THE IMPACT OF INTERNATIONAL TRADE

When a multinational company from a developed country such as the United States chooses to produce goods in a developing country such as Mexico (as in the case of the Maquiladora program), the impact is very similar to international trade. Production moves to the country with a comparative advantage in producing those goods. As in the case of trade, this benefits both the country making the investment and the country receiving the investment. While there are some job losses, typically low-skilled workers in the country making the investment, there are more winners than losers in both countries.

Thus, investment, like trade, is a positive-sum game rather than a zero-sum game. In other words, both countries benefit.

In the end, the Maquiladora program turned out to be so successful that it was a major factor behind the establishment of the North American Free Trade Agreement, or NAFTA (see Case Study 27.3). The combination of the Maquiladora program and NAFTA has helped Mexico to enjoy rapid growth—but not at the expense of the United States, where consumers benefited from lower prices and companies trading with Mexico created new, high-skilled jobs.

International Trade and Individual Markets

We have emphasized that countries can benefit by specializing in the production of goods for which they have a comparative advantage and trading these goods for others for which they have a comparative disadvantage.[2] But how do a

[2] The principle of comparative advantage is useful in explaining and predicting the pattern of world trade, as well as in showing the benefits of trade. For example, consider the exports of the United Kingdom and the United States. Robert Stern, of the University of Michigan (emeritus), compared British and U.S. exports of 39 industries. In 21 of the 24 industries where our labor productivity was more than three times that of the British, our exports exceeded British exports. In 11 of the 15 industries where our labor productivity was less than three times that of the British, our exports were less than British exports. Therefore, in 32 out of 39 industries, the principle of comparative advantage, as interpreted by Stern, predicted correctly which country would export more. This is a high batting average, since labor is not the only input and labor productivity is an imperfect measure of true efficiency. Moreover, as we shall see in subsequent sections, countries raise barriers to foreign trade and so prevent trade from taking place in accord with the principle of comparative advantage.

country's producers know whether they have a comparative advantage or disadvantage in the production of a given commodity? They do not call up the local university and ask the leading professor of economics (although that might not always be such a bad idea). Instead, as we shall see in this section, the market for the good provides the required signals.

To see how this works, we consider a new (and rather whimsical) product, bulletproof suspenders. Suppose that the Mob, having run a scientific survey of mobsters and cops, finds that most wear their suspenders over their bulletproof vests. As a consequence, the Mob's shooters are instructed to render a victim immobile by shooting holes in the victim's suspenders (making his trousers fall down and trip him). Naturally, the producers of suspenders soon find it profitable to produce a new bulletproof variety, an innovation that, it is hoped, will make a solid contribution to law and order. The new suspenders are demanded only in the United States and the United Kingdom, since the rest of the world wears belts. The demand curve in the United States is as shown in panel A of Figure 27.3, and the demand curve in the United Kingdom is as shown in panel B. Suppose further that this product can be manufactured in both the United States and the United Kingdom. The supply curve in the United States is as shown in panel A, and the supply curve in the United Kingdom is as shown in panel B.

Take a closer look at Figure 27.3. Note that prices in the United Kingdom are expressed in pounds (£), and prices in the United States are expressed in dollars ($). This is quite realistic. Each country has its own currency in which prices in that country are expressed. In 2012, £1 was equal to about $1.60. In other words, you could exchange a £1 note for $1.60, or $1.60 for a £1 note. For this reason, the two panels of Figure 27.3 are lined up so that a price of $3.20 is at the same level as a price of £2, $4.80 is at the same level as £3, and so on.

FIGURE 27.3

Determining Quantity Imported and Exported under Free Trade

Under free trade, the price is $4.80, or £3. The United States exports Y–X units, the British import V–U units, and Y–X = V–U.

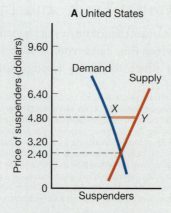

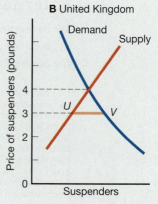

No Foreign Trade

To begin with, suppose that bulletproof suspenders cannot be exported or imported, perhaps because of a very high tariff (tax on imports) imposed on them in both the United States and the United Kingdom. (We can readily imagine members of both Congress and Parliament defending such a tariff on the grounds that a capacity to produce plenty of bulletproof suspenders is important for national defense.) If this happens, the price of bulletproof suspenders is $2.40 in the United States and £4 in Britain. Why? Because as shown in Figure 27.3, these are the prices at which each country's demand curve intersects its supply curve.

Foreign Trade Permitted

Next, suppose that international trade in this product is permitted, perhaps because both countries eliminate the tariff. Now what happens? Since the price is lower in the United States than in the United Kingdom, people can make money by sending this product from the United States to the United Kingdom. After all, they can buy it for $2.40 in this country and sell it for £4 (= $6.40) in the United Kingdom. But they will not be able to do so indefinitely. As more and more suspenders are supplied by the United States for the British market, the price in the United States must go up (to induce producers to produce the additional output) and the price in the United Kingdom must go down (to induce consumers to buy the additional quantity).

When an equilibrium is reached, the price in the United States must equal the price in the United Kingdom. If this did not happen, there would be an advantage in increasing U.S. exports (if the price in the United Kingdom were higher) or in decreasing U.S. exports (if the price in the United States were higher). Only if the prices are equal can an equilibrium exist.

At what level does this price, which is common to both countries, tend to settle? Obviously, the price must end up at the level where the amount of the good one country wants to export equals the amount the other country wants to import. In other words, it must settle at $4.80, or £3 (since this is the price where $Y-X = V-U$). Otherwise, the total amount demanded in both countries would not equal the total amount supplied in both countries. And any reader who has mastered the material in Chapter 2 knows that such a situation cannot be an equilibrium.

The Signal of Market Forces

At this point, we can see how market forces indicate whether a country has a comparative advantage or comparative disadvantage in the production of a certain commodity. If a country has a comparative advantage, it turns out—after the price of the good in various countries is equalized and total world output of the good equals total world demand for it—that the country exports the good under free trade and competition. In Figure 27.3, it turns out that the United States is an exporter of bulletproof suspenders under free trade because the demand and supply curves in the United States and the United Kingdom take the positions they do. The basic reason why the curves take these positions is that the United States has a comparative advantage in the production of this good. To put things in a nutshell, a country's producers can tell (under free trade) whether they have a comparative advantage in the production of a certain commodity by seeing whether it is profitable for them to export it. If they can make a profit, they have a comparative advantage.

Tariffs and Quotas

What Is a Tariff?

Tariff

Despite its advantages, not everyone benefits from free trade. On the contrary, the well-being of some firms and workers may be threatened by foreign competition, and they may press for a **tariff**, a tax the government imposes on imports. The purpose of a tariff is to cut down on imports to protect domestic industry and workers from foreign competition. A secondary reason for tariffs is to produce revenue for the government.

To see how a tariff works, consider the market for wristwatches. Suppose that the demand and supply curves for wristwatches in the United States are as shown in panel A of Figure 27.4 and that the demand and supply curves for wristwatches in Switzerland are as shown in panel B. Clearly, Switzerland

FIGURE 27.4

Effect of a Tariff on Swiss Watches

Under free trade, the price is $10, or 14 Swiss francs. If a tariff of $10 is imposed on each watch imported from Switzerland, imports cease completely. The price in the United States increases to $15, and the price in Switzerland falls to 10 Swiss francs.

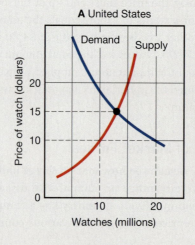

A United States

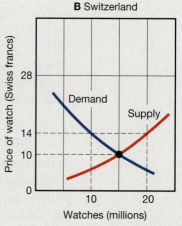

B Switzerland

has a comparative advantage in the production of wristwatches, and under free trade, the price of a wristwatch would tend toward $10 in the United States and 14 Swiss francs in Switzerland. (Note that 1.4 Swiss francs are assumed to equal $1.) Under free trade, the United States would import 10 million wristwatches from Switzerland.

Now, if the United States imposes a tariff of $10 on each wristwatch imported from Switzerland, imports completely cease. Any importers who buy watches in Switzerland at the price of 10 Swiss francs, which equals about $7, must pay a tariff of $10; this makes their total cost about $17 per watch. But this is more than the price of a watch in the United States when there is no foreign trade (which is $15). Consequently, there is no money to be made by importing watches unless Americans can be persuaded to pay more for a Swiss watch than for an identical U.S. watch.

The Social Costs of Tariffs

What is the effect of the tariff? The domestic watch industry receives a higher price than it would without a tariff—$15 rather than $10. And the workers in the domestic watch industry may have more jobs and higher wages than without the tariff. The victim of the tariff is the U.S. consumer, who pays a higher price for wristwatches. Thus, the domestic watch industry benefits at the expense of the rest of the nation. But does the general public lose more than the watch industry gains? In general, the answer is yes. The tariff reduces the welfare of the nation as a whole.

Prohibitive tariff

The tariff in Figure 27.4 is a **prohibitive tariff**, a tariff so high that it stops all imports of the good in question. Not all tariffs are prohibitive. (If they were, the government would receive no revenue at all from tariffs.) In many cases, the tariff is high enough to stop some but not all imports, and as you would expect, the detrimental effect of a nonprohibitive tariff on living standards is less than that of a prohibitive tariff. But this does not mean that nonprohibitive tariffs are harmless. On the contrary, they can do lots of harm to domestic consumption and living standards.

What Is a Quota?

Quotas

Among other barriers to free trade are **quotas**, government-mandated limits on the amount of certain commodities that can be imported annually. The United States sets import quotas on sugar and has exerted pressure on foreign producers to get them to limit the quantity of autos and textiles they export to us. To see how a quota affects trade, production, and prices, we return to the market for wristwatches. Suppose the United States places a quota on the import of wristwatches; no more than 6 million wristwatches can be imported per year. Figure 27.5 shows the effect of the quota. Before it is imposed, the price of wristwatches is $10 (or 14 Swiss francs), and the United States imports

FIGURE 27.5

Effect of a Quota on Swiss Watches

Before the quota is imposed, the price is $10, or 14 Swiss francs. After a quota of 6 million watches is imposed, the price in the United States rises to $12, and the price in Switzerland falls to 12 Swiss francs.

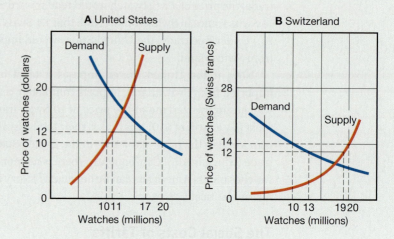

A United States   **B** Switzerland

10 million wristwatches from Switzerland. The quota forces the United States to reduce its imports to 6 million.

What is the effect on the U.S. price? The demand curve shows that if the price is $12, U.S. demand exceeds supply by 6 million watches; in other words, we import 6 million watches. Once the quota is imposed, the price rises to $12, since this is the price that reduces our imports to the amount of the quota. A quota, like a tariff, increases the price of the good. (Note, too, that the price in Switzerland falls to 12 Swiss francs. Therefore, the quota reduces the price in Switzerland.)

The Social Costs of Quotas

Both a quota and a tariff reduce trade, raise prices, protect domestic industry from foreign competition, and reduce the standard of living of the country as a whole. But most economists tend to regard quotas with even less enthusiasm than tariffs. Under many circumstances, a quota insulates local industry from foreign competition even more effectively than a tariff. Foreign producers, if their costs are low enough, can surmount a tariff barrier, but if a quota exists, there is no way they can exceed the quota. Moreover, a (nonprohibitive) tariff provides the government with some revenue, whereas quotas do not even do that. The windfall price increase from a quota accrues to the importer who is lucky enough or influential enough (or sufficiently generous with favors and bribes) to get an import license. (However, if the government auctions off the import licenses, it can obtain revenue from a quota.)

Export Subsidies and Other Nontariff Barriers to Free Trade

Finally, *export subsidies*, another means by which governments try to give their domestic industries an advantage in international competition, are also a major impediment to free trade. Such subsidies may take the form of outright cash disbursements, tax exemptions, preferential financing or insurance arrangements, or other preferential treatment for exports. Export subsidies and other such measures frequently lead to countermeasures. For example, to counter foreign export subsidies on goods sold here, the U.S. government has imposed tariff duties on such goods.

Other nontariff barriers to free trade include licensing requirements and unreasonable product quality standards. By granting few licenses (which are required in some countries to import goods) and imposing unrealistically stringent product quality standards, governments discourage imports.

Arguments for Tariffs and Quotas

Given the disadvantages to society at large of tariffs and other barriers to free trade, why do governments continue to impose them? There are many reasons, some sensible, some irrational.

The National Defense Argument

One of the most convincing arguments is the desirability of maintaining a domestic industry for purposes of national defense. Therefore, even if Sweden had a comparative advantage in producing airplanes, we would not allow free trade to put our domestic producers of aircraft out of business if we felt that a domestic aircraft industry was necessary for national defense. Although the Swedes are by no means unfriendly, we would not want to import our entire supply of such a critical commodity from a foreign country, where the supply might be shut off for reasons of international politics. (Recall the Arab oil embargo of the 1970s.)

This is a perfectly valid reason for protecting certain domestic industries, and many protective measures are defended on these grounds. To the extent that protective measures are, in fact, required for national defense, economists go along with them. The restrictions entail social costs (some of which were described in previous sections), but these costs may well be worth paying for enhanced national security. The trouble is that many barriers to free trade are defended on these grounds when, in fact, they protect domestic industries only tenuously connected with national security. Moreover, even if there is a legitimate case on defense grounds for protecting a domestic industry, subsidies are likely to be a more straightforward and efficient way to do so than tariffs or quotas.

RESTRICTIONS ON U.S. IMPORTS OF JAPANESE AUTOS

When the first Japanese cars arrived on the West Coast in the 1970s, no one saw them as a threat to U.S. jobs. Although they were cheaper and more fuel efficient than U.S.-made cars, most Americans could not be bothered; with gasoline at 30 cents a gallon, the difference in cost between a car that got 30 miles per gallon and one that got 10 was not very great, even for someone who drove a lot.

But all this changed with the Arab oil embargo of 1973. As gas prices climbed, Americans took another look at small foreign cars. With expensive U.S. labor and outmoded facilities on the one side and Japanese efficiency and management techniques on the other, Japan seemed to be winning the war in the showroom.

While imports may create as many jobs as they consume in the long run, in the short run, many smokestack industry workers can be left permanently unemployed or underemployed. Worried U.S. workers wanted protection, and they found a strong advocate in Representative John Dingell, one of the leaders of an emerging protectionist movement in Congress. Dingell spoke with President Reagan and Trade Representative William Brock and warned that if voluntary restrictions on Japanese auto imports were not adopted, Congress would impose mandatory ones. Faced with this choice, the Japanese agreed in negotiations to voluntary restrictions.

The restrictions worked. As the number of Japanese auto imports dropped between 1981 and 1982, domestic auto industry employment rose. But the cost of saving hundreds of thousands of U.S. jobs was restricted choice and higher prices for hundreds of millions of U.S. consumers. Hefty dealer markups were imposed on the scarcer but still-popular imports, and as sticker prices rose on Toyotas and Datsuns, General Motors, Ford, and Chrysler found that they could raise prices, too.

The combined price paid by consumers for trade restrictions is very high; it has been estimated that each job protected from foreign competition with quotas or tariffs in the 1980s cost consumers about $160,000 in higher prices, more than enough to support the holder of that job. While trade restrictions may save jobs in the short run, they lock inefficiencies into the U.S. economy and merely delay needed efforts to divert people and assets into areas of the economy in which the United States has a competitive advantage—and which therefore offer long-term employment and profit possibilities.

Other Arguments for Tariffs

In addition to national defense, several arguments for tariffs or quotas can make sense.

1. *Tariffs or other forms of protection can be justified to foster the growth or development of young industries.* Suppose that Japan has a comparative advantage in the production of a certain semiconductor, but Japan does not presently produce this item. It may take Japanese firms several years to

NAFTA: "JOBS, JOBS, JOBS" OR A "GIANT SUCKING SOUND"?

In the autumn of 1993, as Congress was considering passage of the North American Free Trade Agreement (NAFTA), a fierce debate was raging over the impact of freer trade between the United States, Canada, and Mexico. Members of the Clinton administration claimed that NAFTA would generate a lot of new jobs. Opponents, such as Texas billionaire and one-time presidential candidate for the Reform Party Ross Perot, talked about the "giant sucking sound" of jobs and investment heading south of the border.

In the end, Congress passed NAFTA and the claims on both sides of the debate proved to be egregiously exaggerated. In 1998, the Bank of Montreal (Canada), Harris Bank (United States), and Grupo Financiero Bancomer (Mexico) surveyed 361 companies in the three North American economies to assess the impact of NAFTA on employment. Between early 1994 and the end of 1997, 48 percent of these companies added jobs, 41 percent saw no increase in jobs, and only 11 percent had cut payrolls. More to the point, only 1 out of the 361 companies reported any NAFTA-related jobs losses. Perhaps more to the point, NAFTA did not prevent (and may have even helped) the U.S. unemployment rate from hitting a 30-year low in 2000.

Between 1998 and 2000, all three economies continued to grow rapidly, and in the United States, the unemployment rate reached a 30-year low. Moreover, after a brief dip during the Mexican financial crisis in 1995 and 1996, U.S. exports to Mexico rose to record levels. While NAFTA played only a small part in the U.S. boom, it is also clear that the NAFTA-related losses were minuscule. In other words, there were no sucking sounds.

What about the impact of NAFTA on Mexico? Some analysts have blamed the Mexican financial crisis on NAFTA. However, the crisis had little to do with NAFTA; it was triggered by unsustainable macroeconomic policies in 1994 (basically both fiscal and monetary policies were too stimulative) and political instability (two assassinations and an insurgency in Chiapas Province). In fact, NAFTA, along with a financial rescue package put together by the United States, helped Mexico to enjoy a rapid, export-led recovery.

NAFTA also helped to lock in economic reforms in Mexico. During earlier financial crises, the typical response of the government was to raise tariff barriers and impose capital controls. During 1995, the Mexican government went to great pains to assure foreign investors that it would stay the course on economic reforms and keep its economy open to trade and capital flows. This was truly a paradigm shift. After the debt crisis of the early 1980s, Mexico and other Latin American economies suffered through a "lost decade," and it took foreign investors nine years before they were willing to invest in the region again. After the 1995 Mexican crisis, international investors stayed away for only nine months.

NAFTA also inoculated Mexico against the Asian crisis in 1997 and the Brazilian crisis in 1999. During both of those episodes, Mexico's economy continued to grow. In the final analysis, NAFTA probably has had a bigger positive impact on the Mexican economy than on the U.S. economy. This is to be expected, since the former is one-twentieth the size of the latter. However, NAFTA, like all other free trade agreements, has had a beneficial impact on the United States as well (through lower prices and greater efficiencies).

become proficient in the relevant technology and take advantage of the relevant economies of scale. While this industry is "growing up," Japan may impose a tariff on such semiconductors, shielding its young industry from competition it cannot yet handle. This "infant industry" argument for tariffs has a long history; Alexander Hamilton was one of its early exponents. Needless to say, it is not an argument for permanent tariffs, since infant industries are supposed to grow up—and the sooner the better. (Moreover, a subsidy for the industry would probably be better and easier to remove than a temporary tariff, according to many economists.)

2. *Tariffs may be imposed to protect domestic jobs and reduce unemployment at home.* In the short run, this policy may succeed, but we must recognize that other countries are likely to retaliate by enacting or increasing their own tariffs, so that such a policy may not work very well in the long run. Many economists believe that a more sensible way to reduce domestic unemployment is to use the tools of fiscal and monetary policies rather than tariffs. According to this view, if workers are laid off by industries that cannot compete with foreign producers, proper monetary and fiscal policies, together with retraining programs, should enable these workers to switch to other industries that can compete.

3. *Tariffs may be imposed to prevent a country from being too dependent on only a few industries.* Consider a Latin American country that is a major producer of bananas. Under free trade, this country might produce bananas and little else and so put its entire economy at the mercy of the banana market. If the price of bananas fell, the country's national income would decrease drastically. To promote industrial diversification, this country may establish tariffs to protect other industries, for example, certain types of light manufacturing. In a case like this, the tariff protects the country from having too many of its eggs—or bananas—in a single basket.

4. *Tariffs may improve a country's terms of trade, that is, the ratio of its export prices to its import prices.* The United States is a major importer of bananas. If we impose a tariff on bananas and cut down on the domestic demand for them (because the tariff increases their price), the reduction in our demand is likely to reduce the price of bananas abroad. Consequently, foreign producers of bananas really pay part of the tariff. However, other countries may retaliate, and if all countries pursue such policies, few, if any, are likely to find themselves better off.

REVIEW AND PRACTICE

Summary

1 International trade permits specialization, and specialization increases output. This is the advantage of trade, for both individuals and countries.

2   Country A has an absolute advantage over country B in the production of a good when country A can produce a unit of the good with fewer resources than country B. Trade can be mutually beneficial even if one country has an absolute advantage in the production of all goods.

3   Specialization and trade depend on comparative, not absolute, advantage. A country is said to have a comparative advantage in those products in which its efficiency relative to other countries is higher. Trade can be mutually beneficial if a country specializes in the products in which it has a comparative advantage and imports the products in which it has a comparative disadvantage.

4   If markets are relatively free and competitive, producers automatically are led to produce in accord with comparative advantage. If a country has a comparative advantage in the production of a certain good, after the price of the good in various countries is equalized and total world output of the good equals total world demand, this country will be an exporter of the good under free trade.

5   A tariff is a tax imposed by the government on imports to cut down on imports and protect domestic industry and workers from foreign competition. Tariffs benefit the protected industry at the expense of the general public, and in general, a tariff costs the general public more than the protected industry (and its workers and suppliers) gains.

6   Quotas are another barrier to free trade. They, too, reduce trade, raise prices, protect domestic industry from foreign competition, and reduce the standard of living of the country as a whole.

7   Tariffs, quotas, and other barriers to free trade can sometimes be justified on the basis of national security and other noneconomic considerations. Moreover, tariffs and other forms of protection can sometimes be justified to protect infant industries, prevent a country from being too dependent on only a few industries, and carry out other national objectives.

Problems and Questions

1   Suppose that the United States can produce three supercomputers or 3,000 cases of wine with 1 unit of resources, while France can produce one supercomputer or 2,000 cases of wine with 1 unit of resources. Will specialization increase world output?

2   Suppose the United States has 100 units of resources while France has 50 units. On the basis of the data in question 1, draw the production possibilities curve in each country. (Recall Exploring Further in Chapter 1.) Without international trade, what is the ratio of the price of a computer to the price of a case of wine in each country?

3   Given the information in questions 1 and 2, how do firms in France and the United States know whether they should produce wine or computers? Must the government instruct them on this score? Why or why not?

4   Under the circumstances described in questions 1 and 2, does each country specialize completely in the production of one or the other good? Why or why not? What factors result in incomplete specialization in the real world?

5   Some economists believe that workers get high real income not because they are protected from foreign competition, but because they are highly productive, at least in certain industries. Do you agree? Why or why not?

6   Technological innovation can strengthen the competitive position of a country in which the innovation takes place, either by increasing exports or displacing imports. Give examples of this phenomenon, and discuss various ways that we might measure the effects of technological innovation on a country's competitive position.

7   "The principle of comparative advantage does not work. The United States exports electronic computers to Japan and imports electronic consumer goods like TV sets from Japan." Comment and evaluate.

8   Would you favor a high tariff on imported steel if you were (a) an automobile worker, (b) a steel worker, (c) an automobile buyer, and (d) a plastics worker? Explain your reasoning in each case.

Key Terms

exports

absolute advantage

comparative advantage

terms of trade

tariff

prohibitive tariff

quotas

Viewpoint for Analysis

On June 20, 1997, Sidney Weintraub, of the Center for Strategic and International Studies, in Washington, DC, wrote in an op-ed piece in the *Wall Street Journal*: "In the entire period of NAFTA's existence [a little over three years at the time this op-ed piece appeared], the Department of Labor has certified some 125,000 people as being adversely affected by U.S. investment in, and imports from, Canada and Mexico. This number is about equal to the number of new jobs created in the U.S. every two weeks. About 10,000 of those who were certified took advantage of the benefits in the NAFTA legistlation."[3]

(a) What do the statistics imply about the impact of NAFTA, in particular, and trade, in general, on U.S. employment?

(b) What happened to the workers who did not apply for the compensation benefits available through the NAFTA legislation?

(c) What else can the government do to help those workers who have been displaced by imports from other countries?

[3] "In the Debate about NAFTA, Just the Facts Please," *Wall Street Journal*, June 20, 1997, A19.

Exchange Rates and the Balance of Payments

LEARNING OBJECTIVES

➤ To define exchange rates

➤ To describe the workings of the gold standard, fixed exchange rates, and flexible exchange rates

➤ To discuss the factors underlying recent problems in the international monetary system

➤ To present the arguments for and against trying to stabilize the value of the dollar (relative to other currencies)

The value of the dollar in terms of foreign currencies is highly variable. In 1985, a dollar was worth about 235 Japanese yen; in late 2013, it was worth only about 104 Japanese yen. Why was this change important to U.S. tourists visiting Japan or to exporters or importers? One purpose of this chapter is to answer this question.

In addition, we must consider several other questions. What are exchange rates, and how are they determined? How are international business transactions carried out? Should there be fixed or flexible exchange rates? What problems have afflicted the international monetary system in recent years? These questions, which are both fundamental and timely, are taken up in this chapter.

International Transactions and Exchange Rates

Suppose you want to buy a book from a Japanese publisher, and the book costs 1,650 yen. (The Japanese currency consists of yen, not dollars.) To buy the book, you must somehow get yen to pay the publisher, since this is the currency in which the publisher deals. Or, if the publisher agrees, you might pay in dollars, but the publisher would then have to exchange the dollars for yen, because its bills must be paid in yen. Whatever happens, either you or the publisher must somehow exchange dollars for yen, since international business transactions, unlike transactions within a country, involve two different currencies.

If you decide to exchange dollars for yen to pay the Japanese publisher, how can you make the exchange? The answer is simple. You can buy Japanese yen at a bank, just as you might buy lamb chops at a butcher shop. Just as the lamb chops have a price (expressed in dollars), so the Japanese yen have a price (expressed in dollars). The bank may tell you that each yen you buy costs $0.009. This makes the **exchange rate** between dollars and yen 0.009 to 1, since it takes 0.009 dollar to purchase 1 yen.

Exchange rate

In general, the exchange rate is simply the number of units of one currency that exchanges for a unit of another currency. The obvious question is this: What determines the exchange rate? Why is the exchange rate between Japanese yen and U.S. dollars what it is? Why doesn't a yen exchange for 25 cents, rather than just under 1 cent? These basic questions occupy us in the next several sections.

Exchange Rates under the Gold Standard

Gold standard

As a starter, let us see how exchange rates were determined under the **gold standard**, which prevailed before the 1930s. If a country was on the gold standard, a unit of its currency was convertible into a certain amount of gold. Before World War I, the dollar was convertible into one-twentieth of an ounce of gold, and the British pound was convertible into one-quarter of an ounce of gold. Since the pound exchanged for five times as much gold as the dollar, the pound exchanged for $5. The currency of any other country on the gold standard was convertible into a certain amount of gold in the same way; to see how much its currency was worth in dollars, you divided the amount of gold a unit of its currency was worth by the amount of gold (one-twentieth of an ounce) a dollar was worth.

Why did the exchange rate always equal the ratio between the amount of gold a foreign currency was worth and the amount of gold a dollar was worth? Why did the price of a British pound stay at $5 before World War I? To see why, suppose that the price (in dollars) of a pound rose above this ratio, above $5. Instead of exchanging their dollars directly for pounds, Americans would have done better to exchange them for gold and then exchange the gold for pounds. By this indirect process, Americans could have exchanged $5 for a pound, so they would have refused to buy pounds at a price above $5 per pound.

Similarly, if the price of a pound fell below $5, the British would have refused to sell pounds, since they could have obtained $5 by converting the pound into gold and the gold into dollars. Because Americans would refuse to pay more than $5 and the British would refuse to accept less, the price of a pound had to remain at about $5. (In practice, the pound could be a few cents above or below $5, because it costs money to transport gold to carry out the conversion.)

Balance between Exports and Imports

But what ensured that this exchange rate, dictated by the gold equivalence of currencies, would result in a rough equality of trade between countries? If £1 exchanged for $5, perhaps the British might find our goods so cheap that they would import a great deal from us, while we might find their goods so expensive that we would import little from them. Under these circumstances, the British would have to ship gold to us to pay for the excess of their imports from us over their exports to us, and eventually they could run out of gold. Could this happen? If not, why not? These questions occupied the attention of many early economists. The classic answers were given by David Hume, the Scottish philosopher, in the eighteenth century.

Hume pointed out that under the gold standard, a mechanism ensured that trade would be brought into balance and neither country would run out of gold. This mechanism worked as follows. If, as we assumed, the British bought more from us than we bought from them, they would have to send us gold to pay for the excess of their imports over their exports. As their gold stock declined, their price level would fall. (Recall the quantity theory of money discussed in Chapter 25.) As our gold stock increased, our price level would rise. Because of our rising prices, the British would tend to import less from us; because of their falling prices, we would tend to import more from them. Eventually, when enough gold had left Britain and entered the United States, prices here would have increased enough and prices in Britain would have fallen enough to put imports and exports in balance.

The Foreign Exchange Market

Flexible exchange rates

The gold standard is long gone, and after many decades of fixed exchange rates (discussed in a later section), the major trading countries of the world began to experiment with **flexible exchange rates** in early 1973. Consider a situation where exchange rates are allowed to fluctuate freely, like the price of any commodity in a competitive market. In a case of this sort, exchange rates, like any price, are determined by supply and demand. There is a market for various types of foreign currency—Mexican pesos, British pounds, Japanese yen, and so on—just as there are markets for various types of meat.

In the case of the Japanese yen, the demand and supply curves may look like those shown in Figure 28.1. The demand curve shows the amount of Japanese yen that people with dollars demand at various prices of a yen. The supply curve shows the amount of Japanese yen that people with yen supply at various

FIGURE 28.1

Determining the Exchange Rate between Dollars and Japanese Yen under Freely Fluctuating Exchange Rates

Under freely fluctuating exchange rates, the equilibrium price of a Japanese yen would be $0.009 if the demand and supply curves for dollars are as shown here.

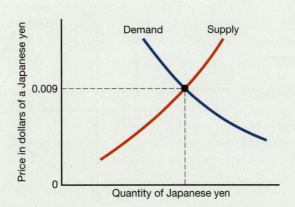

prices of a yen. Since the amount of Japanese currency supplied must equal the amount demanded in equilibrium, the equilibrium price (in dollars) of a Japanese yen is given by the intersection of the demand and supply curves. In Figure 28.1, this intersection is at $0.009.

The Demand and Supply Sides of the Market

We need to look in more detail at the demand and supply sides of this market. On the demand side are people who want to import Japanese goods (like the book you want to buy) into the United States, Americans who want to travel in Japan (where they need Japanese money), Americans who want to build factories in Japan, and others with dollars who want Japanese currency. The people on the supply side are those who want to import U.S. goods into Japan, Japanese who want to travel in the United States (where they need U.S. money), people with yen who want to build factories in the United States, and others with yen who want U.S. currency.

When Americans demand more Japanese VCRs or cars (causing the demand curve to shift upward and to the right), the price (in dollars) of the Japanese yen tends to increase. If the demand curve for yen shifts as shown in Figure 28.2, the result is an increase in the equilibrium price of a yen from $0.009 to $0.011. Conversely, when the Japanese demand more U.S. cars or computers (resulting in a shift of the supply curve downward and to the right), the price (in dollars) of the Japanese yen tends to decrease.

To see why an increase in Japanese demand for U.S. cars or computers shifts the supply curve downward and to the right, recall that the supply curve shows the amount of yen supplied at each price of a yen. Therefore, a shift downward and to the right in the supply curve means that more yen are supplied at a given

FIGURE 28.2

Effect of a Shift in the Demand Curve for Japanese Yen

Because of the demand curve's shift to the right, the equilibrium price of a Japanese yen increases from $0.009 to $0.011.

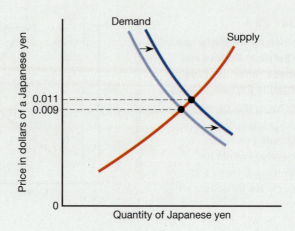

price (in dollars) of the yen. Given the posited increase in Japanese demand for U.S. goods, such a shift in the supply curve would be expected.

Appreciation and Depreciation of a Currency

Appreciation

Depreciation

Two terms frequently encountered in discussions of the foreign exchange market are **appreciation** and **depreciation**. When country A's currency becomes more valuable relative to country B's currency, country A's currency is said to appreciate relative to that of country B, and country B's currency is said to depreciate relative to that of country A. In Figure 28.2, the yen appreciates relative to the dollar, and the dollar depreciates relative to the yen. This use of the terms makes sense. If the number of dollars commanded by a yen increases, the yen becomes more valuable relative to the dollar, and the dollar becomes less valuable relative to the yen.

Note that such a change in exchange rates would not have been possible under the gold standard. Unless a country changed the amount of gold that could be exchanged for a unit of its currency, exchange rates were fixed under the gold standard. Sometimes governments changed the amount of gold that could be exchanged for their currencies. For example, in 1933, the United States increased the price of gold from $21 an ounce to $35 an ounce. When a country increased the price of gold, this was called a **devaluation of currency**.

Devaluation of currency

Determinants of Exchange Rates

Earlier we saw that flexible exchange rates are determined by supply and demand. But what are some of the major factors determining the position of these supply and demand curves?

Relative Price Levels In the long run, the exchange rate between any two currencies may be expected to reflect differences in the price levels in the two countries. To see why, suppose that Japan and the United States are the only exporters or importers of automobiles, and automobiles are the only product they export or import. If an automobile costs $16,000 in the United States and 2,400,000 yen in Japan, what must be the exchange rate between the dollar and the yen? Clearly, a yen must be worth $0.0066, because otherwise the two countries' automobiles would not be competitive in the world market. If a yen were set equal to $0.0091, then a Japanese automobile would cost $21,840 (that is, 2,400,000 × $0.0091), which is far more than what a U.S. automobile would cost. Therefore, foreign buyers would obtain their automobiles in the United States.

Based on this theory, we would expect that if the rate of inflation in country A is higher than in country B, country A's currency is likely to depreciate relative to country B's. Suppose that costs double in the United States but increase by only 25 percent in Japan. After this burst of inflation, an automobile costs $32,000 (that is, 2 times $16,000) in the United States and 3,000,000 yen (that is 1.25 times 2,400,000 yen) in Japan. Hence, the new value of the yen must be $0.0107, rather than the old value of $0.0066. (Why $0.0107? Because this is the exchange rate that makes the new cost of an automobile in the United States, $32,000, equivalent to the new cost of an automobile in Japan, 3,000,000 yen.) Because the rate of inflation is higher in the United States than in Japan, the dollar depreciates relative to the yen.

Relative Rates of Growth Although relative price levels may play an important role in the long run, other factors tend to exert more influence on exchange rates in the short run. In particular, if one country's rate of economic growth is higher than the rest of the world, its currency is likely to depreciate. If a country's economy is booming, this tends to increase its imports. If there is a boom in the United States, Americans tend to import a great deal from other countries. If a country's imports tend to grow faster than its exports, its demand for foreign currency tends to grow more rapidly than the amount of foreign currency supplied to it. Consequently, its currency is likely to depreciate.

Relative Interest Rate Levels If the rate of interest in Japan is higher than in the United States, banks, multinational corporations, and other investors in the United States sell dollars and buy yen to invest in the high-yielding Japanese securities. Also, Japanese investors (and others) are less likely to find U.S. securities attractive. Therefore, the yen tends to appreciate relative to the dollar, since the demand curve for yen shifts to the right and the supply curve for yen shifts to the left. In general, an increase in a country's interest rates leads to an appreciation of its currency, and a decrease in its interest rates leads to a depreciation of its currency. In the short run, interest rate differentials can have a major impact on exchange rates, since a huge amount of funds is moved from country to country in response to differentials in interest rates.

Trade Deficits A country's trade and current account balance can also have a big impact on it currency. When country X runs a trade deficit, its imports exceed its exports. This means that more of its currency is going overseas (to pay for imports) than foreign currency coming in (to pay for exports). This means that the supply of country X's currency increases in the world, and the price (exchange rate) falls. The opposite is true when a country runs a surplus.

The Adjustment Mechanism under Flexible Exchange Rates

Under flexible exchange rates, what ensures a balance in the exports and imports between countries? The situation differs from that described by David Hume, since Hume assumed the existence of the gold standard. Under flexible exchange rates, the balance is achieved through changes in exchange rates. Suppose that the United Kingdom is importing far more from us than we are from the United Kingdom. This means that the British, needing dollars to buy our goods, are willing to supply pounds more cheaply. In other words, the supply curve for British pounds shifts downward and to the right, as shown in Figure 28.3. This causes the price of a pound to decline from P_1 dollars to P_2 dollars. Or, from the United Kingdom's point of view, the price (in pounds) of a dollar is bid up by the swollen demand for imports from the United States.

Because of the increase in the price (in pounds) of a dollar, our goods become more expensive in the United Kingdom. Hence, the British tend to reduce their imports of our goods. At the same time, since the price (in dollars) of a pound has decreased, British goods become cheaper in the United States, and this

FIGURE 28.3

Adjustment Mechanism

If the United Kingdom imports more from us than we do from he United Kingdom, the supply curve for British pounds shifts downward and to the right; this results in a decline of the price of the pound from P_1 to P_2 dollars. If the United Kingdom tries to maintain the price at P_1 dollars, the British government must exchange dollars for $(Q_S - Q_D)$ pounds.

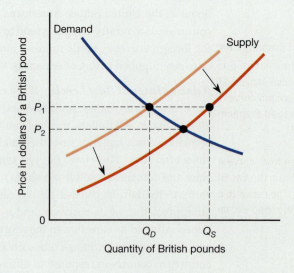

stimulates us to import more from the United Kingdom. Consequently, as our currency appreciates in terms of theirs—or, to put it another way, as theirs depreciates in terms of ours—the British are induced to import less and export more. Hence, there is an automatic mechanism (just as there was under the gold standard) to bring trade between countries into balance.

Fixed Exchange Rates

Fixed exchange rates

Although many economists believed that exchange rates should be allowed to fluctuate, very few exchange rates really did so in the period from the end of World War II up to 1973. Instead, there were mostly **fixed exchange rates** by government action and international agreement. Although they may have varied slightly about the fixed level, the extent to which they were allowed to vary was small. Every now and then, governments changed the exchange rates, for reasons discussed next; but for long periods of time, they remained fixed.

If exchange rates remain fixed, the amount demanded of a foreign currency may not equal the amount supplied. Consider the situation in Figure 28.4. If A is the demand curve for Japanese yen, the equilibrium price of a yen is $0.007. But suppose the fixed exchange rate between dollars and yen is 0.006 to 1; that is, each yen exchanges for $0.006. Unless the government intervenes, more Japanese yen are demanded at a price of $0.006 per yen than are offered. Specifically, the difference between the quantity demanded and the quantity supplied is Q_D-Q_S. Unless the government steps in, a black market for Japanese yen may develop, and the real price may increase toward $0.007 per yen.

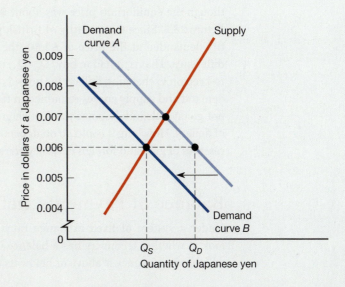

FIGURE 28.4

Fixed Exchange Rate

The equilibrium price of a Japanese yen is $0.007 if A is the demand curve. If $0.006 is the fixed exchange rate, the U.S. government may try to shift the demand curve for yen from curve A to curve B to bring the equilibrium exchange rate into equality with the fixed exchange rate.

Types of Government Intervention

To maintain exchange rates at their fixed levels, governments can intervene in a variety of ways. For example, they may reduce the demand for foreign currencies by reducing defense expenditures abroad, limiting the amount that their citizens can travel abroad, and curbing imports from other countries. In the case depicted in Figure 28.4, the U.S. government might adopt some or all of these measures to shift the demand curve for Japanese yen downward and to the left. If the demand curve can be pushed from curve *A* to curve *B*, the equilibrium price of a Japanese yen can be reduced to $0.006, the fixed exchange rate. For the time being, there no longer is any mismatch between the quantity of yen demanded and the quantity supplied.

When exchange rates are fixed, mismatches of this sort cannot be eliminated entirely and permanently. To deal with such temporary mismatches, governments enter the market and buy and sell their currencies to maintain fixed exchange rates. Take the case of the United Kingdom after World War II. At times, the amount of British pounds supplied exceeded the amount demanded. Then the British government bought up the excess at the fixed exchange rate. At other times, when the quantity demanded exceeded the amount supplied, the British government supplied the pounds desired at the fixed exchange rate. As long as the equilibrium exchange rate was close to (sometimes above and sometimes below) the fixed exchange rate, the amount of its currency the government sold at one time equaled, more or less, the amount it bought at another time.

But in some cases, governments have tried to maintain a fixed exchange rate far from the equilibrium exchange rate. The British government tried during the 1960s to maintain the price (in dollars) of the pound at $2.80, even though the equilibrium price was about $2.40. The situation was as shown in Figure 28.5. Since the quantity of British pounds supplied exceeded the quantity demanded at the price of $2.80, the British government had to buy the difference. That is, it had to buy $(Q_S - Q_D)$ pounds with dollars. Moreover, it had to keep on exchanging dollars for pounds in these quantities for as long as the demand and supply curves remained in these positions. Such a situation could not go on indefinitely, since the British government eventually had to run out of dollars. How long it could go on depended on how big the United Kingdom's reserves of gold and foreign currency were.

Balance of Payments Deficits and Surpluses

Under a system of fixed exchange rates, economists and financial analysts look at whether a country has a balance of payments deficit or surplus to see whether its currency is above or below its equilibrium value. What is a balance

FIGURE 28.5

Balance of Payments Deficit

Because the British pound was overvalued at $2.80, the quantity of pounds demanded (Q_D) was less than the quantity supplied (Q_S). The shortfall—$(Q_S - Q_D)$ pounds—is the balance of payments deficit.

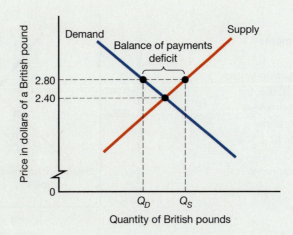

of payments deficit? What is a balance of payments surplus? It is important to understand both of these terms.

Balance of Payments Deficits

Balance of payments deficit

If a country's currency is overvalued (that is, if its fixed price exceeds the equilibrium price), the quantity supplied of its currency exceeds the quantity demanded. This is a **balance of payments deficit**. We return to the case where the price of the British pound was set at $2.80. Under these circumstances, the quantity supplied of pounds exceeded the quantity demanded by $(Q_S - Q_D)$ pounds, as shown in Figure 28.5. This amount—$(Q_S - Q_D)$ pounds—was the United Kingdom's balance of payments deficit. As pointed out in the previous section, it was the number of pounds that the United Kingdom's central bank, the Bank of England, had to purchase. To pay for these pounds, the Bank of England had to give up some of its reserves of foreign currencies or gold.

In a situation of this sort, there may be a run on the overvalued currency. Suppose speculators become convinced that the country with the balance of payments deficit cannot maintain the artificially high price of its currency much longer because its reserves are running low. Because they will suffer losses if they hold onto a currency that is devalued, the speculators are likely to sell the overvalued currency (in Figure 28.5, the British pound) in very large amounts, causing an even bigger balance of payments deficit for the country with the overvalued currency. Faced with the exhaustion of its reserves, the country will likely be forced to allow the price of its currency to fall.

FIGURE 28.6

Balance of Payments Surplus

Because the Japanese yen is undervalued at $0.006, the quantity of yen demanded (Q'_D) is greater than the quantity supplied (Q'_S). The surplus—$(Q'_D - Q'_S)$ yen—is the balance of payments surplus.

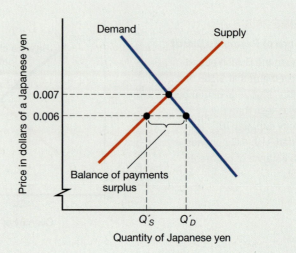

Balance of Payments Surpluses

Balance of payments surplus

If a country's currency is undervalued (that is, if its price is less than the equilibrium price), the quantity demanded of its currency will exceed the quantity supplied. This is a **balance of payments surplus**. What if the price of the Japanese yen is set at $0.006, even though its equilibrium price is about $0.007? As shown in Figure 28.6, the quantity of yen demanded exceeds the quantity supplied by $(Q'_D - Q'_S)$ yen under these circumstances. This amount—$(Q'_D - Q'_S)$ yen—is Japan's balance of payments surplus. Japan can keep the price of the yen at $0.006 only if it provides these $(Q'_D - Q'_S)$ yen in exchange for foreign currencies and gold. By doing so, it increases its reserves.

Whereas a country with an overvalued currency is likely to be forced by the reduction in its reserves to reduce the price of its currency, a country with an undervalued currency is unlikely to be forced by the increase in its reserves to increase the price of its currency. And a country with an undervalued currency often is reluctant to increase the price of its currency because of political pressures by its exporters (and their workers), who point out that such a revaluation would make the country's goods more expensive in foreign markets, reducing its exports. Consequently, when exchange rates were fixed, countries with undervalued currencies were less likely to adjust their exchange rates than countries with overvalued currencies.

Measuring Deficits and Surpluses

If we are given the demand and supply curves for a country's currency, it is a simple matter to determine the deficit or surplus in its balance of payments.

All we have to do is subtract the quantity demanded of the currency from the quantity supplied. However, since we do not observe these demand and supply curves in the real world, this method of determining the deficit or surplus, while fine in principle, is not practical. The available data show only the total amount of the country's currency bought and the total amount of the country's currency sold. Since each unit of the country's currency that is bought must also be sold, it is evident that the total amount bought must equal the total amount sold. Given that this is the case, how can we identify and measure a balance of payments deficit or surplus?

The answer lies in the transactions of the country's central bank. If the central bank's purchases or sales of currency make up for the difference between the quantity demanded and the quantity supplied, it will purchase currency if there is a balance of payments deficit and sell currency if there is a balance of payments surplus. The amount it purchases or sells measures the size of the deficit or surplus. In other words, the official transactions of this country's government with other governments are used to measure the deficit or surplus. Roughly speaking, this is how a balance of payments deficit or surplus was traditionally measured. However, beginning in May 1976, the U.S. government stopped publishing figures on the deficit or surplus in our balance of payments. Under the current regime of flexible exchange rates, changes in demand and supply for foreign exchange generally show up as changes in exchange rates, rather than in the transactions of the central bank. Therefore, figures regarding the deficit or surplus in our balance of payments have lost much of their previous meaning.

Exchange Rates: Pre–World War II Experience

Now that we are familiar with balance of payments deficits and surpluses, we can begin to see how various types of exchange rates have worked out. What has been our experience with the gold standard? With fixed exchange rates? With flexible exchange rates?

During the latter part of the nineteenth century, the gold standard seemed to work very well, but serious trouble developed after World War I. During the war, practically all the warring countries went off the gold standard to keep people from hoarding gold or sending it to neutral countries. After the war, some countries tried to reestablish the old rates of exchange. Because the wartime and postwar rates of inflation were greater in some countries than in others, under the old exchange rates the goods of some countries were underpriced and those of other countries were overpriced. According to the doctrines of David Hume, this imbalance should have been remedied by increases in the general price level in countries where goods were underpriced and reductions in the general price level in countries where goods were overpriced. But wages and prices proved to be inflexible, and as we would expect, it proved especially difficult to adjust them downward. When the adjustment mechanism failed to work quickly enough, the gold standard was abandoned.

During the 1930s, governments tried various schemes. This was the time of the Great Depression, and governments were trying frantically to reduce unemployment. Sometimes a government allowed the exchange rate to be flexible for a while until it found what seemed to be an equilibrium level and then fixed the exchange rate there. Sometimes a government depreciated the value of its own currency relative to those of other countries in an attempt to increase employment by making its goods cheap to other countries. When one country adopted such policies, however, others retaliated; this caused a reduction in international trade and lending but little or no benefit for the country that started the fracas.

The Gold Exchange Standard

In 1944, the Allied governments (in World War II) sent representatives to Bretton Woods, New Hampshire, to work out a more effective system for the postwar era. It was generally agreed that competitive devaluations, such as occurred in the 1930s, should be avoided. Out of the Bretton Woods conference came the *International Monetary Fund (IMF)*, which was set up to maintain a stable system of fixed exchange rates and ensure that when exchange rates had to be changed because of significant trade imbalances, disruption was minimized.

Gold exchange standard
The system developed during the postwar period was generally labeled the **gold exchange standard**, as opposed to the gold standard. Under this system, the dollar, which by this time had taken the place of the British pound as the world's key currency, was convertible (for official monetary purposes) into gold at a fixed price. And since other currencies could be converted into dollars at fixed exchange rates, other currencies were convertible indirectly into gold at a fixed price.

During the early postwar period, the gold exchange standard worked reasonably well. However, it was not too long before problems began to develop. As noted in a previous section, when exchange rates are fixed, a U.S. balance of payments deficit is evidence of pressure on the dollar in foreign exchange markets. During the period from 1950 to 1972 (the last full year when exchange rates were fixed), the United States showed a chronic deficit in its balance of payments. This chronic deficit caused considerable uneasiness and concern, both here and abroad.

In March 1973, representatives of the major trading countries met in Paris to establish a system of fluctuating exchange rates, abandoning the

THE ABANDONMENT OF THE GOLD STANDARD

During the 40 years before World War I, world trade prospered under a system of exchange rates such that currencies were pegged to gold and fixed relative to one another. During World War I, however, as countries expanded their money supplies rapidly to pay for the war effort, every country experienced sharp inflation and different relative rates of inflation. The previous fixed exchange rates could not be honored, so the payment of gold for currency was suspended for the war's duration.

Although relative rates of inflation had changed radically during the war, in 1925, the United Kingdom decided to fix the pound to gold at the prewar level. The primary reason was to preserve the value of bonds and other fixed-income securities, which had lost value during the wartime inflation. Wealthy and influential bondholders pressured the government to reverse the inflation, and pegging the price of the pound to gold was the first step in trying to reestablish the prewar price level.

Countries that had undervalued currencies, such as France and the United States, prospered during the 1920s. France in particular had "export-led" growth, and it accumulated vast reserves of foreign exchange and gold. The British economy, however, stagnated for the six years that it was on the gold standard at the prewar rate. The United Kingdom found itself importing too much and could not compete against foreign producers because its own goods were much higher priced than foreign goods. Only by either devaluing the pound or forcing wages down could the United Kingdom compete. If it failed to do either, it would constantly be sending out more pounds than it

Franklin D. Roosevelt

was collecting in foreign currencies. Foreigners would then exchange those pounds for gold and so drain gold from the country.

The pound weakened in July 1930, and despite efforts to arrange foreign financing to defend the pound and a hike in the British discount rate, gold withdrawals accelerated by September. On September 21, the United Kingdom abandoned the gold standard. The pound fell from $4.86 to $3.25 within a few days but recovered to about $3.50.

Pressure shifted to the dollar as the French withdrew gold from the United States. The United States raised its discount rate from 1.5 to 3.5 percent in October 1930, and this was not offset by open market operations. Bank failures spread. The U.S. money supply, commodity prices, security prices, imports, and (to a lesser extent) industrial production declined faster after the British devaluation than before. The United States lost gold throughout 1932, and the early 1933 banking crises worsened the outflow.

On March 4, President Roosevelt closed the banks and let the dollar float. The dollar fell vis-à-vis the pound, and it was not until 1936 that a stabilization of the dollar, the pound, and the franc was worked out.

Bretton Woods system of fixed exchange rates. This was a major break with the past, and one that was greeted with considerable apprehension as well as hope. However, the major trading countries did not go so far as to establish completely flexible exchange rates. Instead, the float was to be managed. Central banks would step in to buy and sell their currency. The United States agreed that "when necessary and desirable," it would support the value of the dollar. Also, some European countries decided to maintain fixed exchange rates among their own currencies but to float jointly against other currencies.

Fixed versus Flexible Exchange Rates

Why, until 1973, did most countries fix their exchange rates rather than allow them to fluctuate? One important reason was the concern that flexible exchange rates might vary so erratically that it might be difficult to carry out normal trade. U.S. exporters of machine tools to the United Kingdom might not know what British pounds would be worth six months from now, when they would collect a debt in pounds. According to the proponents of fixed exchange rates, fluctuating rates would increase uncertainties for people and firms engaged in international trade and reduce the volume of such trade. Moreover, they argued, the harmful effects of speculation over exchange rates would increase if exchange rates were flexible, because speculators could push a currency's exchange rate up or down and destabilize the exchange market (see Case Study 28.2). They argued further that flexible exchange rates might promote more rapid inflation because countries would be less affected by balance of payments discipline.

Many economists disagreed, feeling that flexible exchange rates would work better. They asked why flexible prices are used and trusted in other areas of the economy but not in connection with foreign exchange. They pointed out that a country would have more autonomy in formulating its fiscal and monetary policies if exchange rates were flexible, and they claimed that speculation regarding exchange rates would not be destabilizing. But until 1973, the advocates of flexible exchange rates persuaded few of the world's central bankers and policy makers.

ARE CURRENCY SPECULATORS TO BLAME FOR THE VOLATILITY IN INTERNATIONAL FINANCIAL MARKETS?

A few years ago, one Western head of state described currency speculation as the "AIDS of our economies." His comments echoed a growing sentiment among some policy makers and analysts that currency speculators are to blame for the volatility in financial markets. While the temptation to find scapegoats may prove irresistible, the reasons behind the financial markets' turmoil in recent years are far more complex than is suggested by such simplistic characterizations.

During the 1990s, there were a surprisingly large number of international financial crises, including two attacks on the European Exchange Rate Mechanism in 1992 and 1993, two runs on the dollar in 1994 and 1995, the Mexican peso devaluation in late 1994, the Asian crisis in 1997, the Russian crisis in 1998, and the Brazilian crisis in 1999. To gain some perspective on the causes of this market turmoil, it is helpful to begin by looking at the size of the world financial markets. The daily turnover in the foreign exchange markets alone is $1.5 trillion, which is about 20 percent of total annual world exports and about 4 percent of total annual world GDP. The total foreign exchange reserves held by the central banks of all the IMF member countries is slightly less than $1 trillion

(less than the turnover in one 24-hour period). Therefore, central bank efforts to go against these markets are doomed to fail. The best that monetary authorities can hope to achieve is to surprise the markets from time to time and inflict losses on a few traders.

The power of the central banks has steadily eroded as the volume in the foreign exchange markets has risen rapidly, increasing five-fold over the past decade. The exponential growth in these markets has been driven by a number of factors, including financial deregulation and the removal of capital controls, the increased use of new technologies to link the 24-hour global markets, financial innovations (for example, derivatives), and increased cross-border diversification.

While speculators are everyone's favorite scapegoat, the truth of the matter is that many thousands of traders hold large positions in the market. No single trader or group of traders can effectively dominate the market for any length of time. Most are driven by market fundamentals or prevailing market psychology. Also, while it is tempting to think of speculative attacks on currencies as a recent phenomenon, such attacks were a regular feature of the Bretton Woods system, especially during its final years.

FIGURE 28.7

Value of the U.S. Dollar in Terms of Major Foreign Currencies, 1967–2012 (March 1973 = 100)

Source: Board of Governors of the Federal Reserve System.

How Well Have Floating Exchange Rates Worked?

Since 1973, exchange rates have been flexible, not fixed. However, there has been some intervention by central banks to keep the movement of exchange rates within broad bounds, although this intervention generally has not been very great. The result has been considerable volatility in exchange rates. The exchange rate between the dollar and the Japanese yen has sometimes varied by 2 percent or more from one day to the next and by 15 percent or more over a period of several months. As shown in Figure 28.7, the value of the dollar (in terms of other major currencies) has gyrated substantially during the past 40 years.

Unquestionably, the variations in exchange rates, some of which are erratic and without fundamental economic significance, have made international transactions more difficult. For example, Renault, the French auto manufacturer, is reported to have hesitated to launch an export drive into the U.S. market because of the erratic behavior of the dollar-franc exchange rate.

During the 1970s, the value of the dollar fell considerably, as shown in Figure 28.7. Between September 1977 and March 1978 and again between June and October 1978, the value of the dollar fell by about 10 percent, in part because of our unfavorable balance of trade (because we pursued a more expansionary policy than our major trading partners) and because interest rates were higher abroad than here.[1]

---

[1] A country is said to have a *favorable* balance of merchandise trade if its exports of merchandise are more than its imports of merchandise and an *unfavorable* balance of merchandise trade if its exports of merchandise are less than its imports of merchandise.

CASE STUDY 28.3

THE RISE AND FALL OF THE BRETTON WOODS SYSTEM

In July 1944, in Bretton Woods, New Hampshire, representatives of 44 countries met for 22 days to create a blueprint for a new world economic order. To ensure stability, the Bretton Woods agreements outlined a new system of international cooperation. The linchpin of the system was the U.S. dollar and its convertibility to gold.

Bretton Woods provided a framework for the rebuilding of Europe. And the United States played the key role in financing Europe's recovery. The Marshall Plan, created in 1947, gave millions of dollars to Europe. This flow of dollars and goods was soon supplemented by loans and private investments from the United States. The U.S. economy reaped immediate benefits from Europe's rebuilding. As fast as the dollars were pumped overseas, they flowed back here to pay for U.S. machinery and goods. In the decade following the war, Europe imported billions of dollars worth of products from the United States. But by the mid-1950s, European economies were no longer so dependent on U.S. goods.

By the 1960s, our payments abroad for imports, investments, and foreign aid had far exceeded our receipts. Whereas there had been an international shortage of dollars during the previous decade, now the world faced a dollar glut. This overwhelming supply of dollars piled up in the vaults of foreign central banks. These banks began to redeem dollars for U.S. gold. Between 1964 and 1966, U.S. gold reserves dropped by $2 billion.

The United States pressured foreign central banks to retain their dollars. The government also tried to restrict the amount of money invested or spent overseas, but to little avail. None of these moves could halt the growing dollar glut or convince currency speculators that the dollar would not be devalued. Speculators dumped billions worth of dollars on the foreign exchange markets. By the time Richard Nixon assumed the presidency, the system carefully crafted at Bretton Woods was on the verge of collapse. Finally, in March 1973, the major developed economies abandoned the Bretton Woods system of fixed exchange rates.

Seven decades after the historic conference, economists and politicians still applaud the goals and the accomplishments of Bretton Woods. It was a historic undertaking to set up rules and procedures to promote world trade that would benefit all countries. Many of the institutions and policies are still in service. But not the exchange rate system. It fell victim to the chronic U.S. balance of payments deficit.

During the early 1980s, the dollar staged a spectacular rebound. Between 1980 and 1985, its value rose by about 60 percent. In large part, this was because inflation in the United States seemed to have moderated, real interest rates here were higher than in other countries (partly the result of huge government borrowing to finance its deficits), and the rates of return from investments here seemed relatively high. This marked appreciation of the dollar hurt

U.S. exporters, since their goods became very expensive to foreigners, but it helped keep a lid on inflation, since imported goods were relatively cheap, and many U.S. firms could not raise their own prices very much without losing business to imported goods.

In the late 1980s, the dollar took a dive; it lost practically all the value it had gained in the early 1980s. In part, this was due to lower interest rates in the United States and the feelings of speculators that the dollar was overvalued. Also, according to many economists, it was partly because a number of governments sold dollars and bought other currencies to bring down the dollar's value. In other words, there was some coordination of major governments' policies to try to reduce the value of the dollar. During the early 1990s, the dollar moved within a much narrower band relative to other currencies, compared with the 1980s. Thanks in large part to the emerging markets crisis and the high-tech boom, the dollar staged a strong rally in the late 1990s. Predictably, the strength of the dollar contributed to a deterioration of the U.S. trade deficit to record levels. In time, this put downward pressure on the dollar, the same way it did in the late 1980s. During much of the 2000s, the dollar remained weak.

CASE STUDY 28.4

THE EURO: EUROPE'S SINGLE CURRENCY

On January 1, 1999, the euro was launched. Preparations for the introduction of the new currency took the better part of a decade. Even the launch itself was phased in. Between January 1999 and January 2002, the euro was used for electronic transactions and official settlements. The new bills and coins began circulation on January 1, 2002. And the local currencies (German marks, French francs, Italian lire, and so on) were phased out by June 30, 2002.

The key features of the European Monetary Union (EMU) were laid out in a treaty signed in the port city of Maastricht, in the Netherlands, in December 1991. The Maastricht Treaty set out a series of stringent preconditions for countries that wanted to join the EMU. These included government deficit and national debt targets that were 3 percent and 60 percent of GDP, respectively. The goal of these preconditions was to rein in profligate governments, such as those in Belgium and Italy. However, the architects of the EMU also wanted to reassure countries with strong currencies, such as Germany, that the new currency would be based on solid foundations.

By spring 1997, all but one European Union member (Greece) qualified to join the EMU. However, 3 of the remaining 14 (Great Britain, Denmark, and Sweden) opted out of the first round of countries joining the monetary union. This left 11 countries (France, Germany, Italy, the Netherlands, Spain, Portugal, Ireland, Belgium, Luxembourg, Austria, and Finland) as the first-round members. Greece joined the EMU in 2001. By 2011, the Eurozone (EMU) had 17 members.

The Maastricht Treaty (and subsequent treaties, especially the Stability and Growth Pact) also established a new European Central Bank (ECB), which now sets monetary policy (primarily short-term interest rates) for all 17 EMU members.

How successful has the euro been? Its launch was very smooth, thanks to the years of preparation. However, almost immediately, the euro began to lose value against other major currencies, falling by 20 percent relative to the U.S. dollar in a little over a year. Some of this weakness was due to an initial lack of confidence in the new currency and the ECB. The currency also suffered because of poor economic fundamentals (especially weak growth) in the European economies during the launch year, 1999. By 2001, the euro had reached an all-time low of close to $0.80. However, the bursting of the high-tech bubble and subsequent recession in the United States, along with the 9/11 terrorist attacks, began to weaken the dollar and strengthen the euro. By early 2004, the euro was up around $1.25 and continued to appreciate through much of the 2000s.

From the outset, there were concerns about how well suited the EMU is to the structure of the European economies. For example, in 1999 and 2000, some economies at the periphery of Europe (Ireland, Spain, Portugal, and Finland) grew much faster than the economies at the core (Germany and France). Interest rates in the peripheral countries should have risen substantially to cool down these economies. At the same time, interest rates in the core countries should have risen much less, if at all. However, thanks to the EMU, short-term interest rates across the member countries are identical; in other words, most of Europe now has a "one size fits all" monetary policy. In the end, the ECB decided to raise interest rates only a little, running the risk that the smaller peripheral countries would overheat.

A related problem concerns asymmetric shocks. For example, what if a global downturn hits Germany and Italy much harder than France (given their greater dependence on exports)? What should the European Central Bank do? In fact the ECB faced exactly this type of dilemma in early 2002 and 2003. Germany and Italy were hit harder by the downturns in the world economy than the other countries in the EMU. As a result, the interest rates set by the ECB were too high for these two countries. In a world of multiple, flexible exchange rates, the adjustment process would have included the depreciation of the exchange rates in Germany and Italy. However, this adjustment mechanism is no longer available to the 12 members of the EMU.

How do the regions of the United States, which also have a single currency, cope with asymmetric shocks? Consider a rise in oil prices that would hurt Massachusetts but boost the economy of Texas. The United States has two adjustment mechanisms that help to equilibrate the impact of such asymmetric shocks. First, the United States has a well-developed system of federal fiscal transfers. As Massachusetts goes into a recession, residents there pay less taxes and receive more unemployment compensation and other federal benefits. The reverse is true in booming Texas. Thus, there is a transfer of funds from Texas to Massachusetts, cooling down the former and helping to boost the latter. Such a system of transfers does not exist in Europe. Second, as people lose jobs in Massachusetts, they often move to other states (for example, Texas), where there are better job opportunities. This type of labor market flexibility does not exist in Europe. Many economists were concerned that if Europe was hit by an asymmetric shock, the impact would be even higher unemployment (see Case Study 10.3) in the hardest-hit countries. This could create large social and political tensions within the EMU.

In fact, an asymmetric shock did hit the Eurozone, starting in 2009. Partly because the financial crisis and Great Recession of 2008–2009 hit some countries harder than others, and partly because of bad policy decisions made by governments, some Eurozone countries (Greece, Ireland, and Portugal) required sovereign bailouts, and others (Italy and Spain) also needed help. The bailouts were very unpopular with voters in countries such as Germany, who were expected to foot the bill.

The sovereign debt crisis, which festered for many years, drove home the serious design flaws in the Eurozone. One (already mentioned) is the inappropriateness of a "one size fits all" monetary policy for countries as diverse as Germany and Greece. In particular, during the decade of the 2000s, interest rates were probably too low for countries in southern Europe (where wage growth was too strong) and too high for countries in northern Europe (which managed to keep wage costs under control).

Another design flaw relates to creating a monetary union without simultaneously creating a banking union and a fiscal union. This means that there is no effective mechanism to rein in profligate governments (such as Greece's) and little political support for bailing out such governments by the voters in countries (such as Germany) whose governments have been much more frugal.

So, in the end, the Eurozone is still a work in progress, and further changes will have to be made if this "grand experiment" is to be a success.

Should the Value of the Dollar Be Stabilized?

According to some economists, like John Williamson, of the Peterson Institute for International Economics, governments should do more to stabilize the value of the dollar. They argue that governments should buy and sell currencies to keep exchange rates within certain target zones, as well as coordinate monetary and fiscal policies. Under the Louvre Accord of 1987, the biggest countries tried to stabilize their currencies within certain ranges that were agreed on, but these ranges were not published as formal targets. In late 1987, when the U.S. government objected to the policies of some of the other countries, it ignored this accord and permitted the dollar to drop.

Other economists, like Harvard's Martin Feldstein, feel that it would be a mistake to try to stabilize the value of the dollar. In their view, attempts of this sort would mean that monetary and fiscal policies would have to be diverted from their proper roles, sacrificing the traditional goals of price stability and high employment. And if the value of the dollar were stabilized, it "would mean harmful distortions in the balance of trade and in the international flow of capital."[2]

Although flexible exchange rates have been in operation for over 40 years, the truth is that a clear assessment of their success— or lack of it—is hard to make because we do not know what would have occurred if some other system of exchange rates had been adopted. Clearly, flexible rates have not lived up to

[2] M. Feldstein, "The Case against Trying to Stabilize the Dollar," *American Economic Review, 79* (May 1989).

the claims of some of their proponents, but neither have they been as disastrous as some of their opponents claimed. So far, they have enabled us to muddle through, although not without substantial problems.

REVIEW AND PRACTICE

Summary

1   An important difference between international business transactions and business transactions within a country is that international business transactions involve more than one currency. The exchange rate is the number of units of one currency that exchanges for a unit of another currency.

2   Under a system of flexible exchange rates, the market for foreign exchange functions like any other free market, where the exchange rate is determined by supply and demand. Under such a system, exchange rates tend to move in a way that removes imbalances among countries in exports and imports. The price of a country's currency tends to fall (or rise) if its inflation rate and growth rate are relatively high (or low) or if its interest rate is relatively low (or high).

3   Until 1973, when exchange rates became more flexible, most exchange rates were fixed by government action and international agreement; exchange rates were allowed to vary slightly, but only slightly, about the official rate.

4   If exchange rates are fixed, the amount of a foreign currency demanded may not equal the amount supplied. To maintain exchange rates at the official levels, governments enter the market and buy and sell their currencies as needed. They also intervene by curbing imports, limiting foreign travel, and other measures.

5   Under a system of fixed exchange rates, a country has a balance of payments deficit if its currency is overvalued and a balance of payments surplus if its currency is undervalued. A balance of payments deficit is the difference between the quantity supplied and the quantity demanded of the currency. A balance of payments surplus is the difference between the quantity demanded and the quantity supplied of the currency.

6   In recent years, variations in exchange rates, some of which were erratic and without fundamental economic significance, have made international transactions more difficult. Although there is no indication that flexible exchange rates will be forsaken, some observers believe that central banks should intervene to a greater extent to influence exchange rates.

Problems and Questions

1   Suppose that the quantity of Japanese yen demanded at each price (in dollars) of a yen is as follows:

Quantity Demanded (billions of yen)	Price of a Yen (in dollars)
20	0.007
15	0.008
10	0.009
5	0.010

Plot this demand curve on a graph. What sorts of groups, organizations, and individuals are part of the demand side of this market?

2   Suppose that the quantity of Japanese yen supplied at each price (in dollars) of a yen is as follows:

Quantity Supplied (billions of yen)	Price of a Yen (in dollars)
8	0.007
9	0.008
10	0.009
11	0.010

Plot this supply curve on the same graph as the demand curve in question 1. What sorts of groups, organizations, and individuals are part of the supply side of this market?

3   On the basis of the information in questions 1 and 2, what is the equilibrium value of the exchange rate if it is completely flexible? Why? Is the exchange rate between the U.S. dollar and the Japanese yen completely flexible at present?

4   Suppose that the exchange rate is fixed and the price (in dollars) of a yen is set at $0.008. On the basis of the data in questions 1 and 2, does the quantity of yen demanded equal the quantity supplied? What sorts of government actions have to be taken?

5   During the 1950s and 1960s, the British government reacted to deficits in its balance of payments by adopting deflationary monetary and fiscal policies (temporarily, at least). Was this sensible? Why or why not?

6   Under what circumstances would you be willing to invest $10,000 (if you had $10,000) in (a) El Salvador, (b) Poland, (c) Japan, and (d) India? What interest rate would you expect? What guarantees would you expect? Why?

7 "Under flexible exchange rates, reserves play a much less important role than under fixed exchange rates." What does this mean? Do you agree? Why or why not?

8 Country X has been confronted with a balance of payments deficit. Explain how it can eliminate this deficit by (a) changing its exchange rate, (b) changing its price level, and (c) adopting controls.

Key Terms

exchange rate
gold standard
flexible exchange rates
appreciation
depreciation

devaluation of currency
fixed exchange rates
balance of payments deficit
balance of payments surplus
gold exchange standard

Viewpoint for Analysis

On December 15, 1999, in an op-ed piece in the *Financial Times*, Connie Mack, then U.S. senator from Florida and chair of the Joint Economic Committee, wrote: "The world economy is becoming a single market. As such, the existence of more than 150 different national currencies makes less and less economic sense. The instability caused by having so many currencies is one of the reasons there is growing interest in official dollarization, whereby emerging market countries abolish their own currencies and adopt the U.S. dollar as legal tender."[3]

(a) What are the advantages of dollarization?

(b) What do countries give up when they adopt the dollar as legal tender?

(c) Under what circumstances would the advantages of dollarization outweigh the disadvantages?

---

[3] "Time to Reap the Dollar's Rewards," *Financial Times*, December 16, 1999, 15.

SHOULD WE BE WORRIED ABOUT THE RISE OF CHINA, INDIA, AND OTHER EMERGING MARKETS?

During the 1984 U.S. presidential campaign, Democratic nominee Walter Mondale asked, "What do we want our kids to do? Sweep up around Japanese computers?" This is a classic example of zero-sum thinking.

Mondale assumed that Japan's prosperity in the 1980s would be at the expense of the United States. His comments echoed the fear of many in business and government who were both fascinated and scared by Japan's rapid growth rates in the 1960s and 1970s. Concerns that Japan would threaten the U.S. dominance in industries such as autos and consumer electronics led to a rise in protectionist sentiment and pressures on Japan to push up its exchange rate and to limit its exports to the United States. Were it not for the damage done to both the U.S. and Japanese economies by these shortsighted policies, the "Japanophobia" of the 1980s would be amusing in retrospect. Not only did the United States continue to thrive in the very same high-tech industries that Mondale was worried about, but Japan's "dominance" was short-lived as other Asian economies (first South Korea and more recently China) became formidable competitors.

There is a sense of déjà vu in the "get tough with China" policies and pronouncements in recent years. Having learned little from the Japan-bashing of the 1980s, the U.S. Congress has been intent on turning China into the new scapegoat. Specifically, there have been numerous bills introduced to "punish" China for its large trade surplus with the United States and, allegedly, its low exchange rate. Assuming that the U.S. trade deficit is all China's fault (it isn't, because it takes two to tango), and assuming that an increase in China's exchange rate will make a big difference (it won't, because other factors are at play, including budget deficits and low household savings in the United States), punishing America's fastest-growing export market could easily end up doing the U.S. economy a lot of harm—especially if China decides to retaliate by imposing restrictions on U.S. exports.

In 1950, Japan's economy was one-tenth the size of the U.S. economy. Fifty years later, it was one-third the size. During those same five decades, the United States enjoyed the fastest growth in per capita income ever! Despite popular fears, Japan's rise was not at America's expense.

The same is true of China's development. China's economy is roughly one-quarter the size of the U.S. economy and at current growth rates could become the biggest economy in the world in the next few decades. This is much more of an opportunity than a threat. Not only was China the third largest economy in the world in 2007, it was also the third largest importer after the United States and Germany.

In contrast, the world's second biggest economy, Japan, imported only about half as much as China. This means that China's growth has been much more open (that is, letting in more imports) than Japan's. Most multinational corporations consider the Chinese market—especially the booming middle-class population—to be a centerpiece of their growth strategies over the next couple of decades.

India is not far behind. Its economy is currently about one-tenth the size of the U.S. economy, but growing at a rate of 6 to 7 percent a year (compared with about 8 percent for China). In some ways it offers even more promising opportunities than China because consumer spending plays a much bigger role in the Indian economy (about 60 percent of total economic activity versus less than 35 percent in China).

People who feel threatened by the rise of Japan, China, and other emerging markets tend to fall into two different types of zero-sum traps.

- First, consider the common misperception that emerging markets compete directly with the United States and other rich countries. They do not. Typically, countries such as China and India produce goods that require low-skilled work. Such jobs have long since left the rich countries, as these economies lost their comparative advantage in low-skilled industries such as textiles, toys, and low-end technologies. The comparative advantage of rich countries is in industries such as aircraft, software, and pharmaceuticals. Trade between rich and poor countries tends to be much more complementary than competitive.

- Second, what about the risk that China and India will "overtake" the rich countries, becoming formidable competitors in high-skilled industries as well? This is a static view of the world and assumes that the United States and other rich countries will not move even further up the development and technology ladders. Time and again, history has shown that rich countries can successfully hold their own (even as some emerging markets are catching up rapidly), as long as they provide the right incentives for investments in human and physical capital and for innovation.

Perhaps one of the most visceral fears triggered by the success of countries such as China and India is the possibility of a "race to the bottom"—that low wages in these countries will force down wages in rich economies, compromise labor and environmental standards, and erode the overall standard of living. Sometimes this is referred to as the "China price"—in other words, low prices in China will put downward pressure on prices (and wages) everywhere. If low wages are the basis of economic competitiveness and strength, why isn't Africa an economic powerhouse? Because wages are only half the story. Productivity is at least as important, if not more. China's true secret is strong productivity growth. While the level of wages and productivity are roughly 20 percent of U.S. levels, the growth rate in productivity has been phenomenal. Productivity has not only been growing faster than wages (roughly twice as fast), but also more rapidly than in most other emerging markets.

The challenge for rich *and* poor countries that feel threatened by the rise of China and India is to not be tempted to block "cheap imports" from these countries or to try to compete on the basis of low wages—moves that will do much more harm than good.

Instead the challenge is to put in place policies that boost productivity—in other words, a "race to the top." In the case of rich countries, this means continued emphasis on education, training, R&D, and innovation in an open, competitive environment. In the case of poor countries, this means learning the real lessons behind the success of so many Asian economies: investment in human and physical capital, openness to trade, foreign investment and technology transfers, good governance, and a strong work ethic. In the long run, there is a high correlation between increases in productivity and increases in wages. This is true for both rich and poor countries.

In the end, Japan's rise in the 1960s to 1980s did not threaten the United States. Nor did Mexico's post-NAFTA success in the 1990s "suck" jobs out of the U.S. economy (see Case Study 27.3). Similarly, the United States will continue to do well even as China, India, and other emerging markets develop rapidly.

In a recent editorial in the *Financial Times*, Michael Bloomberg, then mayor of New York City, made a very eloquent plea against protectionist policies aimed at China and other emerging markets:

> When politicians suggest that the benefits of globalization go primarily to low-wage countries, they are playing into people's fears. In fact, globalization benefits every country that maximizes its strategic advantages—and no country has more strategic advantages than the U.S. We are blessed with many of the best universities in the world; an enormous domestic consumer market; the most cutting-edge technological, medical and scientific research communities; deep capital markets that offer financing to businesses of every kind; and a level of freedom, opportunity and diversity that is unmatched.[1]

Questions

1 What should the United States do to help low-skilled workers whose livelihood is threatened by competition from China, India, and other low-cost emerging markets?

2 Who would be hurt most if the United States were to limit imports from China?

3 What are the similarities between globalization and rapid changes in technologies?

[1] The *Financial Times* editorial by former New York mayor Michael Bloomberg, December 12, 2007.

GLOSSARY

ability-to-pay principle The notion that people should be taxed so as to produce a socially desirable distribution of income.

absolute advantage The ability of one country to produce a commodity more cheaply than another country.

aggregate demand curve A curve, sloping downward to the right, that shows the level of real national output demanded at various economy-wide price levels.

aggregate supply curve A curve, sloping upward to the right, that shows the level of real national output supplied at various economy-wide price levels.

alternative cost The value of what certain resources could have produced had they been used in the best alternative way; also called opportunity cost.

anticipated inflation The rate of inflation expected to occur by consumers and businesses, based on recent trends in the economy.

antitrust laws Legislation (such as the Sherman Act, the Clayton Act, and the Federal Trade Commission Act) intended to promote competition and control monopoly.

appreciation In discussions of exchange rates, an increase in the value of one currency relative to another.

arc elasticity of demand An average measure of elasticity along a demand curve; *see* price elasticity of demand.

automatic stabilizers Structural features of the economy (especially government spending and tax programs) that tend by themselves to stabilize national output without the help of legislation or government policy measures.

autonomous change in spending A change in spending that occurs because of factors other than income or prices.

average fixed cost The firm's total fixed cost divided by its output.

average product of an input Total output divided by the amount of input used to produce this amount of output.

average propensity to consume The fraction of disposable income spent on consumption; equal to personal consumption expenditure divided by disposable income.

average total cost The firm's total cost divided by its output; equal to average fixed cost plus average variable cost.

average variable cost The firm's total variable cost divided by its output.

backward-bending supply curve for labor A supply curve for labor inputs showing that beyond some point, increases in price may result in the supply of smaller amounts of labor.

balance of payments deficit The difference between the quantity supplied and the quantity demanded of a currency when the currency is overvalued (that is, priced above its equilibrium price).

balance of payments surplus The difference between the quantity demanded and the quantity supplied of a currency when the currency is undervalued (that is, priced below its equilibrium price).

barometric firm In an oligopolistic industry, any single firm that is the first to make changes in prices, which are then generally accepted by other firms.

barriers to entry Obstacles (such as high start-up costs, economies of scale, etc.) that make it more difficult for new competitors to enter an area of business.

base year A year chosen as a reference point for comparison with some later or earlier year.

benefit principle The notion that people who receive more from a certain government service should pay more taxes to support it.

budget deficit The amount by which tax revenues fall short of government expenditures.

budget surplus The amount by which tax revenues exceed government expenditures.

business cycle The cyclical fluctuations in national output over time.

$C + I + G + (X - M_i)$ line A curve showing total intended spending (the sum of intended consumption expenditure, investment expenditure, government expenditure, and net exports) at various levels of gross domestic product.

capital formation Investment in plant and equipment.

capital goods Output consisting of plant and equipment that are used to make other goods.

capital-output ratio The ratio of the total capital stock to annual national output.

capitalization A method of computing the value of an asset by calculating the present value of the expected future income this asset will produce.

cartel An open formal collusive arrangement among firms.

central bank A government-established agency that controls the supply of money and supervises the country's commercial banks. The central bank of the United States is the Federal Reserve.

checkoff A system whereby an employer deducts union dues from each worker's pay and hands them over to the union.

closed shop A situation where firms can hire only those workers who are already union members.

collective bargaining A process of negotiation between union and management over wages and working conditions.

collusion A covert arrangement whereby firms agree on price and output levels to decrease competition and increase profits.

comparative advantage The law that states that a country should produce and export the goods it can produce at *relatively* lower costs than other countries.

complements Commodities that tend to be consumed together; that is, commodities with a negative cross elasticity of demand, such that a decrease in the price of one will result in an increase in the quantity demanded of the other.

constant dollars Amounts measured in base-year dollars (that is, according to the purchasing power of the dollar in some earlier year) to express value in a way that corrects for changes in the price level.

constant returns to scale A long-run situation where, if the firm increases the amount of all inputs by the same proportion, output increases by the same proportion as each of the inputs.

consumer An individual or household that purchases the goods and services produced by the economic system.

consumer goods Output consisting of items that consumers purchase, such as clothing, food, and drink.

consumer price index (CPI) A measure of U.S. inflation, calculated by the Bureau of Labor Statistics, originally intended to measure changes in the prices of goods and services purchased by urban wage earners and clerical workers; expanded in 1978 to cover all urban consumers.

consumption function The relationship between consumption spending and disposable income; that is, the amount of consumption expenditure that occurs at various levels of disposable income.

corporate governance The system of checks and balances that guides the decisions of corporate managers.

corporation A fictitious legal person separate and distinct from the stockholders who own it and governed by a board of directors elected by the stockholders.

cost function The relationship between cost and a firm's level of output; that is, what a firm's costs will be at various levels of output.

costs The necessary payments to the owners of resources to get them to provide these resources to a firm.

creeping inflation An increase in the general price level of a few percent per year that gradually erodes the value of money.

cross elasticity of demand The percentage change in the quantity demanded of one commodity resulting from a 1 percent change in the price of another commodity; may be either positive or negative.

crowding-in effect An increase in private investment induced by government deficit spending—something that normally only occurs in recessions, or when there is a lot of slack in the economy.

crowding-out effect The tendency for an increase in public sector expenditure to result in a cut in private sector expenditure.

crude quantity theory of money and prices The theory that if the velocity of circulation of money remains constant and real gross domestic product remains fixed at its full-employment level, it follows from the equation of exchange ($MV = PQ$) that the price level will be proportional to the money supply.

currency Coins and bank notes—also used in a broader sense to denote a country's money (e.g., the U.S. dollar or the Japanese yen).

current dollars Values of key economic variables in today's dollars—not adjusted for inflation.

cyclical unemployment Joblessness that occurs because of business fluctuations.

decreasing returns to scale A long-run situation where, if the firm increases the amount of all inputs by the same proportion, output increases by a smaller proportion than each of the inputs.

deflating   Converting values expressed in current dollars into values expressed in constant dollars to correct for changes in the price level.

demand curve for loanable funds   A curve showing the quantity of loanable funds that is demanded at each interest rate.

demand curve for money   A curve representing the quantity of money that will be demanded at various interest rates (holding constant real GDP and the price level).

demand deposits   Checking accounts; bank deposits subject to payment on demand.

demand-side inflation   An increase in the general price level that occurs because of rightward shifts of the aggregate demand curve. There is too much aggregate spending, too much money chasing too few goods.

depreciation   In discussions of exchange rates, a decrease in the value of one currency relative to another.

depression   A period when national output is well below its potential (full-employment) level; a severe recession.

deregulation   The removal of government controls over pricing and entry barriers in an industry so that market forces can play a larger role.

derived demand   Demand for labor and other inputs not as ends in themselves but as means to produce other things.

devaluation of currency   Under the gold standard, a decrease in the value of a currency as a consequence of an increase in the price of gold.

differentiated oligopoly   A market structure (such as those for automobiles and machinery) where there are only a few sellers of somewhat different products.

diffusion process   The process by which the use of an innovation spreads from firm to firm and from use to use.

direct regulation   Government issue of enforceable rules concerning the conduct of firms.

discount rate   The interest rate the Federal Reserve charges for loans to commercial banks.

discretionary fiscal policy   Fiscal policy that is formulated at the discretion of the policy makers—as opposed to automatic stabilizers.

discretionary policy   Policy that is formulated at the discretion of the policy makers (in contrast to rigid policy rules or feedback policy rules).

discrimination   Barriers that prevent people from having access to the same educational and economic opportunities, depending on their gender, race, or socioeconomic background.

dominant firm   In an oligopolistic industry, a single large firm that sets the price for the industry but lets the small firms sell all they want at that price.

economic growth   The rate at which the economy's total real (inflation-adjusted) output of goods and services is expanding.

economic profits   The excess of a firm's profits over what it could make in other industries.

economic resources   Resources that are scarce and thus command a nonzero price.

economics   The study of how resources are allocated among alternative uses to satisfy human wants.

effluent fee   A fee that a polluter must pay to the government for discharging waste.

entrepreneur   An individual who is willing to take risks in starting a business or developing a new technology or innovation.

equation of exchange   A way of restating the definition of the velocity of circulation of money, such that the amount received for the final goods and services during a period equals the amount spent on those final goods and services during the same period (that is, $MV = PQ$).

equilibrium market basket   The market basket that maximizes consumer satisfaction.

equilibrium price   A price that shows no tendency for change, because it is the price at which the quantity demanded equals the quantity supplied; the price toward which the actual price of a good always tends to move.

excess demand   A situation in which demand exceeds supply at a given price.

excess reserves   The difference between the actual reserve held and the reserves it is required to hold by law, to cover liabilities.

excess supply   A situation in which supply exceeds demand at a given price.

exchange rate   The number of units of one currency that can purchase a unit of another currency.

expansion   The phase in the business cycle after the trough, during which national output rises.

expectations   Beliefs or views on the future values and trends of economic variables, such as GDP and the inflation rate.

expected rate of return   The rate of return (earnings) that investors expect on various types of assets (stocks, bonds, etc.).

expenditures approach The calculation of GDP by adding up its components: consumer spending (C), business fixed investment (I), government spending (G), and exports (X) minus imports (M).

explicit cost The cost of resources for which there is an explicit payment.

exports The goods and services that a country sells to other countries.

external diseconomy A situation that occurs when consumption or production by one person or firm results in uncompensated costs to another person or firm.

external economy A situation that occurs when consumption or production by one person or firm results in uncompensated benefits to another person or firm.

externalities External economies and diseconomies.

featherbedding A practice whereby a union restricts output per worker to increase the amount of labor required to do a certain job.

federal budget The balance sheet of the government, which shows spending by category, revenues by category, and the deficit or surplus.

Federal Open Market Committee (FOMC) A group, composed of the seven members of the Federal Reserve Board plus five presidents of Federal Reserve Banks, that makes decisions concerning the purchase and sale of government securities in order to control bank reserves and the money supply.

Federal Reserve Board The Board of Governors of the Federal Reserve System, composed of seven members appointed by the president for 14-year terms, whose function is to promote the nation's economic welfare by supervising the operations of the U.S. money and banking system.

Federal Reserve System (Fed) A system established by Congress in 1913 that includes commercial banks, the 12 Federal Reserve Banks, and the Board of Governors of the Federal Reserve System.

feedback policy rule A rule allowing the behavior of the variable governed by the policy rule to change, depending on future circumstances.

final goods and services Goods and services destined for the ultimate user (such as flour purchased for family consumption).

firm An organization that produces a good or service for sale in an attempt to make a profit.

firm's demand curve for labor A curve showing the relationship between the price of labor and the amount of labor demanded by a firm; that is, the amount of labor that will be demanded by a firm at various wage rates.

firm's supply curve A curve, usually sloping upward to the right, showing the quantity of output a firm will produce at each price.

fixed exchange rates Exchange rates that are fixed by means of government intervention in the foreign exchange markets.

fixed input A resource used in the production process (such as plant and equipment) whose quantity cannot be changed during the particular period under consideration.

flexible exchange rates Exchange rates determined by market forces.

food programs Federal antipoverty programs that distribute food to the poor, either directly from surpluses produced by farm programs or indirectly via stamps that can be exchanged for food.

45-degree line A line that contains all points where the amount on the horizontal axis equals the amount on the vertical axis.

fractional reserve banking The practice whereby banks hold less cash than the amount they owe their depositors.

free resources Resources (such as air) that are so abundant that they can be obtained without charge.

frictional unemployment Temporary joblessness, such as that occurring among people who have quit jobs, people looking for their first job, and seasonal workers.

full employment The minimum level of joblessness that the economy could achieve without undesirably high inflation, recognizing that there will always be some frictional and structural unemployment.

game A competitive situation where two or more players pursue their own interests, no player can dictate the outcome, and all players are mutually aware.

globalization The closer integration of the world economy through the flow of goods, services, capital, and labor across borders.

gold exchange standard An exchange rate system developed after World War II, under which the dollar was directly convertible into gold at a fixed price, and other currencies, since they could be converted into dollars at fixed exchange rates, were indirectly convertible into gold at a fixed price.

gold standard A method of exchange rate determination prevailing until the 1930s, under which currencies were convertible into a certain amount of gold.

gross domestic product (GDP) The value of the total amount of final goods and services produced by the economy during a period of time; measured either by the expenditure on the final goods and services or by the income generated by the output.

historical cost of assets What a firm actually paid for its assets.

human capital The accumulation of investments in formal education, on-the-job training, and health programs.

human wants The goods, services, and circumstances that people desire.

implicit contract An agreement between the workers and the firm that is not found in any formal, written contract.

implicit cost The cost (for which there is no explicit payment) of the resources provided by the owners of a firm, measured by what these resources could bring if they were used in their best alternative employment.

income approach The calculation of GDP by adding up the sources of income in the economy: wages, corporate profits, interest income, rental income, proprietors income, etc.

income elasticity of demand The percentage change in the quantity demanded of a commodity resulting from a 1 percent increase in total money income (all prices being held constant).

income inequality An unequal distribution of national income that provides a higher than proportional share to richer families.

income redistribution A process by which society helps people who are ill, handicapped, old and infirm, or otherwise unable to provide for themselves.

income tax A federal, state, or local tax imposed on personal income and corporate profits.

income-expenditure analysis An analysis of economic trends using both the income and expenditure components of GDP.

incomes policy A policy to control inflation that sets some targets for wages and prices in the economy as a whole, gives particular firms and industries detailed guides for making wage and price decisions, and provides some inducements for firms and unions to follow these guidelines.

increasing returns to scale A long-run situation where if a firm increases the amount of all inputs by the same proportion, output increases by a larger proportion than each of the inputs.

individual demand curve A curve showing the relationship between individual consumer demand for a good and its price; that is, how much of a good an individual consumer demands at various prices.

induced changes in spending Changes in spending induced by changes in other variables such as income, interest rates, and tax rates.

inflation An increase in the general level of prices economy-wide.

inflationary gap A positive gap between actual and potential output.

innovation The first commercial application of a new technology.

innovator A firm that is first to apply a new technology.

input Any resource used in the production process.

interest The payment of money by borrowers to suppliers of money capital.

interest rate The annual amount that a borrower must pay for the use of a dollar for a year.

intermediate goods Goods not sold to the ultimate user but used as inputs in producing final goods and services (such as flour to be used in manufacturing bread).

labor productivity The amount of output divided by the number of units of labor employed.

Laffer curve A curve representing the relationship between the amount of income tax revenue collected by the government and the marginal tax rate; that is, how much revenue will be collected at various marginal tax rates.

land Natural resources, including minerals as well as plots of ground, used to produce goods and services.

law of diminishing marginal returns The principle that if equal increments of a given input are added (the quantities of other inputs being held constant), the resulting increments of product obtained from the extra unit of input (the marginal product) will begin to decrease beyond some point.

law of diminishing marginal utility The principle that if a person consumes additional units of a given commodity (the consumption of other commodities being held constant), the resulting increments of utility derived from the extra unit of the commodity (the marginal utility) will begin to decrease beyond some point.

legal reserve requirements Regulations imposed by the Federal Reserve System in order to control the money supply, requiring banks (and other institutions) to hold a certain fraction of deposits as cash reserves.

long run The period of time during which all of a firm's inputs are variable, that is, during which the firm could completely change the resources used in the production process.

long-run aggregate supply curve The total quantity of goods and services produced by an economy when all the inputs are fully and efficiently utilized.

long-run average cost function The minimum average cost of producing various output levels when any desired type or scale of plant can be built.

M1 Narrowly defined money supply, which includes coins, currency, demand deposits, and other checkable deposits.

M2 Broadly defined money supply, which includes savings deposits, small time deposits, money market mutual fund balances, and money market deposit accounts, as well as the components of the narrowly defined money supply, Ml (coins, currency, demand deposits, and other checkable deposits).

marginal cost The addition to total cost resulting from the addition of the last unit of output.

marginal product of an input The addition to total output that results from the addition of an extra unit of input (the quantities of all other inputs being held constant).

marginal propensity to consume The fraction of an extra dollar of disposable income spent on consumption.

marginal propensity to save The fraction of an extra dollar of disposable income that is saved.

marginal revenue The addition to total revenue that results from the addition of 1 unit to the quantity sold.

marginal tax rate The proportion of an extra dollar of income that must be paid in taxes.

marginal utility The additional satisfaction derived from consuming an additional unit of a commodity.

market A group of firms and individuals in touch with each other to buy or sell some good or service.

market demand curve A curve, usually sloping downward to the right, showing the relationship between a product's price and the quantity demanded of the product.

market demand curve for labor A curve showing the relationship between the price of labor and the total amount of labor demanded in the market.

market supply curve A curve, usually sloping upward to the right, showing the relationship between a product's price and the quantity supplied of the product.

market supply curve for labor A curve showing the relationship between the price of labor and the total amount of labor supplied in the market.

Medicaid A federal program that pays for the health care of the poor.

Medicare A compulsory hospitalization program plus a voluntary insurance plan for doctors' fees for people over 65, included in the Social Security program.

menu cost A cost incurred when a firm changes its price.

model A theory composed of assumptions that simplify and abstract from reality, from which conclusions or predictions about the real world are deduced.

model of consumer behavior A framework for analyzing consumer behavior that considers tastes and the satisfaction (or utility) that consumers derive from a particular basket of goods and services.

monetarists Economists generally sharing the belief that business cycle fluctuations are due largely to changes in the money supply. Many monetarists think that a free enterprise economy has effective self-regulating mechanisms that activist fiscal and monetary policies tend to disrupt. Some monetarists, like the late Milton Friedman, advocate a rule for stable growth in the money supply of 3 to 5 percent per year.

monetary base The reserves of commercial banks plus currency outside the banks.

monetary policy The exercise of the central bank's control over the quantity of money and the level of interest rates to promote the objectives of national economic policy.

money Anything that serves as a medium of exchange and a standard and store of value; the unit in which the prices of goods and services are measured.

money income Income measured in current dollars (actual money amounts).

monopolistic competition A market structure in which there are many sellers of somewhat differentiated products, entry is easy, and there is no collusion among sellers. Retailing seems to have many of the characteristics of monopolistic competition.

monopoly A market structure (such as those for public utilities) in which there is only one seller of a product.

multiplier The impact on GDP of a change in government spending (or investment or exports)—calculated as the inverse of the marginal propensity to save (the multiplier) times the increase in spending.

national debt The amount owed by the government. To cover the difference between expenditures and tax revenues, the government sells bonds, notes, and other forms of IOUs.

natural monopoly An industry in which the average costs of producing the product reach a minimum at an output rate large enough to satisfy the entire market, so that competition among firms cannot be sustained and one firm becomes a monopolist.

negative income tax A system whereby families with incomes below a certain break-even level would receive, rather than make, a government income tax payment.

network effect A situation where the value of a product to one user increases with the number of other users; also called network externality.

network externality *See* network effect.

new classical macroeconomists A group, led by Robert Lucas, that believes that the government cannot use monetary and fiscal policies to close recessionary and inflationary gaps, because if firms and individuals formulate their expectations rationally, they will tend to frustrate the government's attempts to use activist stabilization policies.

new Keynesians A group that believes, like the Keynesians, that prices and wages tend to be rigid in the short run (but, in contrast to the Keynesians, has developed theories to explain why such wage and price stickiness can be expected).

normative economics Economic propositions about what ought to be or about what a person, organization, or country ought to do.

old-age insurance Benefits paid under the Social Security program to retired workers.

oligopoly A market structure (such as those for autos and steel) in which there are only a few sellers of products that can be either identical or differentiated.

open market operations The purchase and sale of U.S. government securities on the open market by the Federal Reserve to control the quantity of bank reserves.

open shop A situation where a firm can hire both union and nonunion workers, with no requirement that nonunion workers ever join a union.

opportunity cost The value of what certain resources could have produced had they been used in the best alternative way; also called alternative cost.

partnership A form of business organization whereby two or more people agree to own and conduct a business, with each party contributing some proportion of the capital and/or labor and receiving some proportion of the profit or loss.

patent Exclusive rights, given by law, to the inventor of a product or process (usually for 20 years).

payoff matrix A framework for analyzing the outcome of a two-person game, also used to analyze the behavior of oligopolies.

peak The point in the business cycle where national output is highest relative to its potential (full-employment) level.

perfect competition A market structure in which there are many sellers of identical products, no one seller or buyer has control over the price, entry is easy, and resources can switch readily from one use to another. Many agricultural markets have many of the characteristics of perfect competition.

Phillips curve A curve representing the relationship between the rate of increase in the price level and the level of unemployment.

population growth The pace at which a population increases, based on birth and mortality.

positive economics Descriptive statements, propositions, and predictions about the economic world that are generally testable by an appeal to the facts.

potential gross domestic product The total amount of goods and services that could have been produced had the economy been operating at full capacity or full employment.

poverty A situation in which families lack sufficient income to provide for minimal nutritional, housing, and other basic needs.

precautionary demand for money The demand for money because of uncertainty about the timing and size of future disbursements and receipts.

present value The worth of a future stream of income in terms of its value now.

price ceilings Upper limits placed on prices of goods or services, imposed by the government.

price elastic Describing the demand for a good when its price elasticity of demand is greater than 1.

price elasticity of demand The percentage change in quantity demanded resulting from a 1 percent change in price—by convention, always expressed as a positive number.

price floors Price supports imposed by the government on certain goods.

price index The ratio of the value of a set of goods and services in current dollars to the value of the same set of goods and services in constant dollars.

price inelastic Describing the demand for a good when its price elasticity of demand is less than 1.

price leader In an oligopolistic industry, a firm that sets a price that other firms are willing to follow.

price supports Price floors imposed by the government on a certain good.

private cost The price paid by the individual user for the use of a resource.

product differentiation The process by which producers create real or apparent differences between products that perform the same general function.

product group A group of firms that produce similar products that are fairly close substitutes for one another.

product market A market where products are bought and sold.

production function The relationship between the quantities of various inputs used per period of time and the maximum quantity of output that can be produced per period of time; that is, the most output that existing technology permits the firm to produce from various quantities of inputs.

production possibilities curve A curve showing the combinations of amounts of various goods that a society can produce with given (fixed) amounts of resources.

profit The difference between a firm's revenue and its costs.

profit maximization The behavior whereby firms produce the level of output that will give them the most profit.

progressive tax A tax whereby the rich pay a larger proportion of their income for the tax than do the poor.

prohibitive tariff A tariff so high that it prevents imports of a good.

property tax A tax imposed on real estate and/or other property.

proprietorship A firm owned by a single individual.

prosperity A period when national output is close to its potential (full-employment) level.

public goods Goods and services that can be consumed by one person without diminishing the amount of them that others can consume and for which there is no way to prevent citizens from consuming, whether they pay for them or not.

public regulation A set of rules established by the government to reduce the harmful effects of monopolies.

pure oligopoly A market structure (like those for steel, cement, tin cans, and petroleum) in which there are only a few sellers of an identical product.

pure rate of interest The interest rate on a riskless loan.

quota A limit imposed on the amount of a commodity that can be imported annually.

rate of return The annual profit per dollar invested that businesses can obtain by building new structures, adding new equipment, or increasing their inventories; the interest rate earned on the investment in a particular asset.

rational expectations Expectations that are correct on the average (forecasting errors are random). The forecaster makes the best possible use of whatever information is available.

real business cycle models Theories asserting that business fluctuations are due predominantly to shifts in the aggregate supply curve resulting from new technology, good or bad weather, and so on.

real GDP GDP that has been corrected for changes in the price level.

real income Income measured in constant dollars (that is, the amount of goods and services that can be bought with the income).

real interest rate The interest rate adjusted for inflation—calculated by subtracting the actual or expected rate of inflation from any given interest rate.

recession The phase in the business cycle after the peak, during which national output falls.

recessionary gap A negative gap between actual and potential output.

regressive tax A tax whereby the rich pay a smaller proportion of their income for the tax than do the poor.

rent (also called economic rent) The return derived from an input that is fixed in supply.

reproduction cost of assets What the firm would have to pay to replace its assets.

research and development (R&D) Expenditures and activities related to pure scientific research and technological development and innovation.

resource market A market where resources are bought and sold.

resources Inputs used to produce goods and services.

rigid policy rule A rule specifying completely the behavior of the variable governed by the policy rule (for example, Milton Friedman's suggestion that the money supply be set so that it grows at a fixed, agreed-on rate).

risk The uncertainty associated with any activity or innovation whose outcome is unknown.

rule of reason The principle that not all trusts but only unreasonable combinations in restraint of trade require conviction under the antitrust laws.

rules of the game A legal, social, and competitive framework enabling the price system to function as it should.

runaway inflation A very rapid increase in the general price level that wipes out practically all the value of money.

sales tax A tax imposed on the goods consumers buy (with the exception, in some states, of food and medical care).

saving function the relationship between savings and disposable income, that is the amount of saving that occurs at various levels of disposable income.

short run The period during which at least one of a firm's inputs (generally its plant and equipment) is fixed.

short-run aggregate supply curve Shows the level of real national output supplied at each price level, and unlike the long-run aggregate supply curve assumes that not all resources are fully utilized.

social cost The true cost to society (versus the price paid by individuals) for the use of water, air, and nonrenewable resources.

Social Security A program that imposes taxes on wage earners and employers and provides old-age, survivors', disability, and medical benefits to workers covered under the Social Security Act.

stagflation A simultaneous combination of high unemployment and high inflation.

structural deficit The difference between government expenditures and tax revenues that would result if gross domestic product were at its potential, not its actual, level.

structural unemployment Joblessness that occurs when new goods or new technologies call for new skills, and workers with older skills cannot find jobs.

substitutes Commodities with a positive cross elasticity of demand: a decrease in the price of one commodity will result in a decrease in the quantity demanded of the other commodity.

supply curve for loanable funds A curve showing the relationship between the quantity of loanable funds supplied and the pure interest rate.

supply shock An event that suddenly changes the price of a commodity or service and results in a shift in the aggregate supply curve.

supply-side economics A set of propositions concerned with influencing the aggregate supply curve through the use of financial incentives such as tax cuts.

supply-side inflation Inflation resulting from leftward shifts of the aggregate supply curve.

tariff A tax imposed by the government on imported goods (designed to cut down on imports and thus protect domestic industry and workers from foreign competition).

tax credit A credit given directly for the payment of income or corporate taxes, with the goal of encouraging specific activities (for example, energy efficiency).

tax incidence The burden of tax payments (or who actually pays the tax).

technological change New methods of producing existing products, new designs that make it possible to produce new products, and new techniques of organization, marketing, and management.

technology Society's pool of knowledge concerning how goods and services can be produced from a given amount of resources.

terms of trade The ratio of an index of export prices to an index of import prices.

time inconsistency A set of circumstances in which it becomes harder and harder for policy makers to convince people that announced policies will actually be carried out, thus undermining the desired impact of those policies.

total cost The sum of a firm's total fixed cost and total variable cost.

total fixed cost A firm's total expenditure on fixed inputs per period of time.

total revenue A firm's total dollar sales volume.

total utility The amount of satisfaction that a consumer derives from a particular market basket of goods.

total variable cost A firm's total expenditure on variable inputs per period of time.

transactions demand for money The holding of money in cash or in checking accounts to pay for final goods and services.

transfer payments Payments made by the government or private business to individuals who do not contribute to the production of goods and services in exchange for them.

transferable emissions permit A permit that allows the holder of the permit to generate a certain amount of pollution. These permits, limited in number, are sold by the government to the highest bidders at a price set by supply and demand.

trough The point in the business cycle where national output is lowest relative to its potential (full-employment) level.

unanticipated inflation Actual inflation that is above what consumers and businesses expect.

unemployment According to the definition of the Bureau of Labor Statistics, joblessness among people who are actively looking for work and would take a job if one were offered.

union shop A situation where firms can hire nonunion workers who must then become union members within a certain length of time after being hired.

unitary elasticity A price elasticity of demand equal to 1.

utility A number representing the level of satisfaction that a consumer derives from a particular good or group of goods.

value added The amount of value added by a firm or industry to the total worth of a product.

value of the marginal product of labor The marginal product of labor (the additional output resulting from the addition of an extra unit of labor) multiplied by the product's price.

variable input A resource used in the production process (such as labor or raw material) whose quantity can be changed during the particular period under consideration.

velocity of circulation of money Rate at which the money supply is used to make transactions for final goods and services; that is, the average number of times per year that a dollar is used to buy the final goods and services produced. It equals nominal GDP divided by the money supply.

wage and price controls Limits imposed by the government on the amount by which wages and prices can rise, the intent being to reduce the inflation rate at a given unemployment rate.

wage-price spiral A series of steps whereby higher wage demands by workers prompt firms to raise their prices to consumers; this in turn raises the general cost of living and prompts workers to make yet-higher wage demands.

PHOTO CREDITS

Page 16 Paul Zizka/agefotostock; **26** Library of Congress; **31** Bettmann/Corbis; **51** Bettmann/Corbis; **65** Science and Society/ Superstock; **78** Greg Smith/Corbis Saba; **85** Vivek Prakash/Reuters /Landov; **177** Everett Collection/Newscom; **182** Kristin Callahan/ Everett Collection/Alamy Live News; **202** Anna Omelchenko/Dreamstime; **218** Francis Miller/Time Life Pictures/Getty Images; **251** AP Photo; **257** AP Photo; **276** Jim Wilson/The New York Times/Redux; **295** Chuck Kennedy KRT/Newscom; **319** AP Photo; **323** The Art Archive at Art Resource, NY; **338** George Green, U.S. Army Corps of Engineers; **396** World History Archive/Newscom; **399** Album/ Oronoz/Newscom; **447** National Archives; **449** Granger Collection; **452** Abbie Rowe. White House Photographs. John F. Kennedy Presidential Library and Museum, Boston; **470** LBJ Presidential Library; **516** AP Photo; **532** AP Photo; **554** Soren Egeberg/Shutterstock.com; **577** AP Photo; **624** Courtesy Ronald Reagan Library; **679** Library of Congress

INDEX

Page numbers in *italics* refer to illustrations.